Help is available

The Church of Scotland
Stewardship & Finance
To contact your Stewardship Consultant
please phone or email:

Tel: 0131 225 5722
Email: sfadmin@cofscotland.org.uk

VISIT OUR WEBSITE FOR CUSTOMER TESTIMONIALS & COMPLETED PROJECTS

CRAFTWORX

PROFESSIONAL SASH WINDOW RENOVATION

BRUSH DRAFT SEALING
SUBSTANTIAL REPAIRS OR REPLACEMENT
STANDARD GLAZING & OPTIONAL SLIM LINE
DOUBLE GLAZED UNITS
EXTERNAL MASTIC & FINAL PAINT FINISH

W: WWW.CRAFTWORX-RENOVATION.COM

M: 07760 289817 T: 01506 437754

E: LYNN@CRAFTWORX-RENOVATION.COM

UNIT 7, 1 FIRTH ROAD, HOUSTON IND ESTATE, LIVINGSTON, EH54 5DJ

 **70 YEARS OF MOVING MOUNTAINS!**

In 2015 Christian Aid reaches its 70th anniversary of journeying with our partners to overcome poverty. To mark this milestone we are aiming to climb 70 Munros throughout the year. We invite you and your church to join us.

To find out more and to register your interest go to **christianaid.org.uk/70Munros** or call **0141 2217475**

Honour the ones who didn't come home.
Help Erskine care for the ones who did.

Erskine has been providing care, accommodation and employment for ex-Service men and women in Scotland since 1916. We depend heavily on the generosity of people like you to continue our valuable work.

To donate, visit www.erskine.org.uk or call free on 0300 123 1203. Or text ERSKINE to 70707 to donate £3.

ERSKINE
Proud to care

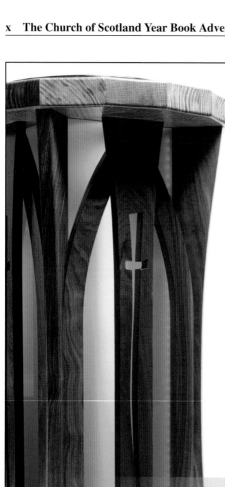

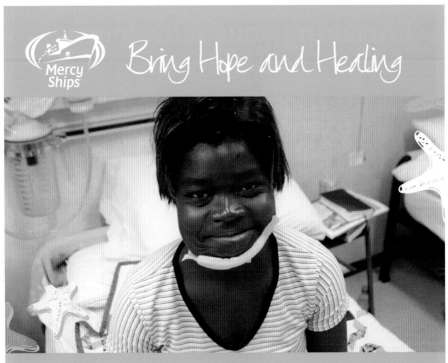

The Right Reverend John P. Chalmers BD CPS

MODERATOR

The Church of Scotland
YEAR BOOK
2014/2015

Editor
Douglas Galbraith

Production Editor
Ivor Normand

Published on behalf of
THE CHURCH OF SCOTLAND
by SAINT ANDREW PRESS
121 George Street, Edinburgh EH2 4YN

THE OFFICES OF THE CHURCH

121 George Street   Tel: 0131-225 5722
Edinburgh EH2 4YN   Fax: 0131-220 3113
                                                          Website: www.churchofscotland.org.uk/

Office Hours: Monday–Friday 9:00am–5:00pm
Facilities Manager: Carole Tait 0131-240 2214

THE COUNCILS OF THE CHURCH

The following five Councils of the Church operate from the Church Offices, 121 George Street, Edinburgh
EH2 4YN (Tel: 0131-225 5722):

- The Council of Assembly
- The Church and Society Council   E-mail: churchandsociety@cofscotland.org.uk
- The Ministries Council   E-mail: ministries@cofscotland.org.uk
- The Mission and Discipleship Council   E-mail: mandd@cofscotland.org.uk
- The World Mission Council   E-mail: world@cofscotland.org.uk

The Social Care Council (CrossReach) operates from Charis House, 47 Milton Road East, Edinburgh
EH15 2SR   Tel: 0131-657 2000
                                                                              Fax: 0131-657 5000
                                                              E-mail: info@crossreach.org.uk
                                                              Website: www.crossreach.org.uk

SCOTTISH CHARITY NUMBERS

The Church of Scotland: unincorporated Councils and Committees   SC011353
The Church of Scotland General Trustees   SC014574
The Church of Scotland Investors Trust   SC022884
The Church of Scotland Trust   SC020269
(For the Scottish Charity Numbers of congregations, see Section 7)

First published in 2014 by SAINT ANDREW PRESS, 121 George Street, Edinburgh EH2 4YN on behalf of THE CHURCH of SCOTLAND

Copyright © THE CHURCH of SCOTLAND, 2014

ISBN 978 0 86153 887 4

It is the Publisher's policy only to use papers that are natural and recyclable and that have been manufactured from timber grown in renewable, properly managed forests. All of the manufacturing processes of the papers are expected to conform to the environmental regulations of the country of origin.

Acceptance of advertisements for inclusion in the *Church of Scotland Year Book* does not imply endorsement of the goods or services or of any views expressed within the advertisements.

British Library Cataloguing in Publication Data
A catalogue record for this book is available from the British Library.

Printed and bound by Bell and Bain Ltd, Glasgow

QUICK DIRECTORY

A.C.T.S. 01259 216980
Christian Aid London...020 7620 4444
Christian Aid Scotland 0141-221 7475
Church and Society Council.......................................0131-240 2275
Church of Scotland Insurance Co. Ltd.............................0131-220 4119
Conforti Institute..01236 607120
Council of Assembly 0131-240 2229
CrossReach..0131-657 2000
Eco-Congregation Scotland 0131-240 2274
Ecumenical Officer...0131-240 2208
Gartmore House 01877 382991
Glasgow Lodging House Mission 0141-552 0285
Iona Community...0141-332 6343
Media Relations Team (Press Office)..............................0131-240 2204/2268
Media Relations Team (after hours)...............................07854 783539
Old Churches House, Dunblane (Scottish Churches House)...........01786 823663
Pension Trustees (E-mail: pensions@cofscotland.org.uk)...........0131-240 2255
Place for Hope 07884 580361
Principal Clerk (E-mail: pcoffice@cofscotland.org.uk)............0131-240 2240
Priority Areas Office..0141-248 2905
Safeguarding Service (item 31 in Assembly Committee list) 0131-240 2256
Scottish Churches Parliamentary Office...........................0131-220 0246
Scottish Storytelling Centre/John Knox House/Netherbow...........0131-556 9579
Trust Housing Association Ltd (formerly Kirk Care) 0131-444 4949
Year Book Editor...01592 752403

Pulpit Supply: Fee and Expenses
Details of the current fee and related expenses in respect of Pulpit Supply will be found as the last item in number 3 (the Ministries Council) on page 13.

**All correspondence regarding the *Year Book* should be sent to
The Editor, *Church of Scotland Year Book*,
Saint Andrew Press, 121 George Street, Edinburgh EH2 4YN
[E-mail: yearbookeditor@cofscotland.org.uk]
Tel: 01592 752403**

GENERAL ASSEMBLY OF 2015
The General Assembly of 2015 will convene on
Saturday, 16 May 2015

CONTENTS

FROM THE MODERATOR

Hardly a day of my working life passes without reference to the *Church of Scotland Year Book*. Behind the statistics, I am made aware of women and men working hard to keep alive the presence of the Church of Scotland in every parish – and, as they do so, they ensure that the presence of Christ permeates the whole of our national life. When I refer to the *Year Book*, I see faces and I remember stories of ministers, deacons, readers and many others who have crossed my path over the years. I picture church buildings, church halls and manses where much of the work of the Church of Scotland is done, and I usually offer a prayer for those that I remember.

Of course, the *Year Book* also tells the story of the challenges that are being faced by the Church of Scotland. On reading the entries this year, there are too many charges facing vacancy; and too many of these vacancies have been medium- to long-term. So, with this year's publication, I am issuing a call to encourage women and men to consider becoming an entry in a future *Year Book*. The Church of Scotland needs accomplished and energetic leadership, and I wonder if you might be someone who would consider serving in one of our variety of ministries?

At the General Assembly this year, I said that this Church of ours has to stop its navel-gazing, get out from under subjects that no one is actually talking about, and get out there and capitalise on the fact that people still want purpose and faith in their lives. They need the Church to be like Jesus: accessible, relevant, generous and forgiving. I'm looking for people who want to be part of that kind of church, and I wonder if you are one who might be encouraged to become a name in this book.

Of course, you'd be more than a name; you'd be enjoying doing with your life one of the best things that a woman or a man could do.

I commend the 2014/15 *Year Book* to you in the prayerful hope that there will be many more entries to read about in future years.

John P. Chalmers

FACAL ON MHODERATOR

Gann gun tèid latha seachad 'nam obair làitheil nach bi mi a' toirt sùil air *Leabhar Bliadhnail Eaglais na h-Alba*. Air cùl nan àireamhan tha mi mothachail air mnathan agus fir a tha ag obair gu cruaidh airson làthaireachd Eaglais na h-Alba a chumail beò anns a h-uile sgìr, agus fhad 's a tha iad a' dèanamh sin tha iad a' dèanamh cinnteach gu bheil làthaireachd Chrìosd a' toirt buaidh air beatha na dùthcha anns an fharsaingeachd. Nuair a bheir mi sùil air an *Leabhar Bhliadhnail* chì mi aodainn agus bidh mi a' cuimhneachadh air naidheachdan mu mhinistearan, deucoin, leughadairean agus iomadh neach eile ris an do choinnich mi rè nam bliadhnachan. Nì mi dealbh air togalaichean, tallaichean-eaglais agus mansaichean far a bheil torr de dh'obair Eaglais na h-Alba a' dol air adhart agus mar as trice cuiridh mi suas ùrnaighean air an son-san air a bheil cuimhne agam.

Gun teagamh sam bith, tha an *Leabhar Bliadhnail* cuideachd a' dèanamh iomradh air na duilgheadasan a tha mu choinneamh Eaglais na h-Alba. Ann a bhith a' leughadh an fhiosrachaidh air a' bhliadhna seo chì mi cus sgìrean a tha bàn agus tha cus a bharrachd de na sgìrean sinn air a bhith gun mhinistear airson ùine mhòr. Mar sin, le leabhar na bliadhna seo tha a' gairm mhnathan agus fir gu bhith a' beachdachadh air a bhith air an cunntas ann an *Leabhar Bliadhnail* a thig a-mach anns na bliadhnachan air thoiseach. Tha feum aig Eaglais na h-Alba air ceannardan a tha sgileil agus èasgaidh, agus saoil a bheil thusa am measg nan daoine a dh'fhaodadh seirbheis a dhèanamh anns na diofar sheòrsachan ministrealachd a tha againn?

Aig an Àrd-sheanadh am bliadhna thubhairt mi gum feum an Eaglais againne sgur a bhith a' sealltainn a-steach oirnn fhèin, cùl a chur ri cuspairean air nach eil daoine a' beachdachadh co-dhiùbh agus a dhol a-mach a ghabhail cothroim air an fhìrnn seo gu bheil daoine fhathast a' lorg creidimh agus dòigh-beatha anns a bheil luach. Tha feum aca air an Eaglais a bhith coltach ri Crìosd – fosgailte, freagarrach, fialaidh agus tròcaireach. Tha mi a' lorg dhaoine a tha airson a bhith 'nan luchd compàirt ann an eaglais den t-seòrsa sin, agus saoil a bheil thusa air cuideigin a bhiodh deònach a bhith air d'ainmeachadh anns an leabhar seo?

Gun teagamh, cha e a-mhàin ainm a bhios annad; gheibheadh tu toileachadh le bhith a' caitheamh do bheatha ann an rud cho math agus as urrainn do mhnathan no do dh'fhir a dhèanamh.

Tha mi a' moladh *Leabhar Bliadhnail* 2014/15 dhuibh leis an ùrnaigh agus leis an dòchas gum bi mòran a bharrachd ainmeannan ri leughadh anns na bliadhnachan air thoiseach.

Iain P. Chalmers

FROM THE EDITOR

Year Books act as a mirror for the Church for their time, both in what is on the page and what is written between the lines. In the centenary year of the start of the Great War, editions from 1914 to 1919 are of interest, giving an insight into the situation in Church and nation during what was seen even in the 1914 edition as 'the most gigantic war of all history'. They chart the progression from a 'curious elevation of spirit' to the breaking-in of the realities of the conflict – so much so that the report given in 1916 of the previous year's Assembly remarked that, 'no matter what the subject under discussion might be, it had not proceeded far before it veered round to one all-absorbing theme'. All pageantry and unnecessary expense were eschewed. The Lord High Commissioner appeared in uniform, and no social events were held at Holyrood. That year also, all three separated Assemblies meeting simultaneously in Edinburgh came together in what is now the Assembly Hall for a common act of intercession. The War impacted on the Assembly in a personal way also: the retiring Moderator and the Vice-Convener of the Business Committee were separately called away on the deaths of their sons.

Early on, the Assembly had begun to talk of the need for a fresh survey of fundamental Christian truth, noting that 'it cannot be the will of God that Christians should slay one another'. Following overtures from Presbyteries, in 1916 a 'Commission on the War in Relation to its Spiritual and Moral Issues' was set up to listen to the God who was 'pleading with his people through recent events and the present distress' with the aim of calling the nation 'with penitence, faith and hope to hear and obey his Word'. The 1918 Assembly reported a wide-ranging programme of conferences and public meetings, mission weeks, forms of prayer and accompanying literature. From out of this experience, plans were made for a closer relationship between Church and the armed forces; and it was at this time also that the office of Reader was restored.

This new edition of the *Year Book* also holds a mirror to its time, shown in the incorporation of a few additional subsections. Before his call to the moderatorial chair, the Principal Clerk had circulated advice on the position of the Church of Scotland and of individual ministers and deacons in respect of the Marriage and Civil Partnership (Scotland) Act 2014, should it become law, together with 'frequently asked questions' on the matter. This can now be found in Section 3, 'Church Procedure'.

We have also tried to clarify the matter of Practising Certificates for ministers who are not in a charge – a matter whose mysteries can challenge even those Presbytery clerks whose holiday reading is Weatherhead's *The Constitution and Laws of the Church of Scotland*. There are three places where such ministers may find their name. One is in the lower list of a Presbytery, where those named would normally renew their certificate annually (except for ministers who retired before 2006, the date of the amendment regarding annual renewal, who do not need to reapply.) In a revamped List I in Section 6, ministers who have resigned their seat (or who are not eligible for a seat) in Presbytery but who renew their certificate are listed, while in List J (formerly List H) are those, fully ministers of Word and Sacrament, who have resigned their seat (or who are not eligible for a seat) and do not wish, or do not have, a practising certificate.

Another sign of the times is the great increase in mobile-phone numbers. If people have offered them, we have put them in. Sometimes, these now replace landlines altogether, continuing the movement towards constant connectedness. The distance yawns between Thoreau's incredulous remark (1849) on hearing of the new telegraph line connecting the two states: 'Maine and Texas, it may be, have nothing important to communicate!' and the order of service in an Oxford church: 'Welcome to the service. Please switch off.' Some, indeed, have multiple telephones to distinguish between their different functions. The wife of one Presbytery clerk refers to his mounted array of phones as his 'Batman utility belt'.

Another new subsection, 'Organist Training Schemes', is found at the end of Section 2, 'General Information'. It stems from the difficulties of some Presbyteries in sourcing organists, and gathers together various approaches to the matter, by Presbyteries themselves as well as other bodies who share the same aim. The desire is still to 'keep music live' in our churches and not to rely on the impersonal 'hymn karaoke' device with its borrowed sounds from cavernous cathedrals in the USA. A colleague, a gifted organist, who is now precentor of an English cathedral, found himself taking services in a country church where there was such a device. However, standing silent was a splendid pipe organ that no-one knew how to play. Thinking the congregation might be delighted to have the live accompaniment from a real instrument for once, he offered to play. The scarcely concealed dismay of the person whose job it was to work the machine warned him he was straying on to someone's jealously defended territory. 'We always do it this way', he was told. There was no live music that day either, but it wasn't a musical matter!

The Very Rev. Dr Gilleasbuig Macmillan KCVO, formerly minister of St Giles' Cathedral, tells of a predecessor in Portree, the Rev. John Mackay, inducted to the North Church in 1927, who every Monday met with his Free Presbyterian counterpart in the town. In both churches, psalms had been led by the voice of the precentor; but the parish church had recently decided to break with tradition, and news had got around. 'I hear', said his colleague drily, 'that you are to get an organ.' He went on: 'All you'll need now is a monkey in the pulpit'. Mackay did not let that pass. 'And all *you'll* need', he countered, 'is an organ!'

Douglas Galbraith
July 2014

ACKNOWLEDGEMENTS

The Editor thanks Dr Roddy MacLeod, who provided the Gaelic material, coining in the process a Gaelic circumlocution for 'navel-gazing'; Roy Pinkerton, whose historical knowledge of the Church assisted Sections 8 and 9 on church buildings and discontinued parish names; Douglas Aitken, who made available the transcripts from his broadcasts from the General Assembly; Sandy Gemmill, who painstakingly assembled the statistics for Section 10; and Jennifer Hamilton for her assistance in Section 7 on legal names and charity numbers. He is also most grateful for the willingness of Presbytery clerks, who, if they minded being continually badgered for the comings and goings of those in their charge, did not show it; and to production editor Ivor Normand, whose trained eye and habit of frequently asking questions makes for a more accurate book than if the Editor had been left to his own devices.

SECTION 1

Assembly Councils,
Committees, Departments and Agencies

[Note: Years, where given, indicate the year of appointment]

1. THE COUNCIL OF ASSEMBLY

The voting members of the Council of Assembly act as the Charity Trustees for the Unincorporated Councils and Committees of the General Assembly: Scottish Charity No. SC011353.

Remit (as amended May 2014)

Introduction
1. The Council of Assembly's main function is to support the Councils and Committees of the Church in seeking to inspire the people of Scotland and beyond with the Good News of Jesus Christ through enthusiastic, worshipping, witnessing, nurturing and serving communities.
2. The Council helps the General Assembly to determine strategy for the Church of Scotland, ensures that the strategic priorities, policies and decisions of the Assembly are implemented effectively and efficiently and supports, resources and nurtures the people of the Church in their work of mission, witness, worship and service.
3. The Council of Assembly is a standing committee of the General Assembly, to which it is directly accountable and to which it reports annually. The General Assembly-appointed members of the Council and the Conveners of the six major Councils are designated as the Charity Trustees of the Unincorporated Councils and Committees of the Church of Scotland (Scottish Charity Number SC011353). The Trustees have 'general control and management of the administration' of the Unincorporated Councils and Committees.
4. The Council has been given authority by the General Assembly to take necessary administrative decisions between General Assemblies and to coordinate, monitor and evaluate the work done by the Councils, Committees and central administrative offices of the Church. The General Assembly has also authorised it to attend to the general interests of the Church in matters which are not covered by the remit of any other Agency.
5. The Senior Management Team exists to support the coordinating and decision-making work of the Council of Assembly and to ensure the efficient implementation of the decisions of it and the General Assembly. The Senior Management Team is accountable to the Council of Assembly, and its minutes are submitted to the Council for information.
6. The Council has committed to displaying in its work and in the behaviour of its members and staff:
    *   confidence in God
    *   trust in each other
    *   servant leadership
    *   collaborative working
    *   enthusiasm.
7. The Council, while exercising a supervisory role, nonetheless commits to working cooperatively and inclusively with Councils, Committees, Presbyteries, Kirk Sessions and all others in the Church, consulting widely where possible. Having regard to the international, evangelical and catholic nature of the Church, the Council of Assembly is committed to working with other churches, at home and overseas, and to encouraging all Agencies to work ecumenically where possible.

Strategy
1. To encourage vision among the members and the Councils and Committees of the Church.

2. To monitor, evaluate and coordinate the work of the Agencies of the General Assembly within the context of policy determined by the Assembly, encouraging the achievement of objectives and the wise use of resources.

3. To oversee the implementation of the Strategic Framework as from time to time agreed by the General Assembly.

4. To advise the General Assembly on the relative priority of work being undertaken by its various Agencies.

5. To keep under review the central administration of the Church, with particular regard to resolving issues of duplication of resources.

6. To advise the General Assembly on matters of reorganisation and structural change, including adjustments to the membership and remits of relevant Agencies of the General Assembly.

7. To advise and work with the Panel on Review and Reform on its priorities and also on the resourcing and implementation of policy decisions arising from its work.

8. To deal with urgent issues arising between meetings of the General Assembly, provided that (a) these do not fall within the jurisdiction of the Commission of Assembly or of any Presbytery or Kirk Session, (b) they are not of a legislative or judicial nature and (c) any action taken in terms of this clause shall be reported to the next General Assembly.

9. To attend to the general interests of the Church in matters which are not covered by the remit of any other Agency.

Governance

10. To exercise the supervisory function required by the Church's Designated Religious Charity status.

11. To ensure adherence to an approved Code of Conduct by the Charity Trustees of the Unincorporated Councils and Committees and to encourage and supervise compliance with such a Code of all other members of Councils and Committees.

12. To advise, support and oversee compliance by Councils, Committees and Presbyteries in the proper discharge of their duties and responsibilities under charity and accounting legislation.

Finance and Stewardship

13. To oversee the management of the finances of the Unincorporated Councils and Committees, ensuring that Church resources are used wisely and effectively and in accordance with the policies, priorities and strategic objectives of the General Assembly.

14. To set appropriate standards of financial management for the Unincorporated Councils and Committees, and to oversee compliance.

15. To supervise and assist Presbyteries and congregations in adhering to financial standards required by charity law and by Regulations of the General Assembly, and to oversee compliance.

16. To oversee the provision of financial services for the Councils and Committees, Statutory Corporations and other Agencies of the General Assembly.

17. To determine policy in relation to the teaching and promotion of Christian stewardship throughout the Church.

18. To provide support to Presbyteries and congregations in the promotion of stewardship with a view to generating sufficient income to resource the worship, mission, nurture and service of the Church.

19. To determine policy in relation to Ministries and Mission Contributions from congregations, subject to the approval of Regulations by the General Assembly and to determine with Presbyteries the Ministries and Mission Contributions required annually from congregations.

20. To determine annually the stipend rate, having regard to the recommendation of the Ministries Council, the determination to be made by the voting members of the Council of Assembly with the exception of those members in receipt of either a salary or stipend from the Parish Ministries Fund.

21. To determine the types and rates of expenses which may be claimed by members serving on Councils, Committees and Statutory Corporations.

22. To bring recommendations to the General Assembly concerning the total amount of the Church's Coordinated Budget for the Parish Ministries Fund and the Mission and Renewal Fund for the following financial year, and to determine the allocation of the budget for the Mission and Renewal Fund among the relevant Agencies of the General Assembly and Ecumenical Bodies.

23. To prepare and present to the General Assembly an indicative Rolling Budget and outline Financial Plan for the following five years.

24. To receive and distribute unrestricted legacies and donations among the Agencies of the General Assembly with power to specify the use to which these funds are to be applied.

25. To reallocate, following upon consultation with the Agency or Agencies affected, unrestricted funds held by or on behalf of any of the Agencies of the General Assembly to another Agency or Agencies with power to specify the use to which the same are to be applied.

26. To prepare, approve and submit annually to the General Assembly the audited Annual Report and Financial Statements of the Unincorporated Councils and Committees of the General Assembly.

Property and Contracts

27. To facilitate strategic property planning across the Unincorporated Councils and Committees to ensure that the best use is made of the property portfolio.

28. To consider and decide on proposals from Agencies of the General Assembly to purchase heritable property or any other asset (except investments) valued in excess of £50,000 or to lease any heritable property where the annual rental is greater than £25,000 per annum. No Agency except those referred to in section 31 of this remit shall purchase or lease such property without prior approval from the Council of Assembly.

29. To consider and decide on proposals from Agencies of the General Assembly, except for those referred to in section 31 of this remit, to sell or lease for a period in excess of five years or otherwise dispose of any heritable property, or to sell or otherwise dispose of any asset (except investments) valued above £50,000, held by or on behalf of that Agency. The Council of Assembly shall have power to allocate all or part of the sale or lease proceeds to another Agency or Agencies in terms of sections 22 and 25 of this remit.

30. To consider and decide on proposals from Agencies of the General Assembly to enter into an agreement or contract for receipt of goods or services (with the exception of contracts of employment or those relating to property transactions) with a total actual or potential financial commitment in excess of £50,000. No Agency shall proceed to enter into such an agreement or contract without prior approval from the Council.

31. To assume ownership of the Church Offices at 117–123 George Street, Edinburgh, title to which shall be held by the Church of Scotland General Trustees for behoof of the Council.

32. To be responsible for the proper maintenance and insurance of the Church Offices at 117–123 George Street.

33. To be responsible for policy matters relating to Health and Safety within the Church Offices.

34. For the avoidance of doubt, sections 28, 29 and 30 shall not apply to the Church of Scotland General Trustees and the Church of Scotland Housing and Loan Fund for Retired Ministers and Widows and Widowers of Ministers, both of which may deal with heritable property and other assets without the approval of the Council.

Staffing and Management

35. To receive reports from, offer guidance to and issue instructions to Agencies of the General Assembly as required from time to time on matters of management, resourcing, organisation, governance and administration.

36. To determine staffing and resourcing requirements of Agencies of the General Assembly, including inter-Departmental sharing or transfer of staff, in accordance with policies drawn up by the Council of Assembly in line with priorities approved by the General Assembly, it being declared that the term 'staffing' shall not include those directly employed by the Ministries Council, the Social Care Council or the World Mission Council.

37. To consult with the relative Councils and Agencies in their appointment of Council Secretaries to the Church and Society, Ministries, Mission and Discipleship, Social Care and World Mission Councils, to appoint the Ecumenical Officer, the Head of Stewardship, the Head of Communications and the Head of Human Resources and Information Technology and to nominate individuals to the General Assembly for appointment to the offices of Principal Clerk of the General Assembly, Depute Clerk of the General Assembly, Secretary to the Council of Assembly, General Treasurer of the Church and Solicitor of the Church.

38. To act as one of the employing agencies of the Church and to assume and exercise the whole rights, functions and responsibilities of the Central Services Committee in that regard.

39. To have responsibility for determining the terms and conditions of the staff for which it is the employing agency.

40. To have responsibility for policy matters relating to Data Protection within the Church Offices and with respect to the General Assembly Councils based elsewhere.

41. To oversee the delivery of central services to departments within the Church Offices, to Councils of the General Assembly and, where appropriate, to the Statutory Corporations, Presbyteries and Congregations, namely:
     (a) Those facilities directly managed by the Facilities Manager;
     (b) Information Technology (including the provision of support services to Presbytery Clerks);
     (c) Human Resources;
     (d) Legal Services (as delivered by the Law Department and subject to such oversight not infringing principles of 'client/solicitor' confidentiality);
     (e) Property Services.

Communication

42. To oversee the development and implementation of the General Assembly's Communication Strategy across the Church.

43. To oversee and manage any major reputational opportunities and risks for the Church, working with other Agencies as appropriate.

44. To oversee effective communication with members and courts of the Church, encouraging good practice.

For the purposes only of this remit, the term 'Agencies' shall mean the following bodies being Standing Committees of the General Assembly, namely:

- *The following Councils: Church and Society, Ministries, Mission and Discipleship, Social Care, World Mission.*
- *The following Committees: Assembly Arrangements, Central Services, Chaplains to Her Majesty's Forces, Ecumenical Relations, Legal Questions, Panel on Review and Reform, Safeguarding, Theological Forum.*

Membership
The Council shall comprise the following:
1. Convener, Vice-Convener and ten members appointed by the General Assembly on the Report of the Nomination Committee.
2. The Conveners of the Councils, namely Church and Society, Ministries, Mission and Discipleship, Social Care and World Mission together with the Convener of the Panel on Review and Reform.
3. The Secretaries of the following Councils, namely Church and Society, Ministries, Mission and Discipleship, Social Care and World Mission, all with a right to speak on matters affecting the interest of their Council, but not to vote or make a motion.
4. The Principal Clerk, the General Treasurer and the Solicitor of the Church without a right to vote or make a motion.
5. The Secretary to the Council of Assembly without a right to vote or make a motion.
6. Other officials, as required by the Council, to be in attendance from time to time without a right to vote or make a motion.

Powers and Framework (Trusteeship)
1. The General Assembly of 2011 approved a Strategic Framework to be used to help to identify priorities and to assist with the process of budgeting and resource allocation. The framework identifies the context in which we work and sets out core strategic priorities for the Church of Scotland, in particular for its Councils and Committees. It also sets out the core values. The Framework makes it clear both what the Church's Councils and Committees should be doing and how they should be doing it. The Council of Assembly uses the Framework to help it to monitor and evaluate progress and commends it to other Councils and Committees and to the wider Church.
2. The General Assembly of 2010 appointed the voting members of the Council of Assembly to act as charity trustees for the Unincorporated Councils and Committees of the General Assembly (the Church of Scotland, Scottish Charity Number SC011353). 'Charity trustees' means the persons having the general control and management of the administration of a charity. A charity trustee must act in the interests of the charity and must, in particular, seek in good faith to ensure that the charity acts in a manner which is consistent with its purposes. All trustees must act with the care and diligence that it is reasonable to expect of a person who is managing the affairs of another person. The Conveners of the Church and Society Council, Ministries Council, Mission and Discipleship Council, Social Care Council and World Mission Council, and of the Panel on Review and Reform, are voting members of the Council and therefore charity trustees. Their first duty is to the interests of the Church of Scotland as a whole and not to their individual Councils.
3. The General Assembly decided that all trustees should:
    * possess an understanding of the life and culture of the Church of Scotland; and
    * be committed to developing and implementing the vision and mission of the General Assembly; and
    * possess an understanding of Scotland's contemporary culture.
    In addition, the Assembly requires that the Council has the following specific areas of expertise among its trustees:
    * communication
    * finance
    * governance
    * law (civil and church)
    * management
    * strategic planning

- theology
- training.

4. The Assembly recommended that trustees in receipt of a salary or stipend from the Church ought not to be in a majority; and the Nomination Committee takes account of this as it seeks to fill vacancies. The Council maintains a register of trustees' interests; this helps to ensure public confidence and also acts as a protection for individual trustees should there ever be allegations of impropriety. A Code of Conduct is in place. It sets out the key principles of trusteeship, advises on confidentiality and declaration of interests, provides a framework for expenses and contains provision for dealing with breaches of the Code.

5. Regular opportunities are given for voting members of the Council of Assembly to meet alone as charity trustees. This applies, for example, when significant staffing matters are under consideration.

6. Trustees may be personally liable in law for the actions of the Unincorporated Councils and Committees. The Council of Assembly, aided by the Audit Committee, has established a framework of realistic and robust risk assessments for all areas of Council and Committee work, across the Church. This helps trustees to exercise their duties under charity law and would also help to protect them against unexpected liabilities.

7. The Council has drawn up a Scheme of Delegation. This details the extent of and limits to the decision-making powers of the Council of Assembly, its groups and subcommittees, other Councils and Committees and senior staff. The Scheme is based on the formal remit of the Council of Assembly but sets out more clearly how those broad powers operate in practice.

Convener: Rev. S. Grant Barclay LLB DipLP BD MSc PhD (2012)
Vice-Convener: Iain Johnston BA (2012)
Secretary: Mrs Pauline Weibye MA DPA Chartered FCIPD

2. THE CHURCH AND SOCIETY COUNCIL

Remit

The remit of the Church and Society Council is to facilitate the Church of Scotland's engagement with, and comment upon, national, political and social issues through:

- the development of theological, ethical and spiritual perspectives in the formulation of policy on such issues;
- the effective representation of the Church of Scotland in offering on its behalf appropriate and informed comment on political and social issues;
- the building, establishing and maintaining of a series of networks and relationships with leaders and influence-shapers in civic society, and engaging long-term in dialogue and the exchange of ideas with them;
- the support of the local church in its mission and engagement by offering professional and accessible resources on contemporary issues;
- the conducting of an annual review of progress made in discharging the remit and the provision of a written report to the Council of Assembly.

   The Church and Society Council also has oversight of a number of other specialised parts of the Church's work:

- **Education**: the oldest standing committee of the Church, working to ensure that chaplains to schools and further-education colleges are appropriately supported and resourced, and to encourage both religious education and religious observance (time for reflection) in schools.

  Policy Officer: Rev. Ken Coulter (E-mail: kcoulter@cofscotland.org.uk)

- **Responding to Climate Change Project (RCCP)**: helping the Church locally, nationally and internationally to respond to the challenge of climate change. The Project also works with partner organisations to engage in debate with government and other decision-makers. (See also Eco-Congregation Scotland, p. 61.)

  Project Officer: Adrian Shaw (E-mail: ashaw@cofscotland.org.uk)

- **Society, Religion and Technology Project (SRTP):** helping the Church to engage with ethical issues in relation to science, and seeking to bring a Christian ethical reflection on the impact of technology on society.

  Policy Officer: Dr Murdo Macdonald (E-mail: mmacdonald@cofscotland.org.uk)

Membership

Convener, Vice-Convener, 28 members appointed by the General Assembly, one of whom will also be appointed to the Ecumenical Relations Committee, and one member appointed from and by the Social Care Council and the Guild. The Nomination Committee will ensure that the Council membership contains at least five individuals with specific expertise in each of the areas of Education, Societal/Political, Science and Technology and Social/Ethical. This number may include the Convener and Vice-Convener of the Council.

Convener: Rev. Sally Foster-Fulton BA BD (2012)
Vice-Convener: Rev. J. Christopher Wigglesworth MBE BSc PhD BD (2012)
Acting Secretary: Rev. Graham K. Blount LLB BD PhD

---

3. THE MINISTRIES COUNCIL
Tel: 0131-225 5722; Fax: 0131-240 2201
E-mail: ministries@cofscotland.org.uk

Ministries Council Remit

The remit of the Ministries Council is the enabling of ministries in every part of Scotland, giving special priority to the poorest and most marginalised, through the recruitment, training and support of recognised ministries of the Church and the assessment and monitoring of patterns of deployment of those ministries. Further details on the recognised ministries of the Church are available on the Church's website (http://www.churchofscotland.org.uk/serve/ministries_in_the_church) as well as information on other aspects of the work of the Council (http://www.churchofscotland.org.uk/about_us/councils_committees_and_departments/councils/ministries_council).

In the fulfilment of this remit, the Council offers strategic leadership in the development of patterns of collaborative ministry which enable the Church of Scotland to be effective in its missionary calling and faithful in its participation in the one ministry of Jesus Christ, and operates within the following spheres of work:

Priority Areas – following the Gospel imperative of priority to the poor
(http://www.churchofscotland.org.uk/serve/priority_areas/about_priority_areas)

- Working directly in support of the poorest parishes in Scotland to enable and resource ministries and to build communities of hope;
- Assisting the whole Church in fulfilling its responsibility to the Gospel imperative of giving priority to the poorest and most marginalised in society;
- Enabling and supporting work in partnership with ecumenical, inter-faith and statutory agencies to achieve the goal of alleviating poverty in Scotland.

Education and Support – recruitment, training and support of ministries personnel
(http://www.churchofscotland.org.uk/serve/ministries_in_the_church/training_for_ministries)
- Promoting and publicising the ministries of the Church at a programme of local and national events;
- Developing and implementing patterns of discernment and assessment and vocational guidance which enable the identification of appropriately called and gifted people to train for recognised ministries;
- Developing and implementing training patterns for those accepted into training for the recognised ministries of the Church;
- Enabling the transfer of people from other denominations into the ministries of the Church;
- Delivering pastoral support to those involved in the recognised ministries of the Church through the development and resourcing of local pastoral networks, direct one-to-one engagement and the provision of occupational health support, counselling, mediation and conflict-resolution services;
- Promoting and providing vocational guidance and lifelong learning opportunities for ministries personnel through in-service events, self-appraisal processes, Continuing Ministerial Development and a study-leave programme.

Partnership Development – working with Presbyteries and other partners in planning and resourcing ministries
(http://www.churchofscotland.org.uk/serve/ministries_in_the_church/ministries_for_communities)
- Working with Presbyteries for effective deployment of ministries to meet the needs of the parishes of Scotland and beyond, including consulting with congregations and other denominations where appropriate;
- Working in partnership with other agencies of the Church and ecumenical partners, to enable the emergence of ministries to meet the needs of the people of Scotland in every part;
- Supporting those engaged in chaplaincy services both directly employed by the Council and employed by other agencies;
- Engaging in partnership with Presbyteries in the deployment of Interim and Transition Ministries;
- Overseeing locum arrangements and Temporary Assistance.

Finance – ensuring good management of funds and monitoring budgets
- Planning strategically for the future funding of the recognised ministries of the Church;
- Managing the funds and overseeing the budgeting processes of the Council to ensure that maximum benefit is derived for the Church's ministries through the use of income and capital;
- Preparing recommendations on the level of stipends and salaries and liaising with Pension Trustees on matters relating to the setting of the Standard Annuity and discretionary increases in pension, and negotiating and reaching agreement with Pension Trustees on funding rates.

Membership
Convener, four Vice-Conveners, 38 members appointed by the General Assembly, one of whom will also be appointed to the Ecumenical Relations Committee, and one member appointed from and by the General Trustees, the Housing and Loan Fund, the Committee on Chaplains to Her Majesty's Forces and the Diaconate Council. For the avoidance of doubt, where a representative of these other bodies is a member of staff, he or she will have no right to vote.

Convener:	Rev. Neil J. Dougall BD
Vice-Conveners:	Rev. Colin M. Brough BSc BD
	Rev. Neil M. Glover
	Rev. Marjory A. MacLean LLB BD PhD RNR
	Rev. Derek H.N. Pope BD

Staff

Council Secretary:	Rev. Martin Scott DipMusEd RSAM BD PhD
	(Tel: ext. 2389; E-mail: mscott@cofscotland.org.uk)
Education and Support Secretary:	Rev. Marjory McPherson LLB BD
	(Tel: ext. 2315; E-mail: mmcpherson@cofscotland.org.uk)
Partnership Development Secretary:	Rev. Angus R. Mathieson MA BD
	(Tel: ext. 2312; E-mail: amathieson@cofscotland.org.uk)
Priority Areas Secretary:	Rev. H. Martin J. Johnstone MA BD MTh PhD
	(Tel: 0141-248 2905; E-mail: mjohnstone@cofscotland.org.uk)
Strategic Projects Manager:	Ms Catherine Skinner BA MA
	(Tel: ext. 2274; cskinner@cofscotland.org.uk)
Ministries Support Officers:	Rev. Jane Denniston MA BD MTh
	(Tel: ext. 2204; E-mail: jdenniston@cofscotland.org.uk)
	Rev. Gavin J. Elliott MA BD
	(Tel: ext. 2255; E-mail: gelliott@cofscotland.org.uk)
	Mr Noel Mathias BA BTh MA
	(Tel: 0141-248 2905; E-mail: nmathias@cofscotland.org.uk)
	Mr John Thomson
	(Tel: ext. 2248; E-mail: jthomson@cofscotland.org.uk)
	Mrs Joyce Watkinson CQSW COSCA, Accredited Counsellor
	(Tel: ext. 2225; E-mail: jwatkinson@cofscotland.org.uk)
	Mrs Moira Whyte MA
	(Tel: ext. 2266; E-mail: mwhyte@cofscotland.org.uk)
Go For It Manager:	Ms Shirley Grieve BA PGCE
	(Tel: ext. 2438; E-mail: sgrieve@cofscotland.org.uk)
Go For It Training and Development Officer:	Miss Catherine McIntosh MA
	(Tel: ext. 2319; E-mail: cmcintosh@cofscotland.org.uk)
The Chance to Thrive Project Co-ordinator:	Rev. Russell McLarty MA BD
	(Tel: 0141-248 2905; E-mail: rmclarty@cofscotland.org.uk)

Ministries Council
Further information about the Council's work and services is available on the Church's website (http://www.churchofscotland.org.uk/about_us/councils_committees_and_departments/councils/

ministries_council) as well as from the Ministries Council staff team at the Church Offices. Information is available on a wide range of matters including the Consolidated Stipend Fund, National Stipend Fund, endowment grants, travelling and other expenses, pulpit supply, study leave, ministries development conferences, pastoral care services (including occupational health), discernment and assessment, education and training, Presbytery Planning, Priority Areas, New Charge Development, Interim and Transition Ministries, Readership, Chaplaincies, the Diaconate, Ministries Development Staff (MDS), the *Go For It* Fund, Emerging Church, and all aspects of work connected with ministers and the ministry of word and sacrament.

Committees
The policy development and implementation of the work of the Ministries Council is managed under the following committees:

1.   Strategic Planning Group
Convener: Rev. Neil J. Dougall BD
The Strategic Planning Group comprises the Convener, Vice-Conveners and senior staff of all four areas (including Finance) of the Council and is empowered by the Council to engage in broad-ranging thinking regarding the future outlook and plans of the Council. It reports directly to Council and brings forward to it ideas and consultation papers offering options as to the future strategic direction of the Council's work. Though a key part of the Council's work, it is a consultative and advisory group rather than a decision-making one.

2.   Priority Areas Committee
Convener: Rev. Derek H.N. Pope BD
The Priority Areas Committee implements the policy of the Council in developing, encouraging and overseeing strategy within Priority Area parishes. It is empowered to develop resources to enable congregations to make appropriate responses to the needs of people living in poverty in their parishes, and to raise awareness of the effects of poverty on people's lives in Scotland. It also co-ordinates the strategy of the wider Church in its priority to Scotland's poorest parishes.

3.   Education and Support Committee
Convener: Rev. Marjory A. MacLean LLB BD PhD RNR
The Education and Support Committee is responsible for the development and oversight of policy in relation to the discernment and assessment process for ministers of Word and Sacrament (full-time and ordained local ministry), Deacons and Readers, together with the admission and readmission of ministers. It is further responsible for the supervision of those in training for those recognised ministries of the Church and operates with powers in relation to both of these areas of work to make recommendations on suitability for training and readiness to engage in ministries at the end of a training period. It also implements Council policies on pastoral care for all recognised ministries, the integration of Occupational Health with ministries support services, and the oversight of the working of those Acts relating to long-term illness of ministers in charges. It promotes development opportunities for those engaged in recognised ministries, including study leave and accompanied reviews.

4.   Partnership Development Committee
Convener: Rev. Colin M. Brough BSc BD
The Partnership Development Committee is responsible for maintaining and developing relationships with Presbyteries and other agencies and partners in the planning and resourcing of ministries. This includes the overall planning of the deployment of the Church's ministries,

primarily through the ongoing monitoring of the development of Presbytery Plans. The Committee also oversees work on emerging ministries (including Fresh Expressions and New Charge Development work). It deals further with the work of Interim Ministry and with all aspects of chaplaincy work. The Committee also oversees the Church of Scotland *Go For It* Fund.

The Committee also provides 50% of the funding towards the work of the Fresh Expressions Development Worker, the Rev. David McCarthy, and contributes, as partners with the Mission and Discipleship Council, towards the Church of Scotland's engagement with the UK-wide Fresh Expressions movement.

5. Finance Committee
Convener: Rev. Neil M. Glover

The Finance Committee maintains an oversight of the budgets for the Council. It also operates with powers to deal with the Parish Ministries Fund, the National Stipend Scheme, Maintenance Allowances, Hardship Grants and Bursaries, Stipend Advances, management of investments, writing-off shortfalls and the granting of further endowments.

The Council also has several *ad hoc* Groups, which report to the Committees and implement specific policies of the Council, as follows:

The Chance to Thrive Steering Group
Leader: Mr Raymond K. Young CBE BArch FRIAS

Recruitment Task Group
Leader: Rev. Andrea E. Price

Training Task Group
Leader: Rev. A. Leslie Milton MA BD PhD

Pastoral and Vocational Care Task Group
Leader: Rev. Mhorag Macdonald MA BD

Go For It Fund Committee (see below)
Convener: Rev. Rolf H. Billes BD

Presbytery Planning Task Group
Leader: Rev. Alison A. Meikle BD

Interim Ministries Task Group
Leader: Rev. Scott Raby LTh

Joint Emerging Church Group (with Mission and Discipleship Council)
Leader: Rev. Norman A. Smith MA BD

Chaplaincies Forum
Leader: Mr W. Alan Imrie BA

Other related bodies:
Chaplains to HM Forces
See separate entry at number 10.

The Church of Scotland Housing and Loan Fund
See separate entry at number 12.

Go For It: Funding Change in Church and Community
The Committee comprises members appointed by the Nominations Committee to the Ministries Council, as well as a number of co-opted members with appropriate skills and knowledge. The Mission and Discipleship Council and the Church and Society Council are also represented.

Convener: Rev. Rolf H. Billes BD
Manager: Ms Shirley Grieve BA PGCE
Training and Development Officer: Miss Catherine McIntosh MA
Administrator: Mrs Susan Calderhead

Go For It is about funding change in church and community. The Fund aims to encourage creative ways of working which develop the life and mission of the local church and are transformative for both communities and congregations. The focus is very much on 'the local'; and any application must be able to demonstrate clearly its association with at least one Church of Scotland congregation. Part of a successful application to Go For It will be the demonstration of a commitment to good partnership working.

There are five criteria for funding, and successful applicants will meet at least two of these:
•   meeting identified needs in a community
•   nurturing Christian faith within and beyond the Church
•   tackling poverty and/or social injustice
•   developing new ecclesial/Christian communities
•   creating work which is genuinely innovative, developing good practice that can be shared.

The Fund gives grants totalling in the region of £1 million per annum. Awards of up to £45,000 (over a three-year period) are available to part-fund locally based work. Additional support is available for projects which can clearly demonstrate that they are engaged with the very poorest members of Scottish society.

We want to encourage local Christians to have creative ideas and then, with the support and help of the Fund, to turn these ideas into practice – to really Go For It.

Full information is available at www.churchofscotland.org.uk/serve/go_for_it. You can contact the Go For It Team on 0131-225 5722 or by e-mailing goforit@cofscotland.org.uk

Pulpit Supply: Fee and Expenses
The General Assembly of 2011 approved new regulations governing the amount of Supply Fee and Expenses. These were effective from 1 April 2012 and are as follows:
1.   In Charges where there is only one diet of worship, the Pulpit Supply Fee shall be a Standard Fee of £55 (or as from time to time agreed by the Ministries Council).
2.   In Charges where there are additional diets of worship on a Sunday, the person fulfilling the Supply shall be paid £15 for each additional Service (or as from time to time agreed by the Ministries Council).
3.   Where the person is unwilling to conduct more than one diet of worship on a given Sunday, he or she shall receive a pro-rata payment based on the total available Fee shared on the basis of the number of Services conducted.
4.   The Fee thus calculated shall be payable in the case of all persons permitted to conduct Services under Act II 1986.
5.   In all cases, Travelling Expenses shall be paid. Where there is no convenient public conveyance, the use of a private car shall be paid for at the rate of 25p per mile for Travelling Expenses. In exceptional circumstances, to be approved in advance, the cost of hiring a car may be met.

6. Where weekend board and lodging are agreed as necessary, these may be claimed for the weekend at a maximum rate of that allowed when attending the General Assembly. The Fee and Expenses should be paid to the person providing the Supply before he or she leaves on the Sunday.

4. THE MISSION AND DISCIPLESHIP COUNCIL
E-mail: mandd@cofscotland.org.uk; Website: www.resourcingmission.org.uk

Remit
The remit of the Mission and Discipleship Council is:
*   to take a lead role in developing and maintaining an overall focus for mission in Scotland, and to highlight its fundamental relationships with worship, service, education and nurture;
*   to take a lead role in developing strategies, resources and services in Christian education and nurture, recognising these as central to both mission and discipleship;
*   to offer appropriate servicing and support nationally, regionally and locally in the promotion of nurturing, worshipping and witnessing communities of faith;
*   to introduce policy on behalf of the Church in the following areas: adult education and elder training, church art and architecture, congregational mission and development, resourcing youth and children's work, worship;
*   to establish and support the Mission Forum with representatives of relevant Councils;
*   to encourage appropriate awareness of, and response to, the requirements of people with particular needs including physical, sensory and/or learning disabilities;
*   to conduct an annual review of progress made in discharging the remit and provide a written report to the Council of Assembly.

Statement of Purpose
The purpose of the Mission and Discipleship Council is to resource God's people in the Church of Scotland for worship, witness, mission and discipleship, enabling and empowering the Church to share God's love in the name of the Father, Son and Holy Spirit, mindful of the changing contemporary culture of Scotland and beyond. Specifically, we will stimulate and support the Church:
*   to reflect critically on our practice and places of worship, and bring about creative change;
*   to communicate the good news of Christ's message;
*   to engage in mission beyond our walls;
*   to nurture in all a discipleship of learning and service;
*   to have a renewed vision that understands what it is to be the body of Christ through the Holy Spirit.

Membership
Convener, three Vice-Conveners and 24 members appointed by the General Assembly, one of whom will also be appointed to the Ecumenical Relations Committee, the Director of Stewardship, one member appointed from and by the General Trustees and the Guild, and the Convener of the Committee on Church Art and Architecture. The Nomination Committee will ensure that the Council membership contains individuals with specific expertise in the areas of Mission, Education, Worship and Media.

Convener: Rev. Colin A.M. Sinclair BA BD
Vice-Conveners: Rev. Daniel J.M. Carmichael MA BD
                                           Rev. Norman A. Smith MA BD
                                           Mr John Hawthorn BSc

Staff
Council Secretary: Rev. Alister W. Bull BD DipMin MTh PhD
                                           (E-mail: abull@cofscotland.org.uk)
Church Without Walls Team Leader: Mrs Lesley Hamilton-Messer MA
                                           (E-mail: lhamilton-messer@cofscotland.org.uk)
Congregational Learning Team Leader: Mr Ronald H. Clarke BEng MSc PGCE
                                           (E-mail: rhclarke@cofscotland.org.uk)
Resourcing Worship Team Leader: Mr Graham Fender-Allison BA
                                           (E-mail: gfender-allison@cofscotland.org.uk)

Mission Development Workers
Mission Development Workers are tasked with supporting local congregations to help them become more resourceful so that they can engage effectively with their communities. They are:

Mr Steve Aisthorpe BA   (E-mail: saisthorpe@cofscotland.org.uk)
Mr Robert Rawson BA   (E-mail: rrawson@cofscotland.org.uk)
Mr Iain Campbell BA PGDE   (E-mail: icampbell@cofscotland.org.uk)

Specialist Development Workers
The following staff members provide specialist advice and support to congregations on key areas of work:

Vacancy   Worship Development Worker
Ms Suzi Farrant BSc BA   Children and Young People Development Worker
                                           (E-mail: sfarrant@cofscotland.org.uk)
Mr David Plews MA MTh   Learning Development Worker
                                           (E-mail: dplews@cofscotland.org.uk)
Rev. David McCarthy BSc BD   Fresh Expressions Development Worker
                                           (E-mail: dmccarthy@cofscotland.org.uk)

The Netherbow: Scottish Storytelling Centre: The integrated facilities of the **Netherbow Theatre** and the **John Knox House Museum**, together with the outstanding conference and reception areas, are an important cultural and visitor centre on the Royal Mile in Edinburgh and provide advice and assistance nationally in the use of the arts in mission, education and worship. 'Story Source', 'Scriptaid' and other resources are available. Contact the Netherbow: Scottish Storytelling Centre, 43–45 High Street, Edinburgh EH1 1SR (Tel: 0131-556 9579; E-mail; reception@scottishstorytellingcentre.com; Website: www.scottishstorytellingcentre.co.uk).

Life and Work
(Tel: 0131-225 5722; Fax: 0131-240 2207; E-mail: magazine@lifeandwork.org)
Life and Work is the Church of Scotland's monthly magazine. Its purpose is to keep the Church informed about events in church life at home and abroad and to provide a forum for Christian opinion and debate on a variety of topics. It has an independent editorial policy. Contributions which are relevant to any aspect of the Christian faith are welcome.

The price of *Life and Work* this year is £2.00. With a circulation of around 25,000, it also offers advertisers a first-class opportunity to reach a discerning readership in all parts of Scotland.

Saint Andrew Press

Saint Andrew Press is managed on behalf of the Church of Scotland by Hymns Ancient and Modern. New titles include the recently published *Reflections on Eldership: Insights from Practising Elders*, compiled by Laurence Wareing. This book is packed with insights from elders that will enthral anyone who is an elder or who wants to understand the vital 'silent army' of the Church. Other titles include *Freedom and Faith: A Question of Scottish Identity* by Donald Smith; *A Simple Life: Roland Walls and the Community of the Transfiguration* by John Miller; *Iona: The Other Island* by Kenneth Steven and Iain Sarjeant; *Scots Worship: Advent, Christmas and Epiphany*; *Black Diamonds and the Blue Brazil* by Ron Ferguson; and *Barclay on the Lectionary Year B* by William Barclay. A paperback edition of the acclaimed *Looking for Mrs Livingstone* by Julie Davidson has also been released.

As Saint Andrew Press celebrates its sixtieth birthday, forthcoming titles include the exciting new practical worship resource *Where Two or Three Are Gathered* by the Rev. Lezley Stewart; a wonderful celebration of Scottish spirituality, *Soul of Scotland* by Harry Reid; and the definitive book about Scotland's pilgrim routes, *The Pilgrim Guide to Scotland* by Donald Smith.

All books, CDs and Church of Scotland stationery can be ordered by telephoning 01603 785925 or by e-mail to orders@norwichbooksandmusic.co.uk

Saint Andrew Press invites readers to visit its website at www.standrewpress.com for a full list of publications, news of helpful new resources, competitions, special events, author news, exclusive offers and information on how to submit proposals for publication. Please contact Ann Crawford (ann@hymnsam.co.uk) with any queries about proposals. Saint Andrew Press is also on Twitter @standrewpress.

Committee on Church Art and Architecture

Convener: Dr J.G. Roberts MA

Membership
The Committee shall comprise a Convener, Vice-Convener and 15 members appointed by the General Assembly.

Remit
This Committee replaced the Committee on Artistic Matters and takes forward that Committee's remit, which is in the following terms:

The Committee advises congregations and Presbyteries regarding the most appropriate way of carrying out renovations, alterations and reordering of interiors, having regard to the architectural quality of Church buildings. It also advises on the installation of stained glass, tapestries, memorials, furniture and furnishings, and keeps a list of accredited artists and craftsworkers.

Any alteration to the exterior or interior of a Church building which affects its appearance must be referred to the Committee for approval, which is given through the General Trustees. Congregations contemplating alterations are urged to consult the Committee at an early stage.

Members of the Committee are prepared, when necessary, to visit churches and meet office-bearers. The Committee's services are given free.

The Committee seeks the conservation of the nation's heritage as expressed in its Church buildings, while at the same time helping to ensure that these buildings continue to serve the worship and witness of the Church in the present day.

In recent years, the General Assembly has conferred these additional duties on the Committee:

1. preparation of reports on the architectural, historical and aesthetic merit of the buildings of congregations involved in questions of readjustment
2. verification of the propriety of repair and renovation work forming the basis of grant applications to public bodies
3. the offering of advice on the maintenance and installation of organs
4. the processing of applications from congregations for permission to dispose of surplus communion plate, and the carrying out of an inventory of sacramental vessels held by congregations.

Work with Rural Churches

The Council aims to affirm, support and resource rural churches. It seeks to reflect the full extent of rural experience, encompassing farming, fishing, tourism, forestry and other professions/ industries that have a bearing on rural life. This will involve collaboration with ecumenical partners and responding periodically to requests for submissions to government consultations.

---

5. THE SOCIAL CARE COUNCIL
(CrossReach)
Charis House, 47 Milton Road East, Edinburgh EH15 2SR
Tel: 0131-657 2000; Fax: 0131-657 5000
E-mail: info@crossreach.org.uk; Website: www.crossreach.org.uk

The Social Care Council, known as CrossReach, provides social-care services as part of the Christian witness of the Church to the people of Scotland.

Remit
The remit of the Social Care Council is:

• as part of the Church's mission, to offer services in Christ's name to people in need;
• to provide specialist resources to further the caring work of the Church;
• to identify existing and emerging areas of need, to guide the Church in pioneering new approaches to relevant problems and to make responses on issues arising within the area of the Council's concern through appropriate channels such as the Church's Church and Society Council, the Scottish Government and the like;
• to conduct an annual review of progress made in discharging the remit and provide an annual written report to the General Assembly;
• to oversee an appropriate corporate management and support service to deliver the above and be responsible for funding all salaries and related costs;
• to set and review terms and conditions of staff and establish appropriate internal governance systems.

Membership
Convener, two Vice-Conveners and 28 members appointed by the General Assembly, one of whom will also be appointed to the Ecumenical Relations Committee. The Council shall have power to appoint such Committees and Groups as it may from time to time determine to be appropriate to ensure that the Council's Remit is fulfilled.

Convener: Dr Sally E. Bonnar (2013)
Vice-Conveners: Ian Huggan (2011)
                             Rev. Dr Richard E. Frazer (2011)
                             Rev. Richard Begg (2014)

Staff
Chief Executive Officer: Peter Bailey (peter.bailey@crossreach.org.uk)

Management Structure
The management structure is service-based. There are three Operational Directors, each with a specialist area of responsibility. They are supported by Heads of Service, who have lead roles for particular types of service and client groups.

Director of Services to Older People: Allan Logan (allan.logan@crossreach.org.uk)
Heads of Service: Brenda Fraser (East)
                                         Morag Waring (West)
                                         Annie McDonald (North)

Director of Adult Care Services: Calum Murray (calum.murray@crossreach.org.uk)
Heads of Service: George McNeilly, Ronnie Black, Andy Cashman

Director of Children and Families: Viv Dickenson (viv.dickenson@crossreach.org.uk)
Head of Service Residential Schools: Paul Gilroy

Director of Finance and Resources: Ian Wauchope (ian.wauchope@crossreach.org.uk)
Business Partners: Arthur Akugbo, Eoin McDunphy, Iwona Lesniak,
                                         Connie Robinson

Director of Human Resources and
   Organisational Development: Mari Rennie (mari.rennie@crossreach.org.uk)
Business Partners: Jane Allan, Corinne Gillies

Head of Estates and Health and Safety: Simon Fitzpatrick (simon.fitzpatrick@crossreach.org.uk)

Health and Safety Manager: Richard Park

Business, Compliance and
   Improvement Head of Service: Claire Hay (claire.hay@crossreach.org.uk)

Business Development Head of Service: Elizabeth Hay (elizabeth.hay@crossreach.org.uk)

List of Services
CrossReach operates 75 services across Scotland, and a list of these can be obtained from Charis House on 0131-657 2000, or from the CrossReach website: www.crossreach.org.uk

---

6. THE WORLD MISSION COUNCIL
Tel: 0131-225 5722
E-mail: world@cofscotland.org.uk

Background
Previously in its history, the Church of Scotland perceived itself to be a large church in a small nation; in today's 'global village', we understand ourselves to be a very small church in world

terms, yet still an integral part of a large worldwide Christian Church. This self-understanding implies that the Church of Scotland's default method of sharing in the mission of God to the whole world must be to work in partnership with others. The World Mission Council (WMC) sees the changing nature of the world Church and wants the Church of Scotland to benefit as widely as possible from the different spiritual experiences that can come from the Church in Europe, South America, Asia, Africa – indeed every corner of the world.

The new remit sets the general direction the WMC wants to travel for the years to come, a journey best described as accompaniment: walking along the road with each other, we find our eyes opened and discover Christ anew as we sit down and eat and talk together, as on the road to Emmaus. WMC wants to see more churches twinned, more people coming to Scotland to visit and enrich our personal, congregational and community lives, and more interactions between Councils of the Church and churches from other countries so that we can learn and grow from involvement with each other.

The strategic aim of the World Mission Council

The aim of the World Mission Council is to enable the Church of Scotland, as part of the holy catholic or universal Church, to participate effectively in the Mission of God in the world, following the example and priorities of Jesus Christ and seeking the guidance of the Holy Spirit.

'*The Spirit of the Lord is on me, because he has anointed me to proclaim good news to the poor. He has sent me to proclaim freedom for the prisoners and recovery of sight for the blind, to set the oppressed free, to proclaim the year of the Lord's favour*' (Luke 4:18–19, NIV).

The World Mission Council seeks to fulfil that aim through the following strategy:

- engaging in a process of attentive accompaniment with the Church of Scotland's partners worldwide (that is, listening to and walking with our partners on our shared journey of faith);
- developing flexible models of partner relationships and service opportunities with the world Church;
- maximising the available human and financial resources;
- maximising the benefits to the Church in Scotland of involvement in the world Church and communicating these benefits to the members and congregations of the Church.

Remit

The remit (approved by the General Assembly 2013) of the World Mission Council is:

- to enable the Church of Scotland, as part of the holy catholic or universal Church, to participate effectively in the Mission of God in the world, following the example of Jesus Christ;
- to discern priorities and establish policies enabling the Church of Scotland to express God's love for the world through the gospel of Jesus Christ;
- to initiate, develop and maintain mutually enriching relationships with churches and church-related organisations internationally;
- to recruit, train and support paid staff and volunteers, sometimes in collaboration with other churches or church-related organisations, to work abroad;
- to inform, encourage and enable members of the Church of Scotland at local, Presbytery and national levels to become engaged in the life of the world Church;
- to encourage and support local partnerships between congregations, Presbyteries and church-related organisations with those in other parts of the world;
- to be informed, and to keep the Church of Scotland informed, about the cultural, political, social, economic, religious and ecclesiastical issues of relevance to worldwide mission;
- to help the people of Scotland to appreciate the worldwide nature of the Christian faith.

Membership
Convener, two Vice-Conveners and 28 members appointed by the General Assembly, one of whom will also be appointed to the Ecumenical Relations Committee, and one member appointed by the Presbytery of Europe (32 in total). In addition, the Church of Scotland Guild sends a representative.

Convener: Rev. Iain D. Cunningham MA BD (2014)
Vice-Conveners: Rev. Christine Sime BSc BD (2012)
                                     Mrs Valerie Brown

Departmental Staff
Council Secretary: Rev. Ian W. Alexander BA BD STM
Secretaries: Jennie Chinembiri (Africa and Caribbean)
                                     Carol Finlay (Twinning and Local Development)
                                     Kenny Roger (Middle East Secretary)
                                     Sandy Sneddon (Asia)

Administration: Donna Maclean

Finance Manager: Catriona Scrimgeour (Assistant Treasurer)

Human Resources: Angela Ocak
                                     Sarah-Jayne McVeigh

Vacancies Overseas
The Council welcomes enquiries from men and women interested in serving in the Church overseas. Vacancies for mission partner appointments in the volunteer programme and opportunities with other organisations can all be considered. Those interested in more information are invited to contact the Human Resources Department at the Church Offices (E-mail: hr@cofscotland.org.uk).

HIV Programme
The Programme aims to raise awareness in congregations about the impact of HIV and AIDS and seeks to channel support to partner churches. For further information, contact Marjorie Clark or Elena Sarra, Co-ordinators (E-mail: hiv@cofscotland.org.uk).

Christian Aid Scotland
Christian Aid is the official relief and development agency of 41 Churches in Britain and Ireland. Christian Aid's mandate is to challenge and enable us to fulfil our responsibilities to the poor of the world. Half a million volunteers and collectors make this possible, with money given by millions of supporters. The Church of Scotland marks its commitment as a Church to this part of its mission through an annual grant from the Mission and Renewal Fund, transmitted through the World Mission Council, which keeps in close touch with Christian Aid and its work. Up-to-date information about projects and current emergency relief work can be obtained from:
• The Head of Christian Aid Scotland, Rev. Dr Kathy Galloway: Christian Aid Scotland, Sycamore House, 290 Bath Street, Glasgow G2 4JR (Tel: 0141-221 7475)
• The Director: Loretta Minghella, Christian Aid Office, PO Box 100, London SE1 7RT (Tel: 020 7620 4444)

Pilgrimage
The Church of Scotland encourages visitors and pilgrims to visit the Christian Community of Israel and Palestine, to walk with them in fellowship and build relationships to help understand their life, witness and situation.

There are two Church of Scotland Residential Centres in Israel which provide comfortable accommodation for pilgrims and visitors to the Holy Land. Further information on planning a pilgrimage experience which includes meetings with the local Christian community and others is available from Colin Johnston (E-mail: revcdj60@gmail.com) and Kenny Roger (E-mail: kroger@cofscotland.org.uk).

(a)   St Andrew's Guest House, 1 David Remez Street, PO Box 8619, Jerusalem 91086, Israel (Tel: 00 972 2 6732401; Fax: 00 972 2 6731711; E-mail: standjer@netvision.net.il)

(b)   The Scots Hotel, St Andrew's, Galilee: 1 Gdud Barak Street, PO Box 104, Tiberias 14100, Israel (Tel: 00 972 4 671 0759; Fax: 00 972 4 672 5282; E-mail: scottie@ netvision.net.il)

A list of Overseas Appointments will be found in List L in Section 6.
A list of Retired Missionaries will be found in List M in Section 6.

---

7. Assembly Arrangements Committee

Membership
Convener, Vice-Convener and ten members appointed by the General Assembly on the Report of the Nomination Committee; the Convener and Vice-Convener also to serve as Convener and Vice-Convener of the General Assembly's Business Committee.

The Clerks are non-voting members of the Assembly Arrangements Committee, and the Moderator and Moderator Designate are members of the Committee.

Convener:	Rev. Derek Browning MA BD DMin
Vice-Convener:	Mrs Judith J.H. Pearson LLB LLM
Secretary:	Acting Principal Clerk

Remit
The Committee's remit is:
* to make all necessary arrangements for the General Assembly;
* to advise the Moderator on his or her official duties if so required;
* to be responsible to the General Assembly for the care and maintenance of the Assembly Hall and the Moderator's flat;
* to be responsible to the General Assembly for all arrangements in connection with the letting of the General Assembly Hall;
* to conduct an annual review of progress made in discharging the remit and provide a written report to the Council of Assembly.

---

8. Central Properties Department

Staff
Property, Health and Safety Manager:	Colin Wallace
Property, Health and Safety Officer:	Jacqueline Collins
Property Officer:	Eunice Hessell
Support Assistant:	Joyce McMurdo

Remit
The Central Properties Department has the remit to provide Property, Facilities and Health and Safety services to the Councils and Departments of the central administration of the Church. This includes:
* management of properties owned by the Councils and Departments
* procurement of land for new-build projects
* delivery of new-build projects including new church buildings
* delivery of major refurbishment programmes
* management of the furlough housing estate for World Mission
* management of facilities and procurement of work equipment
* development and ongoing review of the Health and Safety policy
* provision of Health and Safety management for employing agencies of the Church
* provision of Health and Safety training
* administration of the Health and Safety Committee
* support for arbitrations in the case of parish readjustment.
  Contact: Central Properties Department, 121 George Street, Edinburgh EH2 4YN (Tel: 0131-240 2254; E-mail: cpd@cofscotland.org.uk).

---

9.   Central Services Committee

See under **The Council of Assembly** (number 1): 'Property and Contracts' (page 4); 'Staffing and Management' (page 5).

---

10.   Chaplains to HM Forces

Convener: Rev. Gordon T. Craig BD DipMin
Vice-Convener: Rev. John A.H. Murdoch BA BD DPSS
Secretary: Mr John K. Thomson, Ministries Council, 121 George Street, Edinburgh EH2 4YN

Recruitment
The Chaplains' Committee is entrusted with the task of recruitment of Chaplains for the Regular, Reserve and Auxiliary Forces. Vacancies occur periodically, and the Committee is happy to receive enquiries from all interested ministers.

Forces Registers
The Committee maintains a register of all those who have been baptised and/or admitted to communicant membership by Service Chaplains.
  Parish ministers are asked to take advantage of the facilities by applying for certificates, where appropriate, from the Secretary of the Committee.
  Full information may be obtained from the Secretary, Mr John K. Thomson (Tel: 0131-225 5722; E-mail: jthomson@cofscotland.org.uk).

A list of Chaplains will be found in List C in Section 6.

11.   The Church of Scotland Guild

National Office-bearers and Executive Staff
Convener: Kay Keith MA
Vice-Convener: Linda Young
General Secretary: Iain W. Whyte BA DCE DMS
Associate Secretary: Fiona J. Punton MCIPR
                             (E-mail: fpunton@cofscotland.org.uk)
                             (Tel: 0131-225 5722 ext. 2317 or 0131-240 2217)

The Church of Scotland Guild is a movement within the Church of Scotland whose aim is '**to invite and encourage both women and men to commit their lives to Jesus Christ and to enable them to express their faith in worship, prayer and action**'. Membership of the Guild is open to all who subscribe to that aim.

Groups at congregational level are free to organise themselves under the authority of the Kirk Session, as best suits their own local needs and circumstances. Large groups with frequent meetings and activities continue to operate with a committee or leadership team, while other, smaller groups simply share whatever tasks need to be done among the membership as a whole. Similarly, at Presbyterial Council level, frequency and style of meetings vary according to local needs, as do leadership patterns. Each Council may nominate one person to serve at national level, where five committees take forward the work of the Guild in accordance with the stated Aim. These committees are:

* National Executive
* Finance and General Purposes
* Projects and Topics
* Programmes and Resources
* Marketing and Publicity.

There has always been a close relationship between the Guild and other Departments of the Church, and members welcome the opportunity to contribute to the Church's wider mission through the Project Partnership Scheme and other joint ventures. The Guild is represented on both the Church and Society Council and the Mission and Discipleship Council, and has observers at others.

The project scheme affords groups at congregational level the opportunity to select a project, or projects, from a range of up to six, selected from proposals submitted by a wide range of Church Departments and other Church-related bodies. A project partner in each group seeks ways of promoting the project locally, increasing awareness of the issues raised by it, and encouraging support of a financial and practical nature. Support is available from the Project Co-ordinator at Council level and the Associate Secretary based at the Guild Office.

The Guild is very aware of the importance of good communication in any large organisation, and regularly sends mailings to its groups to pass on information and resources to the members. In addition, the Newsletter, sent to members three times per session, is a useful communication tool, as is the website (www.cos-guild.org.uk). These are a means of sharing experiences and of communicating something of the wider interest and influence of the Guild, which participates in other national bodies such as the Scottish Women's Convention, the Inter-Faith Group on Domestic Abuse and the ACTS Anti-Human Trafficking Group.

Each year, the Guild follows a Theme and produces a resources pack covering worship and study material. There is also a related Discussion Topic with supporting material and background information. The theme, topic and projects all relate to a common three-year strategy which, for

2012–15, is **'Whose we are and Whom we Serve'**, the Guild's motto being chosen to reflect the fact that the Guild marked its 125th anniversary in 2012–13. Under this strategy, the first annual theme was **'A Faith to Proclaim'**. The one for 2013–14 was **'A Fellowship to Build'**, and the final year will be **'A World to Serve'**. At the same time, the Guild is supporting six partnership projects, each chosen to reflect something of the strategy and themes for the triennium. The related discussion topic for 2013–14 is **'Let's talk about ... finding the right way'**.

Further information is available from the Guild Office (Tel: 0131-225 5722 ext. 2317, or 0131-240 2217) or from the website (www.cos-guild.org.uk).

---

12.   The Church of Scotland Housing and Loan Fund for Retired Ministers and Widows and Widowers of Ministers

Membership
The Trustees shall be a maximum of 11 in number, being:
1.   four appointed by the General Assembly on the nomination of the Trustees, who, having served a term of four years, shall be eligible for reappointment;
2.   three ministers and one member appointed by the Ministries Council;
3.   three appointed by the Baird Trust.

Chairman:	Mr J.G. Grahame Lees MA LLB NP
Deputy Chairman:	Rev. Ian Taylor BD ThM
Secretary:	Miss Lin J. Macmillan MA

Staff

Property Manager:	Miss Hilary J. Hardy
Property Assistant:	Mr John Lunn

Remit
The Fund, as established by the General Assembly, facilitates the provision of housing accommodation for retired ministers and widows, widowers and separated or divorced spouses of Church of Scotland ministers. When provided, help may take the form of either a house to rent or a house-purchase loan.

The Trustees may grant tenancy of one of their existing houses or they may agree to purchase for rental occupation an appropriate house of an applicant's choosing. Leases are normally on very advantageous terms as regards rental levels. Alternatively, the Trustees may grant a housing loan of up to 70 per cent of a house-purchase price but with an upper limit. Favourable rates of interest are charged.

The Trustees are also prepared to consider assisting those who have managed to house themselves but are seeking to move to more suitable accommodation. Those with a mortgaged home on retirement may be granted a loan to enable them to repay such a mortgage and thereafter to enjoy the favourable rates of interest charged by the Fund.

Ministers making application within five years of retirement, upon their application being approved, will be given a fairly firm commitment that, in due course, either a house will be made available for renting or a house-purchase loan will be offered. Only within nine months of a minister's intended retiral date will the Trustees initiate steps to find a suitable house; only within one year of that date will a loan be advanced. Applications submitted about ten years prior to retirement have the benefit of initial review and, if approved, a place on the preliminary applications list for appropriate decision in due time.

Donations and legacies over the years have been significant in building up this Fund. Congregational contributions have been, and will continue to be, an essential backbone. The Board of Trustees is a completely independent body answerable to the General Assembly, and enquiries and applications are dealt with in the strictest confidence.

Further information can be obtained from the Secretary, Miss Lin J. Macmillan MA, at the Church of Scotland Offices, 121 George Street, Edinburgh EH2 4YN (Tel: 0131-225 5722 ext. 2310; E-mail: lmacmillan@cofscotland.org.uk; Website: www.churchofscotland.org.uk).

13. Church of Scotland Investors Trust

Membership
(Trustees are appointed by the General Assembly, on the nomination of the Investors Trust)
Chairman: Mr A.W.T. Gibb BA
Vice-Chairman: Ms C.Y. Alexander
Treasurer: Mr I.W. Grimmond BAcc CA
Deputy Treasurer: Mrs A.F. Macintosh BA CA
Secretary: Mrs Nicola Robertson (E-mail: nrobertson@cofscotland.org.uk)

Remit
The Church of Scotland Investors Trust was established by the Church of Scotland (Properties and Investments) Order Confirmation Act 1994 – Scottish Charity Number SC022884 – and offers investment services to the Church of Scotland and to bodies and trusts within or connected with the Church. It offers simple and economical facilities for investment in its three Funds, and investors receive the benefits of professional management, continuous portfolio supervision, spread of investment risk and economies of scale.

The three Funds are:

1. Deposit Fund
The Deposit Fund is intended for short-term investment and seeks to provide a competitive rate of interest while preserving nominal capital value. It is invested mainly in short-term loans to banks and building societies. Interest is calculated quarterly in arrears and paid gross on 15 May and 15 November. Withdrawals are on demand. The Fund is managed by Thomas Miller Investments Limited, Edinburgh and London.

2. Growth Fund
The Growth Fund is a unitised fund, largely equity-based, intended to provide a growing annual income sufficient to meet the Trustees' target distributions and to provide an increase in the value of capital long term. Units can only be purchased or sold on a monthly dealing date, and income is distributed gross on 15 May and 15 November. The Fund is managed by Newton Investment Management Limited, London.

3. Income Fund
The Income Fund is a unitised fund, invested predominantly in fixed-interest securities, intended to provide a high and sustainable income at a level as agreed between the Trustees and the manager from time to time and to protect the long-term nominal value of capital. Units can only be purchased or sold on a monthly dealing date, and income is distributed gross on 4 April and 4 October. The Fund is managed by Royal London Asset Management, London.

Further information and application forms for investment are available on the Church of Scotland website or by writing to the Secretary, The Church of Scotland Investors Trust, 121 George Street, Edinburgh EH2 4YN (E-mail: nrobertson@cofscotland.org.uk).

14.   The Church of Scotland Pension Trustees

Chairman: Mr W. John McCafferty ACII APFS TEP
Vice-Chairman: Mr Graeme R. Caughey BSc FFIA
Secretary: Mr Steven D. Kaney BSc MPMI

Staff
Pensions Manager: Mr Steven D. Kaney BSc MPMI
Pensions Administrators: Miss Fiona McCulloch
                            Mrs Mary Mackenzie
                            Miss Marshall Paterson
Team Secretary: Mrs Nancy Harper

Remit
The body acts as Trustees for the Church of Scotland's three closed Defined Benefits/Final Salary Pension Schemes:
1.   The Church of Scotland Pension Scheme for Ministers and Overseas Missionaries
2.   The Church of Scotland Pension Scheme for Staff
3.   The Church of Scotland Pension Scheme for Presbytery and Parish Workers.
The Trustees have wide-ranging duties and powers detailed in the Trust Law, Pension Acts and other regulations, but in short the Trustees are responsible for the administration of the Pension Schemes and for the investment of the Scheme Funds. Six Trustees are appointed by the General Assembly, and members nominate up to three Trustees for each Scheme.
    The investment of the Funds is delegated to external Investment Managers under the guidelines and investment principles set by the Trustees: Baillie Gifford & Co., Newton Investment Management Ltd, BlackRock, Kames, Rogge and Legal & General.
    The benefits provided by the three Pension Schemes differ in detail, but all provide a pension to the Scheme member and dependants on death of the member, and a lump-sum death benefit on death in service.
    Further information on any of the Church of Scotland Pension Schemes or on individual benefits can be obtained from the Pensions Manager, Church of Scotland Offices, 121 George Street, Edinburgh EH2 4YN (Tel: 0131-225 5722; E-mail: pensions@cofscotland.org.uk).

15.   The Church of Scotland Trust

Membership
(Members are appointed by the General Assembly, on the nomination of the Trust)
Chairman: Mr John M. Hodge WS
Vice-Chairman: Mr Christopher N. Mackay WS
Treasurer: Mr Iain W. Grimmond BAcc CA
Secretary and Clerk: Mrs Jennifer M. Hamilton BA

Remit
The Church of Scotland Trust was established by Act of Parliament in 1932 and has Scottish Charity Number SC020269. The Trust's function since 1 January 1995 has been to hold properties outwith Scotland and to act as Trustee in a number of third-party trusts.

Further information can be obtained from the Secretary and Clerk of The Church of Scotland Trust, 121 George Street, Edinburgh   EH2 4YN (Tel: 0131-240 2222; E-mail: jhamilton@cofscotland.org.uk).

16. Committee on Church Art and Architecture

See entry under **The Mission and Discipleship Council** (number 4).

The *Exchange and Transfer* service, to enable the transfer of furnishings from one church to another, formerly provided by this committee, is now available through the Church's website (www.churchofscotland.org.uk). Further information from the Communications Department (number 17 below).

17. Communications Department

Head of Communications: Seonag Mackinnon

Communications Manager: Rob Flett

Communications and Media Relations Team
Senior Media Relations Officer: Nick Jury
Communications Officer: Andrew Harris

Programmes Co-ordinator: Virginia Cano

Web Team
Web Editor: Jason Derr
Web Developer: Alan Murray

Design Services
Senior Graphic Designer: Claire Bewsey
Senior Graphic Designer: Chris Flexen

The Communications Department has responsibility for providing and promoting effective internal and external communications across the Church of Scotland.

The Media Relations Team services local, regional, national, UK and international media. News releases are issued on a regular basis to a large network of media contacts, and staff provide advice and information on media matters within the Church. Media Relations staff can be contacted on 0131-240 2204/2268 during office hours, or on 07854 783539 after hours, at weekends and on public holidays.

The Web Team is responsible for developing and updating the Church's website (www.churchofscotland.org.uk) and managing the Church's social-media channels. The Design Team creates printed and online material for the Church.

18.   The Department of the General Assembly

The Department of the General Assembly supports the General Assembly and the Moderator, the Council of Assembly and the Ecumenical Relations Committee. In addition, Departmental staff service the following Committees: Assembly Arrangements, Legal Questions, the Committee to Nominate the Moderator, the Nomination Committee, the Committee on Overtures and Cases, the Committee on Classifying Returns to Overtures and the Central Services Committee. The Clerks of Assembly are available for consultation on matters of Church Law, Practice and Procedure.

Staff*
Co-ordinator of Principal Clerk's Office:	Very Rev. A. David K. Arnott MA BD
Acting Principal Clerk of the General Assembly:	Rev. George J. Whyte BSc BD DMin
Acting Depute Clerk of the General Assembly:	Rev. George S. Cowie BSc BD
Secretary to the Council of Assembly:	Mrs Pauline Weibye MA DPA Chartered FCIPD
Ecumenical Officer:	Very Rev. Sheilagh M. Kesting BA BD DD
Personal Assistant to the Principal Clerk:	Mrs Linda Jamieson
Legal and Learning Resources Officer:	Ms Christine Paterson LLB DipLP
Senior Administration Officer: (Assembly Arrangements and Moderatorial Support)	Mrs Alison Murray MA
Senior Administration Officer: (Council of Assembly, Central Services Committee and Nomination Committee)	Mrs Pauline Wilson
Senior Administrator: (Ecumenical Relations)	Miss Rosalind Milne
Worship Development and Mission Statistics Co-ordinator:	Rev. Fiona Tweedie BSc PhD

Contact Details:
Principal Clerk:	0131-240 2240
Secretary to the Council of Assembly:	0131-240 2229
Ecumenical Officer:	0131-240 2208
Linda Jamieson:	0131-240 2240
Rosalind Milne:	0131-225 5722 ext. 2370
Alison Murray:	0131-225 5722 ext. 2250
Christine Paterson:	0131-225 5722 ext. 2263
Pauline Wilson:	0131-240 2229
Rev. Fiona Tweedie:	0131-240 3007
Office Fax number:	0131-240 2239
Office E-mail address:	pcoffice@cofscotland.org.uk

Note: Between May 2014 and June 2015, initial contact for the Acting Principal Clerk and Acting Depute Clerk, who are both part-time and not based in the Church Offices, should be made through the Co-ordinator.

19.   Design Services

For further details, see Communications Department at number 17.

20.   Ecumenical Relations Committee

Remit
- to advise the General Assembly on matters of policy affecting ecumenical relations;
- to ensure that the members on the Committee serving on the other Councils are appropriately informed and resourced so as to be able to represent the ecumenical viewpoint on the Council on which they serve;
- to ensure appropriate support for the Ecumenical Officer's representative function in the event of his or her absence, whether through illness, holidays or other commitments;
- to nominate people from across the work of the Church of Scotland to represent the Church in Assemblies and Synods of other churches, ecumenical consultations and delegations to ecumenical assemblies and so on;
- to call for and receive reports from representatives of the Church of Scotland attending Assemblies and Synods of other churches and those ecumenical conferences and gatherings which are held from time to time;
- to ensure that appropriate parts of such reports are made available to relevant Councils;
- to ensure that information is channelled from and to ecumenical bodies of which the Church of Scotland is a member;
- to ensure that information is channelled from and to other churches in Scotland and beyond;
- to ensure the continued development of ecumenical relations by means of the Web and other publications;
- to ensure personal support for the Ecumenical Officer;
- to approve guidelines for the setting up and oversight of Local Ecumenical Partnerships.

Membership
a)   Five members appointed by the General Assembly, each to serve as a member of one of the five Councils of the Church.
b)   A Convener who is not a member of any of the other Councils and who will act as a personal support for the Ecumenical Officer, and a Vice-Convener, appointed by the General Assembly.
c)   A representative of the United Free Church of Scotland appointed by that Church.
d)   A representative of the Roman Catholic Church in Scotland appointed by the Bishops' Conference and one representative from each of three churches drawn from among the member churches of ACTS and the Baptist Union of Scotland, each to serve for a period of four years.
e)   The Committee shall co-opt Church of Scotland members elected to the central bodies of Churches Together in Britain and Ireland (CTBI), the Conference of European Churches (CEC), the World Council of Churches (WCC), the World Communion of Reformed Churches (WCRC) and the Community of Protestant Churches in Europe (CPCE, formerly the Leuenberg Fellowship of Churches).
f)   The General Secretary of ACTS shall be invited to attend as a corresponding member.
g)   For the avoidance of doubt, while, for reasons of corporate governance, only Church of Scotland members of the Committee shall be entitled to vote, before any vote is taken the views of members representing other churches shall be ascertained.

Convener:	Rev. Alison P. Mcdonald MA BD (2013)
Vice-Convener:	Rev. Peter H. Donald MA PhD BD (2013)
Secretary and Ecumenical	
Officer:	Very Rev. Sheilagh M. Kesting BA BD DD
Senior Administrator:	Miss Rosalind Milne

INTER-CHURCH ORGANISATIONS

World Council of Churches

The Church of Scotland is a founder member of the World Council of Churches, formed in 1948. As its basis declares, it is 'a fellowship of Churches which confess the Lord Jesus Christ as God and Saviour according to the Scriptures, and therefore seek to fulfil their common calling to the glory of the one God, Father, Son and Holy Spirit'. Its member Churches, which number over 300, are drawn from all continents and include all the major traditions – Eastern and Oriental Orthodox, Reformed, Lutheran, Anglican, Baptist, Disciples, Methodist, Moravian, Friends, Pentecostalist and others. Although the Roman Catholic Church is not a member, there is very close co-operation with the departments in the Vatican.

The World Council holds its Assemblies every seven years. Its tenth Assembly took place in Busan, Republic of Korea, from 30 October to 8 November 2013. The theme of the Assembly, 'God of life, lead us to justice and peace', was inspired by the diversity of Asian contexts and by a growing sense of urgency to care for life and seek justice. It is both a prayer and a statement of faith, calling Christians to engage with God's vision of justice and peace, so that all may have life in fullness.

The WCC is divided into six programme areas:

- WCC and the Ecumenical Movement in the 21st Century
- Unity, Mission, Evangelism and Spirituality
- Public Witness: Addressing Power, Affirming Peace
- Justice, Diakonia and Responsibility for Creation
- Education and Ecumenical Formation
- Inter-Religious Dialogue and Co-operation.

The General Secretary is Rev. Dr Olav Fykse Tveit, PO Box 2100, 150 route de Ferney, CH-1211 Geneva 2, Switzerland (Tel: 0041 22 791 61 11; Fax: 0041 22 791 03 61; E-mail: infowcc@wcc-coe.org; Website: www.oikumene.org).

World Communion of Reformed Churches

The Church of Scotland was a founder member of 'The Alliance of the Reformed Churches Throughout the World Holding the Presbyterian System', which began in 1875. As the World Alliance of Reformed Churches, it included also Churches of the Congregational tradition. In June 2010, WARC merged with the Reformed Ecumenical Council and became the World Communion of Reformed Churches.

The World Communion of Reformed Churches (WCRC) brings together 80 million Reformed Christians in 108 countries around the world – united in their commitment to mission, church unity and justice. WCRC links Presbyterian, Reformed, Congregational, Waldensian, United and Uniting Churches.

The WCRC works in four main areas:

- Communication (fostering church unity and interfaith dialogue)
- Justice (helping churches to act for social and economic rights and care of the environment)
- Mission (facilitating mission renewal and empowerment)
- Partnership (providing funds for church unity, mission and justice projects).

The Uniting General Council was held in Grand Rapids, Michigan, USA from 18–28 June 2010. The theme was 'Unity of the Spirit in the Bond of Peace'.

The General Secretary is Rev. Dr Setri Nyomi, Knochenhauerstr. 42, D-30159 Hannover, Germany (Tel: 0049 511 8973 8310; Fax: 0049 511 8973 8311; E-mail: wcrc@wcrc.eu; Website: www.wcrc.eu).

Conference of European Churches

The Church of Scotland is a founder member of the Conference of European Churches, formed in 1959 and until recently the only body which involved in common membership representatives of every European country (except Albania) from the Atlantic to the Urals. More than 100 Churches, Orthodox and Protestant, are members. Although the Roman Catholic Church is not a member, there is very close co-operation with the Council of European Catholic Bishops' Conferences. With the removal of the long-standing political barriers in Europe, the Conference has now opportunities and responsibilities to assist the Church throughout the continent to offer united witness and service.

CEC held its fourteenth Assembly from 3–8 July 2013 in Budapest, Hungary. Its theme was 'And now what are you waiting for? CEC and its mission in a changing Europe'.

The General Secretary is Rev. Dr Guy Liagre, PO Box 2100, 150 route de Ferney, CH-1211 Geneva 2, Switzerland (Tel: 0041 22 791 61 11; Fax: 0041 22 791 62 27; E-mail: cec@cec-kek.org; Website: www.ceceurope.org).

CEC: Church and Society Commission

The Church of Scotland was a founder member of the European Ecumenical Commission for Church and Society (EECCS). The Commission owed its origins to the Christian concern and vision of a group of ministers and European civil servants about the future of Europe. It was established in 1973 by Churches recognising the importance of this venture. Membership included Churches and ecumenical bodies from the European Union. The process of integration with CEC was completed in 2000, and the name, Church and Society Commission (CSC), established. In Brussels, CSC monitors Community activity, maintains contact with MEPs and promotes dialogue between the Churches and the institutions. It plays an educational role and encourages the Churches' social and ethical responsibility in European affairs. It has a small office in Strasbourg.

The Executive Secretary and Interim Team Co-ordinator is Rev. Frank-Dieter Fischbach, Ecumenical Centre, 174 rue Joseph II, B-1000 Brussels, Belgium (Tel: 0032 2 230 17 32; Fax: 0032 2 231 14 13; E-mail: csc@cec-kek.be).

Community of Protestant Churches in Europe

The Church of Scotland is a founder member of the Community of Protestant Churches in Europe (CPCE), which was formerly known as the Leuenberg Church Fellowship. The Fellowship came into being in 1973 on the basis of the Leuenberg Agreement between the Reformation churches in Europe; the name was changed to the CPCE in 2003. The Leuenberg Agreement stipulates that a common understanding of the Gospel based on the doctrine of Justification by Faith, and interpreted with reference to the proclamation of the Word of God, Baptism and the Lord's Supper, is sufficient to overcome the Lutheran–Reformed church division.

Over 100 Protestant churches in Europe, and a number of South American churches with European origin, have been signatories to the Leuenberg Agreement, including Lutheran, Reformed, United and Methodist Churches, as well as pre-Reformation Waldensian, Hussite and Czech Brethren, and they grant each other pulpit and table fellowship. Most of the CPCE member churches are minority churches, and this imparts a particular character to their life and witness. A General Assembly is held every six years – the seventh General Assembly was held in September 2012 in Florence, Italy – and a thirteen-member Council carries on the work of the CPCE in the intervening period.

The General Secretary is Bishop Professor Dr Michael Bunker, Severin-Schreiber-Gasse 3, A-1180 Vienna, Austria (Tel: 0043 1 4791523 900; Fax: 0043 1 4791523 110; E-mail: geke@leuenberg.eu; Website: www.leuenberg.eu).

Churches Together in Britain and Ireland (CTBI)
In September 1990, Churches throughout Britain and Ireland solemnly committed themselves to one another, promising to one another to do everything possible together. To provide frameworks for this commitment to joint action, the Churches established CTBI for the United Kingdom and Ireland, and, for Scotland, ACTS, with sister organisations for Wales and for England.

Churches Together in Britain and Ireland works with member churches to co-ordinate responses, share resources and learn from each other's experiences.

There are currently eight subject-based work areas:
*   Church and Public Issues
*   Theology and Unity
*   Mission
*   China Desk
*   Inter-Religious
*   International Students
*   Racial Justice
*   Action on Asylum and Refugees.

There are also three theme-based work areas:
*   Environment and Climate Change
*   Culture, Identity and the Public Square
*   Migration and Movements of People.

The General Secretary is Rev. Bob Fyffe, 39 Eccleston Square, London SW1V 1BX (Tel: 0845 680 6851; Fax: 0845 680 6852; E-mail: info@ctbi.org.uk; Website: www.ctbi.org.uk).

Action of Churches Together in Scotland (ACTS)
ACTS is governed by a Board of Trustees which consults with the Members' Meeting. The Members' Meeting is composed of representatives from the nine trustee member Churches.

ACTS is staffed by a General Secretary, an Assistant General Secretary and two Network Officers. Their offices are based in Alloa.

These structures facilitate regular consultation and intensive co-operation among those who frame the policies and deploy the resources of the Churches in Scotland and throughout Britain and Ireland. At the same time, they afford greater opportunity for a wide range of members of different Churches to meet in common prayer and study.

The General Secretary is Rev. Matthew Z. Ross LLB BD MTh FSAScot, 7 Forrester Lodge, Inglewood House, Alloa FK10 2HU (Tel: 01259 216980; Fax: 01259 215964; E-mail: ecumenical@acts-scotland.org; Website: www.acts-scotland.org).

---

21.   Facilities Management Department

Staff
Facilities Manager: Carole Tait (Tel: 0131-240 2214)

The responsibilities of the Facilities Manager's Department include:
*   management of a maintenance budget for the upkeep of the Church Offices at 121 George Street, Edinburgh;
*   responsibility for all aspects of health and safety for staff, visitors and contractors working in the building;

- managing a team of staff providing the Offices with security, reception, mail room, print room, switchboard, day-to-day maintenance services and Committee room bookings;
- overseeing all sub-contracted services to include catering, cleaning, boiler-room maintenance, intruder alarm, fire alarms, lifts and water management;
- maintaining building records in accordance with the requirements of statutory legislation;
- overseeing all alterations to the building and ensuring, where applicable, that they meet DDR, Planning and Building Control regulations.

22. General Treasurer's Department

The General Treasurer's Department and the Stewardship Department have merged to form the Stewardship and Finance Department. See number 31.

23. General Trustees

Membership
(New Trustees are appointed, as required, by the General Assembly, on the recommendation of the General Trustees.)

Chairman:	Mr Iain C. Douglas RD BArch FRIAS (2014)
Vice-Chairman:	Mr Roger G.G. Dodd DipBldgCons(RICS) FRICS (2014)
Secretary and Clerk:	Mr David D. Robertson LLB NP
Depute Secretary and Clerk:	Mr Keith S. Mason LLB NP

Committees:
Fabric Committee
Convener: Mr Roger G.G. Dodd DipBldgCons(RICS) FRICS (2010)

Chairman's Committee
Convener: Mr Iain C. Douglas RD BArch FRIAS (2014)

Glebes Committee
Convener: Mr William M. Lawrie (2012)

Finance Committee
Convener: Mr Peter F. King LLB MCIBS (2010)

Audit Committee
Convener: Dr J. Kenneth Macaldowie LLD CA (2005)

Law Committee
Convener: Prof. Stewart Brymer LLB WS NP (2013)

Staff
Secretary and Clerk: Mr David D. Robertson LLB NP

Depute Secretary and Clerk: Mr Keith S. Mason LLB NP
Assistant Secretaries: Ms Claire L. Cowell LLB (Glebes)
 Mrs Morag J. Menneer BSc MRICS (Glebes)
 Mr Brian D. Waller LLB (Ecclesiastical Buildings)
Treasurer: Mr Iain W. Grimmond BAcc CA
Deputy Treasurer: Mrs Anne F. Macintosh BA CA
Assistant Treasurer: Mr Alex Semple FCCA

Remit

The General Trustees are a Property Corporation created and incorporated under the Church of Scotland (General Trustees) Order Confirmation Act 1921. They have Scottish Charity Number SC014574. Their duties, powers and responsibilities were greatly extended by the Church of Scotland (Property & Endowments) Acts and Orders 1925 to 1995, and they are also charged with the administration of the Central Fabric Fund (see below) and the Consolidated Fabric Fund and the Consolidated Stipend Fund in which monies held centrally for the benefit of individual congregations are lodged.

The scope of the work of the Trustees is broad, covering all facets of property administration, but particular reference is made to the following matters:

1. **ECCLESIASTICAL BUILDINGS.** The Trustees' Fabric Committee considers proposals for work at buildings, regardless of how they are vested, and plans of new buildings. Details of all such projects should be submitted to the Committee before work is commenced. The Committee also deals with applications for the release of fabric monies held by the General Trustees for individual congregations, and considers applications for assistance from the Central Fabric Fund from which grants and/or loans may be given to assist congregations faced with expenditure on fabric. Application forms relating to consents for work and possible financial assistance from the Central Fabric Fund are available from the Secretary of the Trustees and require to be submitted through Presbytery with its approval. The Committee normally meets on the first or second Tuesday of each month, apart from July, when it meets on the second last Tuesday, and August, when there is no meeting.

2. **SALE, PURCHASE AND LETTING OF PROPERTIES.** All sales or lets of properties vested in the General Trustees fall to be carried out by them in consultation with the Financial Board of the congregation concerned, and no steps should be taken towards any sale or let without prior consultation with the Secretary of the Trustees. Where property to be purchased is to be vested in the General Trustees, it is essential that contact be made at the earliest possible stage with the Solicitor to the Trustees, who is responsible for the lodging of offers for such properties and all subsequent legal procedure.

3. **GLEBES.** The Trustees are responsible for the administration of Glebes vested in their ownership. All lets fall to be granted by them in consultation with the minister concerned. It should be noted that neither ministers nor Kirk Sessions may grant lets of Glebe land vested in the General Trustees. As part of their Glebe administration, the Trustees review regularly all Glebe rents.

4. **INSURANCE.** The 2013 General Assembly instructed all congregations to insure the churches, halls and manses for which they are responsible (irrespective of ownership) through the scheme offered by the Church of Scotland Insurance Co. Ltd, which also

covers liabilities and contents. It is a company wholly owned by the Church of Scotland whose profits are applied for Church purposes. Insurance enquiries should be sent directly to the Company at 67 George Street, Edinburgh EH2 2JG (Tel: 0131-220 4119; Fax: 0131-220 4120; E-mail: enquiries@cosic.co.uk).

24. Human Resources Department

Staff

Head of Human Resources and
  Information Technology: Mike O'Donnell Chartered FCIPD
Human Resources Manager: Karen Smith Chartered CIPD

Remit

The Human Resources Department has responsibility for Recruitment and Selection, Learning and Development, and producing and updating HR Policies and Procedures to ensure that the Central Services Committee, the Ministries Council and the World Mission Council, as employing agencies, are in line with current employment-law legislation. The Department produces contracts of employment and advises on any changes to an individual employee's terms and conditions of employment. It also provides professional Human Resources advice to the organisation on Employee Relations matters, Performance Management and Diversity and Equality.

Our main aim is to work closely with Councils within the organisation to influence strategy so that each Council is making best use of its people and its people opportunities. We take a consultancy role that facilitates and supports each Council's own initiatives and help each other share and work together in consultation with Unite.

25. Information Technology Department

Staff

Head of Human Resources and Information Technology: Mike O'Donnell
Information Technology Manager: David Malcolm

The Department provides computer facilities to Councils and Departments within 121 George Street and to Presbytery Clerks and other groups within the Councils. It is also responsible for the telephone service within 121 George Street and the provision of assistance and advice on this to other groups.
  The facilities provided include:
*   the provision and maintenance of data and voice networks
*   the purchase and installation of hardware and software
*   support for problems and guidance on the use of hardware and software
*   development of in-house software
*   maintenance of data within some central systems.

26.   Law Department

Staff

Solicitor of the Church and of the General Trustees:	Mrs Janette Wilson LLB NP
Depute Solicitor:	Miss Mary Macleod LLB NP
Solicitors:	Mrs Jennifer Hamilton BA NP
	Mrs Elspeth Annan LLB NP
	Miss Susan Killean LLB NP
	Mrs Anne Steele LLB NP
	Miss Jennifer Sharp LLB NP
	Mr Gregor Buick LLB WS NP
	Mrs Madelaine Sproule LLB NP

The Department's team of experienced solicitors is available to provide legal advice and assistance to all congregations, Presbyteries, Councils, Committees and Courts of the Church. It also represents the Church of Scotland General Trustees, the Church of Scotland Trust and the Church of Scotland Investors Trust. The solicitors in the Department act exclusively on behalf of Church of Scotland bodies and therefore have an understanding and experience of the law as it relates to the Church which cannot be equalled elsewhere. They also have an awareness of wider policy and financial issues affecting both congregations and central Church bodies.

The Department is committed to meeting the particular needs of the Church. It provides a large number of free resources for congregations, which are available to download from the Church website (www.churchofscotland.org.uk/resources/subjects/law_circulars). These include style documents and circulars covering matters such as contracts of employment; guidance on the Bribery Act 2010 as it affects congregations; guidance on the Data Protection Act; charity law; licensing matters and the letting of church halls.

The solicitors in the Department can offer tailored advice on most areas of the law, including:

- marketing properties for sale
- commercial and residential conveyancing
- commercial and residential leasing
- employment issues
- trusts and executries
- charity law
- litigation and dispute resolution
- data protection
- contract law
- planning law
- agricultural law
- licensing and regulatory matters
- mobile-phone installations.

Contact details: E-mail: lawdept@cofscotland.org.uk; Tel: 0131-225 5722 ext. 2230; Fax: 0131-240 2246.

27. Legal Questions Committee

Membership
Convener, Vice-Convener and ten members appointed by the General Assembly on the Report of the Nomination Committee.

Convener: Rev. Alan J. Hamilton LLB BD
Vice-Convener: Rev. Sheila M. Kirk BA LLB BD
Secretary: Acting Principal Clerk
The Assembly Clerks, Procurator and Solicitor of the Church are non-voting members of the Legal Questions Committee.

Remit
- to advise the General Assembly on questions of Church Law and of Constitutional Law affecting the relationship between Church and State;
- to advise and assist Agencies of the General Assembly in the preparation of proposed legislation and on questions of interpretation, including interpretation of and proposed changes to remits;
- to compile the statistics of the Church, except Youth and Finance; and to supervise on behalf of the General Assembly all arrangements for care of Church Records and for Presbytery visits;
- to conduct an annual review of progress made in discharging the remit and provide a written report to the Council of Assembly.

28. Nomination Committee

Membership
(Convener, Vice-Convener and 24 members)
Convener: Rev. Kenneth Stott MA BD (2014)
Vice-Convener: Miss Ann Lyall DCS (2014)
Secretary: Mrs Pauline Weibye MA DPA Chartered FCIPD

Remit
1. To bring before the General Assembly names of persons to serve on the Councils and Standing Committees of the General Assembly.
2. To identify and interview suitable candidates for membership of the Council of Assembly, bringing before the General Assembly the names of persons to serve as charity trustees of the Unincorporated Councils and Committees.
3. To work with the main Councils of the General Assembly to ensure an open, fair and robust process for identifying suitable persons to serve as Conveners of such Councils, engaging with those so identified to ensure their suitability to serve as charity trustees of the Unincorporated Councils and Committees.

29.   Panel on Review and Reform

Membership
(10 members appointed by the General Assembly)
Convener: Rev. Donald Campbell BD (2011)
Vice-Convener: Rev. David C. Cameron BD CertMin (2014)
(The Ecumenical Officer attends but without the right to vote or make a motion.)

Staff
Senior Administrator: Mrs Valerie A. Cox
                                   (Tel: 0131-225 5722 ext. 2336;
                                   E-mail: vcox@cofscotland.org.uk)

Remit
* to listen to the voices of congregations, Presbyteries, Agencies, and those beyond the Church of Scotland;
* through such interaction, consultation and discussion with congregations, Presbyteries, Councils and Agencies of the Church as may be decided upon by the Panel, to formulate and bring before successive General Assemblies:
  (a) a clear statement of the long-term vision of the Church, and
  (b) paths and developments which might be followed by congregations, Presbyteries, Councils and Agencies of the Church to make such a vision a reality;
* to consider the changing needs, challenges and responsibilities of the Church;
* to have particular regard to the gospel imperative of priority for the poor, needy and marginalised.

---

30.   Stewardship and Finance Department

The General Treasurer's Department and the Stewardship Department merged to form the Stewardship and Finance Department on 1 June 2009. This Department is accountable to the Council of Assembly through its Finance Group.
   The Departmental e-mail address is: sfadmin@cofscotland.org.uk

Staff based at the Church Offices
General Treasurer: Mr Iain W. Grimmond BAcc CA
Deputy Treasurer: Mrs Anne F. Macintosh BA CA
Head of Stewardship: Rev. Alan W. Gibson BA BD
Finance Managers:
   Congregational Finance   Mr Archie McDowall BA CA
   General Trustees   Alex Semple FCCA
   Ministries   Mrs Elaine Macadie BA CA
   World Mission   Mrs Catriona M. Scrimgeour BSc ACA
Management and Pensions Accountant: Mrs Kay C. Hastie BSc CA

Regional Staff
Stewardship Consultants:

- Mrs Margot R. Robertson BA (Tel: 01620 893459) for the Presbyteries of:
  Edinburgh, West Lothian, Lothian, Melrose and Peebles, Duns, Jedburgh
- Mrs Edith Scott (Tel: 01357 520503) for the Presbyteries of:
  Annandale and Eskdale, Dumfries and Kirkcudbright, Wigtown and Stranraer, Ayr, Irvine
  and Kilmarnock, Ardrossan, Lanark, Greenock and Paisley, Hamilton
- Mr Stuart G. Sangster (Tel: 01360 622302) for the Presbyteries of:
  Glasgow, Dumbarton, Argyll, Stirling, Lochaber
- Mrs Sandra Holt BSc (Tel: 07807 477682) for the Presbyteries of:
  Falkirk, Dunfermline, Kirkcaldy, St Andrews, Dunkeld and Meigle, Perth, Dundee
- Mrs Fiona Penny (Tel: 01771 653442) for the Presbyteries of:
  Aberdeen, Kincardine and Deeside, Gordon, Buchan, Moray, Abernethy, Inverness

Stewardship requests from congregations in the Presbyteries of Angus, Ross, Sutherland, Caithness, Lochcarron – Skye, Uist, Lewis, Orkney, Shetland, England and Europe should be addressed to the Head of Stewardship at the Church Offices in the first instance.

Main Responsibilities of the Stewardship and Finance Department
- Teaching and promoting Christian stewardship throughout the Church;
- Planning and delivery of stewardship programmes in congregations;
- Calculating the annual Ministries and Mission Contribution for each congregation, and processing payments;
- Providing support, training and advice on financial and accounting matters to Congregational Treasurers;
- Providing management and financial accounting support for the Councils, Committees and Statutory Corporations;
- Providing banking arrangements and operating a central banking system for the Councils, Committees and Statutory Corporations;
- Receiving and discharging legacies and bequests on behalf of the Councils, Committees and Statutory Corporations;
- Making VAT returns and tax recoveries on behalf of the Councils, Committees and Statutory Corporations;
- Payroll processing for the Ministries Council, Central Services Committee and the Pension Schemes.

31. The Church of Scotland Safeguarding Service
Tel: 0131-240 2256; Fax: 0131-220 3113
E-mail: safeguarding@cofscotland.org.uk
Website: www.churchofscotland.org.uk

Convener: Rev. Karen K. Campbell BD MTh DMin (2014)
Vice-Convener: Sheila Ritchie (2014)

Staff
Head of Safeguarding: Richard Crosse MA MSW CQSW
Assistant Head of Safeguarding: Jennifer Milligan CQSW DipSW

The Church of Scotland Safeguarding Service:
What we aim to do and how we provide the service

Introduction

Harm or abuse of children and 'adults at risk' can happen anywhere – even in church communities. We have a duty 'to ensure a safe church for all'. The Church of Scotland has a zero-tolerance approach to harm or abuse of people: any type or level is unacceptable.

The possibility of harm or abuse cannot be eliminated, but the safeguarding structures in the Church and the work of the Safeguarding Service seek to minimise the risk of harm occurring or not being responded to appropriately. The Safeguarding Committee, with representation from across the Church, ensures accountability back to the General Assembly, and also provides a forum for shaping policy and direction.

Remit

The Church of Scotland Safeguarding Service aims to:
• ensure best practice in preventing harm or abuse, and
• ensure that the Church makes a timely and appropriate response when harm or abuse is witnessed, suspected or reported.

Preventing harm and abuse

The Safeguarding Service aims to prevent harm or abuse through ensuring that there is good recognition and reporting. It does this by providing:
• information, support and advice on everyday safeguarding matters where there is not an incident of suspected or reported harm or abuse
• advice and support for the safe recruitment and selection of all paid staff and volunteers
• the process of applying for membership of the Protection of Vulnerable Groups (Scotland) Act 2007 Scheme for those working with children or 'protected adults'.

Safe recruitment

Safe recruitment is about ensuring that only people suitable to work with children and 'adults at risk' are employed. There is a comprehensive range of safeguarding training programmes to meet the particular learning needs of different groups of people in the Church, including, for example, volunteers, Kirk Sessions, Safeguarding Co-ordinators, Ministries Council, Parish Development Fund and CrossReach services.

Responding to disclosures of harm or abuse or risk of abuse

The Safeguarding Service provides:
• verbal and written advice in situations where harm or abuse is suspected, witnessed or reported to members of the Church. This service is also provided for CrossReach Social Care Council services
• support for Safeguarding Panels working with convicted sex offenders to ensure their safe inclusion in worship.

In summary, harm or abuse in the Church is rare, and thankfully the vast majority of people will have no knowledge or experience of it, but even one case is one too many. Our key message is: *'If you suspect or witness harm or abuse, or it is reported to you, you must immediately report it to your Safeguarding Co-ordinator or line manager'.*

Contact can be made with the Safeguarding Office at the address, telephone number, e-mail address and website shown at the head of this article.

32. Scottish Churches Parliamentary Office
Tel: 0131-220 0246
E-mail: chloe@actsparl.org

The Acting Scottish Churches Parliamentary Officer is David Bradwell. The office is at 44 Hanover Street, Edinburgh EH2 2DR.

---

33. Theological Forum

Membership
Convener, Vice-Convener and ten members appointed by the General Assembly on the report of the Nomination Committee. The membership is selected to provide an appropriate balance of (1) ministers of Word and Sacrament, (2) members of academic staff from the Divinity Schools (or equivalent) of institutions of higher education in Scotland, (3) elders and (4) members drawn from the wider membership of the Church, chosen for their particular expertise, experience or provenance; together with one additional member appointed by the Ecumenical Relations Committee.

Convener:	Very Rev. Prof. Iain R. Torrance TD DPhil DD DTheol LHD FRSE
Vice-Convener:	Rev. Frances M. Henderson BA BD PhD
Secretary (*pro tem.*):	Mrs Pauline Weibye MA DPA Chartered FCIPD

Remit
1. To articulate and develop the doctrinal understanding of the Church in accordance with Holy Scripture and with reference to the confessional standards of the Church of Scotland.
2. To express the theological vision of the Church in its worship, fellowship, witness and mission in and beyond contemporary Scotland.
3. To respond to particular theological requests as and when these arise from the General Assembly, the Council of Assembly and the ecumenical partners of the Church.
4. To draw to the attention of the General Assembly theological matters which the Theological Forum considers to be of pressing contemporary relevance.
5. To stimulate wider theological reflection throughout the Church on key doctrinal, ethical and apologetic matters through the provision of appropriate materials and other activities.

The Church of Scotland and the Gaelic Language

Duilleagan Gàidhlig
Ro-ràdh
Ann an 2008, airson a' chiad turais riamh, bha duilleagan air leth againn ann an Gàidhlig anns an *Leabhar Bhliadhnail*, agus a rèir iomraidh rinn mòran toileachadh ris a' ghluasad ùr seo. Tha sinn fo fhiachan am bliadhna a-rithist don Fhear-dheasachaidh airson a bhith cho deònach cuibhreann Ghàidhlig a bhith an lùib na Beurla. An deidh a bhith a' crìonadh fad ghrunn ghinealach, tha

a' Ghàidhlig a-nis a' dèanamh adhartais. Tha e cudthromach gum bi Eaglais na h-Alba a' toirt cùl-taic don leasachadh seo, agus gu dearbha tha i aig teis-meadhan a' ghluasaid seo. Ma bheir sinn sùil air eachdraidh, chì sinn nuair a bha a' Ghàidhlig a' fulang làmhachais-làidir anns na linntean a dh'fhalbh, gu robh an Eaglais glè shoirbheachail ann a bhith a' gabhail ceum-tòisich airson an cànan a dhìon.

Eachdraidh
Bha na thachair an dèidh Blàr Chùil Lodair 'na bhuille chruaidh don Ghàidhlig. Cha do chuidich Achd an Fhòghlaim ann an 1872 le cùisean, Achd nach tug fiù 's iomradh air a' Ghàidhlig. Mar thoradh air seo bha a' Ghàidhlig air a fuadach à sgoiltean na h-Alba. Ach bha a' Ghàidhlig air a cleachdadh anns an Eaglais agus bha sin na mheadhan air a cumail o bhith a' dol à sealladh mar chainnt làitheil.

Poileataics
Tha Pàrlamaid na h-Eòrpa a' toirt inbhe don Ghàidhlig mar aon de na mion-chànanan Eòrpach a tha i a' smaoineachadh a bu chòir a cuideachadh agus a h-altram. Beagan bhliadhnachan air ais chuir iad lagh an gnìomh a bha a' cur mar dhleasdanas air Pàrlamaid Bhreatainn àite a thoirt don Ghàidhlig. Ann an 2005, thug Pàrlamaid na h-Alba Achd Gàidhlig na h-Alba air adhart a' cur na Gàidhlig air stèidh mar chainnt nàiseanta, leis an aon spèis ris a' Bheurla.

Cultar
Tha An Comunn Gàidhealach agus buidhnean eile air obair ionmholta a dhèanamh bho chionn fada ann a bhith a' cur na Gàidhlig air adhart mar nì cudthromach nar cultar. Bho chionn ghoirid chuir An Comunn air bhonn co-chruinneachadh de riochdairean o na h-Eaglaisean airson dòighean a lorg air a bhith a' cleachdadh na Gàidhlig ann an adhradh follaiseach. Fad còrr is fichead bliadhna chaidh adhartas mòr a dhèanamh ann am fòghlam tro mheadhan na Gàidhlig, an toiseach tro chròileagain, bun-sgoiltean, agus a-nis ann an àrd-sgoiltean. Thàinig seo gu ìre nuair a stèidhicheadh Sabhal Mòr Ostaig ann am fòghlam àrd-ìre. Bidh an Sabhal Mòr mar phàirt chudthromach de dh'Oilthigh ùr na Gàidhealtachd agus nan Eilean. Tha Comann Albannach a' Bhìobaill glè dhealasach ann a bhith a' sìor thoirt taic don Ghàidhlig le bhith a' foillseachadh nan Sgriobtar anns a' chànan. Rinn Gàidheil toileachadh mòr ris an eadar-theangachadh ùr de Shoigeul Eòin ann an Gàidhlig an latha an-diugh.

Eaglais na h-Alba
1. Air feadh na dùthcha, tha adhradh air a chumail ann an Gàidhlig, air Ghàidhealtachd agus air Ghalldachd. (Mar eisimpleir, anns na bailtean mòra tha seirbheis Ghàidhlig air a cumail gach Sàbaid ann an Eaglais Ghàidhealach nam Manach Liatha ann an Dùn Eideann, agus ann an Eaglais Chaluim Chille agus Eaglais Sràid a' Ghàradair ann an Glaschu.) Tha còir gum biodh fios aig Clèireach na Clèire air eaglaisean far a bheil seirbheisean Gàidhlig air an cumail. Thug an t-Àrd-sheanadh ann an 2008 misneachadh do Chlèirean coitheanalan freagarrach ainmeachadh far am bu chòir a' Ghàidhlig a bhith air a cleachdadh ann an adhradh nuair a bha iad a' cur phlànaichean-clèire air bhonn. A bharrachd air sin, tha goireasan ann a bheir cuideachadh don fheadhainn a tha airson Gàidhlig a chleachdadh ann an adhradh.
2. Cha mhòr bho stèidhicheadh *Life and Work* tha *Na Duilleagan Gàidhlig* air a bhith rim faotainn as-asgaidh do neach sam bith a tha gan iarraidh.
3. Tha Eaglais na h-Alba, mar phàirt de dh'Iomairt Chonaltraidh na h-Eaglais, airson a bhith a' brosnachadh cleachdadh na Gàidhlig. Tha duilleagan Gàidhlig air leth air an làraich-lìn.
4. Bho chionn beagan bhliadhnachan tha an t-Àrd-sheanadh air na nithean cudthromach seo a mholadh co-cheangailte ris a' Ghàidhlig.
    (i) Tha an t-Àrd-sheanadh a' cur mealadh-naidheachd air Pàrlamaid na h-Alba airson Achd a' Chànain Ghàidhlig (Alba) a stèidheachadh; tha e a' brosnachadh a' BhBC ach

an toir iad cùl-taic do OFCOM a tha ag iarraidh craoladh na Gàidhlig a leudachadh; tha e duilich gu bheil chleachdadh na Gàidhlig a' dol an lughad anns an Eaglais, agus tha e a' toirt cuiridh do Chomhairlean na h-Eaglais, far a bheil sin freagarrach, rannsachadh a dhèanamh air dòighean a lorg a bheir don Ghàidhlig an t-àite sònraichte a chleachd a bhith aice ann am beatha spioradail na h-Alba.

(ii) Tha an t-Àrd-sheanadh a' cur ìmpidh air Comhairle a' Mhisein agus na Deisciobalachd, ann an co-bhoinn ri Comhairle na Ministrealachd, rannsachadh a dhèanamh air inbhe na Gàidhlig ann an Eaglais na h-Alba ann an dùil ri aithisg a thoirt air beulaibh an Àrd-sheanaidh ann an 2008 air mar a ghabhas leasachadh a dhèanamh air cleachdadh na Gàidhlig anns an Eaglais.

(iii) Tha an t-Àrd-sheanadh a' gabhail beachd air àireamh nan sgìrean Gàidhlig, agus tha e a' cur ìmpidh Comhairle na Ministrealachd slatan-tomhais a thoirt chun an Àrd-sheanaidh ann an 2008 airson gun tèid na sgìrean seo a chomharrachadh anns na bliadhnachan air thoiseach.

(iv) Tha an t-Àrd-sheanadh a' cur ìmpidh air Comhairle an Àrd-sheanaidh cumail romhpa a bhith a' toirt cùl-taic don Ghàidhlig an taobh a-staigh na h-Eaglais, am measg rudan eile a bhith a' còmhradh ri buidhnean maoineachaidh freagarrach.

(v) Tha an t-Àrd-sheanadh a' dèanamh toileachaidh ris an Aithisg air Leasachadh ann an Cleachdadh na Gàidhlig, agus tha e a' brosnachadh Comhairle a' Mhisein agus na Deisciobalachd na plànaichean a tha aca airson an ama air thoiseach a chur an gnìomh.

(vi) Tha an t-Àrd-sheanadh a' dèanamh toileachaidh ris an naidheachd gu bheil Seanal Digiteach Gàidhlig ga chur air bhog, agus tha e a' cur ìmpidh air Comhaire na h-Eaglais agus na Coimhearsnachd, ann an co-bhoinn ri Comhairle an Àrd-sheanaidh, a bhith a' còmhradh ri Comhairle nam Meadhanan Gàidhlig mun àite shònraichte a bu chòir a bhith aig prògraman spioradail anns na prògraman a bhios iad a' cur a-mach.

'S e àm air leth inntinneach a tha seo don Ghàidhlig, agus tha an Eaglais airson a bhith a' gabhail a h-àite anns an iomairt as leth ar cànain. 'S iad na duilleagan seo aon de na dòighean anns a bheil sinn a' dèanamh sin.

An t-Àrd-sheanadh 2014

Bha sinn an dòchas gum biodh an t-Urr. Aonghas Moireasdan 'na Mhoderàtor air Àrd-sheanadh na bliadhna seo, agus gur e a bhiodh a' searmonachadh aig an t-seirbheis Ghàidhlig ann an Eaglais nam Manach Liath. Bha sinn duilich gum b'fheudar dha an dreuchd a leigeil seachad le dìth na slàinte. Air ceann na seirbheis agus a' toirt seachad an t-searmoin bha an t-Oll. Urr. Ruairidh MacLeòid. Air ceann na h-ùrnaigh bha an t-Urr. Uisdean Stiùbhart, ministear Bheàrnaraigh ceangailte ri Uige. Bha na Sgrioptaran air an leughadh le fear de bhuill coitheanal Eaglais nam Manach Liath, Dòmhnall Iain Dòmhnallach. Bha Iain MacLeòid, Dùn Eideann, a' togail an fhuinn. An dèidh na seirbheis bha biadh agus àm conaltraidh ann. Bhruidhinn am Moderàtor ris an luchd-adhraidh aig an tì.

Anns an dealachadh

Tha *Na Duilleagan Gàidhlig* rim faotainn saor agus an-asgaidh an lùib *Life and Work*. Tha *Na Duilleagan Gàidhlig* air a bhith a' tighinn a-mach gach mìos o 1880 agus tha iad air an leughadh air feadh an t-saoghail. Tuilleadh fiosrachaidh on Fhear-dheasachaidh, an t-Oll. Urr. Ruairidh MacLeòid, Creag nam Bàirneach, An Fhùirneis, Earra Ghàidheal PA32 8XU (Fòn: 01499 500629; Post-dealain: mail@revroddy.co.uk).

Introduction
The *Year Book 2008/2009*, for the first time ever, featured dedicated pages in Gaelic; and this innovation was very well received. Again, appreciation is expressed to the Editor for his willing co-operation. After many generations of decline, Gaelic is once more moving forward. It is important that the Church of Scotland is seen to be encouraging this progress and indeed is part of it. History teaches that, in the past, when the Gaelic language has been under political oppression, the Church has stood successfully in the vanguard of the defence of the language.

History
The events of Culloden in 1746, as part of the Jacobite rebellion, dealt a cruel blow to the Gaelic language. This was compounded by the Education (Scotland) Act of 1872, which made no mention of the Gaelic language and, indeed, resulted in the outlawing of Gaelic in Scottish schools. The continued use of Gaelic in the Church proved to be the only formal antidote to the disappearance of Gaelic as a viable language.

Politics
The European Parliament recognises Gaelic as one of the minority European languages it sees as important to support and nurture. Some years ago, it passed appropriate legislation laying some responsibility on the United Kingdom Parliament. In 2005, the Scottish Parliament delivered the Gaelic (Scotland) Act, establishing Gaelic as a national language given the same respect as English.

Culture
Traditionally, An Comunn Gaidhealach has done an excellent job in promoting the cultural importance of Gaelic. In recent years, it convened a gathering of representatives from Churches to research how they could help promote the use of Gaelic in public worship. For over twenty years now, there has been substantial growth in Gaelic-medium education, first of all through nurseries, then primary schools and now secondary schools. This has moved on to the establishing of Sabhal Mòr Ostaig in the tertiary sector. The Church of Scotland welcomes the granting of a charter to the University of the Highlands and Islands, and looks forward to the Sabhal Mòr being a vital part of the University. The Scottish Bible Society is also eager to continue its support of Gaelic through the provision of Scriptures. Gaelic-speakers and learners have warmly welcomed the publication of John's Gospel in modern Gaelic.

The Church of Scotland and its ongoing support for Gaelic
1. Across the nation, public worship continues to be conducted in Gaelic. The General Assembly of 2008 encouraged Presbyteries, as part of their planning, to identify appropriate congregations in which Gaelic must be used regularly in public worship. Furthermore, resources are available to encourage the use of Gaelic in worship in all congregations.
2. Almost since its inception, *Na Duilleagan Gàidhlig*, as part of *Life and Work*, has been available free of charge to any who request it with their *Life and Work* subscription. This is still very much alive.
3. The Church of Scotland, as part of its Communication Strategy, is concerned to promote the use of Gaelic. There are dedicated Gaelic pages on the website.
4. Recent years have seen the General Assembly approve a number of important Deliverances relating to Gaelic. For example:
    (i) The General Assembly congratulate the Scottish Parliament on its passing of the Gaelic Language (Scotland) Bill, encourage the BBC to support OFCOM in its desire for the extension of Gaelic broadcasting, express regret at the substantial decrease in the use of Gaelic in the Church and invite Councils of the Church, where appropriate,

to explore ways in which Gaelic can resume its distinctive place within the religious life of Scotland.

(ii)   The General Assembly instructed the Mission and Discipleship Council, in collaboration with the Ministries Council, to undertake an investigation into the present status of Gaelic in the Church of Scotland with a view to reporting to the 2008 General Assembly on the strategic development of the use of the language in the Kirk.

(iii) The General Assembly note the statistics regarding Gaelic-speaking charges and instructed the Ministries Council to bring to the General Assembly of 2008 an agreed set of criteria for future determination of such designations.

(iv)   The General Assembly instruct the Council of Assembly to continue to support the development of Gaelic within the Church, including discussions with appropriate funding bodies.

(v)   The General Assembly welcome the Report on the Strategic Development of the Use of Gaelic and encourage the Mission and Discipleship Council to develop its future plans.

(vi)   The General Assembly welcome the launch of the Gaelic Digital Broadcasting channel and instruct the Church and Society Council, in co-operation with the Council of Assembly, to discuss with the Gaelic Media Council the significant place of religious programmes in its output.

These are exciting times for the Gaelic language, and the Church is responding to the challenge of our day.

The General Assembly 2014

It had been hoped that Rev. Angus Morrison would be Moderator of this year's General Assembly, and that he would be preaching the sermon at the Gaelic service in Greyfriars Kirk. We were sorry that health problems prevented him from taking up the office of Moderator. Conducting worship and preaching the sermon was Rev. Dr Roderick MacLeod, formerly of Cumlodden, Lochfyneside and Lochgair. Prayers were led by Rev. Hugh M. Stewart, minister of Lochs-in-Bernera linked with Uig. A member of the Gaelic congregation of Greyfriars, Donald John MacDonald, read the Scriptures. The precentor was John MacLeod, Edinburgh. Following the service, a light lunch was served, and there was an opportunity for fellowship. The Moderator, the Right Rev. John P. Chalmers, addressed worshippers.

In conclusion

The Gaelic supplement, *Na Duilleagan Gàidhlig,* has since 1880 been issued free of charge along with *Life and Work,* and is read all over the world. More information from the Editor, Rev. Dr Roderick MacLeod, Creag nam Bàirneach, Furnace, Inveraray PA32 8XU (Tel: 01499 500629; E-mail: mail@revroddy.co.uk).

SECTION 2

General Information

(1) OTHER CHURCHES IN THE UNITED KINGDOM

THE UNITED FREE CHURCH OF SCOTLAND
General Secretary: Rev. John Fulton BSc BD, United Free Church Offices, 11 Newton Place, Glasgow G3 7PR (Tel: 0141-332 3435; E-mail: office@ufcos.org.uk).

THE FREE CHURCH OF SCOTLAND
Principal Clerk: Rev. James MacIver, 15 North Bank Street, The Mound, Edinburgh EH1 2LS (Tel: 0131-226 5286; E-mail: principal.clerk@freechurch.org).

FREE CHURCH OF SCOTLAND (CONTINUING)
Clerk of Assembly: Rev. John MacLeod, Free Church Manse, Portmahomack, Tain IV20 1YL (Tel: 01862 871467; E-mail: principalclerk@fccontinuing.org).

THE FREE PRESBYTERIAN CHURCH OF SCOTLAND
Clerk of Synod: Rev. John MacLeod, 6 Church Avenue, Sidcup, Kent DA14 6BU (E-mail: jmacl265@aol.com).

ASSOCIATED PRESBYTERIAN CHURCHES
Clerk of Presbytery: Rev. Archibald N. McPhail, APC Manse, Polvinister Road, Oban PA34 5TN (Tel: 01631 567076; E-mail: archibald.mcphail@virgin.net).

THE REFORMED PRESBYTERIAN CHURCH OF SCOTLAND
Clerk of Presbytery: Rev. Andrew Quigley, Church Offices, 48 North Bridge Street, Airdrie ML6 6NE (Tel: 01236 620107; E-mail: sandrewq@aol.com).

THE PRESBYTERIAN CHURCH IN IRELAND
Clerk of the General Assembly and General Secretary: Rev. Dr Donald J. Watts, Church House, Fisherwick Place, Belfast BT1 6DW (Tel: 02890 322284; E-mail: clerk@presbyterianireland.org).

THE PRESBYTERIAN CHURCH OF WALES
General Secretary: Rev. Meiron Morris, Tabernacle Chapel, 81 Merthyr Road, Whitchurch, Cardiff CF14 1DD (Tel: 02920 627465; E-mail: swyddfa.office@ebcpcw.org.uk).

THE UNITED REFORMED CHURCH
General Secretary: Rev. John Proctor, 86 Tavistock Place, London WC1H 9RT (Tel: 020 7916 8646; Fax: 020 7916 2021; E-mail: roberta.rominger@urc.org.uk).

UNITED REFORMED CHURCH SYNOD OF SCOTLAND
Synod Clerk: Mr Patrick Smyth, 113 West Regent Street, Glasgow G1 2RU (Tel: 0141-248 5382; E-mail: psmyth@urcscotland.org.uk).

BAPTIST UNION OF SCOTLAND
General Director: Rev. Alan Donaldson, 48 Speirs Wharf, Glasgow G4 9TH (Tel: 0141-423 6169; E-mail: director@scottishbaptist.org.uk).

CONGREGATIONAL FEDERATION IN SCOTLAND
Secretary: Rev. May-Kane Logan, 93 Cartside Road, Busby, Glasgow G76 8QD (Tel: 0141-237 1349; E-mail: maycita@talktalk.net).

RELIGIOUS SOCIETY OF FRIENDS (QUAKERS)
Martin Burnell, Clerk to the General Meeting for Scotland, 25 Learmonth Grove, Edinburgh EH4 1BR (Tel: 0131-343 2592; E-mail: mburnell@mbees.net).

ROMAN CATHOLIC CHURCH
Mgr Hugh Bradley, General Secretary, Bishops' Conference of Scotland, 64 Aitken Street, Airdrie ML6 6LT (Tel: 01236 764061; E-mail: gensec@bpsconfscot.com).

THE SALVATION ARMY
Lt-Col. Carol Bailey, Secretary for Scotland and Divisional Commander East Scotland Division, Headquarters and Scotland Secretariat, 12A Dryden Road, Loanhead EH20 9LZ (Tel: 0131-440 9101; E-mail: carol.bailey@salvationarmy.org.uk).

SCOTTISH EPISCOPAL CHURCH
Secretary General: Mr John F. Stuart, 21 Grosvenor Crescent, Edinburgh EH12 5EL (Tel: 0131-225 6357; E-mail: secgen@scotland.anglican.org).

THE SYNOD OF THE METHODIST CHURCH IN SCOTLAND
District Administrator: Mrs Fiona Inglis, Methodist Church Office, Scottish Churches House, Kirk Street, Dunblane FK15 0AJ (Tel/Fax: 01786 820295; E-mail: meth@scottishchurcheshouse.org).

GENERAL SYNOD OF THE CHURCH OF ENGLAND
Secretary General: Mr William Fittall, Church House, Great Smith Street, London SW1P 3NZ (Tel: 020 7898 1360; E-mail: william.fittall@churchofengland.org).

---

(2) OVERSEAS CHURCHES

PRESBYTERIAN CHURCH IN CANADA
Principal Clerk: 50 Wynford Drive, Toronto, Ontario M3C 1J7, Canada (E-mail: pccadmin@presbyterian.ca; Website: www.presbyterian.ca).

UNITED CHURCH OF CANADA
General Secretary: Suite 300, 3250 Bloor Street West, Toronto, Ontario M8X 2Y4, Canada (E-mail: info@united-church.ca; Website: www.united-church.ca).

PRESBYTERIAN CHURCH (USA)
Stated Clerk: 100 Witherspoon Street, Louisville, KY 40202-1396, USA (E-mail: presbytel@pcusa.org; Website: www.pcusa.org).

UNITING CHURCH IN AUSTRALIA
General Secretary: PO Box A2266, Sydney South, New South Wales 1235, Australia (E-mail: enquiries@nat.uca.org.au; Website: www.uca.org.au).

PRESBYTERIAN CHURCH OF AUSTRALIA
Clerk of Assembly: PO Box 2196, Strawberry Hills, NSW 2012; 168 Chalmers Street, Surry Hills, NSW 2010, Australia (E-mail: general@pcnsw.org.au; Website: www.presbyterian.org.au).

PRESBYTERIAN CHURCH OF AOTEAROA, NEW ZEALAND
Executive Secretary: PO Box 9049, Te Aro, Wellington, Aotearoa/New Zealand (E-mail: info@presbyterian.org.nz; Website: www.presbyterian.org.nz).

EVANGELICAL PRESBYTERIAN CHURCH, GHANA
Synod Clerk: PO Box 18, Ho, Volta Region, Ghana (E-mail: epchurch@ghana.com).

PRESBYTERIAN CHURCH OF GHANA
Synod Clerk: PO Box 1800, Accra, Ghana (E-mail: clerk@pcgonline.org).

PRESBYTERIAN CHURCH OF EAST AFRICA
Secretary General: PO Box 27573, 00506 Nairobi, Kenya (E-mail: info@pcea.or.ke; Website: http://pceaheadoffice.org).

CHURCH OF CENTRAL AFRICA PRESBYTERIAN
Secretary General, General Synod: PO Box 30398, Lilongwe 3, Malawi (E-mail: ccapgeneral@africa-online.net).

IGREJA EVANGELICA DE CRISTO EM MOÇAMBIQUE (EVANGELICAL CHURCH OF CHRIST IN MOZAMBIQUE)
General Secretary: Cx. Postale 284, Nampula 70100, Mozambique (E-mail: mugema@tdm.co.mz).

PRESBYTERIAN CHURCH OF NIGERIA
Principal Clerk: 26–29 Ehere Road, Ogbor Hill, PO Box 2635, Aba, Abia State, Nigeria (E-mail: eme.ndukwe@yahoo.com).

UNITING PRESBYTERIAN CHURCH IN SOUTHERN AFRICA (SOUTH AFRICA)
General Secretary: PO Box 96188, Brixton, Johannesburg 2019, South Africa (E-mail: office@unitingpresbyterian.org).

UNITING PRESBYTERIAN CHURCH IN SOUTHERN AFRICA (ZIMBABWE)
Presbytery Clerk: PO Box CY224, Causeway, Harare, Zimbabwe (E-mail: presbyte@mweb.co.zw).

PRESBYTERIAN CHURCH OF THE SUDAN
Head Office: PO Box 40, Malakal, Sudan (E-mail: pcosgassembly@yahoo.com).

UNITED CHURCH OF ZAMBIA
General Secretary: Nationalist Road at Burma Road, PO Box 50122, 15101 Ridgeway, Lusaka, Zambia (E-mail: info@uczsynod.org).

CHURCH OF BANGLADESH
Moderator: Synod Office, Church of Bangladesh, 54/1 Barobag, Mirpur-2, Dhaka 1216, Bangladesh (E-mail: sarkerps@gmail.com).

BURMA: PRESBYTERIAN CHURCH OF MYANMAR
Tahan, Kalaymyo, Myanmar (E-mail: pcmgao@gmail.com).

CHINA
* Amity Foundation, 71 Hankou Road, Nanjing, JS 210008, China.
* China Christian Council, 219 Jiujiang Road, Shanghai 200002, China.
* Nanjing Union Theological Seminary, 100 Qiaoge Lu, Jiangning, Nanjing 211112, China.

CHURCH OF NORTH INDIA
General Secretary: Synod Office, PO Box 311, 16 Pandit Pant Marg., New Delhi 110 001, India
(E-mail: alwanmasih@cnisynod.org).

CHURCH OF SOUTH INDIA
General Secretary: Synod Office, 5 White's Road, Royapettah, Chennai 600 014, India (E-mail:
csi@vsnl.com).

PRESBYTERIAN CHURCH OF KOREA
General Secretary: 135 Yunji Dong, Chongro-Gu, Seoul 110 470, Korea (E-mail: master@pck.
or.kr).

PRESBYTERIAN CHURCH IN THE REPUBLIC OF KOREA
General Secretary: Academy House San 76, Suyu 6-dong, Kangbuk-Ku, Seoul 142070, Korea
(E-mail: prokshin@hanmail.net).

THE UNITED MISSION TO NEPAL
Executive Director: PO Box 126, Kathmandu, Nepal (E-mail: umn@umn.org.np).

CHURCH OF PAKISTAN
Moderator: Rt Rev. Samuel Azariah, Diocese of Raiwind, 17 Warris Road, Lahore 54000, Pakistan
(E-mail: sammyazariah@yahoo.com).

PRESBYTERY OF LANKA
Moderator: 127/1 D S Senanayake Veedyan, Kandy 2000, Sri Lanka (E-mail: scotskirksaman@
sltnet.lk).

PRESBYTERIAN CHURCH IN TAIWAN
General Secretary: 3 Lane 269 Roosevelt Road, Sec. 3, Taipei, Taiwan 10763, ROC (E-mail:
gs@mail.pct.org.tw).

CHURCH OF CHRIST IN THAILAND
General Secretary: 109 CCT Building, 328 Payathai Road, Ratchathevi, Bangkok 10400,
Thailand (E-mail: cctecume@loxinfo.co.th).

PRESBYTERIAN CHURCH IN SINGAPORE
Synod Office: 132 Sophia Road, Singapore (E-mail: office@presbysing.org.sg).

UNITED CHURCH IN JAMAICA AND THE CAYMAN ISLANDS
General Secretary: 12 Carlton Crescent, PO Box 359, Kingston 10, Jamaica (E-mail:
generalsecretary@ucjci.com).

PRESBYTERIAN CHURCH IN TRINIDAD AND TOBAGO
General Secretary: Box 187, Paradise Hill, San Fernando, Trinidad (E-mail: pctt@tstt.net.tt).

PRESBYTERIAN REFORMED CHURCH IN CUBA
General Secretary: Evangelical Theological Seminary of Matanzas, Apartada 149, Dos de Mayofinal, Matanzas, Cuba (E-mail: publiset@enet.cu).

EVANGELICAL CHURCH OF THE CZECH BRETHREN
Moderator: Jungmannova 9, PO Box 466, CZ-11121 Praha 1, Czech Republic (E-mail: ekumena@srcce.cz; Website: www.srcce.cz).

REFORMED CHURCH IN HUNGARY
General Secretary: Abonyi utca 21, H-1146 Budapest, Hungary (E-mail: oikumene@reformatus. hu; Website: www.reformatus.hu).

WALDENSIAN CHURCH
Moderator: Via Firenze 38, 00184 Rome, Italy (E-mail: moderatore@chiesavaldese.org; Website: www.chiesavaldese.org).

PROTESTANT CHURCH IN THE NETHERLANDS
Joseph Haydnlaan 2A, Postbus 8504, NL-3503 RM Utrecht (Tel/Fax: +31 30 880 1880; E-mail: servicedesk@pkn.nl; Website: www.pkn.nl).

SYNOD OF THE NILE OF THE EVANGELICAL CHURCH OF EGYPT
General Secretary: Synod of the Nile of the Evangelical Church, PO Box 1248, Cairo, Egypt (E-mail: epcegypt@yahoo.com).

DIOCESE OF THE EPISCOPAL CHURCH IN JERUSALEM AND THE MIDDLE EAST
Bishop's Office: PO Box 19122, Jerusalem 91191, Israel (E-mail: perexecassistant@j-diocese.org; Website: www.j.diocese.org).

NATIONAL EVANGELICAL SYNOD OF SYRIA AND LEBANON
General Secretary: PO Box 70890, Antelias, Lebanon (E-mail: nessl@synod-sl.org).

MIDDLE EAST COUNCIL OF CHURCHES
General Secretary: PO Box 5376, Deeb Building, Makhoul Street, Beirut, Lebanon (E-mail: mecc@cyberia.net.lb).

[Full information on Churches overseas may be obtained from the World Mission Council.]

---

(3) SCOTTISH DIVINITY FACULTIES
[* denotes a Minister of the Church of Scotland]
[(R) Reader   (SL) Senior Lecturer   (L) Lecturer]

ABERDEEN
(School of Divinity, History and Philosophy)
50–52 College Bounds, Old Aberdeen AB24 3DS
(Tel: 01224 272366; Fax: 01224 273750; E-mail: divinity@abdn.ac.uk)

Master of Christ's College: Rev. John Swinton* BD PhD RNM RNMD
(E-mail: christs-college@abdn.ac.uk)
Head of School: John Morrison MA PhD
Deputy Head of School: Jutta Leonhardt-Balzer DipTheol PhD

Professors: Tom Greggs MA(Oxon) PhD(Cantab) (Historical and Doctrinal
Theology)
Steve Mason BA MA PhD (New Testament Exegesis)
Paul T. Nimmo MA DipIA BD ThM PhD (Systematic Theology)
Rev. Joachim Schaper DipTheol PhD (Old Testament)
Robert Segal BA MA PhD (Religious Studies)
Rev. John Swinton* BD PhD RNM RNMD (Practical Theology
and Pastoral Care)

Senior Lecturers: Andrew Clarke BA MA PhD (New Testament)
Martin Mills MA PhD (Religious Studies)
Rev. Philip Ziegler BA MA MDiv ThD (Systematic Theology)

Lecturers: Kenneth Aitken BD PhD (Hebrew Bible)
Thomas Bokedal ThD MTh (New Testament)
Rev. Christopher Brittain BA MDiv PhD (Practical Theology)
Brian Brock BS MA DipTheol DPhil (Moral and Practical
Theology)
Marie-Luise Ehrenschwendtner DrTheol PhD (Church History)
Zohar Hadromi-Allouche BA PhD (Religious Studies)
Jutta Leonhardt-Balzer DipTheol PhD (New Testament)
Michael Mawson BA MA PhD (Theological Ethics)
Lukas Pokorny MA PhD (Religious Studies)
Lena-Sofia Tiemeyer BA MA MPhil (Old Testament/Hebrew
Bible)
Will Tuladhar-Douglas BA MA MPhil DPhil (Religious Studies)
Donald Wood BA MA MPhil DPhil (Systematic Theology)

ST ANDREWS
(University College of St Mary)
St Mary's College, St Andrews, Fife KY16 9JU
(Tel: 01334 462850/1; Fax: 01334 462852)

Principal: Very Rev. Dr Ian C. Bradley*
Head of School: Dr Mark W. Elliott
Dean:

Chairs: M.I. Aguilar OSB Cam Obl BA MA STB PhD FRSA FRAS FRAI
FIAI (Religion and Politics)
D.W. Brown MA PhD DLitt FBA FRSE (Theology, Aesthetics and
Culture and Wardlaw Professor)

I.J. Davidson MA PhD MTh (Systematic and Historical Theology)
J.R. Davila BA MA PhD (Early Jewish Studies)
K. De Troyer STB MA STL PhD (Old Testament/Hebrew Bible)
R.A. Piper BA BD PhD (Christian Origins)
A.J. Torrance* MA BD DrTheol (Systematic Theology)
J.B. Webster MA PhD DD FRSE (Divinity)
N.T. Wright MA DPhil DD (New Testament and Early Christianity)

Readers: I.C. Bradley* BA MA BD DPhil (Church History)
M.W. Elliott BA BD PhD (Church History)
S.R. Hafemann BA MA DrTheol (New Testament)

Senior Lecturers: S.R. Holmes BA MA MTh PGDip PhD (Theology)
G. Macaskill BSc DipTh PhD (New Testament)
W.A. Tooman BA MA MA PhD (Old Testament/Hebrew Bible)

Lecturers: G.R. Hopps BA MPhil PhD (Literature and Theology)
W. Hyland BA MA PhD (Teaching Fellow – Church History)
M. Nevader BA MPhil DPhil (Old Testament)
J. Perry BA MDiv PhD (Theological Ethics)
E. Shively BA MDiv ThM PhD (New Testament)
E. Stoddart BD PhD (Practical Theology)
J. Wolfe BA MA MPhil DPhil (Theology and Literature)

EDINBURGH
(School of Divinity and New College)
New College, Mound Place, Edinburgh EH1 2LX
(Tel: 0131-650 8900; Fax: 0131-650 7952; E-mail: divinity.faculty@ed.ac.uk)

Head of School: Graham Paul Foster BD MSt PhD
Principal of New College: Rev. Professor David A.S. Fergusson* MA BD DPhil FBA FRSE
Assistant Principal of
New College: Rev. Alison M. Jack* MA BD PhD
Chairs: Professor Stewart J. Brown BA MA PhD DD FRHistS FRSE
(Ecclesiastical History)
Professor Jane E.A. Dawson BA PhD DipEd
(John Laing Professor of Reformation History)
Rev. Professor David A.S. Fergusson* MA BD DPhil FBA FRSE
(Divinity)
Professor Susan Hardman Moore* BA PGCE MA PhD (Early
Modern Religion)
Professor Timothy Lim BA MPhil DPhil (Biblical Studies)
Professor Jolyon Mitchell BA MA PhD (Communications, Arts
and Religion)
Professor Michael S. Northcott MA PhD (Ethics)

Professor Mona Siddiqui OBE FRSE FRSA DCivil Laws (hon)
DLitt (hon) (Islamic and Interreligious Studies)
Professor Brian Stanley MA PhD (World Christianity)

Readers, Senior Lecturers and Lecturers:

Biblical Studies:

Helen K. Bond MTheol PhD (SL)
Graham Paul Foster BD MSt PhD (SL)
David J. Reimer BTh BA MA DPhil (SL)
Anja Klein PhD (L)
Matthew Novenson BA MDiv ThM PhD (L)

Theology and Ethics:

Nicholas Adams MA PhD (SL)
Rev. Ewan Kelly* MB ChB BD PhD (SL) (part-time)
Alexander Chow MA ThM PhD (L)
James Eglinton LLB BTh PhD (L)
David Grumett BA MPhil PhD (L)
Mark Harris MA PhD MA (L)

History of Christianity:

Sara Parvis BA PhD (L)

Religious Studies:

Afeosemime U. Adogame BA MA PhD (SL)
Hannah Holtschneider MPhil PhD (SL)
Steven Sutcliffe BA MPhil PhD (SL)
Naomi Appleton BA MPhil DPhil (L)
Arko Longkumer PhD (L)

Fulton Lecturer in Speech and Communication:
Richard Ellis BSc MEd LGSM

GLASGOW
School of Critical Studies
Theology and Religious Studies Subject Area
4 The Square, University of Glasgow, Glasgow G12 8QQ
(Tel: 0141-330 6526; Fax: 0141-330 4943;
Website: www.gla.ac.uk/departments/theology)

Head of Subject:

Rev. Canon Dr Charlotte Methuen

Trinity College
Principal of Trinity College:
Clerk to Trinity College:

Rev. Dr Doug Gay*

Chairs:

Rev. Prof. David Jasper (Theology and Literature)
Rev. Prof. George Pattison (Divinity)

Readers, Senior Lecturers, Lecturers and Fellows etc.

Biblical Studies: Dr Sarah Nicholson (L)
Dr Sean Adams (L) (New Testament)

Church History: Rev. Canon Dr Charlotte Methuen (SL)
Rev. Prof.-Emer. W. Ian P. Hazlett* (Hon. Professorial Research Fellow)

Catholic Theology: Ms Julie Clague (L)

Practical Theology: Dr Heather Walton (SL)
Rev. Dr Doug Gay* (L)
Ms Leah Robinson (L)

Religious Studies: Dr Lloyd Ridgeon (SL) (Islamic Studies)
Dr Charles Orzech (SL) (Eastern Traditions)
Dr Scott Spurlock (L) (Religion in Scotland)
Dr Mia Spiro (L) (Jewish Studies)
Dr Saeko Yazaki (Research Fellow: Islamic Studies)

Associate Staff (Free Church of Scotland College, Edinburgh)

Rev. Donald M. MacDonald
Rev. Prof. John R. McIntosh
Rev. Prof. John L. Mackay
Rev. Alasdair I. MacLeod
Rev. Prof. Donald Macleod
Rev. John A. MacLeod
Rev. Neil MacMillan
Rev. Duncan Peters

HIGHLAND THEOLOGICAL COLLEGE UHI
High Street, Dingwall IV15 9HA
(Tel: 01349 780000; Fax: 01349 780201;
E-mail: htc@uhi.ac.uk)

Principal of HTC: Rev. Hector Morrison* BSc BD MTh
Vice-Principal of HTC: Jamie Grant PhD MA LLB

Lecturers: Jamie Grant PhD MA LLB (Biblical Studies)
Jason Maston BA MA PhD (New Testament)
Rev. Hector Morrison* BSc BD MTh (Old Testament and Hebrew)
Rev. Nick Needham BD PhD (Church History)
Robert Shillaker BSc BA PhD (Systematic Theology)
Rev. Bruce Ritchie* BSc BD PhD (Church History)
Rev. Innes Visagie MA BTh BA PhD (Pastoral Theology)

(4) SOCIETIES AND ASSOCIATIONS

The undernoted list shows the name of the Association, along with the name and address of the Secretary.

1. INTER-CHURCH ASSOCIATIONS

The FELLOWSHIP OF ST ANDREW: The fellowship promotes dialogue between Churches of the east and the west in Scotland. Further information available from the Secretary, Rev. John G. Pickles, 1 Annerley Road, Annan DG12 6HE (Tel: 01461 202626; E-mail: jgpickles@hotmail.com).

The FELLOWSHIP OF ST THOMAS: An ecumenical association formed to promote informed interest in and to learn from the experience of Churches in South Asia (India, Pakistan, Bangladesh, Nepal, Sri Lanka and Burma (Myanmar)). Secretary: Rev. Canon Val Nellist, 28 Glamis Gardens, Dalgety Bay, Dunfermline KY11 5TD (Tel: 01383 824066; E-mail: valnellist@btinternet.com).

FRONTIER YOUTH TRUST: Encourages, resources and supports churches, organisations and individuals working with young people (in particular, disadvantaged young people). Through the StreetSpace initiative, the Trust is able to help churches to explore new ways of engaging young people in the community around mission and fresh expressions of church. All correspondence to: Frontier Youth Trust, Office S15b, St George's Community Hub, Great Hampton Row, Newtown, Birmingham B19 3JG (Tel: 0121-687 3505; E-mail: frontier@fyt.org.uk; Website: www.fyt.org.uk). For information on StreetSpace, contact Richard Passmore (07830 197160).

INTERSERVE SCOTLAND: We are part of Interserve, an international, evangelical and interdenominational organisation with 160 years of Christian service. The purpose of Interserve is 'to make Jesus Christ known through *wholistic* ministry in partnership with the global church, among the neediest peoples of Asia and the Arab world', and our vision is 'Lives and communities transformed through encounter with Jesus Christ'. Interserve supports over 800 people in cross-cultural ministry in a wide range of work including children and youth, the environment, evangelism, Bible training, engineering, agriculture, business development and health. We rely on supporters in Scotland and Ireland to join us. Director: Grace Penney, 4 Blairtummock Place, Panorama Business Village, Queenslie, Glasgow G33 4EN (Tel: 0141-781 1982; Fax: 0141-781 1572; E-mail: info@issi.org.uk; Website: www.interservescotlandandireland.org).

IONA COMMUNITY: An ecumenical Christian community of men and women from different walks of life and different traditions in the Church, committed to the gospel of Jesus Christ and to following where that leads, even into the unknown; engaged together, and with people of goodwill across the world, in acting, reflecting and praying for justice, peace and the integrity of creation; convinced that the inclusive community we seek must be embodied in the community we practise. The Iona Community's work with young people, Wild Goose Resource Group and Wild Goose Publications, is based in the Glasgow office. The Community also runs residential centres at the Abbey and MacLeod Centre, Iona and Camas, Mull. Leader: Rev. Peter Macdonald, 4th Floor, Savoy House, 140 Sauchiehall Street, Glasgow G2 3DH (Tel: 0141-332 6343; Fax: 0141-332 1090; E-mail: admin@

iona.org.uk; Website: www.iona.org.uk). Centres Director: Rev. Joanna Anderson, Iona Abbey, Isle of Iona, Argyll PA76 6SN (Tel: 01681 700404).

PLACE FOR HOPE: An initiative with its roots in the Church of Scotland, offering a different way of addressing our differences. It is a network of professionally trained individuals, equipped to facilitate some of our more difficult conversations, offering the means of restoring broken relationships. To Kirk Sessions, Presbyteries and any other groups, we provide training in the skills which can lead to more effective conversations with one another, recognising and valuing our differences. We encourage and enable dialogue – rather than debate – and a means of enabling all voices to be heard. We seek to work across denominations and offer our skills and resources into the community. We operate on a confidential basis, and would be pleased to have a conversation at any time on how we might be of help. Visit www.placeforhope.org.uk, or contact Natalie Barrett (Tel: 07884 580361; E-mail: natalie.barrett@placeforhope.org.uk).

The ST COLM'S FELLOWSHIP: An association for all from any denomination who have trained, studied or been resident at St Colm's, either when it was a college or later as International House. There is an annual retreat and annual lecture; and some local groups meet on a regular basis. Hon. Secretary: Margaret Nutter, 'Kilmorich', 14 Balloch Road, Balloch G83 8SR (Tel: 01389 754505; E-mail: mnutter@blueyonder.co.uk).

SCOTTISH CHURCHES HOUSING ACTION: Unites the Scottish Churches in tackling homelessness; supports local volunteering to assist homeless people; advises on using property for affordable housing. Chief Executive: Alastair Cameron, 44 Hanover Street, Edinburgh EH2 2DR (Tel: 0131-477 4500; E-mail: info@churches-housing.org; Website: www.churches-housing.org).

SCOTTISH JOINT COMMITTEE ON RELIGIOUS AND MORAL EDUCATION: This is an interfaith body that began as a joint partnership between the Educational Institute of Scotland and the Church of Scotland to provide resources, training and support for the work of religious and moral education in schools. Rev. Ken Coulter, 121 George Street, Edinburgh EH2 4YN (Tel: 0131-225 5722; E-mail: kcoulter@cofscotland.org.uk), and Mr Lachlan Bradley, 6 Clairmont Gardens, Glasgow G3 7LW (Tel: 0141-353 3595).

SCRIPTURE UNION SCOTLAND: 70 Milton Street, Glasgow G4 0HR (Tel: 0141-332 1162; Fax: 0141-352 7600; E-mail: info@suscotland.org.uk; Website: www.suscotland.org. uk). Scripture Union Scotland's vision is to see the children and young people of Scotland exploring the Bible and responding to the significance of Jesus. SU Scotland works in schools running Christian Focus Weeks, taking part in assemblies and supporting extra-curricular groups. It also offers 'Classroom Outdoors', an outdoor education programme for school groups that is based around Curriculum for Excellence. These events take place at its two activity centres, Lendrick Muir (near Kinross) and Alltnacriche (near Aviemore), which also cater for church or school groups throughout the year. During the school holidays and at weekends, it runs an extensive programme of events for school-age children – including residential holidays (some focused on disadvantaged children and young people), missions and church-based holiday clubs. In addition, it runs discipleship and training programmes for young people and is committed to promoting prayer for, and by, the young people of Scotland through a range of national prayer events and the *Pray for Schools Scotland* initiative. The *SU Scotland Lounge* is our private, invitation-only Facebook group and public blog, providing a safe space for young people to explore the Bible, discuss issues of faith and encourage each other to follow Jesus.

STUDENT CHRISTIAN MOVEMENT: National Co-ordinator: Hilary Topp, SCM, 504F The Big Peg, 120 Vyse Street, Hockley, Birmingham B18 6NE (Tel: 0121-200 3355; E-mail: scm@movement.org.uk; Website: www.movement.org.uk). The Student Christian Movement (SCM) is a student-led community passionate about living out our faith in the real world. We have a network of groups around the country and organise national events.

UCCF: THE CHRISTIAN UNIONS: Blue Boar House, 5 Blue Boar Street, Oxford OX1 4EE (Tel: 01865 253678; E-mail: email@uccf.org.uk). UCCF is a fellowship of students, staff and supporters. Christian Unions are mission teams operating in universities and colleges, supported by the local church, and resourced by UCCF staff. This fellowship exists to proclaim the gospel of Jesus Christ in the student world.

WORLD DAY OF PRAYER: SCOTTISH COMMITTEE: Convener: Christian Williams, 61 McCallum Gardens, Strathview Estate, Bellshill ML4 2SR. Secretary: Marjorie Paton, Muldoanich, Stirling Street, Blackford, Auchterarder PH4 1QG (Tel: 01764 682234; E-mail: marjoriepaton.wdp@btinternet.com; Website: www.wdpscotland.org.uk).

YMCA SCOTLAND: Offers support, training and guidance to churches seeking to reach out to love and serve community needs. National General Secretary: Mr Peter Crory, James Love House, 11 Rutland Street, Edinburgh EH1 2DQ (Tel: 0131-228 1464; E-mail: ian@ymcascotland.org; Website: www.ymcascotland.org).

2. CHURCH OF SCOTLAND SOCIETIES

CHURCH OF SCOTLAND ABSTAINERS' ASSOCIATION: Recognising that alcohol is a major – indeed a growing – problem within Scotland, the aim of the Church of Scotland Abstainers' Association, with its motto 'Abstinence makes sense', is to encourage more people to choose a healthy alcohol-free lifestyle. Further details are available from 'Blochairn', 17A Culduthel Road, Inverness IV24 4AG (Website: www.kirkabstainers.org.uk).

The CHURCH OF SCOTLAND CHAPLAINS' ASSOCIATION: The Association consists of serving and retired chaplains to HM Forces. It holds an annual meeting and lunch, and organises the annual Service of Remembrance in St Giles' Cathedral on Chaplains' Day of the General Assembly. Hon. Secretary: Rev. Neil N. Gardner MA BD, The Manse of Canongate, Edinburgh EH8 8BR (Tel: 0131-556 3515).

The CHURCH OF SCOTLAND RETIRED MINISTERS' ASSOCIATION: Hon. Secretary: Rev. David Dutton, 13 Acredales, Haddington EH41 4NT (Tel: 01620 825999; E-mail: duttondw@gmail.com).

CHURCH OF SCOTLAND WORLD MISSION COUNCIL OVERSEAS ASSOCIATION (previously AROS): Secretary: Mr Walter Dunlop, 50 Oxgangs Road North, Edinburgh EH13 9DR (Tel: 07925 481523; E-mail: walt.jen@btopenworld.com).

The CHURCH SERVICE SOCIETY: Founded in 1865 to study the development of Christian worship through the ages and in the Reformed tradition, and to work towards renewal in contemporary worship. Secretary: Rev. Dr Douglas Galbraith (Tel: 01592 752403; E-mail: dgalbraith@hotmail.com; Website: www.churchservicesociety.org).

FORUM OF GENERAL ASSEMBLY AND PRESBYTERY CLERKS: Secretary: Rev. David W. Clark, 3 Ritchie Avenue, Cardross, Dumbarton G82 5LL (Tel: 01389 849319; E-mail: dumbarton@cofscotland.org.uk).

FORWARD TOGETHER: An organisation for evangelicals within the Church of Scotland. Contact the Secretary, Rev. Michael S. Goss (Tel: 01241 410194; E-mail: michaelgoss@blueyonder.co.uk), or the Chairman, Kenneth M. MacKenzie (Tel: 07836 365022; E-mail: kennethmmackenzie@btinternet.com; Website: http://ftscotland.wordpress.com).

The FRIENDS OF TABEETHA SCHOOL, JAFFA: President: Miss Eileen Robertson. Hon. Secretary: Rev. Iain F. Paton, Muldoanich, Stirling Street, Blackford, Auchterarder PH4 1QG (Tel: 01764 682234; E-mail: iain.f.paton@btinternet.com).

The IRISH GATHERING: Secretary: Rev. Eric G. McKimmon BA BD MTh PhD, The Manse, Manse Road, Woodside, Blairgowrie PH13 9NQ (Tel: 01828 670744; E-mail: ericmckimmon@gmail.com).

SCOTTISH CHURCH SOCIETY: Founded in 1892 to 'defend and advance Catholic doctrine as set forth in the Ancient Creeds and embodied in the Standards of the Church of Scotland'. Secretary: Rev. W. Gerald Jones MA BD MTh, The Manse, Patna Road, Kirkmichael, Maybole KA19 7PJ (Tel: 01655 750286; E-mail: revgerald@jonesg99.freeserve.co.uk).

SCOTTISH CHURCH THEOLOGY SOCIETY: Rev. Mary M. Cranfield MA BD DMin, The Manse, Daviot, Inverurie AB51 0HY (Tel: 01467 671241; E-mail: marymc@ukgateway. net). The Society encourages theological exploration and discussion of the main issues confronting the Church in the twenty-first century.

SOCIETY OF FRIENDS OF ST ANDREW'S JERUSALEM: Hon. Secretary: Major J.M.K. Erskine MBE, World Mission Council, 121 George Street, Edinburgh EH2 4YN. Hon. Treasurer: Mrs Catriona M. Scrimgeour BSc ACA, Finance Manager, The Church of Scotland, 121 George Street, Edinburgh EH2 4YN (Tel: 0131-225 5722).

3. BIBLE SOCIETIES

The SCOTTISH BIBLE SOCIETY: Chief Executive: Elaine Duncan, 7 Hampton Terrace, Edinburgh EH12 5XU (Tel: 0131-337 9701; E-mail: info@scottishbiblesociety.org).

WEST OF SCOTLAND BIBLE SOCIETY: Secretary: Rev. Finlay Mackenzie, 6 Shaw Road, Milngavie, Glasgow G62 6LU (Tel: 07817 680011; E-mail: f.c.mack51@gmail.com; Website: www.westofscotlandbiblesociety.com).

4. GENERAL

The BOYS' BRIGADE: Scottish Headquarters, Carronvale House, Carronvale Road, Larbert FK5 3LH (Tel: 01324 562008; Fax: 01324 552323; E-mail: scottishhq@boys-brigade.org.uk).

BROKEN RITES: Support group for divorced and separated clergy spouses (Tel: 01896 759254 or 01257 423893; Website: www.brokenrites.org).

CHRISTIAN AID SCOTLAND: Kathy Galloway, Head of Christian Aid Scotland, Sycamore House, 290 Bath Street, Glasgow G2 4JR (Tel: 0141-221 7475; E-mail: glasgow@ christian-aid.org). Edinburgh Office: Tel: 0131-220 1254. Perth Office: Tel: 01738 643982.

CHRISTIAN ENDEAVOUR IN SCOTLAND: Challenging and encouraging children and young people in the service of Christ and the Church, especially through the CE Award Scheme: 16 Queen Street, Alloa FK10 2AR (Tel: 01259 215101; E-mail: admin@cescotland.org; Website: www.cescotland.org).

DAYONE CHRISTIAN MINISTRIES (THE LORD'S DAY OBSERVANCE SOCIETY): Ryelands Road, Leominster, Herefordshire HR6 8NZ. Contact Mark Roberts for further information (Tel: 01568 613740; E-mail: info@dayone.co.uk).

ECO-CONGREGATION SCOTLAND: 121 George Street, Edinburgh EH2 4YN (Tel: 0131-240 2274; E-mail: manager@ecocongregationscotland.org; Website: www.ecocongregationscotland.org). Eco-Congregation Scotland is the largest movement of community-based environment groups in Scotland. We offer a programme to help congregations reduce their impact on climate change and live sustainably in a world of limited resources.

FEED THE MINDS: Park Place, 12 Lawn Lane, London SW8 1UD (Tel: 020 7582 3535; E-mail: asach@feedtheminds.org; Website: www.feedtheminds.org).

GIRLGUIDING SCOTLAND: 16 Coates Crescent, Edinburgh EH3 7AH (Tel: 0131-226 4511; Fax: 0131-220 4828; E-mail: administrator@girlguiding-scot.org.uk; Website: www. girlguidingscotland.org.uk).

The GIRLS' BRIGADE IN SCOTLAND: 11A Woodside Crescent, Glasgow G3 7UL (Tel: 0141-332 1765; E-mail: enquiries@girls-brigade-scotland.org.uk; Website: www.girls-brigade-scotland.org.uk).

The LEPROSY MISSION SCOTLAND: Suite 2, Earlsgate Lodge, Livilands Lane, Stirling FK8 2BG (Tel: 01786 449266; E-mail: contactus@tlmscotland.org.uk; Website: www.tlmscotland.org.uk). National Director: Linda Todd. Communications Manager: Stuart McAra.

RELATIONSHIPS SCOTLAND: Chief Executive: Mr Stuart Valentine, 18 York Place, Edinburgh EH1 3EP (Tel: 0845 119 2020; Fax: 0845 119 6089; E-mail: enquiries@ relationships-scotland.org.uk; Website: www.relationships-scotland.org.uk).

SCOTTISH CHURCH HISTORY SOCIETY: Hon. Secretary: Christine Lumsden BA MA PhD, 80/3 Slateford Road, Edinburgh EH11 1QU (Tel: 0131-337 3644; E-mail: christinaclumsden@gmail.com).

SCOTTISH EVANGELICAL THEOLOGY SOCIETY: Secretary: Rosemary Dowsett, 4 Borden Road, Glasgow G13 1QX (Tel: 0141-959 4976; E-mail: dickandrosedowsett@ googlemail.com; Website: www.s-e-t-s.org.uk).

The SCOTTISH REFORMATION SOCIETY: Chairman: Rev. Dr S. James Millar. Vice-Chairman: Rev. John J. Murray. Secretary: Rev. Dr Douglas Somerset. Treasurer: Rev. Andrew W.F. Coghill, The Magdalen Chapel, 41 Cowgate, Edinburgh EH1

1JR (Tel: 0131-220 1450; E-mail: info@scottishreformationsociety.org; Website: www.scottishreformationsociety.org).

The SCOUT ASSOCIATION: Scottish Headquarters, Fordell Firs, Hillend, Dunfermline KY11 7HQ (Tel: 01383 419073; E-mail: shq@scouts-scotland.org.uk; Website: www.scouts-scotland.org.uk).

The SOCIETY IN SCOTLAND FOR PROPAGATING CHRISTIAN KNOWLEDGE: Chairman: Rev. Scott McKenna; Honorary Secretary: Richard Grahame. Address: SSPCK, c/o Tods Murray LLP, Edinburgh Quay, 133 Fountainbridge, Edinburgh EH3 9AG (Tel: 0131-656 2000; Website: www.sspck.co.uk; E-mail: richard.grahame@todsmurray.com).

TEARFUND: 100 Church Road, Teddington TW11 8QE (Tel: 0845 355 8355). Director: Lynne Paterson, Tearfund Scotland, Challenge House, 29 Canal Street, Glasgow G4 0AD (Tel: 0141-332 3621; E-mail: scotland@tearfund.org; Website: www.tearfund.org).

THEATRE CHAPLAINCY UK (formerly the Actor's Church Union) is an ecumenical scheme providing a Church contact and support to staff and travelling theatre groups in theatres and concert halls throughout the UK. Area Chaplain Scotland: Rev. Thomas Coupar (Tel: 07814 588904; E-mail: chaplain@robinchapel.org.uk).

The WALDENSIAN MISSIONS AID SOCIETY FOR WORK IN ITALY: David A. Lamb SSC, 36 Liberton Drive, Edinburgh EH16 6NN (Tel: 0131-664 3059; E-mail: david@ dlamb.co.uk).

YOUTH SCOTLAND: Balfour House, 19 Bonnington Grove, Edinburgh EH6 4BL (Tel: 0131-554 2561; Fax: 0131-454 3438; E-mail: office@youthscotland.org.uk).

YWCA SCOTLAND: National Co-ordinator: Kim Smith, 4B Gayfield Place, Edinburgh EH7 4AB (Tel: 0131-558 8000; E-mail: reception@ywcascotland.org; Website: www. ywcascotland.org).

---

(5) TRUSTS AND FUNDS

The ABERNETHY TRUST: Offers residential accommodation and outdoor activities for Youth Fellowships, Church family weekends and Bible Classes at four outdoor centres in Scotland. Further details from the Executive Director, Abernethy Trust, Nethy Bridge PH25 3ED (Tel: 01479 821279; Website: www.abernethy.org.uk).

The ARROL TRUST: The Arrol Trust gives small grants to young people between the ages of 16 and 25 for the purposes of travel which will provide education or work experience. Potential recipients would be young people with disabilities or who would for financial reasons be otherwise unable to undertake projects. It is expected that projects would be beneficial not only to applicants but also to the wider community. Application forms are available from Callum S. Kennedy WS, Lindsays WS, Caledonian Exchange, 19A Canning Street, Edinburgh EH3 8HE (Tel: 0131-229 1212).

The BAIRD TRUST: Assists in the building and repair of churches and halls, and generally assists the work of the Church of Scotland. Apply to Iain A.T. Mowat CA, 182 Bath Street, Glasgow G2 4HG (Tel: 0141-332 0476; E-mail: info@bairdtrust.org.uk; Website: www.bairdtrust.org.uk).

The Rev. Alexander BARCLAY BEQUEST: Assists a mother, daughter, sister or niece of a deceased minister of the Church of Scotland who at the time of his/her death was acting as his/her housekeeper and who is in needy circumstances. Applications should be made to the Secretary and Clerk, The Church of Scotland Trust, 121 George Street, Edinburgh EH2 4YN (Tel: 0131-240 2222; E-mail: jhamilton@cofscotland.org.uk).

BELLAHOUSTON BEQUEST FUND: Gives grants to Protestant evangelical denominations in the City of Glasgow and certain areas within five miles of the city boundary for building and repairing churches and halls and the promotion of religion. Apply to Mr Donald B. Reid, Mitchells Roberton, 36 North Hanover Street, Glasgow G1 2AD (Tel: 0141-552 3422; E-mail: info@mitchells-roberton.co.uk).

BEQUEST FUND FOR MINISTERS: Provides financial assistance to ministers in outlying districts towards the cost of manse furnishings, pastoral efficiency aids, and personal and family medical or educational (including university) costs. Apply to A. Linda Parkhill CA, 60 Wellington Street, Glasgow G2 6HJ (Tel: 0141-226 4994; E-mail: mail@parkhillmackie.co.uk).

CARNEGIE TRUST FOR THE UNIVERSITIES OF SCOTLAND: In cases of hardship, the Carnegie Trust is prepared to consider applications by students of Scottish birth or extraction (at least one parent born in Scotland), or who have had at least two years' education at a secondary school in Scotland, for financial assistance with the payment of their fees for a first degree at a Scottish university. For further details, students should apply to the Secretary, Carnegie Trust for the Universities of Scotland, Andrew Carnegie House, Pittencrieff Street, Dunfermline KY12 8AW (Tel: 01383 724990; Fax: 01383 749799; E-mail: admin@carnegie-trust.org; Website: www.carnegie-trust.org).

CHURCH OF SCOTLAND INSURANCE CO. LTD: Arranges Church property and liabilities insurance in its capacity of Insurance Intermediary; also arranges other classes of business including household insurance for members and adherents of the Church of Scotland and insurances for charities. It pays its distributable profits to the Church of Scotland through Gift Aid. It is authorised by the Prudential Regulation Authority and regulated by the Financial Conduct Authority and the Prudential Regulation Authority. Contact at 67 George Street, Edinburgh EH2 2JG (Tel: 0131-220 4119; Fax: 0131-220 4120; E-mail: enquiries@cosic.co.uk; Website: www.cosic.co.uk).

CHURCH OF SCOTLAND MINISTRY BENEVOLENT FUND: Makes grants to retired men and women who have been ordained or commissioned for the ministry of the Church of Scotland and to widows, widowers, orphans, spouses or children of such, who are in need. Apply to the Assistant Treasurer (Ministries), 121 George Street, Edinburgh EH2 4YN (Tel: 0131-225 5722).

The CINTRA BEQUEST: See 'Tod Endowment Trust ...' entry below.

CLARK BURSARY: Awarded to accepted candidate(s) for the ministry of the Church of Scotland whose studies for the ministry are pursued at the University of Aberdeen. Applications or recommendations for the Bursary to the Clerk to the Presbytery of Aberdeen, Mastrick Church, Greenfern Road, Aberdeen AB16 6TR by 16 October annually.

CRAIGCROOK MORTIFICATION: Pensions are paid to poor men and women over 60 years old, born in Scotland or who have resided in Scotland for not less than ten years. At present, pensions amount to £1,000–£1,500 p.a.

Ministers are invited to notify the Clerk and Factor, Mrs Fiona M.M. Watson CA, Exchange Place 3, Semple Street, Edinburgh EH3 8BL (Tel: 0131-473 3500; E-mail: charity@scott-moncrieff. com) of deserving persons and should be prepared to act as a referee on the application form.

CROMBIE SCHOLARSHIP: Provides grants annually on the nomination of the Deans of Faculty of Divinity of the Universities of St Andrews, Glasgow, Aberdeen and Edinburgh, who each nominate one matriculated student who has taken a University course in Greek (Classical or Hellenistic) and Hebrew. Award by recommendation only.

The DRUMMOND TRUST: Makes grants towards the cost of publication of books of 'sound Christian doctrine and outreach'. The Trustees are also willing to receive grant requests towards the cost of audio-visual programme material, but not equipment. Requests for application forms should be made to the Secretaries, Hill and Robb, 3 Pitt Terrace, Stirling FK8 2EY (Tel: 01786 450985; E-mail: douglaswhyte@hillandrobb.co.uk). Manuscripts should *not* be sent.

The David DUNCAN TRUST: Makes grants annually to students for the ministry and students in training to become deacons in the Church of Scotland in the Faculties of Arts and Divinity. Preference is given to those born or educated within the bounds of the former Presbytery of Arbroath. Applications not later than 31 October to Thorntons Law LLP, Brothockbank House, Arbroath DD11 1NE (reference: G.J.M. Dunlop; Tel: 01241 872683; E-mail: gdunlop@ thorntons-law.co.uk).

ERSKINE CUNNINGHAM HILL TRUST: Donates 50% of its annual income to the central funds of the Church of Scotland and 50% to other charities. Individual donations are in the region of £1,000. Priority is given to charities administered by voluntary or honorary officials, in particular charities registered and operating in Scotland and relating to the elderly, young people, ex-service personnel or seafarers. Application forms from the Secretary, Nicola Robertson, 121 George Street, Edinburgh EH2 4YN (Tel: 0131-225 5722; E-mail: nrobertson@cofscotland.org.uk).

ESDAILE TRUST: Assists the education and advancement of daughters of ministers, missionaries and widowed deaconesses of the Church of Scotland between 12 and 25 years of age. Applications are to be lodged by 31 May in each year with the Clerk and Treasurer, Mrs Fiona M.M. Watson CA, Exchange Place 3, Semple Street, Edinburgh EH3 8BL (Tel: 0131-473 3500; E-mail: charity@scott-moncrieff.com).

FERGUSON BEQUEST FUND: Assists with the building and repair of churches and halls and, more generally, with the work of the Church of Scotland. Priority is given to the Counties of Ayr, Kirkcudbright, Wigtown, Lanark, Dunbarton and Renfrew, and to Greenock, Glasgow, Falkirk and Ardrossan; applications are, however, accepted from across Scotland. Apply to Iain A.T. Mowat CA, 182 Bath Street, Glasgow G2 4HG (Tel: 0141-332 0476; E-mail: info@ fergusonbequestfund.org.uk; Website: www.fergusonbequestfund.org.uk).

GEIKIE BEQUEST: Makes small grants to students for the ministry, including students studying for entry to the University, preference being given to those not eligible for SAAS awards. Apply to the Assistant Treasurer (Ministries), 121 George Street, Edinburgh EH2 4YN by September for distribution in November each year.

James GILLAN'S BURSARY FUND: Bursaries are available for male or female students for the ministry who were born or whose parents or parent have resided and had their home for not less than three years continually in the old counties (not Districts) of Moray or Nairn. Apply to R. and R. Urquhart LLP, 117–121 High Street, Forres IV36 1AB.

The GLASGOW SOCIETY OF THE SONS AND DAUGHTERS OF MINISTERS OF THE CHURCH OF SCOTLAND: The Society's primary purpose is to grant financial assistance to children (no matter what age) of deceased ministers of the Church of Scotland. Applications are to be submitted by 1 February in each year. To the extent that funds are available, grants are also given for the children of ministers or retired ministers, although such grants are normally restricted to university and college students. These latter grants are considered in conjunction with the Edinburgh-based Society. Limited funds are also available for individual application for special needs or projects. Applications are to be submitted by 31 May in each year. Emergency applications can be dealt with at any time when need arises. Application forms may be obtained from the Secretary and Treasurer, Mrs Fiona M.M. Watson CA, Exchange Place 3, Semple Street, Edinburgh EH3 8BL (Tel: 0131-473 3500; E-mail: charity@scott-moncrieff.com).

HAMILTON BURSARY TRUST: Awarded, subject to the intention to serve overseas under the Church of Scotland World Mission Council or to serve with some other Overseas Mission Agency approved by the Council, to a student at the University of Aberdeen. Preference is given to a student born or residing in (1) Parish of Skene, (2) Parish of Echt, (3) the Presbytery of Aberdeen, Kincardine and Deeside, or Gordon; failing which to Accepted Candidate(s) for the Ministry of the Church of Scotland whose studies for the Ministry are pursued at Aberdeen University. Applications or recommendations for the Bursary to the Clerk to the Presbytery of Aberdeen by 16 October annually.

Martin HARCUS BEQUEST: Makes annual grants to candidates for the ministry resident within the City of Edinburgh. Applications to the Clerk to the Presbytery of Edinburgh, 10/1 Palmerston Place, Edinburgh EH12 5AA by 15 October (E-mail: edinburgh@cofscotland.org.uk).

The HOPE TRUST: Gives some support to organisations involved in combating drink and drugs, and has as its main purpose the promotion of the Reformed tradition throughout the world. There is also a Scholarship programme for Postgraduate Theology Study in Scotland. Apply to Robert P. Miller SSC LLB, 31 Moray Place, Edinburgh EH3 6BY (Tel: 0131-226 5151).

KEAY THOM TRUST: The principal purposes of the Keay Thom Trust are:
1. To benefit the widows, daughters or other dependent female relatives of deceased ministers, or wives of ministers who are now divorced or separated, all of whom have supported the minister in the fulfilment of his duties and who, by reason of death, divorce or separation, have been required to leave the manse. The Trust can assist them in the purchase of a house or by providing financial or material assistance whether it be for the provision of accommodation or not.
2. To assist in the education or training of the above female relatives or any other children of deceased ministers.

Further information and application forms are available from Miller Hendry, Solicitors, 10 Blackfriars Street, Perth PH1 5NS (Tel: 01738 637311).

LADIES' GAELIC SCHOOLS AND HIGHLAND BURSARY ASSOCIATION: Distributes money to students, preferably with a Highland/Gaelic background, who are training to be ministers in the Church of Scotland. Apply by 15 October in each year to the Secretary, Donald J. Macdonald, 35 Durham Avenue, Edinburgh EH15 1RZ (E-mail: djandanne@btinternet.com).

The LYALL BEQUEST (Scottish Charity Number SC005542): Offers grants to ministers:
1. Grants to individual ministers and to couples for a holiday for a minimum of one week. No reapplication within a three-year period; and thereafter a 50 per cent grant to those reapplying.
2. Grants towards sickness and convalescence costs so far as not covered by the National Health Service. Applications should be made to the Secretary and Clerk, The Church of Scotland Trust, 121 George Street, Edinburgh EH2 4YN (Tel: 0131-240 2222; E-mail: jhamilton@cofscotland.org.uk).

Gillian MACLAINE BURSARY FUND: Open to candidates for the ministry of the Church of Scotland of Scottish or Canadian nationality. Preference is given to Gaelic-speakers. Application forms available from Dr Christopher T. Brett MA PhD, Clerk to the Presbytery of Argyll, Minahey Cottage, Kames, Tighnabruaich PA21 2AD (Tel: 01700 811142; E-mail: argyll@cofscotland.org.uk). Closing date for receipt of applications is 31 October.

The E. McLAREN FUND: The persons intended to be benefited are widows and unmarried ladies, preference being given to ladies above 40 years of age in the following order:
(a) Widows and daughters of Officers in the Highland Regiment, and
(b) Widows and daughters of Scotsmen.
Further details from the Secretary, The E. McLaren Fund, Messrs BMK Wilson, Solicitors, 90 St Vincent Street, Glasgow G2 5UB (Tel: 0141-221 8004; Fax: 0141-221 8088; E-mail: rrs@bmkwilson.co.uk).

MORGAN BURSARY FUND: Makes grants to candidates for the Church of Scotland ministry studying at the University of Glasgow. Apply to the Clerk to the Presbytery of Glasgow, 260 Bath Street, Glasgow G2 4JP (Tel: 0141-332 6606).

NOVUM TRUST: Provides small short-term grants – typically between £200 and £2,500 – to initiate projects in Christian action and research which cannot readily be financed from other sources. Trustees welcome applications from projects that are essentially Scottish, are distinctively new, and are focused on the welfare of young people, on the training of lay people or on new ways of communicating the Christian faith. The Trust cannot support large building projects, staff salaries or individuals applying for maintenance during courses or training. Application forms and guidance notes from novumt@cofscotland.org.uk or Mrs Susan Masterton, Blair Cadell WS, The Bond House, 5 Breadalbane Street, Edinburgh EH6 5JH (Tel: 0131-555 5800).

PARK MEMORIAL BURSARY FUND: Provides grants for the benefit of candidates for the ministry of the Church of Scotland from the Presbytery of Glasgow under full-time training. Apply to the Clerk to the Presbytery of Glasgow, 260 Bath Street, Glasgow G2 4JP (Tel: 0141-332 6606).

PATON TRUST: Assists ministers in ill health to have a recuperative holiday outwith, and free from the cares of, their parishes. Apply to Alan S. Cunningham CA, Alexander Sloan, Chartered Accountants, 38 Cadogan Street, Glasgow G2 7HF (Tel: 0141-204 8989; Fax: 0141-248 9931; E-mail: alan.cunningham@alexandersloan.co.uk).

PRESBYTERY OF ARGYLL BURSARY FUND: Open to students who have been accepted as candidates for the ministry and the readership of the Church of Scotland. Preference is given to applicants who are natives of the bounds of the Presbytery, or are resident within the bounds of the Presbytery, or who have a strong connection with the bounds of the Presbytery. Application forms available from Dr Christopher T. Brett MA PhD, Clerk to the Presbytery of Argyll, Minahey Cottage, Kames, Tighnabruaich PA21 2AD (Tel: 01700 811142; E-mail: argyll@cofscotland.org.uk). Closing date for receipt of applications is 31 October.

Margaret and John ROSS TRAVELLING FUND: Offers grants to ministers and their spouses for travelling and other expenses for trips to the Holy Land where the purpose is recuperation or relaxation. Applications should be made to the Secretary and Clerk, The Church of Scotland Trust, 121 George Street, Edinburgh EH2 4YN (Tel: 0131-240 2222; E-mail: jhamilton@cofscotland.org.uk).

SCOTLAND'S CHURCHES TRUST: Assists, through grants, with the preservation of the fabric of buildings in use for public worship by any denomination. Also supports the playing of church organs by grants for public concerts, and through tuition bursaries for suitably proficient piano or organ players wishing to improve skills or techniques. SCT promotes visitor interest in churches through the trust's Pilgrim Journeys covering Scotland. Criteria and how to apply at www.scotlandschurchestrust.org.uk. Scotland's Churches Trust, 15 North Bank Street, Edinburgh EH1 2LP (E-mail: info@scotlandschurchestrust.org.uk).

SMIETON FUND: Makes small holiday grants to ministers. Administered at the discretion of the pastoral staff, who will give priority in cases of need. Applications to the Education and Support Secretary, Ministries Council, 121 George Street, Edinburgh EH2 4YN.

Mary Davidson SMITH CLERICAL AND EDUCATIONAL FUND FOR ABERDEENSHIRE: Assists ministers who have been ordained for five years or over and are in full charge of a congregation in Aberdeen, Aberdeenshire and the north, to purchase books, or to travel for educational purposes, and assists their children with scholarships for further education or vocational training. Apply to Alan J. Innes MA LLB, 100 Union Street, Aberdeen AB10 1QR (Tel: 01224 428000).

The SOCIETY FOR THE BENEFIT OF THE SONS AND DAUGHTERS OF THE CLERGY OF THE CHURCH OF SCOTLAND: Annual grants are made to assist in the education of the children (normally between the ages of 12 and 25 years) of ministers of the Church of Scotland. The Society also gives grants to aged and infirm daughters of ministers and ministers' unmarried daughters and sisters who are in need. Applications are to be lodged by 31 May in each year with the Secretary and Treasurer, Mrs Fiona M.M. Watson CA, Exchange Place 3, Semple Street, Edinburgh EH3 8BL (Tel: 0131-473 3500; E-mail: charity@scott-moncrieff.com).

The Nan STEVENSON CHARITABLE TRUST FOR RETIRED MINISTERS: Provides houses, or loans to purchase houses, on similar terms to the Housing and Loan Fund, for any retired paid church worker with a North Ayrshire connection. Secretary and Treasurer: Mrs Ann Turner, 42 Keir Hardie Drive, Ardrossan KA22 8PA (Tel: 01294 462834; E-mail: annturner62@ btopenworld.com).

Miss M.E. SWINTON PATERSON'S CHARITABLE TRUST: The Trust can give modest grants to support smaller congregations in urban or rural areas who require to fund essential maintenance or improvement works at their buildings. Apply to Mr Callum S. Kennedy WS, Messrs Lindsays WS, Caledonian Exchange, 19A Canning Street, Edinburgh EH3 8HE (Tel: 0131-229 1212).

SYNOD OF GRAMPIAN CHILDREN OF THE CLERGY FUND: Makes annual grants to children of deceased ministers. Apply to Rev. Iain U. Thomson, Clerk and Treasurer, 4 Keirhill Gardens, Westhill AB32 6AZ (Tel: 01224 746743).

SYNOD OF GRAMPIAN WIDOWS' FUND: Makes annual grants (currently £240 p.a.) to widows or widowers of deceased ministers who have served in a charge in the former Synod. Apply to Rev. Iain U. Thomson, Clerk and Treasurer, 4 Keirhill Gardens, Westhill AB32 6AZ (Tel: 01224 746743).

TOD ENDOWMENT TRUST; CINTRA BEQUEST; MINISTRY BENEVOLENT FUND: The Trustees of the Cintra Bequest and of the Church of Scotland Ministry Benevolent Fund can consider an application for a grant from the Tod Endowment funds from any ordained or commissioned minister or deacon in Scotland of at least two years' standing before the date of application, to assist with the cost of the beneficiary and his or her spouse or partner and dependants obtaining rest and recuperation in Scotland. The Trustees of the Church of Scotland Ministry Benevolent Fund can also consider an application from an ordained or commissioned minister or deacon who has retired. Application forms are available from Mrs J.S. Wilson, Solicitor (for the Cintra Bequest), and from the Assistant Treasurer (Ministries) (for the Ministry Benevolent Fund). The address in both cases is 121 George Street, Edinburgh EH2 4YN (Tel: 0131-225 5722). (Attention is drawn to the separate entry above for the Church of Scotland Ministry Benevolent Fund.)

YOUNG MINISTERS' FURNISHING LOAN FUND: Makes loans (of £1,000) to ministers in their first charge to assist with furnishing the manse. Apply to the Assistant Treasurer (Ministries), 121 George Street, Edinburgh EH2 4YN.

The undernoted hotels provide special terms as described. Fuller information may be obtained from the establishments:

CRIEFF HYDRO Ltd and MURRAYPARK HOTEL: The William Meikle Trust Fund and Paton Fund make provision whereby active ministers and their spouses and members of the Diaconate may enjoy the hotel and self-catering accommodation all year round at a supplemented rate, subject to availability and a maximum number of stays per year. Crieff Hydro offers a wide range of inclusive leisure facilities including leisure pool, gym, cinema and entertainment programme. BIG Country also provides free daily childcare for Crieff Hydro guests only. Over-60 on-site activities and five places to eat are also available at great prices.

Note: a moratorium has been placed on benefits from the Trust. The decision will be reviewed in November 2014. All benefits booked before 17 April 2014 will, however, be honoured.

(6) RECENT LORD HIGH COMMISSIONERS
TO THE GENERAL ASSEMBLY

1969	Her Majesty the Queen attended in person
1970	The Rt Hon. Margaret Herbison PC
1971/72	The Rt Hon. Lord Clydesmuir of Braidwood CB MBE TD
1973/74	The Rt Hon. Lord Ballantrae of Auchairne and the Bay of Islands GCMG GCVO DSO OBE
1975/76	Sir Hector MacLennan Kt FRCPGLAS FRCOG
1977	Francis David Charteris, Earl of Wemyss and March KT LLD
1978/79	The Rt Hon. William Ross MBE LLD
1980/81	Andrew Douglas Alexander Thomas Bruce, Earl of Elgin and Kincardine KT DL JP
1982/83	Colonel Sir John Edward Gilmour BT DSO TD
1984/85	Charles Hector Fitzroy Maclean, Baron Maclean of Duart and Morvern KT GCVO KBE
1986/87	John Campbell Arbuthnott, Viscount of Arbuthnott KT CBE DSC FRSE FRSA
1988/89	Sir Iain Mark Tennant KT FRSA
1990/91	The Rt Hon. Donald MacArthur Ross FRSE
1992/93	The Rt Hon. Lord Macfarlane of Bearsden KT FRSE
1994/95	Lady Marion Fraser LT
1996	Her Royal Highness the Princess Royal LT LG GCVO
1997	The Rt Hon. Lord Macfarlane of Bearsden KT FRSE
1998/99	The Rt Hon. Lord Hogg of Cumbernauld
2000	His Royal Highness the Prince Charles, Duke of Rothesay KG KT GCB OM
2001/02	The Rt Hon. Viscount Younger of Leckie
	Her Majesty the Queen attended the opening of the General Assembly of 2002
2003/04	The Rt Hon. Lord Steel of Aikwood KT KBE
2005/06	The Rt Hon. Lord Mackay of Clashfern KT
2007	His Royal Highness the Prince Andrew, Duke of York KG KCVO
2008/09	The Rt Hon. George Reid KT MA
2010/11	Lord Wilson of Tillyorn KT GCMG PRSE
2012/13	The Rt Hon. Lord Selkirk of Douglas QC MA LLB
2014	His Royal Highness the Prince Edward, Earl of Wessex KG GCVO

(7) RECENT MODERATORS
OF THE GENERAL ASSEMBLY

1969	T.M. Murchison MA DD, Glasgow: St Columba Summertown
1970	Hugh O. Douglas CBE LLD DD, Dundee: St Mary's
1971	Andrew Herron MA BD LLB LLD DD, Clerk to the Presbytery of Glasgow
1972	R.W.V. Selby Wright CVO TD DD FRSE JP, Edinburgh: Canongate
1973	George T.H. Reid MC MA BD DD, Aberdeen: Langstane
1974	David Steel MA BD LLD DD, Linlithgow: St Michael's
1975	James G. Matheson MA BD DD, Portree
1976	Thomas F. Torrance MBE DLitt DD FRSE, University of Edinburgh

1977	John R. Gray VRD MA BD ThM DD, Dunblane: Cathedral
1978	Peter P. Brodie MA BD LLB DD, Alloa: St Mungo's
1979	Robert A.S. Barbour KCVO MC MA BD STM DD, University of Aberdeen
1980	William B. Johnston MA BD DLitt DD, Edinburgh: Colinton
1981	Andrew B. Doig BD STM DD, National Bible Society of Scotland
1982	John McIntyre CVO DLitt DD FRSE, University of Edinburgh
1983	J. Fraser McLuskey MC DD, London: St Columba's
1984	John M.K. Paterson MA BD DD ACII, Milngavie: St Paul's
1985	David M.B.A. Smith MA BD DUniv, Logie
1986	Robert Craig CBE DLitt LLD DD, Emeritus of Jerusalem
1987	Duncan Shaw of Chapelverna *Bundesverdienstkreuz* PhD ThDr Drhc, Edinburgh: Craigentinny St Christopher's
1988	James A. Whyte MA LLD DD DUniv, University of St Andrews
1989	William J.G. McDonald MA BD DD, Edinburgh: Mayfield
1990	Robert Davidson MA BD DD FRSE, University of Glasgow
1991	William B.R. Macmillan MA BD LLD DD, Dundee: St Mary's
1992	Hugh R. Wyllie MA DD FCIBS, Hamilton: Old Parish Church
1993	James L. Weatherhead CBE MA LLB DD, Principal Clerk of Assembly
1994	James A. Simpson BSc BD STM DD, Dornoch Cathedral
1995	James Harkness KCVO CB OBE MA DD, Chaplain General (Emeritus)
1996	John H. McIndoe MA BD STM DD, London: St Columba's linked with Newcastle: St Andrew's
1997	Alexander McDonald BA DUniv CMIWSc, General Secretary, Department of Ministry
1998	Alan Main TD MA BD STM PhD DD, University of Aberdeen
1999	John B. Cairns KCVO LTh LLB LLD DD, Dumbarton: Riverside
2000	Andrew R.C. McLellan CBE MA BD STM DD, Edinburgh: St Andrew's and St George's
2001	John D. Miller BA BD DD, Glasgow: Castlemilk East
2002	Finlay A.J. Macdonald MA BD PhD DD, Principal Clerk of Assembly
2003	Iain R. Torrance TD DPhil DD DTheol LHD FRSE, University of Aberdeen
2004	Alison Elliot OBE MA MSc PhD LLD DD FRSE, Associate Director CTPI
2005	David W. Lacy BA BD DLitt DL, Kilmarnock: Henderson
2006	Alan D. McDonald LLB BD MTh DLitt DD, Cameron linked with St Andrews: St Leonard's
2007	Sheilagh M. Kesting BA BD DD, Secretary of Ecumenical Relations Committee
2008	David W. Lunan MA BD DUniv DLitt DD, Clerk to the Presbytery of Glasgow
2009	William C. Hewitt BD DipPS, Greenock: Westburn
2010	John C. Christie BSc BD MSB CBiol, Interim Minister
2011	A. David K. Arnott MA BD, St Andrews: Hope Park with Strathkinness
2012	Albert O. Bogle BD MTh, Bo'ness: St Andrew's
2013	E. Lorna Hood MA BD DD, Renfrew: North
2014	John P. Chalmers BD CPS, Principal Clerk of Assembly

MATTER OF PRECEDENCE

The Lord High Commissioner to the General Assembly of the Church of Scotland (while the Assembly is sitting) ranks next to the Sovereign and the Duke of Edinburgh and before the rest of the Royal Family.

The Moderator of the General Assembly of the Church of Scotland ranks next to the Lord Chancellor of Great Britain and before the Keeper of the Great Seal of Scotland (the First Minister) and the Dukes.

(8) HER MAJESTY'S HOUSEHOLD IN SCOTLAND
ECCLESIASTICAL

Dean of the Order of the Thistle and Dean of the Chapel Royal:	Very Rev. Prof. Iain R. Torrance TD DPhil DD DTheol LHD FRSE

Domestic Chaplains:
Rev. Kenneth I. Mackenzie DL BD CPS
Rev. Neil N. Gardner MA BD

Chaplains in Ordinary:
Rev. Norman W. Drummond CBE MA BD DUniv FRSE
Rev. Alastair H. Symington MA BD
Very Rev. Finlay A.J. Macdonald MA BD PhD DD
Rev. James M. Gibson TD LTh LRAM
Rev. Angus Morrison MA BD PhD
Rev. E. Lorna Hood MA BD DD
Rev. Alistair G. Bennett BSc BD
Rev. Susan M. Brown BD DipMin
Right Rev. John P. Chalmers BD CPS

Extra Chaplains:
Rev. Kenneth MacVicar MBE DFC TD MA
Very Rev. Prof. Robert A.S. Barbour
    KCVO MC MA BD STM DD
Rev. Alwyn Macfarlane MA
Rev. John MacLeod MA
Very Rev. James L. Weatherhead CBE MA LLB DD
Very Rev. James A. Simpson BSc BD STM DD
Very Rev. James Harkness KCVO CB OBE MA DD
Rev. John L. Paterson MA BD STM
Rev. Charles Robertson LVO MA
Very Rev. John B. Cairns KCVO LTh LLB LLD DD
Very Rev. Gilleasbuig Macmillan
    KCVO MA BD Drhc DD FRSE

(9) LONG SERVICE CERTIFICATES

Long Service Certificates, signed by the Moderator, are available for presentation to elders and others in respect of not less than thirty years of service. It should be noted that the period is years of *service*, not (for example) years of ordination in the case of an elder.

In the case of Sunday School teachers and Bible Class leaders, the qualifying period is twenty-one years of service.

Certificates are not issued posthumously, nor is it possible to make exceptions to the rules, for example by recognising quality of service in order to reduce the qualifying period, or by reducing the qualifying period on compassionate grounds, such as serious illness.

A Certificate will be issued only once to any particular individual.

Applications for Long Service Certificates should be made in writing to the Principal Clerk at 121 George Street, Edinburgh EH2 4YN by the parish minister, or by the session clerk on behalf of the Kirk Session. Certificates are not issued from this office to the individual recipients, nor should individuals make application themselves.

(10) LIBRARIES OF THE CHURCH

GENERAL ASSEMBLY LIBRARY AND RECORD ROOM
Most of the books contained in the General Assembly Library have been transferred to the New College Library. Records of the General Assembly, Synods, Presbyteries and Kirk Sessions are now in HM Register House, Edinburgh.

CHURCH MUSIC
The Library of New College contains a selection of works on Church music.

(11) RECORDS OF THE CHURCH OF SCOTLAND

Church records more than fifty years old, unless still in use, should be sent or delivered to the Principal Clerk for onward transmission to the National Records of Scotland. Where ministers or session clerks are approached by a local repository seeking a transfer of their records, they should inform the Principal Clerk, who will take the matter up with the National Records of Scotland.

Where a temporary retransmission of records is sought, it is extremely helpful if notice can be given three months in advance so that appropriate procedures can be carried out satisfactorily.

(12) ORGANIST TRAINING SCHEMES

This is a list of schemes operated by Presbyteries and other bodies to identify and train organists for Sunday services. The list is by no means exhaustive, and the Editor would be glad to know of any omissions.

1. SCOTTISH CHURCHES ORGANIST TRAINING SCHEME (SCOTS)
Established in 1997 as an initiative of the then Panel on Worship, along with the Royal School of Church Music's Scottish Committee and the Scottish Federation of Organists, this is a self-propelled scheme by which a pianist who seeks competence on the organ – and organists who wish to develop their skills – can follow a three-stage syllabus, receiving a certificate at each stage. Participants each have an Adviser whom they meet occasionally for assessment, and also take part in one of the three or four training days which are held in different parts of

Scotland each year. There is a regular e-newsletter, *Scots Wha Play*. The costs are low: £15 annual subscription, and £25 for a training day. SCOTS is an ecumenical scheme. Information from Douglas Galbraith (E-mail: dgalbraith@hotmail.com).

2. PRESBYTERY SCHEMES

Hamilton: Two scholarships of £300 each to cover one year of three terms, each consisting of ten half-hour lessons (E-mail: hamilton@cofscotland.org.uk).

Dunkeld and Meigle: Four scholarships of ten lessons (each £25) for existing or would-be organists of modest means and who are willing to be available for the accompaniment of church services (E-mail: dunkeldmeigle@cofscotland.org.uk).

Perth: Enables up to four people with the requisite keyboard skills to have tuition for up to two years (E-mail: perth@cofscotland.org.uk).

Dundee: Enables two persons per annum, preferably who have reached Grade 6 on keyboard or equivalent, to have organ lessons. A certificate is given on completion (E-mail: lewis_rose48@yahoo.co.uk).

3. OTHER SCHEMES

Positif Organist: This is a year-long experience, when a group meets for an evening once a month (nine meetings) on subjects ranging from the organ and its terminology, through different traditions and periods of organ music, to playing and registering traditional and modern hymns. The cost is £150 for the year. Contact Sheila Chisholm for an application form (E-mail: coolnote@coolnote.freeserve.co.uk; more details at http://sheilachisholm.weebly.com/positif-organist.htm).

St Andrews University: The **Summer Organ School** is a week-long residential course offering expert tuition, practice time and the chance to try several fine organs. Cost: with accommodation £595, without £295. Contact Ruth Carr, Summer Organ School Co-ordinator (Tel: 01334 462226; E-mail: rac10@st-andrews.ac.uk), or download a brochure (Website: www.st-andrews.ac.uk/music/perform/shortcourses).

Royal School of Church Music (RSCM) Skills Courses: These are designed to help practising church musicians to develop the skills and understanding that they need for their role, and to equip those who want to be able to lead music in worship. The programme is based on distance learning, combining private study at home with practical experience in the student's own church. It is designed for use by students studying alone or with a teacher, and may be complemented by optional attendance at RSCM workshops, masterclasses and short residential courses. There are three levels; and participants choose one of four skills: organist, choir director, cantor, music-group leader. Registration is £135; first level £290, each subsequent level £200. Brochure downloadable (Website: www.rscm.com).

Scotland's Churches Trust: In association with the Inches Carr Trust, SCT plans to offer up to four bursaries a year of £250 for a minimum of six hours' tuition, to be used within a three-month period. SCT (see page 67) has as one of its aims the opening of church buildings to visitors and pilgrims during the week; and it is hoped that the bursaries, as well as equipping church organists, might also lead to the instruments being heard more often by the public. Information from Stuart Muir (E-mail: music@saintpaulscathedral.net), Robin Bell (E-mail: robin.bell_home@hotmail.co.uk) or Douglas Galbraith (E-mail: dgalbraith@hotmail.com).

4. OTHER RESOURCES

Different Voices: An online blog/magazine on church music which publishes articles and videos useful to organists and other church musicians (Website: www.churchofscotland.org. uk/blogs).

Scottish Federation of Organists: The national network of organists (Website: www. scotsorgan.org.uk).

Church Service Society: A Scottish society (founded in 1865) which focuses on worship, including church music (Website: www.churchservicesociety.org). See entry on page 59.

SECTION 3

Church Procedure

(1) THE MINISTER AND BAPTISM

The administration of Baptism to infants is governed by Act V 2000 as amended by Act IX 2003. A Statement and Exposition of the Doctrine of Baptism may be found at page 13/8 in the published volume of Reports to the General Assembly of 2003.

The Act itself is as follows:

3.   Baptism signifies the action and love of God in Christ, through the Holy Spirit, and is a seal upon the gift of grace and the response of faith.
- (a)   Baptism shall be administered in the name of the Father and of the Son and of the Holy Spirit, with water, by sprinkling, pouring, or immersion.
- (b)   Baptism shall be administered to a person only once.

4.   Baptism may be administered to a person upon profession of faith.
- (a)   The minister and Kirk Session shall judge whether the person is of sufficient maturity to make personal profession of faith, where necessary in consultation with the parent(s) or legal guardian(s).
- (b)   Baptism may be administered only after the person has received such instruction in its meaning as the minister and Kirk Session consider necessary, according to such basis of instruction as may be authorised by the General Assembly.
- (c)   In cases of uncertainty as to whether a person has been baptised or validly baptised, baptism shall be administered conditionally.

5.   Baptism may be administered to a person with learning difficulties who makes an appropriate profession of faith, where the minister and Kirk Session are satisfied that the person shall be nurtured within the life and worship of the Church.

6.   Baptism may be administered to a child:
- (a)   where at least one parent, or other family member (with parental consent), having been baptised and being on the communion roll of the congregation, will undertake the Christian upbringing of the child;
- (b)   where at least one parent, or other family member (with parental consent), having been baptised but not on the communion roll of the congregation, satisfies the minister and Kirk Session that he or she is an adherent of the congregation and will undertake the Christian upbringing of the child;
- (c)   where at least one parent, or other family member (with parental consent), having been baptised, professes the Christian faith, undertakes to ensure that the child grows up in the life and worship of the Church and expresses the desire to seek admission to the communion roll of the congregation;
- (d)   where the child is under legal guardianship, and the minister and Kirk Session are satisfied that the child shall be nurtured within the life and worship of the congregation;

and, in each of the above cases, only after the parent(s), or other family member, has received such instruction in its meaning as the minister and Kirk Session consider necessary, according to such basis of instruction as may be authorised by the General Assembly.

7.   Baptism shall normally be administered during the public worship of the congregation in which the person makes profession of faith, or of which the parent or other family member is on the communion roll, or is an adherent. In exceptional circumstances, baptism may be administered elsewhere (e.g. at home or in hospital). Further, a minister may administer baptism to a person resident outwith the minister's parish, and who is not otherwise

connected with the congregation, only with the consent of the minister of the parish in which the person would normally reside, or of the Presbytery.

8. In all cases, an entry shall be made in the Kirk Session's Baptismal Register and a Certificate of Baptism given by the minister. Where baptism is administered in a chaplaincy context, it shall be recorded in the Baptismal Register there, and, where possible, reported to the minister of the parish in which the person resides.

9. Baptism shall normally be administered by an ordained minister. In situations of emergency,
    (a) a minister may, exceptionally, notwithstanding the preceding provisions of the Act, respond to a request for baptism in accordance with his or her pastoral judgement, and
    (b) baptism may be validly administered by a person who is not ordained, always providing that it is administered in the name of the Father and of the Son and of the Holy Spirit, with water.

    In every occurrence of the latter case, of which a minister or chaplain becomes aware, an entry shall be made in the appropriate Baptismal Register and where possible reported to the Clerk of the Presbytery within which the baptism was administered.

10. Each Presbytery shall form, or designate, a committee to which reference may be made in cases where there is a dispute as to the interpretation of this Act. Without the consent of the Presbytery, no minister may administer baptism in a case where to his or her knowledge another minister has declined to do so.

11. The Church of Scotland, as part of the Universal Church, affirms the validity of the sacrament of baptism administered in the name of the Father and of the Son and of the Holy Spirit, with water, in accordance with the discipline of other members of the Universal Church.

(2) THE MINISTER AND MARRIAGE

1. BACKGROUND

Prior to 1939, every marriage in Scotland fell into one or other of two classes: regular or irregular. The former was marriage by a minister of religion after due notice of intention had been given; the latter could be effected in one of three ways: (1) declaration *de presenti*, (2) by promise *subsequente copula*, or (3) by co-habitation with habit and repute.

The Marriage (Scotland) Act of 1939 put an end to (1) and (2) and provided for a new classification of marriage as either religious or civil. Marriage by co-habitation with habit and repute was abolished by the Family Law (Scotland) Act 2006.

The law of marriage as it was thus established in 1939 had two important limitations to the celebration of marriage: (1) certain preliminaries had to be observed; and (2) in respect of religious marriage, the service had to be conducted according to the forms of either the Christian or the Jewish faith.

2. THE MARRIAGE (SCOTLAND) ACT 1977

These two conditions were radically altered by the Marriage (Scotland) Act 1977.

Since 1 January 1978, in conformity with the demands of a multi-racial society, the benefits of religious marriage have been extended to adherents of other faiths, the only requirements being the observance of monogamy and the satisfaction of the authorities with the forms of the vows imposed.

Since 1978, the calling of banns has also been discontinued. The couple themselves must each complete a Marriage Notice form and return this to the District Registrar for the area in which they are to be married, irrespective of where they live, at least fifteen days before the ceremony is due to take place. The form details the documents which require to be produced with it.

If everything is in order, the District Registrar will issue, not more than seven days before the date of the ceremony, a Marriage Schedule. This must be in the hands of the minister officiating at the marriage ceremony before the service begins. Under no circumstances must the minister deviate from this rule. To do so is an offence under the Act.

Ministers should note the advice given by the Procurator of the Church in 1962, that they should not officiate at any marriage until at least one day after the 16th birthday of the younger party.

Furthermore, a marriage involving someone who is not an EU citizen involves extra registration requirements, and initial contact should be made with the local Registrar several months before the intended date of marriage.

3. THE MARRIAGE (SCOTLAND) ACT 2002

Although there have never been any limitations as to the place where a religious marriage can be celebrated, civil marriage originally could take place only in the Office of a Registrar. The Marriage (Scotland) Act 2002 permits the solemnisation of civil marriages at places approved by Local Authorities. Regulations have been made to specify the kinds of place which may be 'approved' with a view to ensuring that the places approved will not compromise the solemnity and dignity of civil marriage and will have no recent or continuing connection with any religion so as to undermine the distinction between religious and civil ceremonies.

4. PROCLAMATION OF BANNS

Proclamation of banns is no longer required in Scotland; but, in the Church of England, marriage is governed by the provisions of the Marriage Act 1949, which requires that the parties' intention to marry has to have been proclaimed and which provides that in the case of a party residing in Scotland a Certificate of Proclamation given according to the law or custom prevailing in Scotland shall be sufficient for the purpose. In the event that a minister is asked to call banns for a person resident within the registration district where his or her church is situated, the proclamation needs only to be made on one Sunday if the parties are known to the minister. If they are not, it should be made on two Sundays. In all cases, the Minister should, of course, have no reason to believe that there is any impediment to the marriage.

Proclamation should be made at the principal service of worship in this form:

> There is a purpose of marriage between AB (Bachelor/Widower/Divorced), residing at .... in this Registration District, and CD (Spinster/Widow/Divorced), residing at .... in the Registration District of ...., of which proclamation is hereby made for the first and only (second and last) time.

Immediately after the second reading, or not less than forty-eight hours after the first and only reading, a Certificate of Proclamation signed by either the minister or the Session Clerk should be issued in the following terms:

> At .... the ...... day of ...... 20 ....
> It is hereby certified that AB, residing at ...., and CD, residing at ...., have been duly proclaimed in order to marriage in the Church of .... according to the custom of the Church of Scotland, and that no objections have been offered.
> Signed .... minister or
> Signed .... Session Clerk

5. MARRIAGE OF FOREIGNERS

Marriages in Scotland of foreigners, or of foreigners with British subjects, are, if they satisfy the requirements of Scots Law, valid within the United Kingdom and the various British overseas territories; but they will not necessarily be valid in the country to which the foreigner belongs. This will be so only if the requirements of the law of his or her country have also been complied with. It is therefore most important that, before the marriage, steps should be taken to obtain from the Consul, or other diplomatic representative of the country concerned, a satisfactory assurance that the marriage will be accepted as valid in the country concerned.

6. REMARRIAGE OF DIVORCED PERSONS

By virtue of Act XXVI 1959, a minister of the Church of Scotland may lawfully solemnise the marriage of a person whose former marriage has been dissolved by divorce and whose former spouse is still alive. The minister, however, must carefully adhere to the requirements of the Act which, as slightly altered in 1985, are briefly as follows:

1. The minister should not accede as a matter of routine to a request to solemnise such a marriage. To enable a decision to be made, he or she should take all reasonable steps to obtain relevant information, which should normally include the following:
   (a) Adequate information concerning the life and character of the parties. The Act enjoins the greatest caution in cases where no pastoral relationship exists between the minister and either or both of the parties concerned.
   (b) The grounds and circumstances of the divorce case.
   (c) Facts bearing upon the future well-being of any children concerned.
   (d) Whether any other minister has declined to solemnise the proposed marriage.
   (e) The denomination to which the parties belong. The Act enjoins that special care should be taken where one or more parties belong to a denomination whose discipline in this matter may differ from that of the Church of Scotland.
2. The minister should consider whether there is danger of scandal arising if he or she should solemnise the remarriage, at the same time taking into careful consideration before refusing to do so the moral and spiritual effect of a refusal on the parties concerned.
3. As a determinative factor, the minister should do all he or she can to be assured that there has been sincere repentance where guilt has existed on the part of any divorced person seeking remarriage. He or she should also give instruction, where needed, in the nature and requirements of a Christian marriage.
4. A minister is not required to solemnise a remarriage against his or her conscience. Every Presbytery is required to appoint certain individuals with one of whom ministers in doubt as to the correct course of action may consult if they so desire. The final decision, however, rests with the minister who has been asked to officiate.

---

(3) CONDUCT OF MARRIAGE SERVICES
(CODE OF GOOD PRACTICE)

The code which follows was submitted to the General Assembly in 1997. It appears, on page 1/10, in the Volume of Assembly Reports for that year within the Report of the Board of Practice and Procedure.

1. *Marriage in the Church of Scotland is solemnised by an ordained minister in a religious ceremony wherein, before God, and in the presence of the minister and at least two competent witnesses, the parties covenant together to take each other as husband and wife as long as they both shall live, and the minister declares the parties to be husband and wife. Before solemnising a marriage, a minister must be assured that the necessary legal requirements are being complied with and that the parties know of no legal impediment to their marriage, and he or she must afterwards ensure that the Marriage Schedule is duly completed.* (Act I 1977)

2. Any ordained minister of the Church of Scotland who is a member of Presbytery or who holds a current Ministerial Certificate may officiate at a marriage service (see Act II 1987).

3. While the marriage service should normally take place in church, a minister may, at his or her discretion, officiate at a marriage service outwith church premises. Wherever conducted, the ceremony will be such as to reflect appropriately both the joy and the solemnity of the occasion. In particular, a minister shall ensure that nothing is done which would bring the Church and its teaching into disrepute.

4. A minister agreeing to conduct a wedding should endeavour to establish a pastoral relationship with the couple within which adequate pre-marriage preparation and subsequent pastoral care may be given.

5. 'A minister should not refuse to perform ministerial functions for a person who is resident in his or her parish without sufficient reason' (Cox, *Practice and Procedure in the Church of Scotland*, sixth edition, page 55). Where either party to the proposed marriage has been divorced and the former spouse is still alive, the minister invited to officiate may solemnise such a marriage, having regard to the guidelines in the Act anent the Remarriage of Divorced Persons (Act XXVI 1959 as amended by Act II 1985).

6. A minister is acting as an agent of the National Church which is committed to bringing the ordinances of religion to the people of Scotland through a territorial ministry. As such, he or she shall not be entitled to charge a fee or allow a fee to be charged for conducting a marriage service. When a gift is spontaneously offered to a minister as a token of appreciation, the above consideration should not be taken to mean that he or she should not accept such an unsolicited gift. The Financial Board of a congregation is at liberty to set fees to cover such costs as heat and light, and in addition Organists and Church Officers are entitled to a fee in respect of their services at weddings.

7. A minister should not allow his or her name to be associated with any commercial enterprise that provides facilities for weddings.

8. A minister is not at liberty to enter the bounds of another minister's parish to perform ministerial functions without the previous consent of the minister of that parish. In terms of Act VIII 1933, a minister may 'officiate at a marriage or funeral by private invitation', but, for the avoidance of doubt, an invitation conveyed through a commercial enterprise shall not be regarded as a 'private invitation' within the meaning of that Act.

9. A minister invited to officiate at a Marriage Service where neither party is a member of his or her congregation or is resident within his or her own parish or has any connection with the parish within which the service is to take place should observe the following courtesies:
   (a) he or she should ascertain from the parties whether either of them has a Church of Scotland connection or has approached the appropriate parish minister(s);
   (b) if it transpires that a ministerial colleague has declined to officiate, then he or she (the invited minister) should ascertain the reasons therefor and shall take these and all other relevant factors into account in deciding whether or not to officiate.

(4) MARRIAGE AND CIVIL PARTNERSHIP (SCOTLAND) ACT 2014 ('THE 2014 ACT')
ADVICE FROM THE PRINCIPAL CLERK

The Law of the Church of Scotland provides only that ministers and deacons are able to marry couples of the opposite sex. The Church's Recognition of Marriage Services Act (Act I 1977) (http://www.churchofscotland.org.uk/__data/assets/pdf_file/0016/1816/1977_act_01. pdf) states that a minister or deacon of the Church of Scotland may solemnise the marriage of parties who 'covenant together to take each other as husband and wife'.

Therefore, the Church of Scotland as a denomination would have to change its own Marriage Act before any decision could be made that led to the Church of Scotland opting in to the conducting of marriages between those of the same sex when the Marriage and Civil Partnership (Scotland) Act 2014 ('the 2014 Act') comes into force. The Church would only change its Marriage Act if it decided to change its theology of marriage. Unless such a decision is made, individual ministers and deacons of the Church of Scotland will not, in terms of either Church or civil law, be able to solemnise marriages between those of the same sex.

When the 2014 Act comes into force, there are two ways in which a Church of Scotland minister or deacon could become eligible to conduct a same-sex marriage:

- **Route 1**: The Church of Scotland could request the Scottish Ministers to prescribe it as a body whose ministers and deacons are authorised to solemnise marriage between persons of same sex, and the Scottish Ministers would have to consider whether to grant that request; **or**
- **Route 2**: Rather than becoming a 'prescribed body' under Route 1, the Church could nominate to the Registrar General individual ministers and deacons who wish to conduct same-sex marriages as persons who it desires should be entitled to solemnise same-sex marriages.

The Scottish Government has indicated that it would not expect Route 1 to be used where a Church has celebrants who object to solemnising same-sex marriage. However, were Route 1 to be followed, so that Church of Scotland ministers and deacons generally became able to conduct same-sex marriages, individual ministers and deacons would have to decide whether they wished to conduct same-sex marriages, and there would be a protection on grounds of conscience for those who did not wish to do so: it is stated in the 2014 Act that these provisions would not impose a duty on any person who is eligible to conduct marriages between persons of the same sex actually to conduct such marriages.

The Church of Scotland has not considered, and as of now has no plans to consider, whether it would change its own marriage law and then take any steps to become a 'prescribed body' or to make nominations under the Act. An examination of whether or not the Church of Scotland should, by either of Route 1 or Route 2, permit its ministers and deacons to conduct same-sex marriages would have to be instructed by the General Assembly; and future General Assemblies, following Barrier Act procedure, would have to approve any proposed change to the present status quo. This would be an internal discussion on the Church's own Recognition of Marriage Services Act and on the theological implications of recognition of same-sex marriage.

In short, as matters stand as at March 2014, the change in civil law made by the 2014 Act will not impact upon ministers and deacons of the Church of Scotland.

FAQs
I am a minister of the Church of Scotland. Once the Marriage and Civil Partnership (Scotland) Act 2014 comes into force, will I be entitled to conduct same-sex marriages?

No, you will not. For that to happen, the Church would have to ask the Scottish Ministers to prescribe it or to nominate ministers who wish to carry out same-sex marriages under the 2014 Act. Before that could happen, the matter would need to have been considered by the General Assembly, and the Assembly would need to have taken a decision in favour of allowing solemnisation of same-sex marriage by some or all of its ministers.

I am a minister of the Church of Scotland and, as a matter of conscience, would not wish to conduct same-sex marriages. What safeguards exist for me?
As noted above, the General Assembly would first need to have considered and taken a decision in favour of allowing solemnisation of same-sex marriage by some or all of its ministers. Even if the Church then made a request to the Scottish Ministers to become a prescribed body, and that request was granted (Route 1), the 2014 Act and the Equality Act as amended provide a protection on grounds of conscience, stating that there is no duty on approved celebrants to solemnise same-sex marriages. If the alternative (Route 2) were to be followed, and the Church were to nominate named ministers and deacons to be authorised to conduct same-sex marriages, then the Scottish Government would expect the Church only to do so in respect of persons who wish to solemnise same-sex marriage.

I am a minister of the Church of Scotland, and, in order to offer a full and inclusive ministry to those who present themselves for marriage, I want to be eligible to conduct same-sex marriages. Can I nominate myself as an approved celebrant?
No. Unless the Church becomes a 'prescribed body', you must be nominated by the Church. As noted above, at the moment the Church has no plans to consider changing its marriage law.

Can I apply for temporary authorisation so as to conduct a particular ceremony?
No. Only those clergy belonging to denominations which are 'prescribed bodies' or which have nominated individuals as celebrants can be temporarily authorised to conduct a same-sex marriage.

How does the Act impact upon deacons?
The Act confirms that deacons will be entitled to conduct marriages between persons of different sex. The provisions for same-sex marriage entitle deacons to conduct same-sex marriages on the same basis as ministers (i.e. if the same Church procedures and then civil-law procedures were first followed).

What is the position in terms of the Act as to whether Church of Scotland ministers and deacons may register civil partnerships?
The Act contains provisions which mirror those on same-sex marriage, i.e. the Church would either need to ask to become a 'prescribed body' or would have to nominate certain persons to the Registrar. As with same-sex marriage, the Church has no current plans to do so.

(5) CONDUCT OF FUNERAL SERVICES: FEES

The General Assembly of 2007 received the Report of the Legal Questions Committee which included a statement regarding fees for funerals. That statement had been prepared in the light of approaches from two Presbyteries seeking guidance on the question of the charging of fees (on behalf of ministers) for the conduct of funerals. It had seemed to the Presbyteries that expectations and practice were unacceptably varied across the country, and that the question was complicated by the fact that, quite naturally and legitimately, ministers other than parish ministers occasionally conduct funeral services.

The full text of that statement was engrossed in the Minutes of the General Assembly, and it was felt that it would be helpful to include it also in the *Year Book*.

The statement
The (Legal Questions) Committee believes that the question is two-fold, relating firstly to parish ministers (including associate and assistant ministers, deacons and the like) within their regular ministry, and secondly to ministers and others taking an occasional funeral, for instance by private invitation or in the course of pastoral cover of another parish.

Ministers in receipt of a living
The Committee believes that the position of the minister of a parish, and of other paid staff on the ministry team of a parish, is clear. The Third Declaratory Article affirms the responsibility of the Church of Scotland to provide the ordinances of religion through its territorial ministry, while the stipend system (and, for other staff members, the salary) provides a living that enables that ministry to be exercised without charging fees for services conducted. The implication of this principle is that no family in Scotland should ever be charged for the services of a Church of Scotland minister at the time of bereavement. Clearly, therefore, no minister in receipt of a living should be charging separately (effectively being paid doubly) for any such service. The Committee is conscious that the position of congregations outside Scotland may be different, and is aware that the relevant Presbyteries will offer appropriate superintendence of these matters.

A related question is raised about the highly varied culture of gift-giving in different parts of the country. The Committee believes it would be unwise to seek to regulate this. In some places, an attempt to quash a universal and long-established practice would seem ungracious, while in other places there is no such practice, and encouragement in that direction would seem indelicate.

A second related question was raised about Funeral Directors charging for the services of the minister. The Committee believes that Presbyteries should make it clear to Funeral Directors that, in the case of Church of Scotland funerals, such a charge should not be made.

Ministers conducting occasional services
Turning to the position of ministers who do not receive a living that enables them to conduct funerals without charge, the Committee's starting point is the principle articulated above that no bereaved person should have to pay for the services of a minister. The territorial ministry and the parish system of this Church mean that a bereaved family should not find itself being contingently charged because the parish minister happens to be unavailable, or because the parish is vacant.

Where a funeral is being conducted as part of the ministry of the local parish, but where for any reason another minister is taking it and not otherwise being paid, it is the responsibility of the congregation (through its financial body) to ensure that appropriate fees and expenses are met. Where that imposes a financial burden upon a congregation because of the weight of pastoral need, the need should be taken into account in calculating the resource-needs of that parish in the course of updating the Presbytery Plan.

It is beyond the remit of the Legal Questions Committee to make judgements about the appropriate level of payment. The Committee suggests that the Ministries Council should give the relevant advice on this aspect of the issue.

The Committee believes that these principles could be applied to the conduct of weddings and are perfectly compatible with the Guidelines on that subject which are reproduced in the *Year Book* at item 3 of section 3 dealing with Church Procedure.

(6) THE MINISTER AND WILLS

The Requirements of Writing (Scotland) Act 1995, which came into force on 1 August 1995, has removed the power of a minister to execute wills notarially. Further clarification, if required, may be obtained from the Solicitor of the Church.

(7) PROCEDURE IN A VACANCY

Procedure in a vacancy is regulated by Act VIII 2003 as amended by Acts IX and X 2004, II 2005, V 2006, I, IV and VI 2008 and II and V 2009. The text of the most immediately relevant sections is given here for general information. Schedules of Intimation referred to are also included. The full text of the Act and subsequent amendments can be obtained from the Principal Clerk.

1. Vacancy Procedure Committee
(1)   Each Presbytery shall appoint a number of its members to be available to serve on Vacancy Procedure Committees and shall provide information and training as required for those so appointed.
(2)   As soon as the Presbytery Clerk is aware that a vacancy has arisen or is anticipated, he or she shall consult the Moderator of the Presbytery and they shall appoint a Vacancy Procedure Committee of five persons from among those appointed in terms of subsection (1), which Committee shall (a) include at least one minister and at least one elder and (b) exclude any communicant member or former minister of the vacant charge or of any constituent congregation thereof. The Vacancy Procedure Committee shall include a Convener and Clerk, the latter of whom need not be a member of the Committee but may be the Presbytery Clerk. The same Vacancy Procedure Committee may serve for more than one vacancy at a time.
(3)   The Vacancy Procedure Committee shall have a quorum of three for its meetings.
(4)   The Convener of the Vacancy Procedure Committee may, where he or she reasonably believes a matter to be non-contentious, consult members individually, provided that reasonable efforts are made to consult all members of the Committee. A meeting shall be held at the request of any member of the Committee.
(5)   Every decision made by the Vacancy Procedure Committee shall be reported to the next meeting of Presbytery, but may not be recalled by Presbytery where the decision was subject to the provisions of section 2 below.

2. Request for Consideration by Presbytery
Where in this Act any decision by the Vacancy Procedure Committee is subject to the provisions of this section, the following rules shall apply:

(1)   The Presbytery Clerk shall intimate to all members of the Presbytery by mailing or at a Presbytery meeting the course of action or permission proposed, and shall arrange for one Sunday's pulpit intimation of the same to be made to the congregation or congregations concerned, in terms of Schedule A. The intimation having been made, it shall be displayed as prominently as possible at the church building for seven days.

(2)   Any four individuals, being communicant members of the congregation or full members of the Presbytery, may give written notice requesting that action be taken in terms of subsection (3) below, giving reasons for the request, within seven days after the pulpit intimation.

(3)   Upon receiving notice in terms of subsection (2), the Presbytery Clerk shall sist the process or permission referred to in subsection (1), which shall then require the approval of the Presbytery.

(4)   The Moderator of the Presbytery shall in such circumstances consider whether a meeting *pro re nata* of the Presbytery should be called in order to avoid prejudicial delay in the vacancy process.

(5)   The Presbytery Clerk shall cause to have served upon the congregation or congregations an edict in terms of Schedule B citing them to attend the meeting of Presbytery for their interest.

(6)   The consideration by Presbytery of any matter under this section shall not constitute an appeal or a Petition, and the decision of Presbytery shall be deemed to be a decision at first instance subject to the normal rights of appeal or dissent-and-complaint.

3. Causes of Vacancy
The causes of vacancy shall normally include:
(a)   the death of the minister of the charge;
(b)   the removal of status of the minister of the charge or the suspension of the minister in terms of section 20(2) of Act III 2001;
(c)   the dissolution of the pastoral tie in terms of Act I 1988 or Act XV 2002;
(d)   the demission of the charge and/or status of the minister of the charge;
(e)   the translation of the minister of the charge to another charge;
(f)   the termination of the tenure of the minister of the charge in terms of Act VI 1984.

4. Release of Departing Minister
The Presbytery Clerk shall be informed as soon as circumstances have occurred that cause a vacancy to arise or make it likely that a vacancy shall arise. Where the circumstances pertain to section 3(d) or (e) above, the Vacancy Procedure Committee shall
(1)   except in cases governed by subsection (2) below, decide whether to release the minister from his or her charge and, in any case involving translation to another charge or introduction to an appointment, instruct him or her to await the instructions of the Presbytery or another Presbytery;
(2)   in the case of a minister in the first five years of his or her first charge, decide whether there are exceptional circumstances to justify releasing him or her from his or her charge and proceeding in terms of subsection (1) above;
(3)   determine whether a vacancy has arisen or is anticipated and, as soon as possible, determine the date upon which the charge becomes actually vacant, and
(4)   inform the congregation or congregations by one Sunday's pulpit intimation as soon as convenient.
(5)   The provisions of section 2 above shall apply to the decisions of the Vacancy Procedure Committee in terms of subsections (1) and (2) above.

5. Demission of Charge

(1)   Subject to the provisions of subsection (2) below, when a vacancy has occurred in terms of section 3(c), (d) or (f) above, the Presbytery shall determine whether the minister is, in the circumstances, entitled to a seat in the Presbytery in terms of section 16 of Act III 2000 (as amended).

(2)   In the case where it is a condition of any basis of adjustment that a minister shall demit his or her charge to facilitate union or linking, and the minister has agreed in writing in terms of the appropriate regulations governing adjustments, formal application shall not be made to the Presbytery for permission to demit. The minister concerned shall be regarded as retiring in the interest of adjustment, and he or she shall retain a seat in Presbytery unless in terms of Act III 2000 (as amended) he or she elects to resign it.

(3)   A minister who demits his or her charge without retaining a seat in the Presbytery shall, if he or she retains status as a minister, be subject to the provisions of sections 5 to 15 of Act II 2000 (as amended).

6. Appointment of Interim Moderator

(1)   At the same time as the Vacancy Procedure Committee makes a decision in terms of section 4 above, or where circumstances pertain to section 3(a), (b), (c) or (f) above, the Vacancy Procedure Committee shall appoint an Interim Moderator for the charge and make intimation thereof to the congregation subject to the provisions of section 2 above. The Interim Moderator shall be either a ministerial member of the Presbytery in terms of Act III 2000 or Act V 2001 or a member of the Presbytery selected from a list of those who have received such preparation for the task as the Ministries Council shall from time to time recommend or provide, and he or she shall not be a member in the vacant charge nor a member of the Vacancy Procedure Committee. The name of the Interim Moderator shall be forwarded to the Ministries Council.

(2)   If the Interim Moderator appointed is a ministerial member of Presbytery, it is understood that, in accepting the appointment, he or she is thereby disqualified from becoming an applicant or accepting an invitation to be considered in the current vacancy.

7. Duties of Interim Moderator

(1)   It shall be the duty of the Interim Moderator to preside at all meetings of the Kirk Session (or of the Kirk Sessions in the case of a linked charge) and to preside at all congregational meetings in connection with the vacancy, or at which the minister would have presided had the charge been full. In the case of a congregational meeting called by the Presbytery in connection with adjustment, the Interim Moderator, having constituted the meeting, shall relinquish the chair in favour of the representative of the Presbytery, but he or she shall be at liberty to speak at such a meeting. In consultation with the Kirk Session and the Financial Court, he or she shall make arrangements for the supply of the vacant pulpit.

(2)   The Interim Moderator appointed in a prospective vacancy may call and preside at meetings of the Kirk Session and of the congregation for the transaction of business relating to the said prospective vacancy. He or she shall be associated with the minister until the date of the actual vacancy; after that date, he or she shall take full charge.

(3)   The Interim Moderator shall act as an assessor to the Nominating Committee, being available to offer guidance and advice. If the Committee so desire, he or she may act as their Convener, but in no case shall he or she have a vote.

(4)   In the event of the absence of the Interim Moderator, the Vacancy Procedure Committee shall appoint a member of the Presbytery who is not a member of the vacant congregation to fulfil any of the rights and duties of the Interim Moderator.

(5)   The Interim Moderator shall have the same duties and responsibilities towards all members of ministry teams referred to in section 16 of Act VII 2003 as if he or she were the parish minister, both in terms of this Act and in respect of the terms and conditions of such individuals.

8. Permission to Call

When the decision to release the minister from the charge has been made and the Interim Moderator appointed, the Vacancy Procedure Committee shall consider whether it may give permission to call a minister in terms of Act VII 2003, and may proceed subject to the provisions of section 2 above. The Vacancy Procedure Committee must refer the question of permission to call to the Presbytery if:

(a)   shortfalls exist which in the opinion of the Committee require consideration in terms of section 9 hereunder;

(b)   the Committee has reason to believe that the vacancy schedule referred to in section 10 below will not be approved;

(c)   the Committee has reason to believe that the Presbytery will, in terms of section 11 below, instruct work to be carried out on the manse before a call can be sustained, and judges that the likely extent of such work warrants a delay in the granting of permission to call, or

(d)   the Committee has reason to believe that the Presbytery may wish to delay or refuse the granting of permission for any reason.

Any decision by Presbytery to refuse permission to call shall be subject to appeal or dissent-and-complaint.

9. Shortfalls

(1)   As soon as possible after intimation of a vacancy or anticipated vacancy reaches the Presbytery Clerk, the Presbytery shall ascertain whether the charge has current or accumulated shortfalls in contributions to central funds, and shall determine whether and to what extent any shortfalls that exist are justified.

(2)   If the vacancy is in a charge in which the Presbytery has determined that shortfalls are to any extent unjustified, it shall not resolve to allow a call of any kind until:

(a)   the shortfalls have been met to the extent to which the Presbytery determined that they were unjustified, or

(b)   a scheme for the payment of the unjustified shortfall has been agreed between the congregation and the Presbytery and receives the concurrence of the Ministries Council and/or the Stewardship and Finance Committee for their respective interests, or

(c)   a fresh appraisal of the charge in terms of Act VII 2003 has been carried out, regardless of the status of the charge in the current Presbytery plan:

(i)   During such appraisal, no further steps may be taken in respect of filling the vacancy, and the Presbytery shall make final determination of what constitutes such steps.

(ii)   Following such appraisal and any consequent adjustment or deferred adjustment, the shortfalls shall be met or declared justifiable or a scheme shall be agreed in terms of subsection (b) above; the Presbytery shall inform the Ministries Council and the Stewardship and Finance Committee of its decisions in terms of this section; and the Presbytery shall remove the suspension-of-vacancy process referred to in sub-paragraph (i).

10. Vacancy Schedule

(1)   When in terms of sections 4 and 6 above the decision to release the minister from the charge has been made and the Interim Moderator appointed, there shall be issued by the Ministries

Council a Schedule or Schedules for completion by the responsible Financial Board(s) of the vacant congregation(s) in consultation with representatives of the Presbytery, setting forth the proposed arrangements for payment of ministerial expenses and for provision of a manse, showing the ministry requirements and details of any endowment income. The Schedule, along with an Extract Minute from each relevant Kirk Session containing a commitment fully and adequately to support the ministry, shall be forwarded to the Presbytery Clerk.

(2) The Schedule shall be considered by the Vacancy Procedure Committee and, if approved, transmitted to the Ministries Council by the Presbytery Clerk. The Vacancy Procedure Committee or Presbytery must not sustain an appointment and call until the Schedule has been approved by them and by the Ministries Council, which shall intimate its decision within six weeks of receiving the schedule from the Presbytery.

(3) The accuracy of the Vacancy Schedule shall be kept under review by the Vacancy Procedure Committee.

(4) The provisions of section 2 above shall apply to the decisions of the Vacancy Procedure Committee.

11. Manse

As soon as possible after the manse becomes vacant, the Presbytery Property Committee shall inspect the manse and come to a view on what work, if any, must be carried out to render it suitable for a new incumbent. The views of the Property Committee should then be communicated to the Presbytery, which should, subject to any modifications which might be agreed by that Court, instruct the Financial Board of the congregation to have the work carried out. No induction date shall be fixed until the Presbytery Property Committee has again inspected the manse and confirmed that the work has been undertaken satisfactorily.

12. Advisory Committee

(1) As soon as possible after intimation of a vacancy or anticipated vacancy reaches the Presbytery Clerk, the Vacancy Procedure Committee shall appoint an Advisory Committee of three, subject to the following conditions:

    (a) at least one member shall be an elder and at least one shall be a minister;

    (b) the Advisory Committee may comprise members of the Vacancy Procedure Committee and act as a support committee to congregations in a vacancy;

    (c) the Advisory Committee may contain individuals who are not members of the Presbytery;

    (d) the appointment shall be subject to section 2 above.

(2) The Advisory Committee shall meet:

    (a) before the election of the Nominating Committee, with the Kirk Session (or Kirk Sessions both separately and together) of the vacant charge, to consider together in the light of the whole circumstances of the parish or parishes (i) what kind of ministry would be best suited to their needs and (ii) which system of election of the Nominating Committee described in paragraph 14(2)(d) hereunder shall be used;

    (b) with the Nominating Committee before it has taken any steps to fill the vacancy, to consider how it should proceed;

    (c) with the Nominating Committee before it reports to the Kirk Session and Presbytery the identity of the nominee, to review the process followed and give any further advice it deems necessary;

    (d) with the Kirk Session(s) as soon as an application is made for permission to proceed in terms of section 25A of this Act, to ensure that the requirements of that section are fulfilled;

(e)   with the Nominating Committee at any other time by request of either the Nominating Committee or the Advisory Committee.

In the case of charges which are in the opinion of the Presbytery remote, it will be adequate if the Interim Moderator (accompanied if possible by a member of the Nominating Committee) meets with the Advisory Committee for the purposes listed in paragraphs (a) to (c) above.

13. Electoral Register

(1)   It shall be the duty of the Kirk Session of a vacant congregation to proceed to make up the Electoral Register of the congregation. This shall contain (1) as communicants the names of those persons (a) whose names are on the communion roll of the congregation as at the date on which it is made up and who are not under Church discipline, (b) whose names have been added or restored to the communion roll on revision by the Kirk Session subsequently to the occurrence of the vacancy, and (c) who have given in valid Certificates of Transference by the date specified in terms of Schedule C hereto; and (2) as adherents the names of those persons who, being parishioners or regular worshippers in the congregation at the date when the vacancy occurred, and not being members of any other congregation, have claimed (in writing in the form prescribed in Schedule D and within the time specified in Schedule C) to be placed on the Electoral Register, the Kirk Session being satisfied that they desire to be permanently connected with the congregation and knowing of no adequate reasons why they should not be admitted as communicants should they so apply.

(2)   At a meeting to be held not later than fourteen days after intimation has been made in terms of Schedule C hereto, the Kirk Session shall decide on the claims of persons to be placed on the Electoral Register, such claims to be sent to the Session Clerk before the meeting. At this meeting, the Kirk Session may hear parties claiming to have an interest. The Kirk Session shall thereupon prepare the lists of names and addresses of communicants and of adherents which it is proposed shall be the Electoral Register of the congregation, the names being arranged in alphabetical order and numbered consecutively throughout. The decision of the Kirk Session in respect of any matter affecting the preparation of the Electoral Register shall be final.

(3)   The proposed Electoral Register having been prepared, the Interim Moderator shall cause intimation to be made on the first convenient Sunday in terms of Schedule E hereto that on that day an opportunity will be given for inspecting the Register after service, and that it will lie for inspection at such times and such places as the Kirk Session shall have determined; and further shall specify a day when the Kirk Session will meet to hear parties claiming an interest and will finally revise and adjust the Register. At this meeting, the list, having been revised, numbered and adjusted, shall on the authority of the court be attested by the Interim Moderator and the Clerk as the Electoral Register of the congregation.

(4)   This Register, along with a duplicate copy, shall without delay be transmitted to the Presbytery Clerk, who, in name of the Presbytery, shall attest and return the principal copy, retaining the duplicate copy in his or her own possession. For all purposes connected with this Act, the congregation shall be deemed to be those persons whose names are on the Electoral Register, and no other.

(5)   If after the attestation of the Register any communicant is given a Certificate of Transference, the Session Clerk shall delete that person's name from the Register and initial the deletion. Such a Certificate shall be granted only when application for it has been made in writing, and the said written application shall be retained until the vacancy is ended.

(6)   When a period of more than six months has elapsed between the Electoral Register being attested and the congregation being given permission to call, the Kirk Session shall have power, if it so desires, to revise and update the Electoral Register. Intimation of this intention shall be given in terms of Schedule F hereto. Additional names shall be added to the Register in the form of an Addendum which shall also contain authority for the deletions which have been made; two copies of this Addendum, duly attested, shall be lodged with the Presbytery Clerk, who, in name of the Presbytery, shall attest and return the principal copy, retaining the duplicate copy in his or her own possession.

14. Appointment of Nominating Committee

(1)   When permission to call has been given and the Electoral Register has been attested, intimation in terms of Schedule G shall be made that a meeting of the congregation is to be held to appoint a Committee of its own number for the purpose of nominating one person to the congregation with a view to the appointment of a minister.

(2)   (a)   The Interim Moderator shall preside at this meeting, and the Session Clerk, or in his or her absence a person appointed by the meeting, shall act as Clerk.

(b)   The Interim Moderator shall remind the congregation of the number of members it is required to appoint in terms of this section and shall call for Nominations. To constitute a valid Nomination, the name of a person on the Electoral Register has to be proposed and seconded, and assurance given by the proposer that the person is prepared to act on the Committee. The Clerk shall take a note of all Nominations in the order in which they are made.

(c)   For the avoidance of doubt, a member of a vacant charge shall not be eligible for nomination to serve on a Nominating Committee, if he or she is:

    (i)   a minister (including a retired minister) of the Church of Scotland,

    (ii)   a member of the diaconate of the Church of Scotland,

    (iii)   an employee of the vacant charge,

    (iv)   an employee of the Ministries Council who works in the vacant charge, or

    (v)   the spouse of any former minister of the charge.

(d)   When it appears to the Interim Moderator that the Nominations are complete, they shall be read to the congregation and an opportunity given for any withdrawals. If the number of persons nominated does not exceed the maximum fixed in terms of subsection (4) below, there is no need for a vote, and the Interim Moderator shall declare that these persons constitute a Nominating Committee.

(e)   If the number exceeds the maximum, the election shall proceed by one of the following means, chosen in advance by the Kirk Session, and being either (i) the submission of the names by the Interim Moderator, one by one as they appear on the list, to the vote of the congregation, each member having the right to vote for up to the maximum number fixed for the Committee, and voting being by standing up, or (ii) a system of written ballot devised by the Kirk Session to suit the size of the congregation and approved by the Vacancy Procedure Committee or the Presbytery. In either case, in the event of a tie for the last place, a further vote shall be taken between or among those tying.

(f)   The Interim Moderator shall, at the same meeting or as soon thereafter as the result of any ballot has been determined, announce the names of those thus elected to serve on the Nominating Committee, and intimate to them the time and place of their first meeting, which may be immediately after the congregational meeting provided that has been intimated along with the intimation of the congregational meeting.

(3) Where there is an agreement between the Presbytery and the congregation or congregations that the minister to be inducted shall serve either in a team ministry involving another congregation or congregations, or in a designated post such as a chaplaincy, it shall be competent for the agreement to specify that the Presbytery shall appoint up to two representatives to serve on the Nominating Committee.

(4) The Vacancy Procedure Committee shall, subject to the provisions of section 2 above, determine the number who will act on the Nominating Committee, being an odd number up to a maximum of thirteen.

(5) When the vacancy is in a linked charge, or when a union or linking of congregations has been agreed but not yet effected, or when there is agreement to a deferred union or a deferred linking, or where the appointment is to more than one post, the Vacancy Procedure Committee shall, subject to the provisions of section 2 above, determine how the number who will act on the Nominating Committee will be allocated among the congregations involved, unless provision for this has already been made in the Basis of Union or Basis of Linking as the case may be.

(6) The Nominating Committee shall not have power to co-opt additional members, but the relevant Kirk Session shall have power when necessary to appoint a replacement for any of its appointees who ceases, by death or resignation, to be a member of the Nominating Committee, or who, by falling ill or by moving away from the area, is unable to serve as a member of it.

15. Constitution of the Nominating Committee

It shall be the duty of the Interim Moderator to summon and preside at the first meeting of the Nominating Committee, which may be held at the close of the congregational meeting at which it is appointed and at which the Committee shall appoint a Convener and a Clerk. The Clerk, who need not be a member of the Committee, shall keep regular minutes of all proceedings. The Convener shall have a deliberative vote (if he or she is not the Interim Moderator) but shall in no case have a casting vote. If the Clerk is not a member of the Committee, he or she shall have no vote. At all meetings of the Committee, only those present shall be entitled to vote.

16. Task of the Nominating Committee

(1) The Nominating Committee shall have the duty of nominating one person to the congregation with a view to the election and appointment of a minister. It shall proceed by a process of announcement in a monthly vacancy list, application and interview, and may also advertise, receive recommendations and pursue enquiries in other ways.

(2) The Committee shall give due weight to any guidelines which may from time to time be issued by the Ministries Council or the General Assembly.

(3) The Committee shall make themselves aware of the roles of the other members of any ministry team as described in section 16 of Act VII 2003 and may meet with them for this purpose, but shall not acquire responsibility or authority for the negotiation or alteration of their terms and conditions.

17. Eligibility for Election

The following categories of persons, and no others, are eligible to be nominated, elected and called as ministers of parishes in the Church of Scotland, but always subject, where appropriate, to the provisions of Act IX 2002:

(1) A minister of a parish of the Church, a minister holding some other appointment that entitles him or her to a seat in Presbytery or a minister holding a current Practising Certificate in terms of Section 5 of Act II 2000 (as amended).

(2)   A minister of the Church of Scotland who has retired from a parish or appointment as above, provided he or she has not reached his or her 65th birthday (or, subject to the provisions of Regulations II 2004, his or her 70th birthday).

(3)   (a)   A licentiate of the Church of Scotland who has satisfactorily completed, or has been granted exemption from, his or her period of probationary service.

      (b)   A graduate candidate in terms of section 22 of Act X 2004.

(4)   A minister, licentiate or graduate candidate of the Church of Scotland who, with the approval of the World Mission Council, has entered the courts of an overseas Church as a full member, provided he or she has ceased to be such a member.

(5)   A minister, licentiate or graduate candidate of the Church of Scotland who has neither relinquished nor been judicially deprived of the status he or she possessed and who has served, or is serving, furth of Scotland in any Church which is a member of the World Alliance of Reformed Churches.

(6)   The holder of a Certificate of Eligibility in terms of Act IX 2002. The holder of a Certificate of Eligibility who is a national outside the European Economic Area and Switzerland shall be eligible to apply for charges only in terms of section 25A of this Act.

(7)   For the avoidance of doubt, anyone who has served as an Interim Moderator in the current vacancy shall not be eligible to apply or to be considered as an applicant.

18. Ministers of a Team

Ministers occupying positions within a team ministry in the charge, or larger area including the charge, and former holders of such positions, shall be eligible to apply and shall not by virtue of office be deemed to have exercised undue influence in securing the call. A *locum tenens* in the vacant charge shall not by virtue of office be deemed to have exercised undue influence in securing the call. Any Interim Moderator in the current vacancy shall not be eligible to apply.

19. Ministers of Other Churches

(1)   Where a minister of a church furth of Scotland, who holds a certificate of eligibility in terms of Act IX 2002, is nominated, the nominee, Kirk Session and Presbytery may agree that he or she shall be inducted for a period of three years only and shall retain status as a minister of his or her denomination of origin.

(2)   Upon induction, such a minister shall be accountable to the Presbytery for the exercise of his or her ministry and to his or her own church for matters of life and doctrine. He or she shall be awarded corresponding membership of the Presbytery.

(3)   With the concurrence of the Presbytery and the Ministries Council, and at the request of the congregation, the period may be extended for one further period of not more than three years.

(4)   The provisions of this section shall apply in the case of an appointment as a member of a ministry team as defined in section 16(2)(a) of Act VII 2003 (as amended), provided that the appointment is one which the Presbytery deems must be held by a Ministry of Word and Sacrament.

20. Nomination

(1)   Before the candidate is asked to accept Nomination, the Interim Moderator shall ensure that the candidate is given an adequate opportunity to see the whole ecclesiastical buildings (including the manse) pertaining to the congregation, and to meet privately with all members of staff of the charge or of any wider ministry team, and shall be provided with a copy of the constitution of the congregation, a copy of the current Presbytery Plan and of any current Basis of Adjustment or Basis of Reviewable Tenure, and the most recent audited accounts and statement of funds, and the candidate shall acknowledge receipt in writing to the Interim Moderator.

(2) Before any Nomination is intimated to the Kirk Session and Presbytery Clerk, the Clerk to the Nominating Committee shall secure the written consent thereto of the nominee.

(3) Before reporting the Nomination to the Vacancy Procedure Committee, the Presbytery Clerk shall obtain from the nominee or Interim Moderator evidence of the eligibility of the nominee to be appointed to the charge.

   (a) In the case of a minister not being a member of any Presbytery of the Church of Scotland, this shall normally constitute an Exit Certificate in terms of Act X 2004, or evidence of status from the Ministries Council, or a current practising certificate, or certification from the Ministries Council of eligibility in terms of Act IX 2002.

   (b) In the case of a minister in the first five years of his or her first charge, this shall consist of an extract minute either from the Vacancy Procedure Committee of his or her current Presbytery, or from that Presbytery, exceptionally releasing the minister.

21. Preaching by Nominee

(1) The Interim Moderator, on receiving notice of the Committee's Nomination, shall arrange that the nominee conduct public worship in the vacant church or churches, normally within four Sundays, and that the ballot take place immediately after each such service.

(2) The Interim Moderator shall thereupon cause intimation to be made on two Sundays regarding the arrangements made in connection with the preaching by the nominee and the ballot thereafter, all in terms of Schedule H hereto.

22. Election of Minister

(1) The Interim Moderator shall normally preside at all congregational meetings connected with the election which shall be in all cases by ballot and shall normally be in charge of the ballot.

(2) The Interim Moderator may invite one or more persons (not being persons whose names are on the Electoral Register of the vacant congregation) to assist him or her in the conduct of a ballot vote when he or she judges this desirable.

(3) When a linking or a deferred union or deferred linking is involved, the Interim Moderator shall consult and reach agreement with the minister or Interim Moderator of the other congregation regarding the arrangements for the conduct of public worship in these congregations by the nominee as in section 21(1) above. The Interim Moderator shall in writing appoint a member of Presbytery to take full charge of the ballot vote for the other congregation. In the case of a deferred union or deferred linking, the minister already inducted shall not be so appointed, nor shall he or she be in any way involved in the conduct of the election.

23. Ballot Procedure

(1) The Kirk Session shall arrange to have available at the time of election a sufficient supply of voting-papers printed in the form of Schedule I hereto, and these shall be put into the custody of the Interim Moderator who shall preside at the election, assisted as in section 22 above. He or she shall issue on request to any person whose name is on the Electoral Register a voting-paper, noting on the Register that this has been done. Facilities shall be provided whereby the voter may mark the paper in secrecy, and a ballot-box shall be available wherein the paper is to be deposited when marked. The Interim Moderator may assist any person who asks for help in respect of completing the voting-paper, but no other person whatever shall communicate with the voter at this stage. The Interim Moderator, or the deputy appointed by him or her, shall be responsible for the safe custody of ballot-box, papers and Electoral Register.

(2) As soon as practicable, and at latest within twenty-four hours after the close of the voting, the Interim Moderator shall constitute the Kirk Session, or the joint Kirk Sessions when

more than one congregation is involved, and in presence of the Kirk Session shall proceed with the counting of the votes, in which he or she may be assisted as provided in section 22 above. When more than one ballot-box has been used and when the votes of more than one congregation are involved, all ballot-boxes shall be emptied and the voting-papers shall be mixed together before counting begins so that the preponderance of votes in one area or in one congregation shall not be disclosed.

(3)   A voting-paper shall only be considered as spoilt and the vote not counted where the intention of the voter is unclear, and in no other circumstances. It shall be for the Kirk Session, on the recommendation of the Interim Moderator, to determine whether the intention of the voter is clear.

(4)   If the number voting For exceeds the number voting Against, the nominee shall be declared elected and the Nominating Committee shall be deemed to be discharged.

(5)   If the number voting For is equal to or less than the number voting Against, the Interim Moderator shall declare that there has been failure to elect and that the Nominating Committee is deemed to have been discharged. He or she shall proceed in terms of section 26(b) without further reference to the Presbytery.

(6)   After the counting has been completed, the Interim Moderator shall sign a declaration in one of the forms of Schedule J hereto, and this shall be recorded in the minute of the Kirk Session or of the Kirk Sessions. An extract shall be affixed to the notice-board of the church, or of each of the churches, concerned. In presence of the Kirk Session, the Interim Moderator shall then seal up the voting-papers along with the marked copy of the Electoral Register, and these shall be transmitted to the Presbytery Clerk in due course along with the other documents specified in section 27 below.

24. Withdrawal of Nominee

(1)   Should a nominee intimate withdrawal before he or she has preached as nominee, the Nominating Committee shall continue its task and seek to nominate another nominee.

(2)   Should a nominee intimate withdrawal after he or she has been elected, the Interim Moderator shall proceed in terms of sections 23(4) above and 26(b) below without further reference to the Presbytery.

25. The Call

(1)   The Interim Moderator shall, along with the intimation regarding the result of the voting, intimate the arrangements made for members of the congregation over a period of not less than eight days to subscribe the Call (Schedule K). Intimation shall be in the form of Schedule L hereto.

(2)   The Call may be subscribed on behalf of a member not present to sign in person, provided a mandate authorising such subscription is produced as in Schedule M. All such entries shall be initialled by the Interim Moderator or by the member of the Kirk Session appending them.

(3)   Those eligible to sign the call shall be all those whose names appear on the Electoral Register. A paper of concurrence in the Call may be signed by regular worshippers in the congregation and by adherents whose names have not been entered on the Electoral Register.

25A. Ministers from Non-EEA Countries excluding Switzerland

(1)   Six months after the vacancy has first appeared in a monthly vacancy list, and provided there are no applications currently under the consideration of the Nominating Committee, the Kirk Session (or in the case of a linkage the Kirk Sessions in agreement) may apply to the Presbytery to have the charge listed for the purposes of this section.

(2)   Such applications shall be considered by the whole Presbytery, and shall not form part of the remit of the Vacancy Procedure Committee.

(3)   The Presbytery must be satisfied that there are no outstanding issues of superintendence, or other factors that would make such listing inappropriate, and must consult with the Ministries Council before deciding whether to permit the listing. The Presbytery Clerk shall within seven days send an extract minute of the decision to the Ministries Council.

(4)   Upon receiving notification of the listing from the Presbytery, the Nominating Committee shall proceed again from section 16 of this Act, and holders of Certificates of Eligibility who are nationals of countries outwith the EEA and Switzerland shall now be eligible to apply.

(5)   For the avoidance of doubt, the Nominating Committee (a) must always dispose of any competent applications received in terms of section 17 of this Act before considering those made in terms of this section, but (b) shall not be obliged to make a nomination from any particular group of applicants.

(6)   When a Presbytery withdraws permission to call, or the permission lapses in terms of section 26 of this Act, the Presbytery shall decide whether permission to proceed in terms of this section remains in force during the ensuing process to make a nomination.

26. Failure to Nominate

The exercise by a congregation of its right to call a minister shall be subject to a time-limit of one year; this period shall be calculated from the date when intimation is given of the agreement to grant leave to call. If it appears that an appointment is not to be made within the allotted time (allowing one further calendar month for intimation to the Presbytery), the congregation may make application to the Presbytery for an extension, which will normally be for a further six months. For clear cause shown, a further extension of six months may be granted. If no election has been made and intimated to the Presbytery by the expiry of that time, the permission to call shall be regarded as having lapsed. The Presbytery may thereupon look afresh at the question of adjustment. If the Presbytery is still satisfied that a minister should be appointed, it shall itself take steps to make such an appointment, proceeding in one of the following ways:

(a)   (i)   The Presbytery may discharge the Nominating Committee, strengthen the Advisory Committee which had been involved in the case by the appointment of an additional minister and elder, instruct that Committee to bring forward to a subsequent meeting the name of an eligible individual for appointment to the charge and intimate this instruction to the congregation. If satisfied with the recommendation brought by the Advisory Committee, the Presbytery shall thereupon make the appointment.

(ii)   The Presbytery Clerk shall thereupon intimate to the person concerned the fact of his or her appointment, shall request him or her to forward a letter of acceptance along with appropriate Certificates if these are required in terms of section 27 below, and shall arrange with him or her to conduct public worship in the vacant church or churches on an early Sunday.

(iii)   The Presbytery Clerk shall cause intimation to be made in the form of Schedule N that the person appointed will conduct public worship on the day specified and that a Call in the usual form will lie with the Session Clerk or other suitable person for not less than eight free days to receive the signatures of the congregation. The conditions governing the signing of the Call shall be as in section 25 above.

(iv)   At the expiry of the time allowed, the Call shall be transmitted by the Session Clerk to the Presbytery Clerk who shall lay it, along with the documents referred to in sub-paragraph (ii) above, before the Presbytery at its first ordinary meeting or at a meeting *in hunc effectum*.

(b)   Otherwise, the Presbytery shall instruct that a fresh Nominating Committee be elected in terms of section 14 above. The process shall then be followed in terms of this Act from the point of the election of the Nominating Committee.

27. Transmission of Documents

(1)   After an election has been made, the Interim Moderator shall secure from the person appointed a letter of acceptance of the appointment.

(2)   The Interim Moderator shall then without delay transmit the relevant documents to the Presbytery Clerk. These are: the minute of Nomination by the Nominating Committee, all intimations made to the congregation thereafter, the declaration of the election and appointment, the voting-papers, the marked copy of the Register and the letter of acceptance. He or she shall also inform the Clerk of the steps taken in connection with the signing of the Call, and shall arrange that, at the expiry of the period allowed for subscription, the Call shall be transmitted by the Session Clerk to the Presbytery Clerk.

(3)   After the person elected has been inducted to the charge, the Presbytery Clerk shall:

(a)   deliver to him or her the approved copy of the Vacancy Schedule referred to in section 10(2) above, and

(b)   destroy the intimations and voting-papers lodged with him or her in terms of subsection (2) above and ensure that confidential documents and correspondence held locally are destroyed.

28. Sustaining the Call

(1)   All of the documents listed in section 27 above shall be laid before the Vacancy Procedure Committee, which may resolve to sustain the call and determine arrangements for the induction of the new minister, subject to (a) a request for the release, if appropriate, of the minister from his or her current charge in terms of this Act and (b) the provisions of section 2 above. The Moderator of the Presbytery shall, if no ordinary meeting of the Presbytery falls before the proposed induction date, call a meeting *pro re nata* for the induction.

(2)   In the event that the matter comes before the Presbytery in terms of section 2 above, the procedure shall be as follows:

(a)   The Call and other relevant documents having been laid on the table, the Presbytery shall hear any person whom it considers to have an interest. In particular, the Advisory Committee shall be entitled to be heard if it so desires, or the Presbytery may ask for a report from it. The Presbytery shall then decide whether to sustain the appointment in terms of subsection (1) above, and in doing so shall give consideration to the number of signatures on the Call. It may delay reaching a decision and return the Call to the Kirk Session to give further opportunity for it to be subscribed.

(b)   If the Presbytery sustain an appointment and Call to a Graduate Candidate, and there be no appeal tendered in due form against its judgement, it shall appoint the day and hour and place at which the ordination and induction will take place.

(c)   If the Presbytery sustain an appointment and Call to a minister of the Church of Scotland not being a minister of a parish, or to a minister of another denomination, and there be no ecclesiastical impediment, the Presbytery shall appoint the day and hour and place at which the induction will take place.

(3)   In the event that the Call is not sustained, the Presbytery shall determine either (a) to give more time for it to be signed in terms of section 25 above or (b) to proceed in terms of subsection (a) or (b) of section 26 above.

29. Admission to a Charge

(1) When the Presbytery has appointed a day for the ordination and induction of a Graduate Candidate, or for the induction of a minister already ordained, the Clerk shall arrange for an edict in the form of Schedule O to be read to the congregation on the two Sundays preceding the day appointed.

(2) At the time and place named in the edict, the Presbytery having been constituted, the Moderator shall call for the return of the edict attested as having been duly served. If the minister is being translated from another Presbytery, the relevant minute of that Presbytery or of its Vacancy Procedure Committee agreeing to translation shall also be laid on the table. Any objection, to be valid at this stage, must have been intimated to the Presbytery Clerk at the objector's earliest opportunity, must be strictly directed to life or doctrine and must be substantiated immediately to the satisfaction of the Presbytery, in which case procedure shall be sisted and the Presbytery shall take appropriate steps to deal with the situation that has arisen. Otherwise, the Presbytery shall proceed with the ordination and induction, or with the induction, as hereunder.

(3) The Presbytery shall proceed to the church where public worship shall be conducted by those appointed for the purpose. The Clerk shall read a brief narrative of the cause of the vacancy and of the steps taken for the settlement. The Moderator, having read the Preamble, shall, addressing him or her by name, put to the person to be inducted the questions prescribed (*see the Ordinal of the Church as authorised from time to time by the General Assembly*). Satisfactory answers having been given, the person to be inducted shall sign the Formula. If he or she has not already been ordained, the person to be inducted shall then kneel, and the Moderator by prayer and the imposition of hands, in which members of the Presbytery, appointed by the Presbytery for the purpose, and other ordained persons associated with it, if invited to share in such imposition of hands, shall join, shall ordain him or her to the office of the Holy Ministry. Prayer being ended, the Moderator shall say: 'I now declare you to have been ordained to the office of the Holy Ministry, and in name of the Lord Jesus Christ, the King and Head of the Church, and by authority of this Presbytery, I induct you to this charge, and in token thereof we give you the right hand of fellowship'. The Moderator with all other members of Presbytery present and those associated with it shall then give the right hand of fellowship. The Moderator shall then put the prescribed question to the members of the congregation. Suitable charges to the new minister and to the congregation shall then be given by the Moderator or by a minister appointed for the purpose.

(4) *[This subsection is to be construed in conformity with Act III 2004.]* When an ordained minister is being inducted to a charge, the act of ordination shall not be repeated, and the relevant words shall be omitted from the declaration. In other respects, the procedure shall be as in subsection (3) above.

(5) When the appointment is for a limited or potentially limited period (including Reviewable Tenure, or an appointment in terms of section 19 above), the service shall proceed as in subsections (3) or (4) above, except that in the declaration the Moderator shall say: 'I induct you to this charge on the Basis of [specific Act and Section] and in terms of Minute of Presbytery of date . . .'.

(6) After the service, the Presbytery shall resume its session, when the name of the new minister shall be added to the Roll of Presbytery, and the Clerk shall be instructed to send certified intimation of the induction to the Session Clerk to be engrossed in the minutes of the first meeting of Kirk Session thereafter, and, in the case of a translation from another Presbytery or where the minister was prior to the induction subject to the supervision of another Presbytery, to the Clerk of that Presbytery.

30. Service of Introduction

(1) When a minister has been appointed to a linked charge, the Presbytery shall determine in which of the churches of the linking the induction is to take place. This shall be a service of induction to the charge, in consequence of which the person inducted shall become minister of each of the congregations embraced in the linking. The edict regarding the induction, which shall be in terms of Schedule O, shall be read in all of the churches concerned. There shall be no other service of induction; but, if the churches are far distant from one another, or for other good reason, the Presbytery may appoint a service of introduction to be held in the other church or churches. Intimation shall be given of such service, but not in edictal form.

(2) In any case of deferred union or deferred linking, the minister elected and appointed shall be inducted 'to the vacant congregation of A in deferred union (or linking) with the congregation of B' and there shall be no need for any further act to establish his or her position as minister of the united congregation or of the linked congregation as the case may be. The Presbytery, however, shall in such a case arrange a service of introduction to the newly united congregation of AB or the newly linked congregation of B. Intimation shall be given of such service, but not in edictal form.

(3) When an appointment has been made to an extra-parochial office wholly or mainly under control of the Church (community ministry, full-time chaplaincy in hospital, industry, prison or university, full-time clerkship and so on), the Presbytery may deem it appropriate to arrange a service of introduction to take place in a church or chapel suitable to the occasion.

(4) When an appointment has been made to a parochial appointment other than that of an inducted minister, the Presbytery may arrange a service of introduction to take place within the parish. If ordination is involved, suitable arrangements shall be made and edictal intimation shall be given in terms of Schedule P.

(5) A service of introduction not involving ordination shall follow the lines of an induction except that, instead of putting the normal questions to the minister, the Moderator shall ask him or her to affirm the vows taken at his or her ordination. Where the service, in terms of subsection (3) or (4) above, includes the ordination of the minister, the vows shall be put in full. In either case, in the declaration, the Moderator in place of 'I induct you to . . .' shall say: 'I welcome you as . . .'.

31. Demission of Status

If a minister seeks to demit his or her status as a minister of the Church of Scotland, any accompanying demission of a charge will be dealt with by the Vacancy Procedure Committee in terms of section 4 of this Act without further delay, but the question of demission of status shall be considered by the Presbytery itself. The Moderator of Presbytery, or a deputy appointed by him or her, shall first confer with the minister regarding his or her reasons and shall report to the Presbytery if there appears to be any reason not to grant permission to demit status. Any decision to grant permission to demit status shall be immediately reported to the Ministries Council.

32. Miscellaneous

For the purposes of this Act, intimations to congregations may be made (a) verbally during every act of worship or (b) in written intimations distributed to the whole congregation provided that the congregation's attention is specifically drawn to the presence of an intimation there in terms of this Act.

For the purposes of this Act, attestation of all intimations to congregations shall consist of certification thereof by the Session Clerk as follows:

(a) Certification that all intimations received have been duly made on the correct number of Sundays shall be sent to the Presbytery Clerk before the service of induction or introduction.

(b)   Certification that any particular intimation received has been duly made on the correct number of Sundays shall be furnished on demand to the Vacancy Procedure Committee or the Presbytery Clerk.

(c)   Intimation shall be made immediately to the Presbytery Clerk in the event that intimation has not been duly made on the appropriate Sunday.

33. Repeals and Amendments

(1)   Act V 1984 (as amended) is hereby repealed; it is hereby provided that all other legislation prior to this Act shall be construed in conformity with this Act.

(2)   Earlier Acts and Regulations are amended as follows:

(a)   In sections 2 and 7 of Act XVIII 1932, delete the latter sentence of section 2 and all of subsection 7(b).

(b)   In Act IV 1999, delete 'Act V 1984 section 25(3)' and substitute 'section 29(3) of Act VIII 2003'.

(c)   In section 19(2) of Act II 2000, delete 'section 2(3) of Act V 1984' and substitute 'section 7 of Act VIII 2003'.

(d)   In section 9 of Act XV 2002, delete 'in terms of section 27 of Act V 1984'.

(e)   In section 12(i) of Act XIII 2000 and in section 2(i) of Regulations V 2000, delete 'sections 6-8 of Act V 1984' and substitute section 13 of Act VIII 2003'.

(f)   In section 2(2) of Act IV 2001, delete 'in terms of Act V 1984 section 27' and 'in terms of the said Act V 1984'.

(g)   In paragraph 1 of Schedule 3 to Act V 2002, delete 'section 13 of Act V 1984' and substitute 'section 17 of Act VIII 2003'.

(h)   In paragraph 2(ii) of Schedule 3 to Act V 2002, delete 'Sections 6 to 8 of Act V 1984' and substitute 'section 13 of Act VIII 2003'.

(i)   In section 2 of Act VII 2002, delete 'Act V 1984 section 25' and substitute 'section 29 of Act VIII 2003'.

(j)   In section 9 of Act XV 2002, delete 'in terms of section 27 of Act V 1984'.

(k)   In Regulations II 1996, delete reference to Act V 1984 (as amended) and substitute Act VIII 2003.

(3)   Notwithstanding subsection (1) above, the repeal of Act V 1984 as amended shall not affect the operation of the said Act (or Deliverances of the General Assembly in pursuance thereof) prior to the repeal of the said Act, or anything done or suffered under the said Act or Deliverances; and any rights or obligations acquired or incurred thereunder shall have effect as if the said Act had not been repealed.

34. Interpretation

For the purposes of this Act, the Interpretation section (section 1) of Act VII 2003 will apply.

SCHEDULES

A INTIMATION OF ACTION OR DECISION OF VACANCY PROCEDURE COMMITTEE – Section 2(1)

To be read on one Sunday

The Vacancy Procedure Committee of the Presbytery of .... proposes [here insert action or permission proposed]....... Any communicant member of the congregation(s) of A [and B] may submit to the Presbytery Clerk a request for this proposal to be considered at the next meeting of the Presbytery: where such requests are received from four individuals, being communicant members of the congregation(s) or full members of the Presbytery, the request shall be met. Such request should be submitted in writing to [name and postal address of Presbytery Clerk] by [date seven days after intimation].

A .... B ....   Presbytery Clerk

B EDICT CITING A CONGREGATION TO ATTEND – Section 2(5)

To be read on one Sunday

Intimation is hereby given that, in connection with the [anticipated] vacancy in this congregation, a valid request has been made for the matter of [here insert action or permission which had been proposed] to be considered by the Presbytery. [The proposed course of action] is in the meantime sisted.

Intimation is hereby further given that the Presbytery will meet to consider this matter at .... on .... the .... day of .... at .... o'clock and that the congregation are hereby cited to attend for their interests.

A .... B ....   Presbytery Clerk

C PREPARATION OF ELECTORAL REGISTER – Section 13(1) and (2)

To be read on two Sundays

Intimation is hereby given that in view of the [1]anticipated vacancy, the Kirk Session is about to make up an Electoral Register of this congregation. Any communicant whose name is not already on the Communion Roll as a member should hand in to the Session Clerk a Certificate of Transference, and anyone wishing his or her name added to the Register as an adherent should obtain from the Session Clerk, and complete and return to him or her, a Form of Adherent's Claim. All such papers should be in the hands of the Session Clerk not later than .... The Kirk Session will meet in .... on .... at .... to make up the Electoral Register, when anyone wishing to support his or her claim in person should attend.

C .... D ....   Interim Moderator

[1] This word to be included where appropriate – otherwise to be deleted

D FORM OF ADHERENT'S CLAIM – Section 13(1)

I, [1] .... of [2] ...., being a parishioner or regular worshipper in the Church of .... and not being a member of any other congregation in Scotland, claim to have my name put on the Electoral Register of the parish of .... as an adherent.

Date ....   (Signed).......................

[1] Here enter full name in block capitals
[2] Here enter address in full

E INSPECTION OF ELECTORAL REGISTER – Section 13(3)

To be read on one Sunday

Intimation is hereby given that the proposed Electoral Register of this congregation has now been prepared and that an opportunity of inspecting it will be given today in .... at the close of this service, and that it will be open for inspection at .... on .... between the hours of .... and .... each day. Any questions regarding entries in the Register should be brought to the notice of the Kirk Session which is to meet in .... on .... at .... o'clock, when it will finally make up the Electoral Register.

C .... D ....   Interim Moderator

F REVISION OF ELECTORAL REGISTER – Section 13(6)

To be read on two Sundays

Intimation is hereby given that, more than six months having elapsed since the Electoral Register of this congregation was finally made up, it is now proposed that it should be revised. An opportunity of inspecting the Register will be given in .... at the close of this service, and also at .... on .... between the hours of .... and .... each day. Anyone wishing his or her name added to the Electoral Register as a member should give in a Transference Certificate, or as an adherent should give in a Form of Adherent's Claim (copies of which may be had from the Session Clerk) not later than .... The Kirk Session will meet in .... on .... at .... o'clock, when it will finally make up the Revised Register.

C .... D ....   Interim Moderator

G INTIMATION OF ELECTION OF NOMINATING COMMITTEE – Section 14(1)

To be read on two Sundays

Intimation is hereby given that a meeting of this congregation will be held in the Church [or other arrangement may be given here] on Sunday .... at the close of morning worship for the purpose of appointing a Nominating Committee which will nominate one person to the congregation with a view to the appointment of a minister.

C .... D ....   Interim Moderator

H MINUTE OF NOMINATION BY NOMINATING COMMITTEE – Section 21

To be read on two Sundays

(1)   The Committee chosen by this congregation to nominate a person with a view to the election and appointment of a minister, at a meeting held at .... on ...., resolved to name and propose [1] ...., and they accordingly do name and propose the said ....

Date ....

E .... F ....   Convener of Committee

[1] The name and designation of the person should at this point be entered in full

(2)   Intimation is therefore hereby given that the Nominating Committee having, as by minute now read, named and proposed [*Name*], arrangements have been made whereby public worship will be conducted in this Church by him or her on Sunday the .... day of .... at .... o'clock; and that a vote will be taken by voting-papers immediately thereafter; and that electors may vote For or Against electing and appointing the said [*Name*] as minister of this vacant charge.

C .... D ....   Interim Moderator

I VOTING-PAPER – Section 23

FOR Electing [*Name*]	
AGAINST Electing [*Name*]	

Directions to Voters: If you are in favour of electing [*Name*], put a cross (x) on the upper right-hand space. If you are not in favour of electing [*Name*], put a cross (x) in the lower right-hand space. Mark your voting-paper in this way with a cross and put no other mark on your voting-paper, or your vote may not be counted.

Note: The Directions to Voters must be printed prominently on the face of the voting-paper.

J DECLARATION OF ELECTION RESULT – Section 23(5)

First Form (Successful Election)

I hereby declare that the following are the results of the voting for the election and appointment of a minister to the vacant charge of [1] .... and that the said [*Name*] has accordingly been elected and appointed subject to the judgement of the courts of the Church.

Date ....   C .... D ....   Interim Moderator

[1] Here enter details

FOR Electing [*Name*]
AGAINST Electing [*Name*]

Second Form (Failure to Elect)

I hereby declare that the following are the results of the voting for the election and appointment of a minister to the vacant charge of [1] .... and that in consequence of this vote there has been a failure to elect, and the Nominating Committee is deemed to have been discharged. [Continue in terms of Schedule G if appropriate.]

Date ....   C .... D ....   Interim Moderator

¹ Here enter details

FOR Electing [*Name*]
AGAINST Electing [*Name*]

K THE CALL – Section 25(1)

Form of Call

We, members of the Church of Scotland and of the congregation known as ……….., being without a minister, address this Call to be our minister to you, ……….., of whose gifts and qualities we have been assured, and we warmly invite you to accept this Call, promising that we shall devote ourselves with you to worship, witness, mission and service in this parish, and also to the furtherance of these in the world, to the glory of God and for the advancement of His Kingdom.

Paper of Concurrence

We, regular worshippers in the congregation of the Church of Scotland known as ………., concur in the Call addressed by that congregation to ………. to be their minister.

Note: The Call and Paper of Concurrence should be dated and attested by the Interim Moderator before they are transmitted to the Clerk of the Presbytery.

L SUBSCRIBING THE CALL – Section 25(1)

To be read on at least one Sunday

Intimation is hereby given that this congregation having elected [*Name*] to be their minister, a Call to the said [*Name*] has been prepared and will lie in ………. on ………. the ………. day of ………. between the hours of ………. and ………., when those whose names are on the Electoral Register of the congregation may sign in person or by means of mandates. Forms of mandate may be obtained from the Session Clerk.

A Paper of Concurrence will also be available for signature by persons who are connected with the congregation but whose names are not on the Electoral Register of the congregation.

C ………. D ……….   Interim Moderator

M MANDATE TO SIGN CALL – Section 25(2)

I, ………. of ………., being a person whose name is on the Electoral Register of the congregation, hereby authorise the Session Clerk, or other member of Session, to add my name to the Call addressed to [*Name*] to be our minister.

(Signed) …..........…….

N CITATION IN CASE OF NOMINATION BY PRESBYTERY – Section 26(a)(iii)

To be read on one Sunday

Intimation is hereby given that [*Name*], whom the Presbytery has appointed to be minister of this congregation, will conduct public worship in the Church on Sunday the .... day of .... at .... o'clock.

Intimation is hereby further given that a Call addressed to the said [*Name*] will lie in .... on .... the .... day of .... between the hours of .... and .... during the day and between the hours of .... and .... in the evening, when members may sign in person or by means of mandates, forms of which may be had from the Session Clerk.

Intimation is hereby further given that the Presbytery will meet to deal with the appointment and Call at .... on .... the .... day of .... at .... o'clock and that the congregation are hereby cited to attend for their interests.

A .... B ....   Presbytery Clerk

O EDICTAL INTIMATION OF ADMISSION – Section 29

To be read on two Sundays

- The Presbytery of .... has received a Call from this congregation addressed to [*Name*] to be their minister, and the Call has been sustained as a regular Call, and has been accepted by him/her[1];
- The Presbytery, having judged the said [*Name*] qualified[2] for the ministry of the Gospel and for this charge, has resolved to proceed to his or her[3] ordination and induction on .... the .... day of .... at .... o'clock unless something occur which may reasonably impede it:

Notice is hereby given to all concerned that if they, or any of them, have anything to object to in the life or doctrine of the said [*Name*], they should intimate their objection at their earliest opportunity to the Presbytery Clerk, with evidence of substantiation of the objection.

The Presbytery is to meet at [*time*] on [*date as above*]. In accordance with section 29 of Act VIII 2003, an objection first brought at that time must be immediately substantiated, and the objector must satisfy the Presbytery that there was no earlier opportunity to bring the objection to the attention of the Presbytery Clerk. Otherwise the Presbytery shall proceed without further delay.

By order of the Presbytery

A .... B .... Presbytery Clerk

[1] add, where appropriate, 'and his or her translation has been agreed to by the Presbytery of ....'
[2] omit 'for the ministry of the Gospel and' if the minister to be inducted has been ordained previously
[3] omit, where appropriate, 'ordination and'

P EDICTAL INTIMATION OF ORDINATION IN CASE OF INTRODUCTION – Section 30(1)

To be read on two Sundays

- Whereas [narrate circumstances requiring service of introduction]
- And whereas the Presbytery, having found the said [*Name*] to have been regularly appointed and to be qualified for the ministry of the Gospel and for the said appointment, has resolved to proceed to his or her ordination to the Holy Ministry and to his or her introduction as [specify appointment] on ………. the ……. day of ………. at ………. o'clock unless something occur which may reasonably impede it:

Notice is hereby given to all concerned that if they, or any of them, have anything to object to in the life or doctrine of the said [*Name*], they may appear at the Presbytery which is to meet at ………. on ………. the ………. day of ………. at ………. o'clock; with certification that if no relevant objection be then made and immediately substantiated, the Presbytery will proceed without further delay.

By order of the Presbytery

A ………. B ……….   Presbytery Clerk

SECTION 4

The
General Assembly
of 2014

(1) THE GENERAL ASSEMBLY

The Lord High Commissioner:	His Royal Highness the Prince Edward, Earl of Wessex KG GCVO
Moderator:	Right Rev. John P. Chalmers BD CPS
Chaplains to the Moderator:	Rev. Ian W. Alexander BA BD STM Rev. MaryAnn R. Rennie BD MTh
Acting Principal Clerk:	Rev. George J. Whyte BSc BD DMin
Depute Clerk:	Rev. George S. Cowie BSc BD
Procurator:	Ms Laura Dunlop QC
Law Agent:	Mrs Janette S. Wilson LLB NP
Convener of the Business Committee:	Rev. Janet S. Mathieson MA BD
Vice-Convener of the Business Committee:	Rev. Derek Browning MA BD DMin
Precentor:	Rev. Douglas Galbraith MA BD BMus MPhil ARSCM PhD
Assembly Officer:	Mr David McColl
Assistant Assembly Officer:	Mr Craig Marshall

---

(2) THE MODERATOR

The Right Reverend John P. Chalmers BD CPS

John Chalmers brings to the role of Moderator an almost unrivalled knowledge of the Church of Scotland, its ministers and ministries. Following parish ministry in Renton: Trinity and in Edinburgh: Palmerston Place, service as Clerk of Dumbarton Presbytery, and service as a member, Vice-Convener and, briefly, Convener of the Board of Ministry, he moved to the Church Offices and served as Depute General Secretary within the Ministries Department, engaging with all the work of this complex department and becoming responsible, in large part, for the pastoral care of all the ministers in the Church. This ongoing concern was echoed during the General Assembly when he emphasised the urgent need to recruit women and men to train to be ministers, to help in the task of letting society know that there is something very meaningful about living the life of faith. He became Principal Clerk to the General Assembly in 2010, and in 2013 he was made a Chaplain to the Queen in Scotland.

Having started out studying Chemical Engineering at Strathclyde University, John changed direction mid-course and moved to Glasgow University to study Divinity. He spent a lot of time also driving buses and fixing up old cars for himself and others.

In all that he has done, John has been consistently sustained by a strong and supportive family. In the General Assembly, he paid tribute to the Christian influence and guidance of his late father Isaac and his mother Mary, as well as of his wife Liz and their family. Liz has given much of herself in serving the Church as the wife of a parish minister and on the Boards of Education and Ministry, where she was 'midwife' to a generation of ministers.

John and Liz have three children, who, with their partners and children, have been of immense support: their daughter Ruth and her husband Brian, with Mara and Luke; son David and his wife Jennifer, with Rory; and John James ('JJ') and Kornelia, who will marry during this Moderatorial year.

Many have been aware of the injuries sustained by JJ in Afghanistan. Reflecting on the experience of dealing with JJ's injuries, John has been honest in highlighting the challenges to his faith. When he found heaven to be silent, and felt a real sense of having his faith tested, the messages of support and prayers of the Church, from people known and unknown, were almost tangible and helped him and the family to realise that, even when the worst things happen, it is possible to know God's presence through the love and care of the people around you. This experience has better equipped John, Liz and their family to understand how to share such burdens when others go through similar or worse tragedies.

John, following in his father's footsteps, has supported the work of Enable, a commitment that came through the love for his sister June, who had Down's Syndrome and needed that extra support to enable her to live as full, interesting and active a life as possible, which she certainly did into her late 50s. He was also a board member, and chairman, of Donaldson's School for the Deaf, helping them to secure the sale of their premises in the west of Edinburgh in order to build a state-of-the-art campus in Linlithgow.

Nominated in most unusual circumstances only six weeks before the General Assembly (on the previous nominee's withdrawal on health grounds), John hit the ground running. With so little time to prepare, he would have been forgiven for skimping on preparation. This he did not do. After commending him for his leadership and his 'clarity and kindness', the General Assembly rose to give a standing ovation – testimony to his thorough preparedness to step up to the Moderatorial Chair.

John's involvement in the creation of Place for Hope, which has enabled churches to address difference and diversity positively and to be faithful to the purposes of the gospel through the message of reconciliation, has further convinced him of the benefits of respectful dialogue which acknowledges that others may have a valid point of view and that our own point of view is never furthered by disparaging our rivals, and that this is a model of how we can discuss issues in the Church on which we may have differing opinions.

John is passionate about the role the Church can play in the modern world – not as an institution favoured above others in national life, but as a respected voice committed to giving its fullest service, and working closely with other faith groups and institutions seeking to contribute to the commonweal. He has spoken of wanting the Church and its ministers and members to be more generous of heart, more liberal of love and more profligate with God's grace; to tell the story of a Church which cares about the values by which Scotland lives, which cares about the conditions in which people live and which puts its money where its faith is in the work it does among the most vulnerable and marginalised, at home and abroad.

John has wide-ranging interests, including golf (he is to steward at the Ryder Cup), old lawnmowers, Robert Burns, travel, reading and music. His common sense, practical faith and robust good humour, and his great capacity for fun, will doubtless sustain him through a year in which his handicap will likely move into double figures.

Ian Alexander and MaryAnn Rennie
Chaplains

(3) GENERAL ASSEMBLY 2014

The predominant mode of this Assembly was 'respectful dialogue'. It was a note first struck by the Moderator prior to the Assembly in an article in the *Sunday Times*, and by the Convener, the Very Rev. Professor Iain Torrance, in introducing the report of the Theological Forum, when he spoke of a 'mixed-economy' church, one 'in which several perspectives exist respectfully alongside each other'. This was to be played out in the contexts of ministers and deacons in civil partnerships and of the forthcoming referendum on independence for Scotland.

Civil partnerships

Enabling the discussion as to whether kirk sessions should be allowed to call or appoint ministers and deacons in a civil partnership were an Overture from the Legal Questions Committee which, instructed by the 2013 Assembly, proposed permissive legislation, and the Theological Forum, which offered a 'space' in which differing convictions could hear from one another. Noting that we in the Church of Scotland read scripture in more than one tradition, the Forum argued that we were dealing with a contested issue *within* the interpretation of Scripture, not with the setting aside of Scripture. The Convener suggested we had been living within 'mixed economies' of various kinds for a very long time, and maintained that 'the kind of "mixed economy" of constrained difference ... is understandable within our practices of Bible reading and may be located within our tradition'. After thoughtful debate, the Assembly agreed by 369 votes to 189 to send to Presbyteries the proposed legislation which, while affirming 'the Church's historic and current doctrine and practice in relation to human sexuality', would enable individual kirk sessions to call and appoint ministers and deacons in civil partnerships. The Forum and the Committee were then instructed, since laws to enable this may have been enacted in Scotland by the time of the next Assembly, to consider whether same-sex marriage should be recognised as equivalent in terms of the Overture.

Imagining Scotland's future

The 'respectful dialogue on the Referendum' was framed by the contributions of four speakers, with Shadow Foreign Secretary Douglas Alexander and Principal Doug Gay putting the cases for and against independence, while former Moderator Dr Alison Elliott explored some unresolved questions, the debate then being summed up by John Sturrock QC. Arising from a joint report (Church and Society, Ecumenical Relations, Legal Questions), the Assembly also discussed the implications for the Church if Scotland became independent.

Church and world

More than one report showed the Church as firmly engaged in issues facing society at home and abroad. World Mission Council continued the Church's tradition of working alongside people of other nations, naming among other things violence towards women, human trafficking, the persecution of Christians, and the situation in South Sudan. The lives of two remarkable women were remembered: Mary Slessor and Jane Haining. The Guild reported on their six ongoing partnership projects, ranging from art therapy for individuals suffering from dementia, to the building of homes for victims of genocide in Rwanda, and in addition the Golden Age Project (seeking how to work *with* older people rather than *for* them). In its turn, the Mission and Discipleship Council, among a wide range of new resources for the support and stimulation of congregational worship and mission, drew attention to the opportunities and challenges offered by the Commonwealth Games. CrossReach as always gave account of a widely based, and highly rated, programme of social care.

Not least was the report of the Church and Society Council, and the debate that followed, where once again there was an account of remarkable work being carried out on social issues: poverty, disadvantage, economics, homelessness, the living wage, racial justice, human trafficking, spiritual care in the health service, sectarianism, climate change (a call by young people in Dalgety Bay), the 'bedroom tax', transplant surgery, the high cost of funeral expenses, credit unions, the ending of corroboration in criminal trials, assisted dying, asylum-seekers and the 'Azure Card', the Middle East, the 100th anniversary of the First World War, nuclear weapons, international development, and recruitment to the army of those as young as 16 years of age.

Ministry and mission

Ministries Council reported that by 2024 the Church would be 200 ministers short, and a quarter to a third of congregations would have no minister. To respond to this, the Assembly preferred the proposal of Dr Doug Gay, Principal of Trinity College, for a 'decade for ministry' from 2015 to 2025 in which the aim would be to find and train thirty candidates per year, and over the period train 100 members in the theology and practice of mission. The final report of the Special Commission on Ministerial Tenure underlined the necessity of a more flexible approach to matching ministry to location, involving not only more integrated review processes but also greater personal accountability. A related issue which gave the Assembly pause was the experience of the retiring Moderator, Lorna Hood, in the context of a wide-ranging, entertaining and encouraging report of her year, in finding that women (including Moderators) were still denied access to the pulpits of some Highland churches, reporting the pain felt by some female ministers and elders she had met.

The Assembly was recalled to the wider context of mission and ministry in the report of the Ecumenical Relations Committee when first-time Convener, Alison McDonald, reminded commissioners that the Church of Scotland cannot fulfil the obligations of the Third Article Declaratory on its own but must move forward with other Churches. The report also noted the high proportion of people at the younger end of the scale who had represented the Church on world ecumenical bodies. In the debate, Ms Miriam Weibye, who had been elected to the Central Committee of the World Council of Churches, spoke of experiencing 'respectful dialogue' among people of greatly diverse theological positions. The contribution of younger members of the Church was highlighted also in the report from the Youth Assembly. As well as Scottish identity and other issues, last year's gathering had consulted an 'ecumenical human library' when members of other Churches and groupings opened their beliefs and experience to delegates.

There was a sombre moment on Tuesday morning when the Moderator called the commissioners to a time of silence and prayer following the tragic death the previous evening in a road traffic accident of well-known Lewis minister and Presbytery clerk, Tom Sinclair, who had been a commissioner to this Assembly.

Space does not allow reference to significant and important work reported by other committees. Several Conveners had come to the end of their term of office and were thanked by the Moderator: Andrew McLellan (World Mission Council), Neil Gardner (Chaplains to HM Forces), Janet Mathieson (Assembly Arrangements), Angus McPherson (Central Services), James Dewar (Nomination) and Ranald Mair (Safeguarding).

Enhancing the life of the Assembly

As usual, the business of the Assembly was both lightened and deepened by events within and without. *Heart and Soul* in the Gardens on Sunday afternoon attracted the usual numbers and enthusiasm. Saturday evening worship was brightened (including visually) by the contribution of the choir of Dunfermline Abbey, the congregation to which the Moderator belongs. The Assembly has come to expect that there will be 'surprise visitors', either in residence in the

Palace as guests of the Lord High Commissioner – this year HRH the Prince Edward, Earl of Wessex (whose appropriate and witty addresses were warmly received) – or introduced by committees. The Archbishop of Canterbury made a cameo appearance by video, with a message directed at the Assembly on credit unions. The Guild Convener introduced Lt Colonel John Charteris, the great-great-great-nephew of the founder of the Guild (and of the order of deaconesses, and of *Life and Work*), the Rev. Professor Archibald Charteris, a household name in the Church. Ecumenical and overseas delegates made welcome contributions and brought first-hand information.

On Friday morning, the Assembly gave a warm welcome to His Grace Bishop Angaelos, General Bishop of the Coptic Orthodox Church in the UK, who, speaking of attacks in Egypt on fifty churches and other Christian bodies, noted that, remarkably, the reaction of the Christian Church had been complete silence – no anger, no revenge, no retribution. The previous day, the Assembly had welcomed Rabbi Ephraim Mirvis, 11th Chief Rabbi of the United Hebrew Congregations of the Commonwealth, who spoke about friendship, mutual respect and peace. The rabbi was able to speak frankly of the effect on relations by a report at last year's Assembly, and remarked that it was necessary to know the facts before making a stand. The Moderator did not let this pass, and affirmed the place of a continuing respectful dialogue which was not afraid to share differences and difficulties, instancing as an example the destruction of trees in an incident in the 'Tent of Nations' (a Palestinian Christian farm), reported earlier in the Assembly, which, prompted by former Moderator David Arnott, recalled the deuteronomic prohibition that if you defeat a city you do not destroy the fruit trees.

Thanks to the Moderator
The relaxed, thoughtful and often hilarious character of this Assembly was in large part due to the presiding of the Moderator, who at short notice had replaced Dr Angus Morrison, who had had, amid widespread regret, to withdraw due to ill health. On Friday morning, former Moderator John Cairns begged leave to express the thanks of the Assembly without waiting, as was the custom, until the following year. He concluded his speech: 'You have moved us by your words and your leadership in worship and in prayer. You have moderated this business with clarity and with incredible kindness. You have truly engendered and provided a setting for that which you most wanted, which was respectful dialogue. So often, you have said exactly the right word to guests and to commissioners. We are all in your debt.'

The Editor

SECTION 5

Presbytery Lists

See overleaf for an explanation of the two parts of each list; a Key to Abbreviations; and a list of the Presbyteries in their numerical order.

SECTION 5 – PRESBYTERY LISTS

In each Presbytery list, the congregations are listed in alphabetical order. In a linked charge, the names appear under the first named congregation. Under the name of the congregation will be found the name of the minister and, where applicable, that of an associate minister, ordained local minister, auxiliary minister and member of the Diaconate. The years indicated after a minister's name in the congregational section of each Presbytery list are the year of ordination (column 1) and the year of current appointment (column 2). Where only one date is given, it is both the year of ordination and the year of appointment. For an ordained local minister, the date is of ordination.

In the second part of each Presbytery list, those named are listed alphabetically. The first date is the year of ordination, and the following date is the year of appointment or retirement. If the person concerned is retired, then the appointment last held will be shown in brackets.

KEY TO ABBREVIATIONS

(E)   Indicates a Church Extension charge. New Charge Developments are separately indicated.
(GD)   Indicates a charge where it is desirable that the minister should have a knowledge of Gaelic.
(GE)   Indicates a charge where public worship must be regularly conducted in Gaelic.
(H)   Indicates that a Hearing Aid Loop system has been installed. In Linked charges, the (H) is placed beside the appropriate building as far as possible.
(L)   Indicates that a Chair Lift has been installed.
(R)   Indicates that the minister has been appointed on the basis of Reviewable Tenure.

PRESBYTERY NUMBERS

1	Edinburgh	18	Dumbarton
2	West Lothian	19	Argyll
3	Lothian	20	
4	Melrose and Peebles	21	
5	Duns	22	Falkirk
6	Jedburgh	23	Stirling
7	Annandale and Eskdale	24	Dunfermline
8	Dumfries and Kirkcudbright	25	Kirkcaldy
9	Wigtown and Stranraer	26	St Andrews
10	Ayr	27	Dunkeld and Meigle
11	Irvine and Kilmarnock	28	Perth
12	Ardrossan	29	Dundee
13	Lanark	30	Angus
14	Greenock and Paisley	31	Aberdeen
15		32	Kincardine and Deeside
16	Glasgow	33	Gordon
17	Hamilton	34	Buchan

35	Moray
36	Abernethy
37	Inverness
38	Lochaber
39	Ross
40	Sutherland
41	Caithness
42	Lochcarron – Skye
43	Uist
44	Lewis
45	Orkney
46	Shetland
47	England
48	Europe
49	Jerusalem

(1) EDINBURGH

The Presbytery meets:
- at Palmerston Place Church, Edinburgh, on 9 September, 4 November and 9 December 2014, and on 3 February, 24 March, 5 May and 23 June 2015;
- in the church of the Moderator on 7 October 2014.

Clerk:	REV. GEORGE J. WHYTE BSc BD DMin	10/1 Palmerston Place, Edinburgh EH12 5AA [E-mail: **edinburgh@cofscotland.org.uk**]	0131-225 9137
Depute Clerk:	HAZEL HASTIE MA CQSW PhD AIWS	17 West Court, Edinburgh EH16 4EB [E-mail: **hazel.hastie29@gmail.com**]	07827 314374 (Mbl)

1   Edinburgh: Albany Deaf Church of Edinburgh (H) (0131-444 2054)

Rosemary A. Addis (Mrs) BD	2014		c/o Ministries Council, 121 George Street, Edinburgh EH2 4YN [E-mail: raddis@cofscotland.org.uk]	07738 983393 (Mbl)

2   Edinburgh: Balerno (H)

Louise J. Duncan (Mrs) BD	2005	2010	3 Johnsburn Road, Balerno EH14 7DN [E-mail: bpc-minister@btconnect.com]	0131-449 3830

3   Edinburgh: Barclay Viewforth (0131-229 6810) (E-mail: admin@barclaychurch.org.uk)

Samuel A.R. Torrens BD	1995	2005	113 Meadowspot, Edinburgh EH10 5UY [E-mail: minister@barclayviewforth.org.uk]	0131-478 2376

4   Edinburgh: Blackhall St Columba's (0131-332 4431) (E-mail: secretary@blackhallstcolumba.org.uk)

Vacant	5 Blinkbonny Crescent, Edinburgh EH4 3NB	0131-343 3708

5   Edinburgh: Bristo Memorial Craigmillar

Drausio Goncalves	2008	2013	72 Blackchapel Close, Edinburgh EH15 3SL [E-mail: drausio@bristochurch.com]	0131-657 3266

6   Edinburgh: Broughton St Mary's (H) (0131-556 4786)

Graham G. McGeoch MA BTh MTh	2009	2013	103 East Claremont Street, Edinburgh EH7 4JA [E-mail: minister@bstmchurch.org.uk]	0131-556 7313

7   Edinburgh: Canongate (H)

Neil N. Gardner MA BD	1991	2006	The Manse of Canongate, Edinburgh EH8 8BR [E-mail: nng22@btinternet.com]	0131-556 3515

8 Edinburgh: Carrick Knowe (H) (0131-334 1505) (E-mail: ckchurch@talktalk.net)
Fiona M. Mathieson (Mrs) BEd BD PGCommEd MTh   1988   2001   21 Traquair Park West, Edinburgh EH12 7AN [E-mail: fiona.mathieson@ukgateway.net]   0131-334 9774

9 Edinburgh: Colinton (H) (0131-441 2232) (E-mail: church.office@colinton-parish.com)
Rolf H. Billes BD   1996   2009   The Manse, Colinton, Edinburgh EH13 0JR [E-mail: rolf.billes@colinton-parish.com]   0131-466 8384
Gayle J.A. Taylor (Mrs) MA BD (Assoc)   1999   2009   Colinton Parish Church, Dell Road, Edinburgh EH13 0JR [E-mail: gayle.taylor@colinton-parish.com]   0131-441 2232

10 Edinburgh: Corstorphine Craigsbank (H) (0131-334 6365)
Stewart M. McPherson BD CertMin   1991   2003   17 Craigs Bank, Edinburgh EH12 8HD [E-mail: smcpherson@blueyonder.co.uk]   0131-467 6826 / 07814 901429 (Mbl)

11 Edinburgh: Corstorphine Old (H) (0131-334 7864) (E-mail: corold@aol.com)
Moira McDonald MA BD   1997   2005   23 Manse Road, Edinburgh EH12 7SW [E-mail: moira-mc@live.co.uk]   0131-476 5893

12 Edinburgh: Corstorphine St Anne's (0131-316 4740) (E-mail: office@stannes.corstorphine.org.uk)
James J. Griggs BD MTh   2011   2013   1/5 Morham Gait, Edinburgh EH10 5GH [E-mail: cstannesminister@gmail.com]   0131-466 3269

13 Edinburgh: Corstorphine St Ninian's (H) (0131-539 6204) (E-mail: office@st-ninians.co.uk)
Alexander T. Stewart MA BD FSAScot   1975   1995   17 Templeland Road, Edinburgh EH12 8RZ [E-mail: alextstewart@blueyonder.co.uk]   0131-334 2978

14 Edinburgh: Craigentinny St Christopher's (0131-258 2759)
Guardianship of the Presbytery   61 Milton Crescent, Edinburgh EH15 3PQ

15 Edinburgh: Craiglockhart (H) (E-mail: office@craiglockhartchurch.org)
Gordon Kennedy BSc BD MTh   1993   2012   20 Craiglockhart Quadrant, Edinburgh EH14 1HD [E-mail: gordonkennedy@craiglockhartchurch.org]   0131-444 1615

16 Edinburgh: Craigmillar Park (H) (0131-667 5862) (E-mail: cpkirk@btinternet.com)
John C.C. Urquhart MA MA BD   2010   14 Hallhead Road, Edinburgh EH16 5QJ [E-mail: jccurquhart@gmail.com]   0131-667 1623

17 Edinburgh: Cramond (H) (E-mail: cramond.kirk@blueyonder.co.uk)
G. Russell Barr BA BD MTh DMin   1979   1993   Manse of Cramond, Edinburgh EH4 6NS [E-mail: rev.r.barr@blueyonder.co.uk]   0131-336 2036

18	**Edinburgh: Currie (H) (0131-451 5141) (E-mail: currie_kirk@btconnect.com)**			
	Vacant		43 Lanark Road West, Currie EH14 5JX	0131-449 4719
19	**Edinburgh: Dalmeny linked with Edinburgh: Queensferry**			
	David C. Cameron BD CertMin	1993	2009	1 Station Road, South Queensferry EH30 9HY	0131-331 1100
				[E-mail: minister@qpcweb.org]	
20	**Edinburgh: Davidson's Mains (H) (0131-312 6282) (E-mail: life@dmainschurch.plus.com)**			
	Jeremy R.H. Middleton LLB BD	1981	1988	1 Hillpark Terrace, Edinburgh EH4 7SX	0131-336 3078
				[E-mail: life@dmainschurch.plus.com]	
21	**Edinburgh: Dean (H)**			
	Guardianship of the Presbytery		1 Ravelston Terrace, Edinburgh EH4 3EF	0131-332 5736
22	**Edinburgh: Drylaw (0131-343 6643)**			
	Vacant		15 House o' Hill Gardens, Edinburgh EH4 2AR	0131-343 1441
23	**Edinburgh: Duddingston (H) (E-mail: dodinskirk@aol.com)**			
	James A.P. Jack	1989	2001	Manse of Duddingston, Old Church Lane, Edinburgh EH15 3PX	0131-661 4240
	BSc BArch BD DMin RIBA ARIAS			[E-mail: jamesjack2829@aol.com]	
24	**Edinburgh: Fairmilehead (H) (0131-445 2374) (E-mail: office@fhpc.org.uk)**			
	John R. Munro BD	1976	1992	c/o Fairmilehead Parish Church, 1 Frogston Road West, Edinburgh EH10 7AA	0131-446 9363
				[E-mail: revjohnmunro@hotmail.com]	
	Hayley O'Connor BS MDiv (Assist)		2009	19 Caiystane Terrace, Edinburgh EH10 6SR	0131-629 1610
				[E-mail: oconnorhe@gmail.com]	
25	**Edinburgh: Gorgie Dalry (H) (0131-337 7936)**			
	Peter I. Barber MA BD	1984	1995	90 Myreside Road, Edinburgh EH10 5BZ	0131-337 2284
				[E-mail: pibarber@toucansurf.com]	
26	**Edinburgh: Granton (H) (0131-552 3033)**			
	Norman A. Smith MA BD	1997	2005	8 Wardie Crescent, Edinburgh EH5 1AG	0131-551 2159
				[E-mail: norm@familysmith.biz]	

27 **Edinburgh: Greenbank (H) (0131-447 9969) (E-mail: greenbankchurch@btconnect.com; Website: www.greenbankchurch.org)**
Alison I. Swindells (Mrs) LLB BD   1998   2007   112 Greenbank Crescent, Edinburgh EH10 5SZ   0131-447 4032
[E-mail: alisonswindells@blueyonder.co.uk]
William H. Stone BA MDiv ThM   2012   19 Caiystane Terrace, Edinburgh EH10 6SR   0131-629 1610
(Youth Minister)   07883 815598 (Mbl)
[E-mail: billstoneiii@gmail.com]

28 **Edinburgh: Greenside (H) (0131-556 5588)**
Guardianship of the Presbytery   80 Pilrig Street, Edinburgh EH6 5AS   0131-554 3277 (Tel/Fax)

29 **Edinburgh: Greyfriars Kirk (GE) (H) (0131-225 1900) (E-mail: enquiries@greyfriarskirk.com)**
Richard E. Frazer BA BD DMin   1986   2003   12 Tantallon Place, Edinburgh EH9 1NZ   0131-667 6610
[E-mail: minister@greyfriarskirk.com]
Lezley J. Stewart BD ThM MTh (Assoc)   2000   2014   Greyfriars Kirk, 1 Greyfriars Place, Edinburgh EH1 2QQ   0131-225 1900
07713 974423 (Mbl)
[E-mail: associateminister@greyfriarskirk.com]
(New charge formed by the union of Edinburgh: Greyfriars Tolbooth and Highland Kirk and Edinburgh: Kirk o' Field)

30 **Edinburgh: High (St Giles') (0131-225 4363) (E-mail: info@stgilescathedral.org.uk)**
Calum I. MacLeod BA BD   1996   2014   St Giles' Cathedral, Edinburgh EH1 1RE   0131-225 4363
[E-mail: calummacleod@me.com]
Helen J.R. Alexander BD DipSW (Assist)   1981   2012   7 Polwarth Place, Edinburgh EH11 1LG   0131-346 0685
[E-mail: st_giles_cathedral@btconnect.com]

31 **Edinburgh: Holyrood Abbey (H) (0131-661 6002)**
Philip R. Hair BD   1980   1998   100 Willowbrae Avenue, Edinburgh EH8 7HU   0131-652 0640
[E-mail: phil@holyroodabbey.f2s.com]

32 **Edinburgh: Holy Trinity (H) (0131-442 3304)**
Kenneth S. Borthwick MA BD   1983   2005   16 Thorburn Road, Edinburgh EH13 0BQ   0131-441 1403
[E-mail: kennysamuel@aol.com]
Ian MacDonald BD MTh (Assoc)   2005   12 Sighthill Crescent, Edinburgh EH11 4QE   0131-442 3304
[E-mail: ianafrica@hotmail.com]
Oliver M.H. Clegg BD (Youth Minister)   2003   4 Blinkbonny Steading, Blinkbonny Road, Currie EH14 6AE   0131-478 5341
[E-mail: ollieclegg@btinternet.com]

33 **Edinburgh: Inverleith St Serf's (H)**
Joanne G. Foster (Mrs)   1996   2012   78 Pilrig Street, Edinburgh EH6 5AS   0131-561 1392
DipTMus BD AdvDipCouns
[E-mail: minister@inverleithsaintserfs.org.uk]

34 Edinburgh: Juniper Green (H)
James S. Dewar MA BD 1983 2000 476 Lanark Road, Juniper Green, Edinburgh EH14 5BQ
[E-mail: jim.dewar@blueyonder.co.uk] 0131-453 3494

35 Edinburgh: Kaimes Lockhart Memorial linked with Edinburgh: Liberton
John N. Young MA BD PhD 1996 7 Kirk Park, Edinburgh EH16 6HZ
[E-mail: LLLjyoung@btinternet.com] 0131-664 3067

36 Edinburgh: Kirkliston
Margaret R. Lane (Mrs) BA BD MTh 2009 43 Main Street, Kirkliston EH29 9AF
[E-mail: margaretlane@btinternet.com] 0131-333 3298 / 07795 481441 (Mbl)

37 Edinburgh: Leith North (H) (0131-553 7378) (E-mail: nlpc-office@btinternet.com)
Alexander T. McAspurren BD MTh 2002 2011 6 Craighall Gardens, Edinburgh EH6 4RJ
[E-mail: alexander.mcaspurren@btinternet.com] 0131-551 5252

38 Edinburgh: Leith St Andrew's (H)
Robert A. Mackenzie LLB BD 1993 2013 30 Lochend Road, Edinburgh EH6 8BS
[E-mail: rob.anne@blueyonder.co.uk] 0131-554 7695

39 Edinburgh: Leith South (H) (0131-554 2578) (E-mail: slpc@dial.pipex.com)
John S. (Iain) May 2012 37 Claremont Road, Edinburgh EH6 7NN
[E-mail: johnsmay@blueyonder.co.uk] 0131-554 3062

40 Edinburgh: Leith Wardie (H) (0131-551 3847) (E-mail: churchoffice@wardie.org.uk)
Brian C. Hilsley LLB BD 1990 35 Lomond Road, Edinburgh EH5 3JN
[E-mail: minister@wardie.org.uk] 0131-552 3328

41 Edinburgh: Liberton (H) See Edinburgh: Kaimes Lockhart Memorial

42 Edinburgh: Liberton Northfield (H) (0131-551 3847)
Vacant 9 Claverhouse Drive, Edinburgh EH16 6BR 0131-658 1754

43 Edinburgh: London Road (H) (0131-661 1149)
Vacant 26 Inchview Terrace, Edinburgh EH7 6TQ 0131-669 5311

44 **Edinburgh: Marchmont St Giles' (H) (0131-447 4359)**
    Karen K. Campbell BD MTh DMin   1997   2002   2 Trotter Haugh, Edinburgh EH9 2GZ   0131-447 2834
                                                            [E-mail: karen@marchmontstgiles.org.uk]

45 **Edinburgh: Mayfield Salisbury (0131-667 1522)**
    Scott S. McKenna BA BD MTh MPhil   1994   26 Seton Place, Edinburgh EH9 2JT   0131-667 1286
                                                            [E-mail: ScottSMcKenna@aol.com]

46 **Edinburgh: Morningside (H) (0131-447 6745) (E-mail: office@morningsideparishchurch.org.uk)**
    Derek Browning MA BD DMin   1987   2001   20 Braidburn Crescent, Edinburgh EH10 6EN   0131-447 1617
                                                            [E-mail: minister@morningsideparishchurch.org.uk]

47 **Edinburgh: Morningside United (H) (0131-447 3152)**
    Vacant   1 Midmar Avenue, Edinburgh EH10 6BS   0131-447 8724

48 **Edinburgh: Murrayfield (H) (0131-337 1091) (E-mail: mpchurch@btconnect.com)**
    Keith Edwin Graham MA PGDip BD   2008   2014   45 Murrayfield Gardens, Edinburgh EH12 6DH 0131-337 1364
                                                            [E-mail: keithedwingraham@gmail.com]

49 **Edinburgh: Newhaven (H)**
    Peter Bluett   2007   158 Granton Road, Edinburgh EH5 3RF   0131-476 5212
                                                            [E-mail: peterbluett@sky.com]

50 **Edinburgh: New Restalrig (H) (0131-661 5676)**
    Vacant   19 Abercorn Road, Edinburgh EH8 7DP   0131-661 4045

51 **Edinburgh: Old Kirk Muirhouse (H) (0131-332 4354) (E-mail: minister.oldkirk@btinternet.com)**
    Vacant   35 Silverknowes Road, Edinburgh EH4 5LL   0131-312 7773
    Ann Lyall (Miss) DCS   24 Pennywell Road, Edinburgh EH4 4HD   0131-332 4354
                                                            [E-mail: ann.lyall@btinternet.com]
                      (New charge formed by the union of Edinburgh: Old Kirk and Edinburgh: Muirhouse St Andrew's)

52 **Edinburgh: Palmerston Place (H) (0131-220 1690) (E-mail: admin@palmerstonplacechurch.com)**
    Colin A.M. Sinclair BA BD   1981   1996   30B Cluny Gardens, Edinburgh EH10 6BJ   0131-447 9598
                                                            [E-mail: colins.ppc@virgin.net]   0131-225 3312 (Fax)

53 Edinburgh: Pilrig St Paul's (0131-553 1876)
Mark M. Foster BSc BD   1998   2013   78 Pilrig Street, Edinburgh EH6 5AS   0131-332 5736
[E-mail: minister.psp@gmail.com]

54 Edinburgh: Polwarth (H) (0131-346 2711) (E-mail: polwarthchurch@tiscali.co.uk)
Jack Holt BSc BD MTh   1985   2011   88 Craiglockhart Road, Edinburgh EH14 1EP   0131-441 6105
[E-mail: jack9holt@gmail.com]

55 Edinburgh: Portobello and Joppa (H) (0131-669 3641)
Stewart G. Weaver BA BD PhD   2003   2014   6 St Mary's Place, Edinburgh EH15 2QF   0131-669 2410
[E-mail: stewartweaver@btinternet.com]
(New charge formed by the union of Edinburgh: Portobello Old, Edinburgh: Portobello St James' and Edinburgh: Portobello St Philip's Joppa)

56 Edinburgh: Priestfield (H) (0131-667 5644)
Jared W. Hay BA MTh DipMin DMin   1987   2009   13 Lady Road, Edinburgh EH16 5PA   0131-468 1254
[E-mail: jared.hay@blueyonder.co.uk]

57 Edinburgh: Queensferry (H) See Edinburgh: Dalmeny

58 Edinburgh: Ratho
Ian J. Wells BD   1999   2 Freelands Road, Ratho, Newbridge EH28 8NP   0131-333 1346
[E-mail: ianjwells@btinternet.com]

59 Edinburgh: Reid Memorial (H) (0131-662 1203) (E-mail: reid.memorial@btinternet.com)
Brian M. Embleton BD   1976   1985   20 Wilton Road, Edinburgh EH16 5NX   0131-667 3981
[E-mail: brianembleton@btinternet.com]

60 Edinburgh: Richmond Craigmillar (H) (0131-661 6561)
Elizabeth M. Henderson (Mrs)   1985   1997   Manse of Duddingston, Old Church Lane, Edinburgh EH15 3PX   0131-661 4240
MA BD MTh   [E-mail: lizhende@tiscali.co.uk]

61 Edinburgh: St Andrew's and St George's West (H) (0131-225 3847) (E-mail: info@standrewsandstgeorges.org.uk)
Ian Y. Gilmour BD   1985   2011   25 Comely Bank, Edinburgh EH4 1AJ   0131-332 5848
[E-mail: ianyg2@gmail.com]

62 Edinburgh: St Andrew's Clermiston
Alistair H. Keil BD DipMin 1989 87 Drum Brae South, Edinburgh EH12 8TD [E-mail: ahkeil@blueyonder.co.uk] 0131-339 4149

63 Edinburgh: St Catherine's Argyle (H) (0131-667 7220)
Vacant 5 Palmerston Road, Edinburgh EH9 1TL 0131-667 9344

64 Edinburgh: St Cuthbert's (H) (0131-229 1142) (E-mail: office@st-cuthberts.net)
David W. Denniston BD DipMin 1981 2008 34A Murrayfield Road, Edinburgh EH12 6ER [E-mail: denniston.david@googlemail.com] 0131-337 6637 / 07903 926727 (Mbl)

65 Edinburgh: St David's Broomhouse (H) (0131-443 9851)
Michael J. Mair BD 2014 33 Traquair Park West, Edinburgh EH12 7AN [E-mail: mairmj@gmail.com] 0131-334 1730
Liz Crocker (Mrs) DipComEd DCS 77C Craigcrook Road, Edinburgh EH4 3PH 0131-332 0227

66 Edinburgh: St John's Colinton Mains
Iain M. Goring BSc BD (Interim Minister) 1976 2013 17 Swanston Green, Edinburgh EH10 7EW [E-mail: imgoring@tiscali.co.uk] 0131-445 3451 / 07762 254140 (Mbl)
(New charge formed by the union of Edinburgh: Colinton Mains and Edinburgh: St John's Oxgangs)

67 Edinburgh: St Margaret's (H) (0131-554 7400) (E-mail: stm.parish@virgin.net)
Carol H.M. Ford DSD RSAMD BD 2003 43 Moira Terrace, Edinburgh EH7 6TD [E-mail: revcford@btinternet.com] 0131-669 7329
Pauline Rycroft (Mrs) DCS BA CertTheol 6 Ashville Terrace, Edinburgh EH6 8DD [E-mail: pauline70@rocketmail.com] 0131-554 6564 / 07759 436303 (Mbl)

68 Edinburgh: St Martin's
Russel Moffat BD MTh PhD 1986 2008 5 Duddingston Crescent, Edinburgh EH15 3AS [E-mail: rbmoffat@tiscali.co.uk] 0131-657 9894

69 Edinburgh: St Michael's (H) (E-mail: office@stmichaels-kirk.co.uk)
James D. Aitken BD 2002 2005 9 Merchiston Gardens, Edinburgh EH10 5DD [E-mail: james.aitken2@btinternet.com] 0131-346 1970

70 Edinburgh: St Nicholas' Sighthill
Vacant 122 Sighthill Loan, Edinburgh EH11 4NT 0131-442 2510

71 Edinburgh: St Stephen's Comely Bank (0131-315 4616)
Vacant
8 Blinkbonny Crescent, Edinburgh EH4 3NB
0131-332 3364

72 Edinburgh: Slateford Longstone
Michael W. Frew BSc BD   1978   2005
50 Kingsknowe Road South, Edinburgh EH14 2JW
[E-mail: minister@slatefordlongstone.org.uk]
0131-466 5308

73 Edinburgh: Stenhouse St Aidan's
Vacant
65 Balgreen Road, Edinburgh EH12 5UA
0131-337 7711

74 Edinburgh: Stockbridge (H) (0131-552 8738) (E-mail: stockbridgechurch@btconnect.com)
John A. Cowie BSc BD   1983   2013
19 Eildon Street, Edinburgh EH3 5JU
[E-mail: jacowie54@gmail.com]
0131-557 6052
07506 104416 (Mbl)

75 Edinburgh: The Tron Kirk (Gilmerton and Moredun)
Cameron Mackenzie BD   1997   2010
467 Gilmerton Road, Edinburgh EH17 7JG
[E-mail: mackenz550@aol.com]
0131-664 7538

Name			Charge / Role	Address	Phone
Abernethy, William LTh	1979	1993	(Glenrothes: St Margaret's)	120/1 Willowbrae Road, Edinburgh EH8 7HW	0131-661 0390
Aitken, Alexander R. MA	1965	1997	(Newhaven)	36 King's Meadow, Edinburgh EH16 5JW	0131-667 1404
Alexander, Ian W. BA BD STM	1990	2010	World Mission Council	World Mission Council, 121 George Street, Edinburgh EH2 4YN [E-mail: iwalexander@gmail.com]	0131-225 5722
Anderson, Robert S. BD	1988	1997	(Scottish Churches World Exchange)		
Armitage, William L. BSc BD	1976	2006	(Edinburgh: London Road)	Flat 7, 4 Papermill Wynd, Edinburgh EH7 4GJ [E-mail: bill@billarm.plus.com]	0131-558 8534
Baird, Kenneth S. MSc PhD BD MIMarEST	1998	2009	(Edinburgh: Leith North)	3 Maule Terrace, Gullane EH31 2DB	01620 843447
Barrington, Charles W. H. MA BD	1997	2007	(Associate: Edinburgh: Balerno)	502 Lanark Road, Edinburgh EH14 5DH	0131-453 4826
Beckett, David M. BA BD	1964	2002	(Edinburgh: Greyfriars, Tolbooth and Highland Kirk)	1F1, 31 Sciennes Road, Edinburgh EH9 1NT [E-mail: davidbeckett3@aol.com]	0131-667 2672
Blakey, Ronald S. MA BD MTh	1962	2000	(Assembly Council)	5 Moss Side Road, Biggar ML12 6GF	01899 229226
Booth, Jennifer (Mrs) BD	1996	2004	(Associate: Leith South)	39 Lilyhill Terrace, Edinburgh EH8 7DR	0131-661 3813
Boyd, Kenneth M. MA BD PhD FRCPE	1970	1996	University of Edinburgh: Medical Ethics	1 Doune Terrace, Edinburgh EH3 6DY	0131-225 6485
Brady, Ian D. BSc ARCST BD	1967	2001	(Edinburgh: Corstorphine Old)	28 Frankfield Crescent, Dalgety Bay, Dunfermline KY11 9LW [E-mail: pidb@dbay28.fsnet.co.uk]	01383 825104
Brown, William D. MA	1963	1989	(Wishaw: Thornlie)	9/3 Craigend Park, Edinburgh EH16 5XY [E-mail: wdbrown@surefish.co.uk]	0131-672 2936
Brown, William D. BD CQSW	1987	2013	(Edinburgh: Murrayfield)	79 Carnbee Park, Edinburgh EH16 6GG [E-mail: wdb@talktalk.net]	0131-261 7297

Name	Role			Address	Telephone
Cameron, G. Gordon MA BD STM	(Juniper Green)	1957	1997	10 Beechwood Gardens, Stirling FK8 2AX	01786 472934
Cameron, John W.M. MA BD	(Liberton)	1957	1996	10 Plewlands Gardens, Edinburgh EH10 5JP	0131-447 1277
Chalmers, Murray MA	(Hospital Chaplain)	1965	2006	8 Easter Warriston, Edinburgh EH7 4QX	0131-552 4211
Clark, Christine M. (Mrs) BA BD MTh	(Aberlady with Gullane)	2006	2013	40 Pentland Avenue, Edinburgh EH13 0HY [E-mail: christine.clark7@aol.co.uk]	
Clinkenbeard, William W. BSc BD STM	(Edinburgh: Carrick Knowe)	1966	2000	3/17 Western Harbour Breakwater, Edinburgh EH6 6PA [E-mail: bjclinks@compuserve.com]	
Cook, John MA BD	(Edinburgh: Leith St Andrew's)	1967	2005	26 Silverknowes Court, Edinburgh EH4 5NR	0131-312 8447
Curran, Elizabeth M. (Miss) BD	(Aberlour)	1995	2008	27 Captain's Road, Edinburgh EH17 8HR	0131-664 1358
Cuthell, Tom C. MA BD MTh	(Edinburgh: St Cuthbert's)	1965	2007	Flat 10, 2 Kingsburgh Crescent, Waterfront, Edinburgh EH5 1JS	0131-476 3864
Davidson, D. Hugh MA	(Edinburgh: Inverleith)	1965	2009	Flat 1/2, 22 Summerside Place, Edinburgh EH6 4NZ [E-mail: hdavidson35@btinternet.com]	0131-554 8420
Davidson, Ian M.P. MBE MA BD	(Stirling: Allan Park South with Church of the Holy Rude)	1957	1994	13/8 Craigend Park, Edinburgh EH16 5XX	0131-664 0074
Dawson, Michael S. BTech BD	(Associate: Edinburgh: Holy Trinity)	1979	2005	9 The Broich, Alva FK12 5NR [E-mail: mixpen.dawson@btinternet.com]	01259 769309
Denniston, Jane M. MA BD MTh	(Ministries Council)	2002		34A Murrayfield Road, Edinburgh EH12 6ER	0131-337 6637
Dilbey, Mary D. (Miss) BD	(West Kirk of Calder)	1997	2002	41 Bonaly Rise, Edinburgh EH13 0QU	0131-441 9092
Donald, Alistair P. MA PhD BD	(Chaplain: Heriot-Watt University)	1999	2009	The Chaplaincy, Heriot-Watt University, Edinburgh EH14 4AS [E-mail: a.p.donald@hw.ac.uk]	0131-451 4508
Dougall, Elspeth G. (Mrs) MA BD	(Edinburgh: Marchmont St Giles')	1989	2001	60B Craigmillar Park, Edinburgh EH16 5PU	0131-668 1342
Douglas, Alexander B. BD	(Edinburgh: Blackhall St Columba's)	1979	2014	15 Inchview Gardens, Dalgety Bay, Dunfermline KY11 9SA	01383 242872
Douglas, Colin R. MA BD STM	(Livingston Ecumenical Parish)	1969	2007	34 West Pilton Gardens, Edinburgh EH4 4EQ [E-mail: colindouglas@btinternet.com]	0131-551 3808
Doyle, Ian B. MA BD PhD	(Department of National Mission)	1946	1991	21 Lygon Road, Edinburgh EH16 5QD	0131-667 2697
Drummond, Rhoda (Miss) DCS	(Deacon)	1998		Flat K, 23 Grange Loan, Edinburgh EH9 2ER	0131-668 3631
Dunn, W. Iain C. DA LTh	(Pilrig and Dalmeny Street)	1983	1998	10 Fox Covert Avenue, Edinburgh EH12 6UQ	0131-334 1665
Elliott, Gavin J. MA BD	(Ministries Council)	1976	2004	c/o 121 George Street, Edinburgh EH2 4YN	0131-225 5722
Embleton, Sara R. (Mrs) BA BD MTh	(Edinburgh: Leith St Serf's)	1988	2010	20 Wilton Road, Edinburgh EH16 5NX [E-mail: sara.embleton@blueyonder.co.uk]	0131-478 1624
Evans, Mark BSc MSc DCS	(Chaplain: Queen Margaret Hospital, Dunfermline)	2006		13 Easter Drylaw Drive, Edinburgh EH4 2QA [E-mail: mark.evans59@nhs.net]	(Home) 0131-343 3089 (Office) 01383 674136
Farquharson, Gordon MA BD DipEd	(Stonehaven: Dunnottar)	1998	2007	26 Learmonth Court, Edinburgh EH4 1PB [E-mail: gfarqu@talktalk.net]	0131-343 1047
Faulds, Norman L. MA BD FSAScot	(Aberlady with Gullane)	1968	2000	10 West Fenton Court, West Fenton, North Berwick EH39 5AE	01620 842331
Fergusson, David A.S. (Prof.) MA BD DPhil FBA FRSE	(University of Edinburgh)	1984	2000	23 Riselaw Crescent, Edinburgh EH10 6HN	
Foggitt, Eric W. MA BSc BD	(Dunbar)	1991	2009	Christiaan de Wet Straat 19/2, 1091 NG Amsterdam, The Netherlands [E-mail: ericleric3@btinternet.com]	0131-447 4022

Name			Role	Address	Phone
Forrester, Margaret R. (Mrs) MA BD	1974	2003	(Edinburgh: St Michael's)	25 Kingsburgh Road, Edinburgh EH12 6DZ [E-mail: margaret@rosskeen.org.uk]	0131-337 5646
Fraser, Shirley A. (Miss) MA BD	1992	2008	(Scottish Field Director: Friends International)	6/50 Roseburn Drive, Edinburgh EH12 5NS	0131-347 1400
Gardner, John V.	1997	2003	(Glamis, Inverarity and Kinnettles)	75/1 Lockharton Avenue, Edinburgh EH14 1BD [E-mail: jvgardner66@googlemail.com]	0131-443 7126
Gordon, Margaret (Mrs) DCS	1974	2009	(Edinburgh: Currie)	92 Lanark Road West, Currie EH14 5LA	0131-449 2554
Gordon, Tom MA BD	1967	2008	(Chaplain: Marie Curie Hospice, Edinburgh)	22 Gosford Road, Port Seton, Prestonpans EH32 0HF	01875 812262
Graham, W. Peter MA BD			(Presbytery Clerk)	23/6 East Comiston, Edinburgh EH10 6RZ	0131-445 5763
Hardman Moore, Susan (Prof.) BA PGCE MA PhD	2013		Ordained Local Minister	c/o New College, Mound Place, Edinburgh EH1 2LX [E-mail: s.hardmanmoore@ed.ac.uk]	0131-650 8908 (Mbl) 07811 345699
Harkness, James CB OBE QHC MA DD	1961	1995	(Chaplain General: Army)	13 Saxe Coburg Place, Edinburgh EH3 5BR	0131-343 1297
Hill, J. William BA BD	1967	2001	(Edinburgh: Corstorphine St Anne's)	33/9 Murrayfield Road, Edinburgh EH12 6EP	
Irving, William D. LTh	1985	2005	(Golspie)	122 Swanston Muir, Edinburgh EH10 7HY	0131-441 3384
Jeffrey, Eric W.S. JP MA	1954	1994	(Edinburgh: Bristo Memorial)	18 Gillespie Crescent, Edinburgh EH10 4HT	0131-229 7815
Kelly, Ewan R. MB ChB BD PhD	1994	2006	NHS Education for Scotland	15 Boswall Road, Edinburgh EH5 3RW [E-mail: ewan.kelly@nes.scot.nhs.uk]	0131-551 7706
Kingston, David V.F. BD DipPTh	1993		Chaplain: Army	4 Regt RA RHQ, Alanbrooke Barracks, Topcliffe, Thirsk YO7 3EQ [E-mail: d.v.f.k@btinternet.com]	(Mbl) 07802 417947
Lawson, Kenneth C. MA BD	1963	1999	(Adviser in Adult Education)	56 Easter Drylaw View, Edinburgh EH4 2QP	0131-539 3311
Logan, Anne T. (Mrs) MA BD MTh DMin	1981	2012	(Edinburgh: Stockbridge)	Sunnyside Cottage, 18 Upper Broomieknowe, Lasswade EH18 1LP [E-mail: annetlogan@blueyonder.co.uk]	0131-663 9550
McCaskill, George I.L. MA BD	1953	1990	(Religious Education)	19 Tyler's Acre Road, Edinburgh EH12 7HY	0131-334 7451
Macdonald, Finlay A.J. MA BD PhD DD	1971	2010	(Principal Clerk)	8 St Ronan's Way, Innerleithen EH44 6RG [E-mail: finlay_macdonald@btinternet.com]	01896 831631
Macdonald, Peter J. BD	1986	2009	Leader of the Iona Community	63 Jim Bush Drive, Prestonpans EH32 9GB [E-mail: petermacdonald@iona.org.uk] [E-mail: petermacdonald166@btinternet.com]	(Office) 0141-332 6343 (Mbl) 07946 715166 / 01875 819655
Macdonald, William J. BD	1976	2002	(Board of National Mission: New Charge Development)	1/13 North Werber Park, Edinburgh EH4 1SY	0131-332 0254
MacGregor, Margaret S. (Miss) MA BD DipEd	1985	1994	(Calcutta)	16 Learmonth Court, Edinburgh EH4 1PB	0131-332 1089
McGregor, Alistair G.C. QC BD	1987	2002	(Edinburgh: Leith North)	22 Primrose Bank Road, Edinburgh EH5 3JG	0131-551 2802
McGregor, T. Stewart MBE MA BD	1957	1998	(Chaplain: Edinburgh Royal Infirmary)	19 Lonsdale Terrace, Edinburgh EH3 9HL [E-mail: cetsm@uwclub.net]	0131-229 5332
MacKay, Stewart A.	2009		Chaplain: Army	2 Bn The Parachute Regiment, Merville Barracks, Colchester CO2 7UT	
Mackenzie, James G. BA BD	1980	2005	(Jersey: St Columba's)	26 Drylaw Crescent, Edinburgh EH4 2AU [E-mail: jgmackenzie@jerseymail.co.uk]	0131-332 3720
MacLaughlan, Grant BA BD	1998	2013	Workplace Chaplain	54 Crieff Road, Perth PH1 2RS [E-mail: grm6871@gmail.com]	
Maclean, Ailsa G. (Mrs) BD DipCE	1979	1988	Chaplain: George Heriot's School	28 Swan Spring Avenue, Edinburgh EH10 6NJ	0131-445 1320
Macmillan, Gilleasbuig KCVO MA BD Drhc DD FRSE	1969	2013	(Edinburgh: High (St Giles'))	207 Dalkeith Road, Edinburgh EH16 5DS [E-mail: gmacmillan1@btinternet.com]	

Name			Position	Address	Tel.
MacMurchie, F. Lynne LLB BD	1998	2003	Healthcare Chaplain	Edinburgh Community Mental Health Chaplaincy, 41 George IV Bridge, Edinburgh EH1 1EL	0131-220 5150
McNab, John L. MA BD	1997	2014	Ministries Council		0131-658 1754
McPake, John M. LTh	2000	2014	(Edinburgh: Liberton Northfield)	9 Claverhouse Drive, Edinburgh EH16 6BR [E-mail: john_mcpake9@yahoo.co.uk]	0131-554 4143
McPheat, Elspeth DCS			Deaconess: CrossReach	11/5 New Orchardfield, Edinburgh EH6 5ET	0131-552 6784
McPhee, Duncan C. MA BD	1953	1993	(Department of National Mission)	8 Belvedere Park, Edinburgh EH6 4LR	0131-667 1456
Macpherson, Colin C.R. MA BD	1958	1996	(Dunfermline St Margaret's)	7 Eva Place, Edinburgh EH9 3ET	0131-467 6826
McPherson, Marjory (Mrs) LLB BD MTh	1990	2012	Ministries Council	17 Craigs Walk, Edinburgh EH12 8HD [E-mail: mmcpherson@cofscotland.org.uk]	
Mathieson, Angus R. MA BD	1988	1998	Ministries Council	21 Traquair Park West, Edinburgh EH12 7AN	0131-334 9774
Moir, Ian A. MA BD	1962	2000	(Adviser for Urban Priority Areas)	28/6 Comely Bank Avenue, Edinburgh EH4 1EL	0131-332 2748
Monteith, W. Graham BD PhD	1974	1994	(Flotta and Fara with Hoy and Walls)	203 Grandfield, Edinburgh EH6 4TL	0131-552 2564
Morrice, William G. MA BD STM PhD	1957	1991	(St John's College Durham)	Flat 37, The Cedars, 2 Manse Road, Edinburgh EH12 7SN [E-mail: w.g.morrice@btinternet.com]	0131-316 4845
Morrison, Mary B. (Mrs) MA BD DipEd	1978	2000	(Edinburgh: Stenhouse St Aidan's)	174 Craigcrook Road, Edinburgh EH4 3PP	0131-316 4706
Morton, Andrew R. MA BD DD	1956	1994	(Board of World Mission and Unity)	7A Laverockbank Terrace, Edinburgh EH5 3DJ	0131-538 7049
Moyes, Sheila A. (Miss) DCS			(Deacon)	158 Pilton Avenue, Edinburgh EH5 2JZ [E-mail: sheilamoyes@btinternet.com]	0131-551 1731
Mulligan, Anne MA DCS			(Deacon: Hospital Chaplain)	27A Craigour Avenue, Edinburgh EH17 1NH [E-mail: mulliganne@aol.com]	0131-664 3426
Munro, George A.M.	1968	2000	(Edinburgh: Cluny)	108 Caiyside, Edinburgh EH10 7HR	0131-445 5829
Munro, John P.L. MA BD PhD	1977	2007	(Kinross)	5 Marchmont Crescent, Edinburgh EH9 1HN [E-mail: jplmunro@yahoo.co.uk]	0131-623 0198
Murrie, John BD	1953	1996	(Kirkliston)	31 Nicol Road, The Whins, Broxburn EH52 6JJ	01506 852464
Page, Ruth MA BD DPhil	1976	2000	(University of Edinburgh)	22/5 West Mill Bank, West Mill Road, Edinburgh EH13 0QT	0131-441 3740
Paterson, Douglas S. MA BD	1976	2010	(Edinburgh: St Colm's)	4 Ards Place, High Street, Aberlady EH32 0DB	01875 870192
Plate, Maria A.G. (Miss) LTh BA	1983	2000	(South Ronaldsay and Burray)	Flat 29, 77 Barnton Park View, Edinburgh EH4 6EL	0131-339 8539
Rennie, Agnes M. (Miss) DCS			(Deacon)	3/1 Craigmillar Court, Edinburgh EH16 4AD	0131-661 8475
Ridland, Alistair K. MA BD	1982	2000	Chaplain: Western General Hospital	13 Stewart Place, Kirkliston EH29 0BQ	0131-333 2711
Robertson, Charles LVO MA	1965	2005	(Edinburgh: Canongate)	3 Ross Gardens, Edinburgh EH9 3BS [E-mail: canongate1@aol.com]	0131-662 9025
Robertson, Norma P. (Miss) BD DMin MTh	1993	2002	(Kincardine O'Neil with Lumphanan)	Flat 5, 2 Bumbrae Drive, Grovewood Hill, Edinburgh EH12 8AS	0131-339 6701
Ronald, Norma A. (Miss) MBE DCS	1960	2000	(Deacon)	2B Saughton Road North, Edinburgh EH12 7HG	0131-334 8736
Schofield, Melville F. MA	1965	2006	(Chaplain: Western General Hospitals)	25 Rowantree Grove, Currie EH14 5AT	0131-449 4745
Scott, Ian G. BSc BD STM	1986	2000	(Edinburgh: Greenbank)	50 Forthview Walk, Tranent EH33 1FE [E-mail: igscott50@btinternet.com]	01875 612907
Scott, Martin DipMusEd RSAM BD PhD	1970	2005	Ministries Council	The Manse, Culross, Dunfermline KY12 8JD	01383 880231
Shewan, Frederick D. MA BD	1965	2006	(Edinburgh: Muirhouse St Andrew's)	36 Glendinning Road, Kirkliston EH29 9HE	0131-333 2631
Smith, Angus MA LTh	1965	2006	(Chaplain to the Oil Industry)	3/7 West Powburn, West Savile Gait, Edinburgh EH9 3EW	0131-667 1761
Stark, Suzie BD		2013	Assistant: Edinburgh: St Cuthbert's	St Cuthbert's Church, 5 Lothian Road, Edinburgh EH1 2EP [E-mail: sstark1962@btinternet.com]	0131-229 1142

Name	Years	Position	Address / E-mail	Tel
Steele, Marilynn J. (Mrs) BD DCS	1962 2001	(Deacon)	2 Northfield Gardens, Prestonpans EH32 9LQ [E-mail: marilynnsteele@aol.com]	01875 811497
Stephen, Donald M. TD MA BD ThM		(Edinburgh: Marchmont St Giles')	10 Hawkhead Crescent, Edinburgh EH16 6LR [E-mail: donaldmstephen@aol.com]	0131-658 1216
Stevenson, John MA BD PhD	1963 2001	(Department of Education)	12 Swanston Gardens, Edinburgh EH10 7DL	0131-445 3960
Stirling, A. Douglas BSc	1956 1994	(Rhu and Shandon)	162 Avontoun Park, Linlithgow EH49 6QH	01506 845021
Tait, John M. BSc BD	1985 2012	(Edinburgh: Pilrig St Paul's)	82 Greenend Gardens, Edinburgh EH17 7QH [E-mail: j.m.tait@blueyonder.co.uk]	0131-258 9105
Taylor, William R. MA BD MTh	1983 2004	Chaplaincy Adviser (Church of Scotland): Scottish Prison Service	Calton House, 5 Redheughs Rigg, South Gyle, Edinburgh EH12 9DQ [E-mail: bill.taylor@sps.pnn.gov.uk]	0131-244 8640
Teague, Yvonne (Mrs) DCS		(Board of Ministry)	46 Craigcrook Avenue, Edinburgh EH4 3PX [E-mail: y.teague.1@blueyonder.co.uk]	0131-336 3113
Telfer, Iain J.M. BD DPS	1978 2001	Chaplain: Royal Infirmary	Royal Infirmary of Edinburgh, 51 Little France Crescent, Edinburgh EH16 4SA	0131-242 1997
Thom, Helen (Miss) BA DipEd MA DCS		(Deacon)	84 Great King Street, Edinburgh EH3 6QU	0131-556 5687
Thomson, Donald M. BD	1975 2013	(Tullibody: St Serf's)	50 Sighthill Road, Edinburgh EH11 4NY [E-mail: donniethomson@tiscali.co.uk]	
Tweedie, Fiona BSc PhD	2011	Ordained Local Minister: Mission Statistics Co-ordinator	121 George Street, Edinburgh EH2 4YN [E-mail: ffweedie@cofscotland.org.uk]	0131-225 5722
Watson, Nigel G. MA	1998 2012	(Associate: East Kilbride: Old/Stewartfield/West)	7 St Catherine's Place, Edinburgh EH9 1NU [E-mail: nigel.g.watson@gmail.com]	0131-662 4191
Webster, Peter BD	1977 2014	(Edinburgh: Portobello St James')	51 Kempock Street, Gourock PA19 1ND [E-mail: peterwebster101@hotmail.com]	
Whyte, George J. BSc BD DMin	1981 2008	Presbytery Clerk	4 Baberton Mains Lea, Edinburgh EH14 3HB [E-mail: edinburgh@cofscotland.org.uk]	0131-466 1674
Whyte, Iain A. BA BD STM PhD	1968 2005	(Community Mental Health Chaplain)	14 Carlingnose Point, North Queensferry, Inverkeithing KY11 1ER [E-mail: iainisabel@whytes28.fsnet.co.uk]	01383 410732
Wigglesworth, J. Christopher MBE BSc PhD BD	1968 1999	(St Andrew's College, Selly Oak)	12 Leven Terrace, Edinburgh EH3 9LW [E-mail: wiggles@talk21.com]	0131-228 6335
Wilkinson, John BD MD FRCP DTM&H BSc CQSW BD	1946 1975	(Kikuyu)	70 Craigleith Hill Gardens, Edinburgh EH4 2JH	0131-332 2994
Williams, Jenny M. (Miss)	1996 1997	Greyfriars Nitekirk Joint Co-ordinator	16 Blantyre Terrace, Edinburgh EH10 5AE	0131-447 0050
Wilson, John M. MA	1964 1995	(Adviser in Religious Education)	27 Bellfield Street, Edinburgh EH15 2BR	0131-669 5257
Wishart, William DCS		(Deacon)	1 Brunstane Road North, Edinburgh EH15 2DL [E-mail: bill@wishartfamily.com]	(Mbl) 07846 555654
Wynne, Alistair T.E. BA BD	1982 2009	(Nicosia Community Church, Cyprus)	Flat 6, 14 Burnbrae Drive, Edinburgh EH12 8AS [E-mail: awynne2@googlemail.com]	0131-339 6462
Young, Alexander W. BD DipMin	1988 1999	Lead Chaplain: NHS Lothian	32 Lindsay Circus, The Hawthorns, Rosewell EH24 9EP	(Work) 0131-242 1997

EDINBURGH ADDRESSES

Albany	82 Montrose Terrace
Balerno	Johnsburn Road, Balerno
Barclay Viewforth	Barclay Place
Blackhall St Columba's	Queensferry Road
Bristo Memorial	Peffermill Road, Craigmillar
Broughton St Mary's	Bellevue Crescent
Canongate	Canongate
Carrick Knowe	North Saughton Road
Colinton	Dell Road
Corstorphine	
Craigsbank	Craig's Crescent
Old	Kirk Loan
St Anne's	Kaimes Road
St Ninian's	St John's Road
Craigentinny	
St Christopher's	Craigentinny Road
Craiglockhart	Craiglockhart Avenue
Craigmillar Park	Craigmillar Park
Cramond	Cramond Glebe Road
Currie	Kirkgate, Currie
Davidson's Mains	Quality Street
Dean	Dean Path
Drylaw	Groathill Road North
Duddingston	Old Church Lane, Duddingston
Fairmilehead	Frogston Road West, Fairmilehead
Gorgie Dalry	Gorgie Road

Granton	Boswall Parkway
Greenbank	Braidburn Terrace
Greenside	Royal Terrace
Greyfriars Kirk	Greyfriars Place
High (St Giles')	High Street
Holyrood Abbey	Dalziel Place x London Road
Holy Trinity	Hailesland Place, Wester Hailes
Inverleith St Serf's	Ferry Road
Juniper Green	Lanark Road, Juniper Green
Kaimes Lockhart Memorial	Gracemount Drive
Kirkliston	The Square, Kirkliston
Leith	
North	Madeira Street off Ferry Road
St Andrew's	Easter Road
South	Kirkgate, Leith
Wardie	Primrosebank Road
Liberton	Kirkgate, Liberton
Northfield	Gilmerton Road, Liberton
London Road	London Road
Marchmont St Giles'	Kilgraston Road
Mayfield Salisbury	Mayfield Road x West Mayfield
Morningside	Cluny Gardens
Morningside United	Bruntsfield Place x Chamberlain Rd
Murrayfield	Abinger Gardens
Newhaven	Craighall Road
New Restalrig	Willowbrae Road
Old Kirk Muirhouse	Pennywell Gardens
Palmerston Place	Palmerston Place
Pilrig St Paul's	Pilrig Street

Polwarth	Polwarth Terrace x Harrison Road
Portobello	
Old	Bellfield Street
St James'	Rosefield Place
St Philip's Joppa	Abercorn Terrace
Priestfield	Dalkeith Road x Marchhall Place
Queensferry	The Loan, South Queensferry
Ratho	Baird Road, Ratho
Reid Memorial	West Savile Terrace
Richmond Craigmillar	Niddrie Mains Road
St Andrew's and	
St George's West	George Street and Shandwick Place
St Andrew's Clermiston	Clermiston View
St Catherine's Argyle	Grange Road x Chalmers Crescent
St Cuthbert's	Lothian Road
St David's Broomhouse	Broomhouse Crescent
St John's Colinton Mains	Oxgangs Road North
St Margaret's	Restalrig Road South
St Martin's	Magdalene Drive
St Michael's	Slateford Road
St Nicholas' Sighthill	Calder Road
St Stephen's Comely Bank	Comely Bank
Slateford Longstone	Kingsknowe Road North
Stenhouse St Aidan's	Chesser Avenue
Stockbridge	Saxe Coburg Street
The Tron Kirk	Craigour Gardens and
(Gilmerton and Moredun)	Ravenscroft Street

(2) WEST LOTHIAN

Meets in the church of the incoming Moderator on the first Tuesday of September and in St John's Church Hall, Bathgate, on the first Tuesday of every other month, except December, when the meeting is on the second Tuesday, and January, July and August, when there is no meeting.

Clerk: REV. DUNCAN SHAW BD MTh   St John's Manse, Mid Street, Bathgate EH48 1QD   01506 653146
[E-mail: westlothian@cofscotland.org.uk]

Abercorn (H) linked with Pardovan, Kingscavil (H) and Winchburgh (H)
A. Scott Marshall DipComm BD   1984   1998   The Manse, Winchburgh, Broxburn EH52 6TT   01506 890919
[E-mail: pkwla@aol.com]

Armadale (H)
Julia C. Wiley (Ms) MA(CE) MDiv 1998 2010 70 Mount Pleasant, Armadale, Bathgate EH48 3HB 01501 730358
[E-mail: preachergrace@gmail.com]

Margaret Corrie (Miss) DCS 44 Sunnyside Street, Camelon, Falkirk FK1 4BH 01324 670656
[E-mail: deakcorr@virginmedia.com] 07955 633969 (Mbl)

Avonbridge (H) linked with Torphichen (H)
Sandi McGill (Ms) BD 2002 2012 Manse Road, Torphichen, Bathgate EH48 4LT 01506 676803
[E-mail: sandimac376@gmail.com]

Bathgate: Boghall (H)
Christopher Galbraith BA LLB BD 2012 1 Manse Place, Ash Grove, Bathgate EH48 1NJ 01506 652715
[E-mail: chrisgalbraith@phonecoop.coop]

Bathgate: High (H)
Vacant 19 Hunter Grove, Bathgate EH48 1NN 01506 652654

Bathgate: St John's (H)
Duncan Shaw BD MTh 1975 1978 St John's Manse, Mid Street, Bathgate EH48 1QD 01506 653146
[E-mail: westlothian@cofscotland.org.uk]

Blackburn and Seafield (H)
Robert A. Anderson MA BD DPhil 1980 1998 The Manse, 5 MacDonald Gardens, Blackburn, Bathgate EH47 7RE 01506 652825
[E-mail: robertanderson307@btinternet.com]

Blackridge (H) linked with Harthill: St Andrew's (H)
Vacant East Main Street, Harthill, Shotts ML7 5QW 01501 751239

Breich Valley (H)
Robert J. Malloch BD 1987 2013 Breich Valley Manse, Stoneyburn, Bathgate EH47 8AU 01501 763142
[E-mail: rojama@live.com]

Broxburn (H)
Vacant 2 Church Street, Broxburn EH52 5EL 01506 852825

Fauldhouse: St Andrew's (H)
Robert Sloan BD 1997 2011 7 Glebe Court, Fauldhouse, Bathgate EH47 9DX 01501 771190
[E-mail: robertsloan@scotnet.co.uk]

Harthill: St Andrew's See Blackridge

Kirknewton (H) and East Calder (H)
Andre Groenewald BA BD MDiv DD   1994 2009   8 Manse Court, East Calder, Livingston EH53 0HF   01506 884585 / 07588 845814 (Mbl)
[E-mail: groenstes@yahoo.com]
Brenda Robson PhD (Aux)   2005 2014   2 Baird Road, Ratho, Newbridge EH28 8RA   0131-333 2746
[E-mail: brendarobson@hotmail.co.uk]

Kirk of Calder (H)
John M. Povey MA BD   1981   19 Maryfield Park, Mid Calder, Livingston EH53 0SB   01506 882495
[E-mail: revjpovey@aol.com]
Kay McIntosh (Mrs) DCS   4 Jacklin Green, Livingston EH54 8PZ   01506 440543
[E-mail: kay@backedge.co.uk]

Linlithgow: St Michael's (H) (E-mail: info@stmichaels-parish.org.uk)
D. Stewart Gillan BSc MDiv PhD   1985 2004   St Michael's Manse, Kirkgate, Linlithgow EH49 7AL   01506 842195
[E-mail: stewart@stmichaels-parish.org.uk]
Cheryl McKellar-Young (Mrs) BA BD (Assoc)   2013   c/o Cross House, The Cross, Linlithgow EH49 7AL   01506 842188
[E-mail: cheryl1@stmichaels-parish.org.uk]
Thomas S. Riddell BSc CEng FIChemE (Aux)   1993 1994   4 The Maltings, Linlithgow EH49 6DS   01506 843251
[E-mail: tsriddell@blueyonder.co.uk]

Linlithgow: St Ninian's Craigmailen (H)
W. Richard Houston BSc BD   1998 2004   29 Philip Avenue, Linlithgow EH49 7BH   01506 202246
[E-mail: wrichardhouston@blueyonder.co.uk]

Livingston Ecumenical Parish
Robin R. Hine MA (Team Leader)   21 Bankton Gardens, Livingston EH54 9DZ   01506 207360
(The United Reformed Church)
[E-mail: robin@hiner.com]
Ronald G. Greig MA BD   1987 2008   2 Eastcroft Court, Livingston EH54 7ET   01506 467426
[E-mail: rgglep@gmail.com]
Helen Jenkins BSc MRES PhD BA MA   13 Eastcroft Court, Livingston EH54 7ET   01506 464567
(The Methodist Church)
[E-mail: revhelen@chjenkins.plus.com]
Darren Philip BSc   72 Pinebank, Ladywell, Livingston EH54 6EX   01506 797712
(Youth and Children's Worker)
[E-mail: darren@lepyouth.com]

Livingston: Old (H)
Graham W. Smith BA BD FSAScot   1995   Manse of Livingston, Charlesfield Lane, Livingston EH54 7AJ   01506 420227
[E-mail: gsmith2014@hotmail.com]

Pardovan, Kingscavil and Winchburgh See Abercorn

Polbeth Harwood linked with West Kirk of Calder (H)
Jonanda Groenewald BA BD MTh DD   1999 2014
8 Manse Court, East Calder, Livingston EH53 0HF
[E-mail: jonandagroenewald@gmail.com]
01506 884802

Strathbrock (H)
Marc B. Kenton BTh MTh   1997 2009
1 Manse Park, Uphall, Broxburn EH52 6NX
[E-mail: marc@kentonfamily.co.uk]
01506 852550

Torphichen See Avonbridge

Uphall: South (H)
Ian D. Maxwell MA BD PhD   1977 2013
8 Fernlea, Uphall, Broxburn EH52 6DF
[E-mail: i.d.maxwell@quista.net]
01506 239840

West Kirk of Calder (H) See Polbeth Harwood

Whitburn: Brucefield (H)
Alexander M. Roger BD PhD   1982 2014
48 Gleneagles Court, Whitburn, Bathgate EH47 8PG
[E-mail: s.roger@btinternet.com]

Whitburn: South (H)
Angus Kerr BD CertMin ThM DMin   1983 2013
5 Mansewood Crescent, Whitburn, Bathgate EH47 8HA
[E-mail: revdrkerr@gmail.com]
01501 740333

Black, David W. BSc BD   1968 2008   (Strathbrock)
66 Bridge Street, Newbridge EH28 8SH
[E-mail: dw.black666@yahoo.co.uk]
0131-333 2609

Cameron, Ian MA BD   1953 1981   (Kilbrandon and Kilchattan)
Craigellen, West George Street, Blairgowrie PH10 6DZ
01250 872087

Darroch, Richard J.G.   1993 2010   (Whitburn: Brucefield)
BD MTh MA(CMS)
23 Barnes Green, Livingston EH54 8PP
[E-mail: richdarr@aol.com]
01506 436648

Dundas, Thomas B.S. LTh   1969 1996   (West Kirk of Calder)
35 Coolkill, Sandyford, Dublin 18, Republic of Ireland
[E-mail: deitom35@yahoo.com]
00353 12953061

Jamieson, Gordon D. MA BD   1974 2012   (Head of Stewardship)
41 Goldpark Place, Livingston EH54 6LW
[E-mail: gdj1949@talktalk.net]
01506 412020

Kelly, Isobel J.M. (Miss)   1974 2010   (Greenock: St Margaret's)
MA BD DipEd
76 Bankton Park East, Livingston EH54 9BN
01506 438511

Mackay, Kenneth J. MA BD   1971 2007   (Edinburgh: St Nicholas' Sighthill)
46 Chuckethall Road, Livingston EH54 8FB
[E-mail: knnth_mackay@yahoo.com]
01506 410884

MacRae, Norman I. LTh   1966 2003   (Inverness: Trinity)
144 Hope Park Gardens, Bathgate EH48 2QX
[E-mail: normanmacrae@talktalk.com]
01506 635254

Merrilees, Ann (Miss) DCS   (Deaconess)
23 Cuthill Brae, West Calder EH55 8QE
[E-mail: ann@merrilees.freeserve.co.uk]
01501 762909

Morrison, Iain C. BA BD	1990	2003	(Linlithgow: St Ninian's Craigmailen)	Whaligoe, 53 Eastcroft Drive, Polmont, Falkirk FK2 0SU [E-mail: iain@kirkweb.org]	01324 713249
Nelson, Georgina (Mrs) MA BD PhD DipEd	1990	1995	Hospital Chaplain	63 Hawthorn Bank, Seafield, Bathgate EH47 7EB	01506 670391
Nicol, Robert M.	1984	1996	(Jersey: St Columba's)	59 Kinloch View, Blackness Road, Linlithgow EH49 7HT [E-mail: revrob.nicol@tiscali.co.uk]	01506 840515
Orr, J. McMichael MA BD PhD	1949	1986	(Aberfoyle with Port of Menteith)	17a St Ninians Way, Linlithgow EH49 7HL [E-mail: mikeandmargorr@googlemail.com]	
Thomson, Phyllis (Miss) DCS	2003	2010	(Deaconess)	63 Caroline Park, Mid Calder, Livingston EH53 0SJ	01506 883207
Trimble, Robert DCS			(Deacon)	5 Templar Rise, Dedridge, Livingston EH54 6PJ	01506 412504
Walker, Ian BD MEd DipMS	1973	2007	(Rutherglen: Wardlawhill)	92 Carseknowe, Linlithgow EH49 7LG [E-mail: walk102822@aol.com]	01506 844412
Whitson, William S. MA	1959	1999	(Cumbernauld: St Mungo's)	2 Chapman's Brae, Bathgate EH48 4LH [E-mail: william_whitson@tiscali.co.uk]	01506 650027

(3) LOTHIAN

Meets at Musselburgh: St Andrew's High Parish Church at 7pm on the last Thursday in February, April, June and November, and in a different church on the last Thursday in September.

| Clerk: | **MR JOHN D. McCULLOCH DL** | **20 Tipperwell Way, Howgate, Penicuik EH26 8QP** [E-mail: lothian@cofscotland.org.uk] | **01968 676300** |

Aberlady (H) linked with Gullane (H)
Vacant | | | The Manse, Hummel Road, Gullane EH31 2BG | 01620 843192

Athelstaneford linked with Whitekirk and Tyninghame
Joanne H.G. Evans-Boiten BD | 2004 2009 | The Manse, Athelstaneford, North Berwick EH39 5BE [E-mail: joanne.evansboiten@gmail.com] | 01620 880378

Belhaven (H) linked with Spott
Laurence H. Twaddle MA BD MTh | 1977 1978 | The Manse, Belhaven Road, Dunbar EH42 1NH [E-mail: revtwaddle@aol.com] | 01368 863098

Bilston linked with Glencorse (H) linked with Roslin (H)
John R. Wells BD DipMin | 1991 2005 | 31A Manse Road, Roslin EH25 9LG [E-mail: wellsjr3@aol.com] | 0131-440 2012

Bolton and Saltoun linked with Humbie linked with Yester (H)
Vacant — The Manse, Tweeddale Avenue, Gifford, Haddington EH41 4QN — 01620 810515

Bonnyrigg (H)
John Mitchell LTh CMin — 1991 — 9 Viewbank View, Bonnyrigg EH19 2HU [E-mail: jmitchell1511@gmail.com] — 0131-663 8287 (Tel/Fax)

Cockenzie and Port Seton: Chalmers Memorial (H)
Kristina M. Herbold Ross (Mrs) — 2008 2011 — 2 Links Road, Port Seton, Prestonpans EH32 0HA [E-mail: rev.khross@btinternet.com] — 01875 819254

Cockenzie and Port Seton: Old (H)
Guardianship of the Presbytery

Cockpen and Carrington (H) linked with Lasswade (H) and Rosewell (H)
Vacant — 11 Pendreich Terrace, Bonnyrigg EH19 2DT — 0131-663 6392

Dalkeith: St John's and King's Park (H)
Keith L. Mack BD MTh DPS — 2002 — 13 Weir Crescent, Dalkeith EH22 3JN [E-mail: kthmacker@aol.com] — 0131-454 0206

Dalkeith: St Nicholas' Buccleuch (H)
Alexander G. Horsburgh MA BD — 1995 2004 — 116 Bonnyrigg Road, Dalkeith EH22 3HZ [E-mail: alexanderhorsburgh@gmail.com] — 0131-663 3036

Dirleton (H) linked with North Berwick: Abbey (H) (Office: 01620 892800) (E-mail: abbeychurch@btconnect.com)
David J. Graham BSc BD PhD — 1982 1998 — Sydserff, Old Abbey Road, North Berwick EH39 4BP [E-mail: dirletonkirk@btinternet.com] — 01620 840878

Dunbar (H)
Gordon Stevenson BSc BD — 2010 — The Manse, 10 Bayswell Road, Dunbar EH42 1AB [E-mail: gstev@btconnect.com] — 01368 865482

Dunglass
Suzanne G. Fletcher (Mrs) BA MDiv MA — 2001 2011 — The Manse, Cockburnspath TD13 5XZ [E-mail: revfletcher@btinternet.com] — 01368 830713

Garvald and Morham linked with Haddington: West (H)
John Vischer — 1993   2011 — 15 West Road, Haddington EH41 3RD
[E-mail: j_vischer@yahoo.co.uk] — 01620 822213

Gladsmuir linked with Longniddry (H)
Robin E. Hill LLB BD PhD — 2004 — The Manse, Elcho Road, Longniddry EH32 0LB
[E-mail: robinailsa@btinternet.com] — 01875 853195

Glencorse (H) See Bilston

Gorebridge (H)
Mark S. Nicholas MA BD — 1999 — 100 Hunterfield Road, Gorebridge EH23 4TT
[E-mail: mark@gorepc.com] — 01875 820387

Gullane See Aberlady

Haddington: St Mary's (H)
Jennifer Macrae (Mrs) MA BD — 1998   2007 — 1 Nungate Gardens, Haddington EH41 4EE
[E-mail: minister@stmaryskirk.co.uk] — 01620 823109

Haddington: West See Garvald and Morham

Howgate (H) linked with Penicuik: South (H)
Ian A. Cathcart BSc BD — 1994   2007 — 15 Stevenson Road, Penicuik EH26 0LU
[E-mail: reviac@yahoo.co.uk] — 01968 674692
Frederick Harrison
(Ordained Local Minister) — 2013 — 33 Castle Avenue, Gorebridge EH23 4TH
[E-mail: fred@1st-aid.abelgratis.com] — 01875 820908

Humbie See Bolton and Saltoun
Lasswade and Rosewell See Cockpen and Carrington

Loanhead
Graham L. Duffin BSc BD DipEd — 1989   2001 — 120 The Loan, Loanhead EH20 9AJ
[E-mail: gduffin@talktalk.net] — 0131-448 2459

Longniddry See Gladsmuir

Musselburgh: Northesk (H)
Alison P. McDonald MA BD 1991 1998 16 New Street, Musselburgh EH21 6JP 0131-665 2128
[E-mail: alisonpmcdonald@btinternet.com]

Musselburgh: St Andrew's High (H) (0131-665 7239)
Yvonne E.S. Atkins (Mrs) BD 1997 2004 8 Ferguson Drive, Musselburgh EH21 6XA 0131-665 1124
[E-mail: yesatkins@hotmail.co.uk]

Musselburgh: St Clement's and St Ninian's
Guardianship of the Presbytery The Manse, Wallyford Loan Road, Wallyford, 0131-653 6588
Musselburgh EH21 8BU

Musselburgh: St Michael's Inveresk
Andrew B. Dick BD DipMin 1986 1999 8 Hope Place, Musselburgh EH21 7QE 0131-665 0545
[E-mail: dixbit@aol.com]

Newbattle (H) (Website: http://freespace.virgin.net/newbattle.focus)
Sean Swindells BD DipMin MTh 1996 2011 112 Greenbank Crescent, Edinburgh EH10 5SZ 0131-447 4032
[E-mail: minister@newbattleparish.org] 07791 755976 (Mbl)
Michael D. Watson 2013 47 Crichton Terrace, Pathhead EH37 5QZ 01875 320043
(Ordained Local Minister) [E-mail: mikewatson225@btinternet.com]

Newton
Guardianship of the Presbytery The Manse, Newton, Dalkeith EH22 1SR 0131-663 3845
Andrew Don MBA 2006 5 Eskvale Court, Penicuik EH26 8HT 01968 675766
(Ordained Local Minister) [E-mail: a.a.don@btinternet.com]

North Berwick: Abbey See Dirleton

North Berwick: St Andrew Blackadder (H) (E-mail: admin@standrewblackadder.org.uk) (Website: www.standrewblackadder.org.uk)
Neil J. Dougall BD 1991 2003 7 Marine Parade, North Berwick EH39 4LD 01620 892132
[E-mail: neil@neildougall.co.uk]

Ormiston linked with Pencaitland
David J. Torrance BD DipMin 1993 2009 The Manse, Pencaitland, Tranent EH34 5DL 01875 340963
[E-mail: torrance@talktalk.net]

Pencaitland See Ormiston

Penicuik: North (H) (Website: www.pnk.org.uk)
Ruth D. Halley BEd BD PGCM 2012 93 John Street, Penicuik EH26 8AG 01968 675761
[E-mail: ruth.halley@gmail.com] 07530 307413 (Mbl)

Penicuik: St Mungo's (H)
Vacant

Penicuik: South See Howgate

Prestonpans: Prestongrange
Vacant The Manse, East Loan, Prestonpans EH32 9ED 01875 571579

Roslin See Bilston
Spott See Belhaven

Tranent
Vacant 1 Toll House Gardens, Tranent EH33 2QQ 01875 824604

Traprain
David D. Scott BSc BD 1981 2010 The Manse, Preston Road, East Linton EH40 3DS 01620 860227 (Tel/Fax)
[E-mail: revdd.scott@gmail.com]

Tyne Valley Parish (H)
Alan R. Cobain BD 2000 2013 Cranstoun Cottage, Ford, Pathhead EH37 5RE 01875 320314
[E-mail: erinbro44@yahoo.co.uk]
June E. Johnston BSc MEd BD 2013 49 Braeside Road South, Gorebridge EH23 4DL 01875 823086
(Ordained Local Minister) [E-mail: johnston330@btinternet.com] 07754 448889 (Mbl)

Whitekirk and Tyninghame See Athelstaneford
Yester See Bolton and Saltoun

Andrews, J. Edward	1985	2005	(Armadale)	Dunnichen, 1B Cameron Road, Nairn IV12 5NS 01667 459466
MA BD DipCG FSAScot				[E-mail: edward.andrews@btinternet.com] (Mbl) 07808 720708
Bayne, Angus L. LTh BEd MTh	1969	2005	(Edinburgh: Bristo Memorial Craigmillar)	14 Myredale, Bonnyrigg EH19 3NW 0131-663 6871
				[E-mail: angus@mccookies.com]
Berry, Geoff T. BD BSc	2009	2011	Chaplain: Army	38 Muirfield Drive, Gullane EH31 2HJ
				[E-mail: geofftalk@yahoo.co.uk]
Black, A. Graham MA	1964	2003	(Gladsmuir with Longniddry)	26 Hamilton Crescent, Gullane EH31 2HR 01620 843899
				[E-mail: grablack@btinternet.com]
Brown, Ronald H.	1974	1998	(Musselburgh: Northesk)	6 Monktonhall Farm Cottages, Musselburgh EH21 6RZ 0131-653 2531

Name	Years	Charge/Role	Address	Telephone
Brown, William BD	1972 1997	(Edinburgh: Polwarth)	13 Thornyhall, Dalkeith EH22 2ND	0131-654 0929
Buchanan, John DCS		(Deacon)	19 Gillespie Crescent, Edinburgh EH10 4HZ	0131-229 0794
Burt, Thomas W. BD	1982 2013	(Carlops with Kirkurd and Newlands with West Linton: St Andrew's)	7 Arkwright Court, North Berwick EH39 4RT [E-mail: tomburt@westlinton.com]	01620 895494
Cairns, John B. KCVO LTh LLB LLD DD	1974 2009	(Aberlady with Gullane)	Bell House, Roxburghe Park, Dunbar EH42 1LR [E-mail: johncairns@mail.com]	01368 862501
Coltart, Ian O. CA BD	1988 2010	(Arbirlot with Carmyllie)	25 Bothwell Gardens, Dunbar EH42 1PZ	01368 860064
Forbes, Iain M. BSc BD	1964 2005	(Aberdeen: Beechgrove)	69 Dobbie's Road, Bonnyrigg EH19 2AY [E-mail: panama.forbes@tiscali.co.uk]	0131-454 0717
Fraser, John W. MA BD	1974 2011	(Penicuik: North)	66 Camus Avenue, Edinburgh EH10 6QX [E-mail: jjjjj2005@hotmail.co.uk]	0131-623 0647
Glover, Robert L. BMus BD MTh ARCO	1971 2010	(Cockenzie and Port Seton: Chalmers Memorial)	12 Seton Wynd, Port Seton, Prestonpans EH32 0TY [E-mail: rlglover@btinternet.com]	01875 818759
Hutchison, Alan E.W.		(Deacon)	132 Lochbridge Road, North Berwick EH39 4DR	01620 894077
Jones, Anne M. (Mrs) BD	1998 2002	(Hospital Chaplain)	7 North Elphinstone Farm, Tranent EH33 2ND [E-mail: revamjones@aol.com]	01875 614442
Kellock, Chris N. MA BD	1998 2012	Army Chaplain	7 Para RHA, Merville Barracks, Colchester CO2 7UT	01620 810341
Macdonell, Alasdair W. MA BD	1955 1992	(Haddington: St Mary's)	St Andrews Cottage, Duns Road, Gifford, Haddington EH41 4QW [E-mail: alasdair.macdonell@btinternet.com]	
Manson, James A. LTh	1981 2004	(Glencorse with Roslin)	31 Nursery Gardens, Kilmarnock KA1 3JA [E-mail: james.manson@virgin.net]	01563 535430
Pirie, Donald LTh	1975 2006	(Bolton and Saltoun with Humbie with Yester)	46 Caiystane Avenue, Edinburgh EH10 6SH	0131-445 2654
Ritchie, James McL. MA BD MPhil	1950 1985	(Coalsnaughton)	Flat 2/25, Croft-an-Righ, Edinburgh EH8 8EG [E-mail: jasritch_77@msn.com]	0131-557 1084
Ross, Matthew Z. LLB BD MTh FSAScot	1998 2014	General Secretary, ACTS	Braemar Villa, 2 Links Road, Port Seton, Prestonpans EH32 0HA [E-mail: mzross@btinternet.com]	01875 819544 (Mbl) 07711 706950
Simpson, Robert R. BA BD	1994 2014	(Callander)	10 Bellsmains, Gorebridge EH23 4QD [E-mail: robert@pansmanse.co.uk]	01875 820843
Stein, Jock MA BD	1973 2008	(Tulliallan and Kincardine)	35 Dunbar Road, Haddington EH41 3PJ [E-mail: jstein@handselpress.org.uk]	01620 824896
Stein, Margaret E. (Mrs) DA BD DipRE	1984 2008	(Tulliallan and Kincardine)	35 Dunbar Road, Haddington EH41 3PJ [E-mail: margaretestein@hotmail.com]	01620 824896
Steven, Gordon R. BD DCS		(Deacon)	51 Nantwich Drive, Edinburgh EH7 6RB [E-mail: grsteven@btinternet.com]	0131-669 2054 (Mbl) 07904 385256
Swan, Andrew F. BD	1983 2000	(Loanhead)	Park View, 2 Park Place, Lanark ML11 9HH	
Torrance, David W. MA BD	1955 1991	(Earlston)	38 Forth Street, North Berwick EH39 4JQ [E-mail: torrance103@btinternet.com]	(Tel/Fax) 01620 895109
Underwood, Florence A. (Mrs) BD	1992 2006	(Assistant: Gladsmuir with Longniddry)	18 Covenanters Rise, Pitreavie Castle, Dunfermline KY11 8SQ [E-mail: gunderwood@tesco.net]	01383 740745
Underwood, Geoffrey H. BD DipTh FPhS	1964 1992	(Cockenzie and Port Seton: Chalmers Memorial)	18 Covenanters Rise, Pitreavie Castle, Dunfermline KY11 8SQ [E-mail: gunderwood@tesco.net]	01383 740745

(4) MELROSE AND PEEBLES

Meets at Innerleithen on the first Tuesday of February, March, May, October, November and December, and on the fourth Tuesday of June, and in places to be appointed on the first Tuesday of September.

Clerk:	REV. VICTORIA LINFORD LLB BD		The Manse, 209 Galashiels Road, Stow, Galashiels TD1 2RE [E-mail: melrosepeebles@cofscotland.org.uk]	01578 730237

Ashkirk linked with Selkirk (H)

Margaret D.J. Steele (Miss) BSc BD	2000	2011	1 Loanside, Selkirk TD7 4DJ [E-mail: mdjsteele@gmail.com]	01750 23308

Bowden (H) and Melrose (H)

Alistair G. Bennett BSc BD	1978	1984	Tweedmount Road, Melrose TD6 9ST [E-mail: agbennettmelrose@aol.com]	01896 822217

Broughton, Glenholm and Kilbucho (H) linked with Skirling linked with Stobo and Drumelzier linked with Tweedsmuir (H)

Robert B. Milne BTh	1999	2009	The Manse, Broughton, Biggar ML12 6HQ [E-mail: rbmilne@aol.com]	01899 830331

Caddonfoot (H) linked with Galashiels: Trinity (H)

Elspeth Harley BA MTh	1991	2014	8 Mossilee Road, Galashiels TD1 1NF [E-mail: eharley@hotmail.co.uk]	01896 752420

Carlops linked with Kirkurd and Newlands (H) linked with West Linton: St Andrew's (H)

Linda J. Dunbar BSc BA BD PhD FRHS	2000	2013	The Manse, Main Street, West Linton EH46 7EE [E-mail: revljd@gmail.com]	01968 660221 / 07939 496360 (Mbl)

Channelkirk and Lauder

Vacant			The Manse, Brownsmuir Park, Lauder TD2 6QD	01578 722616

Earlston

Julie M. Woods (Ms) BTh	2005	2011	The Manse, High Street, Earlston TD4 6DE [E-mail: missjulie@btinternet.com]	01896 849236

Eddleston (H) linked with Peebles: Old (H)

Malcolm M. Macdougall BD MTh DipCE	1981	2001	7 Clement Gunn Square, Peebles EH45 8LW [E-mail: calum.macdougall@btopenworld.com]	01721 720568

Ettrick and Yarrow
Samuel Siroky BA MTh   2003   Yarrow Manse, Yarrow, Selkirk TD7 5LA   01750 82336
[E-mail: sesiroky@tiscali.co.uk]

Galashiels: Old and St Paul's (H) linked with Galashiels: St John's (H)
Vacant   Woodlea, Abbotsview Drive, Galashiels TD1 3SL   01896 752320

Galashiels: St John's See Galashiels: Old and St Paul's
Galashiels: Trinity See Caddonfoot

Innerleithen (H), Traquair and Walkerburn
Janice M. Faris (Mrs) BSc BD   1991   2001   The Manse, 1 Millwell Park, Innerleithen, Peebles EH44 6JF   01896 830309
[E-mail: revjfaris@hotmail.com]

Kirkurd and Newlands See Carlops

Lyne and Manor linked with Peebles: St Andrew's Leckie (H) (01721 723121)
Malcolm S. Jefferson   2012   Mansefield, Innerleithen Road, Peebles EH45 8BE   01721 721148
[E-mail: jeffersons02@btinternet.com]

Maxton and Mertoun linked with Newtown linked with St Boswells
Sheila W. Moir (Ms) MTheol   2008   7 Strae Brigs, St Boswells, Melrose TD6 0DH   01835 822255
[E-mail: sheila377@btinternet.com]

Newtown See Maxton and Mertoun
Peebles: Old See Eddleston
Peebles: St Andrew's Leckie See Lyne and Manor
St Boswells See Maxton and Mertoun
Selkirk See Ashkirk
Skirling See Broughton, Glenholm and Kilbucho
Stobo and Drumelzier See Broughton, Glenholm and Kilbucho

Stow: St Mary of Wedale and Heriot
Victoria J. Linford (Mrs) LLB BD   2010   The Manse, 209 Galashiels Road, Stow, Galashiels TD1 2RE   01578 730237
[E-mail: victorialinford@yahoo.co.uk]

Tweedsmuir See Broughton, Glenholm and Kilbucho
West Linton: St Andrew's See Carlops

Name			Charge / Position	Address	Tel.
Arnott, A. David K. MA BD	1971	2010	(St Andrews: Hope Park with Strathkinness)	53 Whitehaugh Park, Peebles EH45 9DB [E-mail: adka53@btinternet.com]	01721 725979 (Mbl) 07759 709205
Bowie, Adam McC.	1976	1996	(Cavers and Kirkton with Hobkirk and Southdean)	Glenbield, Redpath, Earlston TD4 6AD	01896 848173
Cashman, P. Hamilton BSc	1985	1998	(Dirleton with North Berwick: Abbey)	38 Abbotsford Road, Galashiels TD1 3HR [E-mail: mcashman@tiscali.co.uk]	01896 752711
Cutler, James S.H. BD CEng MIStructE	1986	2011	(Black Mount with Culter with Libberton and Quothquan)	12 Kittlegairy Place, Peebles EH45 9LW [E-mail: revjc@btinternet.com]	01721 723950
Devenny, Robert P.	2002		Hospital Chaplain	Blakeburn Cottage, Wester Housebyres, Melrose TD6 9BW	01896 822350
Dick, J. Ronald BD	1973	1996	(Hospital Chaplain)	5 Georgefield Farm Cottages, Earlston TD4 6BH	01896 848956
Dobie, Rachel J.W. (Mrs) LTh	1991	2008	(Broughton, Glenholm and Kilbucho with Skirling with Stobo and Drumelzier with Tweedsmuir)	20 Moss Side Crescent, Biggar ML12 6GE [E-mail: revracheldobie@talktalk.net]	01899 229244
Dodd, Marion E. (Miss) MA BD LRAM	1988	2010	(Kelso: Old and Sprouston)	Esdaile, Tweedmount Road, Melrose TD6 9ST [E-mail: mariondodd@btinternet.com]	01896 822446
Duncan, Charles A. MA	1956	1992	(Heriot with Stow: St Mary of Wedale)	10 Elm Grove, Galashiels TD1 3JA	01896 753261
Hardie, H. Warner BD	1979	2005	(Blackridge with Harthill: St Andrew's)	Keswick Cottage, Kingsmuir Drive, Peebles EH45 9AA [E-mail: hardies@bigfoot.com]	01721 724003
Hogg, Thomas M. BD	1986	2007	(Tranent)	22 Douglas Place, Galashiels TD1 3BT	01896 759381
Howitt, Jane M. MA BD	1996	2014	(Galashiels: St John's)	St John's Manse, Hawthorn Road, Galashiels TD1 2JZ [E-mail: jane_m_howitt@yahoo.co.uk]	01896 752573
Hughes, Barry MA	2011		Ordained Local Minister	Dunslair, Cardrona Way, Cardrona, Peebles EH45 9LD [E-mail: gill_baz@hotmail.com]	01896 831197
Kellet, John M. MA	1962	1995	(Leith: South)	4 High Cottages, Walkerburn EH43 6AZ	01896 870351
Kennon, Stanley BA BD RN	1992	2000	Chaplain: Royal Navy	Britannia Royal Naval College, Dartmouth, Devon TQ6 0HJ [E-mail: brnc-csf@fleetfost.mod.uk]	
Laing, William F. DSC VRD MA	1952	1986	(Selkirk: St Mary's West)	10 The Glebe, Selkirk TD7 5AB	01750 21210
Lawrie, Bruce B. BD	1974	2012	(Duffus, Spynie and Hopeman)	5 Thorncroft, Scotts Place, Selkirk TD7 4LN [E-mail: thorncroft54@gmail.com]	01750 725427
MacFarlane, David C. MA	1957	1997	(Eddleston with Peebles: Old)	Lorimer House Nursing Home, 491 Lanark Road, Edinburgh EH14 5DQ	
Milloy, A. Miller DPE LTh DipTrMan	1979	2012	(General Secretary: United Bible Societies)	18 Kittlegairy Crescent, Peebles EH45 9NJ [E-mail: ammilloy@aol.com]	01721 723380
Moore, W. Haisley MA	1966	1996	(Secretary: The Boys' Brigade)	26 Tweedbank Avenue, Tweedbank, Galashiels TD1 3SP	01896 668577
Munson, Winnie (Ms) BD	1996	2006	(Delting with Northmavine)	6 St Cuthbert's Drive, St Boswells, Melrose TD6 0DF	01835 823375
Norman, Nancy M. (Miss) BA MDiv MTh	1988	2012	(Lyne and Manor)	25 March Street, Peebles EH45 8EP [E-mail: nancy.norman1@googlemail.com]	01721 721699
Rae, Andrew W.	1951	1987	(Annan: St Andrew's Greenknowe Erskine)	Roseneuk, Tweedside Road, Newtown St Boswells TD6 0PQ	01835 823783
Rennie, John D. MA	1962	1996	(Broughton, Glenholm and Kilbucho with Skirling with Stobo and Drumelzier with Tweedsmuir)	29/1 Rosetta Road, Peebles EH45 8HJ [E-mail: tworennies@talktalk.net]	01721 720963

Riddell, John A. MA BD	1967 2006	(Jedburgh: Trinity)	Orchid Cottage, Gingham Row, Earlston TD4 6ET	01896 848784
Steele, Leslie M. MA BD	1973 2013	(Galashiels: Old and St Paul's)	25 Bardfield Road, Colchester CO2 8LW	01206 621939
			[E-mail: lms@hotmail.co.uk]	(Mbl) 07786 797974
Taverner, Glyn R. MA BD	1957 1995	(Maxton and Mertoun with St Boswells)	Woodcot Cottage, Waverley Road, Innerleithen EH44 6QW	01896 830156
Wallace, James H. MA BD	1973 2011	(Peebles: St Andrew's Leckie)	52 Waverley Mills, Innerleithen EH44 6RH	01896 831637
			[E-mail: jimwallace121@btinternet.com]	

(5) DUNS

Meets at Duns, in the Parish Church hall, normally on the first Tuesday of February, March, April, May, October, November and December, on the last Tuesday in June, and in places to be appointed on the first Tuesday of September.

Clerk: MRS HELEN LONGMUIR   7 Station Cottages, Chirnside, Duns **TD11 3LQ**   **01890 819849**
[E-mail: duns@cofscotland.org.uk]

Ayton (H) and Burnmouth linked with Foulden and Mordington linked with Grantshouse and Houndwood and Reston
Norman R. Whyte BD MTh DipMin   1982   2006   The Manse, Beanburn, Ayton, Eyemouth TD14 5QY   01890 781333
[E-mail: burraman@msn.com]

Berwick-upon-Tweed: St Andrew's Wallace Green (H) and Lowick
Adam J.J. Hood MA BD DPhil   1989   2012   3 Meadow Grange, Berwick-upon-Tweed TD15 1NW   01289 332787
[E-mail: minister@sawg.org.uk]

Bonkyl and Edrom linked with Duns (H)
Stephen A. Blakey BSc BD   1977   2012   The Manse, Castle Street, Duns TD11 3DG   01361 883755
[E-mail: stephenablakey@icloud.com]

Chirnside linked with Hutton and Fishwick and Paxton
Vacant   Parish Church Manse, The Glebe, Chirnside, Duns TD11 3XL   01890 819109

Coldingham and St Abbs linked with Eyemouth
Andrew Haddow BEng BD   2012   The Manse, Victoria Road, Eyemouth TD14 5JD   01890 750327
[E-mail: andy@blakkie.co.uk]

Coldstream (H) linked with Eccles
David J. Taverner MCIBS ACIS BD   1996   2011   36 Bennecourt Drive, Coldstream TD12 4BY   01890 883887
[E-mail: rahereuk@hotmail.com]

Duns See Bonkyl and Edrom
Eccles See Coldstream
Eyemouth See Coldingham and St Abbs

Fogo and Swinton linked with Ladykirk and Whitsome linked with Leitholm (H)
Alan C.D. Cartwright BSc BD   1976   The Manse, Swinton, Duns TD11 3JJ   01890 860228
[E-mail: merse.minister@btinternet.com]

Foulden and Mordington See Ayton and Burnmouth

Gordon: St Michael's linked with Greenlaw (H) linked with Legerwood linked with Westruther
Thomas S. Nicholson BD DPS   1982 1995   The Manse, Todholes, Greenlaw, Duns TD10 6XD   01361 810316
[E-mail: nst54@hotmail.com]

Grantshouse and Houndwood and Reston See Ayton and Burnmouth
Greenlaw See Gordon: St Michael's
Hutton and Fishwick and Paxton See Chirnside
Ladykirk and Whitsome See Fogo and Swinton

Langton and Lammermuir Kirk
Ann Inglis (Mrs) LLB BD   1986   2003   The Manse, Cranshaws, Duns TD11 3SJ   01361 890289
[E-mail: revainglis@btinternet.com]

Legerwood See Gordon: St Michael's
Leitholm See Fogo and Swinton
Westruther See Gordon: St Michael's

Gaddes, Donald R.	1961	1994	(Kelso: North and Ednam)	2 Teindhill Green, Duns TD11 3DX [E-mail: drgaddes@btinternet.com]	01361 883172
Gale, Ronald A.A. LTh	1982	1995	(Dunoon: Old and St Cuthbert's)	55 Lennel Mount, Coldstream TD12 4NS [E-mail: rgale89@aol.com]	01890 883699
Graham, Jennifer D. (Mrs) BA MDiv PhD	2000	2011	(Eday with Stronsay: Moncur Memorial)	Lodge, Stronsay, Orkney KW17 2AN [E-mail: jdgraham67@gmail.com]	01857 616487
Hay, Bruce J.L.	1957	1997	(Makerstoun and Smailholm with Stichill, Hume and Nenthorn)	Tweedmouth House, 4 Main Street, Tweedmouth, Berwick-upon-Tweed TD15 2HD	

Name	Years	(Previous charge)	Address	Tel
Higham, Robert D. BD	1985 2002	(Tiree)	36 Low Greens, Berwick-upon-Tweed TD15 1LZ	01289 302392
Hope, Geraldine H. (Mrs) MA BD	1986 2007	(Foulden and Mordington with Hutton and Fishwick and Paxton)	4 Well Court, Chirnside, Duns TD11 3UD [E-mail: geraldine.hope@virgin.net]	01890 818134
Kerr, Andrew MA BLitt	1948 1991	(Kilbarchan: West)	4 Lairds Gate, Port Glasgow Road, Kilmacolm PA13 4EX	01505 874852
Landale, William S.	2005	Auxiliary Minister	Green Hope Guest House, Ellemford, Duns TD11 3SG [E-mail: bill@greenhope.co.uk]	01361 890242
Lindsay, Daniel G. BD	1978 2011	(Coldingham and St Abbs with Eyemouth)	18 Hallidown Crescent, Eyemouth TD14 5TB	01890 751389
Murray, Duncan E. BA BD	1970 2012	(Bonkyl and Preston with Chirnside with Edrom Allanton)	Beech Cottage, York Road, Knaresborough HG5 0TT [E-mail: duncanemurray@tiscali.co.uk]	01423 313287
Neill, Bruce F. MA BD	1966 2007	(Maxton and Mertoun with Newtown with St Boswells)	18 Brierydean, St Abbs, Eyemouth TD14 5PQ [E-mail: bneill@phonecoop.coop]	01890 771569
Paterson, William BD	1977 2001	(Bonkyl and Preston with Chirnside with Edrom Allanton)	Benachie, Gavinton, Duns TD11 3QT [E-mail: billdm.paterson@btinternet.com]	01361 882727
Sherrard, H. Dane BD DMin	1971 2013	(Arrochar with Luss)	The Granary, Mount Pleasant, Duns TD11 4HU [E-mail: dane@mountpleasantgranary.net]	01361 882254 (Mbl) 07801 939138
Walker, Kenneth D.F. MA BD PhD	1976 2008	(Athelstaneford with Whitekirk and Tyninghame)	Allanbank Kothi, Allanton, Duns TD11 3PY [E-mail: walkerkenneth49@gmail.com]	01890 817102

(6) JEDBURGH

Meets at various venues on the first Wednesday of February, March, May, September, October, November and December and on the last Wednesday of June.

Clerk   REV. FRANK CAMPBELL   22 The Glebe, Ancrum, Jedburgh TD8 6UX   **01835 830318**
[E-mail: jedburgh@cofscotland.org.uk]

Ale and Teviot United (H) (Website: www.aleandteviot.org.uk)
Frank Campbell   1989   1991   22 The Glebe, Ancrum, Jedburgh TD8 6UX   01835 830318
[E-mail: jedburgh@cofscotland.org.uk]

Cavers and Kirkton linked with Hawick: Trinity (H)
Michael D. Scouler MBE BSc BD   1988   2009   Kerrscroft, Howdenburn, Hawick TD9 8PH   01450 378248
[E-mail: michaelscouler@hotmail.co.uk]

Cheviot Churches (H) (Website: www.cheviotchurches.org)
Robin D. McHaffie BD   1979   1991   The Manse, Main Street, Kirk Yetholm, Kelso TD5 8PF   01573 420308
[E-mail: robinmchaffie@btinternet.com]
(New name for the charge formerly known as Linton, Morebattle, Hownam and Yetholm)

Hawick: Burnfoot (Website: www.burnfootparishchurch.org.uk)
Charles J. Finnie LTh DPS   1991   1997
29 Wilton Hill, Hawick TD9 8BA   01450 373181
[E-mail: charles.finnie@gmail.com]

Hawick: St Mary's and Old (H) linked with Hawick: Teviot (H) and Roberton
Neil R. Combe BSc MSc BD   1984
The Manse, Buccleuch Road, Hawick TD9 0EL   01450 372150
[E-mail: neil.combe@btinternet.com]

Hawick: Teviot and Roberton See Hawick: St Mary's and Old
Hawick: Trinity See Cavers and Kirkton

Hawick: Wilton linked with Teviothead
Lisa-Jane Rankin (Miss) BD CPS   2003
4 Wilton Hill Terrace, Hawick TD9 8BE   01450 370744 (Tel/Fax)
[E-mail: revlj@talktalk.net]

Hobkirk and Southdean (Website: www.hobkirkruberslaw.org) linked with Ruberslaw (Website: www.hobkirkruberslaw.org)
Douglas A.O. Nicol MA BD   1974   2009
The Manse, Denholm, Hawick TD9 8NB   01450 870268
[E-mail: daon@lineone.net]

Jedburgh: Old and Trinity (Website: www.jedburgh-parish.org.uk)
Graham D. Astles BD MSc   2007
The Manse, Honeyfield Drive, Jedburgh TD8 6LQ   01835 863417
[E-mail: minister@jedburgh-parish.org.uk]   07906 290568 (Mbl)

Kelso Country Churches linked with Kelso: Old (H) and Sprouston (Website: www.kelsolinkedchurchescofs.org)
Jenny Earl MA BD   2007
The Manse, 1 The Meadow, Stichill, Kelso TD5 7TG   01573 470607
[E-mail: jennyearl@btinternet.com]
Anna S. Rodwell (Mrs) BD DipMin (Assoc)   1998   2014
The Old Mill House, Hownam Howgate, Kelso TD5 8AJ   01573 440761
[E-mail: anna.rodwell@gmail.com]

Kelso: North (H) and Ednam (H) (01573 224154) (E-mail: office@kelsonorthandednam.org.uk) (Website: www.kelsonorthandednam.org.uk)
Tom McDonald BD   1994
20 Forestfield, Kelso TD5 7BX   01573 224677
[E-mail: revtom@20thepearlygates.co.uk]

Kelso: Old and Sprouston See Kelso Country Churches

Oxnam (Website: www.oxnamkirk.co.uk)
Guardianship of the Presbytery

Ruberslaw See Hobkirk and Southdean
Teviothead See Hawick: Wilton

Auld, A. Graeme (Prof.) MA BD PhD DLitt FSAScot FRSE	1973	2008	(University of Edinburgh)	Nether Swanshiel, Hobkirk, Bonchester Bridge, Hawick TD9 8IU [E-mail: a.g.auld@ed.ac.uk]	01450 860636
McNicol, Bruce	1967	2006	(Jedburgh: Old and Edgerston)	42 Dounehill, Jedburgh TD8 6LJ [E-mail: mcnicol942@gmail.com]	01835 862991
Shields, John M. MBE LTh	1972	2007	(Channelkirk and Lauder)	12 Eden Park, Ednam, Kelso TD5 7RG [E-mail: john.shields118@btinternet.com]	01573 229015

HAWICK ADDRESSES

Burnfoot	Fraser Avenue	St Mary's and Old	Wilton	Princes Street
		Teviot	off Buccleuch Road	
		Trinity	Central Square	
			Kirk Wynd	

(7) ANNANDALE AND ESKDALE

Meets on the first Tuesday of February, May, September and December, and the third Tuesday of March, June and October. The September meeting is held in the Moderator's charge. The other meetings are held in Dryfesdale Church Hall, Lockerbie, except for the June meeting, which is separately announced.

Clerk: REV. C. BRYAN HASTON LTh   The Manse, Gretna Green, Gretna DG16 5DU   **01461   338313**
                                                 [E-mail: annandaleeskdale@cofscotland.org.uk]
                                                 [E-mail: cbhaston@cofs.demon.co.uk]

Annan: Old (H) linked with Dornock
Vacant   12 Plumdon Park Avenue, Annan DG12 6EY   01461   201405

Annan: St Andrew's (H) linked with Brydekirk
John G. Pickles BD MTh MSc   2011   1 Annerley Road, Annan DG12 6HE   01461   202626
                                                 [E-mail: jgpickles@hotmail.com]

Applegarth, Sibbaldbie (H) and Johnstone linked with Lochmaben (H)
Paul R. Read BSc MA(Th)   2000   2013   The Manse, Barrashead, Lochmaben, Lockerbie DG11 1QF   01387 810640
[E-mail: p.read@btinternet.com]

Brydekirk See Annan: St Andrew's

Canonbie United (H) linked with Liddesdale (H)
William Jackson BD CertMin   1994   2014   23 Langholm Street, Newcastleton TD9 0QX   01387 375242
[E-mail: wiljcksn4@aol.com]

Dalton linked with Hightae linked with St Mungo
Morag A. Dawson BD MTh   1999   2011   The Manse, Hightae, Lockerbie DG11 1JL   01387 811499
[E-mail: moragdawson@yahoo.co.uk]

Dornock See Annan: Old

Gretna: Old (H), Gretna: St Andrew's (H), Half Morton and Kirkpatrick Fleming
C. Bryan Haston LTh   1975   The Manse, Gretna Green, Gretna DG16 5DU   01461 338313
[E-mail: cbhaston@cofs.demon.co.uk]
[E-mail: cbhaston@gretnagreen.eu]
Martyn S. Sanders BA CertEd MA   2013   26 Wood Avenue, Annan DG12 6DA   07830 697976 (Mbl)
(Ordained Local Minister)   [E-mail: martyn.sanders@furtherministriesteam.com]

Hightae See Dalton

Hoddom, Kirtle-Eaglesfield and Middlebie
Frances M. Henderson BA BD PhD   2006   2013   The Manse, Main Road, Ecclefechan, Lockerbie DG11 3BU   01576 300108
[E-mail: f-henderson@hotmail.co.uk]

Kirkpatrick Juxta linked with Moffat: St Andrew's (H) linked with Wamphray
Adam J. Dillon BD ThM   2003   2008   The Manse, 1 Meadowbank, Moffat DG10 9LR   01683 220128
[E-mail: adamdillon@btinternet.com]

Langholm Eskdalemuir Ewes and Westerkirk
I. Scott McCarthy BD   2010   The Manse, Langholm DG13 0BL   01387 380252
[E-mail: iscottmccarthy@gmail.com]

Liddesdale See Canonbie United
Lochmaben See Applegarth, Sibbaldbie and Johnstone

Lockerbie: Dryfesdale, Hutton and Corrie
Alexander C. Stoddart BD   2001   2008   The Manse, 5 Carlisle Road, Lockerbie DG11 2DW   01576 202361
[E-mail: sandystoddart@supanet.com]

Moffat: St Andrew's See Kirkpatrick Juxta
St Mungo See Dalton

The Border Kirk (Church office: Chapel Street, Carlisle CA1 1JA; Tel: 01228 591757)
David G. Pitkeathly LLB BD   1996   2007   95 Pinecroft, Carlisle CA3 0DB   01228 593243
[E-mail: david.pitkeathly@btinternet.com]

Tundergarth
Guardianship of the Presbytery

Wamphray See Kirkpatrick Juxta

Name			Role	Address	Tel
Annand, James M. MA BD	1955	1995	(Lockerbie: Dryfesdale)	Dere Cottage, 48 Main Street, Newstead, Melrose TD6 9DX	0131-225 3393
Beveridge, S. Edwin P. BA	1959	2004	(Brydekirk with Hoddom)	19 Rothesay Terrace, Edinburgh EH3 7RY	01461 206512
Byers, Mairi C. (Mrs) BTh CPS	1992	1998	(Jura)	Meadowbank, Plumdon Road, Annan DG12 6SJ [E-mail: aljbyers@hotmail.com]	
Gibb, J. Daniel M. BA LTh	1994	2006	(Aberfoyle with Port of Menteith)	21 Victoria Gardens, Eastriggs, Annan DG12 6TW [E-mail: dannygibb@hotmail.co.uk]	01461 40560
Harvey, P. Ruth (Ms) MA BD	2009	2012	Place for Hope	Croslands, Beacon Street, Penrith CA11 7TZ [E-mail: ruth.harvey@placeforhope.org.uk]	01768 840749 (Mbl) 07403 638339
MacMillan, William M. LTh	1980	1998	(Kilmory with Lamlash)	Balskia, 61 Queen Street, Lochmaben, Lockerbie DG11 1PP	01387 811528
Macpherson, Duncan J. BSc BD	1993	2002	Chaplain: Army	HQ Hereford Garrison, Hereford HR4 7DD	
Ross, Alan C. CA BD	1988	2007	(Eskdalemuir with Hutton and Corrie with Tundergarth)	Yarra, Ettrickbridge, Selkirk TD7 5JN [E-mail: alkaross@aol.com]	01750 52324
Sanders, Martyn S. BA CertEd MA	2013		Parish Assistant: Annan: Old with Dornock; Annan: St Andrew's with Brydekirk	26 Wood Avenue, Annan DG12 6DA [E-mail: martyn.sanders@furtherministriesteam.com]	(Mbl) 07830 697976
Seaman, Ronald S. MA	1967	2007	(Dornock)	1 Springfield Farm Court, Springfield, Gretna DG16 5EH	01461 337228
Steenbergen, Pauline (Ms) MA BD	1996	2012	Hospice Chaplain	Eden Valley Hospice, Durdar Road, Carlisle CA2 4SD [E-mail: pauline.steenbergen@edenvalleyhospice.co.uk]	01228 817609
Swinburne, Norman BA	1960	1993	(Sauchie)	Damerosehay, Birch Hill Lane, Kirkbride, Wigton CA7 5HZ	01697 351497
Vivers, Katherine A.	2004		Auxiliary Minister	Blacket House, Eaglesfield, Lockerbie DG11 3AA [E-mail: katevivers@yahoo.co.uk]	01461 500412 (Mbl) 07748 233011

Williams, Trevor C. LTh   1990 2007   (Hoddom with Kirtle-Eaglesfield with Middlebie with Waterbeck)   c/o Presbytery Clerk [E-mail: revtrev@btinternet.com]

(8) DUMFRIES AND KIRKCUDBRIGHT

Meets at Dumfries on the last Wednesday of February, June, September and November.

Clerk: REV. WILLIAM T. HOGG MA BD   St Bride's Manse, Glasgow Road, Sanquhar DG4 6BZ [E-mail: dumfrieskirkcudbright@cofscotland.org.uk]   **01659 50247**

Balmaclellan and Kells (H) linked with Carsphairn (H) linked with Dalry (H)
David S. Bartholomew BSc MSc PhD BD   1994   The Manse, Dalry, Castle Douglas DG7 3PJ [E-mail: dhbart@care4free.net]   01644 430380

Balmaghie linked with Tarff and Twynholm (H)
Vacant   The Manse, Manse Road, Twynholm, Kirkcudbright DG6 4NY   01557 860381

Borgue linked with Gatehouse of Fleet
Valerie J. Ott (Mrs) BA BD   2002   The Manse, Planetree Park, Gatehouse of Fleet, Castle Douglas DG7 2EQ [E-mail: valanddav98@btinternet.com]   01557 814233

Caerlaverock linked with Dumfries: St Mary's-Greyfriars' (H)
Vacant   4 Georgetown Crescent, Dumfries DG1 4EQ   01387 253877

Carsphairn See Balmaclellan and Kells

Castle Douglas (H) linked with The Bengairn Parishes
Stephen Ashley-Emery BD DPS   2006   2014   1 Castle View, Castle Douglas DG7 1BG [E-mail: revstephenae@gmail.com]   01556 502171

Closeburn
Guardianship of the Presbytery

Colvend, Southwick and Kirkbean James F. Gatherer BD	1984	2003	The Manse, Colvend, Dalbeattie DG5 4QN [E-mail: james@gatherer.net]	01556 630255
Corsock and Kirkpatrick Durham linked with Crossmichael and Parton Sally Russell BTh MTh		2006	Knockdrocket, Clarebrand, Castle Douglas DG7 3AH [E-mail: rev.sal@btinternet.com]	01556 503645
Crossmichael and Parton See Corsock and Kirkpatrick Durham				
Cummertrees, Mouswald and Ruthwell (H) Vacant			The Manse, Ruthwell, Dumfries DG1 4NP	01387 870217
Dalbeattie (H) and Kirkgunzeon linked with Urr (H) Vacant			36 Mill Street, Dalbeattie DG5 4HE	01556 610029
Dalry See Balmaclellan and Kells				
Dumfries: Maxwelltown West (H) Vacant			Maxwelltown West Manse, 11 Laurieknowe, Dumfries DG2 7AH	01387 252929
Dumfries: Northwest Neil G. Campbell BA BD	1988	2006	c/o Church Office, Dumfries Northwest Church, Lochside Road, Dumfries DG2 0DZ [E-mail: neilcampbell@dumfriesnorthwest.org.uk]	01387 249964
Dumfries: St George's (H) Donald Campbell BD	1997		9 Nunholm Park, Dumfries DG1 1JP [E-mail: minister@saint-georges.org.uk]	01387 252965
Dumfries: St Mary's-Greyfriars' See Caerlaverock				
Dumfries: St Michael's and South Maurice S. Bond MTh BA DipEd PhD	1981	1999	39 Cardoness Street, Dumfries DG1 3AL [E-mail: mauricebond399@btinternet.com]	01387 253849

Dumfries: Troqueer (H)
William W. Kelly BSc BD   1994   Troqueer Manse, Troqueer Road, Dumfries DG2 7DF   01387 253043
[E-mail: wwkelly@yahoo.com]

Dunscore linked with Glencairn and Moniaive
Joachim J.H. du Plessis BA BD MTh   1975   2013   Wallaceton, Auldgirth, Dumfries DG2 0TJ   01387 820245
[E-mail: jjhduplessis@gmail.com]

Durisdeer linked with Penpont, Keir and Tynron linked with Thornhill (H)
J. Stuart Mill MA MBA BD   1976   2013   The Manse, Manse Park, Thornhill DG3 5ER   01848 331191
[E-mail: stuartmill1@hotmail.co.uk]

Gatehouse of Fleet See Borgue
Glencairn and Moniaive See Dunscore

Irongray, Lochrutton and Terregles
Vacant   Shawhead Road, Dumfries DG2 9SJ   01387 730287

Kirkconnel (H)
Alistair J. MacKichan MA BD   1984   2009   The Manse, 31 Kingsway, Kirkconnel, Sanquhar DG4 6PN   01659 67241
[E-mail: alistairjmck@btinternet.com]

Kirkcudbright (H)
Douglas R. Irving LLB BD WS   1984   1998   6 Bourtree Avenue, Kirkcudbright DG6 4AU   01557 330489
[E-mail: douglasirving05@tiscali.co.uk]

Kirkmahoe
David M. Almond BD   1996   2008   The Manse, Kirkmahoe, Dumfries DG1 1ST   01387 710572
[E-mail: almond.david138@googlemail.com]

Kirkmichael, Tinwald and Torthorwald
Willem J. Bezuidenhout BA BD MHEd MEd   1977   2010   Manse of Tinwald, Tinwald, Dumfries DG1 3PL   01387 710246
[E-mail: willembezuidenhout@btinternet.com]

Lochend and New Abbey
Maureen M. Duncan (Mrs) BD   1996   2014   New Abbey Manse, 32 Main Street, New Abbey, Dumfries DG2 8BY   01387 850490
[E-mail: revmo@talktalk.net]

Penpont, Keir and Tynron See Durisdeer

Sanquhar: St Bride's (H)
William T. Hogg MA BD 1979 2000 St Bride's Manse, Glasgow Road, Sanquhar DG6 6BZ 01659 50247
[E-mail: wthogg@yahoo.com]

Tarff and Twynholm See Balmaghie
The Bengairn Parishes See Castle Douglas
(New charge formed by the union of Auchencairn and Rerrick and Buittle and Kelton)

Thornhill See Durisdeer
Urr See Dalbeattie and Kirkgunzeon

Name	Years	Parish	Address	Telephone
Bennett, David K.P. BA	1974 2000	(Kirkpatrick Irongray with Lochrutin with Terregles)	53 Anne Arundel Court, Heathhall, Dumfries DG1 3SL	01387 257755
Dee, Oonagh (Mrs)	2014	Ordained Local Minister	'Kendoon', Merse Way, Kippford, Dalbeattie DG5 4LL [E-mail: oonaghdee@gmail.com]	01556 620001
Greer, A. David C. LLB DMin DipAdultEd	1956 1996	(Barra)	17 Duthac Wynd, Tain IV19 1LP [E-mail: greer2@talktalk.net]	01862 892065
Hamill, Robert BA	1956 1989	(Castle Douglas: St Ringan's)	11 St Andrew Drive, Castle Douglas DG7 1EW	01556 502962
Hammond, Richard J. BA BD	1993 2007	(Kirkmahoe)	3 Marchfield Mount, Marchfield, Dumfries DG1 1SE [E-mail: libby.hammond@virgin.net]	(Mbl) 07764 465783
Holland, William MA	1967 2009	(Lochend and New Abbey)	Ardshean, 55 Georgetown Road, Dumfries DG1 4DD [E-mail: billholland55@btinternet.com]	01387 256131
Hutcheson, Norman M. MA BD	1973 2012	(Dalbeattie with Urr)	66 Maxwell Park, Dalbeattie DG5 4LS [E-mail: norman.hutcheson@gmail.com]	(Mbl) 07766 531732
Kirk, W. Logan MA BD MTh	1988 2000	(Dalton with Hightae with St Mungo)	2 Raecroft Avenue, Collin, Dumfries DG1 4LP	01387 750489
Leishman, James S. LTh BD MA(Div)	1969 1999	(Kirkmichael with Tinwald with Torthorwald)	24 Hunter Avenue, Heathhall, Dumfries DG1 3UX	01387 249241
Mack, Elizabeth A. (Miss) DipEd	1994 2011	(Auxiliary Minister)	24 Roberts Crescent, Dumfries DG2 7RS [E-mail: mackliz@btinternet.com]	01387 264847
McKay, David M. MA BD	1979 2007	(Kirkpatrick Juxta with Moffat: St Andrew's with Wamphray)	20 Auld Brig View, Auldgirth, Dumfries DG2 0XE [E-mail: davidmckay20@tiscali.co.uk]	01387 740013
McKenzie, William M. DA	1958 1993	(Dumfries: Troqueer)	41 Kingholm Road, Dumfries DG1 4SR [E-mail: mckenzie.dumfries@btinternet.com]	01387 253688
McLauchlan, Mary C. (Mrs) LTh	1997 2013	(Mochrum)	3 Ayr Street, Moniaive, Thornhill DG3 4HP [E-mail: mary@revmother.co.uk]	01848 200786
Owen, John J.C. LTh	1967 2001	(Applegarth and Sibbaldbie with Lochmaben)	5 Galla Avenue, Dalbeattie DG5 4JZ [E-mail: jj.owen@onetel.net]	01556 612125
Robertson, Ian W. MA BD	1956 1995	(Colvend, Southwick and Kirkbean)	10 Marjoriebanks, Lochmaben, Lockerbie DG11 1QH	01387 810541

Strachan, Alexander E. MA BD	1974 2012	(Healthcare Chaplain)	2 Leafield Road, Dumfries DG1 2DS	01387 279460

Strachan, Alexander E. MA BD	1974 2012	(Healthcare Chaplain)	2 Leafield Road, Dumfries DG1 2DS [E-mail: aestrachan@aol.com]	01387 279460
Sutherland, Colin A. LTh	1995 2007	(Blantyre: Livingstone Memorial)	71 Caulstran Road, Dumfries DG2 9FJ [E-mail: colin.csutherland@btinternet.com]	01387 279954
Wallace, Mhairi (Mrs)	2013	Ordained Local Minister		(Mbl) 07880 546743
Wilkie, James R. MA MTh	1957 1993	(Penpont, Keir and Tynron)	[E-mail: tobythewestie@msn.com] 31 West Morton Street, Thornhill DG3 5NF	01848 331028
Williamson, James BA BD	1986 2009	(Cummertrees with Mouswald with Ruthwell)	12 Mulberry Drive, Dunfermline KY11 8BZ [E-mail: jimwill@rcmkirk.fsnet.co.uk]	01383 734872
Wotherspoon, Robert C. LTh	1976 1998	(Corsock and Kirkpatrick Durham with Crossmichael and Parton)	7 Hillowton Drive, Castle Douglas DG7 1LL [E-mail: robert.wotherspoon@tiscali.co.uk]	01556 502267
Young, John MTh DipMin	1963 1999	(Airdrie: Broomknoll)	Craigview, North Street, Moniaive, Thornhill DG3 4HR	01848 200318

DUMFRIES ADDRESSES

Maxwelltown West	Laurieknowe	Northwest	St Michael's and South	St Michael's Street
		St George's	Troqueer	Troqueer Road
		St Mary's-Greyfriars	St Mary's Street	

(9) WIGTOWN AND STRANRAER

Meets at Glenluce, in the church hall, on the first Tuesday of March, October and December for ordinary business; on the first Tuesday of September for formal business followed by meetings of committees; on the first Tuesday of November, February and May for worship followed by meetings of committees; and at a church designated by the Moderator on the first Tuesday of June for Holy Communion followed by ordinary business.

Clerk:	**MR SAM SCOBIE**	**40 Clenoch Parks Road, Stranraer DG9 7QT** **[E-mail: wigtownstranraer@cofscotland.org.uk]**	**01776 703975**

Ervie Kirkcolm linked with Leswalt

Michael J. Sheppard BD	1997	Ervie Manse, Stranraer DG9 0QZ [E-mail: mjs@uwclub.net]	01776 854225

Glasserton and Isle of Whithorn linked with Whithorn: St Ninian's Priory

Alexander I. Currie BD CPS	1990	The Manse, Whithorn, Newton Stewart DG8 8PT	01988 500267

Charge / Minister			Address	Telephone
Inch linked with Portpatrick linked with Stranraer: Trinity (H) John H. Burns BSc BD	1985	1988	Bayview Road, Stranraer DG9 8BE	01776 702383
Kirkcowan (H) linked with Wigtown (H) Eric Boyle BA MTh	2006		Seaview Manse, Church Lane, Wigtown, Newton Stewart DG8 9HT [E-mail: ecthered@aol.com]	01988 402314
Kirkinner linked with Sorbie (H) Jeffrey M. Mead BD	1978	1986	The Manse, Kirkinner, Newton Stewart DG8 9AL	01988 840643
Kirkmabreck linked with Monigaff (H) Stuart Farmes	2011	2014	Creebridge, Newton Stewart DG8 6NR [E-mail: thefarmesfamily@tiscali.co.uk]	01671 403361
Kirkmaiden (H) linked with Stoneykirk Vacant			Church Road, Sandhead, Stranraer DG9 9JJ	01776 830548
Leswalt See Ervie Kirkcolm				
Mochrum (H) Vacant			Manse of Mochrum, Port William, Newton Stewart DG8 9QP	01988 700871
Monigaff See Kirkmabreck				
New Luce (H) linked with Old Luce (H) Thomas M. McWhirter MA MSc BD	1992	1997	Glenluce, Newton Stewart DG8 0PU	01581 300319
Old Luce See New Luce				
Penninghame (H) Edward D. Lyons BD MTh	2007		The Manse, 1A Corvisel Road, Newton Stewart DG8 6LW [E-mail: edwardlyons@hotmail.com]	01671 404425
Portpatrick See Inch **Sorbie** See Kirkinner **Stoneykirk** See Kirkmaiden				

Stranraer: High Kirk (H)
Ian McIlroy BSS BD   1996   2009   Stoneleigh, Whitehouse Road, Stranraer DG9 0JB   01776 700616

Stranraer: Trinity See Inch
Whithorn: St Ninian's Priory See Glasserton and Isle of Whithorn
Wigtown See Kirkcowan

Aiken, Peter W.I.	1996 2013	(Kirkmabreck with Monigaff)	Garroch, Viewhills Road, Newton Stewart DG8 6JA [E-mail: revpetevon@gmail.com]	
Baker, Carolyn M. (Mrs) BD	1997 2008	(Ochiltree with Stair)	Clanary, 1 Maxwell Drive, Newton Stewart DG8 6EL [E-mail: cncbaker@btinternet.com]	01988 700590
Bellis, Pamela A. BA	2014	Ordained Local Minister	Maughold, Low Killantrae, Port William, Newton Stewart DG8 9QR [E-mail: pam@bellisconsultancy.co.uk]	
Binks, Mike	2007 2009	Auxiliary Minister	5 Maxwell Drive, Newton Stewart DG8 6EL [E-mail: mike@hollybank.net]	01671 402201 (Mbl) 07590 507917
Harvey, Joyce (Mrs)	2013	Ordained Local Minister	4A Allanfield Place, Newton Stewart DG8 6BS [E-mail: joyceharvey01@btinternet.com]	01671 403693
Munro, Mary (Mrs) BA	1993 2004	(Auxiliary Minister)	14 Auchneel Crescent, Stranraer DG9 0JH	01776 702305

(10) AYR

Meets in Alloway Church Hall on the first Tuesday of every month from September to May, excluding January and April. The June meeting takes place on the third Tuesday of the month in the newly installed Moderator's church. The October meeting is held in a venue determined by the Business Committee.

Clerk: **REV. KENNETH C. ELLIOTT   68 St Quivox Road, Prestwick KA9 1JF   01292 478788**
BD BA CertMin   [E-mail: ayr@cofscotland.org.uk]

Presbytery Office: **Prestwick South Parish Church, 50 Main Street,   01292 678556**
Prestwick KA9 1NX
[E-mail: ayroffice@cofscotland.org.uk]

Alloway (H)
Neil A. McNaught BD MA   1987   1999   1A Parkview, Alloway, Ayr KA7 4QG   01292 441252
[E-mail: nandjmcnaught@btinternet.com]

Name			Address	Telephone
Annbank (H) linked with Tarbolton P. Jill Clancy (Mrs) BD DipMin	2000	2014	The Manse, Tarbolton, Mauchline KA5 5QL [E-mail: jgibson@totalise.co.uk]	01292 540969
Auchinleck (H) linked with Catrine Stephen F. Clipston MA BD	1982	2006	28 Mauchline Road, Auchinleck KA18 2BN [E-mail: steveclipston@btinternet.com]	01290 424776
Ayr: Auld Kirk of Ayr (St John the Baptist) (H) David R. Gemmell MA BD	1991	1999	58 Monument Road, Ayr KA7 2UB [E-mail: drgemmell@hotmail.com]	01292 262580 (Tel/Fax)
Ayr: Castlehill (H) Elizabeth A. Crumlish (Mrs) BD	1995	2008	3 Old Hillfoot Road, Ayr KA7 3LW [E-mail: lizcrumlish@aol.com]	01292 263001
Ayr: Newton Wallacetown (H) Abi T. Ngunga GTh LTh MDiv MTh PhD	2001	2014	9 Nursery Grove, Ayr KA7 3PH [E-mail: abi.t.ngunga@gmail.com]	01292 264251
Ayr: St Andrew's (H) Morag Garrett (Mrs) BD	2011	2013	31 Bellevue Crescent, Ayr KA7 2DP [E-mail: morag_garrett@yahoo.co.uk]	01292 261472
Ayr: St Columba (H) Fraser R. Aitken MA BD	1978	1991	3 Upper Crofts, Alloway, Ayr KA7 4QX [E-mail: frasercolumba@msn.com]	01292 443747
Ayr: St James' (H) Vacant			1 Prestwick Road, Ayr KA8 8LD	01292 262420
Ayr: St Leonard's (H) linked with Dalrymple Vacant			35 Roman Road, Ayr KA7 3SZ	01292 283825
Ayr: St Quivox (H) Rona M. Young (Mrs) BD DipEd	1991	2009	11 Springfield Avenue, Prestwick KA9 2HA [E-mail: revronyoung@hotmail.com]	01292 478306
Douglas T. Moore (Aux)	2003	2012	9 Midton Avenue, Prestwick KA9 1PU [E-mail: douglastmoore@hotmail.com]	01292 671352

Ballantrae (H) linked with St Colmon (Arnsheen Barrhill and Colmonell)
Stephen Ogston MPhys MSc BD   2009   The Manse, 1 The Vennel, Ballantrae, Girvan KA26 0NH
[E-mail: ogston@macfish.com]   01465 831252

Barr linked with Dailly linked with Girvan: South
Ian K. McLachlan MA BD   1999   30 Henrietta Street, Girvan KA26 9AL
[E-mail: iankmclachlan@yetiville.freeserve.co.uk]   01465 713370

Catrine See Auchinleck

Coylton linked with Drongan: The Schaw Kirk
David Whiteman BD   1998   2008   4 Hamilton Place, Coylton, Ayr KA6 6IQ
[E-mail: davesoo@sky.com]   01292 571442

Craigie Symington
Glenda J. Keating (Mrs) MTh   1996   2008   16 Kerrix Road, Symington, Kilmarnock KA1 5QD
[E-mail: kirkglen@btinternet.com]   01563 830205
(New charge formed by the union of Craigie and Symington)

Crosshill (H) linked with Maybole
Brian Hendrie BD   1992   2010   The Manse, 16 McAdam Way, Maybole KA19 8FD
[E-mail: hendrie962@btinternet.com]   01655 883710

Dailly See Barr

Dalmellington linked with Patna Waterside
Fiona A. Wilson (Mrs) BD   2008   2012   4 Carsphairn Road, Dalmellington, Ayr KA6 7RE
[E-mail: weefi12b@hotmail.co.uk]   01292 551503

Dalrymple See Ayr: St Leonard's
Drongan: The Schaw Kirk See Coylton

Dundonald (H)
Robert Mayes BD   1982   1988   64 Main Street, Dundonald, Kilmarnock KA2 9HG
[E-mail: bobmayes@fsmail.net]   01563 850243

Fisherton (H) linked with Kirkoswald (H)
Vacant
The Manse, Kirkoswald, Maybole KA19 8HZ
01655 760210

Girvan: North (Old and St Andrew's) (H)
Richard G. Moffat BD   1994   2013
38 The Avenue, Girvan KA26 9DS
[E-mail: moffatclan@me.com]
01465 713203

Girvan: South See Barr

Kirkmichael linked with Straiton: St Cuthbert's
W. Gerald Jones MA BD MTh   1984   1985
The Manse, Patna Road, Kirkmichael, Maybole KA19 7PJ
[E-mail: revgerald@jonesg99.freeserve.co.uk]
01655 750286

Kirkoswald See Fisherton

Lugar linked with Old Cumnock: Old (H)
John W. Paterson BSc BD DipEd   1994
33 Barrhill Road, Cumnock KA18 1PJ
[E-mail: ocochurchwow@hotmail.com]
01290 420769

Mauchline (H) linked with Sorn
David A. Albon BA MCS   1991   2011
4 Westside Gardens, Mauchline KA5 5DJ
[E-mail: albon@onetel.com]
01290 518528

Maybole See Crosshill

Monkton and Prestwick: North (H)
David Clarkson BSc BA MTh   2010
40 Monkton Road, Prestwick KA9 1AR
[E-mail: revdavidclarkson@gmail.com]
01292 471379

Muirkirk (H) linked with Old Cumnock: Trinity
Scott M. Rae MBE BD CPS   1976   2008
46 Ayr Road, Cumnock KA18 1DW
[E-mail: scottrae1@btopenworld.com]
01290 422145

New Cumnock (H)
Helen E. Cuthbert MA MSc BD   2009
37 Castle, New Cumnock, Cumnock KA18 4AG
[E-mail: helencuthbert@mypostoffice.co.uk]
01290 338296

Ochiltree linked with Stair
William R. Johnston BD 1998 2009 10 Mauchline Road, Ochiltree, Cumnock KA18 2PZ 01290 700365

Old Cumnock: Old See Lugar
Old Cumnock: Trinity See Muirkirk
Patna Waterside See Dalmellington

Prestwick: Kingcase (H) (E-mail: office@kingcase.freeserve.co.uk)
Vacant 15 Bellrock Avenue, Prestwick KA9 1SQ 01292 479571

Prestwick: St Nicholas' (H)
George R. Fiddes BD 1979 1985 3 Bellevue Road, Prestwick KA9 1NW
[E-mail: gfiddes@stnicholasprestwick.org.uk] 01292 477613

Prestwick: South (H) (E-mail: office@pwksouth.plus.com)
Kenneth C. Elliott BD BA CertMin 1989 68 St Quivox Road, Prestwick KA9 1JF
[E-mail: kcelliott@tiscali.co.uk] 01292 478788

St Colmon (Arnsheen Barrhill and Colmonell) See Ballantrae
Sorn See Mauchline
Stair See Ochiltree
Straiton: St Cuthbert's See Kirkmichael
Tarbolton See Annbank

Troon: Old (H)
David B. Prentice-Hyers BA MDiv 2003 2013 85 Bentinck Drive, Troon KA10 6HZ
[E-mail: daveph@troonold.org.uk] 01292 313644

Troon: Portland (H)
Jamie Milliken BD 2005 2011 89 South Beach, Troon KA10 6EQ
[E-mail: troonportlandchurch@gmail.com] 01292 318929 07929 349045 (Mbl)

Troon: St Meddan's (H) (E-mail: st.meddan@virgin.net)
Derek Peat BA BD MTh 2013 27 Bentinck Drive, Troon KA10 6HX
[E-mail: stmeddansminister@btinternet.com] 01292 319163

Birse, G. Stewart CA BD BSc 1980 2013 (Ayr: Newton Wallacetown) 43 Donald Wynd, Largs KA30 8TH
[E-mail: axhp44@dsl.pipex.com] 01475 329081

Name	Years	Charge / Appointment	Address	Telephone
Black, Sandra (Mrs)	2013	Ordained Local Minister	5 Doon Place, Troon KA10 7EQ [E-mail: blacks_troon@hotmail.com]	01292 220075
Blyth, James G.S. BSc BD	1963 1986	(Glenmuick)	40 Robsland Avenue, Ayr KA7 2RW	01292 261276
Bogle, Thomas C. BD	1983 2003	(Fisherton with Maybole: West)	38 McEwan Crescent, Mossblown, Ayr KA6 5DR	01292 521215
Boyd, Ronald M.H. BD DipTh	1995 2010	Chaplain and Teacher of RMPS: Queen Victoria School, Dunblane	6 Victoria Green, Queen Victoria School, Dunblane FK15 0IY	01786 822288
Brown, Jack M. BSc BD	1977 2012	(Applegarth, Sibbaldbie and Johnstone with Lochmaben)	69 Berelands Road, Prestwick KA9 1ER [E-mail: jackm.brown@tiscali.co.uk]	01292 477151
Cranston, George BD	1976 2001	(Rutherglen: Wardlawhill)	20 Capperview, Prestwick KA9 1BH	01292 476627
Crichton, James MA BD MTh	1969 2010	(Crosshill with Dalrymple)	4B Garden Court, Ayr KA8 0AT [E-mail: crichton.james@btinternet.com]	01292 288978
Dickie, Michael M. BSc	1955 1994	(Ayr: Castlehill)	8 Noltmire Road, Ayr KA8 9ES	01292 618512
Geddes, Alexander J. MA BD	1960 1998	(Stewarton: St Columba's)	2 Gregory Street, Mauchline KA5 6BY [E-mail: sandy270736@gmail.com]	01290 518597
Glencross, William M. LTh	1968 1999	(Bellshill: Macdonald Memorial)	1 Lochay Place, Troon KA10 7HH	01292 317097
Grant, J. Gordon MA BD PhD	1957 1997	(Edinburgh: Dean)	33 Fullarton Drive, Troon KA10 6LE	01292 311852
Guthrie, James A.	1969 2005	(Corsock and Kirkpatrick Durham with Crossmichael and Parton)	2 Barhill Road, Pinwherry, Girvan KA26 0QE [E-mail: p.h.m.guthrie@btinternet.com]	01465 841236
Hannah, William BD MCAM MIPR	1987 2001	(Muirkirk)	8 Dovecote View, Kirkintilloch, Glasgow G66 3HY [E-mail: revbillnews@btinternet.com]	0141-776 1337
Harper, David L. BSc BD	1972 2012	(Troon: St Meddan's)	19 Calder Avenue, Troon KA10 7JT [E-mail: d.l.harper@btinternet.com]	01292 312626
Harris, Samuel McC. OStJ BA BD	1974 2010	(Rothesay: Trinity)	36 Adam Wood Court, Troon KA10 6BP	01292 319603
Helon, George G. BA BD	1984 2000	(Barr linked with Dailly)	9 Park Road, Maxwelltown, Dumfries DG2 7PW	01387 259255
Jackson, Nancy	2009 2013	Auxiliary Minister	35 Auchentrae Crescent, Ayr KA7 4BD	01292 262034
Kent, Arthur F.S.	1966 1999	(Monkton and Prestwick: North)	17 St David's Drive, Evesham, Worcs WR11 2AS [E-mail: afskent@onetel.com]	01386 421562
Laing, Iain A. MA BD	1971 2009	(Bishopbriggs: Kenmuir)	9 Annfield News, Prestwick KA9 1PP [E-mail: iandrlaing@yahoo.co.uk]	01292 471732
Lennox, Lawrie I. MA BD DipEd	1991 2006	(Cromar)	7 Carwinshoch View, Ayr KA7 4AY [E-mail: lennox127@btinternet.com]	
Lochrie, John S. BSc BD MTh PhD	1967 2008	(St Colmon)	Cosyglen, Kilkerran, Maybole KA19 8LS	01465 811262 (Mbl) 07771 481698
Lynn, Robert MA BD	1984 2011	(Ayr: St Leonard's with Dalrymple)	8 Kirkbrae, Maybole KA19 7ER	01292 288854
McCrorie, William	1965 1999	(Free Church Chaplain: Royal Brompton Hospital)	12 Shieling Park, Ayr KA7 2UR [E-mail: billevemccrorie@btinternet.com]	
Macdonald, Ian U.	1960 1997	(Tarbolton)	18 Belmont Road, Ayr KA7 2PF	01292 283085
McGurk, Andrew F. BD	1983 2011	(Largs: St John's)	15 Fraser Avenue, Troon KA10 6XF [E-mail: afmcg.largs@talk21.com]	01292 676008
McNidder, Roderick H. BD	1987 1997	Chaplain: NHS Ayrshire and Arran Trust	6 Hollow Park, Alloway, Ayr KA7 4SR	01292 442554
McPhail, Andrew M. BA	1968 2002	(Ayr: Wallacetown)	25 Maybole Road, Ayr KA7 2QA	01292 282108
Mathews, John C. MA BD OBE	1992 2010	(Glasgow: Ruchill Kelvinside)	12 Arrol Drive, Ayr KA7 4AF [E-mail: mejohnmatthews@gmail.com]	01292 264382
Mealyea, Harry B. BArch BD	1984 2011	(Ayr: St Andrew's)	38 Rosamunde Pilcher Drive, Longforgan, Dundee DD2 5EF [E-mail: mealyeal@sky.com]	

Name	Dates	Position	Address	Phone
Mitchell, Sheila M. (Miss) BD MTh	1995 2002	Chaplain: NHS Ayrshire and Arran Trust (Paisley: St Mark's Oldhall)	Ailsa Hospital, Ayr KA6 6BQ	01292 513197
Morrison, Alistair H. BTh DipYCS	1985 2004		92 St Leonard's Road, Ayr KA7 2PU [E-mail: alistairmorrison@supanet.com]	01292 266021
Ness, David T. LTh	1972 2008	(Ayr: St Quivox)	17 Winston Avenue, Prestwick KA9 2EZ [E-mail: dtness@tiscali.co.uk]	
Russell, Paul R. MA BD	1984 2006	Chaplain: NHS Ayrshire and Arran Trust (Craigie with Symington)	23 Nursery Wynd, Ayr KA7 3NZ	01292 618020
Sanderson, Alastair M. BA LTh	1971 2007		26 Main Street, Monkton, Prestwick KA9 2QL [E-mail: alel@sanderson29.fsnet.co.uk]	01292 475819
Simpson, Edward V. BSc BD	1972 2009	(Glasgow: Giffnock South)	8 Paddock View, Thorntoun, Crosshouse, Kilmarnock KA2 0BH [E-mail: eddie.simpson3@talktalk.net]	01563 522841
Smith, Elizabeth (Mrs) BD	1996 2009	(Fauldhouse: St Andrew's)	16 McIntyre Road, Prestwick KA9 1BE [E-mail: smithrevb@btinternet.com]	01292 471588
Stirling, Ian R. BSc BD	1990 2002	Chaplain: The Ayrshire Hospice (Troon: Old)	Ayrshire Hospice, 35–37 Racecourse Road, Ayr KA7 2TG	01292 269200
Symington, Alastair H. MA BD	1972 2012		1 Cavendish Place, Troon KA10 6JG [E-mail: revdahs@btinternet.com]	01292 312556
Wilkinson, Arrick D. BSc BD	2000 2013	(Fisherton with Kirkoswald)	Dunwhinny, Main Street, Ballantrae, Girvan KA26 0NB [E-mail: arrick@dunwhinny-plus.com]	01465 831704
Yorke, Kenneth B.	1982 2009	(Dalmellington with Patna Waterside)	13 Annfield Terrace, Prestwick KA9 1PS [E-mail: kenneth.yorke@googlemail.com]	(Mbl) 07766 320525

AYR ADDRESSES

Ayr

Auld Kirk	Kirkport (116 High Street)
Castlehill	Castlehill Road x Hillfoot Road
Newton Wallacetown	Main Street
St Andrew's	Park Circus
St Columba	Midton Road x Carrick Park
St James'	Prestwick Road x Falkland Park Road
St Leonard's	St Leonard's Road x Monument Road

Girvan

North	Montgomerie Street
South	Stair Park

Prestwick

Kingcase	Waterloo Road

Monkton and Prestwick North	Monkton Road
St Nicholas	Main Street
South	Main Street

Troon

Old	Ayr Street
Portland	St Meddan's Street
St Meddan's	St Meddan's Street

(11) IRVINE AND KILMARNOCK

The Presbytery meets ordinarily at 7:00pm in the Howard Centre, Portland Road, Kilmarnock, on the first Tuesday in September, December, March and on the fourth Tuesday in June for ordinary business, and at different locations on the first Tuesday in October, November, February and May for mission. The September meeting commences with the celebration of Holy Communion.

Clerk:	MR I. STEUART DEY LLB	72 Dundonald Road, Kilmarnock KA1 1RZ [E-mail: irvinekilmarnock@cofscotland.org.uk]	01563 521686 (Home) 01563 526295 (Office)
Depute Clerk:	REV. S. GRANT BARCLAY LLB DipLP BD MSc PhD	1 Thirdpart Place, Kilmarnock KA1 1UL [E-mail: steuart.dey@btinternet.com] [E-mail: minister@stkentigern.org.uk]	01563 571280
Treasurer:	MR JAMES McINTOSH BA CA	15 Dundonald Road, Kilmarnock KA1 1RU	01563 523552

The Presbytery office is staffed each Tuesday, Wednesday and Thursday from 9am until 12:30pm. The office telephone number is 01563 526295.

Caldwell linked with Dunlop
David Donaldson MA BD DMin   1969 2010   4 Dampark, Dunlop, Kilmarnock KA3 4BZ   01560 483268
[E-mail: jd.donaldson@talktalk.net]

Crosshouse (H)
T. Edward Marshall BD   1987 2007   27 Kilmarnock Road, Crosshouse, Kilmarnock KA2 0EZ   01563 524089
[E-mail: marshall1654@hotmail.com]

Darvel (01560 322924)
Charles Lines BA   2010   46 West Main Street, Darvel KA17 0AQ   01560 322924
[E-mail: cmdlines@tiscali.co.uk]

Dreghorn and Springside
Gary E. Horsburgh BA   1977 1983   96A Townfoot, Dreghorn, Irvine KA11 4EZ   01294 217770
[E-mail: garyhorsburgh@hotmail.co.uk]

Dunlop See Caldwell

Fenwick (H)
Geoffrey Redmayne BSc BD MPhil   2000   2 Kirkton Place, Fenwick, Kilmarnock KA3 6DW   01560 600217
[E-mail: gnredmayne@gmail.com]

Galston (H) (01563 820136)
Vacant
60 Brewland Street, Galston KA4 8DX
01563 535673

Hurlford (H)
James D. McCulloch BD MIOP MIP3 FSAScot 1996
12 Main Road, Crookedholm, Kilmarnock KA3 6JT
[E-mail: mccullochmanse1@btinternet.com]
01294 279909

Irvine: Fullarton (H) (Website: www.fullartonchurch.co.uk)
Neil Urquhart BD DipMin 1989
48 Waterside, Irvine KA12 8QJ
[E-mail: minister@fullartonchurch.co.uk]

Irvine: Girdle Toll (H) (Website: www.girdletoll.fsbusiness.co.uk)
Vacant
2 Littlestane Rise, Irvine KA11 2BJ
01294 213565

Irvine: Mure (H)
Vacant
9 West Road, Irvine KA12 8RE
01294 279916

Irvine: Old (H) (01294 273503)
Robert Travers BA BD 1993 1999
22 Kirk Vennel, Irvine KA12 0DQ
[E-mail: robert.travers@live.co.uk]
01294 279265

Irvine: Relief Bourtreehill (H)
Andrew R. Black BD 1987 2003
4 Kames Court, Irvine KA11 1RT
[E-mail: andrewblack@tiscali.co.uk]
01294 216939

Irvine: St Andrew's (H) (01294 276051)
Ian W. Benzie BD 1999 2008
St Andrew's Manse, 206 Bank Street, Irvine KA12 0YD
[E-mail: revianb@gmail.com]
01294 216139

Fiona Blair (Miss) DCS
Mure Church Manse, 9 West Road, Irvine KA12 8RE
[E-mail: fiobla12@aol.com]
07977 235168 (Mbl)

Kilmarnock: Kay Park (H) (07818 550606) (Website: www.kayparkparishchurch.co.uk)
David W. Lacy BA BD DLitt DL 1976 2012
52 London Road, Kilmarnock KA3 7AJ
[E-mail: thelacys@tinyworld.co.uk]
01563 523113 (Tel/Fax)

Kilmarnock: New Laigh Kirk (H)
David S. Cameron BD — 2001 — 2009 — 1 Holmes Farm Road, Kilmarnock KA1 1TP [E-mail: dvdcam5@msn.com] — 01563 525416

Barbara Urquhart (Mrs) DCS — 9 Standalane, Kilmaurs, Kilmarnock KA3 2NB [E-mail: barbaraurquhart1@gmail.com] — 01563 538289

Colin Ogilvie DCS — 32 Upper Bourtree Court, Rutherglen, Glasgow G73 4HT [E-mail: colinogilvie2@gmail.com] — 0141-569 2725 / 07837 287804 (Mbl)

Kilmarnock: Riccarton (H)
Colin A. Strong BSc BD — 1989 — 2007 — 2 Jasmine Road, Kilmarnock KA1 2HD [E-mail: colinastrong@aol.com] — 01563 549490

Kilmarnock: St Andrew's and St Marnock's
James McNaughtan BD DipMin — 1983 — 2008 — 35 South Gargieston Drive, Kilmarnock KA1 1TB [E-mail: jmcnaughtan@gmail.com] — 01563 521665

Kilmarnock: St John's Onthank (H)
Vacant
Colin Ogilvie DCS — 84 Wardneuk Drive, Kilmarnock KA3 2EX / 32 Upper Bourtree Court, Rutherglen, Glasgow G73 4HT [E-mail: colinogilvie2@gmail.com] — 01563 521815 / 0141-569 2725 / 07837 287804 (Mbl)

Anne C. McAllister (Mrs) BSc DipEd CCS (Ordained Local Minister) — 2013 — 39 Bowes Rigg, Stewarton, Kilmarnock KA3 5EN [E-mail: annecmcallister@btinternet.com] — 01560 483191

Kilmarnock: St Kentigern's (Website: www.stkentigern.org.uk)
S. Grant Barclay LLB DipLP BD MSc PhD — 1995 — 1 Thirdpar Place, Kilmarnock KA1 1UL [E-mail: minister@stkentigern.org.uk] — 01563 571280

Kilmarnock: South (01563 524705)
H. Taylor Brown BD CertMin — 1997 — 2012 — 14 McLelland Drive, Kilmarnock KA1 1SE [E-mail: kspc@live.co.uk] — 01563 529920

Kilmaurs: St Maur's Glencairn (H) (Website: www.jimcorbett.freeserve.co.uk/page2.html)
John A. Urquhart BD — 1993 — 9 Standalane, Kilmaurs, Kilmarnock KA3 2NB [E-mail: john.urquhart@talktalk.net] — 01563 538289

Newmilns: Loudoun (H)
Vacant — Loudoun Manse, 116A Loudoun Road, Newmilns KA16 9HH — 01560 320174

Stewarton: John Knox
Gavin A. Niven BSc MSc BD   2010   27 Avenue Street, Stewarton, Kilmarnock KA3 5AP   01560 482418
[E-mail: minister@johnknox.org.uk]

Stewarton: St Columba's (H)
George K. Lind BD MCIBS   1998 2010   1 Kirk Glebe, Stewarton, Kilmarnock KA3 5BJ   01560 485113
[E-mail: gklind@talktalk.net]

Ayrshire Mission to the Deaf
Richard C. Durno DSW CQSW   1989 2013   31 Springfield Road, Bishopbriggs,
Glasgow G64 1PJ   (Voice/Text/Fax) 0141-772 1052
[E-mail: richard.durno@btinternet.com]   (Voice/Text/Voicemail) (Mbl) 07748 607721

Name			Position	Address / E-mail	Telephone
Brockie, Colin G.F. BSc(Eng) BD SOSc	1967	2007	(Presbytery Clerk)	36 Braehead Court, Kilmarnock KA3 7AB [E-mail: revcol@revcol.demon.co.uk]	01563 559960
Campbell, John A. JP FIEM	1984	1998	(Irvine: St Andrew's)	Flowerdale, Balmoral Road, Rattray, Blairgowrie PH10 7AF [E-mail: exrevjack@aol.com]	01250 872795
Cant, Thomas M. MA BD	1965	2004	(Paisley: Laigh Kirk)	3 Meikle Cutstraw, Stewarton, Kilmarnock KA3 5HU [E-mail: revtmcant@aol.com]	01560 480566
Christie, Robert S. MA BD ThM	1964	2001	(Kilmarnock: West High)	24 Homeroyal House, 2 Chalmers Crescent, Edinburgh EH9 1TP	01294 312515
Davidson, James BD DipAFH	1989	2002	(Wishaw: Old)	13 Redburn Place, Irvine KA12 9BQ	01563 573994
Davidson Kelly, Thomas A. MA BD FSAScot	1975	2002	(Glasgow: Govan Old)	2 Springhill Stables, Portland Road, Kilmarnock KA1 2EJ [E-mail: ktdks33@gmail.com]	
Gillon, C. Blair BSc BD	1975	2007	(Glasgow: Ibrox)	East Muirshiel Farmhouse, Dunlop, Kilmarnock KA3 4EJ [E-mail: blair.gillon2@btinternet.com]	01560 483778
Godfrey, Linda BSc BD	2012	2014	(Ayr: St Leonard's with Dalrymple)	9 Taybank Drive, Ayr KA7 4RL [E-mail: godfreykayak@aol.com]	(Mbl) 07825 663866
Hall, William M. BD	1972	2010	(Kilmarnock: Old High Kirk)	33 Cairns Terrace, Kilmarnock KA1 2JG [E-mail: revwillie@talktalk.net]	01563 525080
Hare, Malcolm M.W. BA BD	1956	1994	(Kilmarnock: St Kentigern's)	Flat 5, The Courtyard, Auchlochan, Lesmahagow, Lanark ML11 0GS	
Hay, W.J.R. MA BD	1959	1995	(Buchanan with Drymen)	18 Jamieson Place, Stewarton, Kilmarnock KA3 3HX	01560 482799
Hosain Lamarti, Samuel BD MTh PhD	1979	2006	(Stewarton: John Knox)	7 Dalwhinnie Crescent, Kilmarnock KA3 1QS [E-mail: samlamar@pobroadband.co.uk]	01563 529632
Huggett, Judith A. (Miss) BA BD	1990	1998	Hospital Chaplain	4 Westmoor Crescent, Kilmarnock KA1 1TX [E-mail: judith.huggett@aaaht.scotnhs.uk]	
McAlpine, Richard H.M. BA FSAScot	1968	2000	(Lochgoilhead and Kilmorich)	7 Kingsford Place, Kilmarnock KA3 6FG	01563 572075
MacDonald, James M. BD ThM	1964	1987	(Kilmarnock: St John's Onthank)	29 Carmel Place, Kilmaurs, Kilmarnock KA3 2QU	01563 525254
Scott, Thomas T.	1968	1989	(Kilmarnock: St Marnock's)	6 North Hamilton Place, Kilmarnock KA1 2QN [E-mail: tomtscott@btinternet.com]	01563 531415

Shaw, Catherine A.M. MA	1998 2006	(Auxiliary Minister)	40 Merrygreen Place, Stewarton, Kilmarnock KA3 5EP [E-mail: catherine.shaw@tesco.net]	01560 483352
Welsh, Alex. M. MA BD	1979 2007	Hospital Chaplain	8 Greenside Avenue, Prestwick KA9 2HB [E-mail: alexandevelyn@hotmail.com]	01292 475341

IRVINE and KILMARNOCK ADDRESSES

Irvine

Dreghorn and Springside	Townfoot x Station Brae
Fullarton	Marress Road x Church Street
Girdle Toll	Bryce Knox Court
Mure	West Road
Old	Kirkgate
Relief Bourtreehill	Crofthead, Bourtreehill
St Andrew's	Caldon Road x Oaklands Ave

Kilmarnock

Ayrshire Mission to the Deaf	
Kay Park	10 Clark Street
Kilmarnock South	London Road
New Laigh Kirk	Whatriggs Road
Riccarton	John Dickie Street
	Old Street

St Andrew's and St Marnock's	St Marnock Street
St John's Onthank	84 Wardneuk Street

(12) ARDROSSAN

Meets at Saltcoats, New Trinity, on the first Tuesday of February, March, April, May, September, October, November and December, and on the second Tuesday of June.

Clerk:	MR ALAN K. SAUNDERSON	17 Union Street, Largs KA30 8DG [E-mail: ak.dj.saunderson@hotmail.co.uk]	01475 687217 07866 034355 (Mbl)

Ardrossan: Park (01294 463711)

Tanya Webster BCom DipAcc BD	2011	35 Ardneil Court, Ardrossan KA22 7NQ [E-mail: parkchurchminister@mail.com]	01294 538903
Mandy R. Hickman RGN (Ordained Local Minister)	2013	Lagnaleon, 4 Wilson Street, Largs KA30 9AQ [E-mail: mandyrhickman@gmail.com]	01475 675347

Ardrossan and Saltcoats: Kirkgate (H) (01294 472001) (Website: www.kirkgate.org.uk)

Dorothy A. Granger BA BD	2009	10 Seafield Drive, Ardrossan KA22 8NU [E-mail: dorothygranger61@gmail.com]	01294 463571 07918 077877 (Mbl)

(New charge formed by the union of Ardrossan: Barony St John's and Saltcoats: New Trinity)

Beith (H) (01505 502686)
Roderick I.T. MacDonald BD CertMin   1992   2005   2 Glebe Court, Beith KA15 1ET   01505 503858
                                                                    [E-mail: rodannmac@btinternet.com]

Brodick linked with Corrie linked with Lochranza and Pirnmill linked with Shiskine (H)
Angus Adamson BD   2006   4 Manse Crescent, Brodick, Isle of Arran KA27 8AS   01770 302334
                                                                    [E-mail: adamsonangus@btinternet.com]

Corrie See Brodick

Cumbrae linked with Largs: St John's (H) (01475 674468)
Markus Thane BTh MDiv MTh   2009   2014   1 Newhaven Grove, Largs KA30 8NS   01475 329933
                                                                    [E-mail: markus.thane@yahoo.co.uk]   07445 705172 (Mbl)

Dalry: St Margaret's
James R. Teasdale BA BD   2009   33 Templand Crescent, Dalry KA24 5EZ   01294 832747
                                                                    [E-mail: jamesrteasdale@hotmail.com]

Dalry: Trinity (H)
Martin Thomson BSc DipEd BD   1988   2004   Trinity Manse, West Kilbride Road, Dalry KA24 5DX   01294 832363
                                                                    [E-mail: martin.thomson40@btinternet.com]

Fairlie (H)
Vacant   14 Fairlieburne Gardens, Fairlie, Largs KA29 0ER   01475 568342

Kilbirnie: Auld Kirk (H)
Vacant   49 Holmhead, Kilbirnie KA25 6BS   01505 682348

Kilbirnie: St Columba's (H) (01505 685239)
Fiona C. Ross (Miss) BD DipMin   1996   2004   Manse of St Columba's, Dipple Road, Kilbirnie KA25 7JU   01505 683342
                                                                    [E-mail: fionaross@calvin78.freeserve.co.uk]

Kilmory linked with Lamlash
Vacant   Lamlash, Isle of Arran KA27 8LE   01770 600318

Kilwinning: Mansefield Trinity (01294 550746)
Alan H. Ward MA BD (Interim Minister)   1978   2013   47 Meadowfoot Road, West Kilbride KA23 9BU   01294 822224
                                                                    [E-mail: alanhward@hotmail.co.uk]   07709 906130 (Mbl)

Kilwinning: Old
Jeanette Whitecross BD | 2002 | 2011 | 54 Dalry Road, Kilwinning KA13 7HE
[E-mail: jwx@hotmail.co.uk] | 01294 552606

Lamlash See Kilmory

Largs: Clark Memorial (H) (01475 675186)
T. David Watson BSc BD | 1988 | 2014 | 31 Douglas Street, Largs KA30 8PT
[E-mail: !davidwatson@btinternet.com] | 01475 672370

Largs: St Columba's (01475 686212)
Vacant | | | 17 Beachway, Largs KA30 8QH

Largs: St John's See Cumbrae
Lochranza and Pirnmill See Brodick

Saltcoats: North (01294 464679)
Alexander B. Noble MA BD ThM | 1982 | 2003 | 25 Longfield Avenue, Saltcoats KA21 6DR | 01294 604923

Saltcoats: St Cuthbert's (H)
Arthur Sherratt BD | 1994 | 2014 | 10 Kennedy Road, Saltcoats KA21 5SF
[E-mail: asherratt@sky.com] | 01294 696030

Shiskine See Brodick

Stevenston: Ardeer linked with Stevenston: Livingstone (H)
Vacant | | | 32 High Road, Stevenston KA20 3DR | 01294 464180

Stevenston: High (H) (Website: www.highkirk.com)
M. Scott Cameron MA BD | 2002 | | Glencairn Street, Stevenston KA20 3DL
[E-mail: revhighkirk@btinternet.com] | 01294 463356

Stevenston: Livingstone See Stevenston: Ardeer

West Kilbride (H) (Website: www.westkilbrideparishchurch.org.uk)
James J. McNay MA BD | 2008 | | The Manse, Goldenberry Avenue, West Kilbride KA23 9LJ
[E-mail: minister@westkilbrideparishchurch.org.uk] | 01294 823186

Whiting Bay and Kildonan

Elizabeth R.L. Watson (Miss) BA BD   1981 1982   The Manse, Whiting Bay, Brodick, Isle of Arran KA27 8RE   01770 700289
[E-mail: revewatson@btinternet.com]

Name			Position	Address	Phone
Cruickshank, Norman BA BD	1983	2006	(West Kilbride: Overton)	24D Faulds Wynd, Seamill, West Kilbride KA23 9FA	01294 822239
Currie, Ian S. MBE BD	1975	2010	(The United Church of Bute)	15 Northfield Park, Largs KA30 8NZ	(Mbl) 07764 254300
				[E-mail: ianscurrie@tiscali.co.uk]	
Dailly, John R. BD DipPS	1979	2007	(Chaplain: Army)	2 Curtis Close, Pound Street, Warminster, Wiltshire BA12 9NN	
Drysdale, James H. LTh	1987	2006	(Blackbraes and Shieldhill)	10 John Clark Street, Largs KA30 9AH	01475 674870
Falconer, Alan D. MA BD DLitt	1972	2011	(Aberdeen: St Machar's Cathedral)	18 North Crescent Road, Ardrossan KA22 8NA	01294 472991
				[E-mail: alanfalconer@gmx.com]	
Ford, Alan A. BD	1977	2013	(Glasgow: Springburn)	14 Corsankell Wynd, Saltcoats KA21 6HY	01294 465740
				[E-mail: alan.andy@btinternet.com]	
Gordon, David C.	1953	1988	(Gigha and Cara)	South Beach House, South Crescent Road, Ardrossan KA22 8DU	
Harbison, David J.H.	1958	1998	(Beith: High with Beith: Trinity)	42 Mill Park, Dalry KA24 5BB	01294 834092
				[E-mail: djh@harbi.fsnet.co.uk]	
Hebenton, David J. MA BD	1958	2002	(Ayton and Burnmouth with Grantshouse and Houndwood and Reston)	22B Faulds Wynd, Seamill, West Kilbride KA23 9FA	01294 829228
Howie, Marion L.K. (Mrs) MA ACRS	1992		Auxiliary Minister	51 High Road, Stevenston KA20 3DY	01294 466571
				[E-mail: marion@howiefamily.net]	
McCallum, Alexander D. BD	1987	2005	(Saltcoats: New Trinity)	59 Woodcroft Avenue, Largs KA30 9EW	01475 670133
				[E-mail: sandyandjose@madasafish.com]	
McCance, Andrew M. BSc	1986	1995	(Coatbridge: Middle)	6A Douglas Place, Largs KA30 8PU	01475 673303
Mackay, Marjory H. (Mrs) BD DipEd CCE	1998	2008	(Cumbrae)	4 Golf Road, Millport, Isle of Cumbrae KA28 0HB	01475 530388
				[E-mail: marjory.mackay@gmail.com]	
MacLeod, Ian LTh BA MTh PhD	1969	2006	(Brodick with Corrie)	Cronla Cottage, Corrie, Isle of Arran KA27 8JB	01770 810237
				[E-mail: i.macleod829@btinternet.com]	
Mitchell, D. Ross BA BD	1972	2007	(West Kilbride: St Andrew's)	11 Dunbar Gardens, Saltcoats KA21 6GJ	
				[E-mail: ross.mitchell@virgin.net]	
Paterson, John H. BD	1977	2000	(Kirkintilloch: St David's Memorial Park)	Creag Bhan, Golf Course Road, Whiting Bay, Isle of Arran KA27 8QT	01770 700569
Roy, Iain M. MA BD	1960	1997	(Stevenston: Livingstone)	2 The Fieldings, Dunlop, Kilmarnock KA3 4AU	01560 483072
Taylor, Andrew S. BTh FPhS	1959	1992	(Greenock Union)	9 Raillies Avenue, Largs KA30 8QY	01475 674709
				[E-mail: andrew.taylor_123@btinternet.com]	
Thomson, Margaret (Mrs)	1988	1993	(Saltcoats: Erskine)	7 Glen Farg, St Leonards, East Kilbride, Glasgow G74 2JW	

(13) LANARK

Meets on the first Tuesday of February, March, May, September, October, November and December, and on the third Tuesday of June.

Clerk:	REV. MRS HELEN E. JAMIESON BD DipEd	120 Clyde Street, Carluke ML8 5BG [E-mail: lanark@cofscotland.org.uk]	01555 771218
Depute Clerk:	REV. BRYAN KERR BA BD	Greyfriars Manse, 3 Bellefield Way, Lanark ML11 7NW	01555 663363

Biggar (H) linked with Black Mount
Mike Fucella BD MTh   1997   2013   'Candlemas', 6C Leafield Road, Biggar ML12 6AY   01899 229291
[E-mail: mike@fishwrapper.net]

Black Mount See Biggar

Cairngryffe linked with Libberton and Quothquan (H) linked with Symington (The Tinto Parishes)
George C. Shand MA BD   1981   2014   16 Abington Road, Symington, Biggar ML12 6JX   01899 309400
[E-mail: georgeshand@live.co.uk]

Carluke: Kirkton (H) (Church office: 01555 750778) (Website: www.kirktonchurch.co.uk)
Iain D. Cunningham MA BD   1979   1987   9 Station Road, Carluke ML8 5AA   01555 771262
[E-mail: iaindc@btconnect.com]

Carluke: St Andrew's (H)
Helen E. Jamieson (Mrs) BD DipEd   1989   120 Clyde Street, Carluke ML8 5BG   01555 771218
[E-mail: helenejamieson@o2.co.uk]

Carluke: St John's (H) (Website: www.carluke-stjohns.org.uk)
Vacant   18 Old Bridgend, Carluke ML8 4HN

Carnwath (H) linked with The United Church of Carstairs and Carstairs Junction
Vacant   11 Range View, Kames, Carstairs, Lanark ML11 8TF

Carstairs and Carstairs Junction, The United Church of See Carnwath

Coalburn (H) linked with Lesmahagow: Old (H) (Church office: 01555 892425)
Vacant   9 Elm Bank, Lesmahagow, Lanark ML11 0EA

Crossford (H) linked with Kirkfieldbank
Steven Reid BAcc CA BD — 1989 1997 — 74 Lanark Road, Crossford, Carluke ML8 5RE [E-mail: steven.reid@sky.com] — 01555 860415

Forth: St Paul's (H) (Website: www.forthstpauls.com)
Vacant — 22 Lea Rig, Forth, Lanark ML11 8EA — 01555 812832

Kirkfieldbank See Crossford

Kirkmuirhill (H)
Vacant — The Manse, 2 Lanark Road, Kirkmuirhill, Lanark ML11 9RB — 01555 892409

Lanark: Greyfriars (Church office: 01555 661510) (Website: www.lanarkgreyfriars.com)
Bryan Kerr BA BD — 2002 2007 — Greyfriars Manse, 3 Bellefield Way, Lanark ML11 7NW [E-mail: bryan@lanarkgreyfriars.com] — 01555 663363

Lanark: St Nicholas' (H)
Alison A. Meikle (Mrs) BD — 1999 2002 — 2 Kaimhill Court, Lanark ML11 9HU [E-mail: alison-meikle@sky.com] — 01555 662600

Law
Una B. Stewart (Ms) BD DipEd — 1995 2009 — 3 Shawgill Court, Law, Carluke ML8 5SJ [E-mail: rev.ubs@virgin.net] — 01698 373180

Lesmahagow: Abbeygreen
David S. Carmichael — 1982 — Abbeygreen Manse, Lesmahagow, Lanark ML11 0DB [E-mail: david.carmichael@abbeygreen.org.uk] — 01555 893384

Lesmahagow: Old See Coalburn
Libberton and Quothquan See Cairngryffe
Symington See Cairngryffe

The Douglas Valley Church (Church office: 01555 850000) (Website: www.douglasvalleychurch.org)
Vacant — The Manse, Douglas, Lanark ML11 0RB — 01555 851213

Upper Clyde
Vacant — 66 Carlisle Road, Crawford, Biggar ML12 6TW

Clelland, Elizabeth (Mrs) BD	2002	2012	Chaplain, Divine Healing Fellowship (Scotland)	Braehead House Christian Healing and Retreat Centre, Braidwood Road, Crossford, Carluke ML8 5NQ [E-mail: liz_clelland@yahoo.co.uk]	01555 860716
Cowell, Susan G. (Miss) BA BD	1986	1998	(Budapest)	3 Gavel Lane, Regency Gardens, Lanark ML11 9FB	01555 665509
Craig, William BA LTh	1974	1997	(Cambusbarron: The Bruce Memorial)	31 Heathfield Drive, Blackwood, Lanark ML11 9SR	01555 893710
Easton, David J.C. MA BD	1965	2005	(Burnside-Blairbeth)	Rowanbank, Cormiston Road, Quothquan, Biggar ML12 6ND [E-mail: deaston@btinternet.com]	01899 308459
Findlay, Henry J.W. MA BD	1965	2005	(Wishaw: St Mark's)	2 Alba Gardens, Carluke ML8 5US	01555 759995
Fox, George H.	1959	1977	(Coalsnaughton)		
Gibson, Alan W. BA BD	2001	2012	Head of Stewardship	c/o 121 George Street, Edinburgh EH2 4YN [E-mail: agibson@cofscotland.org.uk]	0131-225 5722
Houston, Graham R. BSc BD MTh PhD	1978	2011	(Cairngryffe with Symington)	3 Alder Lane, Beechtrees, Lanark ML11 9FT [E-mail: gandih6156@btinternet.com]	01555 678004
McLarty, R. Russell MA BD	1985	2011	*The Chance to Thrive* – Project Co-ordinator	9 Sanderson's Wynd, Tranent EH33 1DA	01875 614496
Pacitti, Stephen A. MA	1963	2003	(Black Mount with Culter with Libberton and Quothquan)	157 Nithsdale Road, Glasgow G41 5RD	0141-423 5972
Seath, Thomas J.G.	1980	1992	(Motherwell: Manse Road)	Flat 11, Wallace Court, South Vennel, Lanark ML11 7LL	01555 665399
Young, David A.	1972	2003	(Kirkmuirhill)	15 Mannachie Rise, Forres IV36 2US [E-mail: youngdavid@aol.com]	01309 672849

(14) GREENOCK AND PAISLEY

Meets on the second Tuesday of September, October, November, December, February, March, April and May, and on the third Tuesday of June.

Clerk:	REV. PETER McENHILL BD PhD	
Presbytery Office:	The Presbytery Office as detailed below [E-mail: greenockpaisley@cofscotland.org.uk] 'Homelea', Faith Avenue, Quarrier's Village, Bridge of Weir PA11 3SX	01505 615033 (Tel) 01505 615088 (Fax)

Barrhead: Bourock (H) (0141-881 9813)
| Vacant | | | 14 Maxton Avenue, Barrhead, Glasgow G78 1DY | 0141-881 1462 |

Barrhead: St Andrew's (H) (0141-881 8442)
| James S.A. Cowan BD DipMin | 1986 | 1998 | 10 Arthurlie Avenue, Barrhead, Glasgow G78 2BU [E-mail: jim_cowan@ntlworld.com] | 0141-881 3457 |

Bishopton (H) (Office: 01505 862583)
Daniel Manastireanu BA MTh | 2010 | The Manse, Newton Road, Bishopton PA7 5JP [E-mail: daniel@bishoptonkirk.org.uk] | 01505 862161

Bridge of Weir: Freeland (H) (01505 612610)
Kenneth N. Gray BA BD | 1988 | 15 Lawmarnock Crescent, Bridge of Weir PA11 3AS [E-mail: aandkgray@btinternet.com] | 01505 690918

Bridge of Weir: St Machar's Ranfurly (01505 614364)
Suzanne Dunleavy (Miss) BD DipEd | 1990 1992 | 9 Glen Brae, Bridge of Weir PA11 3BH [E-mail: suzanne.dunleavy@btinternet.com] | 01505 612975

Elderslie Kirk (H) (01505 323348)
Robin N. Allison BD DipMin | 1994 2005 | 282 Main Road, Elderslie, Johnstone PA5 9EF [E-mail: revrobin@sky.com] | 01505 321767

Erskine (0141-812 4620)
Jonathan Fleming MA BD | 2012 | The Manse, 7 Leven Place, Linburn, Erskine PA8 6AS [E-mail: jonathancfleming@me.com] | 0141-570 8103

Gourock: Old Gourock and Ashton (H)
Vacant | | 331 Eldon Street, Gourock PA16 7QN [E-mail: minister@ogachurch.org.uk] | 01475 635578

Gourock: St John's (H)
Glenn A. Chestnutt BA DASE MDiv ThM PhD | 2009 | 6 Barrhill Road, Gourock PA19 1JX [E-mail: glenn.chestnutt@gmail.com] | 01475 632143

Greenock: East End linked with Greenock: Mount Kirk
Francis E. Murphy BEng DipDSE BD | 2006 | 76 Finnart Street, Greenock PA16 8HJ [E-mail: francis_e_murphy@hotmail.com] | 01475 722338

Greenock: Lyle Kirk
Vacant | | 39 Fox Street, Greenock PA16 8PD | 01475 888277
Eileen Manson (Mrs) DipCE (Aux) | 1994 2014 | 1 Cambridge Avenue, Gourock PA19 1XT [E-mail: rev.eileen@ntlworld.com] | 01475 632401

Greenock: Mount Kirk See Greenock: East End

Greenock: St Margaret's (R) (01475 781953) Morris C. Coull BD	1974	2014	Flat 0/1 Toward, The Lighthouses, Greenock Road, Wemyss Bay PA18 6DT	01475 522677
Greenock: St Ninian's Allan G. McIntyre BD	1985		5 Auchmead Road, Greenock PA16 0PY [E-mail: agmcintyre@lineone.net]	01475 631878
Greenock: Wellpark Mid Kirk Alan K. Sorensen BD MTh DipMin FSAScot	1983	2000	101 Brisbane Street, Greenock PA16 8PA [E-mail: alan.sorensen@ntlworld.com]	01475 721741
Greenock: Westburn Karen E. Harbison (Mrs) MA BD	1991	2014	50 Ardgowan Street, Greenock PA16 8EP [E-mail: calumkaren@yahoo.co.uk]	01475 721048
Houston and Killellan (H) Donald Campbell BD	1998	2007	The Manse of Houston, Main Street, Houston, Johnstone PA6 7EL [E-mail: houstonmanse@btinternet.com]	01505 612569
Howwood linked with Lochwinnoch Vacant			The Manse, Beith Road, Howwood, Johnstone PA9 1AS	01505 703678
Inchinnan (H) (0141-812 1263) Alison McBrier MA BD	2011		The Manse, Inchinnan, Renfrew PA4 9PH	0141-812 1688
Inverkip (H) linked with Skelmorlie and Wemyss Bay Archibald Speirs BD	1995	2013	3a Montgomery Terrace, Skelmorlie PA17 5DT [E-mail: archiespeirs1@aol.com]	01475 529320
Johnstone: High (H) (01505 336303) Ann C. McCool (Mrs) BD DSD IPA ALCM	1989	2001	76 North Road, Johnstone PA5 8NF [E-mail: ann.mccool@ntlworld.com]	01505 320006

Johnstone: St Andrew's Trinity
Charles M. Cameron BA BD PhD

1980   2013

45 Woodlands Crescent, Johnstone PA5 0AZ
[E-mail: charlescameron@hotmail.co.uk]

01505 672908

Johnstone: St Paul's (H) (01505 321632)
Alistair N. Shaw MA BD MTh

1982   2003

9 Stanley Drive, Brookfield, Johnstone PA5 8UF
[E-mail: ans2006@talktalk.net]

01505 320060

Kilbarchan: East
Stephen J. Smith BSc BD

1993   2013

East Manse, Church Street, Kilbarchan, Johnstone PA10 2JQ
[E-mail: stephenrevsteve@aol.com]

01505 702621

Kilbarchan: West
Vacant

West Manse, Shuttle Street, Kilbarchan, Johnstone PA10 2JR

01505 342930

Kilmacolm: Old (H) (01505 873911)
Peter McEnhill BD PhD

1992   2007

The Old Kirk Manse, Glencairn Road, Kilmacolm PA13 4NJ
[E-mail: petermcenhill@btinternet.com]

01505 873174

Kilmacolm: St Columba (H)
R. Douglas Cranston MA BD

1986   1992

6 Churchill Road, Kilmacolm PA13 4LH
[E-mail: robert.cranston@sccmanse.plus.com]

01505 873271

Langbank (R) linked with Port Glasgow: St Andrew's (H)
Andrew T. MacLean BA BD

1980   1993

St Andrew's Manse, Barr's Brae, Port Glasgow PA14 5QA
[E-mail: standrews.pg@me.com]

01475 741486

Linwood (H) (01505 328802)
Eileen M. Ross (Mrs) BD MTh

2005   2008

1 John Neilson Avenue, Paisley PA1 2SX
[E-mail: revemr@yahoo.co.uk]

0141-887 2801

Lochwinnoch See Howwood

Neilston (0141-881 9445)
Fiona E. Maxwell BA BD

2004   2013

The Manse, Neilston Road, Neilston, Glasgow G78 3NP
[Email: fiona.maxwell@aol.co.uk]

0141-258 0805

Paisley: Abbey (H) (Tel: 0141-889 7654; Fax: 0141-887 3929)
Alan D. Birss MA BD — 1979 1988 — 15 Main Road, Castlehead, Paisley PA2 6AJ
[E-mail: alan.birss@paisleyabbey.com] — 0141-889 3587

Paisley: Glenburn (0141-884 2602)
Iain M.A. Reid MA BD — 1990 2014 — 10 Hawick Avenue, Paisley PA2 9LD
[E-mail: reviain.reid@ntlworld.com] — 0141-884 4903

Paisley: Lylesland (H) (0141-561 7139)
Alistair W. Cook BSc CA BD — 2008 — 36 Potterhill Avenue, Paisley PA2 8BA
[E-mail: alistaircook@ntlworld.com] — 0141-561 9277

Paisley: Martyrs' Sandyford (0141-889 6603)
Kenneth A.L. Mayne BA MSc CertEd — 1976 2007 — 27 Acer Crescent, Paisley PA2 9LR — 0141-884 7400

Paisley: Oakshaw Trinity (H) (Tel: 0141-889 4010; Fax: 0141-848 5139)
Gordon B. Armstrong BD FIAB BRC — 2010 2012 — The Manse, 16 Golf Drive, Paisley PA1 3LA
[E-mail: revgordon@ntlworld.com] — 0141-887 0884

Paisley: St Columba Foxbar (H) (01505 812377)
Vacant — 13 Corsebar Drive, Paisley PA2 9QD — 0141-848 5826

Paisley: St James' (0141-889 2422)
Ivan C. Warwick TD MA BD — 1980 2012 — 38 Woodland Avenue, Paisley PA2 8BH
[E-mail: L70rev@btinternet.com] — 0141-884 7978 / 07787 535083 (Mbl)

Paisley: St Luke's (H)
D. Ritchie M. Gillon BD DipMin — 1994 — 31 Southfield Avenue, Paisley PA2 8BX
[E-mail: revgillon@hotmail.com] — 0141-884 6215

Paisley: St Mark's Oldhall (H) (0141-882 2755)
Robert G. McFarlane BD — 2001 2005 — 36 Newtyle Road, Paisley PA1 3JX
[E-mail: robertmcf@hotmail.com] — 0141-889 4279

Paisley: St Ninian's Ferguslie (New Charge Development) (0141-887 9436)
Vacant — 10 Stanely Drive, Paisley PA2 6HE — 0141-884 4177
Duncan Ross DCS — 1 John Neilson Avenue, Paisley PA1 2SX
[E-mail: duncan@saintninians.co.uk] — 0141-887 2801

Paisley: Sherwood Greenlaw (H) (0141-889 7060)
John Murning BD   1988   5 Greenlaw Drive, Paisley PA1 3RX   0141-889 3057
[E-mail: revjohnmurning@hotmail.com]

Paisley: Stow Brae Kirk
Robert Craig BA BD DipRS   2008   2012   25 John Neilson Avenue, Paisley PA1 2SX   0141-328 6014
[E-mail: stowbraekirk@gmail.com]

Paisley: Wallneuk North (0141-889 9265)
Peter G. Gill MA BA   2008   5 Glenville Crescent, Paisley PA2 8TW   0141-884 4429
[E-mail: petergill18@hotmail.com]

Port Glasgow: Hamilton Bardrainney
Vacant   80 Bardrainney Avenue, Port Glasgow PA14 6HD   01475 701213

Port Glasgow: St Andrew's See Langbank

Port Glasgow: St Martin's
Vacant   Clunebraehead, Clune Brae, Port Glasgow PA14 5SL   01475 704115

Renfrew: North (0141-885 2154)
E. Lorna Hood (Mrs) MA BD DD   1978   1979   1 Alexandra Drive, Renfrew PA4 8UB   0141-886 2074
[E-mail: revlornahood@gmail.com]

Renfrew: Trinity (H) (0141-885 2129)
Vacant   25 Paisley Road, Renfrew PA4 8JH   0141-886 2131

Skelmorlie and Wemyss Bay See Inverkip

Alexander, Douglas N. MA BD	1961	1999	(Bishopton)	West Morningside, Main Road, Langbank, Port Glasgow PA4 6XP	01475 540249
Armstrong, William R. BD	1979	2008	(Skelmorlie and Wemyss Bay)	25A The Lane, Skelmorlie PA17 5AR [E-mail: warmstrong17@tiscali.co.uk]	01475 520891
Bell, Ian W. LTh	1990	2011	(Erskine)	40 Brueacre Drive, Wemyss Bay PA18 6HA [E-mail: riwbepc@ntlworld.com]	01475 529312
Bell, May (Mrs) LTh	1998	2012	(Johnstone: St Andrew's Trinity)	40 Brueacre Drive, Wemyss Bay PA18 6HA [E-mail: may.bell@ntlbusiness.com]	01475 529312

Name			Role	Address	Phone
Black, Janette M.K. (Mrs) BD	1993	2006	(Assistant: Paisley: Oakshaw Trinity)	5 Craigiehall Avenue, Erskine PA8 7DB	0141-812 0794
Breingan, Mhairi	2011		Ordained Local Minister	6 Park Road, Inchinnan, Renfrew PA4 4QJ	0141-812 1425
Cameron, Margaret (Miss) DCS	1973	2009	(Deacon)	2 Rowans Gate, Paisley PA2 6RD	0141-840 2479
Campbell, John MA BA BSc			(Caldwell)	96 Boghead Road, Lenzie, Glasgow G66 4EN [E-mail: johncampbell.lenzie@gmail.com]	0141-776 0874
Chestnut, Alexander MBE BA	1948	1987	(Greenock: St Mark's Greenbank)	5 Douglas Street, Largs KA30 8PS	01475 674168
Copland, Agnes M. (Mrs) MBE DCS			(Deacon)	3 Craigmuschat Road, Gourock PA19 1SE	01475 631870
Cubie, John P. MA BD	1961	1999	(Caldwell)	36 Winram Place, St Andrews KY16 8XH	01334 474708
Easton, Lilly C. (Mrs)	1999	2012	(Renfrew: Old)	Flat 0/2, 90 Beith Street, Glasgow G11 6DG [E-mail: revlillyeaston@hotmail.co.uk]	0141-586 7628
Erskine, Morag (Miss) DCS			(Deacon)	111 Mains Drive, Park Mains, Erskine PA8 7JJ [E-mail: morag.erskine@ntlworld.com]	0141-812 6096
Forrest, Kenneth P. CBE BSc PhD	2006		Auxiliary Minister	5 Carruth Road, Bridge of Weir PA11 3HQ [E-mail: kenpforrest@hotmail.com]	01505 612651
Fraser, Ian C. BA BD	1983	2008	(Glasgow: St Luke's and St Andrew's)	62 Kingston Avenue, Neilston, Glasgow G78 3JG [E-mail: ianandlindafraser@gmail.com]	0141-563 6794
Gardner, Frank J. MA	1966	2007	(Gourock: Old Gourock and Ashton)	1 Levanne Place, Gourock PA16 1AX [E-mail: fjg@clyde-mail.co.uk]	(Tel/Fax) 01475 630187
Geddes, Elizabeth (Mrs)	2013		Ordained Local Minister	9 Shillingworth Place, Bridge of Weir PA11 3DY [E-mail: geddes_liz@hotmail.com]	01505 612639
Gray, Greta (Miss) DCS			(Deacon)	67 Crags Avenue, Paisley PA3 6SG [E-mail: greta.gray@ntlworld.com]	0141-884 6178
Hamilton, W. Douglas BD	1975	2009	(Greenock: Westburn)	5 Corse Road, Penilee, Glasgow G52 4DG [E-mail: douglas.hamilton44@hotmail.co.uk]	0141-810 1194
Hetherington, Robert M. MA BD	1966	2002	(Barrhead: South and Levern)	31 Brodie Park Crescent, Paisley PA2 6EU [E-mail: r-hetherington@sky.com]	0141-848 6560
Irvine, Euphemia H.C. (Mrs) BD	1972	1988	(Milton of Campsie)	32 Baird Drive, Bargarran, Erskine PA8 6BB	0141-812 2777
Johnston, Mary (Miss) DCS	1989	2001	(Deacon)	19 Lounsdale Drive, Paisley PA2 9ED	0141-849 1615
Kay, David BA BD MTh	1974	2008	(Paisley: Sandyford: Thread Street)	36 Donaldswood Park, Paisley PA2 8RS [E-mail: david.kay500@o2.co.uk]	0141-884 2080
Leitch, Maureen (Mrs) BA BD	1995	2011	(Barrhead: Bourock)	Rockfield, 92 Paisley Road, Barrhead G78 1NW [E-mail: maureen.leitch@ntlworld.com]	0141-580 2927
Lodge, Bernard P. BD	1967	2004	(Glasgow: Govanhill Trinity)	6 Darluith Park, Brookfield, Johnstone PA5 8DD [E-mail: bernardlodge@yahoo.co.uk]	01505 320378
McBain, Margaret (Miss) DCS	1985	2014	Mission and Discipleship Council	33 Quarry Road, Paisley PA2 7RD	0141-884 2920
McCarthy, David J. BSc BD				121 George Street, Edinburgh EH2 4YN [E-mail: dmccarthy@cofscotland.org.uk]	0131-225 5722
MacColl, James C. BSc BD	1966	2002	(Johnstone: St Andrew's Trinity)	Greenways, Winton, Kirkby Stephen, Cumbria CA17 4HL	01768 372290
MacColl, John BD DipMin	1989	2001	Teacher: Religious Education	1 Birch Avenue, Johnstone PA5 0DD	01505 326506
McCully, M. Isobel (Miss) DCS			(Deacon)	10 Broadstone Avenue, Port Glasgow PA14 5BB [E-mail: mi.mccully@btinternet.com]	01475 742240
Macdonald, Alexander MA BD	1966	2006	(Neilston)	35 Lochore Avenue, Paisley PA3 4BY [E-mail: alexmacdonald42@aol.com]	0141-889 0066
McDonald, Alexander BA CMIWSC DUniv	1968	2000	(Department of Ministry)	36 Alloway Grove, Paisley PA2 7DQ [E-mail: amcdonald1@ntlworld.com]	0141-560 1937

Name			Parish	Address	Phone
McKaig, William G. BD	1979	2011	(Langbank)	54 Brisbane Street, Greenock PA16 8NT [E-mail: bill.mckaig@virgin.net]	01506 400619
MacLaine, Marilyn (Mrs) LTh	1995	2009	(Inchinnan)	37 Bankton Brae, Livingston EH54 9LA	01475 723235
Nicol, Joyce M. (Mrs) BA DCS			(Deacon)	93 Brisbane Street, Greenock PA16 8NY [E-mail: joycenicol@hotmail.co.uk]	(Mbl) 07957 642709 / 01505 326254
Noonan, Pam (Mrs)	2013		Ordained Local Minister	18 Woodburn Place, Houston, Johnstone PA6 7NA	
Page, John R. BD DipMin	1988	2003	(Gibraltar)	1 The Walton Building, North Street, Mere, Warminster, Wiltshire BA12 6HU	
Palmer, S.W. BD	1980	1991	(Kilbarchan: East)	4 Bream Place, Houston PA6 7ZJ	01505 615280
Prentice, George BA BTh	1964	1997	(Paisley: Martyrs')	46 Victoria Gardens, Corsebar Road, Paisley PA2 9AQ [E-mail: g-prentice04@talktalk.net]	0141-842 1585
Simpson, James H. BD LLB	1964	2004	(Greenock: Mount Kirk)	82 Harbourside, Inverkip, Greenock PA16 0BF [E-mail: jameshsimpson@yahoo.co.uk]	01475 520582
Smillie, Andrew M. LTh	1990	2005	(Langbank)	7 Turnbull Avenue, West Freeland, Erskine PA8 7DL [E-mail: andrewsmillie@talktalk.net]	0141-812 7030
Stevenson, Stuart	2011		Ordained Local Minister	143 Springfield Park, Johnstone PA5 8JT	0141-886 2131
Stewart, David MA DipEd BD MTh	1977	2013	(Howwood)	72 Glen Avenue, Largs KA30 8QQ [E-mail: revdavidst@aol.com]	
Whiteford, Alexander LTh	1996	2013	(Ardersier with Petty)	Cumbrae, 17 Netherburn Gardens, Houston, Johnstone PA6 7NG [E-mail: alex.whiteford@hotmail.co.uk]	01505 229611
Whyte, John H. MA	1946	1986	(Gourock: Ashton)	6 Castle Levan Manor, Cloch Road, Gourock PA19 1AY	01475 636788
Whyte, Margaret A. (Mrs) BA BD	1988	2011	(Glasgow: Pollokshaws)	4 Springhill Road, Barrhead G78 2AA [E-mail: tdpwhyte@tiscali.co.uk]	0141-881 4942
Young, David T. BA BD	2007	2012	Chaplain: University of Strathclyde	51 Marchfield Avenue, Paisley PA3 2QE [E-mail: david.t.young@strath.ac.uk]	0141-237 5128 (Work) 0141-553 4144

GREENOCK ADDRESSES

Gourock
Old Gourock and Ashton — 41 Royal Street
St John's — Bath Street x St John's Road

Greenock
Lyle Kirk — 31 Union Street; Newark Street x Bentinck Street; Esplanade x Campbell Street
(Lyle Kirk is continuing meantime to retain all three buildings)

Mount Kirk — Dempster Street at Murdieston Park
St Margaret's — Finch Road x Kestrel Crescent
St Ninian's — Warwick Road, Larkfield
Wellpark Mid Kirk — Cathcart Square
Westburn — 9 Nelson Street

Port Glasgow
Hamilton Bardrainney — Bardrainney Avenue x Auchenbothie Road
St Andrew's — Princes Street
St Martin's — Mansion Avenue

PAISLEY ADDRESSES

Abbey	Town Centre	Oakshaw Trinity	Churchill
Glenburn	Nethercraigs Drive off Glenburn Road	St Columba Foxbar	Amochrie Road, Foxbar
Lylesland	Rowan Street off Neilston Road	St James'	Underwood Road
Martyrs'	King Street	St Luke's	Neilston Road
		St Mark's Oldhall	Glasgow Road, Ralston
		St Ninian's Ferguslie	Blackstoun Road

Sandyford (Thread St)	Montgomery Road	
Sherwood Greenlaw	Glasgow Road	
Stow Brae Kirk	Causeyside Street	
Wallneuk North	off Renfrew Road	

(16) GLASGOW

Meets at Govan and Linthouse Parish Church, Govan Cross, Glasgow (unless otherwise intimated), on the following Tuesdays: 2014: 9 September, 14 October, 11 November, 9 December; 2015: 10 February, 10 March, 14 April, 12 May, 16 June.

Clerk:	**VERY REV. WILLIAM C. HEWITT BD DipPS**	**260 Bath Street, Glasgow G2 4JP** [E-mail: glasgow@cofscotland.org.uk] [Website: www.presbyteryofglasgow.org.uk]	**0141-332 6606** **0141-352 6646 (Fax)**
Treasurer:	**DOUGLAS BLANEY**	[E-mail: treasurer@presbyteryofglasgow.org.uk]	

1 Banton linked with Twechar
Vacant
Manse of Banton and Twechar, Banton, Glasgow G65 0QL
01236 826129

2 Bishopbriggs: Kenmure
James Gemmell BD MTh   1999   2010
5 Marchfield, Bishopbriggs, Glasgow G64 3PP
[E-mail: revgemmell@hotmail.com]
0141-772 1468

3 Bishopbriggs: Springfield Cambridge (0141-772 1596)
Ian Taylor BD ThM   1995   2006
64 Miller Drive, Bishopbriggs, Glasgow G64 1FB
[E-mail: taylorian@btinternet.com]
0141-772 1540

4 Broom (0141-639 3528)
James A.S. Boag BD CertMin   1992   2007
3 Laigh Road, Newton Mearns, Glasgow G77 5EX
[E-mail: office@broomchurch.org.uk]
0141-639 2916 (Tel)
0141-639 3528 (Fax)

5 Burnside Blairbeth (0141-634 4130)
William T.S. Wilson BSc BD   1999   2006
59 Blairbeth Road, Burnside, Glasgow G73 4JD
[E-mail: william.wilson@burnsideblairbethchurch.org.uk]
0141-583 6470

#	Name	Ord.	Ind.	Address	Telephone
6	**Busby (0141-644 2073)** Jeremy C. Eve BSc BD	1998		17A Carmunnock Road, Busby, Glasgow G76 8SZ [E-mail: j-eve@sky.com]	0141-644 3670
7	**Cadder (0141-772 7436)** Graham S. Finch MA BD	1977	1999	231 Kirkintilloch Road, Bishopbriggs, Glasgow G64 2JB [E-mail: gsf1957@ntlworld.com]	0141-772 1363
8	**Cambuslang: Flemington Hallside** Neil M. Glover	2005		59 Hay Crescent, Cambuslang, Glasgow G72 6QA [E-mail: neilmglover@gmail.com]	0141-641 1049 07779 280074 (Mbl)
9	**Cambuslang Parish Church** A. Leslie Milton MA BD PhD	1996	2008	74 Stewarton Drive, Cambuslang, Glasgow G72 8DG [E-mail: alesliemilton.milton@gmail.com]	0141-641 2028
	Karen Hamilton (Mrs) DCS	1995	2014	6 Beckfield Gate, Glasgow G33 1SW [E-mail: k.hamilton6@btinternet.com]	0141-558 3195 07514 402612 (Mbl)
10	**Campsie (01360 310939)** Alexandra Farrington LTh	2003	2011	19 Redhills View, Lennoxtown, Glasgow G66 7BL [E-mail: revsfarrington@aol.co.uk]	01360 238126
11	**Chryston (H) (0141-779 4188)** Mark Malcolm MA BD	1999	2008	The Manse, 109 Main Street, Chryston, Glasgow G69 9LA [E-mail: mark.minister@btinternet.com]	0141-779 1436 07731 737377 (Mbl)
	Mark W.J. McKeown MEng MDiv (Assoc)	2013	2014	6 Glenapp Place, Moodiesburn, Glasgow G69 0HS [E-mail: mark.mck@chrystonparishchurch.co.uk]	01236 263406
12	**Eaglesham (01355 302047)** Lynn M. McChlery BA BD	2005		The Manse, Cheapside Street, Eaglesham, Glasgow G76 0NS [E-mail: lsmcchlery@btinternet.com]	01355 303495
13	**Fernhill and Cathkin** Margaret McArthur BD DipMin	1995	2002	82 Blairbeth Road, Rutherglen, Glasgow G73 4JA [E-mail: revmaggiemac@hotmail.co.uk]	0141-634 1508

14	**Gartcosh (H) (01236 873770) linked with Glenboig**			
	David G. Slater BSc BA DipThRS	2011	26 Inchnock Avenue, Gartcosh, Glasgow G69 8EA [E-mail: minister@gartcoshchurch.co.uk] [E-mail: minister@glenboigchurch.co.uk]	01236 870331 01236 872274 (Office)
15	**Giffnock: Orchardhill (0141-638 3604)**			
	Chris Vermeulen DipLT BTh MA	1986	2005	23 Huntly Avenue, Giffnock, Glasgow G46 6LW [E-mail: chris@orchardhill.org.uk]	0141-620 3734
16	**Giffnock: South (0141-638 2599)**			
	Catherine J. Beattie (Mrs) BD	2008	2011	164 Ayr Road, Newton Mearns, Glasgow G77 6EE [E-mail: catherinejbeat@aol.com]	0141-258 7804
17	**Giffnock: The Park (0141-620 2204)**			
	Calum D. Macdonald BD	1993	2001	41 Rouken Glen Road, Thornliebank, Glasgow G46 7JD [E-mail: parkchurch@hotmail.co.uk]	0141-638 3023
18	**Glenboig** See Gartcosh			
19	**Greenbank (H) (0141-644 1841)**			
	Jeanne Roddick BD	2003	Greenbank Manse, 38 Eaglesham Road, Clarkston, Glasgow G76 7DJ [E-mail: jeanne.roddick@ntlworld.com]	0141-644 1395
20	**Kilsyth: Anderson**			
	Allan S. Vint BSc BD MTh	1989	2013	Anderson Manse, Kingston Road, Kilsyth, Glasgow G65 0HR [E-mail: allan@vint.co.uk]	01236 822345 07795 483070 (Mbl)
21	**Kilsyth: Burns and Old**			
	Stuart C. Steell BD CertMin	1992	2014	The Grange, 17 Glasgow Road, Kilsyth, Glasgow G65 9AE [E-mail: ssren@tiscali.co.uk]	01236 823116
22	**Kirkintilloch: Hillhead**			
	Lily F. McKinnon MA BD PGCE	1993	2011	The Manse, 64 Waverley Park, Kensington Gate, Kirkintilloch, Glasgow G66 2BP [E-mail: lily.mckinnon@yahoo.co.uk]	0141-776 4785

23 Kirkintilloch: St Columba's (H) (0141-578 0016)
David M. White BA BD DMin   1988   1992   14 Crossdykes, Kirkintilloch, Glasgow G66 3EU   0141-578 4357
[E-mail: write.to.me@ntlworld.com]

24 Kirkintilloch: St David's Memorial Park (H) (0141-776 4989)
Bryce Calder MA BD   1995   2001   2 Roman Road, Kirkintilloch, Glasgow G66 1EA   0141-776 1434
[E-mail: ministry100@aol.com]   07986 144834 (Mbl)

25 Kirkintilloch: St Mary's (0141-775 1166)
Mark E. Johnstone MA BD   1993   2001   St Mary's Manse, 60 Union Street, Kirkintilloch, Glasgow G66 1DH   0141-776 1252
[E-mail: markjohnstone@me.com]

26 Lenzie: Old (H)
Douglas W. Clark LTh   1993   2000   41 Kirkintilloch Road, Lenzie, Glasgow G66 4LB   0141-776 2184
[E-mail: douglaswclark@hotmail.com]

27 Lenzie: Union (H) (0141-776 1046)
Daniel J.M. Carmichael MA BD   1994   2003   1 Larch Avenue, Lenzie, Glasgow G66 4HX   0141-776 3831
[E-mail: minister@lupc.org]

28 Maxwell Mearns Castle (Tel/Fax: 0141-639 5169)
Scott R.McL. Kirkland BD MAR   1996   2011   122 Broomfield Avenue, Newton Mearns, Glasgow G77 5JR   0141-560 5603
[E-mail: scottkirkland@maxwellmearns.org.uk]

29 Mearns (H) (0141-639 6555)
Joseph A. Kavanagh BD DipPTh MTh MTh   1992   1998   11 Belford Grove, Newton Mearns, Glasgow G77 5FB   0141-384 2218
[E-mail: revjoe@hotmail.co.uk]

30 Milton of Campsie (H)
Julie H.C. Moody BA BD PGCE   2006   Dunkeld, 33 Birdston Road, Milton of Campsie, Glasgow G66 8BX   01360 310548
[E-mail: jhcwilson@msn.com]   07787 184800 (Mbl)

31 Netherlee (H) (0141-637 2503)
Thomas Nelson BSc BD   1992   2002   25 Ormonde Avenue, Netherlee, Glasgow G44 3QY   0141-585 7502 (Tel/Fax)
[E-mail: tomnelson@ntlworld.com]
David Maxwell   2014   248 Old Castle Road, Glasgow G44 5EZ   0141-569 6379
(Ordained Local Minister)   [E-mail: david.maxwell7@ntlworld.com]

32 **Newton Mearns (H) (0141-639 7373)**
Esther J. Ninian (Miss) MA BD — 1993   2009 — 28 Waterside Avenue, Newton Mearns, Glasgow   G77 6TJ
[E-mail: estherninian5194@btinternet.com] — 0141-616 2079

33 **Rutherglen: Old (H)**
Vacant — 31 Highburgh Drive, Rutherglen, Glasgow   G73 3RR — 0141-647 6178

34 **Rutherglen: Stonelaw (0141-647 5113)**
Alistair S. May LLB BD PhD — 2002 — 80 Blairbeth Road, Rutherglen, Glasgow   G73 4JA
[E-mail: alistair.may@ntlworld.com] — 0141-583 0157

35 **Rutherglen: West and Wardlawhill (0844 736 1470)**
Vacant — 12 Albert Drive, Rutherglen, Glasgow   G73 3RT — 0141-569 8547

36 **Stamperland (0141-637 4999) (H)**
Vacant — 109 Ormonde Avenue, Netherlee, Glasgow   G44 3SN — 0141-637 4976   (Tel/Fax)

37 **Stepps (H)**
Gordon MacRae BD MTh — 1985   2014 — 112 Jackson Drive, Crowwood Grange, Stepps, Glasgow   G33 6GF
[E-mail: ge.macrae@btopenworld.com] — 0141-779 5742

38 **Thornliebank (H)**
Vacant — 19 Arthurlie Drive, Giffnock, Glasgow   G46 6UR

39 **Torrance (R) (01360 620970)**
Nigel L. Barge BSc BD — 1991 — 1 Atholl Avenue, Torrance, Glasgow   G64 4JA
[E-mail: nigel.barge@sky.com] — 01360 622379

40 **Twechar** See Banton

41 **Williamwood (0141-638 2091)**
Vacant — 125 Greenwood Road, Clarkston, Glasgow   G76 7LL — 0141-571 7949

42 **Glasgow: Anderston Kelvingrove (0141-221 9408)**
Vacant — 16 Royal Terrace, Glasgow   G3 7NY — 0141-332 7704

43 Glasgow: Baillieston Mure Memorial (0141-773 1216) linked with Glasgow: Baillieston St Andrew's (0141-771 6629)
Malcolm Cuthbertson BA BD 1984 2010 28 Beech Avenue, Baillieston, Glasgow G69 6LF 07740 868181 (Mbl)
[E-mail: malcuth@aol.com]
Alex P. Stuart 2014 107 Baldorran Crescent, Cumbernauld, Glasgow G68 9EX 01236 727710
(Ordained Local Minister) [E-mail: alexpstuart@btopenworld.com]

44 Glasgow: Baillieston St Andrew's See Glasgow: Baillieston Mure Memorial

45 Glasgow: Balshagray Victoria Park
Campbell Mackinnon BSc BD 1982 2001 20 St Kilda Drive, Glasgow G14 9JN 0141-954 9780
[E-mail: campbellbvp@live.com]

46 Glasgow: Barlanark Greyfriars (0141-771 6477)
Vacant 4 Rhindmuir Grove, Glasgow G69 6NE 0141-771 1240

47 Glasgow: Blawarthill
G. Melvyn Wood MA BD 1982 2009 46 Earlbank Avenue, Glasgow G14 9HL 0141-579 6521
[E-mail: gmelvynwood@gmail.com]

48 Glasgow: Bridgeton St Francis in the East (H) (L) (0141-556 2830) (Church House: Tel: 0141-554 8045)
Howard R. Hudson MA BD 1982 1984 10 Albany Drive, Rutherglen, Glasgow G73 3QN 0141-587 8667
[E-mail: howard.hudson@ntlworld.com]
Margaret S. Beaton (Miss) DCS 64 Gardenside Grove, Carmyle, Glasgow G32 8EZ 0141-646 2297
(Deacon and Leader of Centre) [E-mail: margaret@churchhouse.plus.com] 07796 642382 (Mbl)

49 Glasgow: Broomhill (0141-334 2540) linked with Glasgow: Hyndland (H) (Website: www.hyndlandparishchurch.org)
George C. MacKay 1994 2014 27 St Kilda Drive, Glasgow G14 9LN 0141-959 3204
BD CertMin CertEd DipPC [E-mail: g.mackay3@btinternet.com]

50 Glasgow: Calton Parkhead (0141-554 3866)
Alison Davidge MA BD 1990 2008 98 Drumover Drive, Glasgow G31 5RP 07843 625059 (Mbl)
[E-mail: adavidge@sky.com]

51 Glasgow: Cardonald (0141-882 6264)
Calum MacLeod BA BD 1979 2007 133 Newtyle Road, Paisley PA1 3LB 0141-887 2726
[E-mail: pangur@sky.com]

52 Glasgow: Carmunnock (0141-644 0655)
G. Gray Fletcher BSc BD   1989   2001   The Manse, 161 Waterside Road, Carmunnock, Glasgow G76 9AJ   0141-644 1578 (Tel/Fax)
[E-mail: gray.fletcher@virgin.net]

53 Glasgow: Carmyle linked with Glasgow: Kenmuir Mount Vernon
Murdo Maclean BD CertMin   1997   1999   3 Meryon Road, Glasgow G32 9NW   0141-778 2625
[E-mail: murdo.maclean@ntlworld.com]

54 Glasgow: Carnwadric
Graeme K. Bell BA BD   1983   62 Loganswell Road, Thornliebank, Glasgow G46 8AX   0141-638 5884
[E-mail: graemekbell@googlemail.com]

Mary Gargrave (Mrs) DCS   90 Mount Annan Drive, Glasgow G44 4RZ   0141-561 4681
[E-mail: mary.gargrave@btinternet.com]   07896 866618 (Mbl)

55 Glasgow: Castlemilk (H) (0141-634 1480)
Sarah Brown (Ms)   2012   156 Old Castle Road, Glasgow G44 5TW   0141-637 5451
  MA BD ThM DipYW/Theol PDCCE   [E-mail: ministercastlemilk@gmail.com]   07532 457245 (Mbl)
Isobel Beck DCS   16 Patrick Avenue, Stevenston KA20 4AW   07919 193425 (Mbl)
[E-mail: deaconcastlemilk@aol.co.uk]

56 Glasgow: Cathcart Old (0141-637 4168)
Neil W. Galbraith BD CertMin   1987   1996   21 Courthill Avenue, Cathcart, Glasgow G44 5AA   0141-633 5248 (Tel/Fax)
[E-mail: revneilgalbraith@hotmail.com]

57 Glasgow: Cathcart Trinity (H) (0141-637 6658)
Vacant   82 Merrylee Road, Glasgow G43 2QZ   0141-633 3744
Wilma Pearson (Mrs) BD (Assoc)   2004   90 Newlands Road, Glasgow G43 2JR   0141-632 2491
[E-mail: wilma.pearson@ntlworld.com]

58 Glasgow: Cathedral (High or St Mungo's) (0141-552 6891)
Laurence A.B. Whitley MA BD PhD   1975   2007   41 Springfield Road, Bishopbriggs, Glasgow G64 1PL   0141-762 2719
[E-mail: labwhitley@btinternet.com]

Ada MacLeod MA BD PGCE (Assist)   2013   133 Newtyle Road, Paisley PA1 3LB   0141-887 2726
[E-mail: ada@uk7.net]

59 Glasgow: Clincarthill (H) (0141-632 4206)
Mike R. Gargrave BD   2008   2010   90 Mount Annan Drive, Glasgow G44 4RZ   0141-561 4681
[E-mail: mike.gargrave@btinternet.com]

No.	Congregation / Minister	Year	Year	Address / E-mail	Phone
60	**Glasgow: Colston Milton (0141-772 1922)** Christopher J. Rowe BA BD	2008		118 Birsay Road, Milton, Glasgow G22 7QP [E-mail: ministercolstonmilton@yahoo.co.uk]	0141-564 1138
61	**Glasgow: Colston Wellpark (H)** Vacant			16 Bishopsgate Gardens, Colston, Glasgow G21 1XS	0141-589 8866
62	**Glasgow: Cranhill (H) (0141-774 3344)** Muriel B. Pearson (Ms) MA BD PGCE	2004		31 Lethamhill Crescent, Glasgow G33 2SH [E-mail: murielpearson@btinternet.com]	0141-770 6873 07951 888860 (Mbl)
63	**Glasgow: Croftfoot (H) (0141-637 3913)** Robert M. Silver BA BD	1995	2011	4 Inchmurrin Gardens, High Burnside, Rutherglen, Glasgow G73 5RU [E-mail: rob.silver@talktalk.net]	0141-258 7268
64	**Glasgow: Dennistoun New (H) (0141-550 2825)** Ian M.S. McInnes BD DipMin	1995	2008	31 Pencaitland Drive, Glasgow G32 8RL [E-mail: ian.liz1@ntlworld.com]	0141-564 6498
65	**Glasgow: Drumchapel St Andrew's (0141-944 3758)** John S. Purves LLB BD	1983	1984	6 Firdon Crescent, Old Drumchapel, Glasgow G15 6QQ [E-mail: john.s.purves@talk21.com]	0141-944 4566
66	**Glasgow: Drumchapel St Mark's** Audrey Jamieson BD MTh	2004	2007	146 Garscadden Road, Glasgow G15 6PR [E-mail: audrey.jamieson2@btinternet.com]	0141-944 5440
67	**Glasgow: Easterhouse St George's and St Peter's (0141-771 8810)** Vacant			3 Barony Gardens, Baillieston, Glasgow G69 6TS	0141-573 8200
68	**Glasgow: Eastwood** Graham R.G. Cartlidge MA BD STM	1977	2010	54 Mansewood Road, Eastwood, Glasgow G43 1TL [E-mail: cartlidge262@btinternet.com]	0141-649 0463
69	**Glasgow: Gairbraid (H)** Donald Michael MacInnes BD	2002	2011	4 Blackhill Gardens, Summerston, Glasgow G23 5NE [E-mail: revdmmi@gmail.com]	0141-946 0604

70	**Glasgow: Gallowgate** Peter L.V. Davidge BD MTh	2003	2009	98 Drumover Drive, Glasgow G31 5RP [E-mail: rev_dav46@yahoo.co.uk]	07765 096599 (Mbl)
71	**Glasgow: Garthamlock and Craigend East** Vacant Marion Buchanan (Mrs) MA DCS			9 Craigievar Court, Glasgow G33 5DJ 16 Almond Drive, East Kilbride, Glasgow G74 2HX [E-mail: marion.buchanan@btinternet.com]	0141-774 6364 01355 228776 07999 889817 (Mbl)
72	**Glasgow: Gorbals** Ian F. Galloway BA BD	1976	1996	44 Riverside Road, Glasgow G43 2EF [E-mail: ianfgalloway@msn.com]	0141-649 5250
73	**Glasgow: Govan and Linthouse** Moyna McGlynn (Mrs) BD PhD	1999	2008	19 Dumbreck Road, Glasgow G41 5LJ [E-mail: moyna_mcglynn@hotmail.com]	0141-419 0308
	Andrew Thomson BA (Assist)			3 Laurel Wynd, Drumsagard Village, Cambuslang, Glasgow G72 7BH [E-mail: thethomsons@hotmail.co.uk]	0141-641 2936 07772 502774 (Mbl)
	John Paul Cathcart DCS	1976	2010	9 Glen More, East Kilbride, Glasgow G74 2AP [E-mail: paulcathcart@msn.com]	01355 243970 07708 396074 (Mbl)
74	**Glasgow: High Carntyne (0141-778 4186)** Joan Ross (Miss) BSc BD PhD	1999	2005	163 Lethamhill Road, Glasgow G33 2SQ [E-mail: joan@highcarntyne.plus.com]	0141-770 9247
	Patricia A. Carruth (Mrs) BD (Assoc)	1998	2014	38 Springhill Farm Road, Baillieston, Glasgow G69 6GW [E-mail: patrevanne@aol.com]	0141-771 3758
75	**Glasgow: Hillington Park (H)** John B. MacGregor BD	1999	2004	61 Ralston Avenue, Glasgow G52 3NB [E-mail: johnmacgregorof61@hotmail.co.uk]	0141-882 7000
76	**Glasgow: Hyndland** See Glasgow: Broomhill				
77	**Glasgow: Ibrox (H) (0141-427 0896)** Elisabeth G.B. Spence (Miss) BD DipEd	1995	2008	59 Langhaul Road, Glasgow G53 7SE [E-mail: revelisabeth@spenceweb.net]	0141-883 7744

78 **Glasgow: John Ross Memorial Church for Deaf People**
(Voice Text: 0141-420 1391; Fax: 0141-420 3778)
Richard C. Durno DSW CQSW   1989   1998   31 Springfield Road, Bishopbriggs,   (Voice/Text/Fax) 0141-772 1052
                                                              Glasgow G64 1PJ   (Voice/Text/Voicemail) (Mbl) 07748 607721
                                                              [E-mail: richard.durno@btinternet.com]

79 **Glasgow: Jordanhill (Tel: 0141-959 2496)**
Vacant   96 Southbrae Drive, Glasgow G13 1TZ   0141-959 1310

80 **Glasgow: Kelvinbridge (0141-339 1750)**
Gordon Kirkwood BSc BD PGCE MTh   1987   2013   Flat 2/2, 94 Hyndland Road, Glasgow G12 9PZ   0141-334 5352
                                                              [E-mail: gordonkirkwood@hotmail.co.uk]
Cathie H. McLaughlin (Mrs)   2014   8 Lamlash Place, Glasgow G33 3XH   0141-774 2483
(Ordained Local Minister)   [E-mail: chmclaughlin@talktalk.net]
          (New charge formed by the union of Glasgow: Kelvin Stevenson Memorial and Glasgow: Lansdowne)

81 **Glasgow: Kelvinside Hillhead (0141-334 2788)**
Vacant   39 Athole Gardens, Glasgow G12 9BQ   0141-339 2865
Roger Sturrock (Prof.) BD MD FCRP   2014   36 Thomson Drive, Bearsden, Glasgow G61 3PA   0141-942 7412
(Ordained Local Minister)   [E-mail: rogersturrock@mac.com]

82 **Glasgow: Kenmuir Mount Vernon** See Carmyle

83 **Glasgow: King's Park (H) (0141-636 8688)**
Sandra Boyd (Mrs) BEd BD   2007   1101 Aikenhead Road, Glasgow G44 5SL   0141-637 2803
                                                              [E-mail: sandraboyd.bofa@btopenworld.com]

84 **Glasgow: Kinning Park (0141-427 3063)**
Margaret H. Johnston BD   1988   2000   168 Arbroath Avenue, Cardonald, Glasgow G52 3HH   0141-810 3782
                                                              [E-mail: marniejohnston7@aol.com]

85 **Glasgow: Knightswood St Margaret's (H)**
Alexander M. Fraser BD DipMin   1985   2009   26 Airthrey Avenue, Glasgow G14 9LJ   0141-959 7075
                                                              [E-mail: sandyfraser2@hotmail.com]

86 **Glasgow: Langside (0141-632 7520)**
David N. McLachlan BD   1985   2004   36 Madison Avenue, Glasgow G44 5AQ   0141-637 0797
                                                              [E-mail: dmclachlan77@hotmail.com]

87	**Glasgow: Lochwood (H) (0141-771 2649)**		
	Vacant	42 Rhindmuir Road, Swinton, Glasgow G69 6AZ	0141-773 2756
88	**Glasgow: Maryhill (H) (0141-946 3512)**		
	Stuart C. Matthews BD MA	2006	251 Mingavie Road, Bearsden, Glasgow G61 3DQ	0141-942 0804
			[E-mail: stuart.maryhill@gmail.com]	
	James Hamilton DCS		6 Beckfield Gate, Glasgow G33 1SW	0141-558 3195
			[E-mail: j.hamilton111@btinternet.com]	07584 137314 (Mbl)
89	**Glasgow: Merrylea (0141-637 2009)**		
	David P. Hood BD CertMin DipIOB(Scot)	1997	4 Pilmuir Avenue, Glasgow G44 3HX	0141-637 6700
		2001	[E-mail: dphood3@ntlworld.com]	
90	**Glasgow: Mosspark (H) (0141-882 2240)**		
	Vacant	396 Kilmarnock Road, Glasgow G43 2DJ	0141-632 1247
91	**Glasgow: Newlands South (H) (0141-632 3055)**		
	John D. Whiteford MA BD	1989	24 Monreith Road, Glasgow G43 2NY	0141-632 2588
		1997	[E-mail: jwhiteford@hotmail.com]	
92	**Glasgow: Partick South (H)**		
	James Andrew McIntyre BD	2010	3 Branklyn Crescent, Glasgow G13 1GJ	0141-959 3732
			[E-mail: revpartisouth@hotmail.co.uk]	
93	**Glasgow: Partick Trinity (H)**		
	Stuart J. Smith BEng BD MTh	1994	99 Balshagray Avenue, Glasgow G11 7EQ	0141-576 7149
			[E-mail: ssmith99@ntlworld.com]	
94	**Glasgow: Penilee St Andrew (H) (0141-882 2691)**		
	Lyn Peden (Mrs) BD	2010	80 Tweedsmuir Road, Glasgow G52 2RX	0141-883 9873
			[E-mail: psa.minister@yahoo.co.uk]	
95	**Glasgow: Pollokshaws (0141-649 1879)**		
	Roy J.M. Henderson MA BD DipMin	1987	33 Mannering Road, Glasgow G41 3SW	0141-649 0458
		2013	[E-mail: royhenderson1@gmail.com]	

96 Glasgow: Pollokshields (H)
David R. Black MA BD   1986   1997   36 Glencairn Drive, Glasgow G41 4PW   0141-423 4000
[E-mail: davidrblack@btinternet.com]

97 Glasgow: Possilpark (0141-336 8028)
Linda E. Pollock (Miss) BD ThM ThM   2001   2014   108 Erradale Street, Lambhill, Glasgow G22 6PT   0141-336 6909
[E-mail: fantazomi@yahoo.co.uk]

98 Glasgow: Queen's Park Govanhill (0141-423 3654)
Vacant   17 Linndale Drive, Carmunnock Grange, Glasgow G45 0QE   0141-634 1097
(New charge formed by the union of Glasgow: Queen's Park and Glasgow: Govanhill Trinity)

99 Glasgow: Renfield St Stephen's (Tel: 0141-332 4293; Fax: 0141-332 8482)
Peter M. Gardner MA BD   1988   2002   101 Hill Street, Glasgow G3 6TY   0141-353 0349
[E-mail: peter@rsschurch.org.uk]
Iain A. MacLeod   2012   6 Hallydown Drive, Glasgow G13 1UF   07795 014889 (Mbl)
(Ordained Local Minister)   [E-mail: iainamacleod@googlemail.com]

100 Glasgow: Robroyston (New Charge Development) (0141-558 8414)
Jonathan A. Keefe BSc BD   2009   7 Beckfield Drive, Glasgow G33 1SR   0141-558 2952
[E-mail: jonathanakeefe@aol.com]

101 Glasgow: Ruchazie (0141-774 2759)
Vacant   18 Borthwick Street, Glasgow G33 3UU   0141-774 6860

102 Glasgow: Ruchill Kelvinside (0141-946 0466)
Mark Lowey BD DipTh   2012   2013   9 Kirklee Road, Glasgow G12 0RQ   0141-357 3249
[E-mail: marklowey@ymail.com]

103 Glasgow: St Andrew's East (0141-554 1485)
Barbara D. Quigley (Mrs) MTheol ThM DPS   1979   2011   43 Broompark Drive, Glasgow G31 2JB   0141-237 7982
[E-mail: bdquigley@aol.com]

104 Glasgow: St Christopher's Priesthill and Nitshill (0141-881 6541)
Douglas M. Nicol BD CA   1987   1996   36 Springkell Drive, Glasgow G41 4EZ   0141-427 7877
[E-mail: dougiennicol@aol.com]

105 Glasgow: St Columba (GE) (0141-221 3305)
Vacant
1 Reelick Avenue, Peterson Park, Glasgow G13 4NF   0141-952 0948

106 Glasgow: St David's Knightswood (0141-954 1081)
Graham M. Thain LLB BD   1988   1999
60 Southbrae Drive, Glasgow G13 1QD   0141-959 2904
[E-mail: graham_thain@btopenworld.com]

107 Glasgow: St Enoch's Hogganfield (H) (Tel: 0141-770 5694; Fax: 0870 284 0084) (E-mail: church@st-enoch.org.uk)
(Website: www.stenochshogganfield.org.uk)
Graham K. Blount LLB BD PhD   1976   2010
43 Smithycroft Road, Glasgow G33 2RH   0141-770 7593
[E-mail: graham.blount@yahoo.co.uk]

108 Glasgow: St George's Tron (0141-221 2141)
Alastair S. Duncan MA BD   1989   2013
(Transition Minister)
27 Kelvindale Court, Glasgow G12 0IG   07968 852083   (Mbl)
[E-mail: stgeorgestroncofs@gmail.com]

109 Glasgow: St James' (Pollok) (0141-882 4984)
John W. Mann BSc MDiv DMin   2004
30 Ralston Avenue, Glasgow G52 3NA   0141-883 7405
[E-mail: drjohnmann@hotmail.com]

110 Glasgow: St John's Renfield (0141-339 7021) (Website: www.stjohns-renfield.org.uk)
Fiona L. Lillie (Mrs) BA BD MLitt   1995   2009
26 Leicester Avenue, Glasgow G12 0LU   0141-339 4637
[E-mail: fionalillie@btinternet.com]

111 Glasgow: St Margaret's Tollcross Park
Vacant
31 Kenmuir Avenue, Sandyhills, Glasgow G32 9LE   0141-778 5060

112 Glasgow: St Nicholas' Cardonald
Eleanor J. McMahon BEd BD   1994   2013
(Interim Minister)
81 Moorpark Square, Renfrew PA4 8DB   0141-886 1351
[E-mail: e.mcmahon212@btinternet.com]

113 Glasgow: St Paul's (0141-770 8559)
Vacant

114 Glasgow: St Rollox (0141-558 1809)
Vacant
42 Melville Gardens, Bishopbriggs, Glasgow G64 3DE   0141-562 6296

115 Glasgow: Sandyford Henderson Memorial (H) (L)
Jonathan de Groot BD MTh CPS   2007   2014
66 Woodend Drive, Glasgow G13 1TG   0141-954 9013

116 Glasgow: Sandyhills (0141-778 3415)
Graham T. Atkinson MA BD MTh   2006
60 Wester Road, Glasgow G32 9JJ   0141-778 2174
[E-mail: gtatkinson75@yahoo.co.uk]

117 Glasgow: Scotstoun (R)
Richard Cameron BD DipMin   2000
15 Northland Drive, Glasgow G14 9BE   0141-959 4637
[E-mail: rev.rickycam@live.co.uk]

118 Glasgow: Shawlands (0141-649 1773) linked with Glasgow: South Shawlands (R) (0141-649 4656)
Valerie J. Duff (Miss) DMin   1993   2014
29 St Ronan's Drive, Glasgow G41 3SQ   0141-258 6782
[E-mail: valduff@tiscali.co.uk]

119 Glasgow: Sherbrooke St Gilbert's (H) (0141-427 1968)
Thomas L. Pollock   1982   2003
BA BD MTh FSAScot JP
114 Springkell Avenue, Glasgow G41 4EW   0141-427 2094
[E-mail: tompollock06@aol.com]

120 Glasgow: Shettleston New (0141-778 0857)
Ronald A.S. Craig BAcc BD   1983   2007
211 Sandyhills Road, Glasgow G32 9NB   0141-778 1286
[E-mail: rascraig@ntlworld.com]

121 Glasgow: Shettleston Old (R) (H) (0141-778 2484)
Vacant
57 Mansionhouse Road, Mount Vernon, Glasgow G32 0RP   0141-778 8904

122 Glasgow: South Carntyne (H) (0141-778 1343)
Vacant
47 Broompark Drive, Glasgow G31 2JB   0141-554 3275

123 Glasgow: South Shawlands See Glasgow: Shawlands

124 Glasgow: Springburn (H) (0141-557 2345)
Brian M. Casey MA BD   2014
22 Warden Drive, Bishopbriggs, Glasgow G64 1GF   0141-557 3668
[E-mail: brian.casey925@btinternet.com]

125 Glasgow: Temple Anniesland (0141-959 1814)
Fiona Gardner (Mrs) BD MA MLitt   1997   2011   76 Victoria Park Drive North, Glasgow G14 9PJ   0141-959 5647
[E-mail: fionandcolin@hotmail.com]

126 Glasgow: Toryglen (H)
Vacant

127 Glasgow: Trinity Possil and Henry Drummond
Richard G. Buckley BD MTh   1990   1995   50 Highfield Drive, Glasgow G12 0HL   0141-339 2870
[E-mail: richardbuckleyis@hotmail.com]

128 Glasgow: Tron St Mary's (0141-558 1011)
Vacant   6 Broomfield Drive, Glasgow G21 3HE   0141-558 1011

129 Glasgow: Victoria Tollcross
Monica Michelin Salomon BD   1999   2007   228 Hamilton Road, Glasgow G32 9QU   0141-778 2413
[E-mail: monica@michelin-salomon.freeserve.co.uk]

130 Glasgow: Wallacewell (New Charge Development)
Daniel Frank BA MDiv DMin   1984   2011   8 Streamfield Gate, Glasgow G33 1SJ   0141-585 0283
[E-mail: daniellouis106@gmail.com]

131 Glasgow: Wellington (H) (0141-339 0454)
David I. Sinclair BSc BD PhD DipSW   1990   2008   31 Hughenden Gardens, Glasgow G12 9YH   0141-334 2343
[E-mail: davidsinclair@btinternet.com]
Roger Sturrock (Prof.) BD MD FCRP   2014   36 Thomson Drive, Bearsden, Glasgow G61 3PA   0141-942 7412
(Ordained Local Minister)   [E-mail: rogersturrock@mac.com]

132 Glasgow: Whiteinch (Website: www.whiteinchcofs.co.uk)
Alan McWilliam BD MTh   1993   2000   65 Victoria Park Drive South, Glasgow G14 9NX   0141-576 9020
[E-mail: alan@whiteinchurch.org]

133 Glasgow: Yoker (R)
Karen E. Hendry BSc BD   2005   15 Coldingham Avenue, Glasgow G14 0PX   0141-952 3620
[E-mail: karen@hendry-k.fsnet.co.uk]

Name	Charge			Address	Tel
Alexander, Eric J. MA BD	(Glasgow: St George's Tron)	1958	1997	77 Norwood Park, Bearsden, Glasgow G61 2RZ	0141-942 4404
Allen, Martin A.W. MA BD ThM	(Chryston)	1977	2007	Lealenge, 85 High Barrwood Road, Kilsyth, Glasgow G65 0EE	01236 826616
Allison, May M. (Mrs) BD	(Glasgow: Househillwood St Christopher's)	1988	2012	12 Levendale Court, Crookston, Glasgow G53 7SJ [E-mail: revmayallison@hotmail.com]	0141-810 5953
Alston, William G.	(Glasgow: North Kelvinside)	1961	2009	Flat 0/2, 5 Knightswood Court, Glasgow G13 2XN [E-mail: williamalston@hotmail.com]	0141-959 3113
Barr, Alexander C. MA BD	(Glasgow: St Nicholas' Cardonald)	1950	1992	25 Fisher Drive, Phoenix Park, Paisley PA1 2TP	0141-848 5941
Bayes, Muriel C. (Mrs) DCS	(Deacon)			Flat 6, Carlton Court, 10 Fenwick Road, Glasgow G46 6AN	0141-633 0865
Bell, John L. MA BD FRSCM DUniv	(Iona Community)	1978	1988	Flat 2/1, 31 Lansdowne Crescent, Glasgow G20 6NH	0141-334 0688
Bell, Sandra (Mrs) DCS	(Hospital Chaplain)			62 Loganswell Road, Glasgow G42 8AX [E-mail: slbellmrs@yahoo.co.uk]	0141-638 5884
Birch, James PgDip FRSA FIOC	(Auxiliary Minister)	2001	2007	1 Kirkhill Grove, Cambuslang, Glasgow G72 8EH	0141-583 1722
Black, William B. MA BD	(Stornoway: High)	1972	2011	33 Tankerland Road, Glasgow G44 4EN [E-mail: revwillieblack@gmail.com]	0141-637 4717
Blount, A. Sheila (Mrs) BD BA	(Cupar: St John's and Dairsie United)	1978	2010	43 Smithycroft Road, Glasgow G33 2RH [E-mail: asblount@orange.net]	0141-770 7593
Brain, Isobel J. (Mrs) MA	(Ballantrae)	1987	1997	10/11 Maxwell Street, Edinburgh EH10 5GZ	0131-466 6115
Brice, Dennis G. BSc BD	(Taiwan)	1981		8 Parkwood Close, Broxbourne, Herts EN10 7PF [E-mail: dbrice1@comcast.net]	
Bryden, William A. BD	(Yoker: Old with St Matthew's)	1977	1984	145 Bearsden Road, Glasgow G13 1BS	0141-959 5213
Bull, Alister W. BD DipMin MTh PhD	Mission and Discipleship Council	1994	2001	121 George Street, Edinburgh EH2 4YN [E-mail: abull@cofscotland.org.uk]	0131-225 5722
Campbell, A. Iain MA DipEd	(Busby)	1961	1997	430 Clarkston Road, Glasgow G44 3QF [E-mail: bellmac@sagainternet.co.uk]	0141-637 7460
Cunningham, Alexander MA BD	(Presbytery Clerk)	1961	2002	18 Lady Jane Gate, Bothwell, Glasgow G71 8BW	01698 811051
Cunningham, James S.A. MA BD BLit PhD	(Glasgow: Barlanark Greyfriars)	1992	2000	'Kirkland', 5 Inveresk Place, Coatbridge ML5 2DA	01236 421541
Drummond, John W. MA BD	(Rutherglen: West and Wardlawhill)	1971	2011	25 Kingsburn Drive, Rutherglen, Glasgow G73 2AN	0141-571 6002
Duff, T. Malcolm F. MA BD	(Glasgow: Queen's Park)	1985	2009	54 Hawkhead Road, Paisley PA1 3NB	0141-570 0614 (Mbl) 07846 926584
Ferguson, James B. LTh	(Lenzie: Union)	1972	2002	3 Bridgeway Place, Kirkintilloch, Glasgow G66 3HW	0141-588 5868
Ferguson, William B. BA BD	(Glasgow: Broomhill)	1971	2012	20 Swift Crescent, Knightswood Gate, Glasgow G13 4QL [E-mail: revferg@btinternet.com]	0141-954 6655
Finlay, William P. MA BD	(Glasgow: Townhead Blochairn)	1969	2000	High Corrie, Brodick, Isle of Arran KA27 8JB	01770 810689
Fleming, Alexander F. MA BD	(Strathblane)	1966	1995	11 Bankwood Drive, Kilsyth, Glasgow G65 0GZ	01236 821461
Forrest, Martin R. BA MA BD	Prison Chaplain	1988	2012	4/1, 7 Blochairn Place, Glasgow G21 2EB [E-mail: martinrforrest@gmail.com]	0141-552 1132
Forsyth, Sandy LLB BD DipLP PhD	(Associate: Kirkintilloch: St David's Memorial Park)	2009	2013	48 Kerr Street, Kirkintilloch, Glasgow G66 1JZ [E-mail: sandyforsyth67@hotmail.co.uk]	0141-777 8194 (Mbl) 07739 639037
Galloway, Kathy (Mrs) BD DD	(Leader: Iona Community)	1977	2002	20 Hamilton Park Avenue, Glasgow G12 8UU	0141-357 4079
Gay, Douglas C. MA BD PhD	University of Glasgow	1998	2005	1F, 16 Royal Terrace, Glasgow G3 7NY [E-mail: douggay@mac.com]	0141-332 4040 (Mbl) 07971 321452

Name			Position	Address / E-mail	Tel.
Getliffe, Dot (Mrs) DCS BA BD DipEd	2006	2013	Families Worker, West Mearns	3 Woodview Terrace, Hamilton ML3 9DP [E-mail: dgetliffe@aol.co.uk]	01698 423504 07766 910171 (Mbl)
Gibson, H. Marshall MA BD	1957	1996	(Glasgow: St Thomas' Gallowgate)	39 Burntbroom Drive, Glasgow G69 7XG	0141-771 0749
Grant, David I.M. MA BD	1969	2003	(Dalry: Trinity)	8 Mossbank Drive, Glasgow G33 1LS	0141-770 7186
Gray, Christine M. (Mrs)	1986	2010	(Deacon)	11 Woodside Avenue, Thornliebank, Glasgow G46 7HR	0141-571 1008
Green, Alex H. MA BD			(Strathblane)	44 Laburnum Drive, Milton of Campsie, Glasgow G66 8HY [E-mail: lesvert@btinternet.com]	01360 313001
Gregson, Elizabeth M. (Mrs) BD	1996	2001	(Glasgow: Drumchapel St Andrew's)	17 Westfields, Bishopbriggs, Glasgow G64 3PL	0141-563 1918
Haley, Derek BD DPS	1960	1999	(Chaplain: Gartnavel Royal)	9 Kinnaird Crescent, Bearsden, Glasgow G61 2BN	0141-942 9281
Harvey, W. John BA BD DD	1965	2002	(Edinburgh: Corstorphine Craigsbank)	501 Shields Road, Glasgow G41 2RF	0141-429 3774
Hazlett, W. Ian P. (Prof.-Emer.) BA BD Dr theol DLitt DD		2009	University of Glasgow	587 Shields Road, Glasgow G41 2RW [E-mail: ian.hazlett@glasgow.ac.uk]	0141-423 7461 0141-330 5155 (Work)
Hewitt, William C. BD DipPS	1977	2012	Presbytery Clerk	60 Woodlands Grove, Kilmarnock KA3 1TZ [E-mail: billhewitt1@btinternet.com]	01563 533312
Hope, Evelyn P. (Miss) BA BD	1990	1998	(Wishaw: Thornlie)	Flat 0/1, 48 Moss Side Road, Glasgow G41 3UA	0141-649 1522
Houston, Thomas C. BA	1975	2004	(Glasgow: Priesthill and Nitshill)	63 Broomhouse Crescent, Uddingston, Glasgow G71 7RE	0141-771 0577
Hughes, Helen (Miss) DCS			(Deacon)	2/2, 43 Burnbank Terrace, Glasgow G20 6UQ [E-mail: helhug35@gmail.com]	0141-333 9459 07752 604817 (Mbl)
Hunter, Alastair G. MSc BD	1976	1980	(University of Glasgow)	487 Shields Road, Glasgow G41 2RG	0141-429 1687
Johnston, Robert W.M. MA BD STM	1964	1999	(Glasgow: Temple Anniesland)	13 Kilmardinny Crescent, Bearsden, Glasgow G61 3NP	0141-931 5862
Johnstone, H. Martin J. MA BD MTh PhD	1989	2000	Priority Areas Secretary	3/1, 952 Pollokshaws Road, Glasgow G41 2ET [E-mail: mjohnstone@cofscotland.org.uk]	0141-636 5819
Keddie, David A. MA BD	1966	2005	(Glasgow: Linthouse St Kenneth's)	21 Ilay Road, Bearsden, Glasgow G61 1QG [E-mail: revkeddie@gmail.com]	0141-942 5173
Lang, I. Pat (Miss) BSc	1996	2003	(Dunoon: The High Kirk)	37 Crawford Drive, Glasgow G15 6TW	0141-944 2240
Levison, Chris L. MA BD	1972	1998	(Health Care Chaplaincy Training and Development Officer)	Gardenfield, Nine Mile Burn, Penicuik EH26 9LT	
Lloyd, John M. BD CertMin	1984	2009	(Glasgow: Croftfoot)	17 Acacia Way, Cambuslang, Glasgow G72 7ZY	07879 812816 (Mbl)
Love, Joanna (Ms) BSc DCS	1992	2009	Iona Community: Wild Goose Resource Group	92 Everard Drive, Glasgow G21 1XQ [E-mail: jo@iona.org.uk]	0141-772 0149 0141-332 6343 (Office)
Lunan, David W. MA BD DUniv DLitt DD	1970	2002	(Presbytery Clerk)	30 Mill Road, Banton, Glasgow G65 0RD	01236 824110
MacBain, Ian W. BD	1971	1993	(Coatbridge: Coatdyke)	24 Thornyburn Drive, Baillieston, Glasgow G69 7ER	0141-771 7030
MacDonald, Anne (Miss) BA DCS			Healthcare Chaplain: Leverndale Hospital	c/o Leverndale Hospital, Glasgow G53 7TU [E-mail: anne.macdonald2@ggc.scot.nhs.uk]	0141-211 6695 07976 786174 (Mbl)
MacDonald, Kenneth MA BA	2001	2006	(Auxiliary Minister)	5 Henderland Road, Bearsden, Glasgow G61 1AH	0141-943 1103
McDougall, Hilary N. (Mrs) MA PGCE BD (Assoc)	2002	2013	Congregational Facilitator: Presbytery of Glasgow	6 Inchmurrin Gardens, High Burnside, Glasgow G73 5RU [E-mail: hilary@presbyteryofglasgow.org.uk]	0141-384 4428 07539 321832 (Mbl)
MacFadyen, Anne M. (Mrs) BSc BD FSAScot		1995	(Auxiliary Minister)	295 Mearns Road, Glasgow G77 5LT	0141-639 3605
MacKay, Alan H. BD	1974	2010	(Glasgow: Mosspark)	Flat 1/1, 18 Newburgh Street, Glasgow G43 2XR [E-mail: alanhmackay@aol.com]	0141-632 0527
MacKinnon, Charles M. BD	1989	2009	(Kilsyth: Anderson)	36 Hilton Terrace, Bishopbriggs, Glasgow G64 3HB [E-mail: cm.ccmackinnon@tiscali.co.uk]	0141-772 3811

Name			Charge	Address	Tel.
McLachlan, Eric BD MTh	1978	2005	(Glasgow: Cardonald)	16 Kinpurnie Road, Paisley PA1 3HH [E-mail: eric.janis@btinternet.com]	0141-810 5789
McLachlan, Fergus C. BD	1982	2009	(Hospital Chaplain)	46 Queen Square, Glasgow G41 2AZ	0141-423 3830
McLachlan, T. Alastair BSc	1972	2009	(Craignish with Kilbrandon and Kilchattan with Kilninver and Kilmelford)	9 Alder Road, Milton of Campsie, Glasgow G66 8HH	01360 319861
McLaren, D. Muir MA BD MTh PhD	1971	2001	(Glasgow: Mosspark)	House 44, 145 Shawhill Road, Glasgow G43 1SX [E-mail: talastair@btinternet.com]	(Mbl) 07931 155779
McLay, Alastair D. BSc BD	1989	2004	(Glasgow: Shawlands)	183 King's Park Avenue, Glasgow G44 4HZ [E-mail: muir44@yahoo.co.uk]	0141-569 5503
Macleod, Donald BD LRAM DRSAM	1987	2008	(Blairgowrie)	9 Millersneuk Avenue, Lenzie G66 5HJ [E-mail: donmac2@sky.com]	0141-776 6235
MacLeod-Mair, Alisdair T. MEd DipTheol	2001	2012	(Glasgow: Baillieston St Andrew's)	2/2, 44 Leven Street, Pollokshields, Glasgow G41 2JE [E-mail: revalisdair@hotmail.com]	0141-423 9600
MacMahon, Janet P.H. (Mrs) MSc BD	1992	2010	(Kilmaronock Gartocharn)	14 Hillfoot Drive, Bearsden, Glasgow G61 3QQ [E-mail: janetmacmahon@yahoo.co.uk]	0141-942 8611
Macnaughton, J.A. MA BD	1949	1989	(Glasgow: Hyndland)	Lilyburn Care Home, 100 Birdston Road, Milton of Campsie, Glasgow G66 8BY	(Mbl) 07811 621671
MacPherson, James B. DCS	1984	2001	(Deacon)	0/1, 104 Cartside Street, Glasgow G42 9TQ	0141-616 6468
MacQuarrie, Stuart JP BD BSc MBA	1988		Chaplain: Glasgow University	The Chaplaincy Centre, University of Glasgow, Glasgow G12 8QQ	0141-330 5419
MacQuien, Duncan DCS			(Deacon)	35 Criffel Road, Mount Vernon, Glasgow G32 9JE	0141-575 1137
Martindale, John P.F. BD	1994	2005	(Glasgow: Sandyhills)	Flat 3/2, 25 Albert Avenue, Glasgow G42 8RB	0141-433 4367
Miller, John D. BA BD DD	1971	2007	(Glasgow: Castlemilk East)	98 Kirkcaldy Road, Glasgow G41 4LD [E-mail: rev.john.miller@zol.co.zw]	0141-423 0221
Moffat, Thomas BSc BD	1976	2008	(Culross and Torryburn)	Flat 8/1, 8 Cranston Street, Glasgow G3 8GG [E-mail: tom@gallus.org.uk]	0141-248 1886
Moore, William B.	1968	2002	(Prison Chaplain: Low Moss)	10 South Dumbreck Road, Kilsyth, Glasgow G65 9LX	01236 821918
Morrice, Alastair M. MA BD	1991	2013	(Rutherglen: Stonelaw)	5 Brechin Road, Kirriemuir DD8 4BX	
Morrison, Iain BD			(Glasgow: Cathcart Trinity)	11 Ralston Path, Glasgow G52 3LW [E-mail: imorrison144@gmail.com]	(Mbl) 07812 435012
Muir, Fred C. MA BD ThM ARCM	1961	1997	(Stepps)	20 Alexandra Avenue, Stepps, Glasgow G33 6BP	0141-779 2504
Murray, George M. LTh	1995	2011	(Glasgow: St Margaret's Tollcross Park)	6 Mayfield, Lesmahagow ML11 0FH [E-mail: george.murray7@gmail.com]	
Philip, George M. MA	1953	1996	(Glasgow: Sandyford Henderson Memorial)	44 Beech Avenue, Bearsden, Glasgow G61 3EX	0141-942 1327
Raeburn, Alan C. MA BD	1971	2010	(Glasgow: Battlefield East)	3 Orchard Gardens, Strathaven ML10 6UN [E-mail: acraeburn@hotmail.com]	(Mbl) 07709 552161
Ramsay, W.G.	1967	1999	(Glasgow: Springburn)	53 Kelvinvale, Kirkintilloch, Glasgow G66 1RD [E-mail: billram@btopenworld.com]	0141-776 2915
Robertson, Archibald MA BD	1957	1999	(Glasgow: Eastwood)	19 Canberra Court, Braidpark Drive, Glasgow G46 6NS	0141-637 7572
Robertson, Blair MA BD ThM	1990	1998	Chaplain: Southern General Hospital	c/o Chaplain's Office, Southern General Hospital, 1345 Govan Road, Glasgow G51 4TF	0141-201 2357
Ross, Donald M. MA	1953	1994	(Industrial Mission Organiser)	14 Cartsbridge Road, Busby, Glasgow G76 8DH	0141-644 2220
Ross, James MA BD	1968	1998	(Kilsyth: Anderson)	53 Turnberry Gardens, Westwood, Cumbernauld, Glasgow G68 0AY	01236 730501

Name			Position / Charge	Address	Telephone
Saunders, Keith BD	1983	1999	Hospital Chaplain	Western Infirmary, Dumbarton Road, Glasgow G11 6NT	0141-211 2000
Shackleton, William	1960	1996	(Greenock: Wellpark West)	3 Tynwald Avenue, Burnside, Glasgow G73 4RN	0141-569 9407
Shanks, Norman J. MA BD DD	1983	2007	(Glasgow: Govan Old)	1 Marchmont Terrace, Glasgow G12 9LT [E-mail: rufuski@btinternet.com]	0141-339 4421
Simpson, Neil A. BA BD PhD	1992	2001	(Glasgow: Yoker Old with Yoker St Matthew's)	c/o Glasgow Presbytery Office	
Smeed, Alex W. MA BD	2008	2013	(Glasgow: Whiteinch: Associate)	3/1, 24 Thornwood Road, Glasgow G11 7RB [E-mail: alexsmeed@yahoo.co.uk]	0141-337 3878 (Mbl) 07709 756495
Smith, G. Stewart MA BD STM	1966	2006	(Glasgow: King's Park)	33 Brent Road, Stewartfield, East Kilbride, Glasgow G74 4RA [E-mail: stewartandmary@googlemail.com]	(Tel/Fax) 01355 226718
Smith, James S.A.	1956	1991	(Drongan: The Schaw Kirk)	146 Aros Drive, Glasgow G52 1TJ	0141-883 9666
Spencer, John MA BD	1962	2001	(Dumfries: Lincluden with Holywood)	10 Kinkell Gardens, Kirkintilloch, Glasgow G66 2HJ	0141-777 8935
Spiers, John M. LTh MTh	1972	2004	(Giffnock: Orchardhill)	58 Woodlands Road, Thornliebank, Glasgow G46 7JQ	(Tel/Fax) 0141-638 0632
Stewart, Diane E. BD	1988	2006	(Milton of Campsie)	4 Miller Gardens, Bishopbriggs, Glasgow G64 1FG [E-mail: destewart@givemail.co.uk]	0141-762 1358
Stewart, Norma D. (Miss) MA MEd BD MTh	1977	2000	(Glasgow: Strathbungo Queen's Park)	127 Nether Auldhouse Road, Glasgow G43 2YS	0141-637 6956
Sutherland, David A.	2001		Auxiliary Minister	3/1, 145 Broomhill Drive, Glasgow G11 7ND [E-mail: dave.a.sutherland@gmail.com]	0141-357 2058
Sutherland, Denis I.	1963	1995	(Glasgow: Hutchesontown)	56 Lime Crescent, Cumbernauld, Glasgow G67 3PQ	01236 731723
Sutherland, Elizabeth W. (Miss) BD	1972	1996	(Glasgow: Balornock North with Barmulloch)	20 Kirkland Avenue, Blanefield, Glasgow G63 9BZ	01360 770154
Turner, Angus BD	1976	1998	(Industrial Chaplain)	46 Keir Street, Pollokshields, Glasgow G41 2LA [E-mail: ewsutherland@aol.com]	0141-424 0493
Tuton, Robert M. MA	1957	1995	(Glasgow: Shettleston Old)	6 Holmwood Gardens, Uddingston, Glasgow G71 7BH	01698 321108
Walker, Linda	2008	2013	Auxiliary Minister	18 Valeview Terrace, Glasgow G42 9LA [E-mail: walkerlinda@hotmail.com]	0141-649 1340
Walton, Ainslie MA MEd	1954	1995	(University of Aberdeen)	501 Shields Road, Glasgow G41 2RF [E-mail: revainslie@aol.com]	0141-420 3327
White, C. Peter BVMS BD MRCVS	1974	2011	(Glasgow: Sandyford Henderson Memorial)	2 Hawthorn Place, Torrance, Glasgow G64 4EA [E-mail: revcpw@gmail.com]	01360 622680
Whyte, James BD	1981	2011	(Fairlie)	32 Torburn Avenue, Giffnock, Glasgow G46 7RB [E-mail: jameswhyte89@btinternet.com]	
Wilson, John BD	1985	2010	(Glasgow: Temple Anniesland)	4 Carron Crescent, Bearsden, Glasgow G61 1HJ [E-mail: revjwilson@btinternet.com]	0141-931 5609
Younger, Adah (Mrs) BD	1978	2004	(Glasgow: Dennistoun Central)	Flat 0/1, 101 Greenhead Street, Glasgow G40 1HR	0141-550 0878

GLASGOW ADDRESSES

Banton	Kelvinhead Road, Banton
Bishopbriggs	
Kenmure	Viewfield Road, Bishopbriggs
Springfield	The Leys, off Springfield Road
Cambridge	Mearns Road, Newton Mearns
Broom	Church Avenue, Burnside
Burnside Blairbeth	Kirkriggs Avenue, Blairbeth
Busby	Church Road, Busby
Cadder	Cadder Road, Bishopbriggs
Cambuslang	
Flemington Hallside	Hutchinson Place
Parish	Arnott Way
Campsie	Main Street, Lennoxtown
Chryston	Main Street, Chryston
Eaglesham	Montgomery Street, Eaglesham
Fernhill and Cathkin	Neilvaig Drive
Gartcosh	113 Lochend Road, Gartcosh
Giffnock	
Orchardhill	Church Road
South	Eastwood Toll
The Park	Ravenscliffe Drive
Glenboig	Main Street, Glenboig
Greenbank	Eaglesham Road, Clarkston
Kilsyth	
Anderson	Kingston Road, Kilsyth
Burns and Old	Church Street, Kilsyth
Kirkintilloch	
Hillhead	Newdyke Road, Kirkintilloch
St Columba's	Waterside Road nr Auld Aisle Road
St David's Mem Pk	Alexandra Street
St Mary's	Cowgate
Lenzie	
Old	Kirkintilloch Road x Garngaber Ave
Union	65 Kirkintilloch Road
Maxwell	
Mearns Castle	Waterfoot Road
Mearns	Mearns Road, Newton Mearns
Milton of Campsie	Antermony Road, Milton of Campsie

Netherlee	Ormonde Drive x Ormonde Avenue
Newton Mearns	Ayr Road, Newton Mearns
Rutherglen	
Old	Main Street at Queen Street
Stonelaw	Stonelaw Road x Dryburgh Avenue
West and Wardlawhill	3 Western Avenue
Stamperland	Stamperland Gardens, Clarkston
Stepps	Whitehill Avenue
Thornliebank	61 Spiersbridge Road
Torrance	School Road, Torrance
Twechar	Main Street, Twechar
Williamwood	4 Vardar Avenue, Clarkston

Glasgow

Anderston Kelvingrove	759 Argyle St x Elderslie St
Baillieston	
Mure Memorial	Maxwell Drive, Garrowhill
St Andrew's	Bredisholm Road
Balshagray Victoria Pk	218–230 Broomhill Drive
Barlanark Greyfriars	Edinburgh Rd x Halfhill Rd (365)
Blawarthill	Millbrix Avenue
Bridgeton St Francis in the East	26 Queen Mary Street
Broomhill	64–66 Randolph Rd (x Marlborough Ave)
Calton Parkhead	122 Helenvale Street
Cardonald	2155 Paisley Road West
Carmunnock	Kirk Road, Carmunnock
Carmyle	155 Carmyle Avenue
Carnwadric	556 Boydstone Road, Thornliebank
Castlemilk	Carmunnock Road
Cathcart	
Old	119 Carmunnock Road
Trinity	90 Clarkston Road
Cathedral	Cathedral Square, 2 Castle Street
Clincarthill	1216 Cathcart Road
Colston Milton	Egilsay Crescent
Colston Wellpark	1378 Springburn Road
Cranhill	109 Bellrock St (at Bellrock Cr)
Croftfoot	Croftpark Ave x Crofthill Road

Dennistoun New	9 Armadale Street
Drumchapel	
St Andrew's	153 Garscadden Road
St Mark's	281 Kinfauns Drive
Easterhouse St George's and St Peter's	Boyndie Street
Eastwood	Mansewood Road
Gairbraid	1517 Maryhill Road
Gallowgate	David Street
Garthamlock and Craigend East	46 Porchester Street
Gorbals	1 Errol Gardens
Govan and Linthouse	Govan Cross
High Carntyne	358 Carntynehall Road
Hillington Park	24 Berryknowes Road
Hyndland	79 Hyndland Rd, opp Novar Dr
Ibrox	Carillon Road x Clifford Street
John Ross Memorial	100 Norfolk Street
Jordanhill	28 Woodend Drive (x Munro Road)
Kelvinbridge	Belmont Street at Belmont Bridge
Kelvinside Hillhead	Observatory Road
Kenmuir Mount Vernon	2405 London Road, Mount Vernon
King's Park	242 Castlemilk Road
Kinning Park	Eaglesham Place
Knightswood	
St Margaret's	2000 Great Western Road
Langside	167–169 Ledard Road (x Lochleven Road)
Lochwood	2A Liff Place, Easterhouse
Maryhill	1990 Maryhill Road
Merrylea	78 Merrylee Road
Mosspark	167 Ashkirk Drive
Newlands South	Riverside Road x Langside Drive
Partick	
South	259 Dumbarton Road
Trinity	20 Lawrence Street
Penilee St Andrew's	Bowfield Cres x Bowfield Avenue
Pollokshaws	223 Shawbridge Street

Pollokshields	Albert Drive x Shields Road
Possilpark	124 Saracen Street
Queen's Park Govanhill	170 Queen's Drive
Renfield St Stephen's	260 Bath Street
Robroyston	34 Saughs Road
Ruchazie	4 Elibank Street (x Milncroft Road)
Ruchill Kelvinside	Shakespeare Street nr Maryhill Rd and 10 Kelbourne Street (two buildings)
St Andrew's East	681 Alexandra Parade
St Christopher's Priesthill and Nitshill	
Priesthill building	100 Priesthill Rd (x Muirshiel Cr)
Nitshill building	36 Dove Street
St Christopher's	Meikle Road
St Columba	300 St Vincent Street
St David's Knightswood	66 Boreland Drive (nr Lincoln Avenue)
	860 Cumbernauld Road
St Enoch's Hogganfield	163 Buchanan Street
St George's Tron	
St James' (Pollok)	Lyoncross Road x Byrebush Road
St John's Renfield	22 Beaconsfield Road
St Margaret's Tollcross Pk	179 Braidfauld Street
St Nicholas' Cardonald	Hartlaw Crescent nr Gladsmuir Road
St Paul's	30 Langdale St (x Greenrig St)
St Rollox	9 Fountainwell Road
Sandyford Henderson Memorial	Kelvinhaugh Street at Argyle Street
Sandyhills	28 Baillieston Rd nr Sandyhills Rd
Scotstoun	Earlbank Avenue x Ormiston Avenue
Shawlands	Shawlands Cross (1114 Pollokshaws Road)
Sherbrooke St Gilbert's	Nithsdale Rd x Sherbrooke Avenue
Shettleston New	679 Old Shettleston Road
Shettleston Old	99–111 Killin Street
South Carntyne	538 Carntyne Road
South Shawlands	Regwood Street x Deanston Drive
Springburn	180 Springburn Way
Temple Anniesland	869 Crow Road
Toryglen	Glenmore Ave nr Prospecthill Road
Trinity Possil and Henry Drummond	2 Crowhill Street (x Broadholm Street)
Tron St Mary's	128 Red Road
Victoria Tollcross	1134 Tollcross Road
Wallacewell New Charge Development	no building yet obtained
Wellington	University Ave x Southpark Avenue
Whiteinch	35 Inchlee Street
Yoker	10 Hawick Street

(17) HAMILTON

Meets at Motherwell: Dalziel St Andrew's Parish Church Halls, on the first Tuesday of February, March, May, September, October, November and December, and on the third Tuesday of June.

Presbytery Office: 353 Orbiston Street, Motherwell ML1 1QW   01698 259135
[E-mail: hamilton@cofscotland.org.uk]
[E-mail: clerk@presbyteryofhamilton.co.uk]

Clerk: REV. JOHN L. McPAKE BA BD PhD   c/o The Presbytery Office
Depute Clerk: REV. ROBERT A. HAMILTON BA BD   c/o The Presbytery Office
Presbytery Treasurer: MR ROBERT A. ALLAN   7 Graham Place, Ashgill, Larkhall ML9 3BA   01698 883246
[E-mail: Fallan3246@aol.com]

1   Airdrie: Broomknoll (H) (01236 762101) linked with Calderbank
Vacant   38 Commonhead Street, Airdrie ML6 6NS   01236 609584

2   Airdrie: Clarkston
F. Derek Gunn BD   1986   2009   Clarkston Manse, Forrest Street, Airdrie ML6 7BE   01236 603146

#	Charge / Minister			Address / E-mail	Telephone
3	**Airdrie: Flowerhill (H)** Gary J. Caldwell BSc BD	2007		31 Victoria Place, Airdrie ML6 9BU [E-mail: garyjcaldwell@btinternet.com]	01236 754430
4	**Airdrie: High** Ian R.W. McDonald BSc BD PhD	2007		17 Etive Drive, Airdrie ML6 9QL [E-mail: ian@spingetastic.freeserve.co.uk]	01236 760023
5	**Airdrie: Jackson** Kay Gilchrist (Miss) BD	1996	2008	48 Dunrobin Road, Airdrie ML6 8LR [E-mail: gilky61@yahoo.co.uk]	01236 760154
6	**Airdrie: New Monkland (H) linked with Greengairs** Vacant			3 Dykehead Crescent, Airdrie ML6 6PU	01236 763554
7	**Airdrie: St Columba's** Margaret F. Currie BEd BD	1980	1987	52 Kennedy Drive, Airdrie ML6 9AW [E-mail: margaret_currie250@o2.co.uk]	01236 763173
8	**Airdrie: The New Wellwynd** Robert A. Hamilton BA BD	1995	2001	20 Arthur Avenue, Airdrie ML6 9EZ [E-mail: revrob13@blueyonder.co.uk]	01236 763022
9	**Bargeddie (H)** John Fairful BD	1994	2001	The Manse, Manse Road, Bargeddie, Baillieston, Glasgow G69 6UB [E-mail: johnfairful@yahoo.co.uk]	0141-771 1322
10	**Bellshill: Central** Vacant			32 Adamson Street, Bellshill ML4 1DT (New charge formed by the union of **Bellshill: Macdonald Memorial and Bellshill: Orbiston**)	01698 849114
11	**Bellshill: West (H) (01698 747581)** Vacant			16 Croftpark Street, Bellshill ML4 1EY	01698 842877
12	**Blantyre: Livingstone Memorial** Vacant			286 Glasgow Road, Blantyre, Glasgow G72 9DB	01698 823794

13	**Blantyre: Old (H)**				
	Sarah L. Ross (Mrs) BD MTh PGDip	2004	2013	The Manse, Craigmuir Road, High Blantyre, Glasgow G72 9UA [E-mail: revsarahlynsey@gmail.com]	01698 769046
14	**Blantyre: St Andrew's**				
	Vacant			332 Glasgow Road, Blantyre, Glasgow G72 9LQ	01698 828633
15	**Bothwell (H)**				
	James M. Gibson TD LTh LRAM	1978	1989	Manse Avenue, Bothwell, Glasgow G71 8PQ [E-mail: jamesmgibson@msn.com]	01698 853189 (Tel) 01698 854903 (Fax)
16	**Calderbank** See Airdrie: Broomknoll				
17	**Caldercruix and Longriggend (H)**				
	George M. Donaldson MA BD	1984	2005	Main Street, Caldercruix, Airdrie ML6 7RF [E-mail: g.donaldson505@btinternet.com]	01236 842279
18	**Chapelhall (H)**				
	Vacant			The Manse, Russell Street, Chapelhall, Airdrie ML6 8SG	01236 763439
19	**Chapelton linked with Strathaven: Rankin (H)**				
	Shaw J. Paterson BSc BD MSc	1991		15 Lethame Road, Strathaven ML10 6AD [E-mail: s.paterson195@btinternet.com]	01357 520019 (Tel) 01357 529316 (Fax)
	Maxine Buck (Aux)	2007		Brownlee House, Mauldslie Road, Carluke ML8 5HW [E-mail: maxinebuck01@aol.com]	01555 759063
20	**Cleland (H)**				
	Vacant			The Manse, Bellside Road, Cleland, Motherwell ML1 5NP	01698 860260
21	**Coatbridge: Blairhill Dundyvan (H)**				
	Vacant			18 Blairhill Street, Coatbridge ML5 1PG	01236 432304
22	**Coatbridge: Calder (H) linked with Coatbridge: Old Monkland**				
	Vacant			26 Bute Street, Coatbridge ML5 4HF	01236 421516
23	**Coatbridge: Middle**				
	Vacant			47 Blair Road, Coatbridge ML5 1JQ	01236 432427

24	**Coatbridge: New St Andrew's** Fiona Nicolson BA BD	1996	2005	77 Eglinton Street, Coatbridge ML5 3JF	01236 437271
25	**Coatbridge: Old Monkland** See Coatbridge: Calder				
26	**Coatbridge: Townhead (H)** Ecilo Selemani LTh MTh	1993	2004	Crinan Crescent, Coatbridge ML5 2LH [E-mail: eciloselemani@msn.com]	01236 702914
27	**Dalserf** D. Cameron McPherson BSc BD DMin	1982		Manse Brae, Dalserf, Larkhall ML9 3BN [E-mail: revcam@talktalk.net]	01698 882195
28	**East Kilbride: Claremont (H) (01355 238088)** Gordon R. Palmer MA BD STM	1986	2003	17 Deveron Road, East Kilbride, Glasgow G74 2HR [E-mail: gkrspalmer@blueyonder.co.uk]	01355 248526
29	**East Kilbride: Greenhills (E) (01355 221746)** John Brewster MA BD DipEd	1988		21 Turnberry Place, East Kilbride, Glasgow G75 8TB [E-mail: johnbrewster@blueyonder.co.uk]	01355 242564
30	**East Kilbride: Moncreiff (H) (01355 223328)** Neil Buchanan BD	1991	2011	16 Almond Drive, East Kilbride, Glasgow G74 2HX [E-mail: neil.buchanan@talk21.com]	01355 238639
31	**East Kilbride: Mossneuk (01355 260954)** John L. McPake BA BD PhD	1987	2000	30 Eden Grove, Mossneuk, East Kilbride, Glasgow G75 8XU [E-mail: jlm1961@hotmail.co.uk]	01355 234196
32	**East Kilbride: Old (H) (01355 279004)** Anne S. Paton BA BD	2001		40 Maxwell Drive, East Kilbride, Glasgow G74 4HJ [E-mail: annepaton@fsmail.net]	01355 220732
33	**East Kilbride: South (H)** Sandra Black (Mrs) BSc BD (Interim Minister)	1988	2013	36 Glencairn Drive, Glasgow G41 4PW [E-mail: revsblack@btinternet.com]	0141-423 4000

34 **East Kilbride: Stewartfield (New Charge Development)** 1981 2001
Douglas W. Wallace MA BD
8 Thistle Place, Stewartfield, East Kilbride, Glasgow G74 4RH
01355 260879

35 **East Kilbride: West (H)**
Mahboob Masih BA MDiv MTh 1999 2008
4 East Milton Grove, East Kilbride, Glasgow G75 8FN
[E-mail: m_masih@sky.com]
01355 224469

36 **East Kilbride: Westwood (H) (01355 245657)**
Kevin Mackenzie BD DPS 1989 1996
16 Inglewood Crescent, East Kilbride, Glasgow G75 8QD
[E-mail: kevin@westwoodmanse.freeserve.co.uk]
01355 223992

37 **Glassford linked with Strathaven: East**
William T. Stewart BD 1980
68 Townhead Street, Strathaven ML10 6DJ
01357 521138

38 **Greengairs** See Airdrie: New Monkland

39 **Hamilton: Cadzow (H) (01698 428695)**
John Carswell BS MDiv 1996 2009
3 Carlisle Road, Hamilton ML3 7BZ
[E-mail: revcarswell@gmail.com]
01698 426682

40 **Hamilton: Gilmour and Whitehill (H)**
Vacant

41 **Hamilton: Hillhouse**
David W.G. Burt BD DipMin 1989 1998
66 Wellhall Road, Hamilton ML3 9BY
[E-mail: dwgburt@blueyonder.co.uk]
01698 422300

42 **Hamilton: Old (H) (01698 281905)**
Vacant
1 Chateau Grove, Hamilton ML3 7DS
(This congregation has united with the congregation of Hamilton: North)
01698 422511

43 **Hamilton: St John's (H) (01698 283492)**
Joanne C. Hood (Miss) MA BD 2003 2012
9 Shearer Avenue, Ferniegair, Hamilton ML3 7FX
[E-mail: hood137@btinternet.com]
01698 425002

44 **Hamilton: South (H) (01698 281014) linked with Quarter**
Donald R. Lawrie 2012
The Manse, Limekilnburn Road, Quarter, Hamilton ML3 7XA
01698 424511

45	**Hamilton: Trinity (01698 284254)** Vacant			69 Buchan Street, Hamilton ML3 8JY	01698 425326
46	**Hamilton: West (H) (01698 284670)** Vacant			43 Bothwell Road, Hamilton ML3 0BB	01698 458770
47	**Holytown linked with New Stevenston: Wrangholm Kirk** Caryl A.E. Kyle (Mrs) BD DipEd	2008		The Manse, 260 Edinburgh Road, Holytown, Motherwell ML1 5RU [E-mail: caryl_kyle@hotmail.com]	01698 832622
48	**Kirk o' Shotts (H)** Vacant			The Manse, Kirk o' Shotts, Salsburgh, Shotts ML7 4NS	01698 870208
49	**Larkhall: Chalmers (H)** Andrea M. Boyes	2013		Quarry Road, Larkhall ML9 1HH	01698 882238
50	**Larkhall: St Machan's (H)** Alastair McKillop BD DipMin	1995	2004	2 Orchard Gate, Larkhall ML9 1HG [E-mail: revicar@blueyonder.co.uk]	01698 321976
51	**Larkhall: Trinity** Lindsay Schluter ThE CertMin PhD	1995		13 Machan Avenue, Larkhall ML9 2HE [E-mail: lindsay.schluter@o2.co.uk]	01698 881401
52	**Motherwell: Crosshill (H) linked with Motherwell: St Margaret's** Gavin W.G. Black BD	2006		15 Orchard Street, Motherwell ML1 3JE [E-mail: gavin.black12@blueyonder.co.uk]	01698 263410
53	**Motherwell: Dalziel St Andrew's (H) (01698 264097)** Derek W. Hughes BSc BD DipEd	1990	1996	4 Pollock Street, Motherwell ML1 1LP [E-mail: derekthecleric@btinternet.com]	01698 263414
54	**Motherwell: North** Derek H.N. Pope BD	1987	1995	35 Birrens Road, Motherwell ML1 3NS [E-mail: derekpopemotherwell@hotmail.com]	01698 266716
55	**Motherwell: St Margaret's** See Motherwell: Crosshill				

56 Motherwell: St Mary's (H)
David W. Doyle MA BD — 1977 — 1987 — 19 Orchard Street, Motherwell ML1 3JE — 01698 263472

57 Motherwell: South (H)
Vacant — 62 Manse Road, Motherwell ML1 2PT — 01698 239245

58 Newarthill and Carfin
Elaine W. McKinnon MA BD — 1988 — 2014 — Church Street, Newarthill, Motherwell ML1 5HS
[E-mail: elaine.mckinnon@me.com] — 01698 296850

59 Newmains: Bonkle (H) linked with Newmains: Coltness Memorial (H)
Graham Raeburn MTh — 2004 — 5 Kirkgate, Newmains, Wishaw ML2 9BT
[E-mail: grahamraeburn@tiscali.co.uk] — 01698 383858

60 Newmains: Coltness Memorial See Newmains: Bonkle
61 New Stevenston: Wrangholm Kirk See Holytown

62 Overtown
Bruce H. Sinclair BA BD — 2009 — The Manse, 146 Main Street, Overtown, Wishaw ML2 0QP
[E-mail: brucehsinclair@btinternet.com] — 01698 352090

63 Quarter See Hamilton: South

64 Shotts: Calderhead Erskine
Allan B. Brown BD MTh — 1995 — 2010 — The Manse, 9 Kirk Road, Shotts ML7 5ET — 01501 823204 / 07578 448655 (Mbl)

65 Stonehouse: St Ninian's (H)
Paul G.R. Grant BD MTh — 2003 — 4 Hamilton Way, Stonehouse, Larkhall ML9 3PU
[E-mail: minister@st-ninians-stonehouse.org.uk] — 01698 792587

66 Strathaven: Avendale Old and Drumclog (H) (01357 529748)
Alan B. Telfer BA BD — 1983 — 2010 — 4 Fortrose Gardens, Strathaven ML10 6SH
[E-mail: minister@avendale-drumclog.com] — 01357 523031

67 Strathaven: East See Glassford
68 Strathaven: Rankin See Chapelton

69	**Uddingston: Burnhead (H)** Les Brunger BD	2010	90 Laburnum Road, Uddingston, Glasgow G71 5DB [E-mail: lesbrunger@hotmail.co.uk]	01698 813716
70	**Uddingston: Old (H) (01698 814015)** Fiona L.J. McKibbin (Mrs) MA BD	2011	1 Belmont Avenue, Uddingston, Glasgow G71 7AX [E-mail: fionamckibbin@sky.com]	01698 814757
71	**Uddingston: Viewpark (H)** Michael G. Lyall BD	1993 2001	14 Holmbrae Road, Uddingston, Glasgow G71 6AP [E-mail: michaellyall@blueyonder.co.uk]	01698 813113
72	**Wishaw: Cambusnethan North (H)** Mhorag Macdonald (Ms) MA BD	1989	350 Kirk Road, Wishaw ML2 8LH [E-mail: mhoragmacdonald@btinternet.com]	01698 381305
73	**Wishaw: Cambusnethan Old and Morningside** Iain C. Murdoch MA LLB DipEd BD	1995	22 Coronation Street, Wishaw ML2 8LF [E-mail: iaincmurdoch@btopenworld.com]	01698 384235
74	**Wishaw: Craigneuk and Belhaven (H) linked with Wishaw: Old** Alan Greig BSc BD (Interim Minister)	1977 2013	130 Glen Road, Wishaw ML2 7NP	01698 375134
75	**Wishaw: Old (H) (01698 376080)** See Wishaw: Craigneuk and Belhaven			
76	**Wishaw: St Mark's** Graham Austin BD	1997 2008	The Manse, 302 Coltness Road, Wishaw ML2 7EY [E-mail: graham.austin4@btinternet.com]	01698 384596
77	**Wishaw: South Wishaw (H)** Vacant		3 Walter Street, Wishaw ML2 8LQ	01698 387292

Name			Charge	Address	Tel
Barrie, Arthur P. LTh	1973	2007	(Hamilton: Cadzow)	30 Airbles Crescent, Motherwell ML1 3AR [E-mail: elizabethbarrie@ymail.com]	01698 261147
Baxendale, Georgina M. (Mrs) BD	1981	2014	(Motherwell: South)	32 Meadowhead Road, Plains, Airdrie ML6 7HG [E-mail: georgiebaxendale6@tiscali.co.uk]	
Colvin, Sharon E.F. (Mrs) BD LRAM LTCL	1985	2007	(Airdrie: Jackson)	25 Balblair Road, Airdrie ML6 6GQ [E-mail: dibleycol@hotmail.com]	01236 590796
Cook, J. Stanley BD Dip PSS	1974	2001	(Hamilton: West)	Mansend, 137A Old Manse Road, Netherton, Wishaw ML2 0EW [E-mail: stancook@blueyonder.co.uk]	01698 299600
Cullen, William T. BA LTh	1984	1996	(Kilmarnock: St John's Onthank)	6 Laurel Wynd, Cambuslang, Glasgow G72 7BA	0141-641 4337
Currie, David E.P. BSc BD	1983	2012	(Congregational Development Consultant)	69 Kethers Street, Motherwell ML1 3HN	01698 323424
Currie, R. David BSc BD	1984	2004	(Cambuslang: Flemington Hallside)	11 St Mary's Place, Saltcoats KA21 5NY	
Davidson, Amelia (Mrs) BD	2004	2011	(Coatbridge: Calder)	27 Easter Crescent, Wishaw ML2 8XB	01698 383453
Dick, Roddy S.	2010		Auxiliary Minister	[E-mail: roddy.dick@btopenworld.com]	
Dunn, W. Stuart LTh	1970	2006	(Motherwell: Crosshill)	10 Macrostie Gardens, Crieff PH7 4LP	01764 655178
Fraser, James P.	1951	1988	(Strathaven: Avendale Old and Drumclog)	26 Hamilton Road, Strathaven ML10 6JA	01357 522758
Gordon, Alasdair B. BD LLB EdD	1970	1980	(Aberdeen: Summerhill)	Flat 1, 13 Auchingramont Road, Hamilton ML3 6JP [E-mail: alasdairbgordon@hotmail.com]	01698 200561 / 07768 897843 (Mbl)
Grier, James BD	1991	2005	(Coatbridge: Middle)	14 Love Drive, Bellshill ML4 1BY	01698 742545
Hunter, James E. LTh	1974	1997	(Blantyre: Livingstone Memorial)	57 Dalwhinnie Avenue, Blantyre, Glasgow G72 9NQ	01698 826177
Jackson, John A. BD	1997	2014	(Cleland)	49 Lesmahagow Road, Boghead, Lesmahagow ML11 0JA [E-mail: johnajackson932@btinternet.com]	01555 890596
Kent, Robert M. MA BD	1973	2011	(Hamilton: St John's)	48 Fyne Crescent, Larkhall ML9 2UX [E-mail: robertmkent@talktalk.net]	01698 769244
Lusk, Alastair S. BD	1974	2010	(East Kilbride: Moncreiff)	9 MacFie Place, Stewartfield, East Kilbride, Glasgow G74 4TY	01698 384610
McAlpine, John BSc	1988	2004	(Auxiliary Minister)	Braeside, 201 Bonkle Road, Newmains, Wishaw ML2 9AA	
McCabe, George	1963	1996	(Airdrie: High)	Flat 8, Park Court, 2 Craighouse Park, Edinburgh EH10 5LD	0131-447 9522
McDonald, John A. MA BD	1978	1997	(Cumbernauld: Condorrat)	17 Thomson Drive, Bellshill ML4 3ND	
McKee, Norman B. BD	1987	2010	(Uddingston: Old)	148 Station Road, Blantyre, Glasgow G72 9BW [E-mail: normanmckee946@btinternet.com]	01698 827358
Mackenzie, Gordon R. BScAgr BD	1977	2014	(Chapelhall)	16 Crowhill Road, Bishopbriggs, Glasgow G64 1QY [E-mail: rev.g.mackenzie@btopenworld.com]	
MacKenzie, Ian C. MA BD	1970	2011	(Interim Minister)	21 Wilson Street, Motherwell ML1 1NP [E-mail: iancmac@blueyonder.co.uk]	01698 301230
McKenzie, Raymond D. BD	1978	2012	(Hamilton: Burnbank with Hamilton: North)	25 Austine Drive, Hamilton ML3 7YE [E-mail: rdmackenzie@hotmail.co.uk]	
MacLeod, Norman BTh	1999	2013	(Hamilton: St Andrew's)	15 Bent Road, Hamilton ML3 6QB [E-mail: normanmacleod@blueyonder.co.uk]	01698 283264
Martin, James MA BD DD	1946	1987	(Glasgow: High Carntyne)	9 Magnolia Street, Wishaw ML2 7EQ	01698 385825
Melrose, J.H. Loudon MA BD MEd	1955	1996	(Gourock: Old Gourock and Ashton [Assoc])	1 Laverock Avenue, Hamilton ML3 7DD	01698 427958
Moore, Agnes A. (Miss) BD	1987	2014	(Bellshill: West)	10 Carr Quadrant, Mossend, Bellshill ML4 1HZ [E-mail: revamoore2@tiscali.co.uk]	01698 841558
Munton, James G. BA	1969	2002	(Coatbridge: Old Monkland)	2 Moorcroft Drive, Airdrie ML6 8ES [E-mail: jacjim@supanet.com]	01236 754848

Name			Charge	Address	Tel
Price, Peter O. CBE QHC BA FPhS	1960	1996	(Blantyre: Old)	22 Old Bothwell Road, Bothwell, Glasgow G71 8AW [E-mail: petorprice@aol.com]	01698 854032
Rogerson, Stuart D. BSc BD	1980	2001	(Strathaven: West)	17 Westfield Park, Strathaven ML10 6XH [E-mail: srogerson@cnetwork.co.uk]	01357 523321
Ross, Keith W. MA BD	1984	2007	Congregational Development Officer for the Presbytery of Hamilton	Easter Bavelaw House, Pentland Hills Regional Park, Balerno EH14 7JS [E-mail: keithross.hamiltonpresbytery@googlemail.com]	(Mbl) 07855 163449
Salmond, James S. BA BD MTh ThD	1979	2003	(Holytown)	165 Torbothie Road, Shotts ML7 5NE	01698 870598
Spence, Sheila M. (Mrs) MA BD	1979	2010	(Kirk o' Shotts)	6 Drumbowie Crescent, Salsburgh, Shotts ML7 4NP	
Stevenson, John LTh	1998	2006	(Cambuslang: St Andrew's)	20 Knowehead Gardens, Uddingston, Glasgow G71 7PY [E-mail therev20@sky.com]	01698 817582
Stitt, Ronald J. Maxwell LTh BA ThM BREd DMin FSAScot	1977	2012	(Hamilton: Gilmour and Whitehill)	413 Gilmerton Road, Edinburgh EH17 7JJ	
Thomson, John M.A. TD JP BD ThM	1978	2014	(Hamilton: Old)	8 Skylands Place, Hamilton ML3 8SB [E-mail: jt@john1949-plus.com]	01698 422511
Thorne, Leslie W. BA LTh	1987	2001	(Coatbridge: Clifton)	'Hatherleigh', 9 Chatton Walk, Coatbridge ML5 4FH [E-mail: lesthorne@tiscali.co.uk]	01236 432241
Waddell, Elizabeth A. (Mrs) BD	1999	2014	(Hamilton: West)	114 Branchalfield, Wishaw ML2 8QD [E-mail: elizabethwaddell@tiscali.co.uk]	(Mbl) 07963 199921 01698 382909
Wilson, James H. LTh	1970	1996	(Cleland)	21 Austine Drive, Hamilton ML3 7YE [E-mail: wilsonjh@blueyonder.co.uk]	01698 457042
Wyllie, Hugh R. MA DD FCIBS	1962	2000	(Hamilton: Old)	18 Chantinghall Road, Hamilton ML3 8NP	01698 420002
Zambonini, James LIADip		1997	Auxiliary Minister	100 Old Manse Road, Wishaw ML2 0EP	01698 350889

HAMILTON ADDRESSES

Airdrie
Broomknoll — Broomknoll Street
Clarkston — Forrest Street
Flowerhill — 89 Graham Street
High — North Bridge Street
Jackson — Glen Road
New Monkland — Glenmavis
St Columba's — Thrashbush Road
The New Wellwynd — Wellwynd

Coatbridge
Blairhill Dundyvan — Blairhill Street
Calder — Calder Street
Middle — Bank Street
New St Andrew's — Church Street
Old Monkland — Woodside Street
Townhead — Crinan Crescent

East Kilbride
Claremont — High Common Road, St Leonard's
Greenhills — Greenhills Centre
Moncreiff — Calderwood Road
Mossneuk — Eden Drive
Old — Montgomery Street
South — Baird Hill, Murray
West — Kittoch Street
Westwood — Belmont Drive, Westwood

Hamilton
Cadzow — Woodside Walk
Gilmour and Whitehill — Glasgow Road, Burnbank
Hillhouse — Abbotsford Road, Whitehill
Old — Clerkwell Road
St John's — Leechlee Road
South — Duke Street
Trinity — Strathaven Road
West — Neilsland Square off North Road
Burnbank Road

Motherwell
Crosshill — Windmillhill Street x Airbles Street
Dalziel St Andrew's — Merry Street and Muir Street
North — Chesters Crescent
St Margaret's — Shields Road
St Mary's — Avon Street
South — Gavin Street

Uddingston
Burnhead   Laburnum Road   Kirk Road
Old   Old Glasgow Road   Kirk Road
Viewpark   Old Edinburgh Road

Wishaw
Cambusnethan
North
Old

Craigneuk and   Craigneuk Street
Belhaven   Main Street
Old   Coltness Road
St Mark's   East Academy Street
South Wishaw

(18) DUMBARTON

Meets at Dumbarton, in Riverside Church Halls, on the first Tuesday of February, March, April (if required), May (if required), June, September, October (if required), November and December, and on the third Tuesday of June at the incoming Moderator's church for the installation of the Moderator.

Clerk:	REV. DAVID W. CLARK MA BD		3 Ritchie Avenue, Cardross, Dumbarton G82 5LL [E-mail: dumbarton@cofscotland.org.uk]	01389 849319

Alexandria

Elizabeth W. Houston MA BD DipEd	1985	1995	32 Ledrish Avenue, Balloch, Alexandria G83 8JB [E-mail: cleric2@hotmail.com]	01389 751933

Arrochar linked with Luss

Vacant			The Manse, Luss, Alexandria G83 8NZ	01436 860240

Baldernock (H)

Andrew P. Lees BD	1984	2002	The Manse, Bardowie, Milngavie, Glasgow G62 6ES [E-mail: andrew.lees@yahoo.co.uk]	01360 620471

Bearsden: Baljaffray (H)

Ian McEwan BSc PhD BD FRSE	2008		5 Fintry Gardens, Bearsden, Glasgow G61 4RJ [E-mail: mcewan7@btinternet.com]	0141-942 0366

Bearsden: Cross (H)

Graeme R. Wilson MCIBS BD ThM	2006		61 Drymen Road, Bearsden, Glasgow G61 2SU [E-mail: graeme.wilson@gmail.com]	0141-942 0507

Bearsden: Killermont (H)

Alan J. Hamilton LLB BD	2003		8 Clathic Avenue, Bearsden, Glasgow G61 2HF [E-mail: ajh63@o2.co.uk]	0141-942 0021

Bearsden: New Kilpatrick (H) (0141-942 8827) (E-mail: mail@nkchurch.org.uk)
Roderick G. Hamilton MA BD   1992   2011   51 Manse Road, Bearsden, Glasgow G61 3PN   0141-942 0035
[E-mail: rghamilton@ntlworld.com]

Bearsden: Westerton Fairlie Memorial (H) (0141-942 6960)
Christine M. Goldie LLB BD MTh DMin   1984   2008   3 Canniesburn Road, Bearsden, Glasgow G61 1PW   0141-942 2672
[E-mail: christinegoldie@talktalk.net]

Bonhill (H) (01389 756516) linked with Renton: Trinity (H)
Vacant   1 Glebe Gardens, Bonhill, Alexandria G83 9NZ

Cardross (H) (01389 841322)
Vacant

Clydebank: Abbotsford linked with Dalmuir: Barclay (0141-941 3988)
Ruth Morrison MA BD   2009   2014   16 Parkhall Road, Dalmuir, Clydebank G81 3RJ   0141-941 3317
[E-mail: ruthie225@hotmail.com]

Clydebank: Faifley
Gregor McIntyre BSc BD   1991   Kirklea, Cochno Road, Hardgate, Clydebank G81 6PT   01389 876836
[E-mail: mail@gregormcintyre.com]

Clydebank: Kilbowie St Andrew's linked with Clydebank: Radnor Park (H)
Margaret J.B. Yule BD   1992   11 Tiree Gardens, Old Kilpatrick, Glasgow G60 5AT   01389 875599
[E-mail: mjbyule@yahoo.co.uk]

Clydebank: Radnor Park See Clydebank: Kilbowie St Andrew's

Clydebank: St Cuthbert's linked with Duntocher (H)
Guardianship of the Presbytery

Craigrownie linked with Garelochhead (01436 810589) linked with Rosneath: St Modan's (H)
Vacant

Dalmuir: Barclay See Clydebank: Abbotsford

Dumbarton: Riverside (H) (01389 742551) linked with Dumbarton: West Kirk (H)
C. Ian W. Johnson MA BD   1997   2014   18 Castle Road, Dumbarton G82 1JF   01389 726685
                                                                [E-mail: ian.ciw.johnson@btinternet.com]

Dumbarton: St Andrew's (H) linked with Old Kilpatrick Bowling
Vacant   17 Mansewood Drive, Dumbarton G82 3EU   01389 726715

Dumbarton: West Kirk See Dumbarton: Riverside
Duntocher See Clydebank: St Cuthbert's
Garelochhead See Craigrownie

Helensburgh: Park (H) (01436 674825)
Vacant

Helensburgh: St Andrew's Kirk (H) (01436 676880) linked with Rhu and Shandon (H)
George Vidits BD MTh   2000   2006   46 Suffolk Street, Helensburgh G84 9QZ   01436 672054
                                                                [E-mail: george.vidits@btinternet.com]

Associate minister: to be appointed

Jamestown (H)
Norma Moore MA BD   1995   2004   26 Kessog's Gardens, Balloch, Alexandria G83 8QJ   01389 756447
                                                                [E-mail: norma-moore@sky.com]

Kilmaronock Gartocharn
Guardianship of the Presbytery

Luss See Arrochar

Milngavie: Cairns (H) (0141-956 4868)
Andrew Frater BA BD MTh   1987   1994   4 Cairns Drive, Milngavie, Glasgow G62 8AJ   0141-956 1717
                                                                [E-mail: office@cairnschurch.org.uk]

Milngavie: St Luke's (0141-956 4226)
Ramsay B. Shields BA BD   1990   1997   70 Hunter Road, Milngavie, Glasgow G62 7BY   0141-577 9171 (Tel)
                                                                [E-mail: rbs@minister.com]   0141-577 9181 (Fax)

Milngavie: St Paul's (H) (0141-956 4405)
Fergus C. Buchanan MA BD MTh   1982   1988   8 Buchanan Street, Milngavie, Glasgow G62 8DD   0141-956 1043
                                                                [E-mail: f.c.buchanan@ntlworld.com]

Old Kilpatrick Bowling See Dumbarton: St Andrew's
Renton: Trinity See Bonhill
Rhu and Shandon See Helensburgh: St Andrew's Kirk
Rosneath: St Modan's See Craigrownie

Name			Charge	Address [E-mail]	Telephone
Booth, Frederick M. LTh	1970	2005	(Helensburgh: St Columba)	Achnashie Coach House, Clynder, Helensburgh G84 0QD [E-mail: boothef@btinternet.com]	01436 831858
Christie, John C. BSc BD MSB CBiol	1990	2014	(Interim Minister)	10 Cumberland Avenue, Helensburgh G84 8QG [E-mail: rev.jcc@btinternet.com]	01436 674078 (Mbl) 07711 336392
Clark, David W. MA BD	1975	2014	(Helensburgh: St Andrew's Kirk with Rhu and Shandon)	3 Ritchie Avenue, Cardross, Dumbarton G82 5LL [E-mail: clarkdw@talktalk.net]	01389 849319
Crombie, William D. MA BD	1947	1987	(Glasgow: Calton New with St Andrew's)	9 Fairview Court, 46 Main Street, Milngavie, Glasgow G62 6BU	0141-956 1898
Dalton, Mark BD DipMin RN		2002	Chaplain: Royal Navy	HM Naval Base Clyde, Faslane, Helensburgh G84 8HL [E-mail: mark.dalton242@mod.uk]	01436 674321 ext. 6216
Donaghy, Leslie G. BD DipMin PGCE FSAScot	1990	2004	(Dumbarton: St Andrew's)	53 Oak Avenue, East Kilbride, Glasgow G75 9ED [E-mail: leslie@donaghy.org.uk]	(Mbl) 07809 484812
Ferguson, Archibald M. MSc PhD CEng FRINA	1989	2004	(Auxiliary Minister)	The Whins, 2 Borrowfield, Station Road, Cardross, Dumbarton G82 5NL [E-mail: drarchiefferguson@gmail.com]	01389 841517
Hamilton, David G. MA BD	1971	2004	(Braes of Rannoch with Foss and Rannoch)	79 Finlay Rise, Milngavie, Glasgow G62 6QL [E-mail: davidhamilton40@googlemail.com]	0141-956 4202
Harris, John W.F. MA	1967	2012	(Bearsden: Cross)	68 Mitre Road, Glasgow G14 9LL [E-mail: jwfh@sky.com]	0141-321 1061
Hudson, Eric V. LTh	1971	2007	(Bearsden: Westerton Fairlie Memorial)	2 Murrayfield Drive, Bearsden, Glasgow G61 1JE [E-mail: evhudson@hotmail.co.uk]	0141-942 6110
Kemp, Tina MA		2005	Auxiliary Minister	12 Oaktree Gardens, Dumbarton G82 1EU [E-mail: tinakemp@blueyonder.co.uk]	01389 730477
McCutcheon, John		2014	Ordained Local Minister	Flat 2/6 Parkview, Milton Brae, Milton, Dumbarton G82 2TT [E-mail: JMccutc933@aol.com]	01389 739034
McIntyre, J. Ainslie MA BD	1963	1984	(University of Glasgow)	60 Bonnaughton Road, Bearsden, Glasgow G61 4DB [E-mail: jamcintyre@hotmail.com]	0141-942 5143 (Mbl) 07050 295103
Miller, Ian H. BA BD	1975	2012	(Bonhill)	Derand, Queen Street, Alexandria G83 0AS [E-mail: revianmiller@btinternet.com]	01389 753039
Munro, David P. MA BD STM	1953	1996	(Bearsden: North)	14 Birch Road, Killearn, Glasgow G63 9SQ [E-mail: david.munro1929@btinternet.com]	01360 550098
Murdoch, Christine	1999	2012	(Lochwinnoch)	Flat 2, The Ponderosa, Shore Road, Kilcreggan, Helensburgh G84 0HQ [E-mail: rev.christine@btinternet.com]	01436 842565 (Mbl) 07973 331890
Nutter, Margaret		2014	Ordained Local Minister	Kilmorich, 14 Balloch Road, Balloch, Alexandria G83 8SR [E-mail: mnutter@blueyonder.co.uk]	01389 754505
O'Donnell, Barbara		2007	Auxiliary Minister	Ashbank, 258 Main Street, Alexandria G83 0NU	01389 752356

Ramage, Alastair E. MA BA ADB CertEd	1996	Auxiliary Minister	16 Claremont Gardens, Milngavie, Glasgow G62 6PG [E-mail: sueandalastairramage@btinternet.com]	0141-956 2897
Robertson, Ishbel A.R. MA BD	2013	Ordained Local Minister	Oakdene, 81 Bonhill Road, Dumbarton G82 2DU [E-mail: ishbelrobertson@blueyonder.co.uk]	01389 763436
Speed, David K. LTh	1969 2004	(Glasgow: Shettleston Old)	153 West Princes Street, Helensburgh G84 8EZ [E-mail: dkspeed@btinternet.com]	01436 674493
Steven, Harold A.M. MSJJ LTh FSA Scot	1970 2001	(Baldernock)	9 Cairnhill Road, Bearsden, Glasgow G61 1AT [E-mail: harold.allison.steven@gmail.com]	0141-942 1598
Stewart, Charles E. BSc BD MTh PhD	1976 2000	(Chaplain of the Fleet)	105 Sinclair Street, Helensburgh G84 9HY [E-mail: c.e.stewart@btinternet.com]	01436 678113
West, Richard B.	1994 2013	(Craigrownie with Rosneath: St Modan's)	Carriden, Shore Road, Kilcreggan, Helensburgh G84 0HG [E-mail: rickangelawest@yahoo.co.uk]	(Mbl) 07751 834832
Wright, Malcolm LTh	1970 2003	(Craigrownie with Rosneath: St Modan's)	30 Clairinsh, Drumkinnon Gate, Balloch, Alexandria G83 8SE [E-mail: malcolmcatherine@msn.com]	01389 720338

DUMBARTON ADDRESSES

Bearsden
Baljaffray	Grampian Way
Cross	Drymen Road
Killermont	Rannoch Drive
New Kilpatrick	Manse Road
Westerton	Crarae Avenue

Clydebank
Abbotsford	Town Centre
Faifley	Faifley Road
Kilbowie St Andrew's	Kilbowie Road
Radnor Park	Radnor Street
St Cuthbert's	Linnvale

Dumbarton
Riverside	High Street
St Andrew's	Aitkenbar Circle
West Kirk	West Bridgend

Helensburgh
Park	Charlotte Street
St Andrew's Kirk	Colquhoun Square

Milngavie
Cairns	Buchanan Street
St Luke's	Kirk Street
St Paul's	Strathblane Road

(19) ARGYLL

Meets in the Village Hall, Tarbert, Loch Fyne, Argyll on the first Tuesday or Wednesday of March, June, September and December. For details, contact the Presbytery Clerk.

Clerk:	DR CHRISTOPHER T. BRETT MA PhD	Minahey Cottage, Kames, Tighnabruaich PA21 2AD [E-mail: argyll@cofscotland.org.uk]	01700 811142
Treasurer:	MRS PAMELA A. GIBSON	Allt Ban, Portsonachan, Dalmally PA33 1BJ [E-mail: justpam1@tesco.net]	01866 833344

Appin linked with Lismore

Vacant	The Manse, Appin PA38 4DD	01631 730143

Ardchattan (H)
Jeffrey A. McCormick BD   1984   Ardchattan Manse, North Connel, Oban PA37 1RG   01631 710364
[E-mail: jeff.mcc@virgin.net]

Ardrishaig (H) linked with South Knapdale
David Carruthers BD   1998   The Manse, Park Road, Ardrishaig, Lochgilphead PA30 8HE   01546 603269

Barra (GD) linked with South Uist (GD)
Vacant   Cuithir, Castlebay, Isle of Barra HS9 5XD   01871 810230

Campbeltown: Highland (H)
Vacant   Highland Church Manse, Kirk Street, Campbeltown PA28 6BN   01586 551146

Campbeltown: Lorne and Lowland (H)
Philip D. Wallace BSc BTh DTS   1998   2004   Lorne and Lowland Manse, Castlehill, Campbeltown PA28 6AN   01586 552468
[E-mail: pdwallace10@btinternet.com]
Kristian Wallace (Mrs)
BA BD CertTheol DRM PhD (Aux)   2007   Lorne and Lowland Manse, Castlehill, Campbeltown PA28 6AN   01586 552468
[E-mail: pdwallace10@btinternet.com]

Coll linked with Connel
George G. Cringles BD   1981   2002   St Oran's Manse, Connel, Oban PA37 1PJ   (Connel) 01631 710242
[E-mail: george.cringles@btinternet.com]   (Coll) 01879 230366

Colonsay and Oronsay (Website: www.islandchurches.org.uk)
Vacant

Connel See Coll

Craignish linked with Kilbrandon and Kilchattan linked with Kilninver and Kilmelford (Netherlorn)
Kenneth R. Ross BA BD PhD   1982   2010   The Manse, Kilmelford, Oban PA34 4XA   01852 200565
[E-mail: kennethr.ross@btinternet.com]

Cumlodden, Lochfyneside and Lochgair linked with Glenaray and Inveraray (West Lochfyneside)
Vacant   The Manse, Inveraray PA32 8XT   01499 302060

Dunoon: St John's linked with Kirn (H) linked with Sandbank (H) (Central Cowal)
Vacant
The Manse, 13 Dhailling Park, Hunter Street, Kirn, Dunoon
PA23 8FB

Glenda M. Wilson (Mrs) DCS   1990   2006
Ardlayne, 23 Bullwood Road, Dunoon PA23 7QJ
[E-mail: deacglendamwilson@gmail.com]   01369 700848

01369 702256

Dunoon: The High Kirk (H) linked with Innellan (H) linked with Toward (H) (South-East Cowal)
Aileen M. Robson (Miss) BD   2003   2011
7A Mathieson Lane, Innellan, Dunoon PA23 7SH
[E-mail: am65robson@ymail.com]   01369 830276

Ruth I. Griffiths (Mrs) (Aux)   2004
Kirkwood, Mathieson Lane, Innellan, Dunoon PA23 7TA
[E-mail: ruthigriffiths@googlemail.com]   01369 830145

Gigha and Cara (H) (GD) linked with Kilcalmonell linked with Killean and Kilchenzie (H)
David J. Thom BD PgDipMin PgDipPSAT   2000   2013
The Manse, Muasdale, Tarbert, Argyll PA29 6XD
[E-mail: revdjt@gmail.com]   01583 421432

Glassary, Kilmartin and Ford linked with North Knapdale
Clifford R. Acklam BD MTh   1997   2010
The Manse, Kilmichael Glassary, Lochgilphead PA31 8QA
[E-mail: clifford.acklam@btinternet.com]   01546 606926

Glenaray and Inveraray See Cumlodden, Lochfyneside and Lochgair

Glenorchy and Innishael linked with Strathfillan
Vacant   The Manse, Dalmally PA33 1AA   01838 200207

Innellan See Dunoon: The High Kirk

Iona linked with Kilfinichen and Kilvickeon and the Ross of Mull
John K. Collard MA BD (Interim Minister)   1986   2013
The Manse, Bunessan, Isle of Mull PA67 6DW   01681 700227

Jura (GD) linked with Kilarrow (H) linked with Kildalton and Oa (GD) (H)
Vacant   The Manse, Bowmore, Isle of Islay PA43 7LH   01496 810271

Kilarrow See Jura
Kilbrandon and Kilchattan See Craignish
Kilcalmonell See Gigha and Cara

Kilchoman (GD) linked with Kilmeny linked with Portnahaven (GD)
Valerie G.C. Watson MA BD STM   1987   2013   The Manse, Port Charlotte, Isle of Islay PA48 7TW   01496 850241
[E-mail: vgcwatson@btinternet.com]

Kilchrenan and Dalavich linked with Muckairn
Robert E. Brookes BD   2009   Muckairn Manse, Taynuilt PA35 1HW   01866 822204
[E-mail: eilanview@uwclub.net]

Kildalton and Oa See Jura

Kilfinan linked with Kilmodan and Colintraive linked with Kyles (H) (West Cowal)
David Mitchell BD DipPTheol MSc   1988   2006   West Cowal Manse, Kames, Tighnabruaich PA21 2AD   01700 811045
[E-mail: revdmitchell@icloud.com]

Kilfinichen and Kilvickeon and the Ross of Mull See Iona
Killean and Kilchenzie See Gigha and Cara
Kilmeny See Kilchoman
Kilmodan and Colintraive See Kilfinan

Kilmore (GD) and Oban (Website: www.obanchurch.com)
Dugald J.R. Cameron BD DipMin MTh   1990   2007   Kilmore and Oban Manse, Ganavan Road, Oban PA34 5TU 01631 566253
[E-mail: obancofs@btinternet.com]
Christine Fulcher BEd   2012   2014   St Blaan's Manse, Southend, Campbeltown PA28 6RQ   01586 830504
(Ordained Local Minister)   [E-mail: chris@pcmanse.plus.com]

Kilmun (St Munn's) (H) linked with Strone (H) and Ardentinny
David Mill KJSJ MA BD   1978   2010   The Manse, Blairmore, Dunoon PA23 8TE   01369 840313
[E-mail: revandevmill@aol.com]

Kilninian and Kilmore linked with Salen (H) and Ulva linked with Tobermory (GD) (H)
linked with Torosay (H) and Kinlochspelvie (North Mull)
John H. Paton BSc BD   1983   2013   The Manse, Gruline Road, Salen, Aros, Isle of Mull PA72 6XF 01680 300001
[E-mail: jpaton160@btinternet.com]

Kilninver and Kilmelford See Craignish
Kirn See Dunoon: St John's

Kyles See Kilfinan
Lismore See Appin

Lochgilphead
Hilda C. Smith (Miss) MA BD MSc | 1992 | 2005 | Parish Church Manse, Manse Brae, Lochgilphead PA31 8QZ | 01546 602238
[E-mail: hilda.smith2@btinternet.com]

Lochgoilhead (H) and Kilmorich linked with Strachur and Strathlachlan (Upper Cowal)
Robert K. Mackenzie MA BD PhD | 1976 | 1998 | The Manse, Strachur, Cairndow PA27 8DG | 01369 860246
[E-mail: rkmackenzie@strachurmanse.fsnet.co.uk]

Muckairn See Kilchrenan and Dalavich
North Knapdale See Glassary, Kilmartin and Ford
Portnahaven See Kilchoman

Rothesay: Trinity (H) (Website: www.rothesaytrinity.org)
Andrew Barrie BSc BD | 1984 | 2010 | 12 Crichton Road, Rothesay, Isle of Bute PA20 9JR | 01700 503010
[E-mail: drew.barrie@btinternet.com]

Saddell and Carradale (H) linked with Southend (H)
Stephen Fulcher BA MA | 1993 | 2012 | St Blaan's Manse, Southend, Campbeltown PA28 6RQ | 01586 830504
[E-mail: steve@pcmanse.plus.com]

Salen and Ulva See Kilninian and Kilmore
Sandbank See Dunoon: St John's

Skipness
Vacant

Southend See Saddell and Carradale
South Knapdale See Ardrishaig
South Uist See Barra
Strachur and Strathlachlan See Lochgoilhead and Kilmorich
Strathfillan See Glenorchy and Innishael
Strone and Ardentinny See Kilmun

Tarbert, Loch Fyne and Kilberry (H)

Thomas M. Bryson BD	1997	2011	The Manse, Campbeltown Road, Tarbert, Argyll PA29 6SX	01880 821012

[E-mail: thomas@bryson3.wanadoo.co.uk]

The United Church of Bute

John Owain Jones MA BD FSAScot	1981	2011	10 Bishop Terrace, Rothesay, Isle of Bute PA20 9HF	01700 504502

[E-mail: johnowainjones@ntlworld.com]

Tiree (GD)

Elspeth J. MacLean (Mrs) BVMS BD	2011	The Manse, Scarinish, Isle of Tiree PA77 6TN	01879 220377

[E-mail: ejmaclean@yahoo.co.uk]

Tobermory See Kilninian and Kilmore
Torosay and Kinlochspelvie See Kilninian and Kilmore
Toward See Dunoon: The High Kirk

Name			Role	Address	Phone
Beautyman, Paul H. MA BD	1993	2009	Youth Adviser	130b John Street, Dunoon PA23 7BN [E-mail: paul.beautyman@argyll-bute.gov.uk]	(Mbl) 07596 164112
Bell, Douglas W. MA LLB BD	1975	1993	(Alexandria: North)	3 Cairnbaan Lea, Cairnbaan, Lochgilphead PA31 8BA	01546 606815
Bristow, W.H.G. BEd HDipRE DipSpecEd	1951	2002	(Chaplain: Army)	Cnoc Ban, Southend, Campbeltown PA28 6RQ	01586 830667
Dunlop, Alistair J. MA	1965	2004	(Saddell and Carradale)	8 Pipers Road, Cairnbaan, Lochgilphead PA31 8UF [E-mail: dunrevn@btinternet.com]	01546 600316
Forrest, Alan B. MA	1956	1993	(Uphall: South)	126 Shore Road, Innellan, Dunoon PA23 7SX	01369 830424
Gibson, Elizabeth A. (Mrs) MA MLitt BD	2003	2013	(Glenorchy and Innishael with Strathfillan)	Mo Dhachaidh, Lochdon, Isle of Mull PA64 6AP	01680 812541
Gibson, Frank S. BL BD STM DSWA DD	1963	1995	(Kilarrow with Kilmeny)	1/7 Joppa Station Place, Edinburgh EH15 2QU [E-mail: lizgibson@phonecoop.coop]	
Goss, Alister J. BD DMin	1975	2009	(Industrial Chaplain)	24 Albert Place, Ardnadam, Sandbank, Dunoon PA23 8QF [E-mail: scimwest@hotmail.com]	01369 704495
Gray, William LTh	1971	2006	(Kilberry with Tarbert)	Lochnagar, Longsdale Road, Oban PA34 5DZ [E-mail: gray98@hotmail.com]	01631 567471
Henderson, Charles M.	1952	1989	(Campbeltown: Highland)	Springbank House, Askomill Walk, Campbeltown PA28 6EP	01586 552759
Henderson, Grahame McL. BD	1974	2008	(Kirn)	6 Gerhallow, Bullwood Road, Dunoon PA23 7QB [E-mail: ghende5884@aol.com]	01369 702433
Hood, Catriona A.	2006		Auxiliary Minister	'Elyside', Dalintober, Campbeltown PA28 6EB [E-mail: catriona.hood@argyll-bute.gov.uk]	01586 551490
Hood, H. Stanley C. MA BD	1966	2000	(London: Crown Court)	10 Dalriada Place, Kilmichael Glassary, Lochgilphead PA31 8QA	01546 606168
Lamont, Archibald	1952	1994	(Kilcalmonell with Skipness)	8 Achlonan, Taynuilt PA35 1JJ	
Lind, Michael J. LLB BD	1984	2012	(Campbeltown: Highland)	Maybank, Station Road, Conon Bridge, Dingwall IV7 8BJ [E-mail: mijylind@btinternet.com]	01866 822385

Name			Congregation	Address	Tel
Macfarlane, James PhD	1991	2011	(Lochgoilhead and Kilmorich)	'Lindores', 11 Bullwood Road, Dunoon PA23 7QJ [E-mail: mac.farlane@btinternet.com]	01369 710626
McIvor, Anne (Miss) SRD BD	1996	2013	(Gigha and Cara)	20 Albyn Avenue, Campbeltown PA28 6LY [E-mail: annemcivor@btinternet.com]	(Mbl) 07901 964825
MacLeod, Roderick MA BD PhD(Edin) PhD(Open)	1966	2011	(Cumlodden, Lochfyneside and Lochgair)	Creag-nam-Bannach, Furnace, Inveraray PA32 8XU [E-mail: mail@revroddy.co.uk]	01499 500629
Marshall, Freda (Mrs) BD FCII	1993	2005	(Colonsay and Oronsay with Kilbrandon and Kilchattan)	Allt Mhaluidh, Glenview, Dalmally PA33 1BE [E-mail: mail@freda.org.uk]	01838 200693
Millar, Margaret R.M. (Miss) BTh	1977	2008	(Kilchrenan and Dalavich with Muckairn)	Fearnoch Cottage, Fearnoch, Taynuilt PA35 1JB [E-mail: macoje@aol.com]	01866 822416
Morrison, Angus W. MA BD	1959	1999	(Kildalton and Oa)	1 Livingstone Way, Port Ellen, Isle of Islay PA42 7EP	01496 300043
Park, Peter B. BD MCIBS	1997	2014	(Fraserburgh: Old)	Hillview, 24 McKelvie Road, Oban PA34 4GB [E-mail: peterpark9@btinternet.com]	01631 565849
Ritchie, Walter M.	1973	1999	(Uphall: South)	Hazel Cottage, Barr Mor View, Kilmartin, Lochgilphead PA31 8UN	01546 510343
Scott, Randolph MA BD	1991	2013	(Jersey: St Columba's)	18 Lochan Avenue, Kirn, Dunoon PA23 8HT [E-mail: rev.rs@hotmail.com]	01369 703175
Shedden, John CBE BD DipPSS	1971	2008	(Fuengirola)	Orchy Cottage, Dalmally PA33 1AX [E-mail: rev.johnshedden@gmx.com]	01838 200535
Stewart, Joseph LTh	1979	2011	(Dunoon: St John's with Sandbank)	7 Glenmorag Avenue, Dunoon PA23 7LG	01369 703438
Taylor, Alan T. BD	1980	2005	(Isle of Mull Parishes)	Erray Road, Tobermory, Isle of Mull PA75 6PS	01688 302496
Wilkinson, W. Brian MA BD	1968	2007	(Glenaray and Inveraray)	3 Achlonan, Taynuilt PA35 1JJ [E-mail: brianwilkinson@f2s.com]	01866 822036

ARGYLL Communion Sundays

Ardrishaig	4th Apr, 1st Nov	Kilarrow	1st Mar, Jun, Sep, Dec	Portnahaven	3rd Jul
Barra	2nd Mar, June, Sep, Easter, Advent	Kilcalmonell	1st Jul, 3rd Nov	Rothesay: Trinity	1st Feb, Jun, Nov
Campbeltown		Kilchoman	1st Jul, 2nd Dec, Easter	Saddell and Carradale	2nd May, 1st Nov
Highland	1st May, Nov	Kildalton and Oa	Last Jan, Jun, Oct, Easter	Sandbank	1st Jan, May, Nov
Lorne and Lowland	1st May, Nov	Kilfinan	Last Apr, Oct	Skipness	2nd May, Nov
Craignish	1st Jun, Nov	Killean and Kilchenzie	1st Mar, Jul, Oct	Southend	1st Jun, Dec
Cumlodden, Lochfyneside and Lochgair	1st May, 3rd Nov	Kilmeny	2nd May, 3rd Nov	South Knapdale	4th Apr, 1st Nov
Dunoon		Kilmodan and Colintraive	1st Apr, Sep	South Uist	
St John's	1st Mar, Jun, Nov	Kilmun	Last Jun, Nov	Howmore	1st Jun
The High Kirk	1st Feb, Jun, Oct	Kilninver and Kilmelford	Last Feb, Jun, Oct	Daliburgh	1st Sep
Gigha and Cara	1st May, Nov	Kirn	2nd Jun, Oct	Strachur and Strathlachlan	1st Mar, Jun, Nov
Glassary, Kilmartin and Ford	1st Apr, Sep	Kyles	1st May, Nov	Strone and Ardentinny	Last Feb, Jun, Oct
Glenaray and Inveraray	1st Apr, Jul, Oct, Dec	Lochgair	Last Apr, Oct	Tarbert and Kilberry	1st May, Oct
Innellan	1st Mar, Jun, Sep, Dec	Lochgilphead	2nd Oct (Gaelic)	Tayvallich	2nd May, Nov
Inverlussa and Bellanoch	2nd May, Nov	Lochgoilhead and Kilmorich	1st Apr, Nov	The United Church of Bute	1st Feb, Jun, Nov
Jura	Passion Sun., 2nd Jul, 3rd Nov	North Knapdale	3rd Oct, 2nd May	Toward	Last Feb, May, Aug, Nov

(22) FALKIRK

Meets at Falkirk Trinity Parish Church on the first Tuesday of September, December, March and May, on the fourth Tuesday of October and January and on the third Tuesday of June.

Clerk:	REV. ROBERT S.T. ALLAN LLB DipLP BD	9 Major's Loan, Falkirk FK1 5QF [E-mail: falkirk@cofscotland.org.uk]	01324 625124
Depute Clerk:	REV. ANDREW SARLE BSc BD	114 High Station Road, Falkirk FK1 5LN [E-mail: depclerk@falkirkpresbytery.org]	01324 621648
Treasurer:	MR ARTHUR PRIESTLY	32 Broomhill Avenue, Larbert FK5 3EH [E-mail: treasurer@falkirkpresbytery.org]	01324 557142

Airth (H)

James F. Todd BD CPS	1984	2012	The Manse, Airth, Falkirk FK2 8LS	01324 831120

Blackbraes and Shieldhill linked with Muiravonside

Louise J.E. McClements RGN BD	2008		81 Stevenson Avenue, Polmont, Falkirk FK2 0GU [E-mail: louise.mcclements@virgin.net]	01324 717757

Bo'ness: Old (H)

Douglas I. Campbell BD DPS	2004	2009	10 Dundas Street, Bo'ness EH51 0DG [E-mail: douglas@bokonline.org.uk]	01506 204585

Bo'ness: St Andrew's (Website: www.standonline.org.uk) (01506 825803)

Albert O. Bogle BD MTh	1981		St Andrew's Manse, 11 Erngath Road, Bo'ness EH51 9DP [E-mail: albertbogle@mac.com]	01506 822195

Bonnybridge: St Helen's (H) (Website: www.bbshnc.com)

George MacDonald BTh	2004	2009	The Manse, 32 Reilly Gardens, High Bonnybridge FK4 2BB [E-mail: georgemacdonald1@virginmedia.com]	01324 874807

Bothkennar and Carronshore

Andrew J. Moore BSc BD	2007		11 Hunter Place, Greenmount Park, Carronshore, Falkirk FK2 8QS [E-mail: theminister@themoores.me.uk]	01324 570525

Brightons (H)
Murdo M. Campbell BD DipMin — 1997 — 2007 — The Manse, Maddiston Road, Brightons, Falkirk FK2 0JP [E-mail: murdocampbell@hotmail.com] — 01324 712062

Carriden (H)
Malcolm Lyon BD — 2007 — 2014 — The Spires, Foredale Terrace, Carriden, Bo'ness EH51 9LW [E-mail: malcolmlyon2@hotmail.com] — 01506 822141

Cumbernauld: Abronhill (H)
Joyce A. Keyes (Mrs) BD — 1996 — 2003 — 26 Ash Road, Cumbernauld, Glasgow G67 3ED — 01236 723833

Cumbernauld: Condorrat (H)
Grace Saunders BSc BTh — 2007 — 2011 — 11 Rosehill Drive, Cumbernauld, Glasgow G67 4EQ [E-mail: rev.grace.saunders@btinternet.com] — 01236 452090

Marion Perry (Mrs) (Aux) — 2009 — 2013 — 17a Tarbolton Road, Cumbernauld, Glasgow G67 2AJ [E-mail: perryask@hotmail.com] — 01236 898519 / 07563 180662 (Mbl)

Cumbernauld: Kildrum (H)
Elinor J. Gordon (Miss) BD — 1988 — 2004 — 64 Southfield Road, Balloch, Cumbernauld, Glasgow G68 9DZ [E-mail: elinorgordon@aol.com] — 01236 723204

David Nicholson DCS — 2D Doonside, Kildrum, Cumbernauld, Glasgow G67 2HX [E-mail: deacdave@btinternet.com] — 01236 732260

Cumbernauld: Old (H) (Website: www.cumbernauldold.org.uk)
Catriona Ogilvie (Mrs) MA BD — 1999 — The Manse, 23 Baronhill, Cumbernauld, Glasgow G67 2SD — 01236 721912
Valerie Cuthbertson (Miss) DCS — 105 Bellshill Road, Motherwell ML1 3SJ — 01698 259001

Cumbernauld: St Mungo's
Vacant — 18 Fergusson Road, Cumbernauld, Glasgow G67 1LS — 01236 721513

Denny: Old
Vacant — 31 Duke Street, Denny FK6 6NR — 01324 824508

Denny: Westpark (H) (Website: www.westparkchurch.org.uk)
Vacant — 13 Baxter Crescent, Denny FK6 5EZ — 01324 876224

Dunipace (H)
Jean W. Gallacher (Miss) BD CMin CTheol DMin — 1989 — The Manse, 239 Stirling Street, Dunipace, Denny FK6 6QJ — 01324 824540

Falkirk: Bainsford linked with Falkirk: St James'

Vacant			
Andrew Sarle BSc BD	2013	1 Valleyview Place, Newcarron Village, Falkirk FK2 7JB	01324 621087
(Ordained Local Minister)		114 High Station Road, Falkirk FK1 5LN	01324 621648

Falkirk: Camelon (Church office: 01324 870011)

Stuart Sharp MTheol DipPA	2001	30 Cotland Drive, Falkirk FK2 7GE	01324 623631

Falkirk: Grahamston United (H)

Ian Wilkie BD PGCE	2001	2007	16 Cromwell Road, Falkirk FK1 1SF	01324 624461
			[E-mail: yanbluejeans@aol.com]	07877 803280 (Mbl)

Falkirk: Laurieston linked with Redding and Westquarter

J. Mary Henderson MA BD DipEd PhD	1990	2009	11 Polmont Road, Laurieston, Falkirk FK2 9QQ	01324 621196
			[E-mail: jmary.henderson@tiscali.co.uk]	

Falkirk: St Andrew's West (H)

Alastair M. Horne BSc BD	1989	1997	1 Maggiewood's Loan, Falkirk FK1 5SJ	01324 623308

Falkirk: St James' See Falkirk: Bainsford

Falkirk: Trinity (H)

Robert S.T. Allan LLB DipLP BD	1991	2003	9 Major's Loan, Falkirk FK1 5QF	01324 625124
Kathryn Brown (Mrs)	2014		1 Callendar Park Walk, Callendar Grange, Falkirk FK1 1TA	01324 617352
(Ordained Local Minister)			[E-mail: kaybrown1cpw@talktalk.net]	

(New charge formed by the union of **Falkirk: Erskine and Falkirk: Old and St Modan's**)

Grangemouth: Abbotsgrange

Aftab Gohar MA MDiv PgDip	1995	2010	8 Naismith Court, Grangemouth FK3 9BQ	01324 482109
			[E-mail: abbotsgrange@aol.com]	07528 143784 (Mbl)

Grangemouth: Kirk of the Holy Rood

David J. Smith BD DipMin	1992	2003	The Manse, Bowhouse Road, Grangemouth FK3 0EX	01324 471595
			[E-mail: davidkhrood@tiscali.co.uk]	

Grangemouth: Zetland (H)
Vacant
Lorna I. MacDougall (Miss) MA DipGC (Aux) 2003 — Ronaldshay Crescent, Grangemouth FK3 9JH — 01324 472868
34 Millar Place, Carron, Falkirk FK2 8QB — 01324 552739

Haggs (H)
Helen F. Christie (Mrs) BD 1998 — 5 Watson Place, Dennyloanhead, Bonnybridge FK4 2BG — 01324 813786

Larbert: East
Melville D. Crosthwaite BD DipEd DipMin 1984 1995 — 1 Cortachy Avenue, Carron, Falkirk FK2 8DH — 01324 562402

Larbert: Old (H)
Vacant — The Manse, 38 South Broomage Avenue, Larbert FK5 3ED — 01324 872760

Larbert: West (H)
Vacant — 11 Carronvale Road, Larbert FK5 3LZ — 01324 562878

Muiravonside See Blackbraes and Shieldhill

Polmont: Old
Vacant — 3 Orchard Grove, Polmont, Falkirk FK2 0XE — 01324 718677

Redding and Westquarter See Falkirk: Laurieston

Slamannan
Vacant — The Manse, Manse Place, Slamannan, Falkirk FK1 3EN — 01324 851307

Stenhouse and Carron (H)
William Thomson BD 2001 2007 — The Manse, 21 Tipperary Place, Stenhousemuir, Larbert FK5 4SX — 01324 416628

Black, Ian W. MA BD 1976 2013 (Grangemouth: Zetland) — Flat 1R, 2 Carrickvale Court, Carrickstone, Cumbernauld, Glasgow G68 0LA — 01236 453370
[E-mail: iwblack@hotmail.com]

Brown, James BA BD DipHSW DipPsychol 1973 2001 (Abercorn with Dalmeny) — 6 Salmon Court, Schoolbrae, Bo'ness EH51 9HF — 01506 822454

Name	Charge			Address	Telephone
Brown, T. John MA BD	(Tullibody: St Serf's)	1995	2006	1 Callendar Park Walk, Callendar Grange, Falkirk FK1 1TA [E-mail: johnbrown1cpw@talktalk.net]	01324 617352
Campbell-Jack, W.C. BD MTh PhD	(Glasgow: Possilpark)	1979	2011	35 Castle Avenue, Airth, Falkirk FK2 8GA [E-mail: c.c-j@homecall.co.uk]	01324 832011
Chalmers, George A. MA BD MLitt	(Catrine with Sorn)	1962	2002	3 Cricket Place, Brightons, Falkirk FK2 0HZ	01324 712030
Hardie, Robert K. MA BD	(Stenhouse and Carron)	1968	2005	33 Palace Street, Berwick-upon-Tweed TD15 1HN	
Heriot, Charles R. JP BA	(Brightons)	1962	1996	Oakbank Nursing Home, Wilson Avenue, Polmont, Falkirk FK2 0QZ	
Holland, John C.	(Strone and Ardentinny)	1976	1985	7 Polmont Park, Polmont, Falkirk FK2 0XT	01324 880109
Job, Anne J. BSc BD	(Kirkcaldy: Viewforth with Thornton)	1993	2010	5 Carse View, Airth, Falkirk FK2 8NY [E-mail: aj@ajjob.co.uk]	01324 832094
Kesting, Sheilagh M. (Miss) BA BD DD	Ecumenical Relations	1980	1993	12 Glenview Drive, Falkirk FK1 5JU	01324 671489
Macaulay, Glendon BD	(Falkirk: Erskine)	1999	2012	43 Gavin's Lee, Tranent EH33 2AP [E-mail: gd.macaulay@btinternet.com]	01875 615851
McCallum, John	(Falkirk: Irving Camelon)	1962	1998	11 Burnbrae Gardens, Falkirk FK1 5SB	01324 619766
MacDonald, Monica (Mrs)	Ordained Local Minister	2014		32 Reilly Gardens, High Bonnybridge, Bonnybridge FK4 2BB [E-mail: monica.macdonald55@googlemail.com]	01324 874807
McDonald, William G. MA BD	(Falkirk: Grahamston United)	1959	1975	14 Priestden Park, St Andrews KY16 8DL	01334 479770
McDowall, Ronald J. BD	(Falkirk: Laurieston with Redding and Westquarter)	1980	2001	'Kailas', Windsor Road, Falkirk FK1 5EJ	01324 871947
MacKinnon, Ronald M. DCS	(Deacon)			12 Mossywood Court, McGregor Avenue, Airdrie ML6 7DY [E-mail: ronnie@ronniemac.plus.com]	01236 763389, 07594 427960 (Mbl)
Mathers, Daniel L. BD	(Grangemouth: Charing Cross and West)	1982	2001	10 Ercall Road, Brightons, Falkirk FK2 0RS	01324 872253
Maxton, Ronald M. MA	(Dollar: Associate)	1955	1995	5 Rulley View, Denny FK6 6QQ	01324 825441
Miller, Elsie M. (Miss) DCS	(Deaconess)			30 Swinton Avenue, Rowansbank, Baillieston, Glasgow G69 6JR	0141-771 0857
Orr, Sheena BA MSc MBA BD	Prison Ministry in Kenya	2011		PO Box 2299-00621, Village Market, Nairobi, Kenya [E-mail: sheens59@gmail.com]	00254 (0)732630215
Ross, Evan J. LTh	(Cowdenbeath: West with Mossgreen and Crossgates)	1986	1998	5 Arneil Place, Brightons, Falkirk FK2 0NJ	01324 719936
Scott, Donald H. BA BD	Chaplain: HMYOI Polmont	1983	2002	14 Gibsongray Street, Falkirk FK2 0AB [E-mail: donaldhscott@hotmail.com]	01324 722241
Smith, Richard BD	(Denny: Old)	1976	2002	Easter Wayside, 46 Kennedy Way, Airth, Falkirk FK2 8GB [E-mail: richards@uklinux.net]	01324 831386
Wandrum, David	Auxiliary Minister	1993		5 Cawder View, Carrickstone Meadows, Cumbernauld, Glasgow G68 0BN	01236 723288
Wilson, Phyllis M. (Mrs) DipCom DipRE	(Motherwell: South Dalziel)	1985	2006	'Landemer', 17 Sneddon Place, Airth, Falkirk FK2 8GH [E-mail: thomas.wilson38@btinternet.com]	01324 832257

FALKIRK ADDRESSES

Church	Address	Church	Address	Church	Address
Blackbraes and Shieldhill	Main St x Anderson Cr	Denny: Old	Denny Cross	Grangemouth: Abbotsgrange	Abbot's Road
Bo'ness: Old	Panbrae Road	Westpark	Duke Street	Kirk of the Holy Rood	Bowhouse Road
St Andrew's	Grahamsdyke Avenue	Dunipace	Stirling Street	Zetland	Ronaldshay Crescent
Carriden	Carriden Brae	Falkirk: Bainsford	Hendry Street, Bainsford	Haggs	Glasgow Road
Cumbernauld: Abronhill	Larch Road	Camelon	Dorrator Road	Larbert: East	Kirk Avenue
Condorrat	Main Road	Grahamston United	Bute Street	Old	Denny Road x Stirling Road
Kildrum	Clouden Road	Laurieston	Main Falkirk Road	West	Main Street
Old	Baronhill	St Andrew's West	Newmarket Street	Muiravonside	off Vellore Road
St Mungo's	St Mungo's Road	St James'	Thornhill Road x Firs Street	Polmont: Old	Kirk Entry/Bo'ness Road
		Trinity	Kirk Wynd	Redding and Westquarter	Main Street
				Slamannan	Manse Place
				Stenhouse and Carron	Church Street

(23) STIRLING

Meets at the Moderator's church on the second Thursday of September, and at Bridge of Allan Parish Church on the second Thursday of February, March, April, May, June, October, November and December.

Clerk:	**REV. ALEXANDER M. MILLAR MA BD MBA MCMI**	
	St Columba's Manse, 5 Clifford Road, Stirling FK8 2AQ	01786 469979
	[E-mail: alexmillar0406@gmail.com]	
Depute Clerk:	**MR ANDREW MUIRHEAD MA MLitt**	
	Ythanglen, Copland Place, Alva FK12 5LN	01259 760143
	[E-mail: andrew.muirhead1@btinternet.com]	
Treasurer:	**MR MARTIN DUNSMORE**	
	60 Brookfield Place, Alva FK12 5AT	01259 762262
	[E-mail: mpgduns@btinternet.com]	
Presbytery Office:	**Bridge of Allan Parish Church, 12 Keir Street, Bridge of Allan FK9 4NW**	
	[E-mail: stirling@cofscotland.org.uk]	

Aberfoyle (H) linked with Port of Menteith (H) (Website: www.aberfoyleportchurches.org.uk)
Terry Ann Taylor BA MTh   2005   2014   The Manse, Lochard Road, Aberfoyle, Stirling FK8 3SZ   01877 382391
[E-mail: terryanntaylor@btinternet.com]

Alloa: Ludgate (Website: www.alloaludgatechurch.org.uk)
Carol Anne Parker (Mrs) BEd BD   2009   2014   28 Alloa Park Drive, Alloa FK10 1QY   01259 212709
[E-mail: ca.parker76@btinternet.com]

Alloa: St Mungo's (H) (Website: www.stmungosparish.org.uk)
Sang Y. Cha BD   2011   37A Claremont, Alloa FK10 2DG   01259 213872
[E-mail: syc@cantab.net]

Alva (Website: www.alvaparishchurch.org.uk)
James N.R. McNeil BSc BD   1990   1997   34 Ochil Road, Alva FK12 5JT   01259 760262
[E-mail: revjim@btinternet.com]

Balfron (Website: www.balfronchurch.org.uk) linked with Fintry (H) (Website: www.fintrykirk.btck.org.uk)
Sigrid Marten   1997   2013   7 Station Road, Balfron, Glasgow G63 0SX   01360 440285
[E-mail: minister@marten.org.uk]

Balquhidder linked with Killin and Ardeonaig (H)
Vacant   The Manse, Killin FK21 8TN   01567 820247

Bannockburn: Allan (H) (Website: www.allanchurch.org.uk)
Jim Landels BD CertMin   1990   The Manse, Bogend Road, Bannockburn, Stirling FK7 8NP   01786 814692
[E-mail: revjimlandels@btinternet.com]

Bannockburn: Ladywell (H) (Website: www.ladywellchurch.co.uk)
Elizabeth M.D. Robertson (Miss) BD CertMin   1997   57 The Firs, Bannockburn FK7 0EG   01786 812467
[E-mail: lizrob@talktalk.net]

Bridge of Allan (H) (01786 834155) (Website: www.bridgeofallanparishchurch.org.uk)
Vacant   29 Keir Street, Bridge of Allan, Stirling FK9 4QJ   01786 832753

Buchanan linked with Drymen (Website: www.drymenchurch.org)
Alexander J. MacPherson BD   1986   1997   Buchanan Manse, Drymen, Glasgow G63 0AQ   01360 870212
[E-mail: revalex.1@gmail.com]

Buchlyvie (H) linked with Gartmore (H)
Elaine H. MacRae (Mrs) BD   1985   2004   112 Jackson Drive, Crowwood Grange, Stepps, Glasgow G33 6GF   0141-779 5742
[E-mail: ge.macrae@btopenworld.com]   07834 269487 (Mbl)

Callander (H) (Tel/Fax: 01877 331409) (Website: www.callanderkirk.org.uk)
Vacant   3 Aveland Park Road, Callander FK17 8FD   01877 330097

Cambusbarron: The Bruce Memorial (H) (Website: www.connectcambusbarron.org)
Graham Nash MA BD   2006   2012   14 Woodside Court, Cambusbarron, Stirling FK7 9PH   01786 442068
[E-mail: gpnash@btopenworld.com]

Clackmannan (H) (Website: www.clackmannankirk.org.uk)
Scott Raby LTh 1991 2007 The Manse, Port Street, Clackmannan FK10 4JH 01259 211255
[E-mail: minister@clackmannankirk.org]

Cowie (H) and Plean linked with Fallin (Website: www.cowiepleanandfallinchurch.com)
Alan L. Dunnett LLB BD 1994 2008 5 Fincastle Place, Cowie, Stirling FK7 7DS 01786 818413
[E-mail: alan.dunnett@sky.com]
Linda Dunnett (Mrs) BA DCS 5 Fincastle Place, Cowie, Stirling FK7 7DS 01786 818413
07838 041683 (Mbl)
[E-mail: lindadunnett@sky.com]

Dollar (H) linked with Glendevon linked with Muckhart (Website: www.dollarparishchurch.org.uk)
Jerome O'Brien BA LLB MTh 2001 2013 2 Princes Crescent East, Dollar FK14 7BU 01259 743593
[E-mail: 1jeromeobrien@gmail.com]

Drymen See Buchanan

Dunblane: Cathedral (H) (Website: www.dunblanecathedral.org.uk)
Colin C. Renwick BMus BD 1989 2014 Cathedral Manse, The Cross, Dunblane FK15 0AQ 01786 822205
[E-mail: c.renwick@btopenworld.com]
Sally Foster-Fulton (Mrs) BA BD (Assoc) 1999 2007 21 Craiglea, Causewayhead, Stirling FK9 5EE 01786 463060
[E-mail: sallyfulton01@gmail.com]

Dunblane: St Blane's (H) linked with Lecropt (H) (Website: www.lecroptkirk.org.uk)
Vacant 49 Roman Way, Dunblane FK15 9DJ 01786 822268

Fallin See Cowie and Plean
Fintry See Balfron

Gargunnock (Website: www.gargunnock.com/church) linked with Kilmadock linked with Kincardine-in-Menteith
Andrew B. Campbell BD DPS MTh 1979 2011 The Manse, Manse Brae, Gargunnock, Stirling FK8 3BQ 01786 860678
[E-mail: andycampbell153@btinternet.com]

Gartmore See Buchlyvie
Glendevon See Dollar

Killearn (H) (Website: www.killearn.org.uk)
Lee Messeder BD PgDipMin   2003   2010   2 The Oaks, Killearn, Glasgow G63 9SF   01360 550045
[E-mail: minister@killearnkirk.org.uk]

Killin and Ardeonaig See Balquhidder
Kilmadock See Gargunnock
Kincardine-in-Menteith See Gargunnock

Kippen (H) linked with Norrieston
Vacant   The Manse, Main Street, Kippen, Stirling FK8 3DN   01786 870229

Lecropt See Dunblane: St Blane's

Logie (H) (Website: www.logiekirk.co.uk)
R. Stuart M. Fulton BA BD   1991   2006   21 Craiglea, Causewayhead, Stirling FK9 5EE   01786 463060
[E-mail: stuart.fulton@btinternet.com]
Anne F. Shearer BA DipEd (Aux)   2010   10 Colsnaur, Menstrie FK11 7HG   01259 769176
[E-mail: anne.f.shearer@btinternet.com]

Menstrie (H) (Website: www.menstrieparishchurch.co.uk)
Vacant   The Manse, 7 Long Row, Menstrie FK11 7BA   01259 761461

Muckhart See Dollar
Norrieston See Kippen
Port of Menteith See Aberfoyle

Sauchie and Coalsnaughton
Margaret Shuttleworth MA BD   2013   62 Toll Road, Kincardine, Alloa FK10 4QZ   01259 731002
[E-mail: revmshuttleworth@gmail.com]

Stirling: Allan Park South (R) (H) (Website: www.apschurch.com)
Alistair Cowper BSc BD   2011   22 Laurelhill Place, Stirling FK8 2JH   01786 355872
[E-mail: minister@apschurch.com]   07791 524504 (Mbl)

Stirling: Church of the Holy Rude (H) (Website: http://holyrude.org) linked with Stirling: Viewfield Erskine (H)
Alan F. Miller BA MA BD   2000   2010   7 Windsor Place, Stirling FK8 2HY   01786 465166
[E-mail: revafmiller@gmail.com]

Stirling: North (H) (01786 463376) (Website: www.northparishchurch.com)
Calum Jack BSc BD   2004   18 Shirras Brae Road, Stirling FK7 0BA   01786 357428
[E-mail: calum@northparishchurch.com]

Stirling: St Columba's (H) (01786 449516) (Website: www.stcolumbasstirling.org.uk)
Alexander M. Millar MA BD MBA MCMI   1980   2010   St Columba's Manse, 5 Clifford Road, Stirling FK8 2AQ   01786 469979
[E-mail: alexmillar0406@gmail.com]

Stirling: St Mark's (Website: www.stmarksstirling.org.uk)
Stuart Davidson BD   2008   176 Drip Road, Stirling FK8 1RR   01786 473716
[E-mail: stuart_davidson1@sky.com]
Jean Porter (Mrs) BD DCS   St Mark's Church, Drip Road, Stirling FK8 1RE   07729 316321 (Mbl)
[E-mail: info@stmarksstirling.org.uk]

Stirling: St Ninians Old (H) (Website: www.stniniansold.org.uk)
Gary J. McIntyre BD DipMin   1993   1998   7 Randolph Road, Stirling FK8 2AJ   01786 474421
[E-mail: gary.mcintyre7@btinternet.com]

Stirling: Viewfield Erskine See Stirling: Church of the Holy Rude

Strathblane (H) (Website: www.strathblanekirk.org.uk)
Richard Begg MA BD   2008   2011   2 Campsie Road, Strathblane, Glasgow G63 9AB   01360 770226
[E-mail: RBEGG711@aol.com]

Tillicoultry (H) (Website: www.tillicoultryparishchurch.btck.co.uk)
Alison E.P. Britchfield (Mrs) MA BD   1987   2013   The Manse, 17 Dollar Road, Tillicoultry FK13 6PD   01259 750340
[E-mail: alibritchfield@gmail.com]

Tullibody: St Serf's (H)
Vacant   16 Menstrie Road, Tullibody, Alloa FK10 2RG   01259 729804

Abeledo, Benjamin J.A. BTh DipTh PTh   1991 2000   Chaplain: Army   30 Dollar Road, Tillicoultry FK13 6PD   01259 752705
[E-mail: benjamin.abeledo@btinternet.com]
Aitken, E. Douglas MA   1961 1998   (Clackmannan)   1 Dolan Grove, Saline, Dunfermline KY12 9UP   01383 852730
[E-mail: douglasaitken14@btinternet.com]

Name	Dates	Position	Address / E-mail	Telephone
Allen, Valerie L. (Ms) BMus MDiv DMin	1990 2013	(Arbroath: Old and Abbey)	16 Pine Court, Doune FK16 6JE [E-mail: vl2allen@btinternet.com]	01786 842577 (Mbl) 07801 291538
Barr, John BSc PhD BD	1958 1979	(Kilmacolm: Old)	6 Ferry Court, Stirling FK9 5GJ [E-mail: kilbrandon@btinternet.com]	01786 472286
Brown, James H. BD	1977 2005	(Helensburgh: Park)	14 Gullipen View, Callander FK17 8HN [E-mail: revjimhbrown@yahoo.co.uk]	01877 339425
Cloggie, June (Mrs)	1997 2006	(Auxiliary Minister)	11A Tulipan Crescent, Callander FK17 8AR [E-mail: david.cloggie@hotmail.co.uk]	01877 331021
Cochrane, James P.N. LTh	1994 2012	(Tillicoultry)	12 Sandpiper Meadow, Alloa Park, Alloa FK10 1QU [E-mail: jamescochrane@pobroadband.co.uk]	01259 218883
Cook, Helen (Mrs) BD	1974 2012	Hospital Chaplain	60 Pelstream Avenue, Stirling FK7 0BG [E-mail: revhcook@btinternet.com]	01786 464128
Gaston, A. Ray C. MA BD	1969 2002	(Leuchars: St Athernase)	'Hamewith', 13 Manse Road, Dollar FK14 7AL [E-mail: gaston.arthur@yahoo.co.uk]	01259 743202
Gillespie, Irene C. (Mrs) BD	1991 2007	(Tiree)	39 King O'Muirs Drive, Tullibody, Alloa FK10 3AY [E-mail: revicg@btinternet.com]	01259 723937
Gilmour, William M. MA BD	1969 2008	(Lecropt)	14 Pine Court, Doune FK16 6JE	01786 842928
Goodison, Michael J. BSc BA	2013	Chaplain: Army	82 Nevis Crescent, Alloa FK10 2BN [E-mail: mike.goodison@btinternet.com]	01259 724333
Izett, William A.F.	1968 2000	(Law)	1 Duke Street, Clackmannan FK10 4EF [E-mail: william.izett@talktalk.net]	01259 724203
Jack, Alison M. MA BD PhD	1998 2001	Assistant: Curse of Gowrie	5 Murdoch Terrace, Dunblane FK15 9JE [E-mail: alisonmjack809@btinternet.com]	01786 825116
MacCormick, Moira G. BA LTh	1986 2003	(Buchlyvie with Gartmore)	12 Rankine Wynd, Tullibody, Alloa FK10 2UW [E-mail: mgmaccormick@o2.co.uk]	01259 724619
McIntosh, Hamish N.M. MA	1949 1987	(Fintry)	9 Abbeyfield House, 17 Allan Park, Stirling FK8 2QG	01786 470294
Mack, Lynne (Mrs)	2013	Ordained Local Minister	36 Middleton, Menstrie FK11 7HD [E-mail: lynne.mack@aol.co.uk]	01259 761465
McKenzie, Alan BSc BD	1988 2013	(Bellshill: Macdonald Memorial with Bellshill: Orbiston)	89 Drip Road, Stirling FK8 1RN [E-mail: rev.a.mckenzie@btopenworld.com]	01786 430450
Malloch, Philip R.M. LLB BD	1970 2009	(Killearn)	8 Michael McParland Drive, Torrance, Glasgow G64 4EE [E-mail: pmalloch@mac.com]	01360 620089
Mathew, J. Gordon MA BD	1973 2011	(Buckie: North)	45 Westhaugh Road, Stirling FK9 5GF [E-mail: jg.matthew@btinternet.com]	01786 445951
Millar, Jennifer M. (Mrs) BD DipMin	1986 1995	Teacher: Religious and Moral Education	5 Clifford Road, Stirling FK8 2AQ [E-mail: ajrmillar@blueyonder.co.uk]	01786 469979
Mitchell, Alexander B. BD	1981 2014	(Dunblane: St Blane's)	24 Hebridean Gardens, Crieff PH7 3BP [E-mail: alex.mitchell6@btopenworld.com]	01764 652241
Ovens, Samuel B. BD	1982 1993	(Slamannan)	21 Bevan Drive, Alva FK12 5PD	01259 763456
Paterson, John L. MA BD STM	1964 2003	(Linlithgow: St Michael's)	'Kirkmichael', 22 Waterfront Way, Stirling FK9 5GH [E-mail: revianpaterson@hotmail.co.uk]	01786 447165
Picken, Stuart D.B. MA BD PhD	1966 2014	(Ardoch with Blackford)	18C Kilbryde Crescent, Dunblane FK15 9BA [E-mail: picken@eikoku.demon.co.uk]	01786 825947

Roderick, Maggie R. BA BD FRSA FTSI	2010 2012	(Associate: Stirling: St Ninians Old)	34 Craiglea, Stirling FK9 5EE [E-mail: revmaggieroderick@btinternet.com]	(Mbl) 07984 604205
Sangster, Ernest G. MA BD ThM	1958 1997	(Alva)	6 Lawhill Road, Dollar FK14 7BG	01259 742344
Scott, James F.	1957 1997	(Dyce)	5 Gullipen View, Callander FK17 8HN	01877 330565
Scoular, J. Marshall	1954 1996	(Kippen)	6 Buccleuch Court, Dunblane FK15 0AR	01786 825976
Sewell, Paul M.N. MA BD	1970 2010	(Berwick-upon-Tweed: St Andrew's Wallace Green and Lowick)	7 Bohun Court, Stirling FK7 7UT [E-mail: paulmsewell@btinternet.com]	01786 489969
Sherry, George T. LTh	1977 2004	(Menstrie)	4 Woodburn Way, Alva FK12 5LB [E-mail: gandms@btinternet.com]	01259 763779
Sinclair, James H. MA BD DipMin	1966 2004	(Auchencairn and Rerrick with Buittle and Kelton)	16 Delaney Court, Alloa FK10 1RB	01259 729001
Thomson, Raymond BD DipMin	1992 2013	(Slamannan)	8 Rhodders Grove, Alva FK12 5ER	01259 769083
Weighton, Gillian (Mrs) BD STM	1992 2014	(Bridge of Allan)	First Presbyterian Church, 716 College Avenue, Racine, Wisconsin, USA [E-mail: gillweighton@aol.com]	

STIRLING ADDRESSES

Allan Park South	Dumbarton Road	North	Springfield Road
Holy Rude	St John Street	St Columba's	Park Terrace
		St Mark's	Drip Road

St Ninians Old	Kirk Wynd, St Ninians
Viewfield Erskine	Barnton Street

(24) DUNFERMLINE

Meets at Dunfermline in St Andrew's Erskine Church, Robertson Road, on the first Thursday of each month, except January, July and August when there is no meeting, and June when it meets on the last Thursday.

Clerk:	REV. IAIN M. GREENSHIELDS BD DipRS ACMA MSc MTh	38 Garvock Hill, Dunfermline KY12 7UU [E-mail: dunfermline@cofscotland.org.uk]	01383 741495 (Office) 01383 723955 (Home)

Aberdour: St Fillan's (H) (Website: www.stfillans.presbytery.org)

Peter S. Gerbrandy-Baird MA BD MSc FRSA FRGS	2004	St Fillan's Manse, 36 Bellhouse Road, Aberdour, Fife KY3 0TL	01383 861522

Beath and Cowdenbeath: North (H)

David W. Redmayne BSc BD	2001	10 Stuart Place, Cowdenbeath KY4 9BN [E-mail: beathandnorth@dunfermlinepresbytery.org.uk]	01383 511033

Cairneyhill (H) (01383 882352) linked with Limekilns (H) (01383 873337)
Norman M. Grant BD   1990   The Manse, 10 Church Street, Limekilns, Dunfermline KY11 3HT   01383 872341
                                                         [E-mail: nmg57@live.com]

Carnock and Oakley (H) linked with Saline and Blairingone
Vacant   The Manse, Main Street, Carnock, Dunfermline KY12 9JG   01383 850327

Cowdenbeath: Trinity (H)
Gavin Boswell BTheol   1993   66 Barclay Street, Cowdenbeath KY4 9LD   01383 515089
John Wyllie   (Pastoral Assistant)   51 Seafar Street, Kelty KY4 0JX   01383 839200

Culross and Torryburn (H)
Jayne E. Scott (Mrs) BA MEd MBA   1988   2009   The Manse, Culross, Dunfermline KY12 8JD   01383 880231
                                                         [E-mail: jayne.scott5@btinternet.com]

Dalgety (H) (01383 824092) (E-mail: office@dalgety-church.co.uk) (Website: www.dalgety-church.co.uk)
Christine Sime (Miss) BSc BD   1994   2012   9 St Colme Drive, Dalgety Bay, Dunfermline KY11 9LQ   01383 822316
                                                         [E-mail: revsime@btinternet.com]

Dunfermline: Abbey (H) (Website: www.dunfabbey.freeserve.co.uk)
MaryAnn R. Rennie (Mrs) BD MTh   1998   2012   3 Perdieus Mount, Dunfermline KY12 7XE   01383 727311
                                                         [E-mail: maryann.r.rennie@gmail.com]

Dunfermline: East (New Charge Development)
Andrew A. Morrice MA BD   1999   2010   9 Dover Drive, Dunfermline KY11 8HQ   01383 621050
                                                         [E-mail: andrew@dunfermlineeastchurch.org.uk]

Dunfermline: Gillespie Memorial (H) (01383 621253) (E-mail: gillespie.church@btopenworld.com)
Vacant   4 Killin Court, Dunfermline KY12 7XF   01383 723329

Dunfermline: North
Ian G. Thom BSc PhD BD   1990   2007   13 Barbour Grove, Dunfermline KY12 9YB   01383 733471
                                                         [E-mail: ianthom58@btinternet.com]

Dunfermline: St Andrew's Erskine (01383 841660)
Muriel F. Willoughby (Mrs) MA BD   2006   2013   71A Townhill Road, Dunfermline KY12 0BN   01383 734657
                                                         [E-mail: muriel.willoughby@btinternet.com]

Dunfermline: St Leonard's (01383 620106) (E-mail: office@stleonardsparishchurch.org.uk) (Website: www.stleonardsparishchurch.org.uk)
Vacant
12 Torvean Place, Dunfermline KY11 4YY
01383 721054

Dunfermline: St Margaret's
Iain M. Greenshields
BD DipRS ACMA MSc MTh
1984   2007
38 Garvock Hill, Dunfermline KY12 7UU
[E-mail: revimaclg@hotmail.co.uk]
01383 723955

Dunfermline: St Ninian's
Elizabeth A. Fisk (Mrs) BD
1996
51 St John's Drive, Dunfermline KY12 7TL
01383 722256

Dunfermline: Townhill and Kingseat (H)
Rosemary A. Smith BD
1997   2010
7 Lochwood Park, Kingseat, Dunfermline KY12 0UX
[E-mail: revrosieann@gmail.com]
01383 626181

Inverkeithing linked with North Queensferry (R)
Colin M. Alston BMus BD BN RN
1975
1 Dover Way, Dunfermline KY11 8HR
[E-mail: ca5884400@gmail.com]
01383 621050

Kelty (Website: www.keltykirk.org.uk)
Hugh D. Steele LTh DipMin
1994   2013
15 Arlick Road, Kelty KY4 0BH
[E-mail: hugdebra@aol.com]
01383 830291

Limekilns See Cairneyhill

Lochgelly and Benarty: St Serf's
Vacant
82 Main Street, Lochgelly KY5 9AA
01592 780435

North Queensferry See Inverkeithing

Rosyth
Violet C.C. McKay (Mrs) BD
1988   2002
42 Woodside Avenue, Rosyth KY11 2LA
[E-mail: vcmckay@btinternet.com]
01383 412776

Morag Crawford (Miss) MSc DCS
118 Wester Drylaw Place, Edinburgh EH4 2TG
[E-mail: morag.crawford.dcs@blueyonder.co.uk]
0131-332 2253
07970 982563 (Mbl)

Saline and Blairingone See Carnock and Oakley

Tulliallan and Kincardine MA BD
Alexander Shuttleworth MA BD   2004 2013   62 Toll Road, Kincardine, Alloa FK10 4QZ   01259 731002
[E-mail: revshuttleworth@aol.com]

Name	Ord.	Ind.	(Previous charge)	Address	Tel
Boyle, Robert P. LTh	1990	2010	(Saline and Blairingone)	43 Dunipace Crescent, Dunfermline KY12 7JE [E-mail: boab.boyle@btinternet.com]	01383 740980
Brown, Peter MA BD FRAScot	1953	1987	(Holm)	24 Inchmickery Avenue, Dalgety Bay, Dunfermline KY11 5NF	01383 822456
Chalmers, John P. BD CPS	1979	1995	Principal Clerk	10 Liggars Place, Dunfermline KY12 7XZ	01383 739130
Donald, Kenneth W. BA BD	1982	2011	Service of the Church	24 Fieldfare View, Dunfermline KY11 4FY [E-mail: kenneth@kdonald.freeserve.co.uk]	
Farquhar, William E. BA BD	1987	2006	(Dunfermline: Townhill and Kingseat)	29 Queens Drive, Middlewich, Cheshire CW10 0DG	01606 835097
Jenkins, Gordon F.C. MA BD PhD	1968	2006	(Dunfermline: North)	20 Lumsden Park, Cupar KY15 5YL [E-mail: jenkinsgordon1@sky.com]	01334 652548
Jessamine, Alistair L. MA BD	1979	2011	(Dunfermline: Abbey)	11 Gallowhill Farm Cottages, Strathaven ML10 6BZ [E-mail: chatty.1@talktalk.net]	01357 520934
Johnston, Thomas N. LTh	1972	2008	(Edinburgh: Priestfield)	71 Main Street, Newmills, Dunfermline KY12 8ST [E-mail: tomjohnston@blueyonder.co.uk]	01383 889240
Kenny, Elizabeth S.S. BD RGN SCM	1989	2010	(Carnock and Oakley)	5 Cobden Court, Crossgates, Cowdenbeath KY4 8AU [E-mail: esskenny@btinternet.com]	(Mbl) 07831 763494
Laidlaw, Victor W.N. BD	1975	2008	(Edinburgh: St Catherine's Argyle)	9 Tern Road, Dunfermline KY11 8GA	01383 620134
Leitch, D. Graham MA BD	1974	2012	(Tyne Valley Parish)	9 St Margaret Wynd, Dunfermline KY12 0UT [E-mail: dgrahamleitch@gmail.com]	01383 249245
McLellan, Andrew R.C. CBE MA BD STM DD	1970	2002	(HM Inspector of Prisons)	4 Liggars Place, Dunfermline KY12 7XZ	01383 725959
Reid, A. Gordon BSc BD	1982	2008	(Dunfermline: Gillespie Memorial)	7 Arkleston Crescent, Paisley PA3 4TG	0141-842 1542 / (Mbl) 07773 300989
Reid, David MSc LTh FSAScot	1961	1992	(St Monans with Largoward)	North Lethans, Saline, Dunfermline KY12 9TE [E-mail: reid501@fsmail.net]	01383 733144
Shewan, Frederick D.F. MA BD	1970	2005	(Edinburgh: Muirhouse St Andrew's)	38 Tremayne Place, Dunfermline KY12 9YH	01383 734354
Stuart, Anne (Miss) DCS			(Deacon)	1 Murrell Terrace, Aberdour, Burntisland KY3 0XH	01383 860049
Sutherland, Iain A. BSc BD	1996	2014	(Dunfermline: Gillespie Memorial)	4 Killin Court, Dunfermline KY12 7XF [E-mail: RevISutherland@aol.com]	01383 723329
Watt, Robert J. BD	1994	2009	(Dumbarton: Riverside)	101 Birrell Drive, Dunfermline KY11 8FA [E-mail: r.watt21@virginmedia.com]	01383 735417 / (Mbl) 07753 683717
Whyte, Isabel H. (Mrs) BD	1993		(Chaplain: Queen Margaret Hospital, Dunfermline)	14 Carlingnose Point, North Queensferry, Inverkeithing KY11 1ER [E-mail: iainisabel@whytes28.fsnet.co.uk]	01383 410732

(25) KIRKCALDY

Meets at Kirkcaldy, in the St Bryce Kirk Centre, on the first Tuesday of March, September and December, and on the last Tuesday of June. It meets also on the first Tuesday of November for Holy Communion and a conference at the church of the Moderator.

Clerk:	REV. ROSEMARY FREW (Mrs) MA BD	83 Milton Road, Kirkcaldy KY1 1TP [E-mail: kirkcaldy@cofscotland.org.uk]	01592 260315
Depute Clerk:	MR DOUGLAS G. HAMILL BEM	41 Abbots Mill, Kirkcaldy KY2 5PE [E-mail: hamilldg@tiscali.co.uk]	01592 267500

Auchterderran Kinglassie
Vacant   7 Woodend Road, Cardenden, Lochgelly KY5 0NE   01592 720202
(New charge formed by the union of Auchterderran: St Fothad's and Kinglassie)

Auchtertool linked with Kirkcaldy: Linktown (H) (01592 641080)
Catriona M. Morrison (Mrs) MA BD   1995   2000   16 Raith Crescent, Kirkcaldy KY2 5NN [E-mail: catriona@linktown.org.uk]   01592 265536
Marc Prowe   16 Raith Crescent, Kirkcaldy KY2 5NN [E-mail: marc@linktown.org.uk]   01592 265536

Buckhaven (01592 715577) and Wemyss
Wilma Cairns (Miss) BD   1999   2004   33 Main Road, East Wemyss, Kirkcaldy KY1 4RE [E-mail: wilcairns@blueyonder.co.uk]   01592 712870
Jacqueline Thomson (Mrs) MTh DCS   1 Barron Terrace, Leven KY8 4DL [E-mail: churchdeacon@blueyonder.co.uk]   01333 301115 / 07806 776560 (Mbl)

Burntisland (H)
Alan Sharp BSc BD   1980   2001   21 Ramsay Crescent, Burntisland KY3 9JL [E-mail: alansharp03@aol.com]   01592 874303

Dysart: St Clair (H)
Maudeen I. MacDougall (Miss) BA BD MTh   1978   2014   1 School Brae, Dysart, Kirkcaldy KY1 2XB [E-mail: rev.maudeen@gmail.com]   01592 561967

Glenrothes: Christ's Kirk (H)
Vacant   12 The Limekilns, Glenrothes KY6 3QJ   01592 620536

Glenrothes: St Columba's (01592 752539) (Rothes Trinity Parish Grouping)
Alan Kimmitt BSc BD   2013   40 Liberton Drive, Glenrothes KY6 3PB
[E-mail: alan@kimmitt.org.uk]   01592 742233

Glenrothes: St Margaret's (H) (01592 328162)
Vacant   8 Alburne Park, Glenrothes KY7 5RB   01592 752241

Glenrothes: St Ninian's (H) (01592 610560) (E-mail: office@stninians.co.uk) (Rothes Trinity Parish Grouping)
Allistair Roy BD DipSW PGDip   2007   1 Cawdor Drive, Glenrothes KY6 2HN
[E-mail: alli@stninians.co.uk]   01592 611963

Kennoway, Windygates and Balgonie: St Kenneth's (01333 351372) (E-mail: stkennethsparish@gmail.com)
Richard Baxter MA BD   1997   2 Fernhill Gardens, Windygates, Leven KY8 5DZ
[E-mail: richard-baxter@msn.com]   01333 352329

Kinghorn
James Reid BD   1985   1997   17 Myre Crescent, Kinghorn, Burntisland KY3 9UB
[E-mail: jim17reid@aol.com]   01592 890269

Kirkcaldy: Abbotshall (H)
Rosemary Frew (Mrs) MA BD   1988   2005   83 Milton Road, Kirkcaldy KY1 1TP
[E-mail: rosiefrew@blueyonder.co.uk]   01592 260315

Kirkcaldy: Bennochy
Robin J. McAlpine BDS BD MTh   1988   2011   25 Bennochy Avenue, Kirkcaldy KY2 5QE
[E-mail: revrobinmcalpine@gmail.com]   01592 643518

Kirkcaldy: Linktown See Auchtertool

Kirkcaldy: Pathhead (H) (Tel/Fax: 01592 204635) (E-mail: pathhead@btinternet.com) (Website: www.pathheadparishchurch.co.uk)
Andrew C. Donald BD DPS   1992   2005   73 Loughborough Road, Kirkcaldy KY1 3DD
[E-mail: andrewcdonald@blueyonder.co.uk]   01592 652215

Kirkcaldy: St Bryce Kirk (H) (01592 640016) (E-mail: office@stbrycekirk.org.uk)
Ken Froude MA BD   1979   6 East Fergus Place, Kirkcaldy KY1 1XT   01592 264480
[E-mail: kenfroude@blueyonder.co.uk]

Kirkcaldy: Templehall (H)
Anthony J.R. Fowler BSc BD   1982 2004   35 Appin Crescent, Kirkcaldy KY2 6EJ   01592 260156
[E-mail: ajrf@btinternet.com]

Kirkcaldy: Torbain
Ian Elston BD MTh   1999   91 Sauchenbush Road, Kirkcaldy KY2 5RN   01592 263015
[E-mail: elston667@btinternet.com]

Leslie: Trinity (Rothes Trinity Parish Grouping)
Guardianship of the Presbytery

Leven
Gilbert C. Nisbet CA BD   1993 2007   5 Forman Road, Leven KY8 4HH   01333 303339
[E-mail: gcn-leven@blueyonder.co.uk]

Markinch and Thornton
Vacant   7 Guthrie Crescent, Markinch, Glenrothes KY7 6AY   01592 758264
(New charge formed by the union of Markinch and Thornton)

Methil: Wellesley (H)
Gillian Paterson (Mrs) BD   2010   10 Vettriano Vale, Leven KY8 4GD   01333 423147
[E-mail: gillianpaterson10@hotmail.co.uk]

Methilhill and Denbeath
Elisabeth F. Cranfield (Miss) MA BD   1988   9 Chemiss Road, Methilhill, Leven KY8 2BS   01592 713142
[E-mail: ecranfield@btinternet.com]

Adams, David G. BD	1991 2011	(Cowdenbeath: Trinity)	13 Fernhill Gardens, Windygates, Leven KY8 5DZ [E-mail: adams.69@btinternet.com]	01333 351214
Collins, Mitchell BD CPS	1996 2005	(Creich, Flisk and Kilmany with Monimail)	6 Netherby Park, Glenrothes KY6 3PL [E-mail: collinsmit@aol.com]	01592 742915
Elston, Peter K.	1963 2000	(Dalgety)	6 Cairngorm Crescent, Kirkcaldy KY2 5RF [E-mail: peterkelston@btinternet.com]	01592 205622
Ferguson, David J.	1966 2001	(Bellie with Speymouth)	4 Russell Gardens, Ladybank, Cupar KY15 7LT	01337 831406

Name				Phone
Forrester, Ian L. MA	1964	1996	(Frieckheim Kinnell with Inverkeilor and Lunan) — 8 Bennochy Avenue, Kirkcaldy KY2 5QE	01592 260251
Forsyth, Alexander R. TD BA MTh	1973	2013	(Markinch) — 49 Scaraben Crescent, Formonthills, Glenrothes KY6 3HL [E-mail: arf11721@outlook.com]	01592 749049 (Mbl) 07756 239021
Galbraith, Douglas MA BD BMus MPhil ARSCM PhD	1965	2005	Editor: *The Year Book* — 34 Balbirnie Street, Markinch, Glenrothes KY7 6DA [E-mail: dgalbraith@hotmail.com]	01592 752403
Gatt, David W.	1981	1995	(Thornton) — 15 Beech Avenue, Thornton, Kirkcaldy KY1 4AT	01592 774328
Gibson, Ivor MA	1957	1993	(Abercorn with Dalmeny) — 15 McInnes Road, Markinch, Glenrothes KY7 6BA	01592 759982
Gisbey, John E. MA BD MSc DipEd	1964	2002	(Thornhill) — Whitemyre House, 28 St Andrews Road, Largoward, Leven KY9 1HZ	01334 840540
Gordon, Ian D. LTh	1972	2001	(Markinch) — 2 Somerville Way, Glenrothes KY7 5GE	01592 742487
Houghton, Christine (Mrs) BD	1997	2010	(Whitburn: South) — 39 Cedar Crescent, Thornton, Kirkcaldy KY1 4BE [E-mail: c.houghton1@btinternet.com]	01592 772823
McLeod, Alistair G.	1988	2005	(Glenrothes: St Columba's) — 13 Greenmantle Way, Glenrothes KY6 3QG [E-mail: aagm@btinternet.com]	01592 744558
McNaught, Samuel M. MA BD MTh	1968	2002	(Kirkcaldy: St John's) — 6 Munro Court, Glenrothes KY7 5GD [E-mail: sjmcnaught@btinternet.com]	01592 742352
Munro, Andrew MA BD PhD	1972	2000	(Glencaple with Lowther) — 7 Dunvegan Avenue, Kirkcaldy KY2 5SG [E-mail: am.smm@blueyonder.co.uk]	01592 566129
Nicol, George G. BD DPhil	1982	2013	(Falkland with Freuchie) — 48 Fidra Avenue, Burntisland KY3 0AZ [E-mail: ggnicol@totalise.co.uk]	01592 873258
Paterson, Maureen (Mrs) BSc	1992	2010	(Auxiliary Minister) — 91 Dalmahoy Crescent, Kirkcaldy KY2 6TA [E-mail: m.e.paterson@blueyonder.co.uk]	01592 262300
Templeton, James L. BSc BD	1975	2012	(Innerleven: East) — 29 Coldstream Avenue, Leven KY8 5TN [E-mail: jamietempleton@btinternet.com]	01333 427102
Thomson, John D. BD	1985	2005	(Kirkcaldy: Pathhead) — 3 Tottenham Court, Hill Street, Dysart, Kirkcaldy KY1 2XY [E-mail: j.thomson10@sky.com]	01592 655313 (Mbl) 07885 414979
Tomlinson, Bryan L. TD	1969	2003	(Kirkcaldy: Abbotshall) — 2 Duddingston Drive, Kirkcaldy KY2 6JP [E-mail: abbkirk@blueyonder.co.uk]	01592 564843
Webster, Elspeth H. (Miss) DCS			(Deaconess) — 82 Broomhill Avenue, Burntisland KY3 0BP [E-mail: abbkirk@blueyonder.co.uk]	01592 873616
Wilson, Tilly (Miss) MTh	1990	2012	(Dysart) — 6 Citron Glebe, Kirkcaldy KY1 2NF [E-mail: tillywilson@blueyonder.co.uk]	01592 263141

KIRKCALDY ADDRESSES

Abbotshall	Abbotshall Road	Templehall	Beauly Place
Bennochy	Elgin Street x High Street	Torbain	Lindores Drive
Linktown	Nicol Street x High Street	Viewforth	Viewforth Street x Viewforth Terrace
Pathhead	Harriet Street x Church Street		
St Bryce Kirk	St Brycedale Avenue x Kirk Wynd		

(26) ST ANDREWS

Meets at Cupar, in St John's Church Hall, on the first Wednesday of February, March, May, September, October, November and December, and on the last Wednesday of May and June.

Clerk:	**REV. NIGEL J. ROBB FCP MA BD ThM MTh**	Hope Park and Martyrs' Church, 1 Howard Place, St Andrews KY16 9UY **[E-mail: standrews@cofscotland.org.uk]**	**01334 478144**
Depute Clerk:	**MRS CATHERINE WILSON**	5 Taeping Close, Cellardyke, Anstruther KY10 3YL **[E-mail: catherine.wilson15@btinternet.com]** **Presbytery Office**	**01333 310936** **01337 858442**

Abdie and Dunbog (H) linked with Newburgh (H)
Lynn Brady (Miss) BD DipMin   1996   2002   2 Guthrie Court, Cupar Road, Newburgh, Cupar KY14 6HA
[E-mail: revbrady1963@yahoo.co.uk]   01337 842228

Anstruther linked with Cellardyke (H) linked with Kilrenny
Arthur A. Christie BD   1997   2009   16 Taeping Close, Cellardyke, Anstruther KY10 3YL
[E-mail: revaac@btinternet.com]   01333 313917

Auchtermuchty (H) linked with Edenshead and Strathmiglo
James G. Redpath BD DipPTh   1988   2006   The Manse, Kirk Wynd, Strathmiglo, Cupar KY14 7QS
[E-mail: james.redpath2@btopenworld.com]   01337 860256

Balmerino (H) linked with Wormit (H)
James Connolly   1982   2004   5 Westwater Place, Newport-on-Tay DD6 8NS
DipTh CertMin MA(Theol) DMin   [E-mail: revconnolly@btinternet.com]   01382 542626

Boarhills and Dunino
Guardianship of the Presbytery (in deferred linking with St Andrews: Holy Trinity)

Cameron linked with St Andrews: St Leonard's (H) (01334 478702) (E-mail: stlencam@btconnect.com)
Alan D. McDonald LLB BD MTh DLitt DD   1979   1998   1 Cairnhill Gardens, St Andrews KY16 8QY
[E-mail: alan.d.mcdonald@talk21.com]   01334 472793

Carnbee linked with Pittenweem
Margaret E.S. Rose BD   2007   29 Milton Road, Pittenweem, Anstruther KY10 2LN
[E-mail: mgt.r@btopenworld.com]   01333 312838

Cellardyke See Anstruther

Ceres, Kemback and Springfield
James W. Campbell BD — 1995 — 2010 — The Manse, St Andrews Road, Ceres, Cupar KY15 5NQ [E-mail: revjimashkirk@aol.com] — 01334 829350

Crail linked with Kingsbarns (H)
Ann Allison BSc PhD BD — 2000 — 2011 — The Manse, St Andrews Road, Crail, Anstruther KY10 3UH [E-mail: revann@sky.com] — 01333 451986

Creich, Flisk and Kilmany linked with Monimail
Vacant — Creich Manse, Brunton, Cupar KY15 4PA — 01337 870332

Cupar: Old (H) and St Michael of Tarvit
Vacant — 76 Hogarth Drive, Cupar KY15 5YH — 01334 653196

Cupar: St John's and Dairsie United
Jan J. Steyn (Mr) — 2011 — The Manse, 23 Hogarth Drive, Cupar KY15 5YH [E-mail: jansteyn464@btinternet.com] — 01334 650751

Edenshead and Strathmiglo See Auchtermuchty

Elie (H) Kilconquhar and Colinsburgh (H)
Emma McDonald — 2013 — 30 Bank Street, Elie, Leven KY9 1BW — 01333 330685

Falkland linked with Freuchie (H)
Vacant — 1 Newton Road, Falkland, Cupar KY15 7AQ — 01337 858557

Freuchie See Falkland

Howe of Fife
William F. Hunter MA BD — 1986 — 2011 — The Manse, 83 Church Street, Ladybank, Cupar KY15 7ND [E-mail: mail@billhunter.plus.com] — 01337 832717

Kilrenny See Anstruther
Kingsbarns See Crail

Largo and Newburn (H) linked with Largo: St David's
John A.H. Murdoch BA BD DPSS | 1979 2006 | The Manse, Church Place, Upper Largo, Leven KY8 6EH [E-mail: jm.largo@btinternet.com] | 01333 360286

Largo: St David's See Largo and Newburn

Largoward (H) linked with St Monans (H)
Peter W. Mills CB BD DD CPS | 1984 2013 | The Manse, St Monans, Anstruther KY10 2DD [E-mail: pwmills@live.co.uk] | 01333 730258

Leuchars: St Athernase
Caroline Taylor (Mrs) MA BD | 1995 2003 | 7 David Wilson Park, Balmullo, St Andrews KY16 0NP [E-mail: caro234@btinternet.com] | 01334 870038

Monimail See Creich, Flisk and Kilmany
Newburgh See Abdie and Dunbog

Newport-on-Tay (H)
Stanley A. Brook BD MTh | 1977 2009 | 8 Gowrie Street, Newport-on-Tay DD6 8ED [E-mail: stan_brook@hotmail.com] | 01382 540009

Pittenweem See Carnbee

St Andrews: Holy Trinity
Rory MacLeod BA MBA BD | 1994 2004 | 5 Cupar Road, Guardbridge, St Andrews KY16 0UA [E-mail: annicerory@gmail.com] | 01334 838038

St Andrews: Hope Park and Martyrs' (H) linked with Strathkinness
Allan McCafferty BSc BD | 1993 2011 | 20 Priory Gardens, St Andrews KY16 8XX [E-mail: minister@hpmchurch.org.uk] | 01334 478287 (Tel/Fax)

St Andrews: St Leonard's See Cameron
St Monans See Largoward
Strathkinness See St Andrews: Hope Park and Martyrs'

Tayport
Brian H. Oxburgh BSc BD   1980   2011   27 Bell Street, Tayport DD6 9AP   01382 553879
                                                [E-mail: b.oxburgh@btinternet.com]

Wormit See Balmerino

Alexander, James S. MA BD BA PhD   1966 1973   (University of St Andrews)   5 Strathkinness High Road, St Andrews KY16 9RP   01334 472680
Bradley, Ian C. MA BD DPhil   1990 1990   University of St Andrews   4 Donaldson Gardens, St Andrews KY16 9DN   01334 475389
Brown, Harry J. LTh   1991 2009   (Dundee: Menzieshill)   6 Hall Street, Kettlebridge, Cupar KY15 7QF   01337 830088
    [E-mail: harrybrown@aol.com]
Brown, Lawson R. MA   1960 1997   (Cameron with St Andrew's: St Leonard's and West)   10 Park Street, St Andrews KY16 8AQ   01334 473413
Cameron, John U.   1974 2008   (Dundee: Broughty Ferry St Stephen's and West)
    BA BSc PhD BD ThD
Douglas, Peter C. JP   1966 1993   (Boarhills with Dunino)   10 Howard Place, St Andrews KY16 9HL   01334 474474
Earnshaw, Philip BA BSc BD   1986 1996   (Glasgow: Pollokshields)   The Old Schoolhouse, Flisk, Newburgh, Cupar KY14 6HN   01337 870218
Fairlie, George BD BVMS MRCVS   1971 2002   (Crail with Kingsbarns)   22 Castle Street, St Monans, Anstruther KY10 2AP   01333 730640
Fraser, Ann G. BD CertMin   1990 2007   (Auchtermuchty)   41 Warrack Street, St Andrews KY16 8DR   01334 475868
                                          24 Irvine Crescent, St Andrews KY16 8LG   (Tel/Fax) 01334 461329
                                          [E-mail: anngilfraser@btinternet.com]
Galloway, Robert W.C. LTh   1970 1998   (Cromarty)   22 Haughgate, Leven KY8 4SG   01333 426223
Gibson, Henry M. MA BD PhD   1960 1999   (Dundee: The High Kirk)   4 Comerton Place, Drumoig, Leuchars, St Andrews KY16 0NQ   01382 542199
Gordon, Peter M. MA BD   1958 1995   (Airdrie: West)   3 Cupar Road, Cuparmuir, Cupar KY15 5RH   01334 652341
                                          [E-mail: machrie@madasafish.com]
Hamilton, Ian W.F.   1978 2012   (Nairn: Old)   Mossneuk, 5 Windsor Gardens, St Andrews KY16 8XL   01334 477745
    BD LTh ALCM AVCM   [E-mail: reviwfh@btinternet.com]
Harrison, Cameron   2006   (Auxiliary Minister)   Woodfield House, Priormuir, St Andrews KY16 8LP   01334 478067
Hegarty, John D. LTh ABSC   1988 2004   (Buckie: South and West with Enzie)   26 Montgomery Way, Kinross KY13 8FD   01577 863829
                                          [E-mail: john.hegarty@tesco.net]
Jeffrey, Kenneth S. BA BD PhD   2002 2014   University of Aberdeen   The North Steading, Dalgairn, Cupar KY15 4PH   01334 653196
                                          [E-mail: ksjeffrey@biopenworld.com]
Lancaster, Craig MA BD   2004 2011   Chaplain: RAF   Station Chaplain, RAF Leuchars, St Andrews KY16 0JX   01334 857782
                                                                                    07968 270391   (Mbl)
MacEwan, Donald G. MA BD PhD   2001 2012   Chaplain: University of St Andrews   Chaplaincy Centre, 3A St Mary's Place, St Andrews KY16 9UY   01334 462865
                                          [E-mail: dgm21@st-andrews.ac.uk]   07713 322036   (Mbl)
McGregor, Duncan J. MIFM   1982 1996   (Channelkirk with Lauder: Old)   14 Mount Melville, St Andrews KY16 8NG   01334 478314
Mackenzie, A. Cameron MA   1955 1995   (Biggar)   Hedgerow, 5 Shiels Avenue, Freuchie, Cupar KY15 7JD   01337 857763
McLean, John P. BSc BPhil BD   1994 2013   (Glenrothes: St Margaret's)   72 Lawmill Gardens, St Andrews KY16 8QS   01334 470803
                                          [E-mail: john@mcleanmail.me.uk]
Meager, Peter   1971 1998   (Elie with Kilconquhar and Colinsburgh)   7 Lorraine Drive, Cupar KY15 5DY   01334 656991
    MA BD CertMgmt(Open)
Neilson, Peter MA BD MTh   1975 2006   Mission Consultant   Linne Bheag, 2 School Green, Anstruther KY10 3HF   01333 310477
                                          [E-mail: neilson.peter@btinternet.com]   07818 418608   (Mbl)

Name			Charge	Address	Telephone
Petrie, Ian D. MA BD	1970	2008	(Dundee: St Andrew's)	27 High Street East, Anstruther KY10 3DQ [E-mail: idp-77@hotmail.com]	01333 310181
Reid, Alan A.S. MA BD STM	1962	1995	(Bridge of Allan: Chalmers)	Wayside Cottage, Bridgend, Ceres, Cupar KY15 5LS	01334 828509
Robb, Nigel J. FCP MA BD ThM MTh	1981	2014	Presbytery Clerk	Presbytery Office, Hope Park and Martyrs' Church, 1 Howard Place, St Andrews KY16 9UY	(Mbl) 07966 286958
Roy, Alan J. BSc BD	1960	1999	(Aberuthven with Dunning)	14 Comerton Place, Drumoig, Leuchars, St Andrews KY16 0NQ [E-mail: a.roy225@btinternet.com]	01382 542225
Salters, Robert B. MA BD PhD	1966	1971	(University of St Andrews)	Vine Cottage, 119 South Street, St Andrews KY16 9UH	01334 473198
Strong, Clifford LTh	1983	1995	(Creich, Flisk and Kilmany with Monimail)	60 Maryknowe, Gauldry, Newport-on-Tay DD6 8SL	01382 330445
Taylor, Ian BSc MA LTh DipEd	1983	1997	(Abdie and Dunbog with Newburgh)	Lundie Cottage, Arncroach, Anstruther KY10 2RN	01333 720222
Thrower, Charles G. BSc	1965	2002	(Carnbee with Pittenweem)	Grange House, Wester Grangemuir, Pittenweem, Anstruther KY10 2RB [E-mail: charlesandsteph@btinternet.com]	01333 312631
Torrance, Alan J. (Prof.) MA BD DrTheol	1984	1999	University of St Andrews	Kincaple House, Kincaple, St Andrews KY16 9SH	(Home) 01334 850755 (Office) 01334 462843
Walker, James B. MA BD DPhil	1975	2011	(Chaplain: University of St Andrews)	5 Priestden Park, St Andrews KY16 8DL	01334 472839
Wotherspoon, Ian G. BA LTh	1967	2004	(Coatbridge: St Andrew's)	12 Cherry Lane, Cupar KY15 5DA [E-mail: wotherspoonrig@aol.com]	01334 650710
Wright, Lynda (Miss) BEd DCS			Chaplain, Cameron Hospital	Chaplain's Office, Cameron Hospital, Cameron Bridge, Windygates, Leven KY8 5RR [E-mail: lynda.keyhouse@tiscali.co.uk]	(Mbl) 07835 303395
Young, Evelyn M. (Mrs) BSc BD	1984	2003	(Kilmun (St Munn's) with Strone and Ardentinny)	2 Priestden Place, St Andrews KY16 8DP	01334 479662

(27) DUNKELD AND MEIGLE

Meets at Pitlochry on the first Tuesday of February, September and December, on the third Tuesday of April and the fourth Tuesday of October, and at the Moderator's church on the third Tuesday of June.

Clerk: **REV. JOHN RUSSELL MA**   **Kilblaan, Gladstone Terrace, Birnam, Dunkeld PH8 0DP**   **01350 728896**
[E-mail: dunkeldmeigle@cofscotland.org.uk]

Aberfeldy (H) linked with Amulree (H) and Strathbraan linked with Dull and Weem (H)
Vacant   The Manse, Taybridge Terrace, Aberfeldy PH15 2BS   01887 820656

Alyth (H)
Michael J. Erskine MA BD   1985   2012   The Manse, Cambridge Street, Alyth, Blairgowrie PH11 8AW   01828 632238
[E-mail: erskinemike@gmail.com]

Amulree and Strathbraan See Aberfeldy

Ardler, Kettins and Meigle
Vacant
The Manse, Dundee Road, Meigle, Blairgowrie PH12 8SB   01828 640074

Bendochy linked with Coupar Angus: Abbey   1997
Bruce Dempsey BD
Caddam Road, Coupar Angus, Blairgowrie PH13 9EF   01828 627331
[E-mail: revbruce.dempsey@btopenworld.com]

Blair Atholl and Struan linked with Tenandry
Vacant
Blair Atholl, Pitlochry PH18 5SX   01796 481213

Blairgowrie   2003   2008
Harry Mowbray BD CA
The Manse, Upper David Street, Blairgowrie PH10 6HB   01250 872146
[E-mail: hmowbray@viewlands.plus.com]

Braes of Rannoch linked with Foss and Rannoch (H)
Vacant
The Manse, Kinloch Rannoch, Pitlochry PH16 5QA   01882 632381

Caputh and Clunie (H) linked with Kinclaven (H)   2003   2011
Peggy Ewart-Roberts BA BD
Cara Beag, Essendy Road, Blairgowrie PH10 6QU   01250 876897
[E-mail: revpeggy.r@googlemail.com]

Coupar Angus: Abbey See Bendochy
Dull and Weem See Aberfeldy

Dunkeld (H)   1984   2001
R. Fraser Penny BA BD
Cathedral Manse, Dunkeld PH8 0AW   01350 727249
[E-mail: fraserpenn@aol.com]

Fortingall and Glenlyon linked with Kenmore and Lawers (H)   1999
Anne J. Brennan BSc BD MTh
The Manse, Balnaskeag, Kenmore, Aberfeldy PH15 2HB   01887 830218
[E-mail: annebrennan@yahoo.co.uk]

Foss and Rannoch See Braes of Rannoch

Grantully, Logierait and Strathtay
Vacant — The Manse, Strathtay, Pitlochry PH9 0PG — 01887 840251

Kenmore and Lawers See Fortingall and Glenlyon
Kinclaven See Caputh and Clunie

Kirkmichael, Straloch and Glenshee linked with Rattray (H) 1996 2012
Linda Stewart (Mrs) BD — The Manse, Alyth Road, Rattray, Blairgowrie PH10 7HF — 01250 872462
[E-mail: lindacstewart@tiscali.co.uk]

Pitlochry (H) (01796 472160)
Mary M. Haddow (Mrs) BD — 2001 2012 — Manse Road, Moulin, Pitlochry PH16 5EP — 01796 472774
[E-mail: mary_haddow@btconnect.com]

Rattray See Kirkmichael, Straloch and Glenshee
Tenandry See Blair Atholl and Struan

Name	Dates	Charge	Address	Telephone
Campbell, Richard S. LTh	1993 2010	(Gargunnock with Kilmadock with Kincardine-in-Menteith)	3 David Farquharson Road, Blairgowrie PH10 6FD [E-mail: revrichards@yahoo.co.uk]	01250 876386
Cassells, Alexander K. MA BD	1961 1997	(Leuchars: St Athernase and Guardbridge)	47 Burghmuir Road, Perth PH1 1JG	01738 637995
Creegan, Christine M. (Mrs) MTh	1993 2005	(Grantully, Logierait and Strathtay)	Lonaig, 28 Lettoch Terrace, Pitlochry PH16 5BA	01796 472422
Duncan, James BTh FSAScot	1980 1995	(Blair Atholl and Struan)	25 Knockard Avenue, Pitlochry PH16 5JE	01796 474096
Ewart, William BSc BD	1972 2010	(Caputh and Clunie with Kinclaven)	Cara Beag, Essendy Road, Blairgowrie PH10 6QU [E-mail: ewe1@btinternet.com]	01250 876897
Henderson, John D. MA BD	1953 1992	(Cluny with Monymusk)	Aldersyde, George Street, Blairgowrie PH10 6HP	01250 875181
Knox, John W. MTheol	1992 1997	(Lochgelly: Macainsh)	Heatherlea, Main Street, Ardler, Blairgowrie PH12 8SR	01828 640731
McAlister, D.J.B. MA BD PhD	1951 1989	(North Berwick: Blackadder)	2 Duff Avenue, Moulin, Pitlochry PH16 5EN	01796 473591
McFadzean, Iain MA BD	1989 2010	National Director: Workplace Chaplaincy (Scotland)	2 Lowfield Crescent, Luncarty, Perth PH1 3FG [E-mail: iain.mcfadzean@wpcscotland.co.uk]	01738 827338 (Mbl) 07969 227696
MacRae, Malcolm H. MA PhD	1971 2010	(Kirkmichael, Straloch and Glenshee with Rattray)	10B Victoria Place, Stirling FK8 2QU [E-mail: malcolm.macrae1@btopenworld.com]	01786 465547
MacVicar, Kenneth MBE DFC TD MA	1950 1990	(Kenmore with Lawers with Fortingall and Glenlyon)	Illeray, Kenmore, Aberfeldy PH15 2HE	01887 830514
Nelson, Robert C. BA BD	1980 2010	(Isle of Mull, Kilninian and Kilmore with Salen and Ulva with Tobermory with Torosay and Kinlochspelvie)	St Colme's, Perth Road, Birnam, Dunkeld PH8 0BH [E-mail: robertnelson@onetel.net]	01350 727455
Ormiston, Hugh C. BSc BD MPhil PhD	1969 2004	(Kirkmichael, Straloch and Glenshee with Rattray)	Cedar Lea, Main Road, Woodside, Blairgowrie PH13 9NP	01828 670539
Oswald, John BSc PhD BD	1997 2011	(Muthill with Trinity Gask and Kinkell)	1 Woodlands Meadow, Rosemount, Blairgowrie PH10 6GZ [E-mail: revdocoz@bigfoot.com]	01250 872598
Ramsay, Malcolm BA LLB DipMin	1986 2011	Overseas service in Nepal	c/o World Mission Council, 121 George Street, Edinburgh EH2 4YN [E-mail: amalcolmramsay@gmail.com]	0131-225 5722

Robertson, Matthew LTh	1968	2002	(Cawdor with Croy and Dalcross)	Inver, Strathay, Pitlochry PH9 0PG	01887 840780
Russell, John MA	1959	2000	(Tillicoultry)	Kilblaan, Gladstone Terrace, Birnam, Dunkeld PH8 0DP	01350 728896
Shannon, W.G. MA BD	1955	1998	(Pitlochry)	19 Knockard Road, Pitlochry PH16 5HJ	01796 473533
Tait, Thomas W. BD MBE	1972	1997	(Rattray)	3 Rosemount Park, Blairgowrie PH10 6TZ	01250 874833
White, Brock A. LTh	1971	2001	(Kirkcaldy: Templehall)	1 Littlewood Gardens, Blairgowrie PH10 6XZ	01250 870399
Whyte, William B. BD	1973	2003	(Nairn: St Ninian's)	The Old Inn, Park Hill Road, Rattray, Blairgowrie PH10 7DS	01250 874401
Wilson, John M. MA BD	1965	2004	(Altnaharra and Farr)	Berbice, The Terrace, Blair Atholl, Pitlochry PH18 5SZ	01796 481619
Wilson, Mary D. (Mrs) RGN SCM DTM	1990	2004	(Auxiliary Minister)	Berbice, The Terrace, Blair Atholl, Pitlochry PH18 5SZ	01796 481619

(28) PERTH

Meets at 10am on the second Saturday of September at Auchterarder, December at Perth: Riverside, March at Kinross, and June at Crieff.

Clerk: REV. ALAN D. REID MA BD

Presbytery Office: **209 High Street, Perth PH1 5PB**   **01738 451177**
      [E-mail: perth@cofscotland.org.uk]

Aberdalgie (H) and Forteviot (H) linked with Aberuthven and Dunning (H)
Vacant   Aberdalgie, Perth PH2 0QD
      (New name for the charge formerly known as The Stewartry of Strathearn)

Abernethy and Dron and Arngask
Moira Herkes BD   1985   2014   3 Manse Road, Abernethy, Perth PH2 9JP   01738 850938
      [E-mail: minister@abernethydronarngaskchurch.org.uk]

Aberuthven and Dunning See Aberdalgie and Forteviot

Almondbank Tibbermore linked with Methven and Logiealmond
Philip W. Patterson BMus BD   1999   2008   The Manse, Pitcairngreen, Perth PH1 3EA   01738 583217
      [E-mail: philip.patterson@btinternet.com]

Ardoch (H) linked with Blackford (H)
Vacant   01786 880217

Auchterarder (H)
Robert D. Barlow 2010 2013 22 Kirkfield Place, Auchterarder PH3 1FP 01764 662399
BA BSc MSc PhD CChem MRSC [E-mail: rob@miragemedia.co.uk]

Auchtergaven and Moneydie linked with Redgorton and Stanley
Adrian J. Lough BD 2012 22 King Street, Stanley, Perth PH1 4ND 01738 827952
[E-mail: revlough@btinternet.com]

Blackford See Ardoch

Cargill Burrelton linked with Collace
Eric G. McKimmon BA BD MTh PhD 1983 2012 The Manse, Manse Road, Woodside, Blairgowrie PH13 9NQ 01828 670352
[E-mail: ericmckimmon@gmail.com]

Cleish (H) linked with Fossoway: St Serf's and Devonside
Elisabeth M. Stenhouse (Ms) BD 2006 2014 31 Burnbank Meadows, Kinross KY13 8GE 01577 862937
[E-mail: lissten@sky.com]

Collace See Cargill Burrelton

Comrie (H) linked with Dundurn (H)
Graham McWilliams BSc BD 2005 The Manse, Strowan Road, Comrie, Crieff PH6 2ES 01764 670076
[E-mail: Themansefamily@aol.com]

Crieff (H)
Andrew J. Philip BSc BD 1996 2013 8 Strathearn Terrace, Crieff PH7 3AQ 01764 218976
[E-mail: minister@crieffparishchurch.org]

Dunbarney (H) and Forgandenny
Allan J. Wilson BSc MEd BD 2007 Dunbarney Manse, Manse Road, Bridge of Earn, Perth PH2 9DY 01738 812211
[E-mail: allanjwilson@dfpchurch.org.uk]

Dundurn See Comrie

Errol (H) linked with Kilspindie and Rait
Vacant South Bank, Errol, Perth PH2 7PZ 01821 642279

Fossoway: St Serf's and Devonside See Cleish

Fowlis Wester, Madderty and Monzie linked with Gask (H)   1986   2008
Eleanor D. Muir (Miss) MTheol DipPTheol
Beechview, Abercairney, Crieff PH7 3NF
[E-mail: eleanordmuir@tiscali.co.uk]
01764 652116

Gask See Fowlis Wester, Madderty and Monzie
Kilspindie and Rait See Errol

Kinross (H) (Office: 01577 862570)
Alan D. Reid MA BD   1989   2009
15 Green Wood, Kinross KY13 8FG
[E-mail: kinrossmanse@tiscali.co.uk]
01577 862952

Methven and Logiealmond See Almondbank Tibbermore

Muthill (H) linked with Trinity Gask and Kinkell
Klaus O.F. Buwert LLB BD DMin   1984   2013
The Manse, Station Road, Muthill, Crieff PH5 2AR
[E-mail: klaus@buwert.co.uk]
01764 681205

Orwell (H) and Portmoak (H) (Office: 01577 862100)
Angus Morrison MA BD PhD   1979   2011
41 Auld Mart Road, Milnathort, Kinross KY13 9FR
[E-mail: angusmorrison3@gmail.com]
01577 863461

Perth: Craigie and Moncreiffe
Carolann Erskine BD   2009
The Manse, 46 Abbot Street, Perth PH2 0EE
[E-mail: erskine13@blueyonder.co.uk]
01738 623748

Robert Wilkie (Aux)   2011
24 Huntingtower Road, Perth PH1 2JS
[E-mail: robert.wilkie.07@aberdeen.ac.uk]
01738 628301

Perth: Kinnoull (H)
David I. Souter BD   1996   2001
The Broch, 34 Monart Road, Perth PH1 5UQ
[E-mail: d.souter@blueyonder.co.uk]
01738 626046

Perth: Letham St Mark's (H) (Office: 01738 446377)
James C. Stewart BD DipMin   1997
35 Rose Crescent, Perth PH1 1NT
[E-mail: diamondboy09@yahoo.com]
01738 624167

Kenneth D. McKay DCS
11F Balgowan Road, Perth PH1 2JG
[E-mail: deakendan@gmail.com]
01738 621169
07843 883042 (Mbl)

Perth: North (Office: 01738 622298)
Hugh O'Brien CSS MTheol
2001 2009 127 Glasgow Road, Perth PH2 0LU
[E-mail: the.manse@btconnect.com]
01738 625728

Perth: Riverside (Office: 01738 622341)
David R. Rankin MA BD
2009 2014 44 Hay Street, Perth PH1 5HS
[E-mail: davebobrankin@gmail.com]
07810 008754 (Mbl)

Perth: St John's Kirk of Perth (H) (01738 626159) linked with Perth: St Leonard's-in-the-Fields (H) (01738 632238)
James K. Wallace MA BD STM
1988 2009 5 Strathearn Terrace, Perth PH2 0LS
[E-mail: jkwministry@hotmail.com]
01738 621709

Patricia Munro (Ms) BSc DCS
4 Hewat Place, Perth PH1 2UD
[E-mail: pat.munrodcs@gmail.com]
01738 443088
07814 836314 (Mbl)

Perth: St Leonard's-in-the-Fields See Perth: St John's Kirk of Perth

Perth: St Matthew's (Office: 01738 636757; Vestry: 01738 630725)
Scott Burton BD DipMin
1999 2007 23 Kincarrathie Crescent, Perth PH2 7HH
[E-mail: minister@stmatts.org.uk]
01738 626828

Redgorton and Stanley See Auchtergaven and Moneydie

St Madoes and Kinfauns
Marc F. Bircham BD MTh
2000 Glencarse, Perth PH2 7NF
[E-mail: mark.bircham@btinternet.com]
01738 860837

Scone and St Martins
Gordon A. McCracken BD CertMin DMin
(Interim Minister)
1988 2013 13 Haddon Road, Perth PH2 7JA
[E-mail: gordonangus@btopenworld.com]
01738 451481

Alan Livingstone
(Ordained Local Minister)
2013 Meadowside, Lawnmuir, Methven, Perth PH1 3SZ
[E-mail: livingstone24@btinternet.com]
01738 840682

Trinity Gask and Kinkell See Muthill

Name	(Parish)			Address	Tel
Ballentine, Ann M. (Miss) MA BD	(Kirknewton and East Calder)	1981	2007	17 Nelfield Road, Crieff PH7 3DU [E-mail: annmballentine@gmail.com]	01764 652567
Barr, George K. ARIBA BD PhD	(Uddingston: Viewpark)	1967	1993	7 Tay Avenue, Comrie, Crieff PH6 2PF [E-mail: gbarr2@compuserve.com]	01764 670454
Barr, T. Leslie LTh	(Kinross)	1969	1997	8 Fairfield Road, Kelty KY4 0BY [E-mail: leslie_barr@yahoo.com]	01383 839330
Bertram, Thomas A.	(Patna Waterside)	1972	1995	3 Scrimgeours Corner, 29 West High Street, Crieff PH7 4AP	01764 652066
Brown, Elizabeth (Mrs) JP RGN	(Auxiliary Minister)	1996	2007	8 Viewlands Place, Perth PH1 1BS [E-mail: liz.brown@blueyonder.co.uk]	01738 552391
Brown, Marina D. (Mrs) MA BD MTh	(Hawick: St Mary's and Old)	2000	2012	Moneydie School Cottage, Luncarty, Perth PH1 3HZ [E-mail: revmdb1711@btinternet.com]	01738 582163
Buchan, William DipTheol BD	(Kilwinning: Abbey)	1987	2001	34 Bridgewater Avenue, Auchterarder PH3 1DQ [E-mail: billbuchan3@btinternet.com]	01764 660306
Cairns, Evelyn BD	(Chaplain: Rachel House)	2004	2012	15 Talla Park, Kinross KY13 8AB [E-mail: revelyn@btinternet.com]	01577 863990
Caskie, J. Colin BA BD	(Rhu and Shandon)	1977	2012	13 Anderson Drive, Perth PH1 1JZ [E-mail: jcolincaskie@gmail.com]	01738 445543
Coleman, Sidney H. BA BD MTh	(Glasgow: Merrylea)	1961	2001	'Blaven', 11 Clyde Place, Perth PH2 0EZ [E-mail: sidney.coleman@blueyonder.co.uk]	01738 565072
Craig, Joan H. (Miss) MTheol	(Orkney: East Mainland)	1986	2005	7 Jedburgh Place, Perth PH1 1SJ [E-mail: joanhcraig@btinternet.com]	01738 580180
Dixon, David S. MA BD	(Inchbrayock with Montrose: Melville South)	1976	2014	20 Anderson Drive, Perth PH1 1JX [E-mail: dsdixon49@gmail.com]	01738 626841
Donaldson, Robert B. BSocSc	(Kilchoman with Portnahaven)	1953	1997	11 Strathearn Court, Crieff PH7 3DS	01764 654976
Drummond, Alfred G. BD DMin	Scottish General Secretary: Evangelical Alliance	1991	2006	10 Errochty Court, Perth PH1 2SU [E-mail: frdrmmnd@aol.com]	01738 621305
Fleming, Hamish K. MA	(Banchory Ternan: East)	1966	2001	36 Earnmuir Road, Comrie, Crieff PH6 2EY [E-mail: hamishnan@gmail.com]	01764 679178
Fletcher, Timothy E.G. BA FCMA	Auxiliary Minister	1998		3 Ardchoille Park, Perth PH2 7TL [E-mail: fletcherts@btinternet.com]	01738 638189 (Mbl) 07747 013985
Graham, Sydney S. DipYL MPhil BD	(Iona with Kilfinichen and Kilvickeon and the Ross of Mull)	1987	2009	'Aspen', Milton Road, Luncarty, Perth PH1 3ES [E-mail: syd@sydgraham.plus.com]	01738 829350
Gregory, J.C. LTh	(Blantyre: St Andrew's)	1968	1992	2 Southlands Road, Auchterarder PH3 1BA	01764 664594
Gunn, Alexander M. MA BD	(Aberfeldy with Amulree and Strathbraan with Dull and Weem)	1967	2006	'Navarone', 12 Cornhill Road, Perth PH1 1LR [E-mail: sandygunn@btinternet.com]	01738 443216
Halliday, Archibald R. BD MTh	(Duffus, Spynie and Hopeman)	1964	1999	8 Turretbank Drive, Crieff PH7 4LW [E-mail: roberthalliday343@btinternet.com]	01764 656464
Kelly, T. Clifford	(Ferintosh)	1973	1995	20 Whinfield Drive, Kinross KY13 8UB	01577 864946
Lawson, James B. MA BD	(South Uist)	1961	2002	4 Cowden Way, Comrie, Crieff PH6 2NW [E-mail: james.lawson7@btopenworld.com]	01764 679180
Lawson, Ronald G. MA BD	(Greenock: Wellpark Mid Kirk)	1964	1999	6 East Brougham Street, Stanley, Perth PH1 4NJ	01738 828871
Low, J.E. Stewart MA	(Tarbat)	1957	1997	8 Dalginross Gardens, Comrie PH6 2HQ	01764 670461

Name			Appointment	Address / E-mail	Tel
McCormick, Alastair F.	1962	1998	(Creich with Rosehall)	14 Balmanno Park, Bridge of Earn, Perth PH2 9RJ	01738 813588
McCrum, Robert BSc BD	1982	2014	(Ayr: St James')	28 Rose Crescent, Perth PH1 1NT [E-mail: robert.mccrum@virgin.net]	01738 447906
MacDonald, James W. BD	1976	2012	(Crieff)	'Mingulay', 29 Hebridean Gardens, Crieff PH7 3BP [E-mail: rev_up@btinternet.com]	01764 654500
McGregor, William LTh	1987	2003	(Auchtergaven and Moneydie)	'Ard Choille', 7 Taypark Road, Luncarty, Perth PH1 3FE [E-mail: bill.mcgregor7@btinternet.com]	01738 827866
McIntosh, Colin G. MA BD	1976	2013	(Dunblane: Cathedral)	Drumhead Cottage, Drum, Kinross KY13 0PR [E-mail: colinmcintosh4@btinternet.com]	01577 840012
MacKenzie, Donald W. MA	1941	1983	(Auchterarder: The Barony)	81 Kingswell Terrace, Perth PH1 2DA	01738 633716
MacMillan, Riada M. (Mrs) BD	1991	1998	(Perth: Craigend Moncreiffe with Rhynd)	73 Muirend Gardens, Perth PH1 1JR	01738 628867
McNaughton, David J.H. BA CA	1976	1995	(Killin and Ardeonaig)	14 Rankine Court, Wormit, Newport-on-Tay DD6 8TA	01738 860867
Main, Douglas M. BD	1986	2014	(Errol with Kilspindie and Rait)	14 Madoch Road, St Madoes, Perth PH2 7TT [E-mail: revdmain@sky.com]	
Malcolm, Alistair BD DPS	1976	2012	(Inverness: Inshes)	11 Kinclaven Gardens, Murthly, Perth PH1 4EX [E-mail: amalcolm067@btinternet.com]	01738 710979
Michie, Margaret (Mrs)	2013		Ordained Local Minister: Loch Leven Parish Grouping	3 Loch Leven Court, Wester Balgedie, Kinross KY13 9NE [E-mail: margaretmichie@btinternet.com]	01592 840602
Millar, Archibald E. DipTh	1965	1991	(Perth: St Stephen's)	7 Maple Place, Perth PH1 1RT	01738 621813
Munro, Gillian (Miss) BSc BD	1989	2003	Head of Spiritual Care, NHS Tayside	Royal Victoria Hospital, Dundee DD2 1SP	01382 423116
Paton, Iain F. BD FCIS	1980	2006	(Elie with Kilconquhar and Colinsburgh)	Muldoanich, Stirling Street, Blackford, Auchterarder PH4 1QG [E-mail: iain.f.paton@btinternet.com]	01764 682234
Patterson, Andrew R.M. MA BD	1985	2013	(Edinburgh: Portobello Old)	Hoolmyre Farm, Balbeggie, Perth PH2 6JD [E-mail: armpatterson@gmail.com]	01821 650864
Pattison, Kenneth J. MA BD STM	1967	2004	(Kilmuir and Logie Easter)	2 Castle Way, St Madoes, Glencarse, Perth PH2 7NY [E-mail: k_pattison@btinternet.com]	01738 860340
Philip, Elizabeth (Mrs) DCS MA BA PGCSE				8 Stratheam Terrace, Crieff PH7 3AQ [E-mail: ephilipstitch@gmail.com]	01764 218976 (Mbl) 07970 767851
Philip, Michael R. BD	1978	2014	(Falkirk: Bainsford)	9 Muir Bank, Scone, Perth PH2 6SZ [E-mail: mrphilip@blueyonder.co.uk]	01738 564533 (Mbl) 07776 011601
Reid, David T. BA BD	1954	1993	(Cleish with Fossoway: St Serf's and Devonside)	Benarty, Wester Balgedie, Kinross KY13 9HE	01592 840214
Russell, Kenneth G. BD CCE	1986	2013	Prison Chaplain	158 Bannockburn Road, Stirling FK7 0EW [E-mail: kenrussell1000@hotmail.com]	01786 812680
Searle, David C. MA DipTh	1965	2003	(Warden: Rutherford House)	Stonefall Lodge, 30 Abbey Lane, Grange, Errol PH2 7GB [E-mail: dcs@davidsearle.plus.com]	01821 641004
Shirra, James MA	1945	1987	(St Martins with Scone: New)	17 Dunbarney Avenue, Bridge of Earn, Perth PH2 9BP	01738 812610
Simpson, James A. BSc BD STM DD	1960	2000	(Dornoch Cathedral)	'Dornoch', Perth Road, Bankfoot, Perth PH1 4ED [E-mail: ja@simpsondornoch.co.uk]	01738 787710
Sloan, Robert P. MA BD	1968	2007	(Braemar and Crathie)	1 Broomhill Avenue, Perth PH1 1EN [E-mail: sloan12@virginmedia.com]	01738 443904
Stenhouse, W. Duncan MA BD	1989	2006	(Dunbarney and Forgandenny)	32 Sandport Gait, Kinross KY13 8FB [E-mail: duncan.stenhouse@btinternet.com]	01577 866992

Name			Charge/Role	Address	Phone
Stewart, Anne E. (Mrs) BD CertMin	1998		Prison Chaplain	35 Rose Crescent, Perth PH1 1NT [E-mail: anne.stewart2@sps.pnn.gov.uk]	01738 624167
Stewart, Gordon G. MA			(Perth: St Leonard's-in-the-Fields and Trinity)	'Balnoe', South Street, Rattray, Blairgowrie PH10 7BZ	01250 870626
Stewart, Robin J. MA BD STM	1961	2000	(Orwell with Portmoak)	'Oakbrae', Perth Road, Murthly, Perth PH1 4HF	01738 710220
Thomson, J. Bruce MA BD	1959	1995	(Scone: Old)	47 Elm Street, Errol, Perth PH2 7SQ [E-mail: RevBruceThomson@aol.com]	01821 641039 (Mbl) 07850 846404
Thomson, Peter D. MA BD	1972	2009	(Comrie with Dundurn)	34 Queen Street, Perth PH2 0EJ [E-mail: peterthomson208@btinternet.com]	01738 622418
Wallace, Catherine PGDipC DCS	1968	2004	Deacon	5 Strathearn Terrace, Perth PH2 0LS [E-mail: samesky2407@aol.com]	01738 621709

PERTH ADDRESSES

Craigie	Abbot Street
Kinnoull	Dundee Rd near Queen's Bridge
Letham St Mark's	Rannoch Road
Moncreiffe	Glenbruar Crescent
North	Mill Street near Kinnoull Street
Riverside	Bute Drive
St John's	St John's Street
St Leonard's-in-the-Fields	Marshall Place
St Matthew's	Tay Street

(29) DUNDEE

Meets at Dundee: Steeple, Nethergate, on the second Wednesday of February, March, May, September, November and December, and on the fourth Wednesday of June.

Clerk:	REV. JAMES L. WILSON BD CPS	[E-mail: dundee@cofscotland.org.uk]	01382 459249 (Home) 07885 618659 (Mobile)
Depute Clerk:	REV. JANET P. FOGGIE MA BD PhD	[E-mail: r3vjw@aol.com] [E-mail: rev.foggie@btinternet.com]	01382 660152
Presbytery Office:		Whitfield Parish Church, Haddington Crescent, Dundee DD4 0NA	01382 503012

Abernyte linked with Inchture and Kinnaird linked with Longforgan (H)
Marjory A. MacLean (Miss) LLB BD PhD RNR 1991 2011 — The Manse, Longforgan, Dundee DD2 5HB [E-mail: mrjrymcln@aol.com] — 01382 360238

Auchterhouse (H) linked with Monikie and Newbigging and Murroes and Tealing (H)
David A. Collins BSc BD 1993 2006 — New Kirk Manse, 25 Ballinard Gardens, Broughty Ferry, Dundee DD5 1BZ [E-mail: revdacollins@btinternet.com] — 01382 778874

Dundee: Balgay (H)
Patricia Ramsay (Mrs) BD — 2005 — 2013 — 150 City Road, Dundee DD2 2PW
[E-mail: patriciaramsay505@btinternet.com] — 01382 669600 / 07813 189776 (Mbl)

Dundee: Barnhill St Margaret's (H) (01382 737294) (E-mail: church.office@btconnect.com)
Susan Sutherland (Mrs) BD — 2009 — 2 St Margaret's Lane, Barnhill, Dundee DD5 2PQ
[E-mail: susan.sutherland@sky.com] — 01382 779278

Dundee: Broughty Ferry New Kirk (H)
Catherine E.E. Collins (Mrs) MA BD — 1993 — 2006 — New Kirk Manse, 25 Ballinard Gardens, Broughty Ferry, Dundee DD5 1BZ
[E-mail: revccollins@dsl.pipex.com] — 01382 778874

Dundee: Broughty Ferry St James' (H)
Vacant — 2 Ferry Road, Monifieth, Dundee DD5 4NT — 01382 534468

Dundee: Broughty Ferry St Luke's and Queen Street (01382 770329)
C. Graham D. Taylor BSc BD FIAB — 2001 — 22 Albert Road, Broughty Ferry, Dundee DD5 1AZ
[E-mail: taystar.taylor@googlemail.com] — 01382 779212

Dundee: Broughty Ferry St Stephen's and West (H) linked with Dundee: Dundee (St Mary's) (H) (01382 226271)
Keith F. Hall MA BD — 1980 — 1994 — 33 Strathern Road, West Ferry, Dundee DD5 1PP — 01382 778808

Dundee: Camperdown (H) (01382 623958)
Vacant — Camperdown Manse, Myrekirk Road, Dundee DD2 4SF — 01382 621383

Dundee: Chalmers-Ardler (H)
Kenneth D. Stott MA BD — 1989 — 1997 — The Manse, Turnberry Avenue, Dundee DD2 3TP
[E-mail: arkstotts@aol.com] — 01382 827439

Dundee: Coldside
Anthony P. Thornthwaite MTh — 1995 — 2011 — 9 Abercorn Street, Dundee DD4 7HY
[E-mail: tony.thornthwaite@sky.com] — 01382 458314

Dundee: Craigiebank (H) (01382 731173) linked with Dundee: Douglas and Mid Craigie
Edith F. McMillan (Mrs) MA BD — 1981 — 1999 — 19 Americanmuir Road, Dundee DD3 9AA
[E-mail: douglas244@tiscali.co.uk] — 01382 812423

Dundee: Douglas and Mid Craigie See Dundee: Craigiebank

Dundee: Downfield Mains (H) (01382 810624/812166)
Vacant
9 Elgin Street, Dundee DD3 8NL
01382 827207

Dundee: Dundee (St Mary's) See Dundee: Broughty Ferry St Stephen's and West

Dundee: Fintry Parish Church (01382 508191)
Colin M. Brough BSc BD   1998   2002
4 Clive Street, Dundee DD4 7AW
[E-mail: colin.brough@blueyonder.co.uk]
01382 458629

Dundee: Lochee (H) (Office: 01382 612549)
Hazel Wilson (Ms) MA BD DipEd DMS   1991   2006
32 Clayhills Drive, Dundee DD2 1SX
[E-mail: hwilson704@btinternet.com]
01382 561989

Willie Strachan MBA DipY&C   2013
(Ordained Local Minister)
Ladywell House, Lucky Slap, Monikie, Dundee DD5 3QG
[E-mail: luckyslapdees@btinternet.com]
01382 370286

Dundee: Logie and St John's Cross (H) (01382 668514)
Vacant
7 Hyndford Street, Dundee DD2 1HQ
01382 641572

Dundee: Meadowside St Paul's (H) (01382 202255)
Vacant
36 Blackness Avenue, Dundee DD2 1HH
01382 668828

Dundee: Menzieshill
Robert Mallinson BD   2010
The Manse, Charleston Drive, Dundee DD2 4ED
[E-mail: bobmalli1975@hotmail.co.uk]
01382 667446
07595 249089 (Mbl)

Dundee: St Andrew's (H) (01382 224860)
Janet P. Foggie MA BD PhD   2003   2009
39 Tullideph Road, Dundee DD2 2JD
[E-mail: rev.foggie@btinternet.com]
01382 660152

Dundee: St David's High Kirk (H)
Marion J. Paton (Miss) MA BMus BD   1991   2007
6 Adelaide Place, Dundee DD3 6LF
[E-mail: sdhkrev@googlemail.com]
01382 322955

Dundee: Steeple (H) (01382 200031) Robert A. Calvert BSc BD DMin	1983	2014	128 Arbroath Road, Dundee DD4 7HR [E-mail: robertacalvert@gmail.com]	01382 455411
Dundee: Stobswell (H) (01382 461397) William McLaren MA BD	1990	2007	23 Shamrock Street, Dundee DD4 7AH [E-mail: williammclaren63@googlemail.com]	01382 459119
Dundee: Strathmartine (H) (01382 825817) Stewart McMillan BD	1983	1990	19 Americanmuir Road, Dundee DD3 9AA [E-mail: mcmillan_strath@btinternet.com]	01382 812423
Dundee: Trinity (H) Vacant			65 Clepington Road, Dundee DD4 7BQ	01382 458764
Dundee: West Andrew T. Greaves BD	1985	2000	Manse of Dundee West Church, Wards of Keithock, by Brechin DD9 7PZ [E-mail: andrewgreaves2@btinternet.com]	01356 624479
Dundee: Whitfield (H) (01382 503012) James L. Wilson BD CPS	1986	2001	53 Old Craigie Road, Dundee DD4 7JD [E-mail: r3vjw@aol.com]	01382 459249
Fowlis and Liff linked with Lundie and Muirhead (H) Donna M. Hays (Mrs) MTheol DipEd DipTMHA	2004		149 Coupar Angus Road, Muirhead of Liff, Dundee DD2 5QN [E-mail: dmhays32@aol.com]	01382 580210
Inchture and Kinnaird See Abernyte				
Invergowrie (H) Robert J. Ramsay LLB NP BD	1986	1997	2 Boniface Place, Invergowrie, Dundee DD2 5DW [E-mail: s3rjr@tiscali.co.uk]	01382 561118
Longforgan See Abernyte **Lundie and Muirhead** See Fowlis and Liff				

Monifieth (H)

Dorothy U. Anderson (Mrs) LLB DipLP BD   2006   2009   8 Church Street, Monifieth, Dundee DD5 4JP   01382 532607
[E-mail: dorothy@kirkyard.plus.com]

Monikie and Newbigging and Murroes and Tealing See Auchterhouse

Name	Years	Role	Address	Phone
Allan, Jean (Mrs) DCS		(Deacon)	12C Hindmarsh Avenue, Dundee DD3 7LW [E-mail: jeanmeallan45@googlemail.com]	01382 827299 (Mbl) 07709 959474
Barrett, Leslie M. BD FRICS	1991 2001	Chaplain: University of Abertay, Dundee	Dunelm Cottage, Logie, Cupar KY15 4SJ [E-mail: l.barrett@abertay.ac.uk]	01334 870396
Campbell, Gordon MA BD CDipAF DipHSM MCMI MIHM AFRIN ARSGS FRGS FSAScot	2001	Auxiliary Minister: Chaplain: University of Dundee	2 Falkland Place, Kingoodie, Invergowrie, Dundee DD2 5DY [E-mail: gordon.campbell@dundeepresbytery.org.uk]	01382 561383
Clark, David M. MA BD	1989 2013	(Dundee: Steeple)	2 Rose Street, St Monans, Anstruther KY10 2BQ [E-mail: dmclark72@gmail.com]	01333 738034
Craik, Sheila (Mrs) BD	1989 2001	(Dundee: Camperdown)	35 Haldane Terrace, Dundee DD3 0HT	01382 802078
Cramb, Erik M. LTh	1973 1989	(Industrial Mission Organiser)	Flat 35, Braehead, Methven Walk, Dundee DD2 3FJ [E-mail: erikcramb@aol.com]	01382 526196
Donald, Robert M. LTh BA	1969 2005	(Kilmodan and Colintraive)	2 Blacklaw Drive, Birkhill, Dundee DD2 5RJ [E-mail: robbie.donald@dundeepresbytery.org.uk]	01382 581337
Douglas, Fiona C. (Ms) MBE MA BD PhD	1989 1997	Chaplain: University of Dundee	10 Springfield, Dundee DD1 4JE	01382 384157
Fraser, Donald W. MA	1958 2010	(Monifieth)	1 Blake Avenue, Broughty Ferry, Dundee DD5 3LH [E-mail: fraserdonald37@yahoo.co.uk]	01382 477491 (Mbl) 07531 863316
Galbraith, W. James L. BSc BD MICE	1973 1996	(Kilchrenan and Dalavich with Muckairn)	586 Brook Street, Broughty Ferry, Dundee DD5 2EA	01382 732110
Hawdon, John E. BA MTh AICS	1961 1995	(Dundee: Clepington)	53 Hillside Road, Dundee DD2 1QT [E-mail: john.hawdon@dundeepresbytery.org.uk]	01382 646212
Ingram, J.R.	1954 1978	(Chaplain: RAF)	48 Marlee Road, Broughty Ferry, Dundee DD5 3EX	01382 736400
Jamieson, David B. MA BD STM	1974 2011	(Monifieth)	8A Albert Street, Monifieth, Dundee DD5 4JS	01382 532772
Kay, Elizabeth (Miss) DipYCS	1993 2007	(Auxiliary Minister)	1 Kintail Walk, Inchture, Perth PH14 9RY [E-mail: liz.kay@dundeepresbytery.org.uk]	01828 686029
Laidlaw, John J. MA	1964 1973	(Adviser in Religious Education)	14 Dalhousie Road, Barnhill, Dundee DD5 2SQ	01382 477458
Laing, David J.H. BD DPS	1976 2014	(Dundee: Trinity)	18 Kerrington Crescent, Barnhill, Dundee DD5 2TN [E-mail: david.laing@live.co.uk]	01382 739586
McLeod, David C. BSc MEng BD	1969 2001	(Dundee: Fairmuir)	6 Carseview Gardens, Dundee DD2 1NE	01382 641371
McMillan, Charles D. LTh	1979 2004	(Elgin: High)	11 Troon Terrace, The Orchard, Ardler, Dundee DD2 3FX	01382 831358
Mair, Michael V.A. MA BD	1967 2007	(Craigiebank with Dundee: Douglas and Mid Craigie)	48 Panmure Street, Monifieth DD5 4EH [E-mail: mvamair@gmail.com]	01382 530538
Martin, Janie (Miss) DCS		(Deacon)	16 Wentworth Road, Ardler, Dundee DD2 8SD	
Mitchell, Jack MA BD CTh	1987 1996	(Dundee: Menzieshill)	29 Carrick Gardens, Ayr KA7 2RT	01382 813786

Name			Role	Address	Phone
Mowat, Gilbert M. MA	1948	1986	(Dundee: Albany-Butterburn)	Abbeyfield House, 16 Grange Road, Bearsden, Glasgow G61 3PL	01575 572503
Powrie, James E. LTh	1969	1995	(Dundee: Chalmers-Ardler)	3 Kirktonhill Road, Kirriemuir DD8 4HU	01382 581790
Rae, Robert LTh	1968	1983	(Chaplain: Dundee Acute Hospitals)	14 Neddertoun View, Liff, Dundee DD3 5RU	01382 520519
Reid, R. Gordon BSc BD MIET	1993	2010	(Carriden)	6 Bayview Place, Monifieth, Dundee DD5 4TN [E-mail: GordonReid@aol.com]	07952 349884 (Mbl)
Robertson, James H. BSc BD	1975	2014	(Culloden: The Barn)	'Far End', 35 Mains Terrace, Dundee DD4 7BZ [E-mail: jimrob838@gmail.com]	01382 522773 / 07595 465838 (Mbl)
Robson, George K. LTh DPS BA	1983	2011	(Dundee: Balgay)	11 Ceres Crescent, Broughty Ferry, Dundee DD5 3JN [E-mail: gkrobson@tiscali.co.uk]	01382 901212
Rogers, James M. BA DB DCult	1955	1996	(Gibraltar)	24 Mansion Drive, Dalclaverhouse, Dundee DD4 9DD	01382 506162
Rose, Lewis (Mr) DCS	1993		(Deacon)	6 Gauldie Crescent, Dundee DD3 0RR [E-mail: lewis_rose48@yahoo.co.uk]	01382 816580 / 07899 790466 (Mbl)
Scott, James MA BD	1973	2010	(Drumoak-Durris)	3 Blake Place, Broughty Ferry, Dundee DD5 3LQ [E-mail: jimscott73@yahoo.co.uk]	01382 739595
Scoular, Stanley	1963	2000	(Rosyth)	31 Duns Crescent, Dundee DD4 0RY	01382 501653
Strickland, Alexander LTh	1971	2005	(Dairsie with Kemback with Strathkinness)	12 Ballumbie Braes, Dundee DD4 0UN	01382 685539

DUNDEE ADDRESSES

Balgay	200 Lochee Road
Barnhill St Margaret's	10 Invermark Terrace
Broughty Ferry	
New Kirk	370 Queen Street
St James'	5 Fort Street
St Luke's and Queen Street	5 West Queen Street
St Stephen's and West	96 Dundee Road
Camperdown	22 Brownhill Road
Chalmers-Ardler	Turnberry Avenue
Coldside	Isla Street
Craigiebank	Craigie Avenue at Greendykes Road
Douglas and Mid Craigie	Balbeggie Place/ Longtown Terrace
Downfield South	Haldane Street off Strathmartine Road
Dundee (St Mary's)	Nethergate
Fintry	Fintry Road x Fintry Drive
Lochee	191 High Street, Lochee
Logie and St John's Cross	Shaftesbury Rd x Blackness Ave
Mains	Foot of Old Glamis Road
Meadowside St Paul's	114 Nethergate
Menzieshill	Charleston Drive, Menzieshill
St Andrew's	2 King Street
St David's High Kirk	119A Kinghorne Road
Steeple	Nethergate
Stobswell	170 Albert Street
Strathmartine	507 Strathmartine Road
Trinity	73 Crescent Street
West	130 Perth Road
Whitfield	Haddington Crescent

(30) ANGUS

Meets at Forfar in St Margaret's Church Hall on the first Tuesday of February, March, May, September, November and December, and on the last Tuesday of June.

Clerk: REV. MICHAEL S. GOSS BD DPS   [E-mail: michaelgoss@blueyonder.co.uk]
Deputy Clerk: REV. IAN A. McLEAN BSc BD DMin [E-mail: iamclean@lineone.net]
Presbytery Office: St Margaret's Church, West High Street, Forfar DD8 1BJ   01307 464224
                                                   [E-mail: angus@cofscotland.org.uk]

Aberlemno (H) linked with Guthrie and Rescobie
Brian Ramsay BD DPS MLitt   1980   1984   The Manse, Guthrie, Forfar DD8 2TP   01241 828243
[E-mail: revdbrianr@hotmail.com]

Arbirlot linked with Carmyllie
Stewart J. Lamont BSc BD   1972   2011   The Manse, Arbirlot, Arbroath DD11 2NX   01241 879800
[E-mail: lamontsj@gmail.com]

Arbroath: Knox's (H) linked with Arbroath: St Vigeans (H)
Nelu I. Balaj BD MA ThD   2010   The Manse, St Vigeans, Arbroath DD11 4RF   01241 873206
[E-mail: nelu@gmx.co.uk]   07954 436879 (Mbl)

Arbroath: Old and Abbey (H) (Church office: 01241 877068)
Dolly Purnell BD   2003   2014   51 Cliffburn Road, Arbroath DD11 5BA   01241 872196 (Tel/Fax)
[E-mail: revdollypurnell@btinternet.com]

Arbroath: St Andrew's (H) (E-mail: office@arbroathstandrews.org.uk)
W. Martin Fair BA BD DMin   1992   92 Grampian Gardens, Arbroath DD11 4AQ   01241 873238 (Tel/Fax)
[E-mail: martin.fair@sky.com]
Stuart D. Irvin BD (Assoc)   2013   67 Brechin Road, Arbroath DD11 1TA   01241 872339
[E-mail: stuart.d.irvin@googlemail.com]

Arbroath: St Vigeans See Arbroath: Knox's

Arbroath: West Kirk (H)
Alasdair G. Graham BD DipMin   1981   1986   1 Charles Avenue, Arbroath DD11 2EY   01241 872244
[E-mail: alasdairggraham@tiscali.co.uk]

Barry linked with Carnoustie
Michael S. Goss BD DPS   1991   44 Terrace Road, Carnoustie DD7 7AR   01241   410194
   [E-mail: michaelgoss@blueyonder.co.uk]   07787   141567 (Mbl)

Dougal Edwards BTh   2013   25 Mackenzie Street, Carnoustie DD7 6HD   01241   852666
(Ordained Local Minister)   [E-mail: dougal.edwards@blueyonder.co.uk]

Brechin: Cathedral (H) (Cathedral office: 01356 629360) (Website: www.brechincathedral.org.uk)
Roderick J. Grahame BD CPS   1991   2010   Chanonry Wynd, Brechin DD9 6JS   01356   624980
   [E-mail: rjgrahame@talktalk.net]

Brechin: Gardner Memorial (H) linked with Farnell
Jane M. Blackley MA BD   2009   15 Caldhame Gardens, Brechin DD9 7JJ   01356   622034
   [E-mail: jmblackley6@aol.com]

Carmyllie See Arbirlot
Carnoustie See Barry

Carnoustie: Panbride (H)
Matthew S. Bicket BD   1989   8 Arbroath Road, Carnoustie DD7 6BL   01241   854478 (Tel)
   [E-mail: matthew@bicket.freeserve.co.uk]   01241   855088 (Fax)

Colliston linked with Friockheim Kinnell linked with Inverkeilor and Lunan (H)
Peter A. Phillips BA   1995   2004   The Manse, Inverkeilor, Arbroath DD11 5SA   01241   830464
   [E-mail: rev.p.phillips@gmail.com]

Dun and Hillside
Vacant   4 Manse Road, Hillside, Montrose DD10 9FB   01674   830288

Dunnichen, Letham and Kirkden
Dale London BTh FSAScot   2011   2013   7 Braehead Road, Letham, Forfar DD8 2PG   01307   818025
   [E-mail: dlondon@hotmail.com]

Eassie, Nevay and Newtyle
Carleen Robertson (Miss) BD   1992   2 Kirkton Road, Newtyle, Blairgowrie PH12 8TS   01828   650461
   [E-mail: carleen.robertson120@btinternet.com]

Edzell Lethnot Glenesk (H) linked with Fern Careston Menmuir
David T. Gray BArch BD 2010
19 Lethnot Road, Edzell, Brechin DD9 7TG
[E-mail: davidgray64@sky.com]
01356 647846
07789 718622 (Mbl)

Ian Gray 2013
(Ordained Local Minister)
'The Mallards', 15 Rossie Island Road, Montrose DD10 9NH
[E-mail: iancelia15@aol.com]
01674 677126

Farnell See Brechin: Gardner Memorial
Fern Careston Menmuir See Edzell Lethnot Glenesk

Forfar: East and Old (H)
Barbara Ann Sweetin BD 2011
The Manse, Lour Road, Forfar DD8 2BB
[E-mail: barbara.ann17@talktalk.net]
01307 248228

Forfar: Lowson Memorial (H)
Karen Fenwick PhD MPhil BSc BD 2006
1 Jamieson Street, Forfar DD8 2HY
[E-mail: kmfenwick@talktalk.net]
01307 468585

Forfar: St Margaret's (H) (Church office: 01307 464224)
Vacant
St Margaret's Manse, 15 Potters Park Crescent, Forfar DD8 1HH
01307 462044

Friockheim Kinnell See Colliston

Glamis (H), Inverarity and Kinnettles
Guardianship of the Presbytery
(See Eassie, Nevay and Newtyle)

Guthrie and Rescobie See Aberlemno

Inchbrayock linked with Montrose: Melville South
Vacant
The Manse, Ferryden, Montrose DD10 9SD
01674 672108

Inverkeilor and Lunan See Colliston

Kirriemuir: St Andrew's (H) linked with Oathlaw Tannadice
John K. Orr BD MTh 2012
26 Quarry Park, Kirriemuir DD8 4DR
[E-mail: minister@standrews-kirriemuir.org.uk]
01575 572610

Montrose: Melville South See Inchbrayock

Montrose: Old and St Andrew's
Ian A. McLean BSc BD DMin   1981   2008   2 Rosehill Road, Montrose DD10 8ST   01674 672447
[E-mail: iamclean@lineone.net]

Oathlaw Tannadice   See Kirriemuir: St Andrew's

The Glens and Kirriemuir: Old (H) (Church office: 01575 572819) (Website: www.gkopc.co.uk)
Malcolm I.G. Rooney DPE BEd BD   1993   1999   20 Strathmore Avenue, Kirriemuir DD8 4DJ   01575 573724
[E-mail: malcolm@gkopc.co.uk]   07909 993233 (Mbl)
Linda Stevens (Mrs) BSc BD PgDip   2006   17 North Latch Road, Brechin DD9 6LE   01356 623415
(Team Minister)   [E-mail: linda@gkopc.co.uk]   07701 052552 (Mbl)

The Isla Parishes
Brian Ian Murray BD   2002   2010   Balduff House, Kilry, Blairgowrie PH11 8HS   01575 560268
[E-mail: bentleymurray@googlemail.com]

Name			(Former charge)	Address	Tel
Anderson, John F. MA BD FSAScot	1966	2006	(Aberdeen: Mannofield)	8 Eider Close, Montrose DD10 9NE	01674 672029
				[E-mail: jfa941@aol.com]	
Brodie, James BEM MA BD STM	1955	1974	(Hurlford)	25A Keptie Road, Arbroath DD11 3ED	01241 873298
Butters, David	1964	1998	(Turriff: St Ninian's and Forglen)	68A Millgate, Friockheim, Arbroath DD11 4TN	01241 828030
Dingwall, Brian BTh CQSW	1999	2013	(Upper Donside)	20 Woodend Drive, Kirriemuir DD8 4TF	01575 573918
				[E-mail: brian.d12@btinternet.com]	07906 656847 (Mbl)
Drysdale, James P.R.	1967	1999	(Brechin: Gardner Memorial)	51 Airlie Street, Brechin DD9 6JX	01356 625201
Duncan, Robert F. MTheol	1986	2001	(Lochgelly: St Andrew's)	25 Rowan Avenue, Kirriemuir DD8 4TB	01575 573973
Gough, Ian G. MA BD MTh DMin	1974	2009	(Arbroath: Knox's with Arbroath: St Vigeans)	23 Keptie Road, Arbroath DD11 3ED	07891 838379 (Mbl)
				[E-mail: ianggough@btinternet.com]	
Hastie, George I. MA BD	1971	2009	(Mearns Coastal)	23 Borrowfield Crescent, Montrose DD10 9BR	01674 672290
Hodge, William N.T.	1966	1995	(Longside)	19 Craigengar Park, Craigshill, Livingston EH54 5NY	01506 435813
Milton, Eric G. RD	1963	1994	(Blairdaff)	16 Bruce Court, Links Parade, Carnoustie DD7 7JE	01241 854928
Morrice, Alastair M. MA BD	1968	2002	(Rutherglen: Stonelaw)	5 Brechin Road, Kirriemuir DD8 4BX	01575 574102
				[E-mail: ambishkek@swissmail.org]	
Norrie, Graham MA BD	1967	2007	(Forfar: East and Old)	'Novar', 14A Wyllie Street, Forfar DD8 3DN	01307 468152
				[E-mail: grahamnorrie@hotmail.com]	
Perry, Joseph B.	1955	1989	(Farnell)	19 Guthrie Street, Letham, Forfar DD8 2PS	01307 818741
Reid, Albert B. BD BSc	1966	2001	(Ardler, Kettins and Meigle)	1 Mary Countess Way, Glamis, Forfar DD8 1RF	01307 840213
				[E-mail: abreid@btinternet.com]	
Robertson, George R. LTh	1985	2004	(Udny and Pitmedden)	3 Slateford Gardens, Edzell, Brechin DD9 7SX	01356 647322
				[E-mail: geomag.robertson@btinternet.com]	
Smith, Hamish G.	1965	1993	(Auchterless with Rothienorman)	11A Guthrie Street, Letham, Forfar DD8 2PS	01307 818973
Thomas, Martyn R.H. CEng MIStructE	1987	2002	(Fowlis and Liff with Lundie and Muirhead of Liff)	14 Kirkgait, Letham, Forfar DD8 2XQ	01307 818084
				[E-mail: martyn.thomas@mypostoffice.co.uk]	

Thomas, Shirley A. (Mrs) DipSocSci AMIA (Aux) MTh CQSW DipCommEd (Auxiliary Minister) 2000 2006 14 Kirkgait, Letham, Forfar DD8 2XQ 01307 818084
[E-mail: martyn.thomas@mypostoffice.co.uk]

Watt, Alan G.N. (Edzell Lethnot Glenesk with Fern Careston Menmuir) 1996 2009 128 Restenneth Drive, Forfar DD8 2DH 01307 461686
[E-mail: watt455@btinternet.com]

Webster, Allan F. MA BD (Workplace Chaplain) 1978 2008 42 McCulloch Drive, Forfar DD8 2EB 01307 464252 (Mbl) 07546 276725
[E-mail: allanfwebster@aol.com]

Youngson, Peter (Kirriemuir: St Andrew's) 1961 1996 'Coreen', Woodside, Northmuir, Kirriemuir DD8 4PG 01575 572832

ANGUS ADDRESSES

Arbroath: Knox's	Howard Street
Old and Abbey	West Abbey Street
St Andrew's	Hamilton Green
West Kirk	Keptie Street
Brechin: Cathedral	Bishops Close
Gardner Memorial	South Esk Street
Carnoustie:	Dundee Street
Panbride	Arbroath Road
Forfar: East and Old	East High Street
Lowson Memorial	Jamieson Street
St Margaret's	West High Street
Kirriemuir: Old	High Street
St Andrew's	Glamis Road
Montrose: Melville South	Castle Street
Old and St Andrew's	High Street

(31) ABERDEEN

Meets on the first Tuesday of February, March, May, September, October, November and December, and on the fourth Tuesday of June. The venue varies.

Clerk: **REV. JOHN A. FERGUSON BD DipMin DMin**
Administrator and Depute Clerk: **MRS MOYRA CAMERON**
Presbytery Office: **Mastrick Church, Greenfern Road, Aberdeen AB16 6TR** **01224 698119**
[E-mail: aberdeen@cofscotland.org.uk]

Aberdeen: Bridge of Don Oldmachar (01224 709299) (Website: www.oldmacharchurch.org)
David J. Stewart BD MTh DipMin 2000 2012 60 Newburgh Circle, Aberdeen AB22 8QZ 01224 701365
[E-mail: brigodon@clara.co.uk]

Aberdeen: Cove (New Charge Development)
David Swan BVMS BD 2005 4 Charleston Way, Cove, Aberdeen AB12 3FA 01224 899933
[E-mail: david@covechurch.org.uk]
Daniel Robertson BA BD (Assoc) 2009 2014 5 Bruce Walk, Nigg, Aberdeen AB12 3LX 01224 878418 07909 840654 (Mbl)
[E-mail: dan_robertson100@hotmail.com]

Aberdeen: Craigiebuckler (H) (01224 315649)
Kenneth L. Petrie MA BD | 1984 | 1999 | 185 Springfield Road, Aberdeen AB15 8AA [E-mail: patandkenneth@aol.com] | 01224 315125

Aberdeen: Ferryhill (H) (01224 213093)
J. Peter N. Johnston BSc BD | 2001 | 2013 | 54 Polmuir Road, Aberdeen AB11 7RT [E-mail: peter.johnston@ferryhillparishchurch.org] | 01224 949192

Aberdeen: Garthdee (H) linked with Aberdeen: Ruthrieston West (H)
Benjamin D.W. Byun BS MDiv MTh PhD | 1992 | 2008 | 53 Springfield Avenue, Aberdeen AB15 8JJ [E-mail: benjamin@byun1.fsnet.co.uk] | 01224 312706

Aberdeen: High Hilton (H) (01224 494717)
G. Hutton B. Steel MA BD | 1982 | 2013 | 24 Rosehill Drive, Aberdeen AB24 4JJ [E-mail: hsteel57@btinternet.com] | 01224 493552

Aberdeen: Holburn West (H) (01224 571120)
Duncan C. Eddie MA BD | 1992 | 1999 | 31 Cranford Road, Aberdeen AB10 7NJ [E-mail: dceddies@tiscali.co.uk] | 01224 325873

Aberdeen: Mannofield (H) (01224 310087) (E-mail: office@mannofieldchurch.org.uk)
Keith T. Blackwood BD DipMin | 1997 | 2007 | 21 Forest Avenue, Aberdeen AB15 4TU [E-mail: minister@mannofieldchurch.org.uk] | 01224 315748

Aberdeen: Mastrick (H) (01224 694121)
Elizabeth J.B. Youngson BD | 1996 | 2011 | 8 Corse Wynd, Kingswells, Aberdeen AB15 8TP [E-mail: elizabeth.youngson@btinternet.com] | 01224 749346

Aberdeen: Middlefield (H)
Vacant

Aberdeen: Midstocket
Sarah E.C. Nicol (Mrs) BSc BD MTh | 1985 | 2013 | 182 Midstocket Road, Aberdeen AB15 5HS [E-mail: sarahmidstocket@btinternet.com] | 01224 561358

Aberdeen: Northfield
Scott C. Guy BD | 1989 | 1999 | 28 Byron Crescent, Aberdeen AB16 7EX [E-mail: scguy55@gmail.com] | 01224 692332

Aberdeen: Queen Street (01224 643567)
Graham D.S. Deans MA BD MTh DMin — 1978 2008 — 51 Osborne Place, Aberdeen AB25 2BX [E-mail: graham.deans@btopenworld.com] — 01224 646429

Aberdeen: Queen's Cross (H) (01224 644742)
Scott Rennie MA BD STM — 1999 2009 — 1 St Swithin Street, Aberdeen AB10 6XH [E-mail: minister@queenscrosschurch.org.uk] — 01224 322549

Aberdeen: Rubislaw (H) (01224 645477)
Robert L. Smith BS MTh PhD — 2000 2013 — 45 Rubislaw Den South, Aberdeen AB15 4BD [E-mail: rubislaw.minister@virginmedia.com] — 01224 314773

Aberdeen: Ruthrieston West See Aberdeen: Garthdee

Aberdeen: St Columba's Bridge of Don (H) (01224 825653)
Louis Kinsey BD DipMin TD — 1991 — 151 Jesmond Avenue, Aberdeen AB22 8UG [E-mail: louis@stcolumbaschurch.org.uk] — 01224 705337

Aberdeen: St George's Tillydrone (H) (01224 482204)
James Weir BD — 1991 2003 — 127 Clifton Road, Aberdeen AB24 4RH [E-mail: minister@saint-georges-tillydrone.org.uk] — 01224 483976

Aberdeen: St John's Church for Deaf People (H) (01224 494566)
Vacant

Aberdeen: St Machar's Cathedral (H) (01224 485988)
Vacant — 18 The Chanonry, Old Aberdeen AB24 1RQ — 01224 483688

Aberdeen: St Mark's (H) (01224 640672)
Diane L. Hobson (Mrs) BA BD — 2002 2010 — 65 Mile-end Avenue, Aberdeen AB15 5PU [E-mail: dianehobson.rev@btinternet.com] — 01224 622470

Aberdeen: St Mary's (H) (01224 487227)
Elsie J. Fortune (Mrs) BSc BD — 2003 — 456 King Street, Aberdeen AB24 3DE [E-mail: eric.fortune@lineone.net] — 01224 633778

Aberdeen: St Nicholas Kincorth, South of
Edward C. McKenna BD DPS   1989   The Manse, Kincorth Circle, Aberdeen AB12 5NX   01224 872820
[E-mail: eddiemckenna@uwclub.net]
Daniel Robertson BA BD (Assoc)   2014   5 Bruce Walk, Nigg, Aberdeen AB12 3LX   01224 878418
07909 840654 (Mbl)
[E-mail: dan_robertson100@hotmail.com]

Aberdeen: St Nicholas Uniting, Kirk of (H) (01224 643494)
B. Stephen C. Taylor BA BBS MA MDiv   1984   2005   12 Louisville Avenue, Aberdeen AB15 4TX   01224 314318
01224 649242 (Fax)
[E-mail: minister@kirk-of-st-nicholas.org.uk]

Aberdeen: St Stephen's (H) (01224 624443)
Maggie Whyte BD   2010   6 Belvidere Street, Aberdeen AB25 2QS   01224 635694
[E-mail: maggiewhyte@aol.com]

Aberdeen: South Holburn (H) (01224 211730)
George S. Cowie BSc BD   1991   2006   54 Woodstock Road, Aberdeen AB15 5JF   01224 315042
[E-mail: gscowie@aol.com]

Aberdeen: Stockethill
Ian M. Aitken MA BD   1999   52 Ashgrove Road West, Aberdeen AB16 5EE   01224 686929
[E-mail: ncdstockethill@uk.uumail.com]

Aberdeen: Summerhill (H) (Website: www.summerhillchurch.org.uk)
Michael R.R. Shewan MA BD CPS   1985   2010   36 Stronsay Drive, Aberdeen AB15 6JL   01224 324669
[E-mail: michaelshewan@btinternet.com]

Aberdeen: Torry St Fittick's (H) (01224 899183)
Edmond Gatima BEng BD MSc MPhil PhD   2013   11 Devanha Gardens East, Aberdeen AB11 7UH   01224 588245

Aberdeen: Woodside (H) (01224 277249)
Markus Auffermann DipTheol   1999   2006   322 Clifton Road, Aberdeen AB24 4HQ   01224 484562
[E-mail: mauffermann@yahoo.com]

Bucksburn Stoneywood (H) (01224 712411)
Nigel Parker BD MTh DMin   1994   23 Polo Park, Stoneywood, Aberdeen AB21 9JW   01224 712635
[E-mail: revdr.n.parker@btinternet.com]

Cults (H)
Ewen J. Gilchrist BD DipMin DipComm   1982   2005   1 Cairnlee Terrace, Bieldside, Aberdeen AB15 9AE   01224 861692
[E-mail: ewengilchrist@btconnect.com]

Dyce (H) (01224 771295)
Manson C. Merchant BD CPS   1992   2008   100 Burnside Road, Dyce, Aberdeen AB21 7HA   01224 722380
[E-mail: mc.merchant@btinternet.com]

Kingswells
Alisa McDonald BA MDiv   2008   2013   Kingswells Manse, Lang Stracht, Aberdeen AB15 8PL   01224 740229

Newhills (H) (Tel/Fax: 01224 716161)
Hugh M. Wallace MA BD   1980   2007   Newhills Manse, Bucksburn, Aberdeen AB21 9SS   01224 712655
[E-mail: revhugh@hotmail.com]

Peterculter (H) (01224 735845)
John A. Ferguson BD DipMin DMin   1988   1999   7 Howie Lane, Peterculter AB14 0LJ   01224 735041
[E-mail: john.ferguson525@btinternet.com]

Barron, Jane L. (Mrs) BA DipEd BD   1999   2013   (Aberdeen: St Machar's Cathedral)   Denhead Old Farm, St Andrews KY16 3PA
[E-mail: janebarron23@hotmail.com]

Beattie, Walter G. MA BD   1956   1995   (Arbroath: Old and Abbey)   126 Seafield Road, Aberdeen AB15 7YQ   01224 329259
Campbell, W.M.M. BD CPS   1970   2003   (Hospital Chaplain)   43 Murray Terrace, Aberdeen AB11 7SA   07761 235815
Cowie, Marian (Mrs) MA BD MTh   1990   2012   (Aberdeen: Midstocket)   54 Woodstock Road, Aberdeen AB15 5JF   01224 315042
[E-mail: mcowieou@aol.com]

Craig, Gordon T. BD DipMin   1998   2012   Chaplain to UK Oil and Gas Industry   c/o Total E and P (UK) plc, Altens Industrial Estate, Crawpeel Road, Aberdeen AB12 3FG   01224 297532
[E-mail: gordon.craig@ukoilandgaschaplaincy.com]

Douglas, Andrew M. MA   1957   1995   (Aberdeen: High Hilton)   219 Countesswells Road, Aberdeen AB15 7RD   01224 311932
Falconer, James B. BD   1982   1991   Hospital Chaplain   3 Brimmond Walk, Westhill AB32 6XH   01224 744621
Garden, Margaret J. (Miss) BD   1993   2009   (Cushnie and Tough)   26 Earns Heugh Circle, Cove Bay, Aberdeen AB12 3PY
[E-mail: mj.garden@btinternet.com]

Gardner, Bruce K. MA BD PhD   1988   2011   (Aberdeen: Bridge of Don Oldmachar)   21 Hopetoun Crescent, Bucksburn, Aberdeen AB21 9QY   (Mbl) 07891 186724
[E-mail: drbruckgardner@aol.com]

Goldie, George D. ALCM   1953   1995   (Aberdeen: Greyfriars)   27 Broomhill Avenue, Aberdeen AB10 6JL   01224 322503
Gordon, Laurie Y.   1960   1995   (Aberdeen: John Knox)   1 Alder Drive, Portlethen, Aberdeen AB12 4WA   01224 782703
Graham, A. David M. BA BD   1971   2005   (Aberdeen: Rosemount)   Elmhill House, 27 Shaw Crescent, Aberdeen AB25 3BT   01224 648041

Grainger, Harvey L. LTh	1975	2004	(Kingswells)	13 St Ronan's Crescent, Peterculter, Aberdeen AB14 0RL [E-mail: harveygrainger@tiscali.co.uk]	01224 739824 (Mbl) 07768 333216
Haddow, Angus H. BSc	1963	1999	(Methlick)	25 Lerwick Road, Aberdeen AB16 6RF	01224 969521
Hamilton, Helen (Miss) BD	1991	2003	(Glasgow: St James' Pollok)	The Cottage, West Tilbouries, Maryculter, Aberdeen AB12 5GD	01224 739632
Hutchison, David S. BSc BD ThM	1991	1999	(Aberdeen: Torry St Fittick's)	51 Don Street, Aberdeen AB24 1UH	01224 276122
Johnstone, William (Prof.) MA BD	1963	2001	(University of Aberdeen)	9/5 Mount Alvernia, Edinburgh EH16 6AW	0131-664 3140
Lundie, Ann V. DCS			(Deacon)	20 Langdykes Drive, Cove, Aberdeen AB12 3HW [E-mail: ann.lundie@btopenworld.com]	01224 898416
McCallum, Moyra (Miss) MA BD DCS			(Deacon)	176 Hilton Drive, Aberdeen AB24 4LT [E-mail: moymac@aol.com]	01224 486240 (Mbl) 07986 581899
Maciver, Norman MA BD DMin	1976	2006	(Newhills)	4 Mundi Crescent, Newmachar, Aberdeen AB21 0LY [E-mail: norirene@aol.com]	01651 869434
Main, Alan (Prof.) TD MA BD STM PhD DD	1963	2001	(University of Aberdeen)	Kirkfield, Barthol Chapel, Inverurie AB51 8TD	01651 806773
Montgomery, Jean B. (Miss) MA BD	1973	2005	(Forfar: St Margaret's)	12 St Ronan's Place, Peterculter, Aberdeen AB14 0QX [E-mail: revjeanb@tiscali.co.uk]	01224 732350
Phillippo, Michael MTh BSc BVetMed MRCVS	2003		(Auxiliary Minister)	25 Deeside Crescent, Aberdeen AB15 7PT [E-mail: phillippo@btinternet.com]	01224 318317
Richardson, Thomas C. LTh ThB	1971	2004	(Cults: West)	19 Kinkell Road, Aberdeen AB15 8HR [E-mail: thomas.richardson7@btinternet.com]	01224 315328
Rodgers, D. Mark BA BD MTh	1987	2003	Hospital Chaplain	152D Gray Street, Aberdeen AB10 6JW	01224 210810
Sefton, Henry R. MA BD STM PhD	1957	1992	(University of Aberdeen)	25 Albury Place, Aberdeen AB11 6TQ	01224 572305
Sheret, Brian S. MA BD DPhil	1982	2009	(Glasgow: Drumchapel Drumry St Mary's)	59 Airyhall Crescent, Aberdeen AB15 7QS	01224 323032
Stewart, James C. MA BD STM	1960	2000	(Aberdeen: Kirk of St Nicholas)	54 Murray Terrace, Aberdeen AB11 7SB	01224 587071
Swinton, John (Prof.) BD PhD	1999		University of Aberdeen	51 Newburgh Circle, Bridge of Don, Aberdeen AB22 8XA [E-mail: j.swinton@abdn.ac.uk]	01224 825637
Torrance, Iain R. (Prof.) TD DPhil DD DTheol LHD FRSE	1982	2012	(President: Princeton Theological Seminary)	17 St Bernard's Crescent, Edinburgh EH4 1NR [E-mail: irt@ptsem.edu]	0131-315 3746
Wilkie, William E. LTh	1978	2001	(Aberdeen: St Nicholas Kincorth, South of)	32 Broomfield Park, Portlethen, Aberdeen AB12 4XT	01224 782052
Wilson, Thomas F. BD	1984	1996	Education	55 Allison Close, Cove, Aberdeen AB12 3WG	01224 873501

ABERDEEN ADDRESSES

Church	Address	Church	Address
Bridge of Don Oldmachar	Ashwood Park	Garthdee	Ramsay Gardens
Cove	Loirston Primary School, Loirston Avenue	High Hilton	Hilton Drive
Craigiebuckler	Springfield Road	Holburn West	Great Western Road
Cults	Quarry Road, Cults	Kingswells	Old Skene Road, Kingswells
Dyce	Victoria Street, Dyce	Mannofield	Great Western Road x Craigton Road
Ferryhill	Fonthill Road x Polmuir Road	Mastrick	Greenfern Road
		Middlefield	Manor Avenue
		Midstocket	Mid Stocket Road
		New Stockethill	
		Northfield	Byron Crescent
		Peterculter	Craigton Crescent

Queen Street	Queen Street
Queen's Cross	Albyn Place
Rubislaw	Queen's Gardens
Ruthrieston West	Broomhill Road
St Columba's	Brachead Way, Bridge of Don
St George's	Hayton Road, Tillydrone
St John's for the Deaf	at St Mark's
St Machar's	The Chanory
St Mark's	Rosemount Viaduct
St Mary's	King Street

| St Nicholas Kincorth, South of | Kincorth Circle | St Stephen's South Holburn Summerhill | Powis Place Holburn Street Stronsay Drive | Torry St Fittick's Woodside | Walker Road Church Street, Woodside |
| St Nicholas Uniting, Kirk of | Union Street | | | | |

(32) KINCARDINE AND DEESIDE

Meets in various locations as arranged on the first Tuesday of September, October, November, December, March and May, and on the last Tuesday of June at 7pm.

Clerk: REV. HUGH CONKEY BSc BD 39 St Ternans Road, Newtonhill, Stonehaven AB39 3PF 01569 739297
[E-mail: kincardinedeeside@cofscotland.org.uk]

Aberluthnott linked with Laurencekirk (H)
Ronald Gall BSc BD 1985 2001 Aberdeen Road, Laurencekirk AB30 1AJ 01561 378838
[E-mail: ronniegall@live.com]

Aboyne-Dinnet (H) (01339 886989) linked with Cromar (E-mail: aboynedinnet.cos@virgin.net)
Frank Ribbons MA BD DipEd 1985 2011 49 Charlton Crescent, Aboyne AB34 5GN 01339 887267
[E-mail: frankribs@gmail.com]

Arbuthnott, Bervie and Kinneff
Dennis S. Rose LTh 1996 2010 10 Kirkburn, Inverbervie, Montrose DD10 0RT 01561 362560
[E-mail: dennis2327@aol.co.uk]

Banchory-Devenick and Maryculter/Cookney (01224 735983) (E-mail: thechurchoffice@tiscali.co.uk)
Melvyn J. Griffiths BTh DipTheol DMin 1978 2014 The Manse, Kirkton of Maryculter, Aberdeen AB12 5FS 01224 730150
[E-mail: thehavyn@btinternet.com]

Banchory-Ternan: East (H) (01330 820380) (E-mail: banchoryeastchurchoffice@btconnect.com)
Alan J.S. Murray BSc BD PhD 2003 2013 East Manse, Station Road, Banchory AB31 5YP 01330 822481
[E-mail: alanjsm54@btopenworld.com]

Banchory-Ternan: West (H)
Antony Stephen MA BD 2001 2011 The Manse, 2 Wilson Road, Banchory AB31 5UY 01330 822811
[E-mail: tony@banchorywestchurch.com]

Charge / Minister			Address	Telephone
Birse and Feughside Anita van der Wal	2008	2013	The Manse, Finzean, Banchory AB31 6PB [E-mail: vanderwal@btinternet.com]	01330 850776
Braemar and Crathie Kenneth I. Mackenzie DL BD CPS	1990	2005	The Manse, Crathie, Ballater AB35 5UL [E-mail: crathiemanse@tiscali.co.uk]	01339 742208
Cromar See Aboyne-Dinnet				
Drumoak (H)-Durris (H) Vacant			26 Sunnyside Drive, Drumoak, Banchory AB31 3EW	01330 811031
Glenmuick (Ballater) (H) Vacant			The Manse, Craigendarroch Walk, Ballater AB35 5ZB	01339 754014
Laurencekirk See Aberluthnott				
Mearns Coastal Colin J. Dempster BD CertMin	1990	2010	The Manse, Kirkton, St Cyrus, Montrose DD10 0BW [E-mail: coldcoast@btinternet.com]	01674 850880
Mid Deeside Alexander C. Wark MA BD STM	1982	2012	The Manse, Torphins, Banchory AB31 4GQ [E-mail: alecwark@yahoo.co.uk]	01339 882276
Newtonhill Hugh Conkey BSc BD	1987	2001	39 St Ternans Road, Newtonhill, Stonehaven AB39 3PF [E-mail: hugh@conkey.plus.com]	01569 730143
Portlethen (H) (01224 782883) Flora J. Munro (Mrs) BD DMin	1993	2004	18 Rowanbank Road, Portlethen, Aberdeen AB12 4NX [E-mail: floramunro@aol.co.uk]	01224 780211
Stonehaven: Dunnottar (H) linked with Stonehaven: South (H) Rosslyn P. Duncan BD MTh		2007	Dunnottar Manse, Stonehaven AB39 3XL [E-mail: rosslynpduncan@gmail.com]	01569 762166

Stonehaven: Fetteresso (H) (01569 767689) (E-mail: fetteresso.office@btinternet.com)

Fyfe Blair BA BD DMin	1989	2009	11 South Lodge Drive, Stonehaven AB39 2PN [E-mail: fyfeblair@talktalk.net]	01569 762876

Stonehaven: South See Stonehaven: Dunnottar

West Mearns

Catherine A. Hepburn (Miss) BA BD	1982	2000	West Mearns Parish Church Manse, Fettercairn, Laurencekirk AB30 1UE [E-mail: cahepburn@btinternet.com]	01561 340203

Broadley, Linda J. (Mrs) LTh DipEd	1996	2013	(Dun and Hillside)	Snaefell, Lochside Road, St Cyrus, Montrose DD10 0DB [E-mail: lindabroadley@btinternet.com]	
Brown, J.W.S. BTh	1960	1995	(Cromar)	10 Forestside Road, Banchory AB31 5ZH [E-mail: iainisobel@aol.com]	01330 824353
Cameron, Ann J. (Mrs) CertCS DCE TEFL	2005		Auxiliary Minister	Currently resident in Qatar [E-mail: anncameron2@googlemail.com]	
Christie, Andrew C. LTh	1975	2000	(Banchory-Devenick and Maryculter/Cookney)	17 Broadstraik Close, Elrick, Aberdeen AB32 6JP	01224 746888
Forbes, John W.A. BD	1973	1999	(Edzell Lethnot with Fern, Careston and Menmuir with Glenesk)	Little Ennochie Steading, Finzean, Banchory AB31 6LX [E-mail: jrbbb@icloud.com]	01330 850785
Kinninburgh, Elizabeth B.F. (Miss) MA BD	1970	1986	(Birse with Finzean with Strachan)	21 Glen Tanar, Allachburn, Low Road, Aboyne AB34 5GW	01339 886757
Lamb, A. Douglas MA	1964	2002	(Dalry: St Margaret's)	9 Luther Drive, Laurencekirk AB30 1FE [E-mail: lamb.edzell@talk21.com]	01561 376816
Smith, Albert E. BD	1983	2006	(Methlick)	42 Haulkerton Crescent, Laurencekirk AB30 1FB [E-mail: aesmith42@googlemail.com]	01561 376111
Taylor, Peter R. JP BD	1977	2001	(Torphins)	42 Beltic Road, Torphins, Banchory AB31 4JT [E-mail: ptaylor850@btinternet.com]	01339 882780
Tierney, John P. MA	1945	1985	(Peterhead: West: Associate)	3 Queenshill Drive, Aboyne AB34 5DG	01339 886741
Wallace, William F. BDS BD	1968	2008	(Wick: Pulteneytown and Thrumster)	Lachan Cottage, 29 Station Road, Banchory AB31 5XX [E-mail: williamwallace39@talktalk.net]	01330 822259
Watt, William D. LTh	1978	1996	(Aboyne-Dinnet)	2 West Toll Crescent, Aboyne AB34 5GB [E-mail: wdwatt22@tiscali.co.uk]	01339 886943
Watts, Anthony BD DipTechEd JP	1999	2013	(Glenmuick (Ballater))	7 Cumiskie Crescent, Forres IV36 2QB [E-mail: tony.watts6@btinternet.com]	
Wilson, Andrew G.N. MA BD DMin	1977	2012	(Aberdeen: Rubislaw)	Auchintarph, Coull, Tarland, Aboyne AB34 4TT [E-mail: agn.wilson@gmail.com]	01339 880918

(33) GORDON

Meets at various locations on the first Tuesday of February, March, April, May, September, October, November and December, and on the last Tuesday of June.

Clerk:	REV. G. EUAN D. GLEN BSc BD		The Manse, 26 St Ninians, Monymusk, Inverurie AB51 7HF [E-mail: gordon@cofscotland.org.uk]	01467 651470

Barthol Chapel linked with Tarves
Vacant

  8 Murray Avenue, Tarves, Ellon AB41 7LZ   01651 851250

Belhelvie (H)
Paul McKeown BSc PhD BD   2000   2005   Belhelvie Manse, Balmedie, Aberdeen AB23 8YR
[E-mail: pmckeown1@btconnect.com]   01358 742227

Blairdaff and Chapel of Garioch
Vacant

  The Manse, Chapel of Garioch, Inverurie AB51 5HE   01467 681619

Cluny (H) linked with Monymusk (H)
G. Euan D. Glen BSc BD   1992   The Manse, 26 St Ninians, Monymusk, Inverurie AB51 7HF
[E-mail: euan.glen_1@btinternet.com]   01467 651470

Culsalmond and Rayne linked with Daviot (H)
Mary M. Cranfield (Miss) MA BD DMin   1989   The Manse, Daviot, Inverurie AB51 0HY
[E-mail: marymc@ukgateway.net]   01467 671241

Cushnie and Tough (R) (H)
Rosemary Legge (Mrs) BSc BD MTh   1992   2010   The Manse, Muir of Fowlis, Alford AB33 8JU
[E-mail: cushnietough@aol.com]   01975 581239

Daviot See Culsalmond and Rayne

Echt linked with Midmar (H)
Vacant

  The Manse, Echt, Westhill AB32 7AB   01330 860004

Ellon
James M. Davies BSc BD (Interim Minister)   1982   2013   27 Buchan Drive, Newmachar, Aberdeen AB21 0NR
[E-mail: daviesjim@btinternet.com]   01651 862281
07921 023144 (Mbl)

Fintray Kinellar Keithhall
Ellen Larson Davidson BA MDiv   2007   20 Kinmohr Rise, Blackburn, Aberdeen AB21 0LJ   01224 791350
[E-mail: larsondavidson@gmail.com]

Foveran
Richard Reid BSc BD MTh   1991   2013   The Manse, Foveran, Ellon AB41 6AP   01358 789288
[E-mail: reidricky8@aol.com]

Howe Trinity
John A. Cook MA BD   1986   2000   The Manse, 110 Main Street, Alford AB33 8AD   01975 562282
[E-mail: john.cook2@homecall.co.uk]

Huntly Cairnie Glass
Thomas R. Calder LLB BD WS   1994   The Manse, Queen Street, Huntly AB54 8EB   01466 792630
[E-mail: cairniechurch@aol.com]

Insch-Leslie-Premnay-Oyne (H)
Vacant   22 Western Road, Insch AB52 6JR   01464 820914

Inverurie: St Andrew's (Website: standrewschurchinverurie.org.uk)
Vacant   St Andrew's Manse, 1 Ury Dale, Inverurie AB51 3XW

Inverurie: West
Ian B. Groves BD CPS   1989   West Manse, 1 Westburn Place, Inverurie AB51 5QS   01467 620468
[E-mail: i.groves@inveruriewestchurch.org]

01467 620285

Kennay
Vacant   Kemnay, Inverurie AB51 9ND   01467 642219   (Tel/Fax)

Kintore (H)
Neil W. Meyer BD MTh   2000   2014   28 Oakhill Road, Kintore, Inverurie AB51 0FH   01467 632219
[E-mail: kintorekirk.minister@gmail.com]

Meldrum and Bourtie
Alison Jaffrey (Mrs) MA BD FSAScot   1990   2010   The Manse, Urquhart Road, Oldmeldrum, Inverurie AB51 0EX   01651 872250
[E-mail: alison@revjaffrey.com]

Methlick
Will Stalder BA MDiv MLitt PhD — 2014 — The Manse, Manse Road, Methlick, Ellon AB41 7DG [E-mail: bostowill@gmail.com] — 01651 806264

Midmar See Echt
Monymusk See Cluny

New Machar
Douglas G. McNab BA BD — 1999 2010 — The New Manse, Newmachar, Aberdeen AB21 0RD [E-mail: dougie.mcnab@btinternet.com] — 01651 862278

Noth
Regine U. Cheyne (Mrs) MA BSc BD — 1988 2010 — Manse of Noth, Kennethmont, Huntly AB54 4NP — 01464 831690

Skene (H)
Stella Campbell MA BD — 2012 — The Manse, Manse Road, Kirkton of Skene, Westhill AB32 6LX [E-mail: minister.skeneparish@mail.com] — 01224 745955
Marion G. Stewart (Miss) DCS — Kirk Cottage, Kirkton of Skene, Westhill AB32 6XE [E-mail: m313stewart@btinternet.com] — 01224 743407

Strathbogie Drumblade
Neil I.M. MacGregor BD — 1995 — 49 Deveron Park, Huntly AB54 8UZ — 01466 792702

Tarves See Barthol Chapel

Udny and Pitmedden
Gillean P. Maclean (Mrs) BD — 1994 2013 — The Manse, Manse Road, Udny Green, Ellon AB41 7RS [E-mail: minister@uppc.org.uk] — 01651 843794

Upper Donside (H) (E-mail: upperdonsideparishchurch@btinternet.com)
Vacant — The Manse, Lumsden, Huntly AB54 4GQ — 01464 861757

Craggs, Sheila (Mrs) — 2001 2008 — (Auxiliary Minister) — 7 Morar Court, Ellon AB41 9GG — 01358 723055
Craig, Anthony J.D. BD — 1987 2009 — (Glasgow: Maryhill) — 4 Hightown, Collieston, Ellon AB41 8RS [E-mail: craig.glasgow@gmx.net] — 01358 751247
Dryden, Ian MA DipEd — 1988 2001 — (New Machar) — 16 Glenhome Gardens, Dyce, Aberdeen AB21 7FG [E-mail: ian@idryden.freeserve.co.uk] — 01224 722820

Hawthorn, Daniel MA BD DMin	1965 2004	(Belhelvie)	7 Crimond Drive, Ellon AB41 8BT [E-mail: donhawthorn@compuserve.com]	01358 723981
Jones, Robert A. LTh CA	1966 1997	(Marnoch)	13 Gordon Terrace, Inverurie AB51 4GT	01467 622691
Lyon, Andrew LTh	1971 2007	(Fraserburgh West with Rathen West)	Barmekyn, Keig, Alford AB33 8BH [E-mail: andrew@lyon60.orangehome.co.uk]	01975 562768
Macalister, Eleanor	1994 2006	(Ellon)	2 Crimond Drive, Ellon AB41 8BT [E-mail: macal1ster@aol.com]	01358 722711
Mack, John C. JP	1985 2008	(Auxiliary Minister)	The Willows, Auchleven, Insch AB52 6QB	01464 820387
McKay, Margaret MA BD MTh	1991 2003	(Auchaber United with Auchterless)	The Smithy, Knowes of Elrick, Aberchirder, Huntly AB54 7PN [E-mail: elricksmithy@yahoo.co.uk]	(Tel) 01466 780208 (Fax) 01466 780015
McLeish, Robert S.	1970 2000	(Insch-Leslie-Premnay-Oyne)	19 Western Road, Insch AB52 6JR	01464 820749
Pryde, W. Kenneth DA BD	1994 2012	(Foveran)	15 Laurel Gardens, Bridge of Don, Aberdeen AB22 8YY [E-mail: wkpryde@hotmail.com]	
Renton, John P. BA LTh	1976 2014	(Kenmay)	2 Fettermear Way, Kemnay, Inverurie AB51 5JH [E-mail: j.m.renton@btinternet.com]	01467 642403
Rodger, Matthew A. BD	1978 1999	(Ellon)	15 Meadowlands Drive, Westhill AB32 6EJ	01224 743184
Scott, Allan D. BD	1977 1989	(Culsalmond with Daviot with Rayne)	Hilbury View, Hill Farm Lane, Duns Tew, Bicester OX25 6JH	
Stoddart, A. Grainger	1975 2001	(Meldrum and Bourtie)	6 Mayfield Gardens, Insch AB52 6XL	01464 821124
Taylor, Jane C. (Miss) BD DipMin	1990 2013	(Insch-Leslie-Premnay-Oyne)	1/2, 72 St Vincent Crescent, Glasgow G3 8NQ [E-mail: jane.c.taylor@btinternet.com]	0141-204 3022
Thomson, Iain U. MA BD	1970 2011	(Skene)	4 Keithill Gardens, Westhill AB32 6AZ [E-mail: iainuthomson@googlemail.com]	01224 746743

(34) BUCHAN

Meets at St Kane's Centre, New Deer, Turriff on the first Tuesday of February, March, May, September, October, November and December, and on the third Tuesday of June.

Clerk:	**REV. SHEILA M. KIRK BA LLB BD**	**The Manse, Old Deer, Peterhead AB42 5JB** [E-mail: buchan@cofscotland.org.uk]	**01771 623582**

Aberdour linked with Pitsligo

William B. Ross LTh CPS	1988 2013	19 Summers Road, Rosehearty, Fraserburgh AB43 7HP [E-mail: williamross278@btinternet.com]	01346 571823

Charge / Minister	Year(s)	Address	Telephone
Auchaber United linked with Auchterless Stephen J. Potts BA	2012	The Manse, Auchterless, Turriff AB53 8BA [E-mail: stevejpotts@hotmail.co.uk]	01888 511058
Auchterless See Auchaber United			
Banff linked with King Edward David I.W. Locke MA MSc BD	2000 2012	7 Colleonard Road, Banff AB45 1DZ [E-mail: davidlockerev@yahoo.co.uk]	01261 812107 07776 448301 (Mbl)
Crimond linked with Lonmay Vacant		The Manse, Crimond, Fraserburgh AB43 8QJ	01346 532431
Cruden (H) Vacant		The Manse, Hatton, Peterhead AB42 0QQ	01779 841229
Deer (H) Sheila M. Kirk BA LLB BD	2007 2010	The Manse, Old Deer, Peterhead AB42 5JB [E-mail: sheilamkirk@googlemail.com]	01771 623582
Fraserburgh: Old Vacant		4 Robbies Road, Fraserburgh AB43 7AF	01346 515332
Fraserburgh: South (H) linked with Inverallochy and Rathen: East Ronald F. Yule	1982	15 Victoria Street, Fraserburgh AB43 9PJ	01346 518244
Fraserburgh: West (H) linked with Rathen: West Vacant		4 Kirkton Gardens, Fraserburgh AB43 8TU	01346 513303
Fyvie linked with Rothienorman Robert J. Thorburn BD	1978 2004	The Manse, Fyvie, Turriff AB53 8RD [E-mail: rjthorburn@aol.com]	01651 891230
Gardenstown Donald N. Martin BD	1996	The Manse, Fernie Brae, Gardenstown, Banff AB45 3YL [E-mail: ferniebrae@gmail.com]	01261 851256

Inverallochy and Rathen: East See Fraserburgh: South
King Edward See Banff

Longside
Robert A. Fowlie BD   2007

The Manse, Old Deer, Peterhead AB42 5JB   01771 623582
[E-mail: bob.fowlie@googlemail.com]

Lonmay See Crimond

Macduff
Calum Stark LLB BD   2011

10 Ross Street, Macduff AB44 1NS   01261 832316
[E-mail: revcstark@gmail.com]

Marnoch
Alan Macgregor BA BD PhD   1992   2013

Marnoch Manse, 53 South Street, Aberchirder, Huntly AB54 7TS   01466 781143
[E-mail: marnochkirk@btconnect.com]

Maud and Savoch linked with New Deer: St Kane's
Vacant

The Manse, New Deer, Turriff AB53 6TD   01771 644216

Monquhitter and New Byth linked with Turriff: St Andrew's
James Cook MA MDiv   1999   2002

St Andrew's Manse, Balmellie Road, Turriff AB53 4SP   01888 560304
[E-mail: jmscook9@aol.com]

New Deer: St Kane's See Maud and Savoch

New Pitsligo linked with Strichen and Tyrie
Andrew Fothergill BA   2012

Kingsville, Strichen, Fraserburgh AB43 6SQ   01771 637365
[E-mail: andrewfothergill@btinternet.com]

Ordiquhill and Cornhill (H) linked with Whitehills
W. Myburgh Verster BA BTh LTh MTh   1981   2011

6 Craigneen Place, Whitehills, Banff AB45 2NE   01261 861317
[E-mail: wverster8910@btinternet.com]

Peterhead: Old Vacant			1 Hawthorn Road, Peterhead AB42 2DW	
Peterhead: St Andrew's (H) Vacant			1 Landale Road, Peterhead AB42 1QN	01779 238200
Peterhead: Trinity Vacant			18 Landale Road, Peterhead AB42 1QP	
Pitsligo See Aberdour				
Portsoy Norman Nicoll BD	2003	2010	The Manse, 4 Seafield Terrace, Portsoy, Banff AB45 2QB [E-mail: minister.portsoychurch@gmail.com]	01261 842272
Rathen: West See Fraserburgh: West **Rothienorman** See Fyvie				
St Fergus Jeffrey Tippner BA MDiv MCS PhD	1991	2012	26 Newton Road, St Fergus, Peterhead AB42 3DD [E-mail: revjeff@btconnect.com]	01779 838287
Sandhaven Vacant				
Strichen and Tyrie See New Pitsligo **Turriff: St Andrew's** See Monquhitter and New Byth				
Turriff: St Ninian's and Forglen Kevin R. Gruer BSc BA		2011	4 Deveronside Drive, Turriff AB53 4SP [E-mail: minister@stniniansandforglen.org.uk]	01888 563850
Whitehills See Ordiquhill and Cornhill				
Blaikie, James BD	1972	1997	(Berwick-on-Tweed: St Andrew's Wallace Green and Lowick)	
			57 Glenugie View, Peterhead AB42 2BW	01779 490625

Coutts, Fred MA BD	1973 1989	(Hospital Chaplain)	Ladebank, 1 Manse Place, Hatton, Peterhead AB42 0UQ [E-mail: fred.coutts@btinternet.com]	01779 841320
Fawkes, G.M. Allan BA BSc JP	1979 2000	(Lonmay with Rathen: West)	3 Northfield Gardens, Hatton, Peterhead AB42 0SW [E-mail: afawkes@aol.com]	01779 841814
Gehrke, Robert B. BSc BD CEng MIEE	1994 2013	(Blackridge with Harthill: St Andrew's)	140 The Green, Gardenstown, Banff AB45 3BD [E-mail: bob.gehrke@gmail.com]	01261 839129
McMillan, William J. CA LTh BD	1969 2004	(Sandsting and Aithsting with Walls and Sandness)	7 Ardinn Drive, Turriff AB53 4PR [E-mail: revbillymcmillan@aol.com]	01888 560727
Macnee, Iain LTh BD MA PhD	1975 2011	(New Pitsligo with Strichen and Tyrie)	Wardend Cottage, Alvah, Banff AB45 3TR [E-mail: macneeiain4@googlemail.com]	01261 815647
Noble, George S. DipTh	1972 2000	(Carfin with Newarthill)	Craigowan, 3 Main Street, Inverallochy, Fraserburgh AB43 8XX	01346 582749
Ross, David S. MSc PhD BD	1978 2013	(Prison Chaplain Service)	3–5 Abbey Street, Old Deer, Peterhead AB42 5LN [E-mail: padsross@btinternet.com]	01771 623994
van Sittert, Paul BA BD	1997 2011	Chaplain: Army	1 Bn The Royal Regiment of Scotland, Dreghorn Barracks, Edinburgh EH13 9QW [E-mail: vansittert@btinternet.com]	

(35) MORAY

Meets at St Andrew's-Lhanbryd and Urquhart on the first Tuesday of February, March, May, September, October, November and December, and at the Moderator's church on the fourth Tuesday of June.

Clerk:	REV. GRAHAM W. CRAWFORD BSc BD STM		The Manse, Prospect Terrace, Lossiemouth IV31 6JS [E-mail: moray@cofscotland.org.uk]	07944 287777 (Mbl)

Aberlour (H)

Shuna M. Dicks BSc BD	2010		The Manse, Mary Avenue, Aberlour AB38 9QU [E-mail: revshuna@btinternet.com]	01340 871687

Alves and Burghead linked with Kinloss and Findhorn

Louis C. Bezuidenhout BA MA BD DD	1978	2014	The Manse, 4 Manse Road, Kinloss, Forres IV36 3GH [E-mail: macbez@gmail.com]	01309 690474

Bellie linked with Speymouth

Alison C. Mehigan BD DPS	2003		11 The Square, Fochabers IV32 7DG [E-mail: alison@mehigan.org]	01343 820256

Birnie and Pluscarden linked with Elgin: High

Stuart M. Duff BA	1997	2014	The Manse, Daisy Bank, 5 Forteath Avenue, Elgin IV30 1TQ [E-mail: stuart.duff@gmail.com]	01343 545703

Buckie: North (H) linked with Rathven
Isabel C. Buchan (Mrs) BSc BD RE(PgCE)   1975   2013   The Manse, 14 St Peter's Road, Buckie   AB56 1DL   01542 832118
[E-mail: revicbuchan@bluebucket.org]

Buckie: South and West (H) linked with Enzie
Vacant   Craigendarroch, 14 Cliff Terrace, Buckie   AB56 1LX   01542 833775

Cullen and Deskford (Website: www.cullen-deskford-church.org.uk)
Douglas F. Stevenson BD DipMin   1991   2010   3 Seafield Place, Cullen, Buckie   AB56 4UU   01542 841963
[E-mail: dstevenson655@btinternet.com]

Dallas linked with Forres: St Leonard's (H) linked with Rafford
Donald K. Prentice BSc BD   1989   2010   St Leonard's Manse, Nelson Road, Forres   IV36 1DR   01309 672380
[E-mail: donald.prentice@tesco.net]
Anne Attenburrow BSc MB ChB (Aux)   2006   2013   4 Jock Inksons Brae, Elgin   IV30 1QE   01343 552330
[E-mail: AAttenburrow@aol.com]
John Morrison BSc BA PGCE   2013   35 Kirkton Place, Elgin   IV30 6JR   01343 550199
(Ordained Local Minister)   [E-mail: shalla57@aol.com]

Duffus, Spynie and Hopeman (H) (Website: www.duffusparish.co.uk)
Jennifer Adams BEng BD   2013   The Manse, Duffus, Elgin   IV30 5QP   01343 830276
[E-mail: jennyadamsbd@gmail.com]

Dyke linked with Edinkillie
Vacant   Manse of Dyke, Brodie, Forres   IV36 2TD   01309 641239

Edinkillie See Dyke
Elgin: High See Birnie and Pluscarden

Elgin: St Giles' (H) and St Columba's South (01343 551501) (Office: Williamson Hall, Duff Avenue, Elgin   IV30 1QS)
Steven Thomson BSc BD   2001   2013   18 Reidhaven Street, Elgin   IV30 1QH   01343 545729
[E-mail: stevie.thomson284@btinternet.com]   07841 368797 (Mbl)

Enzie See Buckie: South and West

Findochty linked with Portknockie
Hilary W. Smith BD DipMin MTh PhD   1999   2014   20 Netherton Terrace, Findochty, Buckie   AB56 4QD   01542 833484
[E-mail: hilaryoxfordsmith1@gmail.com]

Forres: St Laurence (H)
Barry J. Boyd LTh DPS 1993
12 Mackenzie Drive, Forres IV36 2JP
[E-mail: barry.j.boydstlaurence@btinternet.com]
01309 672260
07778 731018 (Mbl)

Forres: St Leonard's See Dallas

Keith: North, Newmill, Boharm and Rothiemay (H) (01542 886390)
Vacant
North Manse, Church Road, Keith AB55 5BR
01542 882559

Keith: St Rufus, Botriphnie and Grange (H)
Kay Gauld (Mrs) BD STM PhD 1999 2014
Church Road, Keith AB55 5BR
[E-mail: kay_gauld@btinternet.com]
01542 882799

Kinloss and Findhorn See Alves and Burghead

Knockando, Elchies and Archiestown (H) linked with Rothes (Website: www.moraykirk.co.uk)
Robert J.M. Anderson BD FInstLM 1993 2000
The Manse, Rothes, Aberlour AB38 7AF
[E-mail: robert@carmanse.freeserve.co.uk]
01340 831381

Lossiemouth: St Gerardine's High (H)
Geoffrey D. McKee BA 1997 2014
The Manse, St Gerardine's Road, Lossiemouth IV31 6RA
[E-mail: geoff.mckee@btinternet.com]
01343 813146

Lossiemouth: St James'
Graham W. Crawford BSc BD STM 1991 2003
The Manse, Prospect Terrace, Lossiemouth IV31 6JS
[E-mail: pictishreiver@aol.com]
07817 504042 (Mbl)

Mortlach and Cabrach (H)
Vacant
Mortlach Manse, Dufftown, Keith AB55 4AR
01340 820380

Portknockie See Findochty
Rafford See Dallas
Rathven See Buckie: North
Rothes See Knockando, Elchies and Archiestown

St Andrew's-Lhanbryd (H) and Urquhart
Andrew J. Robertson BD   2008   2010   39 St Andrews Road, Lhanbryde, Elgin IV30 8PU   01343 843765
[E-mail: ajr247@btinternet.com]

Speymouth See Bellie

Bain, Brian LTh	1980	2007	(Gask with Methven and Logiealmond)	Bayview, 13 Stewart Street, Portgordon, Buckie AB56 5QT [E-mail: brian.bain4@btinternet.com]	01542 831215
Buchan, Alexander MA BD PGCE	1975	1992	(North Ronaldsay with Sanday)	The Manse, 14 St Peter's Road, Buckie AB56 1DL [E-mail: revabuchan@bluebucket.org]	01542 832118
Connolly, Daniel BD DipTheol DipMin	1983	2012	Chaplain: Army	9 Burnside, Kinloss, Forres IV36 3XL	01309 690666
Davidson, A.A.B. MA BD	1960	1997	(Grange with Rothiemay)	11 Sutors Rise, Nairn IV12 5BU	01343 820937
King, Margaret MA DCS	2002	2012	(Deacon in Presbytery)	56 Murrayfield, Fochabers IV32 7EZ	01309 671719
Morton, Alasdair J. MA BD DipEd FEIS	1960	2000	(Bowden with Newtown)	16 St Leonard's Road, Forres IV36 1DW [E-mail: alasgilmor@hotmail.co.uk]	01309 671719
Morton, Gillian M. (Mrs) MA BD PGCE	1983	1996	(Hospital Chaplain)	16 St Leonard's Road, Forres IV36 1DW [E-mail: gillianmorton@hotmail.co.uk]	01309 671719
Munro, Sheila BD	1995	2003	Chaplain: RAF	RAF Lossiemouth, Elgin IV31 6SD [E-mail: sheila.munro781@halton.raf.mod.uk]	
Poole, Ann McColl (Mrs) DipEd ACE LTh	1983	2003	(Dyke with Edinkillie)	Kirkside Cottage, Dyke, Forres IV36 2TF	01309 641046
Robertson, Peter BSc BD	1988	1998	(Dallas with Forres: St Leonard's with Rafford)	17 Ferryhill Road, Forres IV36 2GY [E-mail: peterrobertsonforres@talktalk.net]	01309 676769
Rollo, George B. BD	1974	2010	(Elgin: St Giles' and St Columba's South)	'Struan', 13 Meadow View, Hopeman, Elgin IV30 5PL [E-mail: rollos@gmail.com]	01343 835226
Shaw, Duncan LTh CPS	1984	2011	(Alves and Burghead with Kinloss and Findhorn)	73 Woodside Drive, Forres IV36 0UF	
Smith, Hugh M.C. LTh	1973	2013	(Mortlach and Cabrach)	6 Concraig Walk, Kingswells, Aberdeen AB15 8DU	01224 745275
Smith, Morris BD	1988	2013	(Cromdale and Advie with Dulnain Bridge with Grantown-on-Spey)	1 Urquhart Grove, New Elgin IV30 8TB [E-mail: mosmith.themanse@btinternet.com]	01343 545019
Thomson, James M. BA	1952	2000	(Elgin: St Giles' and St Columba's South: Associate)	48 Mayne Road, Elgin IV30 1PD	01343 547664
Whittaker, Mary	2011		Auxiliary Minister	11 Templand Road, Lhanbryde, Elgin IV30 8BR	
Whyte, David LTh	1993	2011	(Boat of Garten, Duthil and Kincardine)	1 Lemanfield Crescent, Garmouth, Fochabers IV32 7LS [E-mail: whytedj@btinternet.com]	01343 870667
Wright, David L. MA BD	1957	1998	(Stornoway: St Columba)	84 Wyvis Drive, Nairn IV12 4TP	01667 451613

(36) ABERNETHY

Meets at Boat of Garten on the first Tuesday of February, March, May, September, October, November and December, and on the last Tuesday of June.

Clerk: REV. CATHERINE A. BUCHAN MA MDiv   **The Manse, Fort William Road, Newtonmore PH20 1DG**   **01540 673238**
[E-mail: abernethy@cofscotland.org.uk]

Abernethy (H) linked with Boat of Garten (H), Duthil (H) and Kincardine
Donald K. Walker BD   1979   2013   The Manse, Deshar Road, Boat of Garten PH24 3BN   01479 831252
[E-mail: donaldabdk@gmail.com]

Alvie and Insh (R) (H) linked with Rothiemurchus and Aviemore (H)
Vacant   The Manse, 8 Dalfaber Park, Aviemore PH22 1QF   01479 810280

Boat of Garten, Duthil and Kincardine See Abernethy

Cromdale (H) and Advie linked with Dulnain Bridge (H) linked with Grantown-on-Spey (H)
Vacant   The Manse, Golf Course Road, Grantown-on-Spey PH26 3HY   01479 872084

Dulnain Bridge See Cromdale and Advie
Grantown-on-Spey See Cromdale and Advie

Kingussie (H)
Alison H. Burnside (Mrs) MA BD   1991   2013   The Manse, 18 Hillside Avenue, Kingussie PH21 1PA   01540 662327
[E-mail: alisonskyona@btinternet.com]

Laggan (H) linked with Newtonmore: St Bride's (H)
Catherine A. Buchan (Mrs) MA MDiv   2002   2009   The Manse, Fort William Road, Newtonmore PH20 1DG   01540 673238
[E-mail: catherinebuchan567@btinternet.com]

Newtonmore: St Bride's See Laggan
Rothiemurchus and Aviemore See Alvie and Insh

Tomintoul (H), Glenlivet and Inveraven
Christopher Wallace BD DipMin   1988   2014   The Manse, Tomintoul, Ballindalloch AB37 9HA   01807 580254
[E-mail: cw@churchofscotland.onmicrosoft.com]

Bjarnason, Sven S. CandTheol	1975 2011	(Tomintoul, Glenlivet and Inveraven)	14 Edward Street, Dunfermline KY12 0JW [E-mail: sven@bjarnason.org.uk]	01383 724625
Burnside, William A.M. MA BD PGCE	1990 2013	(Stromness)	The Manse, 18 Hillside Avenue, Kingussie PH21 1PA [E-mail: bburnside@btinternet.com]	01540 662327
Duncanson, Mary (Ms)	2013	Ordained Local Minister: Presbytery Pastoral Support	3 Balmenach Road, Cromdale, Grantown-on-Spey PH26 3LJ [E-mail: mary1105@hotmail.co.uk]	01479 872165
MacEwan, James A.I. MA BD	1973 2012	(Abernethy with Cromdale and Advie)	Rapness, Station Road, Nethy Bridge PH25 3DN [E-mail: wurrus@hotmail.co.uk]	01479 821116
Pickering, John M. BSc BD DipEd BD DipMin	1997 2010	(Dundee: Mains)	Oriole House, Ardbroilach Road, Kingussie PH21 1JY	01479 873419
Ritchie, Christine A.Y. (Mrs)	2002 2012	(Braes of Rannoch with Foss and Rannoch)	25 Beachen Court, Grantown-on-Spey PH26 3JD [E-mail: cayritchie@btinternet.com]	
Thomson, Mary Ellen (Mrs)	2013	Ordained Local Minister	Riverside Flat, Gynack Street, Kingussie PH21 1EL [E-mail: marythomson835@btinternet.com]	01540 661772
Wallace, Sheila (Mrs) DCS BA BD		Deacon	Beannach Cottage, Spey Avenue, Boat of Garten PH24 3BE [E-mail: sheilad.wallace53@gmail.com]	01479 831548
Whyte, Ron C. BD CPS	1990 2013	(Alvie and Insh with Rothiemurchus and Aviemore)	13 Hillside Avenue, Kingussie PH21 1PA [E-mail: ron4xst@btinternet.com]	01540 661101 (Mbl) 07979 026973

(37) INVERNESS

Meets at Inverness, in Inverness: Trinity, on the first Tuesday of February, March, May, September, October, November and December; and at the Moderator's church on the fourth Tuesday of June.

Clerk:	REV. TREVOR G. HUNT BA BD	7 Woodville Court, Culduthel Avenue, Inverness IV2 6BX [E-mail: inverness@cofscotland.org.uk]	01463 250355 07753 423333 (Mbl)

Ardersier (H) linked with Petty

Robert Cleland	1997 2014	The Manse, Ardersier, Inverness IV2 7SX [E-mail: cleland810@btinternet.com]	01667 462224

Auldearn and Dalmore linked with Nairn: St Ninian's (H)

Vacant		The Manse, Auldearn, Nairn IV12 5SX	01667 451675

Cawdor (H) linked with Croy and Dalcross (H)

Janet S. Mathieson MA BD	2003	The Manse, Croy, Inverness IV2 5PH [E-mail: mathieson173@btinternet.com]	01667 493217

Croy and Dalcross See Cawdor

Culloden: The Barn (H) Vacant		45 Oakdene Court, Culloden IV2 7XL	01463 790504
Daviot and Dunlichity linked with Moy, Dalarossie and Tomatin Reginald F. Campbell BD BSc DipChEd	1979 2003	The Manse, Daviot, Inverness IV2 5XL [E-mail: campbell578@talktalk.net]	01463 772242
Dores and Boleskine Vacant			
Inverness: Crown (H) (01463 231140) Peter H. Donald MA PhD BD	1991 1998	39 Southside Road, Inverness IV2 4XA [E-mail: peter.donald7@btinternet.com]	01463 230537
Inverness: Dalneigh and Bona (GD) (H) Andrew A. McMillan BD	2012	9 St Mungo Road, Inverness IV3 5AS [E-mail: siberiantiger13@hotmail.com]	01463 232339
Inverness: East (H) Andrew T.B. McGowan (Prof.) BD STM PhD	1979 2009	2 Victoria Drive, Inverness IV2 3QD [E-mail: atbmcgowan@invernesseast.com]	01463 238770
Inverness: Hilton Duncan MacPherson LLB BD	1994	66 Culduthel Mains Crescent, Inverness IV2 6RG [E-mail: duncan@hiltonchurch.org.uk]	01463 231417
Inverness: Inshes (H) David S. Scott MA BD	1987 2013	48 Redwood Crescent, Milton of Leys, Inverness IV2 6HB [E-mail: david@insheschurch.org]	01463 772402
Inverness: Kinmylies (H) Andrew Barrie BD	2013	2 Balnafettack Place, Inverness IV3 8TQ [E-mail: andrewabarrie@hotmail.co.uk]	01463 224307
Inverness: Ness Bank (R) (H) Fiona E. Smith (Mrs) LLB BD	2010	15 Ballifeary Road, Inverness IV3 5PJ [E-mail: fiona.denhead@btopenworld.com]	01463 234653

Inverness: Old High St Stephen's
Peter W. Nimmo BD ThM — 1996 2004 — 24 Damfield Road, Inverness IV2 3HU
[E-mail: peter.nimmo7@btinternet.com] — 01463 250802

Inverness: St Columba (New Charge Development) (H)
Scott A. McRoberts BD MTh — 2012 — 20 Bramble Close, Inverness IV2 6BS
[E-mail: scottmcroberts@stcolumbainverness.org] — 01463 230308 / 07535 290092 (Mbl)

Inverness: Trinity (H)
Alistair Murray BD — 1984 2004 — 60 Kenneth Street, Inverness IV3 5PZ
[E-mail: a.murray111@btinternet.com] — 01463 234756

Kilmorack and Erchless
Vacant — 'Roselynn', Croyard Road, Beauly IV4 7DJ — 01463 782260

Kiltarlity linked with Kirkhill
Vacant — Wardlaw Manse, Wardlaw Road, Kirkhill, Inverness IV5 7NZ — 01463 831662

Kirkhill See Kiltarlity
Moy, Dalarossie and Tomatin See Daviot and Dunlichity

Nairn: Old (H)
Vacant

Nairn: St Ninian's See Auldearn and Dalmore
Petty See Ardersier

Urquhart and Glenmoriston (H)
Hugh F. Watt BD DPS DMin — 1986 1996 — Blairbeg, Drumnadrochit, Inverness IV3 6UG
[E-mail: hugh.watt2@btinternet.com] — 01456 450231

Archer, Morven (Mrs) — 2013 — Ordained Local Minister — 42 Firthview Drive, Inverness IV3 8QE
[E-mail: morvarch@btinternet.com] — 01463 237840

Black, Archibald T. BSc — 1964 1997 — (Inverness: Ness Bank) — 16 Elm Park, Inverness IV2 4WN — 01463 230588

Brown, Derek G. BD DipMin DMin — 1989 1994 — Chaplain: NHS Highland — Cathedral Manse, Cnoc-an-Lobht, Dornoch IV25 3HN
[E-mail: revsbrown@aol.com] — 01862 810296

Buell, F. Bart BA MDiv — 1980 1995 — (Urquhart and Glenmoriston) — 6 Towerhill Place, Cradlehall, Inverness IV2 5FN
[E-mail: bartbuell@talktalk.net] — 01463 794634

Chisholm, Archibald F. MA	1957	1997	(Braes of Rannoch with Foss and Rannoch)	32 Seabank Road, Nairn IV12 4EU	01667 452001
Christie, James LTh	1993	2003	(Dores and Boleskine)	20 Wester Inshes Crescent, Inverness IV2 5HL	01463 710534
Duncan, John C. BD MPhil	1987	2001	Chaplain: Army	3 Bn The Black Watch, The Royal Regiment of Scotland, Fort George, Ardersier, Inverness IV1 2TD [E-mail: john.duncan831@mod.uk]	(Mbl) 07825 119227
Fraser, Jonathan MA(Div) MTh ThM	2012		Associate: Inverness: Hilton	20 Moy Terrace, Inverness IV2 4EL [E-mail: jonathan@hiltonchurch.org.uk]	(Home) 01463 711609 (Work) 01463 233310
Frizzell, R. Stewart BD	1961	2000	(Wick: Old)	98 Boswell Road, Inverness IV2 3EW	01463 231907
Hunt, Trevor G. BA BD	1986	2011	(Evie with Firth with Rendall)	7 Woodville Court, Culduthel Avenue, Inverness IV2 6BX [E-mail: trevorhunt@gmail.com]	01463 250355 (Mbl) 07753 423333
Jeffrey, Stewart D. BSc BD	1962	1997	(Banff with King Edward)	10 Grigor Drive, Inverness IV2 4LP [E-mail: stewart.jeffrey@talktalk.net]	01463 230085
Livesley, Anthony LTh	1979	1997	(Kiltearn)	87 Beech Avenue, Nairn IV12 4ST [E-mail: tonylivesley@googlemail.com]	01667 455126
Logan, Robert J.V. MA BD	1962	2001	(Abdie and Dunbog with Newburgh)	Lindores, 1 Murray Place, Smithton, Inverness IV2 7PX [E-mail: rjvlogan@btinternet.com]	01463 790226
Mackenzie, Seoras L. BD	1996	1998	Chaplain: Army	Carver Barracks, Wimbish, Saffron Walden, Essex CB10 2YA	
MacQuarrie, Donald A. BSc BD	1979	2012	(Fort William: Duncansburgh MacIntosh with Kilmonivaig)	Birch Cottage, 4 Craigrorie, North Kessock, Inverness IV1 3XH [E-mail: pdmacq@ukgateway.net]	01463 731050
Mitchell, Joyce (Mrs) DCS	1994		(Deacon)	Sunnybank, Farr, Inverness IV2 6XG [E-mail: joyce@mitchell71.freeserve.co.uk]	01808 521285
Morrison, Hector BSc BD MTh	1981	1994	Principal: Highland Theological College	24 Oak Avenue, Inverness IV2 4NX	01463 238561
Rettie, James A. BTh	1981	1999	(Melness and Eriboll with Tongue)	2 Trantham Drive, Westhill, Inverness IV2 5QT	01463 798896
Ritchie, Bruce BSc BD PhD	1977	2014	(Dingwall: Castle Street)	16 Brinckman Terrace, Westhill, Inverness IV2 5BL [E-mail: brucezomba@hotmail.com]	01463 791389
Robb, Rodney P.T.	1995	2004	(Stirling: St Mark's)	2A Mayfield Road, Inverness IV2 4AE	01463 230831
Robertson, Fergus A. MA BD	1971	2010	(Inverness: Dalneigh and Bona)	16 Druid Temple Way, Inverness IV2 6UQ [E-mail: faavrobertson@yahoo.co.uk]	01463 718462
Stirling, G. Alan S. MA	1960	1999	(Leochel Cushnie and Lynturk with Tough)	97 Lochlann Road, Culloden, Inverness IV2 7HJ	01463 798313
Turner, Fraser K. LTh	1994	2007	(Kiltarlity with Kirkhill)	20 Caulfield Avenue, Inverness IV2 5GA [E-mail: fraseratq@yahoo.co.uk]	01463 794004
Waugh, John L. LTh	1973	2002	(Ardclach with Auldearn and Dalmore)	58 Wyvis Drive, Nairn IV12 4TP [E-mail: jwaugh334@btinternet.com]	(Tel/Fax) 01667 456397
Younger, Alastair S. BScEcon ASCC	1969	2008	(Inverness: St Columba High)	33 Duke's View, Slackbuie, Inverness IV2 6BB [E-mail: younger873@btinternet.com]	01463 242873

INVERNESS ADDRESSES

Inverness

Crown	Kingsmills Road x Midmills Road
Dalneigh and Bona	St Mary's Avenue
East	Academy Street x Margaret Street
Hilton	Druid Road x Tomatin Road
Inshes	Inshes Retail Park
Kinmylies	Kinmylies Way
Ness Bank	Ness Bank x Castle Road
St Stephen's	Old Edinburgh Road x Southside Road
The Old High	Church Street x Church Lane
Trinity	Huntly Place x Upper Kessock Street

Nairn

Old	Academy Street x Seabank Road
St Ninian's	High Street x Queen Street

(38) LOCHABER

Meets at Caol, Fort William, in Kilmallie Church Hall at 6pm, on the first Tuesday of September and December, on the last Tuesday of October and on the fourth Tuesday of March. The June meeting is held at 6pm on the first Tuesday in the church of the incoming Moderator.

Clerk:	MRS ELLA GILL	5 Camus Inas, Acharacle PH36 4JQ	01967 431834
		[E-mail: lochaber@cofscotland.org.uk]	
Treasurer:	MR ERIC WALKER	Tigh a' Chlann, Inverroy, Roy Bridge PH31 4AQ	01397 712028
		[E-mail: line15@btinternet.com]	

Acharacle (H) linked with Ardnamurchan

Fiona Ogg (Mrs) BA BD   2012   The Manse, Acharacle PH36 4JU   01967 431654
[E-mail: fionaogg@gmail.com]

Ardgour and Kingairloch linked with Morvern linked with Strontian

Donald G.B. McCorkindale BD DipMin   1992   2011   The Manse, 2 The Meadows, Strontian, Acharacle PH36 4HZ   01967 402234
[E-mail: donald.mccorkindale@sky.com]
[E-mail: donald@aksm.org.uk]

Ardnamurchan See Acharacle

Duror (H) linked with Glencoe: St Munda's (H) (R)

Vacant

Fort Augustus linked with Glengarry

Tabea Baader   2012   The Manse, Fort Augustus PH32 4BH   01320 366210
[E-mail: tabeabaader@gmx.de]

Fort William: Duncansburgh MacIntosh (H) linked with Kilmonivaig

Vacant   The Manse of Duncansburgh, The Parade, Fort William PH33 6BA   01397 702297

Glencoe: St Munda's See Duror
Glengarry See Fort Augustus

Kilmallie
Richard T. Corbett BSc MSc PhD BD   1992   2005   Kilmallie Manse, Corpach, Fort William PH33 7JS   01397 772736
[E-mail: richard.t.corbett@btinternet.com]

Kilmonivaig See Fort William: Duncansburgh MacIntosh

Kinlochleven (H) linked with Nether Lochaber (H)
Malcolm A. Kinnear MA BD PhD   2010   The Manse, Lochaber Road, Kinlochleven PH50 4QW   01855 831227
[E-mail: malcolm.kinnear563@btinternet.com]

Morvern See Ardgour
Nether Lochaber See Kinlochleven

North West Lochaber
Edgar J. Ogston BSc BD   1976   2013   Church of Scotland Manse, Annie's Brae, Mallaig PH41 4RG   01687 460042
[E-mail: edgar.ogston@macfish.com]

Strontian See Ardgour

Anderson, David M. MSc FCOptom   1984 2012   (Ordained Local Minister)   'Mirlos', 1 Dumfries Place, Fort William PH33 6UQ   01397 702091
[E-mail: david@mirlos.co.uk]

Lamb, Alan H.W. BA MTh   1959 2005   (Associate Minister)   Smiddy House, Arisaig PH39 4NH   01687 450227
[E-mail: h.a.lamb@handalamb.plus.com]

Millar, John L. MA BD   1981 1990   (Fort William: Duncansburgh with Kilmonivaig)   Flat 0/1, 12 Chesterfield Gardens, Glasgow G12 0BF   0141-339 4098
[E-mail: johnmillar123@btinternet.com]

Muirhead, Morag (Mrs)   2013   Ordained Local Minister   6 Dunbarton Road, Fort William PH33 6UU   01397 703643
[E-mail: mowgli49@aol.com]

Perkins, Mairi   2012   Ordained Local Minister   Ashlea, Cuil Road, Duror, Appin PA38 4DA   01631 740313
[E-mail: m.perkins553@btinternet.com]

Rae, Peter C. BSc BD   1968 2000   (Beath and Cowdenbeath: North)   8 Wether Road, Great Cambourne, Cambridgeshire CB23 5DT   01954 710079
[E-mail: rae.fairview@btinternet.com]

Varwell, Adrian P.J. BA BD PhD   1983 2011   (Fort Augustus with Glengarry)   19 Enrick Crescent, Kilmore, Drumnadrochit, Inverness IV63 6TP   01456 459352
[E-mail: adrian.varwell@btinternet.com]

Winning, A. Ann MA DipEd BD   1984 2006   (Morvern)   'Westering', 13C Carnoch, Glencoe, Ballachulish PH49 4HQ   01855 811929
[E-mail: awinning009@btinternet.com]

LOCHABER Communion Sundays Please consult the Presbytery website: www.cofslochaber.co.uk

(39) ROSS

Meets on the first Tuesday of September in the church of the incoming Moderator, and in Dingwall: Castle Street Church on the first Tuesday of October, November, December, February, March and May, and on the last Tuesday of June.

Clerk: MR RONALD W. GUNSTONE BSc   20 Bellfield Road, North Kessock, Inverness IV1 3XU   01463 731337
[E-mail: ross@cofscotland.org.uk]

Alness
Vacant
Michael Macdonald (Aux)   2004 2014   27 Darroch Brae, Alness IV17 0SD   01349 882238
73 Firhill, Alness IV17 0RT   01349 884268
[E-mail: mike_mary@hotmail.co.uk]

Avoch linked with Fortrose and Rosemarkie
Alan T. McKean BD CertMin   1982 2010   5 Ness Way, Fortrose IV10 8SS   01381 621433
[E-mail: a.mckean2345@btinternet.com]

Contin (H) linked with Fodderty and Strathpeffer (H)
Fanus Erasmus MA LTh MTh ThD   1978 2013   The Manse, Contin, Strathpeffer IV14 9ES   01997 421028
[E-mail: fanuserasmus@yahoo.com]

Cromarty linked with Resolis and Urquhart
Vacant   The Manse, Culbokie, Dingwall IV7 8JN   01349 877452

Dingwall: Castle Street (H)
Stephen Macdonald BD MTh   2008 2014   16 Achany Road, Dingwall IV15 9JB   01349 867315
07570 804193 (Mbl)
[E-mail: sm.2@hotmail.co.uk]

Dingwall: St Clement's (H)
Vacant   8 Castlehill Road, Dingwall IV15 9PB

Fearn Abbey and Nigg linked with Tarbat
David V. Scott BTh — 1994 — 2006 — Church of Scotland Manse, Fearn, Tain IV20 1WN — 01862 832626 (Tel/Fax)

Ferintosh
Andrew F. Graham BTh DPS — 2001 — 2006 — Ferintosh Manse, Leanaig Road, Conon Bridge, Dingwall IV7 8BE [E-mail: afg1960@tiscali.co.uk] — 01349 861275

Fodderty and Strathpeffer See Contin
Fortrose and Rosemarkie See Avoch

Invergordon
Kenneth Donald Macleod BD CPS — 1989 — 2000 — The Manse, Cromlet Drive, Invergordon IV18 0BA [E-mail: kd-macleod@tiscali.co.uk] — 01349 852273

Killearnan (H) linked with Knockbain (H)
Vacant — The Church of Scotland Manse, Coldwell Road, Artafallie, North Kessock, Inverness IV1 3ZE — 01463 731333

Kilmuir and Logie Easter
Fraser M.C. Stewart BSc BD — 1980 — 2011 — The Manse, Delny, Invergordon IV18 0NW [E-mail: fraserstewart1955@hotmail.com] — 01862 842280

Kiltearn (H)
Donald A. MacSween BD — 1991 — 1998 — The Manse, Swordale Road, Evanton, Dingwall IV16 9UZ [E-mail: donaldmacsween@hotmail.com] — 01349 830472

Knockbain See Killearnan

Lochbroom and Ullapool (GD)
Vacant — The New Manse, Garve Road, Ullapool IV26 2SX — 01854 613146

Resolis and Urquhart See Cromarty

Rosskeen
Robert Jones BSc BD — 1990 — Rosskeen Manse, Perrins Road, Alness IV17 0XG [E-mail: rob2jones@btinternet.com] — 01349 882265

Tain
Vacant   01862 894140

Tarbat See Fearn Abbey and Nigg

Urray and Kilchrist
Scott Polworth LLB BD   2009   The Manse, Corrie Road, Muir of Ord IV6 7TL   01463 870259
[E-mail: scottpolworth@btinternet.com]

Archer, Nicholas D.C. BA BD	1971	1992	(Dores and Boleskine)	2 Aldie Cottages, Tain IV19 1LZ [E-mail: na.2ac777@btinternet.com]	01862 821494
Dupar, Kenneth W. BA BD PhD	1965	1993	(Christ's College, Aberdeen)	The Old Manse, The Causeway, Cromarty IV11 8XJ	01381 600428
Forsyth, James LTh	1970	2000	(Fearn Abbey with Nigg Chapelhill)	Rhives Lodge, Golspie, Sutherland KW10 6DD	
Glass, Alexander OBE MA	1998	2009	(Auxiliary Minister)	Craigton, Tulloch Avenue, Dingwall IV15 9TU	01349 863258
Horne, Douglas A. BD	1977	2009	(Tain)	151 Holm Farm Road, Culduthel, Inverness IV2 6BF [E-mail: douglas.horne@talktalk.net]	01463 712677
Liddell, Margaret (Miss) BD DipTh	1987	1997	(Contin)	20 Wyvis Crescent, Conon Bridge, Dingwall IV7 8BZ [E-mail: margaretliddell@talktalk.net]	01349 865997
Lincoln, John MPhil BD	1986	2014	(Balquhidder with Killin and Ardeonaig)	59 Obsdale Park, Alness IV17 0TR [E-mail: johnlincoln@minister.com]	01349 882791
Mackinnon, R.M. LTh	1968	1995	(Kilmuir and Logie Easter)	27 Riverford Crescent, Conon Bridge, Dingwall IV7 8HL	01349 866293
McLean, Gordon LTh	1972	2008	(Contin)	Beinn Dhorain, Kinnettas Square, Strathpeffer IV14 9BD [E-mail: gmaclean@hotmail.co.uk]	01997 421380
MacLennan, Alasdair J. BD DCE	1978	2001	(Resolis and Urquhart)	Airdale, Seaforth Road, Muir of Ord IV6 7TA	01463 870704
Macleod, John MA	1959	1993	(Resolis and Urquhart)	'Benview', 19 Balvaird, Muir of Ord IV6 7RG [E-mail: sheilaandjohn@yahoo.co.uk]	01463 871286
Munro, James A. BA BD DMS	1979	2013	(Port Glasgow: Hamilton Bardrainney)	1 Wyvis Crescent, Conon Bridge, Dingwall IV7 8BZ [E-mail: james781munro@btinternet.com]	01349 865752
Niven, William W. BTh	1982	1995	(Alness)	4 Obsdale Park, Alness IV17 0TP	01349 882427
Ramsden, Iain BTh	1999	2013	(Killearnan with Knockbain)	19 Balvaird Terrace, Muir of Ord IV6 7TR [E-mail: s4rev@sky.com]	01463 870453
Rutherford, Ellen B. (Miss) MBE DCS	1994	2013	(Deacon)	Urray Care Home, Muir of Ord IV6 7SY	
Smith, Russel BD			(Dingwall: St Clement's)	1 School Road, Conon Bridge, Dingwall IV7 8AE [E-mail: russantwo@btinternet.com]	01349 861011
Tallach, John MA MLitt	1970	2010	(Cromarty)	29 Firthview Drive, Inverness IV3 8NS [E-mail: j.tallach@tiscali.co.uk]	01463 418721

(40) SUTHERLAND

Meets at Lairg on the first Tuesday of March, May, September, November and December, and on the first Tuesday of June at the Moderator's church.

Clerk: REV. MARY J. STOBO   **Druim-an-Sgairnich, Ardgay IV24 3BG**   **01863 766868**
[E-mail: sutherland@cofscotland.org.uk]

Altnaharra and Farr
Vacant   The Manse, Bettyhill, Thurso KW14 7SS   01641 521208

Assynt and Stoer
Vacant   Canisp Road, Lochinver, Lairg IV27 4LH   01571 844342

Clyne (H) linked with Kildonan and Loth Helmsdale (H)
John Macgregor BD   2001   2013   Golf Road, Brora KW9 6QS   01408 621239
[E-mail: john_macg@hotmail.com]

Creich See Kincardine Croick and Edderton

Dornoch Cathedral (H)
Susan M. Brown (Mrs) BD DipMin   1985   1998   Cathedral Manse, Cnoc-an-Lobht, Dornoch IV25 3HN   01862 810296
[E-mail: revsbrown@aol.com]

Durness and Kinlochbervie
John T. Mann BSc BD   1990   1998   Manse Road, Kinlochbervie, Lairg IV27 4RG   01971 521287
[E-mail: jtmklb@aol.com]

Eddrachillis
John MacPherson BSc BD   1993   Church of Scotland Manse, Scourie, Lairg IV27 4TQ   01971 502431

Golspie
John B. Sterrett BA BD PhD   2007   The Manse, Fountain Road, Golspie KW10 6TH   01408 633295 (Tel/Fax)
[E-mail: johnbsterrett@yahoo.co.uk]

Kildonan and Loth Helmsdale See Clyne

Kincardine Croick and Edderton linked with Creich linked with Rosehall

Anthony M. Jones BD DPS DipTheol CertMin FRSA	1994	2010	The Manse, Ardgay IV24 3BG [E-mail: revanthonyjones@yahoo.com]	01863 766285
Hilary Gardner (Miss) (Aux)	2010	2012	Cayman Lodge, Kincardine Hill, Ardgay IV24 3DJ [E-mail: gardnerhilary@hotmail.com]	01863 766107

Lairg (H) linked with Rogart (H)

Vacant	The Manse, Lairg IV27 4EH	01549 402373

Melness and Tongue (H)

Stewart Goudie BSc BD	2010	St Andrew's Manse, Tongue, Lairg IV27 4XL [E-mail: stewart@goudie.me.uk]	01847 611230 (Tel/Fax) 07957 237757 (Mbl)

Rogart See Lairg
Rosehall See Kincardine Croick and Edderton

Chambers, John OBE BSc	1972	2009	(Inverness: Ness Bank)	Bannlagan Lodge, 4 Earls Cross Gardens, Dornoch IV25 3NR [E-mail: chambersdornoch@btinternet.com]	01862 811520
Goskirk, J.L. LTh	1968	2010	(Lairg with Rogart)	Rathvilly, Lairgmuir, Lairg IV27 4ED [E-mail: leslie_goskirk@sky.com]	01549 402569
McCree, Ian W. BD	1971	2011	(Clyne with Kildonan and Loth Helmsdale)	Tigh Ardachu, Mosshill, Brora KW9 6NG [E-mail: ian@mccree.f9.co.uk]	01408 621185
Muckart, Graeme W.M. MTh MSc FSAScot	1983	2009	(Kincardine Croick and Edderton)	Kildale, Clashmore, Dornoch IV25 3RG [E-mail: avqt18@dsl.pipex.com]	
Stobo, Mary J. (Mrs)	2013		Ordained Local Minister; Community Healthcare Chaplain	Druim-an-Sgairnich, Ardgay IV24 3BG [E-mail: sutherland@cofscotland.org.uk]	01863 766868

(41) CAITHNESS

Meets alternately at Wick and Thurso on the first Tuesday of February, March, May, September, November and December, and the third Tuesday of June.

Clerk:	REV. RONALD JOHNSTONE BD		2 Comlifoot Drive, Halkirk KW12 6ZA [E-mail: caithness@cofscotland.org.uk]	01847 839033

Bower linked with Halkirk Westerdale linked with Watten
Alastair H. Gray MA BD — 1978 2005 — The Manse, Station Road, Watten, Wick KW1 5YN [E-mail: alastair.h.gray@btinternet.com] — 01955 621220

Canisbay linked with Dunnet linked with Keiss linked with Olrig
Vacant — The Manse, Canisbay, Wick KW1 4YH — 01955 611756

Dunnet See Canisbay
Halkirk Westerdale See Bower
Keiss See Canisbay
Olrig See Canisbay

The North Coast Parish
Vacant — Church of Scotland Manse, Reay, Thurso KW14 7RE

The Parish of Latheron
Gordon Oliver BD — 1979 2010 — Central Manse, Main Street, Lybster KW3 6BN [E-mail: parish-of-latheron@btconnect.com] — 01593 721706

Thurso: St Peter's and St Andrew's (H)
David S.M. Malcolm BD — 2011 2014 — The Manse, 40 Rose Street, Thurso KW14 8RF [E-mail: DavidSMMalcolm@aol.com] — 01847 895186

Thurso: West (H)
Vacant — Thorkel Road, Thurso KW14 7LW — 01847 892663

Watten See Bower

Wick: Pulteneytown (H) and Thrumster
Vacant   The Manse, Coronation Street, Wick KW1 5LS   01955 603166

Wick: St Fergus
John Nugent   1999   2011   Mansefield, Miller Avenue, Wick KW1 4DF   01955 602167
                                  [E-mail: johnnugentis@mail2web.com]

Craw, John DCS	1998 2009	(Deacon)	Liabost, 8 Proudfoot Road, Wick KW1 4PQ	01955 603805
			[E-mail: johncraw607@btinternet.com]	(Mbl) 07544 761653
Duncan, Esme (Miss)	2013	Ordained Local Minister	Avalon, Upper Warse, Canisbay, Wick KW1 4YD	01955 611455
			[E-mail: esmeduncan@btinternet.com]	
Johnstone, Ronald BD	1977 2011	(Thurso: West)	2 Comlifoot Drive, Halkirk KW12 6ZA	01847 839033
			[E-mail: ronaldjohnstone@btinternet.com]	
Nicol, Robert	2013	Ordained Local Minister	3 Castlegreen Road, Thurso KW14 7DN	
			[E-mail: robert.nicol1@btinternet.com]	
Rennie, Lyall	2013	Ordained Local Minister	Ruachmarra, Lower Warse, Canisbay, Wick KW1 4YB	01955 611756
			[E-mail: lyall.rennie@btinternet.com]	
Stewart, Heather (Mrs)	2013	Ordained Local Minister	Burnthill, Thrumster, Wick KW1 5TR	01955 651717
			[E-mail: heatherburnthill@btopenworld.com]	(Work) 01955 603333
Warner, Kenneth BD	1981 2008	(Halkirk and Westerdale)	Kilearnan, Clayock, Halkirk KW12 6UZ	01847 831825
			[E-mail: wrnrkenn@btinternet.com]	

CAITHNESS Communion Sundays

Bower	1st Jul, Dec	Keiss	1st May, 3rd Nov	Watten	4th Mar, Jun, Nov
Canisbay	1st Jun, Nov	Latheron	Apr, Jul, Sep, Nov	West	1st Jul, Dec
Dunnet	last May, Nov	North Coast	Mar, Easter, Jun, Sep, Dec	Wick: Pulteneytown and	1st Mar, Jun, Sep, Dec
Halkirk Westerdale	Apr, Jul, Oct	Olrig	last May, Nov	Thrumster	
		Thurso: St Peter's and St Andrew's	Mar, Jun, Sep, Dec	Wick: St Fergus	Apr, Oct

(42) LOCHCARRON – SKYE

Meets in Kyle on the first Tuesday of each month, except January, May, July and August.

Clerk: REV. ALLAN I. MACARTHUR BD — High Barn, Croft Road, Lochcarron, Strathcarron **IV54 8YA**
[E-mail: lochcarronskye@cofscotland.org.uk]
[E-mail: a.macarthur@btinternet.com]
01520 722278 (Tel)
01520 722674 (Fax)

Applecross, Lochcarron and Torridon (GD)
David Macleod   2008   The Manse, Colonel's Road, Lochcarron, Strathcarron IV54 8YG   01520 722829
[E-mail: david.macleod@me.com]

Bracadale and Duirinish (GD)
Vacant   Duirinish Manse, Dunvegan, Isle of Skye IV55 8WQ   01470 521457

Gairloch and Dundonnell (GD)
Vacant   Church of Scotland Manse, The Glebe, Gairloch IV21 2BT   01445 712053 (Tel/Fax)

Glenelg and Kintail
Roderick N. MacRae BTh   2001   2004   Church of Scotland Manse, Inverinate, Kyle IV40 8HE   01599 511245
[E-mail: barvalous@msn.com]

Kilmuir and Stenscholl (GD)
Vacant   Staffin, Portree, Isle of Skye IV51 9JX   01470 562759 (Tel/Fax)

Lochalsh
Vacant   The Manse, Main Street, Kyle IV40 8DA   01599 534294

Portree (GD)
Sandor Fazakas BD MTh   1976   2007   Viewfield Road, Portree, Isle of Skye IV51 9ES   01478 611868
[E-mail: fazakass52@yahoo.com]

Snizort (H) (GD)
Vacant   The Manse, Kensaleyre, Snizort, Portree, Isle of Skye IV51 9XE   01470 532453

Strath and Sleat (GD)

Vacant

John D. Urquhart BA BD	1998	2003	The Manse, 6 Upper Breakish, Isle of Skye IV42 8PY	01471 820063
(Part-Time: Gaelic Services)			The Manse, The Glebe, Kilmore, Teangue, Isle of Skye IV44 8RG	01471 844469

[E-mail: ministear@hotmail.co.uk]

Name			Role	Address	Tel
Anderson, Janet (Miss) DCS			(Deaconess)	Creagard, 31 Lower Breakish, Isle of Skye IV42 8QA [E-mail: jaskye@hotmail.co.uk]	01471 822403
Beaton, Donald MA BD MTh	1961	2002	(Glenelg and Kintail)	Kilmaluag Croft, North Duntulm, Isle of Skye IV51 9UF	01470 552296
Calhoun, Robert L. BBA MDiv DMin	1974	2012	(Snizort)	145 Lamont, San Antonio, TX 78209, USA [E-mail: drre0911@yahoo.com]	
Kellas, David J. MA BD	1966	2004	(Kilfinan with Kyles)	Buarblach, Glenelg, Kyle IV40 8LA [E-mail: davidkellas@btinternet.com]	01599 522257
Macarthur, Allan I. BD	1973	1998	(Applecross, Lochcarron and Torridon)	High Barn, Croft Road, Lochcarron, Strathcarron IV54 8YA [E-mail: a.macarthur@btinternet.com]	(Mbl) 07909 577764 (Tel) 01520 722278 (Fax) 01520 722674
McCulloch, Alen J.R. MA BD	1990	2012	(Chaplain: Royal Navy)	Aros, 6 Gifford Terrace Road, Plymouth PL3 4JE [E-mail: aviljoen90@hotmail.com]	01752 657290
Mackenzie, Hector M.		2008	Chaplain: Army	3 Bn The Parachute Regiment, Merville Barracks, Colchester CO2 7UT [E-mail: mackenziehector@hotmail.com]	
Macleod, Donald LTh	1988	2000	(Snizort)	Burnside, Upper Galder, Glenelg, Kyle IV40 8JZ [E-mail: donaldpmacleod_7@btinternet.com]	01599 522265
Martin, George M. MA BD	1987	2005	(Applecross, Lochcarron and Torridon)	8(1) Buckingham Terrace, Edinburgh EH4 3AA	0131-343 3937
Morrison, Derek	1995	2013	(Gairloch and Dundonnell)	2 Cliffton Place, Poolewe, Achnasheen IV22 2JU [E-mail: derekmorrison1@aol.com]	01445 781333
Murray, John W.		2003	Auxiliary Minister	1 Totescore, Kilmuir, Portree, Isle of Skye IV51 9YN [E-mail: jwm7@hotmail.co.uk]	01470 542297

LOCHCARRON – SKYE Communion Sundays

Applecross	1st Sep	Glenshiel	1st Jul
Arnisort	3rd Mar, Sep	Kilmuir	1st Mar, Sep
Bracadale	Last Feb	Kintail	3rd Apr, Jul
Broadford	3rd Jan, Easter, 3rd Sep	Kyleakin	Last Sep
Duirinish	4th Jun	Lochalsh and Stromeferry	4th Jan, Jun, Sep, Christmas, Easter
Dundonnell	1st Aug	Lochcarron and Shieldaig	Easter; communion held on a revolving basis when there is a fifth Sunday in the month
Elgol	3rd Jun, Nov		
Gairloch	2nd Jun, Nov		
Glenelg			

Plockton and Kyle	2nd May, 1st Oct
Portree	Easter, Pentecost, Christmas, 2nd Mar, Aug, 1st Nov
Sleat	Last May
Snizort	1st Jan, 4th Mar
Stenscholl	1st Jun, Dec
Strath	4th Jan
Torridon and Kinlochewe	

In the Parish of Strath and Sleat, Easter communion is held on a revolving basis.

(43) UIST

Meets on the first Tuesday of February, March, September and November in Lochmaddy, and on the third Tuesday of June in Leverburgh.

Clerk: MR WILSON McKINLAY   **Heatherburn Cottage, Rhughasnish, Isle of South Uist HS8 5PE**   **01870 610393**
[E-mail: uist@cofscotland.org.uk]

Benbecula (GD) (H)
Vacant   Church of Scotland Manse, Griminish, Isle of Benbecula HS7 5QA   01870 602180

Berneray and Lochmaddy (GD) (H)
Vacant   Church of Scotland Manse, Lochmaddy, Isle of North Uist HS6 5AA   01876 500414

Carinish (GD) (H)
Vacant   Church of Scotland Manse, Clachan, Locheport, Lochmaddy, Isle of North Uist HS6 5HD   01876 580219

Kilmuir and Paible (GE)
Vacant   Paible, Isle of North Uist HS6 5ED   01876 510310

Manish-Scarista (GD) (H)
Vacant   Scarista, Isle of Harris HS3 3HX   01859 550200

Tarbert (GD) (H)
Vacant   The Manse, Manse Road, Tarbert, Isle of Harris HS3 3DF   01859 502231

MacDonald, Angus J. BSc BD	1995	2001	(Lochmaddy and Trumisgarry)	7 Memorial Avenue, Stornoway, Isle of Lewis HS1 2QR	01851 706634
Macdonald, Ishabel	2011		Ordained Local Minister	'Cleat Aíe Ora', 18 Carinish, Isle of North Uist HS6 5HN	01876 580367
MacInnes, David MA BD	1966	1999	(Kilmuir and Paible)	9 Golf View Road, Kinmylies, Inverness IV3 8SZ	01463 717377
MacIver, Norman BD	1976	2011	(Tarbert)	57 Boswell Road, Wester Inshes, Inverness IV2 3EW [E-mail: norman@n-cmaciver.freeserve.co.uk]	
Macpherson, Kenneth J. BD	1988	2002	(Benbecula)	70 Baile na Cille, Balivanich, Isle of Benbecula HS7 5ND	01870 602751
Morrison, Donald John	2001		Auxiliary Minister	22 Kyles, Tarbert, Isle of Harris HS3 3BS	01859 502341
Petrie, Jackie G.	1989	2011	(South Uist)	7B Malaclete, Isle of North Uist HS6 5BX [E-mail: jackiegpetrie@yahoo.com]	01876 560804

Smith, John M.	1956 1992	(Lochmaddy)	Hamersay, Clachan, Locheport, Lochmaddy, Isle of North Uist HS6 5HD	01876 580332
Smith, Murdo MA BD	1988 2011	(Manish-Scarista)	Aisgeir, 15A Upper Shader, Isle of Lewis HS3 3MX	

UIST Communion Sundays

Benbecula	2nd Mar, Sep	Carinish	4th Mar, Aug
Berneray and Lochmaddy	4th Jun, last Oct	Kilmuir and Paible	1st Jun, 3rd Nov
		Manish-Scarista	3rd Apr, 1st Oct
		Tarbert	2nd Mar, 3rd Sep

(44) LEWIS

Meets at Stornoway, in St Columba's Church Hall, on the second Tuesday of February, March, September and November. It also meets if required in April, June and December on dates to be decided.

Clerk:	**MR JOHN CUNNINGHAM**	**1 Raven's Lane, Stornoway, Isle of Lewis HS2 0EG** **[E-mail: lewis@cofscotland.org.uk]**	**01851 709977** **07789 878840 (Mbl)**

Barvas (GD) (H) Paul Amed LTh DPS	1992	2008	Barvas, Isle of Lewis HS2 0QY [E-mail: paulamed@hebrides.net]	01851 840218
Carloway (GD) (H) (Office: 01851 643211) Vacant			Church of Scotland Manse, Knock, Carloway, Isle of Lewis HS2 9AU	01851 643255
Cross Ness (GE) (H) Ian Murdo M. Macdonald DPA BD	2001		Cross Manse, Swainbost, Ness, Isle of Lewis HS2 0TB [E-mail: crosschurch@me.com]	01851 810375
Kinloch (GE) (H) Iain M. Campbell BD	2004	2008	Laxay, Lochs, Isle of Lewis HS2 9LA [E-mail: i455@btinternet.com]	01851 830218
Knock (GE) (H) Guardianship of the Presbytery				

Lochs-Crossbost (GD) (H)
Guardianship of the Presbytery

Lochs-in-Bernera (GD) (H) linked with Uig (GE) (H)
Hugh Maurice Stewart DPA BD   2008
4 Seaview, Knock, Point, Isle of Lewis HS2 0PD   01851 870379
(Temporary Manse)
[E-mail: berneralwuig@btinternet.com]

Stornoway: High (GD) (H)
Vacant
1 Goathill Road, Stornoway, Isle of Lewis HS1 2NJ   01851 703106

Stornoway: Martin's Memorial (H) (Church office: 01851 700820)
Thomas MacNeil MA BD   2002   2006
Matheson Road, Stornoway, Isle of Lewis HS1 2LR   01851 704238
[E-mail: tommymacneil@hotmail.com]

Stornoway: St Columba (GD) (H) (Church office: 01851 701546)
William J. Heenan BA MTh   2012
St Columba's Manse, Lewis Street, Stornoway, Isle of Lewis HS1 2JF   01851 705933
[E-mail: wmheenan@hotmail.co.uk]   07837 770589 (Mbl)

Uig See Lochs-in-Bernera

Name			Address	Telephone
Jamieson, Esther M.M. (Mrs) BD	1984 2002	(Glasgow: Penilee St Andrew)	1 Redburn, Bayview, Stornoway, Isle of Lewis HS1 2UU [E-mail: iandejamieson@btinternet.com]	01851 704789 07867 602963 (Mbl)
Johnstone, Ben MA BD DMin	1973 2013	(Strath and Sleat)	Loch Alainn, 5 Breaclete, Great Bernera, Isle of Lewis HS2 9LT [E-mail: benonbernera@gmail.com]	01851 612445
Macdonald, James LTh CPS	1984 2001	(Knock)	Elim, 8A Lower Bayble, Point, Isle of Lewis HS2 0QA [E-mail: elim8a@hotmail.co.uk]	01851 870173
Maclean, Donald A. DCS	1975 2006	(Deacon)	8 Upper Barvas, Isle of Lewis HS2 0QX	01851 840454
MacLennan, Donald Angus		(Kinloch)	4 Kestrel Place, Inverness IV2 3YH [E-mail: maclennankinloch@btinternet.com]	01463 243750 07799 668270 (Mbl)
Macleod, William	1957 2006	(Uig)	54 Lower Barvas, Isle of Lewis HS2 0QY	01851 840217
Shadakshari, T.K. BTh BD MTh	1998 2006	Healthcare Chaplain	23D Benside, Newmarket, Stornoway, Isle of Lewis HS2 0DZ [E-mail: tk.shadakshari@nhs.net]	01851 701727 (Home) 01851 704704 (Office) 07403 697138 (Mbl)

LEWIS Communion Sundays

Barvas	3rd Mar, Sep	Knock	3rd Apr, 1st Nov
Carloway	1st Mar, last Sep	Lochs-Crossbost	4th Mar, Sep
Cross Ness	2nd Mar, Oct	Lochs-in-Bernera	1st Apr, 2nd Sep
Kinloch	3rd Mar, 2nd Jun, 2nd Sep		

Stornoway: High	3rd Feb, last Aug
Martin's Memorial	3rd Feb, last Aug, 1st Dec, Easter
Stornoway: St Columba	3rd Feb, last Aug
Uig	3rd Jun, 4th Oct

(45) ORKNEY

Normally meets at Kirkwall, in the St Magnus Centre, on the second Tuesday of February, May, September and November. One meeting is usually held outwith the St Magnus Centre.

Clerk: MR DAVID BAKER MSc MCIOB   59 Albert Street, Kirkwall, Orkney KW15 1HQ   01856 878381
[E-mail: orkney@cofscotland.org.uk]   07500 050855 (Mbl)

Birsay, Harray and Sandwick
Vacant   The Manse, North Biggings Road, Dounby, Orkney KW17 2HZ   01856 771803

East Mainland
Wilma A. Johnston MTheol MTh   2006   2014   The Manse, Holm, Orkney KW17 2SB   01856 781772
[E-mail: rev_wilmajohnston@btinternet.com]

Eday linked with Stronsay: Moncur Memorial (H)
Vacant   The Manse, Stronsay, Orkney KW17 2AF   01857 616311

Evie (H) linked with Firth (H) (01856 761117) linked with Rendall linked with Rousay
Roy Cordukes BSc BD   2014   The Manse, Finstown, Orkney KW17 2EG   01856 761328
[E-mail: minister@cordukes.plus.com]

Firth See Evie

Flotta linked with Hoy and Walls linked with Orphir (H) and Stenness (H)
Vacant   Stenness Manse, Stenness, Stromness, Orkney KW16 3HH

Hoy and Walls See Flotta

Kirkwall: East (H) linked with Shapinsay
Julia Meason MTh — 2013 — East Church Manse, Thoms Street, Kirkwall, Orkney KW15 1PF [E-mail: julia.meason@hotmail.com] — 01856 874789

Kirkwall: St Magnus Cathedral (H)
G. Fraser H. Macnaughton MA BD — 1982 2002 — Berstane Road, Kirkwall, Orkney KW15 1NA [E-mail: macnaughton187@btinternet.com] — 01856 873312

North Ronaldsay linked with Sanday (H)
Vacant — The Manse, Sanday, Orkney KW17 2BW — 01857 600429

Orphir and Stenness See Flotta

Papa Westray linked with Westray
Iain D. MacDonald BD — 1993 — The Manse, Hilldavale, Westray, Orkney KW17 2DW [E-mail: idmacdonald@btinternet.com] — 01857 677357 (Tel/Fax) / 07710 443780 (Mbl)

Rendall See Evie
Rousay (Church centre: 01856 821271) See Evie
Sanday See North Ronaldsay
Shapinsay See Kirkwall: East

South Ronaldsay and Burray
Stephen Manners MA BD (Assoc) — 1989 2012 — St Margaret's Manse, Church Road, St Margaret's Hope, Orkney KW17 2SR [E-mail: sk.manners@me.com] — 01856 831670 / 07747 821458 (Mbl)

Stromness (H)
Magdaléna Trgalová — 2013 — 5 Manse Lane, Stromness, Orkney KW16 3AP — 01856 851487

Stronsay: Moncur Memorial See Eday
Westray See Papa Westray

Brown, R. Graeme BA BD — 1961 1998 — (Birsay with Rousay) — Bring Deeps, Orphir, Orkney KW17 2LX [E-mail: graeme_sibyl@btinternet.com] — (Tel/Fax) 01856 811707

Clark, Thomas L. BD	1985 2008	(Orphir with Stenness)	7 Headland Rise, Burghead, Elgin IV30 5HA [E-mail: toml.clark@btinternet.com]	01343 830144
Fidler, David G.	2013	Ordained Local Minister	34 Guardhouse Park, Stromness, Orkney KW16 3DP [E-mail: dvdfid@yahoo.co.uk]	01856 850575 (Mbl) 07900 386473
Prentice, Martin	2013	Ordained Local Minister	Cott of Howe, Cairston, Stromness, Orkney KW16 3JU [E-mail: mwm.prentice@virgin.net]	01856 851139 (Mbl) 07795 817213
Tait, Alexander	1967 1995	(Glasgow: St Enoch's Hogganfield)	Ingermas, Evie, Orkney KW17 2PH [E-mail: jen1957@hotmail.co.uk]	01856 751477
Wishart, James BD	1986 2009	(Deer)	Upper Westshore, Burray, Okney KW17 2TE [E-mail: jwishart06@btinternet.com]	01856 731672

(46) SHETLAND

Meets at Lerwick on the first Tuesday of February, April, June, September, November and December.

| Clerk: | REV. CHARLES H.M. GREIG MA BD | 6 Hayhoull Place, Bigton, Shetland ZE2 9GA [E-mail: shetland@cofscotland.org.uk] | 01950 422468 |

Burra Isle linked with Tingwall

| Deborah Dobby (Mrs) BA BD PGCE RGN RSCN | 2014 | The Manse, 25 Hogalee, East Voe, Scalloway, Shetland ZE1 0UU [E-mail: deborahdobby@gmail.com] | 01595 881157 |

Delting linked with Northmavine

| Vacant | | The Manse, Grindwell, Brae, Shetland ZE2 9QJ | 01806 522219 |
| Robert M. MacGregor CMIOSH DipOSH RSP (Aux) | 2004 | Olna Cottage, Brae, Shetland ZE2 9QS [E-mail: revbobdelting@mypostoffice.co.uk] | 01806 522604 |

Dunrossness and St Ninian's inc. Fair Isle linked with Sandwick, Cunningsburgh and Quarff

| Charles H.M. Greig MA BD | 1976 1997 | 6 Hayhoull Place, Bigton, Shetland ZE2 9GA [E-mail: chm.greig@btopenworld.com] | 01950 422468 |

Fetlar linked with Unst linked with Yell

| David Cooper BA MPhil | 1975 2008 | North Isles Manse, Gutcher, Yell, Shetland ZE2 9DF [E-mail: reverenddavidcooper@googlemail.com] | 01957 744258 |

(David Cooper is a minister of the Methodist Church)

Lerwick and Bressay

| Caroline R. Lockerbie BA MDiv DMin | 2007 2013 | The Manse, 82 St Olaf Street, Lerwick, Shetland ZE1 0ES [E-mail: caroline.lockerbie@btinternet.com] | 01595 692125 |

(Transition Minister)

Nesting and Lunnasting linked with Whalsay and Skerries

| Irene A. Charlton (Mrs) BTh | 1994 | 1997 | The Manse, Marrister, Symbister, Whalsay, Shetland ZE2 9AE
[E-mail: irene.charlton@btinternet.com] | 01806 566767 |

Northmavine See Delting

Sandsting and Aithsting linked with Walls and Sandness

| D. Brian Dobby MA BA | 1999 | 2014 | The Manse, 25 Hogalee, East Voe, Scalloway, Shetland ZE1 0UU
[E-mail: briandobby@googlemail.com] | 07909 452262 (Mbl) |

Sandwick, Cunningsburgh and Quarff See Dunrossness and St Ninian's
Tingwall See Burra Isle
Unst See Fetlar
Walls and Sandness See Sandsting and Aithsting
Whalsay and Skerries See Nesting and Lunnasting
Yell See Fetlar

Kirkpatrick, Alice H. (Miss) MA BD FSAScot	1987	2000	(Northmavine)	1 Daisy Park, Baltasound, Unst, Shetland ZE2 9EA	
Knox, R. Alan MA LTh AInstAM	1965	2004	(Fetlar with Unst with Yell)	27 Killyvalley Road, Garvagh, Co. Londonderry, Northern Ireland BT51 5LX	02829 558925
Macintyre, Thomas MA BD	1972	2011	(Sandsting and Aithsting with Walls and Sandness)	Lappideks, South Voxter, Cunningsburgh, Shetland ZE2 9HF [E-mail: the2macs.macintyre@btinternet.com]	01950 477549
Smith, Catherine (Mrs) DCS	1964	2003	(Presbytery Assistant)	21 Lingaro, Bixter, Shetland ZE2 9NN	01595 810207
Williamson, Magnus J.C.	1982	1999	(Fetlar with Yell)	Creekhaven, Houl Road, Scalloway, Shetland ZE1 0XA	01595 880023

(47) ENGLAND

Meets at London, in Crown Court Church, on the second Tuesday of February, and at St Columba's, Pont Street, on the second Tuesday of June and October.

| Clerk: | REV. ALISTAIR CUMMING MSc CCS FInstLM | 64 Prince George's Avenue, London SW20 8BH
[E-mail: england@cofscotland.org.uk] | 07534 943986 (Mbl) |

Corby: St Andrew's (H)

| Vacant | 43 Hempland Close, Corby, Northants NN18 8LR | 01536 746429 |

Corby: St Ninian's (H) (01536 265245)
Kleber Machado BTh MA MTh | 1998 | 2012 | The Manse, 46 Glyndebourne Gardens, Corby, Northants NN18 0PZ | 01536 669478
[E-mail: klebermachado@ymail.com]

Guernsey: St Andrew's in the Grange (H)
Graeme W. Beebee BD | 1993 | 2003 | The Manse, Le Villocq, Castel, Guernsey GY5 7SB | 01481 257345
[E-mail: beehive@cwgsy.net]

Jersey: St Columba's (H)
David Logan MStJ BD MA CF(V) FRSA | 2009 | 2014 | 18 Claremont Avenue, St Saviour, Jersey JE2 7SF | 01534 730659
[E-mail: minister@castleroy.org] | 07797 742012 (Mbl)

Liverpool: St Andrew's
Guardianship of the Presbytery
Session Clerk: Mr Robert Cottle | 0151-524 1915

London: Crown Court (H) (020 7836 5643)
Philip L. Majcher BD | 1982 | 2007 | 53 Sidmouth Street, London WC1H 8JX | 020 7278 5022
[E-mail: minister@crowncourtchurch.org.uk]

London: St Columba's (H) (020 7584 2321) linked with Newcastle: St Andrew's (H)
C. Angus MacLeod MA BD | 1996 | 2012 | 29 Hollywood Road, Chelsea, London SW10 9HT | 020 7584 2321 (Office)
[E-mail: minister@stcolumbas.org.uk]

Andrea E. Price (Mrs) (Assoc) | 1997 | 2014 | St Columba's, Pont Street, London SW1X 0BD | 020 7610 6994 (Home)
[E-mail: associateminister@stcolumbas.org.uk] | 020 7584 2321 (Office)

Dorothy Lunn (Aux) | 2002 | 2002 | 14 Bellerby Drive, Ouston, Co. Durham DH2 1TW | 0191-492 0647
[E-mail: dorothylunn@hotmail.com]

Newcastle: St Andrew's See London: St Columba's

Anderson, Andrew F. MA BD | 1981 2011 | (Edinburgh: Greenside) | 58 Reliance Way, Oxford OX4 2FG | 01865 778397
[E-mail: andrew.relianceway@gmail.com]

Bowie, A. Glen CBE BA BSc | 1954 1984 | (Principal Chaplain: RAF) | 16 Weir Road, Hemingford Grey, Huntingdon PE18 9EH | 01480 381425
Brown, Scott J. CBE QHC BD | 1993 1993 | Chaplain of the Fleet: Royal Navy | Principal Church of Scotland and Free Churches Chaplain (Naval), | 02392 625552
and Director Naval Chaplaincy Service (Capability), MP 1.2, | (Mbl) 07769 847876
Leach Building, Whale Island, Portsmouth PO2 8BY
[E-mail: scott.brown943@mod.uk]

Cairns, W. Alexander BD | 1978 2006 | (Corby: St Andrew's) | Kirkton House, Kirkton of Craig, Montrose DD10 9TB | (Mbl) 07808 588045
[E-mail: sandy.cairns@btinternet.com]

Cameron, R. Neil | 1975 1981 | (Chaplain: Community)
[E-mail: neilandminacameron@yahoo.co.uk]

Name			Role	Address	Tel
Cherry, Alastair J. BA BD FPLD	1982	2009	(Glasgow: Penilee St Andrew's)	6 Upper Abbey Road, Belvedere, Kent DA17 5AJ [E-mail: alastair.j.cherry@btinternet.com]	01322 402818
Coulter, David G. QHC BA BD MDA PhD CF	1989	1994	Chaplain: Army	8 Ashdown Terrace, Tidworth, Wilts SP9 7SQ [E-mail: padredgcoulter@yahoo.co.uk]	01980 842175
Cumming, Alistair MSc CCS FInstLM	2010		Auxiliary Minister: London: St Columba's	64 Prince George's Avenue, London SW20 8BH [E-mail: afcumming@hotmail.com]	020 8540 7365 07534 943986 (Mbl)
Dowswell, James A.M.	1991	2001	(Lerwick and Bressay)	Mill House, High Street, Staplehurst, Tonbridge, Kent TN12 0AU [E-mail: jdowswell@btinternet.com]	01580 891271
Fields, James MA BD STM	1988	1997	School Chaplain	The Bungalow, The Ridgeway, Mill Hill, London NW7 1QX	020 8201 1397
Frail, Nicola BLE MBA MDiv	2000	2012	Chaplain: Army	9 Regt Army Air Corps, Dishforth Airfield, Thirsk YO7 3EZ [E-mail: nrfscot@hotmail.com]	
Francis, James BD PhD	2002	2009	Chaplain: Army	37 Milburn Road, Coleraine BT52 1QT	02870 353869
Langlands, Cameron H. BD MTh ThM PhD MInstLM	1995	2009	Pastoral and Spiritual Care Manager: Lancashire Teaching Hospitals NHS Trust	Department of Pastoral and Spiritual Care, Lancashire Teaching Hospitals NHS Foundation Trust, Royal Preston Hospital, Sharoe Green Lane, Fulwood, Preston PR2 9HT [E-mail: cameron.langlands@lthtr.nhs.uk]	01772 522350
Lovett, Mairi F. BSc BA DipPS MTh	2005	2013	Hospital Chaplain	Royal Brompton Hospital, Sydney Street, London SW3 6NP [E-mail: m.lovett@rbht.nhs.uk]	020 7352 8121 ext. 4736
Lugton, George L. MA BD	1955	1997	(Guernsey: St Andrew's in the Grange)	6 Clos de Beauvoir, Rue Cohu, Guernsey GY5 7TE	01481 254285 (Tel/Fax)
Macfarlane, Peter T. BA LTh	1970	1994	(Chaplain: Army)	4 rue de Rives, 37160 Abilly, France	
McIndoe, John H. MA BD STM DD	1966	2000	(London: St Columba's with Newcastle: St Andrew's)	5 Dunlin, Westerlands Park, Glasgow G12 0FE [E-mail: johnandeve@mcindoe555.fsnet.co.uk]	0141-579 1366
MacLeod, Rory N. MA BD	1986	1992	Chaplain: Army	39 Regt, Royal Regiment of Artillery, Albemarle Barracks, Harlow Hill, Newcastle-upon-Tyne NE15 0RF	
McMahon, John K.S. MA BD	1998	2012	Head of Spiritual and Pastoral Care, West London Mental Health Trust	Broadmoor Hospital, Crowthorne, Berkshire RG45 7EG [E-mail: john.mcmahonrev@wlmht.nhs.uk]	01344 754098
Mather, James BA DipArch MA MBA	2010		Auxiliary Minister: University Chaplain	24 Ellison Road, Barnes, London SW13 0AD [E-mail: jsm.johnstonmather@btinternet.com]	020 8876 6540 (Home) 020 7361 1670 (Work) 07836 715655 (Mbl)
Middleton, Paul BMus BD ThM PhD	2000		University Lecturer	97B Whipcord Lane, Chester CH1 4DG	01704 543044
Munro, Alexander W. MA BD	1978		Chaplain and Teacher of Religious Studies	Columba House, 12 Alexandra Road, Southport PR9 0NB [E-mail: awmunro@tiscali.co.uk]	
Pickles, Robert G.D.W. BD MPhil ThD	2003	2010	(Orwell and Portmoak)	Chadacres, 49 Rotton Park Road, Birmingham B16 0SG [E-mail: robert.pickles@btopenworld.com]	0121-454 4046
Shackleton, Scott J.S. QCVS BA BD PhD RN	1993	2010	Chaplain: Royal Navy	HQ 3 Commando Brigade, RMB Stonehouse, Durnford Street, Plymouth PL1 3QS [E-mail: shackletonscott@hotmail.com]	01752 836397
Trevorrow, James A. LTh	1971	2003	(Glasgow: Cranhill)	12 Test Green, Corby, Northants NN17 2HA [E-mail: jimtrevorrow@compuserve.com]	01536 264018
Walker, R. Forbes BSc BD ThM	1987	2013	School Chaplain	Flat 5, 18 Northside Wandsworth Common, London SW18 2SL [E-mail: revrfw@gmail.com]	020 8870 0953

Wallace, Donald S.	1950 1980	(Chaplain: RAF)	7 Dellfield Close, Watford, Herts WD1 3BL	01923 223289
Ward, Michael J. BSc BD PhD MA PGCE	1983 2009	Training and Development Officer: Presbyterian Church of Wales	Apt 6, Bryn Hedd, Conwy Road, Penmaen-mawr, Gwynedd LL34 6BS [E-mail: revmw@btopenworld.com]	(Mbl) 07765 598816
Wood, Peter J. MA BD	1993	(College Lecturer)	97 Broad Street, Cambourne, Cambridgeshire CB23 6DH [E-mail: pejowood@tiscali.co.uk]	01954 715558
Wylie, Jonathan	2000 2014	Chaplain: RAF	9 St Edmund's Square, RAF Honington IP31 1LT [E-mail: jonathan.wylie922@mod.uk]	(Mbl) 07818 401402

ENGLAND – Church Addresses

Corby:	St Andrew's St Ninian's	Occupation Road Beanfield Avenue	
Liverpool:			
London:	Crown Court St Columba's	Crown Court WC2 Pont Street SW1	
Newcastle:	The Western Rooms, Anglican Cathedral	Sandyford Road	

(48) EUROPE

Meets over the weekend of the second Sunday of March and October, hosted by congregations in mainland Europe.

Clerk: REV. JAMES SHARP	102 Rue des Eaux-Vives, CH-1207 Geneva, Switzerland [E-mail: europe@cofscotland.org.uk]	**0041 22 786 4847**

Amsterdam

Vacant	Jan Willem Brouwersstraat 9, NL-1071 LH Amsterdam, The Netherlands [E-mail: minister@ercadam.nl]	0031 20 672 2288

Bochum

James M. Brown MA BD	1982	Neustrasse 15, D-44787 Bochum, Germany [E-mail: j.brown56@gmx.de]	0049 234 133 65

Brussels (E-mail: secretary@churchofscotland.be)

Andrew Gardner BSc BD PhD	1997 2004	23 Square des Nations, B-1000 Brussels, Belgium [E-mail: minister@churchofscotland.be]	0032 2 672 40 56

Budapest (Church telephone: 0036 1 373 0725)
Aaron Stevens   2010
H-1143, Stefánia út 32, Budapest, Hungary
[E-mail: revastevens@yahoo.co.uk]
(Mbl) 0036 70 615 5394

Colombo, Sri Lanka: St Andrew's Scots Kirk
Roderick D.M. Campbell   1975   2014
OStJ TD BD DMin FSAScot
73 Galle Road, Colpetty, Colombo 3, Sri Lanka
[E-mail: minister@standrewsscotskirk.org]
0094 (11) 2386774

Costa del Sol
Vacant
The Manse, Avenida Jesus Santos Rein, 24 Edf. Lindamar 4 – 3Q,
Fuengirola, 29640 Malaga, Spain
0034 951 260 982

Geneva
Ian A. Manson BA BD   1989   2001
20 Ancienne Route, 1218 Grand Saconnex, Geneva, Switzerland
[E-mail: cofsg@pingnet.ch]
0041 22 798 29 09
(Office) 0041 22 788 08 31

Gibraltar
Ewen MacLean BA BD   1995   2009
St Andrew's Manse, 29 Scud Hill, Gibraltar
[E-mail: scotskirk@gibraltar.gi]
00350 200 77040

Lausanne
Ian J.M. McDonald MA BD   1984   2010
26 Avenue de Rumine, CH-1005 Lausanne, Switzerland
[E-mail: minister@scotskirklausanne.ch]
0041 21 323 98 28

Lisbon
Vacant
Rua da Arriaga 13, 1200-625 Lisbon, Portugal
[E-mail: cofslx@netcabo.pt]
00351 218 043 410

Malta
T. Douglas McRoberts BD CPS FRSA   1975   2009
La Romagnola, 15 Triq is-Seiqia, Misrah Kola, Attard
ATD 1713, Malta
[E-mail: doug.mcroberts@btinternet.com]
Church address: 210 Old Bakery Street, Valletta, Malta
[E-mail: minister@saintandrewsmalta.com]
(Tel/Fax) 00356 214 15465

Paris
James M. Cowie BD — 1977
10 Rue Thimmonier, F-75009 Paris, France
[E-mail: jimcowie@europe.com]
0033 1 48 78 47 94

Regensburg (University)
Rhona Dunphy (Mrs) BD DPTheol — 2005
Liskircherstrasse 9, D-93049 Regensburg, Germany
[E-mail: rhona@dunphy.de]
(Mbl) 0049 (0) 176 83 10 69 67

Rome: St Andrew's
William B. McCulloch BD — 1997 2002
Via XX Settembre 7, 00187 Rome, Italy
[E-mail: revwbmcculloch@hotmail.com]
(Tel) 0039 06 482 7627
(Fax) 0039 06 487 4370

Rotterdam (Church telephone: 0031 10 412 4779)
Vacant
Church address: Schiedamse Vest 119–121, NL-2012 BH Rotterdam, The Netherlands
Meeuwenstraat 4A, NL-3071 PE Rotterdam, The Netherlands
[E-mail: scotsintchurch@cs.com]
0031 10 220 4199

Trinidad
Garwell Bacchas
50 Frederick Street, Port of Spain, Trinidad
[E-mail: revbacchas@gmail.com]
001 868 627 9312

Turin
Vacant
Via S. Pio V 17, 10125 Torino, Italy
[E-mail: esc.torino@alice.it]
Church address: Via Sant Anselmo 6, 10125 Turin, Italy
0039 011 650 5770
0039 011 650 9467

Warwick, Bermuda: Christ Church
Barry W. Dunsmore MA BD — 1982 2009
Mailing address: PO Box PG88, Paget PG BX, Bermuda
Church address: Christ Church, Middle Road, Warwick, Bermuda
[E-mail: christchurch@logic.bm; Website: www.christchurch.bm]
Manse address: The Manse, 6 Manse Road, Paget PG 01, Bermuda
(Office) 001 441 236 1882

David P. Anderson BSc BD — 2002
Irene Bom (Ordained Local Minister: worship resourcing) — 2008
James S. Dick MA BTh — 1988 1997
SCOTSDG, Wessex Barracks, Fallingbostel, Germany, BFPO 38
Bergpolderstraat 53A, NL-3038 KB Rotterdam, The Netherlands
[E-mail: ibsalem@xs4all.nl]
[E-mail: jim.s.dick@googlemail.com]
0031 10 265 1703

Morris M. Dutch BD BA DipBTI	1998	2013	41 Baronald Drive, Glasgow G12 0HN [E-mail: mmdutch@yahoo.co.uk]	0141-357 2286
Derek G. Lawson LLB BD	1998	2011	2 Rue Joseph Guillemot, F-87210 Oradour St Genest, France [E-mail: derek.lawson@sfr.fr]	0033 5 55 68 53 03
James Sharp (Ordained Local Minister: pastoral training and support)	2005		102 Rue des Eaux-Vives, CH-1207 Geneva, Switzerland [E-mail: jimsharp@bluewin.ch]	0041 22 786 4847
(Turin) Alexander B. Cairns MA	1957	2009	Beechwood, Main Street, Sandhead, Stranraer DG9 9JG	
(Bermuda) T. Alan W. Garrity BSc BD MTh	1969	2008	17 Solomon's View, Dunlop, Kilmarnock KA3 4ES [E-mail: alangarrity@btinternet.com]	01560 486879
(Rome) David F. Huie MA BD	1962	2001	15 Rosebank Gardens, Largs KA30 8TD [E-mail: dfh@davidhuie35.plus.com]	01475 670733
(Brussels) Thomas C. Pitkeathly MA CA BD	1984	2004	1 Lammermuir Court, Gullane EH31 2HU [E-mail: joostpot@gmail.com]	01620 843373
(Rotterdam) Joost Pot BSc (Auxiliary Minister)	1992	2004		
(Colombo) John P.S. Purves MBE BSc BD	1978	2013	37 Hollywood, Largs KA30 8SR	
(Budapest) Bertalan Tamas			Pozsonyi út 34, Budapest H-1137, Hungary [E-mail: bertalantamas@hotmail.com]	0036 1 239 6315 (Mbl) 0036 30 638 6647

(49) JERUSALEM

Clerk:	JOANNA OAKLEY-LEVSTEIN		St Andrew's, Galilee, PO Box 104, Tiberias 14100, Israel	00972 50 5842517

Jerusalem: St Andrew's

Paraic Reamonn BA BD	1982	2014	St Andrew's Scots Memorial Church, 1 David Remez Street, PO Box 8619, Jerusalem 91086, Israel [E-mail: stachjer@netvision.net.il]	00972 2 673 2401

Tiberias: St Andrew's

Colin D. Johnston MA BD	1986	2009	St Andrew's, Galilee, 1 Gdud Barak Street, PO Box 104, Tiberias 14100, Israel [E-mail: revcdj60@gmail.com]	00972 4 671 0759

SECTION 6

Additional Lists of Personnel

LIST A – ORDAINED LOCAL MINISTERS

NAME	ORD	ADDRESS	TEL	PR
Archer, Morven (Mrs)	2013	42 Firthview Drive, Inverness IV3 8QE	01463 237840	37
Bellis, Pamela A. BA	2014	Maughold, Low Killantrae, Port William, Newton Stewart DG8 9QR	01988 700590	9
Black, Sandra (Mrs)	2013	5 Doon Place, Troon KA10 7EQ	01292 220075	10
Bom, Irene	2008	Bergpolderstraat 53A, NL-3038 KB Rotterdam, The Netherlands	0031 10 265 1703	48
Breingan, Mhairi	2011	6 Park Road, Inchinnan, Renfrew PA4 4QJ	0141-812 1425	14
Brown, Kathryn (Mrs)	2014	1 Callendar Park Walk, Callendar Grange, Falkirk FK1 1TA	01324 617352	22
Dee, Oonagh	2014	'Kendoon', Merse Way, Kippford, Dalbeattie DG5 4LL	01556 620001	8
Don, Andrew MBA	2006	5 Eskdale Court, Penicuik EH26 8HT	01968 675766	3
Duncan, Esme (Miss)	2013	Avalon, Upper Warse, Canisbay, Wick KW1 4YD	01955 611455	41
Duncanson, Mary (Ms)	2013	3 Balmenach Road, Cromdale, Grantown-on-Spey PH26 3LJ	01479 872165	36
Edwards, Dougal BTh	2013	25 Mackenzie Street, Carnoustie DD7 6HD	01241 852666	30
Fidler, David G.	2013	34 Guardhouse Park, Stromness, Orkney KW16 3DP	01856 850575	45
Fulcher, Christine	2012	St Blaan's Manse, Southend, Campbeltown PA28 6RQ	01586 830504	19
Geddes, Elizabeth (Mrs)	2013	9 Shillingworth Place, Bridge of Weir PA11 3DY	01505 612639	14
Gray, Ian	2013	'The Mallards', 15 Rossie Island Road, Montrose DD10 9NH	01674 677126	30
Hardman Moore, Susan (Prof.) BA PGCE MA PhD	2013	c/o New College, Mound Place, Edinburgh EH1 2LX	0131-650 8908	1
Harrison, Frederick	2013	33 Castle Avenue, Gorebridge EH23 4TH	01875 820908	3
Harvey, Joyce (Mrs)	2013	4A Allanfield Place, Newton Stewart DG8 6BS	01671 403693	9
Hickman, Mandy R. RGN	2013	Lagnaleon, 4 Wilson Street, Largs KA30 9AQ	01475 675347	12
Hughes, Barry MA	2011	Dunslair, Cardrona Way, Cardrona, Peebles EH45 9LD	01896 831197	4
Johnston, June E. BSc MEd BD	2013	49 Braeside Road South, Gorebridge EH23 4DL	01875 823086	3
Livingstone, Alan	2013	Meadowside, Lawmuir, Methven, Perth PH1 3SZ	01738 840682	28
McAllister, Anne C. (Mrs) BSc DipEd CCS	2013	39 Bowes Rigg, Stewarton, Kilmarnock KA3 5EN	01560 483191	11
McCutcheon, John	2014	Flat 2/6 Parkview, Milton Brae, Milton, Dumbarton G82 2TT	01389 739034	18
Macdonald, Ishabel	2011	'Cleat Afe Ora', 18 Carinish, Isle of North Uist HS6 5HN	01876 580367	43
MacDonald, Monica (Mrs)	2014	32 Reilly Gardens, High Bonnybridge, Bonnybridge FK4 2BB	01324 874807	22
Mack, Lynne (Mrs)	2013	36 Middleton, Menstrie FK11 7HD	01259 761465	23
McLaughlin, Cathie H. (Mrs)	2014	8 Lamlash Place, Glasgow G33 3XH	0141-774 2483	16
MacLeod, Iain A.	2012	6 Hallydown Drive, Glasgow G13 1UF	07795 014889 (Mbl)	16
Maxwell, David	2014	248 Old Castle Road, Glasgow G44 5EZ	0141-569 6379	16
Michie, Margaret (Mrs)	2013	3 Loch Leven Court, Wester Balgedie, Kinross KY13 9NE	01592 840602	28
Morrison, John BSc BA PGCE	2013	35 Kirkton Place, Elgin IV30 6JR	01343 550199	35
Muirhead, Morag (Mrs)	2013	6 Dumbarton Road, Fort William PH33 6UU	01397 703643	38
Nicol, Robert	2013	3 Castlegreen Road, Thurso KW14 7DN		41
Noonan, Pam (Mrs)	2013	18 Woodburn Place, Houston, Johnstone PA6 7NA	01505 326254	14
Nutter, Margaret	2014	Kilmorich, 14 Balloch Road, Balloch, Alexandria G83 8SR	01389 754505	18
Perkins, Mairi (Mrs)	2012	Ashlea, Cuil Road, Duror, Appin PA38 3DA	01631 740313 (Work)	38
Prentice, Martin	2013	Cott of Howe, Cairston, Stromness, Orkney KW16 3JU	01856 851139	45

Rennie, Lyall	2013	Ruachmarra, Lower Warse, Canisbay, Wick KW1 4YB	01955 611756	41
Robertson, Ishbel A.R. MA BD	2013	Oakdene, 81 Bonhill Road, Dumbarton G82 2DU	01389 763436	18
Sanders, Martyn S. BA CertEd MA	2013	26 Wood Avenue, Annan DG12 6DA	(Mbl) 07830 697976	7
Sarle, Andrew BSc BD	2013	114 High Station Road, Falkirk FK1 5LN	01324 621648	22
Sharp, James	2005	102 Rue des Eaux-Vives, CH-1207 Geneva, Switzerland	0041 22 786 4847	48
Stevenson, Stuart	2011	143 Springfield Park, Johnstone PA5 8JT	0141-886 2131	14
Stewart, Heather (Mrs)	2013	Burnthill, Thrumster, Wick KW1 5TR	01955 651717	41
Stobo, Mary J. (Mrs)	2013	Druim-an-Sgairnich, Ardgay IV24 3BG	01863 766868	40
Strachan, Willie MBA DipY&C	2013	Ladywell House, Lucky Slap, Monikie, Dundee DD5 3QG	01382 370286	29
Stuart, Alex P.	2014	107 Baldorran Crescent, Cumbernauld, Glasgow G68 9EX	01236 727710	16
Sturrock, Roger (Prof.) BD MD FCRP	2014	36 Thomson Drive, Bearsden, Glasgow G61 3PA	0141-942 7412	16
Thomson, Mary Ellen (Mrs)	2013	Riverside Flat, Gynack Street, Kingussie PH21 1EL	01540 661772	36
Tweedie, Fiona BSc PhD	2011	121 George Street, Edinburgh EH2 4YN	0131-225 5722	1
Wallace, Mhairi (Mrs)	2013		(Mbl) 07880 546743	8
Watson, Michael D.	2013	47 Crichton Terrace, Pathhead EH37 5QZ	01875 320043	3

ORDAINED LOCAL MINISTERS (Retired List)

Anderson, David M. MSc FCOptom	1984	'Mirlos', 1 Dumfries Place, Fort William PH33 6UQ	01397 702091	38

LIST B – AUXILIARY MINISTERS

NAME	ORD	ADDRESS	TEL	PR
Attenburrow, Anne BSc MB ChB	2006	4 Jock Inksons Brae, Elgin IV30 1QE	01343 552330	35
Binks, Mike	2007	5 Maxwell Drive, Newton Stewart DG8 6EL	01671 402201	9
Buck, Maxine	2007	Brownlee House, Mauldslie Road, Carluke ML8 5HW	01555 759063	17
Cameron, Ann J. (Mrs) CertCS DCE TEFL	2005	Currently resident in Qatar		32
Campbell, Gordon MA BD CDipAF DipHSM MCMI MIHM AFRIN ARSGS FRGS FSAScot	2001	2 Falkland Place, Kingoodie, Invergowrie, Dundee DD2 5DY	01382 561383	29
Cumming, Alistair MSc CCS FInstLM	2010	64 Prince George's Avenue, London SW20 8BH	020 8540 7365 (Mbl) 07534 943986	47
Dick, Roddy S.	2010	27 Easter Crescent, Wishaw ML2 8XB	01698 383453	17
Fletcher, Timothy E.G. BA FCMA	1998	3 Ardchoille Park, Perth PH2 7TL	01738 638189 (Mbl) 07747 013985	28
Forrest, Kenneth P. CBE BSc PhD	2006	5 Carruth Road, Bridge of Weir PA11 3HQ	01505 612651	14
Gardner, Hilary (Miss)	2010	Cayman Lodge, Kincardine Hill, Ardgay IV24 3DJ	01863 766107	40
Griffiths, Ruth I. (Mrs)	2004	Kirkwood, Mathieson Lane, Innellan, Dunoon PA23 7TA	01369 830145	19

NAME	ORD	ADDRESS	TEL	PR
Hood, Catriona A.	2006	'Elyside', Dalintober, Campbeltown PA28 6EB	01586 551490	19
Howie, Marion L.K. (Mrs) MA ARCS	1992	51 High Road, Stevenston KA20 3DY	01294 466571	12
Jackson, Nancy	2009	Cygnet House, Holmfarm Road, Catrine, Mauchline KA5 6TA	01290 550511	10
Kemp, Tina MA	2005	12 Oaktree Gardens, Dumbarton G82 1EU	01389 730477	18
Landale, William S.	2005	Green Hope Guest House, Green Hope, Duns TD11 3SG	01361 890242	5
Lunn, Dorothy	2002	14 Bellerby Drive, Ouston, Co. Durham DH2 1TW	0191-492 0647	47
Macdonald, Michael	2004	73 Firhill, Alness IV17 0RT	01349 884268	39
MacDougall, Lorna I. (Miss) MA DipGC	2003	34 Millar Place, Carron, Falkirk FK2 8QB	01324 552739	22
MacGregor, Robert M. CMIOSH DipOSH RSP	2004	Olna Cottage, Brae, Shetland ZE2 9QS	01806 522604	46
Manson, Eileen (Mrs) DipCE	1994	1 Cambridge Avenue, Gourock PA19 1XT	01475 632401	14
Mather, James	2010	24 Ellison Road, Barnes, London SW13 0AD	(Home) 020 8876 6540 (Work) 020 7361 1670 (Mbl) 07836 715655	47
Moore, Douglas T.	2003	9 Milton Avenue, Prestwick KA9 1PU	01292 671352	10
Morrison, Donald John	2001	22 Kyles, Tarbert, Isle of Harris HS3 3BS	01859 502341	43
Murray, John W.	2003	1 Totescore, Kilmuir, Portree, Isle of Skye IV51 9YN	01470 542297	42
O'Donnell, Barbara	2007	Ashbank, 258 Main Street, Alexandria G83 0NU	01389 752356	18
Paterson, Andrew E. JP	1994	6 The Willows, Kelty KY4 0FQ	01383 830998	24
Perry, Marion (Mrs)	2009	17a Tarbolton Road, Cumbernauld, Glasgow G67 2AJ	01236 898519 (Mbl) 07563 180662	22
Ramage, Alastair E. MA BA ADB CertEd	1996	16 Claremont Gardens, Milngavie, Glasgow G62 6PG	0141-956 2897	18
Riddell, Thomas S. BSc CEng FIChemE	1993	4 The Malings, Linlithgow EH49 6DS	01506 843251	2
Robson, Brenda (Dr)	2005	2 Baird Road, Ratho, Newbridge EH28 8RA	0131-333 2746	2
Shearer, Anne F. BA DipEd	2010	10 Colsnaur, Menstrie FK11 7HG	01259 769176	23
Sutherland, David A.	2001	3/1, 145 Broomhill Drive, Glasgow G11 7ND	0141-357 2058	16
Vivers, Katherine A.	2004	Blacket House, Eaglesfield, Lockerbie DG11 3AA	01461 500412	7
Walker, Linda	2008	18 Valeview Terrace, Glasgow G42 9LA	0141-649 1340	16
Wallace, Kristian (Mrs) BA BD CertTheol DRM PhD	2007	Lorne and Lowland Manse, Castlehill, Campbeltown PA28 6AN	01586 552468	19
Wandrum, David	1993	5 Cawder View, Carrickstone Meadows, Cumbernauld, Glasgow G68 0BN	01236 723288	22
Whittaker, Mary	2011	11 Templand Road, Lhanbryde, Elgin IV30 8BR		35
Wilkie, Robert	2011	24 Huntingtower Road, Perth PH1 2JS	01738 628301	28
Zambonini, James LIADip	1997	100 Old Manse Road, Netherton, Wishaw ML2 0EP	01698 350889	17

AUXILIARY MINISTERS (Retired List)

NAME	ORD	ADDRESS	TEL	PR
Birch, James PgDip FRSA FIOC	2001	1 Kirkhill Grove, Cambuslang, Glasgow G72 8EH	0141-583 1722	16
Brown, Elizabeth (Mrs) JP RGN	1996	8 Viewlands Place, Perth PH1 1BS	01738 552391	28

	ORD		ADDRESS		
Cloggie, June (Mrs)	1997		11A Tulipan Crescent, Callander FK17 8AR	01877 331021	23
Craggs, Sheila (Mrs)	2001		7 Morar Court, Ellon AB41 9GG	01358 723055	33
Ferguson, Archibald M. MSc PhD CEng FRINA	1989		The Whins, 2 Barrowfield, Station Road, Cardross, Dumbarton G82 5NL	01389 841517	18
Glass, Alexander OBE MA	1998		Craigton, Tulloch Avenue, Dingwall IV15 9TU	01349 863258	39
Harrison, Cameron	2006		Woodfield House, Priormuir, St Andrews KY16 8LP	01334 478067	26
Jenkinson, John J. JP LTCL ALCM DipEd DipSen	1991		8 Rosehall Terrace, Falkirk FK1 1PY	01324 625498	22
Kay, Elizabeth (Miss) DipYCS	1993		1 Kintail Walk, Inchture, Perth PH14 9RY	01828 686029	29
McAlpine, John BSc	1988		Braeside, 201 Bonkle Road, Newmains, Wishaw ML2 9AA	01698 384610	17
MacDonald, Kenneth MA BA	2001		5 Henderland Road, Bearsden, Glasgow G61 1AH	0141-943 1103	16
MacFadyen, Anne M. (Mrs) BSc BD FSAScot	1995		295 Mearns Road, Glasgow G77 5LT	0141-639 3605	16
Mack, Elizabeth A. (Miss) DipPEd	1994		24 Roberts Crescent, Dumfries DG2 7RS	01387 264847	8
Mack, John C. JP	1985		The Willows, Auchleven, Insch AB52 6QB	01464 820387	33
Mailer, Colin	1996		Innis Chonain, Back Row, Polmont, Falkirk FK2 0RD	01324 712401	22
Munro, Mary (Mrs) BA	1993		14 Auchneel Crescent, Stranraer DG9 0JH	01776 702305	9
Paterson, Maureen (Mrs) BSc	1992		91 Dalmahoy Crescent, Kirkcaldy KY2 6TA	01592 262300	25
Phillipson, Michael MTh BSc BVetMed MRCVS	2003		25 Deeside Crescent, Aberdeen AB15 7PT	01224 318317	31
Pot, Joost BSc	1992		[E-mail: joostpot@gmail.com]		48
Shaw, Catherine A.M. MA	1998		40 Merrygreen Place, Stewarton, Kilmarnock KA3 5EP	01560 483352	11
Thomas, Shirley A. (Mrs) DipSocSci AMIA	2000		14 Kirkgait, Letham, Forfar DD8 2XQ	01307 818084	30
Wilson, Mary D. (Mrs) RGN SCM DTM	1990		Berbice, The Terrace, Bridge of Tilt, Blair Atholl, Pitlochry PH18 5SZ	01796 481619	27

LIST C – CHAPLAINS TO HM FORCES

The three columns give dates of ordination and commissioning, and where serving: Royal Navy, Army, Royal Air Force, Royal Naval Reserve, Territorial Army, Army Cadet Force, or where the person named is an Officiating Chaplain.

NAME	ORD	COM	BCH	ADDRESS
Abeledo, Benjamin J.A. BTh DipTh PTh	1991	1999	A	HQ 51 (Scottish) Brigade, Forthside, Stirling FK7 7RR
Anderson, David P. BSc BD	2002	2007	A	SCOTSDG, Wessex Barracks, Fallingbostel, Germany, BFPO 38
Berry, Geoff T. BD BSc	2009		OC	4 Bn The Royal Regiment of Scotland, Oerbke-Lager, Fallingbostel, BFPO 38
Blackwood, Keith T. BD DipMin	1997		ACF	Shetland Independent Battery, ACF, TA Centre, Fort Charlotte, Lerwick, Shetland ZE1 0JN
Blakey, Stephen A. BSc BD	1977		TA	6 Bn The Royal Regiment of Scotland, Walcheran Barracks, 122 Hotspur Street, Glasgow G20 8LQ
Blakey, Stephen A. BSc BD	1977		OC	Glasgow Universities Officers' Training Corps
Blakey, Stephen A. BSc BD	1977		ACF	Lothian & Borders Bn ACF, Royal Regiment of Scotland, Drumshoreland House, Broxburn EH52 5PF
Blakey, Stephen A. BSc BD	1977		OC	HQ (Scottish) Brigade, Tayforth University Officers' Training Corps

Name	Year	Service	Posting
Brown, Scott J. CBE QHC BD	1993	RN	The Chaplain of the Fleet, MP 1.2, Navy Command HQ, Whale Island, Portsmouth, Hants PO2 8BY
Bryson, Thomas M. BD	1997	ACF	2 Bn The Highlanders, ACF, Royal Regiment of Scotland, Cadet Training Centre, Rocksley Drive, Boddam, Peterhead AB42 3BA
Bryson, Thomas M. BD	1997	OC	51 Infantry Brigade, Forthside, Stirling FK7 7RR
Campbell, Karen K. BD MTh DMin	1997	OC	Personnel Recovery Centre, Edinburgh
Cobain, Alan R. BD	2000	RAF	71 Engineer Regiment, RAF Leuchars, Fife KY16 0JX
Connolly, Daniel BD DipTheol DipMin	1983	A	39 Engr Regt (Air Support), Kinloss Barracks, Kinloss, Forres IV36 3XL
Coulter, David G. QHC BA BD MDA PhD CF	1989 1994	A	Chaplain General, MoD Chaplains (Army), HQ Land Forces, 2nd Floor Zone 6, Ramillies Building, Marlborough Lines, Andover, Hants SP11 8HJ
Dalton, Mark BD DipMin RN	2002	RN	HM Naval Base Clyde, Faslane, Helensburgh G84 8HL
Davidson, Mark R. MA BD STM PhD RN	2005	RN	The Chaplaincy, 45 Commando RM, RM Condor, Arbroath DD11 3SP
Davidson Kelly, Thomas A. MA BD FSAScot	1975	OC	Army Personnel Centre, Glasgow
Dicks, Shuna M. BSc BD	2010	ACF	2 Bn The Highlanders, ACF, Royal Regiment of Scotland, Cadet Training Centre, Rocksley Drive, Boddam, Peterhead AB42 3BA
Duncan, John C. BD MPhil	1987	A	3 Bn The Black Watch, The Royal Regiment of Scotland, Fort George, Ardersier, Inverness IV1 2TD
Frail, Nicola BLE MBA MDiv	2000	A	9 Regt Army Air Corps, Dishforth Airfield, Thirsk YO7 3EZ
Francis, James BD PhD	2002	A	2 Bn The Rifles, Abercorn Barracks, Ballykinler, BFPO 805
Gardner, Neil N. MA BD	1991	OC	Edinburgh Universities Officers' Training Corps
Goodison, Michael J. BSc BA	2013	A	1 Bn The Duke of Lancaster's Regiment, Somme Barracks, Catterick Garrison DL9 4LD
Irvine, Lisa-Jane BD CPS	2003	OC	2 Bn The Royal Highland Fusiliers, Glencorse Barracks, Penicuik EH26 0QH
Kellock, Chris N. MA BD	1998	A	7 Para RHA, Merville Barracks, Colchester CO2 7UT
Kennon, Stanley BE BD RN	1992	RN	Church of Scotland and Free Churches Chaplain, Britannia Royal Naval College, Dartmouth, Devon TQ6 0HJ
Kingston, David V.F. BD DipPTh	1993	RN	4 Regt RA RHQ, Alanbrooke Barracks, Topcliffe, Thirsk YO7 3EQ
Kinsey, Louis BD DipMin TD	1991	TA	205 (Scottish) Field Hospital (V), Graham House, Whitefield Road, Glasgow G51 6JU
Lancaster, Craig MA BD	2004	RAF	Station Chaplain, RAF Leuchars, St Andrews KY16 0JX
Logan, David BD MA FRSA	2009	ACF	Black Watch Bn, ACF, Royal Regiment of Scotland, Queen's Barracks, 131 Dunkeld Road, Perth PH1 5BT
McCulloch, Alen J.R. MA BD	1990	ACF	Cornwall ACF, 7 Castle Canyke Road, Bodmin PL31 1DX
MacDonald, Roderick I.T. BD CertMin	1992	ACF	West Lowland Bn, ACF, Royal Regiment of Scotland, Fusilier House, Seaforth Road, Ayr KA8 9HX
MacKay, Stewart A.	2009	A	2 Bn The Parachute Regiment, Merville Barracks, Colchester CO2 7UT
Mackenzie, Cameron BD	1997	ACF	Lothian and Borders Bn, ACF, Royal Regiment of Scotland, Drumshoreland House, Broxburn EH52 5PF
Mackenzie, Hector M.	2008	A	3 Bn The Parachute Regiment, Merville Barracks, Colchester CO2 7UT
Mackenzie, Seoras L. BD	1996	A	Carver Barracks, Wimbish, Saffron Walden CB10 2YA
McLaren, William MA BD	1990	ACF	Angus and Dundee Bn, ACF, Royal Regiment of Scotland, Barry Buddon, Carnoustie DD7 7RY
McLaren, William MA BD	1990	OC	225 GS Med Regt
McLay, Neil BA BD	2006	A	QRH, Athlone Barracks, Sennelager, Germany, BFPO 16

MacLean, Marjory A. LLB BD PhD RNR	1991		RNR	HMS *Scotia*, MoD Caledonia, Hilton Road, Rosyth, Dunfermline KY11 2XH
MacLeod, Rory N. MA BD	1986	1992	A	39 Regt, Royal Regiment of Artillery, Albemarle Barracks, Harlow Hill, Newcastle-upon-Tyne NE15 0RF
MacPherson, Duncan J. BSc BD	1993	2002	A	Infantry Training Centre, Vimy Barracks, Catterick DL9 3PS
Mathieson, Angus R. MA BD	1988		OC	Edinburgh Garrison
Munro, Sheila BD	1995	2003	RAF	RAF Lossiemouth, Elgin IV31 6SD
Prentice, Donald K. BSc BD	1989		OC	205 (Scottish) Field Hospital
Rowe, Christopher J. BA BD	2008		TA	32 (Scottish) Signal Regiment, 21 Jardine Street, Glasgow G20 6JU
Selemani, Ecilo LTh MTh	1993		ACF	Glasgow and Lanark Bn, ACF, Royal Regiment of Scotland, Gilbertfield Road, Cambuslang, Glasgow G72 8YP
Selemani, Ecilo LTh MTh	1993	2011	OC	51 Infantry Brigade, Forthside, Stirling FK7 7RR
Shackleton, Scott J.S. QCVS BA BD PhD RN	1993	2010	RN	HQ 3 Commando Brigade, RMB Stonehouse, Durnford Street, Plymouth PL1 3QS
Stewart, Fraser M.C. BSc BD	1980		ACF	1 Bn The Highlanders, ACF, Royal Regiment of Scotland, Gordonville Road, Inverness IV2 4SU
Taylor, Gayle J.A. MA BD	1999		OC	1 Scots, Edinburgh
van Sittert, Paul BA BD	1997		A	3 Bn The Rifles, Dreghorn Barracks, Edinburgh EH13 9QW
Warwick, Ivan C. TD MA BD	1980		ACF	1 Bn The Highlanders, ACF, Royal Regiment of Scotland, Gordonville Road, Inverness IV2 4SU
Warwick, Ivan C. TD MA BD	1980		ACF	Orkney Independent Battery, ACF, Territorial Army Centre, Weyland Park, Kirkwall KW1 5LP
Warwick, Ivan C. TD MA BD	1980		OC	Glasgow and Strathclyde Universities Officers' Training Corps
Whiteford, Alexander LTh	1996		OC	Fort George and Cameron Barracks, Inverness
Wilson, Fiona A. BD	2008		ACF	West Lowland Battalion, ACF, Royal Regiment of Scotland, Fusilier House, Seaforth Road, Ayr KA8 9HX
Wylie, Jonathan	2000	2014	RAF	Staff Chaplain PJHQ, Northwood HQ, Sandy Lane, Northwood, Middlesex HA6 3HP

LIST D – HOSPITAL CHAPLAINS

NHS LOTHIAN

Head of Service, Spiritual Care and Bereavement
Alexander W. Young
Lead Chaplain
Caroline Applegath
Spiritual Care Offices: 0131-242 1990; 0131-537 6516

The Royal Infirmary of Edinburgh
51 Little France Crescent, Edinburgh EH16 4SA (0131-536 1000)

Liberton Hospital
113 Lasswade Road, Edinburgh EH16 6UB (0131-536 7800)
Alexander W. Young   0131-242 1990/1
Caroline Applegath   0131-242 1996
Iain Telfer   0131-242 1997
The Western General Hospital
Crewe Road South, Edinburgh EH4 2XU (0131-537 1000)
Alistair Ridland   0131-537 1400
Liz Markey   0131-537 1401
The Royal Hospital for Sick Children
9 Sciennes Road, Edinburgh EH9 1LF (0131-536 0000)
Caroline Applegath   0131-536 0144
St John's Hospital
Howden Road West, Livingston EH54 6PP (01506 523000)
Georgina Nelson   01506 522188
Joe Gierasik   01506 522187
The Royal Edinburgh Hospital
Morningside Place, Edinburgh EH10 5HF (0131-537 6000)
Lynne MacMurchie   0131-537 6368
Maxwell Reay   0131-537 6366
Edinburgh Community Mental Health (Community Office 0131-220 5159)
Lynne MacMurchie   0131-537 6368
Maxwell Reay   0131-537 6366
Corstorphine
136 Corstorphine Road, Edinburgh EH12 6TT (0131-459 7200)
Rosemary Bayne   0131-537 6516
Findlay House, Seafield Street, Edinburgh EH6 7LN (0131-454 2200)
Alexander W. Young   0131-537 6516
Linlithgow St Michael's
Edinburgh Road, Linlithgow EH49 6QS (01506 842053)
Dr Georgina Nelson   01506 522188
Herdmanflat
Aberlady Road, Haddington EH41 3BU (0131-536 8300)
Rosemary Bayne   0131-537 6516
Roodlands
Hospital Road, Haddington EH41 3PF (0131-536 8300)
Rosemary Bayne   0131-537 6516
Midlothian Community Hospital
70 Eskbank Road, Bonnyrigg EH22 3ND (0131-454 1001)
Trisha Murphy-Black   0131-537 6516
Belhaven
Beveridge Row, Dunbar EH42 1TR (01368 862246)
Laurence H. Twaddle   01368 863098
St Columba's Hospice

Kirklands House, Gogarmuir Road, Gogarbank, Edinburgh EH12 9BZ
Donald Reid   0131-551 1381
Marie Curie Hospice, Edinburgh
Frogston Road West, Edinburgh EH10 7DR
Patrick Ryan   0131-470 2201

For further information and full details of all e-mail/telephone contacts, see www.nhslothian.scot.nhs.uk/Services/A-Z/SpiritualCare

BORDERS

MELROSE –   Rev. Anna Garvie   Chaplaincy Centre, Borders General Hospital,   01896 826564
BORDERS GENERAL HOSPITAL   Mr David Thaw   Melrose TD6 9BS
(These Chaplains also serve the Community Hospitals: Hay Lodge (Peebles), Knoll (Duns), Kelso, Hawick and Eyemouth.)

DUMFRIES AND GALLOWAY

DUMFRIES AND GALLOWAY
ROYAL INFIRMARY
THOMAS HOPE, LANGHOLM
LOCHMABEN
MOFFAT
NEW ANNAN
CASTLE DOUGLAS
KIRKCUDBRIGHT   Rev. Douglas R. Irving   6 Bourtree Avenue, Kirkcudbright DG6 4AU   01557 330489
THORNHILL
NEWTON STEWART
STRANRAER: GALLOWAY COMMUNITY

AYRSHIRE AND ARRAN

Chaplaincy Services and Staff Care Manager   Rev. Sheila M. Mitchell   01292 513197
                                                                                                                     (Mbl) 07748 180302
Chaplaincy Services and Staff Care Office   Ailsa Hospital, Ayr KA6 6AB   01292 513023
Lead Health and Care Chaplain   Rev. Judith A. Huggett   Crosshouse Hospital, Kilmarnock KA2 0BE   (Work) 01563 827301
Health and Care Chaplains   Rev. Roderick H. McNidder 6 Hollow Park, Alloway, Ayr KA7 4SR   01292 442554
                                 Rev. Paul R. Russell   23 Nursery Wynd, Ayr KA7 3NZ   (Work) 01292 614587
WAR MEMORIAL, ARRAN   Rev. Elizabeth R.L. Watson The Manse, Whiting Bay, Brodick, Isle of Arran KA27 8RE   01770 700289
                                 Rev. Alex M. Welsh   8 Greenside Avenue, Prestwick KA9 2HB   01563 826128
                                 Miss Muriel Wilson DCS   28 Bellevue Crescent, Ayr KA7 2DR   (Work) 01292 264939

LANARKSHIRE

Head of Spiritual Care, NHS Lanarkshire	Rev. Robert P. Devenny	Law House, Airdrie Road, Carluke ML8 5ER	01698 377637
LADY HOME	Rev. Susan G. Cowell	3 Gavel Lane, Regency Gardens, Lanark ML11 9FB	01555 665509
LOCKHART	Rev. Alison A. Meikle	2 Kaimhill Court, Lanark ML11 9HU	01555 662600
KELLO	Rev. Susan G. Cowell	3 Gavel Lane, Regency Gardens, Lanark ML11 9FB	01555 665509
WISHAW GENERAL	Rev. Sharon E.F. Colvin	25 Balblair Road, Airdrie ML6 6GQ	01236 590796
	Rev. Mhorag MacDonald	350 Kirk Road, Wishaw ML2 8LH	01698 381305
	Rev. Kathryn Smith-Anderson	Wishaw General Hospital, 50 Nenthorn Street, Wishaw ML2 0DP	01698 366779
STRATHCLYDE	Rev. David W. Doyle	19 Orchard Street, Motherwell ML1 3JE	01698 263472
HAIRMYRES	James S.G. Hastie	Hairmyres Hospital, Eaglesham Road, East Kilbride, Glasgow G75 8RG	01355 584301
(Mental Health)	Rev. Patricia Johnston	Hairmyres Hospital, Eaglesham Road, East Kilbride, Glasgow G75 8RG	01355 584301
	Marian McElhinney	Hairmyres Hospital, Eaglesham Road, East Kilbride, Glasgow G75 8RG	01355 584669
STONEHOUSE	Rev. Marjorie Taylor	25 Balblair Road, Airdrie ML6 6GQ	01698 794000
UDSTON	Rev. Sharon E.F. Colvin	Udston Hospital, Farm Road, Burnbank, Hamilton ML3 9LA	01236 590796
NORTH LANARKSHIRE Community Chaplain	Major James Bryden	Airdrie Community Health Clinic, 84–88 Graham Street, Airdrie ML6 6DE	01698 723200
	Rev. David Parker		01236 772269
COATHILL	Rev. David Parker	Airdrie Community Health Clinic, 84–88 Graham Street, Airdrie ML6 6DE	01236 772269
MONKLANDS	Rev. Helen Mee	Monklands Hospital, Monkscourt Avenue, Airdrie ML6 0JS	01236 712607
	Rev. Christian Okeke	Monklands Hospital, Monkscourt Avenue, Airdrie ML6 0JS	01236 712607
WESTER MOFFAT	Rev. David Parker	Airdrie Community Health Clinic, 84–88 Graham Street, Airdrie ML6 6DE	01236 772269
CRAIGHOUSE AND CLELAND	Rev. Derek Pope	35 Birrens Road, Motherwell ML1 3NS	01698 266716

GREATER GLASGOW AND CLYDE

Head of Chaplaincy and Spiritual Care	Rev. Blair Robertson	Chaplaincy Centre, Southern General Hospital, 1345 Govan Road, Glasgow G51 4TF [E-mail: blair.robertson@ggc.scot.nhs.uk]	0141-201 2156
GLASGOW ROYAL INFIRMARY (GRI); THE PRINCESS ROYAL MATERNITY HOSPITAL; LIGHTBURN HOSPITAL	Rev. Adam Plenderleith Rev. Tim Bennison Mayra Gomez-Sorto	Chaplains' Office, Glasgow Royal Infirmary, Castle Street, Glasgow G4 0SF (all three chaplains)	0141-211 4661

Hospital	Chaplain	Address	Telephone
BEATSON WEST OF SCOTLAND CANCER CENTRE; GARTNAVEL GENERAL HOSPITAL (GGH) and GLASGOW WESTERN INFIRMARY; BLAWARTHILL HOSPITAL; DRUMCHAPEL HOSPITAL; GLASGOW HOMOEOPATHIC HOSPITAL	Rev. Keith Saunders	Chaplains' Office, Glasgow Western Infirmary, Dumbarton Road, Glasgow G11 6NT	0141-211 2812
		Chaplains' Office, Gartnavel General Hospital, 1053 Great Western Road, Glasgow G12 0YN	0141-211 3026
ROYAL HOSPITAL FOR SICK CHILDREN AT YORKHILL	Rev. Jim Meighan	Chaplaincy Centre, Royal Hospital for Sick Children, Dalnair Street, Glasgow G3 8SJ	0141-201 0595
SOUTHERN GENERAL HOSPITAL (SGH)	Rev. Blair Robertson Mr Andrew Gillies Ms Rebekah Sharp	Chaplaincy Centre, Southern General Hospital, 1345 Govan Road, Glasgow G51 4TF [E-mail: blair.robertson@ggc.scot.nhs.uk]	0141-201 2156 / 2357
VICTORIA INFIRMARY (VI); NEW VICTORIA HOSPITAL: MANSIONHOUSE UNIT; MEARNSKIRK HOSPITAL	Rev. Ishaku Bitrus Imam Mohammed Ishaq	Chaplaincy Centre, Victoria Infirmary, Langside Road, Glasgow G42 9TY	0141-201 5164
GARTNAVEL ROYAL HOSPITAL (GRH) and Mental Health units in western Glasgow	Rev. Dr Kevin Franz	Chaplain's Office, Gartnavel Royal Hospital, Great Western Road, Glasgow G12 0XH	0141-211 3686
STOBHILL HOSPITAL SITE; THE ORCHARDS; BIRDSTON HOSPITAL; FOURHILLS NURSING HOME; GREENFIELD PARK NURSING HOME	Rev. Andrew Davis	Chaplain's Office, Parkhead Hospital, 81 Salamanca Street, Glasgow G31 5ES	0141-531 5908
LEVERNDALE HOSPITAL and Mental Health units in southern Glasgow	Anne MacDonald DCS	Chaplain's Office, Leverndale Hospital, 510 Crookston Road, Glasgow G53 7TU	0141-211 6695
RUTHERGLEN ROWANTREE/RODGER PARK NURSING HOME NHS Partnership Beds	Anne MacDonald DCS	(Leverndale Hospital Chaplaincy)	0141-211 6695
ROYAL ALEXANDRA HOSPITAL, PAISLEY; VALE OF LEVEN HOSPITAL; DYKEBAR HOSPITAL; DUMBARTON JOINT HOSPITAL	Rev. Carol Campbell Rev. Gordon Jones	Chaplaincy Centre, Royal Alexandra Hospital, Corsebar Road, Paisley PA2 9PN	0141-314 9561 / 7365
INVERCLYDE ROYAL HOSPITAL (IRH) and RAVENSCRAIG HOSPITAL, GREENOCK	Rev. Philip Craven	Chaplain's Office, Inverclyde Royal Hospital, Larkfield Road, Greenock PA16 0XN	01475 504759

FORTH VALLEY

Head of Spiritual Care	Rev. Margery Collin	Forth Valley Royal Hospital, Larbert FK5 4WR [E-mail: margery.collin@nhs.net]	01324 566072 07824 460882
FORTH VALLEY ROYAL	Mrs Mary Anne Burgoyne Mr Philip Hacking	Forth Valley Royal Hospital, Larbert FK5 4WR Forth Valley Royal Hospital, Larbert FK5 4WR	01324 566071 01324 566071
MENTAL HEALTH UNITS	Rev. Helen Christie Rev. Timothy Njuguna	5 Watson Place, Dennyloanhead, Bonnybridge FK4 2BG Forth Valley Royal Hospital, Larbert FK5 4WR	01324 813786 01324 566075

Location / Role	Name	Address	Telephone
BO'NESS HOSPITAL			
FALKIRK COMMUNITY	Mr Frank Hartley	49 Argyll Place, Kilsyth, Glasgow G65 0PY	01236 824135
	Rev. Helen Christie	5 Watson Place, Dennyloanhead, Bonnybridge FK4 2BG	01324 813786
CLACKMANNAN COMMUNITY	Rev. Helen Cook	Forth Valley Royal Hospital, Larbert FK5 4WR	01324 566072
STIRLING COMMUNITY	Rev. James Landels	Allan Manse, Bogend Road, Bannockburn, Stirling FK7 8NP	01786 814692

FIFE

Head of Spiritual Care	Mr Mark Evans DCS	Department of Spiritual Care, Queen Margaret Hospital, Whitefield Road, Dunfermline KY12 0SU [E-mail: mark.evans59@nhs.net]	01383 674136
VICTORIA HOSPITAL, KIRKCALDY: Healthcare Chaplains (Acute)	Mr Damian Murray	Victoria Hospital, Hayfield Road, Kirkcaldy KY2 5AH	01592 648158
	Miss Sharon Dick	Victoria Hospital, Hayfield Road, Kirkcaldy KY2 5AH	01592 648158
STRATHEDEN HOSPITAL, CUPAR; WHYTEMAN'S BRAE, KIRKCALDY; LYNEBANK, DUNFERMLINE	Mr Allan Grant	Chaplain's Office, Stratheden Hospital, Stratheden, Cupar KY15 5RR [E-mail: allan.grant@nhs.net]	07795 627697
ADAMSON HOSPITAL, CUPAR: Community Healthcare Chaplain	Rev. Lynn Brady	Adamson Hospital, Bank Street, Cupar KY15 4JG [E-mail: lynn.brady@nhs.net]	07815 922889
CENTRAL FIFE (CAMERON; GLENROTHES; RANDOLPH WEMYSS): Community Healthcare Chaplain	Miss Lynda Wright DCS	Chaplain's Office, Main Administration Block, Cameron Hospital, Cameron Bridge, Windygates, Leven KY8 5RR [E-mail: lynda.wright1@nhs.net]	07835 303395
ST ANDREWS: Community Healthcare Chaplain	Rev. Dr James Connolly	St Andrews Community Hospital and Health Centre, Largo Road, St Andrews KY16 8AR [E-mail: jamesconnolly@nhs.net]	07711 177655
Community Chaplaincy Listening (Scotland): National Coordinator	Miss Lynda Wright DCS	[E-mail: lynda.wright1@nhs.net]	07835 303395

TAYSIDE

Location / Role	Name	Address	Telephone
Head of Spiritual Care	Rev. Gillian Munro	Wellbeing Cottage, Royal Victoria Hospital, Dundee DD2 1SP	01382 423116
Staff Support	Rev. David Gordon	Wellbeing Cottage, Royal Victoria Hospital, Dundee DD2 1SP	01382 423116
DUNDEE NINEWELLS HOSPITAL	Mr Andrew Bennett	Chaplain's Office, Ninewells Hospital, Dundee DD1 9SY	01382 632755
ROXBURGHE HOUSE	Mr Andrew Bennett	Chaplain's Office, Roxburghe House	01382 740804
PERTH ROYAL INFIRMARY	Rev. Anne Findlay	Chaplain's Office, Perth Royal Infirmary	01738 473896
MURRAY ROYAL, PERTH	Rev. Geoff Williams		01382 423110
ABERFELDY COMMUNITY	Rev. Anne Brennan		01382 423110
BLAIRGOWRIE COMMUNITY	Rev. Geoff Williams		01382 423110
PITLOCHRY COMMUNITY	Rev. Geoff Williams		01382 423110
CRIEFF COMMUNITY	Rev. Geoff Williams		01382 423110
CORNHILL MACMILLAN CENTRE	Rev. Anne Findlay	Chaplain's Office, Perth Royal Infirmary	01738 473896

ST MARGARET'S COMMUNITY	Rev. James MacDonald
ARBROATH INFIRMARY	Rev. Alasdair Graham
ANGUS CHAPLAIN	Rev. Rona Phillips
(Little Cairnie Hospital, Montrose Infirmary, Brechin Infirmary, Stracathro Hospital)	Susan Carnegie Centre, Stracathro Hospital
CARSE VIEW CENTRE; DUNDEE	Rev. Alan Gibbon
COMMUNITY	

ST MARGARET'S COMMUNITY — 01382 423110
ARBROATH INFIRMARY — 01382 423110
ANGUS CHAPLAIN — 01382 423110
CARSE VIEW CENTRE; DUNDEE — 01382 835504

GRAMPIAN

Head of Spiritual Care
Rev. Mark Rodgers, Chaplains' Office, Aberdeen Royal Infirmary, Foresterhill, Aberdeen   AB25 2ZN   01224 553166

1. ACUTE SECTOR
ABERDEEN ROYAL INFIRMARY; ABERDEEN MATERNITY HOSPITAL
Chaplains' Office, Aberdeen Royal Infirmary, Foresterhill, Aberdeen   AB25 2ZN
Rev. Mark Rodgers   01224 553316
Rev. James Falconer   01224 554905
Rev. Sylvia Spencer   01224 559214
Miss Mairearad Ros   01224 553271
Mrs Katrina Blackwood   01224 551016

ROYAL ABERDEEN CHILDREN'S HOSPITAL
Chaplain's Office, Royal Aberdeen Children's Hospital, Westburn Drive, Aberdeen   AB25 2ZG
Rev. James Falconer   01224 554905

ROXBURGHE HOUSE
Chaplain's Office, Roxburghe House, Ashgrove Road, Aberdeen   AB25 2ZH
Rev. Sylvia Spencer   01224 557077

WOODEND HOSPITAL
Chaplain's Office, Woodend Hospital, Eday Road, Aberdeen   AB15 6XS
Mrs Gillian Douglas   01224 556788
Rev. John Duthie (Assistant Chaplain)   01224 556006
          01224 556007

DR GRAY'S HOSPITAL, ELGIN
Rev. Andrew Willis, Deanshaugh Croft, Mulben, Keith   AB55 6YJ   01343 567262
Rev. David A. Young, 15 Mannachie Rise, Forres   IV36 2US   01542 860240
          01309 672849

THE OAKS, ELGIN
Rev. David A. Young, 15 Mannachie Rise, Forres IV36 2US — 01309 672849

2. MENTAL HEALTH
ROYAL CORNHILL HOSPITAL
Chaplain's Office, Royal Cornhill Hospital, Cornhill Road, Aberdeen AB25 2ZH
Rev. Jim Simpson — 01224 557293
Miss Pamela Adam (Assistant Chaplain) — 01224 557484
Mr Donald Meston (Assistant Chaplain) — 01224 557231

3. COMMUNITY HOSPITALS

Hospital	Chaplain	Address	Telephone
ABOYNE	Rev. John Duthie	Moraine, Inchmarlo, Banchory AB31 4BR	01330 824108
GLEN O' DEE, BANCHORY	Rev. John Duthie	Moraine, Inchmarlo, Banchory AB31 4BR	01330 824108
CHALMERS, BANFF	Mrs Margaret Robb	Chrislouan, Keith Hall, Inverurie AB51 0LN	01651 882310
FLEMING, ABERLOUR	Rev. Andrew Willis	Deanshaugh Croft, Mulben, Keith AB55 6YJ	01542 860240
FRASERBURGH	Rev. Dr David S. Ross	3–5 Abbey Street, Deer, Peterhead AB42 5LN	01771 623994
INVERURIE	Rev. Ian B. Groves	1 Westburn Place, Inverurie AB51 5QS	01467 620285
INSCH	Mrs Margaret Robb	Chrislouan, Keith Hall, Inverurie AB51 0LN	01651 882310
JUBILEE, HUNTLY	Rev. Norma Milne	26 Green Road, Huntly AB54 8BE	01466 793841
KINCARDINE COMMUNITY, STONEHAVEN	Rev. Margaret Jackson	3 Ramsay Road, Stonehaven AB39 2HJ	07936 366626
LEANCHOIL, FORRES	Rev. David A. Young	15 Mannachie Rise, Forres IV36 2US	01309 672284
MUIRTON	Rev. Andrew Willis	Deanshaugh Croft, Mulben, Keith AB55 6YJ	01542 860240
PETERHEAD COMMUNITY	Rev. David S. Ross	3–5 Abbey Street, Deer, Peterhead AB42 5LN	01771 623994
SEAFIELD, BUCKIE	Rev. Andrew Willis	Deanshaugh Croft, Mulben, Keith AB55 6YJ	01542 860240
STEPHEN, DUFFTOWN			
TURNER, KEITH	Rev. Dr Kay Gauld	The Manse, Church Road, Keith AB55 5BR	01542 882799
TURRIFF	Mrs Margaret Robb	Chrislouan, Keith Hall, Inverurie AB51 0LN	01651 882310
UGIE, PETERHEAD	Rev. Dr David S. Ross	3–5 Abbey Street, Deer, Peterhead AB42 5LN	01771 623994

HIGHLAND

Lead Chaplain
THE RAIGMORE HOSPITAL [01463 704000]

	Chaplain	Address	Telephone
	Rev. Dr Derek Brown	Raigmore Hospital	01463 704463
	Rev. Dr Derek Brown	Cathedral Manse, Cnoc-an-Lobht, Dornoch IV25 3HN	
	Mrs Lindsay Rodgers	Raigmore Hospital	01463 704463
	Rev. Maureen Wilson	Raigmore Hospital	01463 704463

IAN CHARLES			
ST VINCENT, KINGUSSIE	Janet Davidson		01667 422710 ext. 8811
NEW CRAIGS	Rev. Dr Iain Macritchie		01463 704000
NAIRN TOWN AND COUNTY	Janet Davidson		01667 422710 ext. 8811

Location	Name	Address	Phone
BELFORD	Sheena MacLean		01397 702481
ROSS MEMORIAL, DINGWALL	Rev. Russel Smith	Ross Memorial Hospital, Ferry Road, Dingwall IV15 9QT	01349 863313
INVERGORDON COUNTY	Rev. Kenneth D. Macleod	The Manse, Cromlet Drive, Invergordon IV18 0BA	01349 852273
LAWSON MEMORIAL	Mr Karl Weidner		01408 664029
MIGDALE	Mr Karl Weidner		01863 766211
CAITHNESS GENERAL	Rev. Alastair H. Gray	The Manse, Station Road, Watten, Wick KW1 5YN	01955 621220
DUNBAR	Rev. Alastair H. Gray	The Manse, Station Road, Watten, Wick KW1 5YN	01955 621220
BROADFORD MACKINNON MEMORIAL	Janet Anderson		01471 822491
PORTREE	Rev. Donald G. MacDonald	Free Church Manse, 3 Sluggans, Portree, Isle of Skye IV51 9LY	01478 613256
CAMPBELTOWN	Mrs Andrea Holden		01586 552224
LOCHGILPHEAD	Mr Raymond Deans	60 Ardmory Road, Rothesay, Isle of Bute PA20 0PG	(Mbl) 07580 533400
ISLAY			01496 301000
DUNOON	Mr Raymond Deans	60 Ardmory Road, Rothesay, Isle of Bute PA20 0PG	(Mbl) 07580 533400
ROTHESAY	Mr Raymond Deans	60 Ardmory Road, Rothesay, Isle of Bute PA20 0PG	(Mbl) 07580 533400
LORN AND THE ISLANDS DISTRICT GENERAL	Rev. William Gray	Liogh, Glengallan Road, Oban PA34	01631 567500
Community Healthcare Chaplain (East Sutherland)	Rev. Mary J. Stobo	Druim-an-Sgairnich, Ardgay IV24 3BG	01863 766868

WESTERN ISLES HEALTH BOARD

UIST AND BARRA HOSPITAL WESTERN ISLES, STORNOWAY	Rev. T.K. Shadakshari	23D Benside, Newmarket, Stornoway, Isle of Lewis HS2 0DZ [E-mail: tk.shadakshari@nhs.net]	(Home) 01851 701727 (Office) 01851 704704 (Mbl) 07403 697138
	Rev. Ishabel Macdonald	18 Carinish, Isle of North Uist HS6 5HN	01876 580367

LIST E – FULL-TIME WORKPLACE CHAPLAINS

Location	Name	Address	Phone
CHIEF EXECUTIVE OFFICER	Rev. Iain McFadzean	iain.mcfadzean@wpcscotland.co.uk	(Mbl) 07969 227696
EDINBURGH AND CENTRAL			
Regional Organiser	Mr Paul Wilson	paul.wilson@wpcscotland.co.uk	(Mbl) 07703 585987
Edinburgh City Centre	Rev. Tony Bryer	tony.bryer@wpcscotland.co.uk	(Mbl) 07834 748129
Edinburgh West	Rev. Grant MacLaughlan	grant.maclaughlan@wpcscotland.co.uk	(Mbl) 07814 093235

WEST OF SCOTLAND			
Regional Organiser	Rev. Jack Quinn	jack.quinn@wpcscotland.co.uk	(Mbl) 07999 485109
Team Leader	Mrs Cate Adams	cate.adams@wpcscotland.co.uk	(Mbl) 07944 334659
EAST OF SCOTLAND			
Regional Organiser	Rev. Chic Lidstone	chic.lidstone@wpcscotland.co.uk	01738 623022
(Chic Lidstone is not a member of the Church of Scotland but has Corresponding membership of Dundee Presbytery)			
ABERDEEN – City Centre	Rev. Ron Flett	ron.flett@wpcscotland.co.uk	(Mbl) 07508 654423
UK OIL AND GAS INDUSTRY	Rev. Gordon Craig	gordon.craig@ukoilandgaschaplaincy.com	01224 297532

LIST F – PRISON CHAPLAINS

ADVISER TO SCOTTISH PRISON SERVICE (NATIONAL)	Rev. William R. Taylor	SPS HQ, Calton House, 5 Redheughs Rigg, South Gyle, Edinburgh EH12 9DQ [E-mail: bill.taylor@sps.pnn.gov.uk]	0131-244 8640
ADDIEWELL	Rev. Bob Paterson Rev. Peter Hall Mrs Terry Paterson	HM Prison, Addiewell, West Calder EH55 8QA	01506 874500 ext. 3606
CORNTON VALE	Rev. William R. Taylor Ms Deirdre Yellowlees	HM Prison and YOI Cornton Vale, Stirling FK9 5NU	01786 835365
DUMFRIES	Rev. Neil Campbell Rev. Calum Smith	HM Prison, Dumfries DG2 9AX	01387 274214
EDINBURGH: SAUGHTON	Rev. Prof. Bob Akroyd Rev. Keith Graham Major David Betteridge Rev. Sam Torrens	HM Prison, Edinburgh EH11 3LN	0131-444 3115

GLASGOW: BARLINNIE	Rev. Douglas Clark Rev. Alex Wilson Rev. Jonathan Keefe Rev. Ian McInnes Rev. John Murfin	HM Prison, Barlinnie, Glasgow G33 2QX	0141-770 2059
GLENOCHIL	Rev. Graham Bell Rev. Elizabeth Kenny	HM Prison, Glenochil FK10 3AD	01259 760471 ext. 7211 or 7431
GRAMPIAN	Rev. Alison Harvey Rev. Louis Kinsey	HMP Grampian, South Road, Peterhead AB42 2YY	01779 485744
GREENOCK	Rev. Douglas Cranston	HM Prison, Gateside, Greenock PA16 9AH	01475 787801 ext. 287
INVERNESS	Rev. Dr Peter Donald Rev. Alexander Shaw Rev. Christopher Smart	HM Prison, Inverness IV2 3HN	01463 229020 ext. 244
KILMARNOCK	Rev. Jill Clancy	HMP Kilmarnock, Bowhouse, Mauchline Road, Kilmarnock KA1 5AA	01563 548928
LOW MOSS	Rev. Martin Forrest Mr Craig Bryan Rev. John Craib	HMP Low Moss, 190 Crosshill Road, Bishopbriggs, Glasgow G64 2QB	0141-762 9727
OPEN ESTATE: CASTLE HUNTLY	Rev. Anne E. Stewart	HMP Open Estate, Castle Huntly, Longforgan, Dundee DD2 5HL	01382 319388
PERTH	Rev. Kenneth G. Russell Ms Deirdre Yellowlees	Chaplaincy Centre, HM Prison, Perth PH2 7JH	01738 458216
POLMONT	Rev. Donald H. Scott Mr Craig Bryan	Chaplaincy Centre, HMYOI Polmont, Falkirk FK2 0AB	01324 722241
SHOTTS	Ms Dorothy Russell Rev. Murdo Maclean	Chaplaincy Centre, HM Prison, Shotts ML7 4LE	01501 824071

LIST G – UNIVERSITY CHAPLAINS

ABERDEEN	Easter Smart MDiv DMin	01224 488396
ABERTAY, DUNDEE	Leslie M. Barrett BD FRICS	01382 308447
CAMBRIDGE	Nigel Uden (U.R.C. and C. of S.)	01223 314586
DUNDEE	Fiona C. Douglas MBE MA BD PhD	01382 384157
EDINBURGH	Richard E. Frazer BA BD DMin (Honorary)	0131-650 2595
GLASGOW	Stuart D. MacQuarrie JP BD BSc	0141-330 5419
GLASGOW CALEDONIAN	Peter M. Gardner MA BD (E-mail: peter@rsschurch.org.uk)	0141-331 8576
HERIOT-WATT	Alistair P. Donald MA PhD BD	0131-451 4508
NAPIER	John R. Smith MA BD (Honorary)	0131-447 8724
OXFORD	Carla Grosch-Miller (U.R.C. and C. of S.)	0865 554358
ROBERT GORDON	Isaac M. Poobalan	01224 591527
ST ANDREWS	Donald G. MacEwan MA BD PhD	01334 462866
STIRLING		01786 832753
STRATHCLYDE	David T. Young BA BD	0141-553 4144

LIST H – THE DIACONATE

NAME	COM	APP	ADDRESS	TEL	PRES
Beaton, Margaret (Miss) DCS	1989	1988	64 Gardenside Grove, Carmyle, Glasgow G32 8EZ [E-mail: margaret@churchhouse.plus.com]	0141-646 2297	16
Beck, Isobel DCS	2014	2014	16 Patrick Avenue, Stevenston KA20 4AW [E-mail: deaconcastlemilk@aol.co.uk]	(Mbl) 07796 642382 (Mbl) 07919 193425	16
Bell, Sandra (Mrs) DCS	2001	2004	62 Loganswell Road, Thornliebank, Glasgow G46 8AX	0141-638 5884	16
Black, Linda (Miss) BSc DCS	1993	2004	148 Rowan Road, Abronhill, Cumbernauld, Glasgow G67 3DA [E-mail: lnan@blueyonder.co.uk]	01236 786265	22
Blair, Fiona (Miss) DCS	1994	2010	Mure Church Manse, 9 West Road, Irvine KA12 8RE [E-mail: fiobla12@aol.com]	(Mbl) 07977 235168	11
Buchanan, Marion (Mrs) MA DCS	1983	2006	16 Almond Drive, East Kilbride, Glasgow G74 2HX [E-mail: marion.buchanan@btinternet.com]	(Mbl) 07999 889817	16
Burns, Marjory (Mrs) DCS	1997	1998	22 Kirklee Road, Mossend, Bellshill ML4 2QN [E-mail: mburns8070@aol.co.uk]	01698 292685 (Mbl) 07792 843922	17
Carson, Christine (Miss) MA DCS	2006		36 Upper Wellhead, Limekilns, Dunfermline KY11 3JQ	01383 873131 (Mbl) 07919 137294	24
Cathcart, John Paul (Mr) DCS	2000		9 Glen More, East Kilbride, Glasgow G74 2AP [E-mail: paulcathcart@msn.com]	01355 243970 (Mbl) 07708 396074	16

Name			Address / E-mail	Telephone	No.
Corrie, Margaret (Miss) DCS	1989	2013	44 Sunnyside Street, Camelon, Falkirk FK1 4BH [E-mail: deakcorr@virginmedia.com]	01324 670656; (Mbl) 07955 633969	2
Crawford, Morag (Miss) MSc DCS	1977	1998	118 Wester Drylaw Place, Edinburgh EH4 2TG [E-mail: morag.crawford.dcs@blueyonder.co.uk]	(Tel/Fax) 0131-332 2253; (Mbl) 07970 982563	24
Crocker, Liz (Mrs) DipComEd DCS	1985	2003	77C Craigcrook Road, Edinburgh EH4 3PH	0131-332 0227	1
Cunningham, Ian (Mr) DCS	1994	2002	110 Nelson Terrace, Keith AB55 5FD [E-mail: icunninghamdcs@btinternet.com]		35
Cuthbertson, Valerie (Miss) DipTMus DCS	2003		105 Bellshill Road, Motherwell ML1 3SJ [E-mail: v.cuthbertson333@btinternet.com]	01698 259001	22
Deans, Raymond (Mr) DCS	1994	2003	60 Ardmory Road, Rothesay, Isle of Bute PA20 0PG [E-mail: r.deans93@btinternet.com]	01700 504893	19
Dunnett, Linda (Mrs) BA DCS	1976	2000	5 Fincastle Place, Cowie, Stirling FK7 7DS [E-mail: lindadunnett@sky.com]	01786 818413; (Mbl) 07838 041683	23
Evans, Mark (Mr) BSc MSc DCS	1988	2006	13 Easter Drylaw Drive, Edinburgh EH4 2QA [E-mail: mark.evans59@nhs.net]	0131-343 3089; (Office) 01383 674136	1
Gargrave, Mary (Mrs) DCS	1989	2002	The Manse, 90 Mount Annan Drive, Glasgow G44 4RZ [E-mail: mary_gargrave@btinternet.com]	0141-561 4681; (Mbl) 07896 866618	16
Getliffe, Dot (Mrs) DCS BA BD DipEd	2006	2013	3 Woodview Terrace, Hamilton ML3 9DP [E-mail: dgetliffe@aol.co.uk]	01698 423504; (Mbl) 07766 910171	16
Hamilton, James (Mr) DCS	1997	2000	6 Beckfield Gate, Glasgow G33 1SW [E-mail: j.hamilton111@btinternet.com]	0141-558 3195; (Mbl) 07584 137314	16
Hamilton, Karen (Mrs) DCS	1995	2009	6 Beckfield Gate, Glasgow G33 1SW [E-mail: k.hamilton6@btinternet.com]	0141-558 3195; (Mbl) 07514 402612	16
Love, Joanna (Ms) BSc DCS	1992	2009	92 Everard Drive, Glasgow G21 1XQ [E-mail: jo@iona.org.uk]	0141-772 0149; (Office) 0141-332 6343	16
Lyall, Ann (Miss) DCS	1980	2013	24 Pennywell Road, Edinburgh EH4 4HD [E-mail: ann.lyall@btinternet.com]	0131-332 4354	1
MacDonald, Anne (Miss) BA DCS	1980	2002	502 Castle Gait, Paisley PA1 2PA [E-mail: anne.macdonald2@ggc.scot.nhs.uk]	0141-840 1875; (Mbl) 07976 786174	16
McIntosh, Kay (Mrs) DCS	2008	2013	4 Jacklin Green, Livingston EH54 8PZ [E-mail: kay@backedge.co.uk]	01506 440543	2
McKay, Kenneth D. (Mr) DCS	1996	1998	11F Balgowan Road, Letham, Perth PH1 2JG [E-mail: deakendan@gmail.com]	01738 621169; (Mbl) 07843 883042	28
McPheat, Elspeth (Miss) DCS	1985	2001	11/5 New Orchardfield, Edinburgh EH6 5ET	0131-554 4143	1
Munro, Patricia (Ms) BSc DCS	1986	2012	4 Hewat Place, Perth PH1 2UD [E-mail: pat.munrodcs@gmail.com]	01738 443088; (Mbl) 07814 836314	28
Nicholson, David (Mr) DCS	1994	1993	2D Doonside, Kildrum, Cumbernauld, Glasgow G67 2HX [E-mail: deacdave@btinternet.com]	01236 732260	22
Ogilvie, Colin (Mr) DCS	1998	2003	32 Upper Bourtree Court, Rutherglen, Glasgow G73 4HT [E-mail: colinogilvie2@gmail.com]	0141-569 2725; (Mbl) 07837 287804	11
Philip, Elizabeth (Mrs) DCS MA BA PGCSE	2007		8 Strathearn Terrace, Crieff PH7 3AQ [E-mail: ephilipstitch@gmail.com]	01764 218976; (Mbl) 07970 767851	28
Porter, Jean (Mrs) BD DCS	2006	2008	St Mark's Church, Drip Road, Stirling FK8 1RE [E-mail: info@stmarksstirling.org.uk]	(Mbl) 07729 316321	23
Ross, Duncan (Mr) DCS	1996	2006	1 John Neilson Avenue, Paisley PA1 2SX [E-mail: duncan@saintninians.co.uk]	0141-887 2801	14

NAME	COM	ORD	ADDRESS	TEL	PRES
Rycroft, Pauline (Mrs) DCS BA CertTheol PGDipC DCS	2003	2006	6 Ashville Terrace, Edinburgh EH6 8DD [E-mail: pauline70@rocketmail.com]	0131-554 6564 (Mbl) 07759 436303	1
Stewart, Marion G. (Miss) DCS	1991	1994	Kirk Cottage, Kirkton of Skene, Westhill, Skene AB32 6XE [E-mail: m313stewart@btinternet.com]	01224 743407	33
Thomson, Jacqueline (Mrs) MTh DCS	2004	2004	1 Barron Terrace, Leven KY8 4DL [E-mail: churchdeacon@blueyonder.co.uk]	01333 301115 (Mbl) 07806 776560	25
Urquhart, Barbara (Mrs) DCS	1986	2006	9 Standalane, Kilmaurs, Kilmarnock KA3 2NB [E-mail: barbaraurquhart1@gmail.com]	01563 538289	11
Wallace, Catherine (Mrs) PGDipC DCS	1987		5 Strathearn Terrace, Perth PH2 0LS [E-mail: samesky2407@aol.com]	01738 621709	28
Wallace, Sheila (Mrs) DCS BA BD	2009	2011	Beanach Cottage, Spey Avenue, Boat of Garten PH24 3BE [E-mail: sheilad.wallace53@gmail.com]	01479 831548 (Mbl) 07733 243046	36
Wilson, Glenda (Mrs) DCS	1990	2006	Ardlayne, 23 Bullwood Road, Dunoon PA23 7QJ [E-mail: deacglendamwilson@gmail.com]	01369 700848	19
Wright, Lynda (Miss) BEd DCS	1979	1992	Key Cottage, High Street, Falkland, Cupar KY15 7BU [E-mail: lynda.keyhouse@tiscali.co.uk]	01337 857705 (Mbl) 07835 303395	26

THE DIACONATE (Retired List)

NAME	COM	ADDRESS	TEL	PRES
Allan, Jean (Mrs) DCS	1989	12C Hindmarsh Avenue, Dundee DD3 7LW [E-mail: jeanmieallan45@googlemail.com]	01382 827299 (Mbl) 07709 959474	29
Anderson, Janet (Miss) DCS	1979	Creagard, 31 Lower Breakish, Isle of Skye IV42 8QA [E-mail: jaskye@hotmail.co.uk]	01471 822403	42
Bayes, Muriel C. (Mrs) DCS	1963	Flat 6, Carleton Court, 10 Fenwick Road, Glasgow G46 4AN	0141-633 0865	16
Buchanan, John (Mr) DCS	2010	19 Gillespie Crescent, Edinburgh EH10 4HZ	0131-229 0794	3
Cameron, Margaret (Miss) DCS	1961	2 Rowans Gate, Paisley PA2 6RD	0141-840 2479	14
Copland, Agnes M. (Mrs) MBE DCS	1950	Altnacraig House, Lyle Road, Greenock PA16 7XT		14
Craw, John (Mr) DCS	1998	Liabost, 8 Proudfoot Road, Wick KW1 4PQ	01955 603805 (Mbl) 07544 761653	41
Cunningham, Alison W. (Miss) DCS	1961	23 Strathblane Road, Milngavie, Glasgow G62 8DL	0141-563 9232	18
Drummond, Rhoda (Miss) DCS	1960	Flat K, 23 Grange Loan, Edinburgh EH9 2ER	0131-668 3631	1
Erskine, Morag (Miss) DCS	1979	111 Mains Drive, Park Mains, Erskine PA8 7JJ	0141-812 6096	14
Flockhart, Andrew (Mr) DCS	1988	Flat 0/1, 8 Hardie Avenue, Rutherglen, Glasgow G73 3AS	0141-569 0716	16
Forrest, Janice (Mrs)	1990	4/1, 7 Blochairn Place, Glasgow G21 2EB	0141-552 1132	16
Gordon, Fiona S. (Mrs) MA DCS	1958	Machrie, 3 Cupar Road, Cuparmuir, Cupar KY15 5RH [E-mail: machrie@madasafish.com]	01334 652341	26
Gordon, Margaret (Mrs) DCS	1998	92 Lanark Road West, Currie EH14 5LA	0131-449 2554	1

Name	Year	Address / E-mail	Telephone	No.
Gray, Catherine (Miss) DCS	1969	10C Eastern View, Gourock PA19 1RJ [E-mail: gray_catherine2@sky.com]	01475 637479	14
Gray, Christine M. (Mrs) DCS	1969	11 Woodside Avenue, Thorniebank, Glasgow G46 7HR	0141-571 1008	16
Gray, Greta (Miss) DCS	1992	67 Crags Avenue, Paisley PA2 6SG [E-mail: greta.gray@ntlworld.com]	0141-884 6178	14
Howden, Margaret (Miss) DCS	1954	38 Munro Street, Kirkcaldy KY11 1PY	01592 205913	25
Hughes, Helen (Miss) DCS	1977	2/2, 43 Burnbank Terrace, Glasgow G20 6UQ [E-mail: helhug35@gmail.com]	0141-333 9459 (Mbl) 07752 604817	16
Hutchison, Alan E.W. (Mr) DCS	1988	132 Lochbridge Road, North Berwick EH39 4DR	01620 894077	3
Johnston, Mary (Miss) DCS	1988	19 Lounsdale Drive, Paisley PA2 9ED	0141-849 1615	14
King, Chris (Mrs) DCS	2002	28 Kilnford, Dundonald, Kilmarnock KA2 9ET [E-mail: chrisking99@tiscali.co.uk]	01563 851197	10
King, Margaret MA DCS	2002	56 Murrayfield, Fochabers IV32 7EZ	01343 820937	35
Lundie, Ann V. (Miss) DCS	1972	20 Langdykes Drive, Cove, Aberdeen AB12 3HW	01224 898416	31
McBain, Margaret (Miss) DCS	1974	33 Quarry Road, Paisley PA2 7RD	0141-884 2920	14
McCallum, Moyra (Miss) MA BD DCS	1965	176 Hilton Drive, Aberdeen AB24 4LT [E-mail: moymac@aol.com]	01224 486240 (Mbl) 07986 581899	31
McCully, M. Isobel (Miss) DCS	1974	10 Broadstone Avenue, Port Glasgow PA14 5BB [E-mail: mi.mccully@btinternet.com]	01475 742240	14
MacKinnon, Ronald (Mr) DCS	1996	12 Mossywood Court, McGregor Avenue, Airdrie ML6 7DY [E-mail: ronnie@ronniemac.plus.com]	01236 763389 (Mbl) 07594 427960	22
MacLean, Donald A. (Mr) DCS	1988	8 Upper Barvas, Isle of Lewis HS2 0QX	01851 840454	44
McNaughton, Janette (Miss) DCS	1982	4 Dunellan Avenue, Moodiesburn, Glasgow G69 0GB	01236 870180	22
MacPherson, James B. (Mr) DCS	1988	0/1, 104 Cartside Street, Glasgow G42 9TQ	0141-616 6468	16
MacQuien, Duncan (Mr) DCS	1988	35 Criffel Road, Mount Vernon, Glasgow G32 9JE	0141-575 1137	14
Martin, Janie (Miss) DCS	1979	16 Wentworth Road, Dundee DD2 3SD [E-mail: janimar@aol.com]	01382 813786	29
Merrilees, Ann (Miss) DCS	1994	23 Cuthill Brae, Willow Wood Residential Park, West Calder EH55 8QE [E-mail: ann@merrilees.freeserve.co.uk]	01501 762909	2
Miller, Elsie M. (Miss) DCS	1974	30 Swinton Avenue, Rowanbank, Baillieston, Glasgow G69 6JR	0141-771 0857	22
Mitchell, Joyce (Mrs) DCS	1994	Sunnybank, Farr, Inverness IV2 6XG [E-mail: joyce@mitchell71.freeserve.co.uk]	01808 521285	37
Morrison, Jean (Dr) DCS	1964	45 Corslet Road, Currie EH14 5LZ [E-mail: jean.morrison@blueyonder.co.uk]	0131-449 6859	1
Moyes, Sheila (Miss) DCS	1957	158 Pilton Avenue, Edinburgh EH5 2JZ [E-mail: sheilamoyes@btinternet.com]	0131-551 1731	1
Mulligan, Anne MA DCS	1974	27A Craigour Avenue, Edinburgh EH17 7NH [E-mail: mulliganne@aol.com]	0131-664 3426	1
Nicol, Joyce (Mrs) BA DCS	1974	93 Brisbane Street, Greenock PA16 8NY [E-mail: joycenicol@hotmail.co.uk]	01475 723235 (Mbl) 07957 642709	14
Palmer, Christine (Ms) DCS	2003	Flat 4, Carissima Court, 99 Elmer Road, Elmer, Bognor Regis PO22 6LH	01243 85641	28
Rennie, Agnes M. (Miss) DCS MBE DCS	1974	3/1 Craigmillar Court, Edinburgh EH16 4AD	0131-661 8475	1
Ronald, Norma A. (Miss)	1961	2B Saughton Road North, Edinburgh EH12 7HG	0131-334 8736	1
Rose, Lewis (Mr) DCS	1993	6 Gauldie Crescent, Dundee DD3 0RR [E-mail: lewis_rose48@yahoo.co.uk]	01382 816580 (Mbl) 07899 790466	29

NAME	ORD	ADDRESS	TEL	PRES
Rutherford, Ellen B. (Miss) MBE DCS	1962	Urray Care Home, Muir of Ord IV6 7SY		39
Smith, Catherine (Mrs) DCS	1964	21 Lingaro, Bixter, Shetland ZE2 9NN	01595 810207	46
Steele, Marilynn J. (Mrs) BD DCS	1999	2 Northfield Gardens, Prestonpans EH32 9LQ	01875 811497	1
Steven, Gordon R. BD DCS	1997	51 Nantwich Drive, Edinburgh EH7 6RB [E-mail: grsteven@btinternet.com]	0131-669 2054	3
Stuart, Anne (Miss) DCS	1966	1 Murrell Terrace, Aberdour, Burntisland KY3 0XH	(Mbl) 07904 385256 / 01383 860049	24
Tait, Agnes (Mrs) DCS	1995	10 Carnoustie Crescent, Greenhills, East Kilbride, Glasgow G75 8TE	01389 873196	17
Teague, Yvonne (Mrs) DCS	1965	46 Craigcrook Avenue, Edinburgh EH4 3PX [E-mail: y.teague.1@blueyonder.co.uk]	0131-336 3113	1
Thom, Helen (Miss) BA DipEd MA DCS	1959	84 Great King Street, Edinburgh EH3 6QU	0131-556 5687	1
Thomson, Phyllis (Miss) DCS	2003	63 Caroline Park, Mid Calder, Livingston EH53 0SJ	01506 883207	2
Trimble, Robert DCS	1988	5 Templar Rise, Livingston EH54 6PJ	01506 412504	2
Webster, Elspeth H. (Miss) DCS	1950	82 Broomhill Avenue, Burntisland KY3 0BP	01592 873616	25
Wilson, Muriel (Miss) MA BD DCS	1997	28 Bellevue Crescent, Ayr KA7 2DR [E-mail: muriel.wilson4@btinternet.com]	01292 264939	10
Wishart, William (Mr) DCS	1994	1 Brunstane Road North, Edinburgh EH15 2DL [E-mail: bill@wishartfamily.co.uk]	(Mbl) 07846 555654	1

THE DIACONATE (Supplementary List)

NAME	ORD	ADDRESS	TEL
Gilroy, Lorraine (Mrs) DCS	1988	5 Bluebell Drive, Cheverel Court, Bedward CO12 0GE	02476 366031
Guthrie, Jennifer M. (Miss) DCS		14 Eskview Terrace, Ferryden, Montrose DD10 9RD	01674 674413
Harris, Judith (Mrs) DCS	1993	243 Western Avenue, Sandfields, Port Talbot, West Glamorgan SA12 7NF	01639 884855
Hood, Katrina (Mrs) DCS	1988	67C Farquhar Road, Edgbaston, Birmingham B18 2QP	
Hudson, Sandra (Mrs) DCS	1982	10 Albany Drive, Rutherglen, Glasgow G73 3QN	
Muir, Alison M. (Mrs) DCS	1969	77 Arthur Street, Dunfermline KY12 0JJ	
Ramsden, Christine (Miss) DCS	1978	2 Wykeham Close, Bassett, Southampton SO16 7LZ	
Walker, Wikje (Mrs) DCS	1970	24 Brodie's Yard, Queen Street, Coupar Angus PH13 9RA	01828 628251

LIST I – MINISTERS WHO HOLD PRACTISING CERTIFICATES (in accordance with Act II (2000), but who are not members of a Presbytery)

NAME	ORD	ADDRESS	TEL	PRES
Adamson, Hugh M. BD	1976	38F Maybole Road, Ayr KA7 4SF [E-mail: hmadamson768@btinternet.com]	01292 440958	11

Name	Ord.	Address	Tel	No.
Aitken, Ewan R. BA BD	1992	159 Restalrig Avenue, Edinburgh EH7 6PJ	0131-467 1660	1
Alexander, William M. BD	1971	110 Fairview Circle, Danestone, Aberdeen AB22 8YR	01224 703752	31
Anderson, David MA BD	1975	Rowan Cottage, Aberlour Gardens, Aberlour AB38 9LD	01340 871906	35
Anderson, Kenneth G. MA BD	1967	8 School Road, Arbroath DD11 2LT	01241 874825	30
Anderson, Susan M. (Mrs) BD	1997	32 Murrayfield, Bishopbriggs, Glasgow G64 3DS [E-mail: susanbbriggs32@gmail.com]	0141-772 6338	11
Barbour, Robert A.S. (Prof.) KCVO MC MA BD STM DD	1954	Old Fincastle, Pitlochry PH16 5RJ	01796 473209	27
Barclay, Neil W. BSc BEd BD	1986	4 Gibsongray Street, Falkirk FK2 7LN	01324 874681	22
Bardgett, Frank D. MA BD PhD	1987	Tigh an Iasgair, Street of Kincardine, Boat of Garten PH24 3BY [E-mail: tigh@bardgett.plus.com]	01479 831751	36
Bartholomew, Julia (Mrs) BSc BD	2002	Kippenhill, Dunning, Perth PH2 0RA	01764 684929	28
Beattie, Warren R. BSc BD MSc PhD	1991	Director for Mission Research, OMF International, 2 Cluny Road, Singapore 259570 [E-mail: beattiewarren@omf.net]	0065 6319 4550	1
Biddle, Lindsay (Ms)	1991	30 Ralston Avenue, Glasgow G52 3NA [E-mail: lindsaybiddle@hotmail.com]	0141-883 7405	
Birrell, John M. MA LLB BD	1974	'Hiddlehame', 5 Hewat Place, Perth PH1 2UD [E-mail: john.birrell@nhs.net]	01738 443335	28
Black, James S. BD DPS	1976	7 Breck Terrace, Penicuik EH26 0RJ [E-mail: jsb.black@btopenworld.com]	01968 677559	3
Boyd, Ian R. MA BD PhD	1989	33 Castleton Drive, Newton Mearns, Glasgow G77 3LE	0141-931 5344	16
Bradley, Andrew W. BD	1975	Flat 1/1, 38 Cairnhill View, Bearsden, Glasgow G61 1RP	01224 491451	31
Brown, Robert F. MA BD ThM	1971	55 Hilton Drive, Aberdeen AB24 4NJ [E-mail: Bjacob546@aol.com]		
Caie, Albert LTh	1983	34 Ringwell Gardens, Stonehouse, Larkhall ML9 3QW	01698 792187	17
Coogan, J. Melvyn LTh	1992	19 Glen Grove, Largs KA30 8QQ		12
Cowieson, Roy J. BD	1979	2160-15 Hawk Drive, Courtenay, BC V9N 9B2, Canada [E-mail: arjay1232@gmail.com]		13
Davidson, John F. BSc DipEdTech	1970	49 Craigmill Gardens, Carnoustie DD7 6HX [E-mail: davidson900@btinternet.com]	01241 854566	30
Davidson, Mark R. MA BD STM PhD RN	2005	20 Kinmohr Rise, Blackburn, Aberdeen AB21 0LJ [E-mail: mark.davidson122@mod.uk]	01224 791350	33
Dick, John H.A. MA MSc BD	1982	18 Fairfield Road, Kelty KY4 0BY	01506 237597	31
Dickson, Graham T. MA BD	1985	43 Hope Park Gardens, Bathgate EH48 2QT [E-mail: gtd22@blueyonder.co.uk]		2
Donaldson, Colin V.	1982	3A Playfair Terrace, St Andrews KY16 9HX	01334 472889	3
Drake, Wendy F. (Mrs) BD	1978	21 William Black Place, South Queensferry EH30 9QR [E-mail: revwdrake@hotmail.co.uk]	0131-331 1520	1
Drummond, Norman W. (Prof.) CBE MA BD DUniv FRSE	1976	c/o Columba 1400 Ltd, Staffin, Isle of Skye IV51 9JY	01478 611400	42
Ellis, David W. GIMechE GIProdE	1962	4 Wester Tarsappie, Rhynd Road, Perth PH2 8PT	01738 449618	16
Espie, Howard	2011	1 Sprucebank Avenue, Langbank, Port Glasgow PA14 6YX [E-mail: howardespie.me.com]	01475 540391	1
Ferguson, Ronald MA BD ThM DUniv	1972	Vinbreck, Orphir, Orkney KW17 2RE [E-mail: ronbluebrazil@aol.com]	01856 811353	45
Fowler, Richard C.A. BSc MSc BD	1978	4 Gardentown, Whalsay, Shetland ZE2 9AB	01806 566538	46

Name	Year	Address	Tel	No.
Fraser, Ian M. MA BD PhD	1946	Ferndale, Gargunnock, Stirling, FK8 3BW	01786 860612	23
Frew, John M. MA BD	1946	17 The Furrows, Walton-on-Thames KT12 3JQ		16
Gammack, George BD	1985	13A Hill Street, Broughty Ferry, Dundee DD5 2JP	01382 778636	29
Gauld, Beverly G.D.D. MA BD	1972	7 Rowan View, Lanark ML11 9FQ	01555 665765	13
Gillies, Janet E. BD	1998	18 McIntyre Lane, Macmerry, Tranent EH33 1QL	01875 824607	3
Grainger, Alison J. BD	1995	2 Hareburn Avenue, Avonbridge, Falkirk FK1 2NR [E-mail: revajrgrainger@btinternet.com]	01324 861632	2
Grubb, George D.W. BA BD BPhil DMin	1962	10 Wellhead Close, South Queensferry EH30 9WA	0131-331 2072	1
Harper, Anne J.M. (Miss) BD STM MTh CertSocPsych	1979	122 Greenock Road, Bishopton PA7 5AS	01505 862466	16
Haslett, Howard J. BA BD	1972	26 The Mallings, Haddington EH41 4EF [E-mail: howard.haslett@btinternet.com]	01620 820292	3
Hendrie, Yvonne (Mrs) MA BD	1995	The Manse, 16 McAdam Way, Maybole KA19 8FD	01655 883710	10
Hibbert, Frederick W. BD	1986	4 Cemydd Terrace, Senghenydd, Caerphilly, Mid Glamorgan CF83 4HL	02920 831653	47
Homewood, Ivor Maxwell MSc BD	1997	An der Fließwiese 26, D-14052 Berlin, Germany [E-mail: maxhomewood@me.com]	0049 30 3048722	48
Hosie, James MA BD MTh	1959	Hilbre, Baycrofts, Strachur, Cairndow PA27 8BY	01369 860634	19
Hutchison, Alison M. (Mrs) BD DipMin	1988	Ashfield, Drumoak, Banchory AB31 5AG [E-mail: amhutch62@aol.com]	01330 811309	31
Jenkinson, John J. JP LTCL ALCM DipEd DipSen (Aux)	1991	8 Rosehall Terrace, Falkirk FK1 1PY	01324 625498	22
Kenny, Celia G. BA MTh MPhil PhD	1995	37 Grosvenor Road, Rathgar, Dublin 6, Ireland [E-mail: cgkenny@tcd.ie]		5
Kerr, Hugh F. MA BD	1968	134C Great Western Road, Aberdeen AB10 6QE	01224 580091	31
Lawrie, Robert M. BD MSc DipMin LLCM(TD) MCMI	1994	18/1 John's Place, Edinburgh EH6 7EN [E-mail: robert.lawrie@ed.ac.uk]	0131-554 9765	1
Ledgard, J. Christopher BA	1969	Streonshalh, 8 David Hume View, Chirnside, Duns TD11 3SX [E-mail: ledgard07@btinternet.com]	01890 817124	5
Liddiard, F.G.B. MA	1957	34 Trinity Fields Crescent, Brechin DD9 6YF	01356 622966	30
Lindsay, W. Douglas BD CPS	1978	3 Drummond Place, Calderwood, East Kilbride, Glasgow G74 3AD	01355 234169	16
Lithgow, Anne R. (Mrs) MA BD	1992	14 Thorntonloch Holdings, Dunbar EH42 1QT [E-mail: anne.lithgow@btinternet.com]		3
Logan, Thomas M. LTh	1971	3 Duncan Court, Kilmarnock KA3 7TF	01563 524398	11
Lyall, David BSc BD STM PhD	1965	16 Brian Crescent, Tunbridge Wells, Kent TN4 0AP [E-mail: lyall3@gmail.com]	01892 670323	47
McAdam, David J. BSc BD (Assoc)	1990	12 Dunellan Crescent, Moodiesburn, Glasgow G69 0GA [E-mail: dmca29@hotmail.co.uk]	01236 870472	16
McDonald, Ross J. BA BD ThM RNR	1998	HMS *Dalriada*, Navy Buildings, Eldon Street, Greenock PA16 7SL [E-mail: rossjmcdonald@tiscali.co.uk]	(Mbl) 0141-883 7545 07952 558767	16
McFadyen, Gavin BEng BD	2006	20 Tennyson Avenue, Bridlington YO15 2EP [E-mail: mcfadyen.gavin@gmail.com]	(Mbl) 01262 608659 07503 971068	18
McGillivray, A. Gordon MA BD STM	1951	36 Larchfield Neuk, Balerno EH14 7NL		1
Maciver, Iain BD	2007	5 MacLeod Road, Stornoway, Isle of Lewis HS1 2HJ [E-mail: iain.maciver@hebrides.net]		44

Name		Address	Tel	No.
McKay, Johnston R. MA BA PhD	1969	15 Montgomerie Avenue, Fairlie, Largs KA29 0EE [E-mail: johnston.mckay@btopenworld.com]	01475 568802	16
McKean, Martin J. BD DipMin	1984	56 Kingsknowe Drive, Edinburgh EH14 2JX	0131-466 1157	1
MacPherson, Gordon C.	1963	203 Capelrig Road, Patterton, Newton Mearns, Glasgow G77 6ND	0141-616 2107	16
McPherson, William BD DipEd	1993	83 Laburnum Avenue, Port Seton, Prestonpans EH32 0UD	01875 812252	22
McWilliam, Thomas M. MA BD	1964	Flat 3, 13 Culduthel Road, Inverness IV2 4AG [E-mail: tommcwilliam@btconnect.com]	01463 718981	39
Mailer, Colin (Aux)	1996	Innis Chonain, Back Row, Polmont, Falkirk FK2 0RD	01324 712401	22
Main, Arthur W.A. BD	1954	13/3 Eildon Terrace, Edinburgh EH3 5NL	0131-556 1344	16
Masson, John D. MA BD PhD BSc	1984	2 Beechgrove, Craw Hall, Brampton CA8 1TS [E-mail: jmasson96@btinternet.com]	ex-directory	7
Melville, David D. BD	1989	28 Porterfield, Comrie, Dunfermline KY12 9HJ	01383 850075	24
Millar, Peter W. MA BD PhD	1971	6/5 Ettrickdale Place, Edinburgh EH3 5JN [E-mail: ionacottage@hotmail.com]	0131-557 0517	1
Moodie, Alastair R. MA BD	1978	4 Burnbrae Road, Auchinloch, Glasgow G66 5DQ		16
Morton, Andrew Q. MA BSc BD FRSE	1949	Sunnyside, 4A Manse Street, Aberdour, Burntisland KY3 0TY		18
Muir, Margaret A. (Miss) MA LLB BD	1989	59/4 South Beechwood, Edinburgh EH12 5YS	0131-313 3240	13
Newell, Alison M. (Mrs) BD	1986	1A Inverleith Terrace, Edinburgh EH3 5NS [E-mail: alinewell@aol.com]	0131-556 3505	1
Newell, J. Philip MA BD PhD	1982	1A Inverleith Terrace, Edinburgh EH3 5NS	0131-556 3505	1
Newlands, George M. (Prof.) MA BD PhD DLitt FRSA FRSE	1970	731 16th Street North, Lethbridge, Alberta, Canada T1H 3B3		16
Nicolson, John Murdo	1997	5 Dovecote Road, Bromsgrove, Worcs B61 7BN		42
Notman, John R. BSc BD	1990	5 Osborne Terrace, Port Seton, Prestonpans EH32 0BZ	01875 814358	47
Ostler, John H. MA LTh	1975	10 Waverley Park, Kirkintilloch, Glasgow G66 2BP	0141-776 0407	3
Owen, Catherine W. MTh	1984	6 The Willows, Kelty KY4 0FQ	01383 830998	16
Paterson, Andrew E. JP	1994	33/5 Carnbee Avenue, Edinburgh EH16 6GA	0131-664 0673	24
Penman, Iain D. BD	1977	Regent College, 5800 University Boulevard, Vancouver BC V6T 2E4, Canada [E-mail: iainpenmanklm@aol.com]	(Mbl) 07931 993427	1
Provan, Iain W. MA BA PhD	1991	Tigh an Achaidh, 21 Fernoch Crescent, Lochgilphead PA31 8AE	001 604 224 3245	1
Risby, Lesley P. (Mrs) BD	1994	[E-mail: mrsrisby@hotmail.com]	01546 600464	19
Roy, Alistair A. MA BD	1955	1 Broaddykes Close, Kingswells, Aberdeen AB15 8UF	01224 743310	31
Sawers, Hugh BA	1968	2 Rosemount Meadows, Castlepark, Bothwell, Glasgow G71 8EL	01698 853960	17
Scotland, Ronald J. BD	1993	7A Rose Avenue, Elgin IV30 1NX [E-mail: ronnieandjill@thescotlands.co.uk]	01343 543086	35
Scouller, Hugh BSc BD	1985	11 Kirk View, Haddington EH41 4AN [E-mail: h.scouller@btinternet.com]		3
Shaw, D.W.D. BA BD LLB WS DD	1960	4/13 Succoth Court, Edinburgh EH12 6BZ	0131-337 2130	26
Smith, Ronald W. BA BEd BD	1979	1F1, 2 Middlefield, Edinburgh EH7 4PF	0131-553 1174 (Mbl) 07900 896954	23
Stewart, Margaret L. (Mrs) BSc MB ChB BD	1985	28 Inch Crescent, Bathgate EH48 1EU	01506 653428	2

NAME	ORD	ADDRESS	TEL	PRES
Storrar, William F. (Prof.) MA BD PhD	1984	Director, Center of Theological Inquiry, 50 Stockton Street, Princeton, NJ 08540, USA		1
Strachan, David G. BD DPS	1978	1 Deeside Park, Aberdeen AB15 7PQ	01224 324101	31
Strachan, Ian M. MA BD	1959	'Cardenwell', Glen Drive, Dyce, Aberdeen AB21 7EN	01224 772028	31
Thomas, W. Colville ChLJ BTh BPhil DPS DSc	1964	11 Muirfield Crescent, Gullane EH31 2HN	01620 842415	3
Tollick, Frank BSc DipEd	1958	3 Bellhouse Road, Aberdour, Burntisland KY3 0TL	01383 860559	24
Turnbull, John LTh	1994	4 Rathmor Road, Biggar ML12 6QG	01899 221502	13
Turnbull, Julian S. BSc BD MSc CEng MBCS	1980	25 Hamilton Road, Gullane EH31 2HP [E-mail: jules@turnbull25.plus.com]	01620 842958	3
Watson, James B. BSc	1968 2009	(Coldstream with Eccles) 3 Royal Terrace, Hutton, Berwick-upon-Tweed TD15 1TP [E-mail: jimwatson007@hotmail.com]	01289 386282	
Watson, John M. LTh	1989	20 Greystone Place, Newtonhill, Stonehaven AB39 3UL [E-mail: watson-john18@sky.com]	01569 730604 (Mbl) 07733 334380	31
Weatherhead, James L. CBE MA LLB DD	1960	59 Brechin Road, Kirriemuir DD8 4DE	01575 572237	30
Webster, Brian G. BSc BD CEng MIET	1998	3/1 Cloch Court, 57 Albert Road, Gourock PA19 1NJ [E-mail: revwebby@aol.com]	01475 638332	23
Weir, Mary K. (Mrs) BD PhD	1968	1249 Millar Road RR1, SITEH-46, BC V0N 1G0, Canada	001 604 947 0636	1
Whitton, John P.	1977	115 Sycamore Road, Farnborough, Hants GU14 6RE	01252 674488	47
Wilkie, James L. MA BD	1959	7 Comely Bank Avenue, Edinburgh EH4 1EW [E-mail: jl.wilkie@btinternet.com]	0131-343 1552	1
Wood, James L.K.	1967	1 Glen Drive, Dyce, Aberdeen AB21 7EN	01224 722543	31

LIST J – MINISTERS WHO ARE NOT MEMBERS OF A PRESBYTERY AND WHO DO NOT CURRENTLY HOLD A PRACTISING CERTIFICATE (in terms of Act II (2000))

NAME	ORD	ADDRESS	TEL	PRES
Aitchison, James W. BD	1993	84 Wakefords Park, Church Crookham, Fleet, Hampshire GU52 8EZ		31
Arbuthnott, Joan E. (Mrs) MA BD	1993	139/1 New Street, Musselburgh EH21 6DH	0131-665 6736	3
Beck, John C. BD	1975	31 The Woodlands, Stirling FK8 2LB		35
Birrell, Isobel (Mrs) BD	1994	'Hiddlehame', 5 Hewat Place, Perth PH1 2UD [E-mail: isobel@ibmail.org.uk]	01738 443335 (Mbl) 07540 797945	17
Black, W. Graham MA BD	1983	72 Linksview, Linksfield Road, Aberdeen AB24 5RG [E-mail: graham.black@virgin.net]	01224 492491	31
Bonar, Alexander F. LTh LRIC	1988	7 Westbank Court, Westbank Terrace, Macmerry, Tranent EH33 1QS [E-mail: sandybonar@tiscali.co.uk]	01875 615165	3
Breakey, Judith (Ms) LizTheol MTh DipEd	2010	[E-mail: judith.breakey@gmail.com]		16
Brown, Alastair BD	1986	52 Henderson Drive, Kintore, Inverurie AB51 0FB	01467 632787	32
Brown, Joseph MA	1954	The Orchard, Hermitage Lane, Shedden Park Road, Kelso TD5 7AN	01573 223481	6

Name	Year	Address / E-mail	Phone	No.
Burgess, Paul C.J. MA	1968	Springvale, Halket Road, Lugton, Kilmarnock KA3 4EE [E-mail: paulandcathie@gmail.com]	01505 850254	2
Campbell, J. Ewen R. MA BD	1967	20 St Margaret's Road, North Berwick EH39 4PJ	01620 893814	25
Cooper, George MA BD	1943	8 Leighton Square, Alyth, Blairgowrie PH11 8AQ	01828 633746	1
Craig, Eric MA BD BA	1959	5 West Relugas Road, Edinburgh EH9 2PW	0131-667 8210	1
Craig, Gordon W. MBE MA BD	1972	1 Beley Bridge, Dunino, St Andrews KY16 8LT	01334 880285	26
Crawford, Michael S.M. LTh	1966	Brownside of Strichen, New Pitsligo, Fraserburgh AB43 6NY		31
Crawford, S.G. Victor	1980	Crofton, 65 Main Road, East Wemyss, Kirkcaldy KY1 4RL	01592 712325	25
Cumming, David P.L. MA	1957	Shillong, Tarbat Ness Road, Portmahomack, Tain IV20 1YA	01862 871794	19
Currie, Gordon C.M. MA BD	1975	43 Deanburn Park, Linlithgow EH49 6HA	01506 842759	2
Davies, Gareth W. BA BD	1979	Pitadro House, Fordell Gardens, Dunfermline KY11 7EY	01383 417634	24
Dean, Roger A.F. LTh	1983	0/2, 20 Ballogie Road, Glasgow G44 4TA [E-mail: roger.dean4@btopenworld.com]		16
Dutton, David W. BA	1973	13 Acredales, Haddington EH41 4NT [E-mail: duttondw@gmail.com]	01620 825999	9
Finlay, Quintin BA BD	1975	Ivy Cottage, Greenlees Farm, Kelso TD5 8BT	(Mbl) 07901 981171	6
Flockhart, D. Ross OBE BA BD DUniv	1955	Longwood, Humbie EH36 5PN [E-mail: rossflock@btinternet.com]	01875 833208	3
Forrester, Duncan B. (Prof.) MA BD DPhil DD FRSE	1962	25 Kingsburgh Road, Edinburgh EH12 6DZ [E-mail: dbforrester@rosskeen.org.uk]	0131-337 5646	1
Gow, Neil BSc MEd BD	1996	Hillhead Lodge, Portknockie, Buckie AB56 4PB [E-mail: n.gow334@btinternet.com]	01542 840625	35
Greig, James C.G. MA BD STM	1955	Block 2, Flat 2, Station Lofts, Strathblane, Glasgow G63 9BD [E-mail: james.greig12@btinternet.com]	01360 771915	16
Hamilton, David S.M. MA BD STM	1958	49 Paddocks Lane, Cheltenham GL50 4NU	01242 254917	47
Howie, William MA BD STM	1964	26 Morgan Road, Aberdeen AB16 5JY	01224 483669	31
Hurst, Frederick R. MA	1965	Flat 6, 21 Bulldale Place, Glasgow G14 0NE	0141-959 2604	40
Inglis, Donald B.C. MA MEd BD	1975	39 Thomson Drive, Bearsden, Glasgow G61 3PA	0141-942 1387	18
Lynn, Joyce (Mrs) MIPM BD	1995	Flat 8, 131 St Vincent Street, Broughty Ferry, Dundee DD5 2DA	01382 690556	29
Macaskill, Donald MA BD PhD	1994			16
McClenaghan, L. Paul BA	1973	4 Glendale Gardens, Randalstown, Co. Antrim BT41 3EJ [E-mail: paul.mcclenaghan@gmail.com]	02894 478545	34
McCreadie, David W.	1961	23 Willoughby Place, Callander PH17 8DG	01877 330785	23
Macdonald, Murdo C. MA BD	2002	[E-mail: murdocmacdonald@gmail.com]		2
McDonald, William J.C. DD	1953	7 Blacket Place, Edinburgh EH9 1RN	0131-667 2100	1
Macfarlane, Alwyn J.C. MA	1951	Flat 12, Homeburn House, 177 Fenwick Road, Giffnock, Glasgow G46 6JD	0141-620 3235	1
Macfarlane, Thomas G. BSc PhD BD	1956	12 Elphinstone Court, Lochwinnoch Road, Kilmacolm PA13 4DW	01505 874962	14
McGill, Thomas W.	1972	Westfell, Monreith, Newton Stewart DG8 9LT	01988 700449	9
McKenzie, Mary O. (Miss)	1976	4 Dunellan Avenue, Moodiesburn, Glasgow G69 0GB	01236 870180	16
Mackie, John F. BD	1979	1A Halls Close, Weldon, Corby, Northants NN17 3HH		40
Mackinnon, Thomas J.R. LTh DipMin	1996	4 Flashadder, Arnisort, Portree, Isle of Skye IV51 9PT	01470 582377	39
McLean, John MA BD	1967	16 Eastside Drive, Westhill AB32 6QN	01224 747701	33
Mair, John BSc	1965	21 Kenilworth Avenue, Helensburgh G84 7JR	01436 671744	18
Miller, Irene B. (Mrs) MA BD	1984	5 Braeside Park, Aberfeldy PH15 2DT	01887 829396	27
Murray, Douglas R. MA BD	1965	32 Forth Park, Bridge of Allan, Stirling FK9 5NT [E-mail: d-smurray@supanet.com]	01786 831081	23

Name	Year	Address	Telephone	No.
Neilson, Rodger BSc BD	1972	4 Waulkmill Steading, Charlestown, Dunfermline KY12 8ZS	01383 873336	34
O'Leary, Thomas BD	1983	1 Carter's Place, Irvine KA12 0BU	01294 313274	11
Osbeck, John R. BD	1979	15 Deeside Crescent, Aberdeen AB15 7PT	01224 315595	31
Park, Christopher BSc BD	1977	65 Moubray Road, Dalgety Bay, Dunfermline KY11 9JP [E-mail: chrispark8649@hotmail.com]	01383 821111	24
Patterson, James BSc BD	2003	c/o 9 Oakview, Balmedie, Aberdeen AB23 8SR		1
Peacock, Heather M. BSc PhD BD	2009	9 Frankscroft, Peebles EH45 9DX [E-mail: hmpeacock@btinternet.com]		32
Pryce, Stuart F.A.	1963	36 Forth Park, Bridge of Allan, Stirling FK9 5NT	01786 831026	23
Ramsay, Alan MA	1967	12 Riverside Grove, Lochyside, Fort William PH33 7RD	01397 702054	38
Reid, Janette G. (Miss) BD	1991	c/o Glasgow Presbytery Office, 260 Bath Street, Glasgow G2 4JP		16
Reid, William M. MA BD	1966	10 Rue Rossini, F-75009 Paris, France		48
Ritchie, Garden W.M.	1961	23 Croft Road, Kelso TD5 7EP	01573 224419	6
Robertson, John M. BSc BD	1975	8 North Green Drive, The Wilderness, Airth, Falkirk FK2 8RA	01324 832244	16
Robertson, Thomas G.M. LTh	1971	23 Muirend Avenue, Perth PH1 1JL	01738 624432	28
Roy, James A. MA BD	1965	'Beechwood', 7 Northview Terrace, Wormit, Newport-on-Tay DD6 8PP [E-mail: jim.roy@dundeepresbytery.org.uk]	01382 543578	29
Duncan Shaw of Chapelverna Bundesverdienstkreuz PhD ThDr Dthc	1951	4 Sydney Terrace, Edinburgh EH7 6SL	0131-663 1234	19
Smith, Ralph C.P. MA STM	1960	2A Waverley Road, Eskbank, Dalkeith EH22 3DJ [E-mail: rcpsmith@waitrose.com]		1
Spowart, Mary G. (Mrs) BD	1978	Aldersyde, St Abbs Road, Coldingham, Eyemouth TD14 5NR	01890 771697	26
Stone, W. Vernon MA BD	1949	36 Woodrow Court, Port Glasgow Road, Kilmacolm PA13 4QA [E-mail: stone@kilmacolm.fsnet.co.uk]	01505 872644	14
Sutcliffe, Clare B. BSc BD	2000	4 Dalmailing Avenue, Dreghorn, Irvine KA11 4HX		11
Taylor, David J. MA BD	1982	32 Croft an Righ, Inverkeithing KY11 1PF	01383 413227	24
Thomson, Alexander BSc BD MPhil PhD	1973	4 Munro Street, Dornoch IV25 3RA [E-mail: alexander.thomson6@btopenworld.com]	01862 811650	40
Thomson, Gilbert L. BA	1965	3 Fortharfield, Freuchie, Cupar KY15 7JJ	01337 857431	25
Watson, James B. BSc	1968	3 Royal Terrace, Hutton, Berwick-upon-Tweed TD15 1TP [E-mail: jimwatson007@hotmail.com]	01289 386282	5
Webster, John G. BSc	1964	Plane Tree, King's Cross, Brodick, Isle of Arran KA27 8RG	01770 700747	16
Wedderburn, A.J.M. (Prof.) MA BA PhD	1975	Therese-Danner-Platz 3, D-80636 Munich, Germany [E-mail: ajmw42@gmx.de]	0049 89 1200 3726	
Westmarland, Colin A.	1971	PO Box 5, Cospicua, CSPOL, Malta	00356 216 923552	48
Wilkie, George D. OBE BL	1948	2/37 Barnton Avenue West, Edinburgh EH4 6EB	0131-339 3973	1

LIST K – MINISTRIES DEVELOPMENT STAFF

In addition, some ministers and deacons employed by the Ministries Council in this capacity are listed in Section 5 (Presbyteries), with deacons also in List H of Section 6.

NAME	APP	ADDRESS	APPOINTMENT	TEL
Adam, Pamela BD	2009	Basement Left Flat, 409 Holburn Street, Aberdeen AB10 7GS [E-mail: thekirk@btinternet.com]	Gordon: Ellon	01358 725690 (Work) 07712 674614 (Mbl)
Anderson, Christopher	2008	14 Edmonstone Drive, Danderhall, Dalkeith EH22 1QQ	Newton and Loanhead	0131-663 0819
Archibald, Trish BD PGCE	2014	St Quivox Church, Dalmilling Road, Ayr KA8 0GP [E-mail: trishdalmilling@gmail.com]	North Ayr Family Development Worker	07508 992591 (Mbl)
Baker, Paula (Mrs)	2007	Kernow, 18 Main Street, Buckpool, Buckie AB56 1XQ [E-mail: paulabakerkernow@yahoo.co.uk]	Birnie and Pluscarden linked with Elgin: High: Parish Assistant	01542 832662
Boland, Susan (Mrs) DipHE (Theol)	2001	8 Menzies Drive, Balornock, Glasgow G21 3NB [E-mail: susan.reford@btopenworld.com]	Cumbernauld: Abronhill	0141-558 4945
Broere, Teresa (Mrs)	2014	3 Balnastraid Cottages, Dinnet, Aboyne AB34 5NE [E-mail: broere@btinternet.com]	Aberdeen: Mastrick	01339 880058
Bruce, Nicola (Mrs) BD MTh	2009	11 South Chesters Lane, Bonnyrigg EH19 3GL [E-mail: overhills@hotmail.com]	Lothian Presbytery: Tranent Cluster: Family and Youth Development Worker	0131-663 5252 07711 223100 (Mbl)
Bruce, Stuart	2009	1 Craighill Drive, Clarkston, Glasgow G76 7TG [E-mail: stuart.bruce7@ntl.world.com]	Glasgow: Govanhill Trinity: Parish Assistant	07850 039593 (Mbl)
Campbell, Alasdair BA	2000	3 Gellatly Road, Dunfermline KY11 4BH [E-mail: adcam@talktalk.net]	Forth Churches Group: Parish Assistant	01383 726238
Campbell, Neil MA	2010	36 Clovis Duveau Drive, Dundee DD2 5JB [E-mail: neilcampbell98@btinternet.com]	Dundee: Craigiebank with Douglas and Mid Craigie: Youth and Young Adult Development Worker	01382 561171 (Home) 01382 731173 (Work) 07999 349587 (Mbl)
Crossan, Morag BA	2010	1A Church Hill, Dalmellington, Ayr KA6 7QP [E-mail: morag.crossan@gmail.com]	Dalmellington with Patna Waterside: Youth and Children's Worker	01292 550984 07861 736071 (Mbl)
Crumlin, Melodie (Mrs) BA PGMgt DipBusMgt	2000	Abercromby Business Centre, Suite 2, 279 Abercromby Street, Glasgow G40 2DD [E-mail: projectmanager@peekproject.co.uk]	PEEK (Possibilities for Each and Every Kid): Project Development Manager	0141-558 2589 (Home) 0141-554 3968 (Work) 07904 672891 (Mbl)
Dale-Pimentil, Sheila (Mrs) MA BD	1999/2007	3 Golf Road, Lundin Links, Leven KY8 6BB [E-mail: sdale.pimentil@btinternet.com]	Kennoway, Windygates and Balgonie: St Kenneth's: Parish Assistant	01333 329618 (Home) 01333 351372 (Mbl)
Finch, John BA		231 Kirkintilloch Road, Bishopbriggs, Glasgow G64 2JB [E-mail: johnfinch75@hotmail.com]	Gorbals Parish Church: Community Development Worker	0141-429 0253 (Work) 07715 119263 (Mbl)
Gray, Ian	2011	The Mallards, 15 Rossie Island Road, Montrose DD10 9NH [E-mail: iancelia15@aol.com]	Esk Parish Grouping – Angus Presbytery: Pastoral Assistant	01674 677126 (Home) 07757 888233 (Mbl)
Gunn, Phil BSc	2014	Mannofield Parish Church, Great Western Road, Aberdeen AB10 6UZ	Aberdeen: Mannofield: Parish Assistant	01224 310087 07763 135618 (Mbl)

Guy, Helen J. (Miss)	2013	16/9 Craigend Park, Edinburgh EH16 5XX [E-mail: helenjguy@googlemail.com]	Edinburgh: The Tron Kirk	0131-664 3406 07923 177392 (Mbl)
Hardie, Petra BA	2014	98 Lincoln Avenue, Glasgow G13 3HS [E-mail: petra.drumchapel.standrews@gmail.com]	Glasgow: Drumchapel St Andrew's	0141-387 4870 (Mbl) 07776 074335 (Mbl)
Haringman, Paul MSc	2010	11 Tower Gardens, Westhill, Inverness IV2 5DQ [E-mail: paul.haringman@barnchurch.org.uk]	Inverness: Culloden: The Barn: Community Worker	01463 798946 (Home) 01463 795428 (Work) 07837 903277 (Mbl)
Harper, Kirsty (Mrs) BA	2009	Granton Parish Church, 55 Boswall Parkway, Edinburgh EH5 2BR [E-mail: kirsty@granton.org.uk]	Edinburgh: Granton	07974 425369 (Mbl)
Hunter, Jean (Mrs)	2006	Manse, Shiskine, Isle of Arran KA27 8EP [E-mail: j.hunter744@btinternet.com]	Brodick with Corrie with Lochranza: Parish Assistant	01770 860380
Hutchison, John BA	2014	30/4 West Pilton Gardens, Edinburgh EH4 4EG [E-mail: john@rothestrinity.org.uk]	Glenrothes: Rothes Trinity Parish Grouping	0131-258 5162 01592 366008 (Office) 01506 491498
Johnston, Ashley (Miss)	2014	4 Craigallan Park, Bo'ness EH51 9QY [E-mail: ajohnston10992@gmail.com]	Abercorn with Pardovan, Kingscavil and Winchburgh: Family Development Worker	07974 632112 (Mbl)
Johnstone, Christine	2009	25 Brockley View, Kilbirnie KA25 7HQ [E-mail: ceejae51@yahoo.co.uk]	East Kilbride: Claremont and South Parishes: Parish Assistant	
Keenan, Deborah	2009	St George's and St Peter's Church, 40 Boyndie Street, Easterhouse, Glasgow G34 9JE [E-mail: debbiedkeenan@gmail.com]	Glasgow: Easterhouse St George's and St Peter's	0141-771 8810 (Work) 07928 116142 (Mbl)
McEwen, Craig	2010	c/o Church Office, Dumfries Northwest Church, Lochside Road, Dumfries DG2 0DZ [E-mail: craigmcewen@dumfriesnorthwest.org.uk]	Dumfries: Northwest: Parish Assistant	01387 249964
McGreechin, Anne	2014	112 Longstone Road, Glasgow G33 3JY [E-mail: annemcgreechin@hotmail.com]	Cranhill, Ruchazie and Garthamlock and Craigend East Parish Grouping	
McIlreavy, Gillian (Mrs)		Church House, 796 Govan Road, Glasgow G51 2YL [E-mail: glpcglasgow@googlemail.com]	Glasgow: Govan and Linthouse	0141-445 2010 07811 332632 (Mbl)
McKay, Angus		35 East Campbell Street, Glasgow G1 5DT	Lodging House Mission	0141-552 0285
Mackenzie, Lynn		1990 Maryhill Road, Glasgow G20 0EF [E-mail: l.mackenzie@gmopbuzz.org]	Greater Maryhill Outreach Project	0141-946 3512
Montgomery, Rilza (Ms)	2009	71 Glendinning Crescent, Edinburgh EH16 6DN	Edinburgh: Muirhouse St Andrew's	0131-440 4442
Morrocco, Ellie	2014	Christ's Kirk, Pitcoudie Avenue, Glenrothes KY7 6SU [E-mail: elliemorrocco@gmail.com]	Edinburgh: Christ's Kirk and St Margaret's Churches, Glenrothes	07976 834977 (Mbl)
Moyo, Fabulous BTh MTh PhD	2014	St Quivox Church, Dalmilling Road, Ayr KA8 0GP [E-mail: fabmoyo@gmail.com]	North Ayr Family Development Worker	07508 992635 (Mbl)
Murphy, Lucy	2014	54 Duddingston View, Edinburgh EH15 3LZ [E-mail: ljmurphy@blueyonder.co.uk]	Edinburgh: Richmond Craigmillar	
Orr, Gillian BA	2009	'Zippity Do Da', Loch Alvie, Aviemore PH22 1QB [E-mail: gillianorr.cosyouth@googlemail.com]	Presbytery of Abernethy: Youth Worker	01479 811699 07969 457191 (Mbl)

Philip, Darren BSc	2009	Livingston United Parish Church, Nether Dechmont Community Centre, Fells Rigg, Livingston EH54 8AX [E-mail: darren@lepyouth.com]	Livingston Ecumenical Parish: Youth and Children's Worker	07861 455121 (Mbl)
Pryde, Erica	2014	46 Newbattle Abbey Crescent, Dalkeith EH22 3LN	Newbattle Parish Church	
Reynolds, Jessica (Mrs)	2009	12 Queen Street, Portnahaven, Isle of Islay PA47 7SJ [E-mail: jessica_reynolds@btinternet.com]	Youth and Children's Worker, Argyll	07445 491132 (Mbl)
Robertson, Douglas BEng BA(Th) MTh	2009	Robroyston Parish Church, 34 Saugh Drive, Glasgow G33 1HG [E-mail: dougie.robroyston@hotmail.co.uk]	Robroyston NCD: Church Development Worker	07825 397018 (Mbl)
Safrany, Zoltan (Rev.)		30 Thomson Road, Armadale, Bathgate EH48 3GJ [E-mail: safiref@gmail.com]	Bathgate: St John's: Parish Development Worker	07411 444743 (Mbl)
Smith, David	2003	66 Hendry Road, Kirkcaldy KY2 5DB [E-mail: dave-lpc@hotmail.com]	Dundee: Lochee	01382 612549 (Office) 07443 621237 (Mbl)
Stark, Alastair BA	2014	36 Norman View, Leuchars, St Andrews KY16 0ES [E-mail: alastair-stark@live.co.uk]	Glenrothes and Leslie: Youth and Children's Worker	01592 366009
Stark, Jennifer MA MATheol	2010	South Leith Parish Halls, 6 Henderson Street, Edinburgh EH6 6BS [E-mail: outreach@leithchurchestogether.org.uk]	Edinburgh: Leith Churches Outreach Project: Leader	0131-554 2578
Stewart, Peter	2009	5 Craigievar Crescent, Glasgow G33 5DN [E-mail: pete@clanstewart.co.uk]	Glasgow: Barlanark Greyfriars	07855 424633 (Mbl)
Stirling, Diane (Miss) BSc DipCPC BTh	2009	Douglas and Mid Craigie Church, Balbeggie Place, Dundee DD4 8RD [E-mail: parish.assistant@yahoo.co.uk]	Parish Assistant	01382 731173 07762 744606 (Mbl)
Taylor, Valerie AssocCIPD PgDip	2010	372 Victoria Road, Torry, Aberdeen AB11 9PA [E-mail: vtaylor.torrystfitticks@gmail.com]	Aberdeen: Torry St Fittick's: MDS	07723 778788 (Mbl)
Thomas, Jay MA BA	2009	1 Mahon Court, Moodiesburn, Glasgow G69 0QE [E-mail: jasonthomas21@hotmail.com]	Glasgow: St James' Pollok	07475 040886 (Mbl)
Wellstood, Keith PGDip MICG	2009	47 Carrington Terrace, Crieff PH7 4DZ [E-mail: keithw2011@btinternet.com]	Perth: Riverside: Community Worker	01764 655678 (Home) 01738 622341 (Office) 07963 766782 (Mbl)
Willis, Mags	2008	Chalmers-Ardler Church, Turnberry Avenue, Dundee DD2 3TP [E-mail: magswillis@hotmail.com]	Dundee: Chalmers-Ardler	01382 858283 07776 995146 (Mbl)
Young, Neil James	2001	31 Craigendmuir Street, Blackhill, Glasgow G33 1LG [E-mail: neil@stpaulsyouthforum.co.uk]	Glasgow: St Paul's: Youth Worker	0141-770 8559 07748 808488 (Mbl)

LIST L – OVERSEAS LOCATIONS

PRESBYTERY OF EUROPE

AMSTERDAM
The English Reformed Church, The Begijnhof (off the Spui). Service each Sunday at 10:30am.
[Website: www.ercadam.nl]

BERMUDA
Christ Church Warwick, Middle Road, Warwick. Sunday services: 8:00am and 11:00am.
[Website: www.christchurch.bm]

BRUSSELS
St Andrew's Church, Chaussée de Vleurgat 181 (off Ave. Louise). Service each Sunday at 11:00am.
[Website: www.churchofscotland.be]

BUDAPEST
St Columba's Scottish Mission, Vörösmarty utca 51, H-1064 Budapest.   (Church Tel) 0036 1 373 0725
Service in English and Sunday School each Sunday at 11:00am.   (Tel/Fax) 0036 1 460 0708
[Website: www.scotskirkhungary.com]

COLOMBO
St Andrew's Scots Kirk, 73 Galle Road, Colombo 3, Sri Lanka. Service each Sunday at 9:30am.
[Website: www.standrewsscotskirk.org]

COSTA DEL SOL
Services at Lux Mundi Ecumenical Centre, Calle Nueva 7, Fuengirola, Malaga.   (Tel) 0034 952 474840
Service each Sunday at 10:30am.
[Website: www.churchofscotlandcostadelsol.eu]

GENEVA
The Calvin Auditoire, Place de la Taconnerie (beside Cathedral of St Pierre). Service each Sunday at 11:00am.
[Website: www.churchofscotlandgeneva.com]

GIBRALTAR
St Andrew's Church, Governor's Parade. Service each Sunday at 10:30am.
[Website: www.scotskirkgibraltar.com]

LAUSANNE
26 Avenue de Rumine, CH-1005 Lausanne. Service each Sunday at 10:30am.
[Website: www.scotskirklausanne.ch]

LISBON
St Andrew's Church, Rua da Arriaga 13–15, Lisbon. Service each Sunday at 11:00am.
[Website: www.saintandrewslisbon.com]

MALTA
St Andrew's Church, 210 Old Bakery Street, Valletta. Service each Sunday at 10:30am.
[Website: www.saintandrewsmalta.com]

PARIS
The Scots Kirk, 17 Rue Bayard, F-75008 Paris (Metro: Roosevelt).
Service each Sunday at 11:00am.
[Website: www.scotskirkparis.com]

ROME
Via XX Settembre 7, 00187 Rome. Service each Sunday at 11:00am.
[Website: www.presbyterianchurchrome.org]

ROTTERDAM
The Scots Kirk, Schiedamsevest 121, Rotterdam. Service each Sunday at 10:30am.
Informal service at 9:15am.
[Website: www.scotsintchurch.com]

| TRINIDAD | Church of Scotland Greyfriars St Ann's, 50 Frederick Street, Port of Spain, Trinidad | (Tel) 001 868 627 9312 |

Associated with Presbytery

BOCHUM	English-speaking Christian congregation – ECC Bochum: Pauluskirche, Grabenstraße 9, D-44787 Bochum. Service each Sunday at 12:30pm. [Website: www.ecc-bochum.de]	
REGENSBURG	English-language congregation: Alumneum, Am Olberg 2, D-93047 Regensburg. Sunday service: second Sunday 10:30am; fourth Sunday 6:00pm. [Website: www.esg-regensburg.de]	
TURIN	English-speaking congregation of the Waldensian Church in co-operation with the Church of Scotland. Via Principe Tommaso 1, 10125 Torino. Service each Sunday at 10:30am. [Website: www.torinovaldese.org]	

AFRICA

MALAWI   **Church of Central Africa Presbyterian**

Synod of Blantyre

| Dr Ruth Shakespeare (2011) | Mulanje Mission Hospital, PO Box 45, Mulanje, Malawi [E-mail: shakespeareruth@gmail.com] | (Tel) 00265 9922 61569 (Fax) 00265 1 467 022 |

Synod of Livingstonia

| Miss Helen Scott (2000, held previous appointment) | CCAP Girls' Secondary School, PO Box 2, Ekwendeni, Malawi [E-mail: helenms1960@yahoo.co.uk] | (Tel) 00265 1929 1932 |

Synod of Nkhoma

| Dr David Morton (2009) | Nkhoma Hospital, PO Box 48, Nkhoma, Malawi [E-mail: kuluva2@gmail.com] | (Tel) 00265 9940 74022 |
| Mr Rob Jones (2010) | Nkhoma Hospital, PO Box 48, Nkhoma, Malawi [E-mail: robert@thejonesfamily.org.uk] | (Tel) 00265 998 951500 |

ZAMBIA   **United Church of Zambia**

Mr Keith and Mrs Ida Waddell (Ecum) (2008)	Mwandi UCZ Mission, PO Box 60693, Livingstonia, Zambia [E-mail: keithida2014@gmail.com]	(Tel) 00260 977 328 767
Ms Jenny Featherstone (Ecum) (2007)	c/o Chodort Training Centre, PO Box 630451, Choma, Zambia [E-mail: jenny.featherstone@googlemail.com]	(Tel) 00260 979 703 130
Mr Glen Lund (2010)	UCZ Theological College, PO Box 20429, Kitwe, Zambia [E-mail: redhair.community@googlemail.com]	(Tel) 00260 978 363 400

ASIA

BANGLADESH

Church of Bangladesh (Ecum) (2010)
Miss Pat Jamieson (Ecum) (2010)
Flat 5N, Quamroon Noor Apartments, 9/1 Sir Sayed Ahmed Road, Block A Mohammadpur, Dhaka 1207, Bangladesh
[E-mail: patjamieson30@gmail.com]

NEPAL

Mr Joel Githinji (2010)
c/o United Mission to Nepal, PO Box 126, Kathmandu, Nepal
(Tel: 00 977 1 4228 118)
[E-mail: joelkavari2003@gmail.com]

Rev. Malcolm and Mrs Cati Ramsay (Ecum) (2011)
c/o United Mission to Nepal, PO Box 126, Kathmandu, Nepal
(Tel: 00 977 1 4228 118)
[E-mail: amalcolmramsay@gmail.com]

MIDDLE EAST

ISRAEL AND OCCUPIED PALESTINIAN TERRITORY

[NOTE: Church Services are held in St Andrew's Scots Memorial Church, Jerusalem, each Sunday at 10:00am, and at St Andrew's, Galilee each Sunday at 6:00pm]

Jerusalem
Rev. Parraic and Mrs Vivien Reamonn (2014)
St Andrew's, Jerusalem, 1 David Remez Street, PO Box 8619, Jerusalem 91086, Israel
(Tel: 00 972 2 673 2401; Fax: 00 972 2 673 1711)
[E-mail: stachjer@netvision.net.il]

Mr Kenny and Mrs Alison Roger (2013)
St Andrew's, Jerusalem, 1 David Remez Street, PO Box 8619, Jerusalem 91086, Israel
(Tel: 00 972 2 673 2401; Fax: 00 972 2 673 1711; Mobile: 00 972 50 542 2262)
[E-mail: kroger@cofscotland.org.uk]
[Website: www.scotsguesthouse.com]

Tiberias
Rev. Colin D. Johnston (2009)
St Andrew's, Galilee, 1 Gdud Barak Street, PO Box 104, Tiberias 14100, Israel
(Tel: 00 972 4 671 0759; Fax: 00 972 4 672 5282)
[E-mail: revcdj60@gmail.com]
[Website: www.scotshotels.co.il]

Jaffa
Mr Anthony and Mrs Darya Short (2006)
Tabeetha School, 21 Yefet Street, PO Box 8170, Jaffa 61081, Israel
(Tel: 00 972 3 682 1581; Fax: 00 972 3 681 9357; Mobile: 00 972 54 757 2104)
[E-mail: principal@tabeethaschool.org]
[Website: www.tabeethaschool.org]

LIST M – OVERSEAS RESIGNED AND RETIRED MISSION PARTNERS (ten or more years' service)

NAME	APP	RET	AREA	ADDRESS
Anderson, Karen (Mrs)	1992	2006	Israel	23 Allanpark Street, Largs KA30 9AG
Anderson, Kathleen (Mrs)	1955	1968	Pakistan	37 Bowling Green Court, Brook Street, Chester CH1 3DP
Archibald, Mary L. (Miss)	1964	1982	Nigeria/Ghana	490 Low Main Street, Wishaw ML2 7PL
Baxter, Mrs Ray	1954	1969	Malawi	91/17 Morningside Road, Edinburgh EH10 4AY
Berkeley, Dr John	1967	1977	Bhutan	Drumbeg, Coylumbridge, Aviemore PH22 1QU
and Dr Muriel	1995	1998	Yemen	
Bone, Mr David and Mrs Isobel	1977	1988	Malawi	315 Blackness Road, Dundee DD2 1SH
Boyle, Lexa (Miss)	1959	1992	Aden/Yemen/Sudan	7 Maxwell Grove, Glasgow G41 5JP
Brodie, Rev. Jim	1955	1974	North India	25A Keptie Road, Arbroath DD11 3ED
	1996	1998	Nepal	
Brown, Janet H. (Miss)	1967	1980	Pakistan	6 Baxter Park Terrace, Dundee DD4 6NL
Burnett, Dr Fiona	1988	1998	Zambia	The Glenholm Centre, Broughton, Biggar ML12 6JF
Burnett, Dr Robin	1964	1967	Nigeria	79 Bank Street, Irvine KA12 0LL
and Mrs Storm	1968	1977	South Africa	
Byers, Rev. Mairi	1960	1971	Ghana	Meadowbank, Plumdon Road, Annan DG12 6SJ
Coltart, Rev. Ian O.	1967	1985	North India	25 Bothwell Gardens, Dunbar EH42 1PZ
Conacher, Marion (Miss)	1963	1993	India	41 Magdalene Drive, Edinburgh EH15 3BG
Cooper, Rev. George	1966	1986	Kenya	8 Leighton Square, Alyth, Blairgowrie PH11 8AQ
Crosbie, Ann R. (Miss)	1955	1967	Nigeria	Flat 3-11, 40 Shawholm Crescent, Glasgow G43 1NZ
Dawson, Miss Anne	1976	2000	Malawi	31 Colville Gardens, Alloa FK10 1DU
Dodman, Rev. Roy				
and Mrs Jane	1983	2006	Jamaica	8 Malthouse Drive, Belper, Derbyshire DE56 1RU
Drever, Dr Bryan	1962	1982	Aden/Yemen/Pakistan	188 Addison Road, King's Head, Birmingham
Duncan, Mr David				
and Mrs Allison	1952	1969	Nigeria	7 Newhailes Avenue, Musselburgh EH21 6DW
Duncan, Rev. Graham	1977	1987	South Africa	56 Daphne Road, Maroelana, 0081 Pretoria, South Africa
and Mrs Sandra	1998	2006		
Dunlop, Mr Walter T.				
and Mrs Jennifer	1979	1994	Malawi/Israel	50 Oxgangs Road, Edinburgh EH13 9DR
Fauchelle, Mrs Margaret	1991	1999	Zambia, Malawi, Zimbabwe	Flat 3, 22 North Avenue, Devonport, Auckland 1309, New Zealand
Ferguson, Mr John K.P.	1977	1989	Pakistan	15 Ashgrove, Craigshill, Livingston EH54 5IQ
Finlay, Carol (Ms)	1990	2001	Malawi	96 Broomfield Crescent, Edinburgh EH12 7LX
Fischbacher, Dr Colin M.				
and Mrs Sally	1986	1998	Malawi	11 Barclay Square, Gosforth, Newcastle-upon-Tyne NE3 2JB
Foster, Joyce (Miss) BSc	1968	1972	Kenya	99 Sixth Street, Newtongrange EH22 4LA
	1972	1981	Malawi	
Fowler, Rev. Margaret	1988	2007	Jamaica	PO Box 3097, Negril, Westmorland, Jamaica

Gaston, Dr Andrew and Mrs Felicity	1997	2008	Malawi	25 Kimberley Drive, Crown Hill, Plymouth, Devon PL6 5WA
Irvine, Mr Clive and Mrs Su	1984	1999	Nepal	McGregor Flat, 92 Blackford Avenue, Edinburgh EH9 3ES
Karam, Ishbel (Mrs)	1968	1985	Pakistan	Hillsgarth, Baltasound, Unst, Shetland ZE2 9DY
King, Mrs Betty	1955	1971	North India	23 Main Street, Newstead, Melrose TD6 9DX
Knowles, Dr John K. and Mrs Heather	1976	1992	Malawi	Trollopes Hill, Monton Combe, Bath BA2 7HX
Laidlay, Mrs Una	1961	1968	Yemen	Isles View, 5 Bell's Road, Lerwick, Shetland ZE1 0QB
	1968	1971	Pakistan	
	1971	1978	Yemen	
Liddell, Margaret (Miss)	1964	1980	Zambia	20 Wyvis Crescent, Conon Bridge, Dingwall IV7 8BZ
Logie, Robina (Mrs)	1950	1960	North India	23 Stonefield Drive, Inverurie AB51 9DZ
McCulloch, Lesley (Mrs)	1982	1992	Malawi/Pakistan	824 Caroline Street, Port Angeles, WA 98362-3504, USA
McCutcheon, Agnes W.F. (Miss)	1957	1989	India	10A Hugh Murray Grove, Cambuslang, Glasgow G72 7NG
MacDonald, Dr Alistair and Mrs Freda	1949	1962	Nigeria	10 Millside, Morpeth, Northumberland NE61 1PN
McGoff, A.W. (Miss)	1954	1974	Kolhapur	6 Mossvale Walk, Craigend, Glasgow G33 5PF
MacGregor, Rev. Margaret S.	1959	1994	India	16 Learmonth Court, Edinburgh EH4 1PB
McKenzie, Rev. William M.	1958	1974	Zambia	41 Kingholm Road, Dumfries DG1 4SR
MacKinnon, Emma L. (Miss)	1952	1972	Nigeria	142 Glencairn Street, Stevenston KA20 3BU
McMahon, Mrs Jessie	1959	1976	North India	7 Ridgepark Drive, Lanark ML11 7PG
Malley, Beryl Stevenson (Miss)	1982	1992	Malawi	272/2 Craigcrook Road, Edinburgh EH4 7TF
Millar, Mrs Margaret R.M.	1967	1996	Malawi/Zambia	Fearnoch Cottage, Fearnoch, Taynuilt PA35 1JB
Millar, Rev. Peter W.	1976	1989	South India	6/5 Ettrickdale Place, Edinburgh EH3 5JN
Moir, Rev. Ian A. and Mrs Elsie	1962	1973	South Africa	28/6 Comely Bank Avenue, Edinburgh EH4 1EL
Morrice, Mrs Margaret	1971	1998	Buenos Aires/Kenya	104 Baron's Hill Avenue, Linlithgow EH49 7JG
Morton, Rev. Alasdair J. and Mrs Gillian M.	1960	1973	Zambia	16 St Leonard's Road, Forres IV36 1DW
Munro, Harriet (Miss)	1959	1969	Malawi	26 The Forge, Braidpark Drive, Glasgow G46 6LB
Murray, Rev. Douglas R. and Mrs Sheila	1994	2004	Switzerland	32 Forth Park, Bridge of Allan, Stirling FK9 5NT
Murray, Mr Ian and Mrs Isabel	1962	2000	Pakistan	17 Piershill Terrace, Edinburgh EH8 7EY
Musgrave, Mrs Joan	1966	1980	Zambia	4 Ravelston Heights, Edinburgh EH4 3LX
	2000	2006	Jerusalem	
Musk, Mrs Lily	1959	1959	Malawi	1 Tulloch Place, St Andrews KY16 8XJ
	1959	1974	Zambia	
Nelson, Mrs Anne	1947	1952	Pakistan	7 Manse Road, Roslin EH25 9LF
	1952	1959	North India	
	1970	1973	North India	
Nicholson, Rev. Thomas S.	1981	1995	Taiwan	The Manse, Todholes, Greenlaw, Duns TD10 6XD
Nicol, Catherine (Miss)	1960	2000	Pakistan	St Columba Christian Girls' RTC, Barah Patthar, Sialkot 2, Pakistan
Nutter, Margaret (Miss)	1966	1979	Pakistan	Kilmorich, 14 Balloch Road, Balloch, Alexandria G83 8SR
Pacitti, Rev. Stephen A.	1977	1996	Taiwan	157 Nithsdale Road, Glasgow G41 5RD

Pattison, Rev. Kenneth J. and Mrs Susan	1966	Malawi	2 Castle Way, St Madoes, Glencarse, Perth PH2 7NY	
Philip, Mrs Margaret	1951	Nigeria	Penlan, Holm Farm Road, Catrine, Mauchline KA5 6TA	
Philpot, Rev. David	1981	WCC Geneva	2/27 Pentland Drive, Edinburgh EH10 6PX	
Reid, Dr Ann	1988	Ghana	36 Kingshill Court, Standish, Wigan WN6 0AR	
Reid, Margaret I. (Miss)	1982	Malawi	3/1 Coxfield Lane, Edinburgh EH11 2RF	
Ritchie, Ishbel M. (Miss)	1964	Eastern Himalaya	8 Ross Street, Dunfermline KY12 0AN	
Ritchie, Rev. James M.	1955	Yemen	Flat 2/25, Croft-an-Rìgh, Edinburgh EH8 8EG	
Ritchie, Mary Scott (Miss)	1977	Malawi/Zambia/Israel	Afton Villa, 1 Afton Bridgend, New Cumnock KA18 4AX	
Ross, Rev. Prof. Kenneth R. and Mrs Hester	1968 1988	Malawi	The Manse, Kilmelford, Oban PA34 4XA	
Rough, Mary E. (Miss)	1966	Blantyre	6 Glebe Street, Dumfries DG1 2LF	
Roy, Rev. Alan J.	1960	Zambia	14 Comerton Place, Drumoig, Leuchars, St Andrews KY16 0NQ	
Russell, M.M. (Miss)	1946	Nigeria	14 Hozier Street, Carluke ML8 5DW	
Samuel, Lynda (Mrs)	1974	Madras	28 Braehead, Methven Walk, Dundee DD2 3FJ [E-mail: rasam42@onetel.com]	
Shepherd, Dr Clyne	1956	Nigeria	10 Kingsknowe Road South, Edinburgh EH14 2JE	
Smith, Mr Harry and Mrs Margaret	1959	Nigeria	31 Woodville Crescent, Sunderland SR4 8RE	
Sneddon, Mr Sandy and Mrs Marie	1968	Malawi		
Steedman, Martha (Mrs) (née Hamilton)	1986	Pakistan	84 Greenend Gardens, Edinburgh EH17 7QH	
Stewart, Marion G. (Miss)	1955	North India	Muir of Blebo, Blebo Craigs, Cupar KY15 5TZ	
Stone, Rev. W.V. MA BD	1976	Malawi/Israel	Kirk Cottage, Kirkton of Skene, Westhill, Skene AB32 6XX	
Tennant, Frances (Miss)	1949	Zambia	36 Woodrow Court, Port Glasgow Road, Kilmacolm PA13 4QA	
Wallace, A. Dorothy (Miss)	1965	Pakistan	101 St John's Road, Edinburgh EH12 6NN	
Walker, Rev. Donald K. and Mrs Judith	1953	North India	Amberley, Mill Lane, Nethy Bridge PH25 3DR	
Westmarland, Rev. Colin A.	1981	Zambia	The Manse, Deshar Road, Boat of Garten PH24 3BN	
Wilkie, Rev. James L.	1975	Malta	PO Box 5, Cospicua, CSPO1, Malta	
Wilkinson, Dr Alison	1959	Zambia	7 Comely Bank Avenue, Edinburgh EH4 1EW	
Wilkinson, Rev. John	1992	Kenya	5 Birch Avenue, Stirling FK8 2PL	
Wilson, Irene (Ms)	1946	Kenya	70 Craigleith Hill Gardens, Edinburgh EH4 2JH	
Wilson, Rev. Mark	1993 1953	Israel Nagpur	37 Kings Avenue, Longniddry EH32 0QN	

LIST N – READERS

1. EDINBURGH

Brown, Ivan   4 St Cuthberts Court, Edinburgh EH13 0LG   0131-441 1245
[E-mail: j.ivanb@btinternet.com]   (Mbl) 07730 702860

Christie, Gillian L. (Mrs)
32 Allan Park Road, Edinburgh EH14 1LJ
[E-mail: mrsglchristie@aol.com]
0131-443 4472
(Mbl) 07914 883354

Davies, Ruth (Ms) (attached to Liberton)
4 Hawkhead Grove, Edinburgh EH16 6LS
[E-mail: ruth@mdavies.me.uk]
0131-664 3608

Farrant, Yvonne (Ms)
Flat 7, 14 Duddingston Mills, Edinburgh EH8 7NF
[E-mail: yvonne.farrant@crossreach.org.uk]
0131-661 0672
(Mbl) 07747 766405

Farrell, William J.
50 Ulster Crescent, Edinburgh EH8 7JS
[E-mail: w.farrell154@btinternet.com]
0131-661 1026

Farrow, Edmund
14 Brunswick Terrace, Edinburgh EH7 5PG
[E-mail: edmundfarrow@blueyonder.co.uk]
0131-558 8210

Johnston, Alan
8/19 Constitution Street, Edinburgh EH6 7BT
[E-mail: alanacj@cairnassoc.wanadoo.co.uk]
0131-554 1326
(Mbl) 07901 510819

Kerrigan, Herbert A. (Prof.) MA LLB QC
Airdene, 20 Edinburgh Road, Dalkeith EH22 1JY
[E-mail: kerrigan@kerriganqc.com]
0131-660 3007
(Mbl) 07725 953772

McKenzie, Janet (Mrs)
80C Colinton Road, Edinburgh EH14 1DD
[E-mail: jintymck@talktalk.net]
0131-444 2054

McPherson, Alistair
77 Bonaly Wester, Edinburgh EH13 0RQ
[E-mail: amjhmcpherson@blueyonder.co.uk]
0131-478 5384

Pearce, Martin
4 Corbiehill Avenue, Edinburgh EH4 5DR
[E-mail: martin.j.pearce@blueyonder.co.uk]
0131-336 4864
(Mbl) 07801 717222

Sherriffs, Irene (Mrs)
22/2 West Mill Bank, Edinburgh EH13 0QT
[E-mail: reenie.sherriffs@blueyonder.co.uk]
0131-466 9530

Tew, Helen (Mrs)
318 Lanark Road, Edinburgh EH14 2LJ
[E-mail: helentew9@gmail.com]
0131-478 1268
(Mbl) 07986 170802

Wyllie, Anne (Miss)
2F3, 46 Jordan Lane, Edinburgh EH10 4QX
[E-mail: anne.wyllie@tiscali.co.uk]
0131-447 9035

2. WEST LOTHIAN

Coyle, Charlotte (Mrs)
28 The Avenue, Whitburn EH47 0DA
[E-mail: paulcharlotte@talktalk.net]
01501 740687

Elliott, Sarah (Miss)
105 Seafield Rows, Seafield, Bathgate EH47 7AW
[E-mail: sarah.elliott6@btopenworld.com]
01506 654950

Galloway, Brenda (Dr)
Lochend, 58 St Ninians Road, Linlithgow EH49 7BN
[E-mail: bhgallo@yahoo.com]
01506 842028

Middleton, Alex
36 Fivestanks Place, Broxburn EH52 6BJ
[E-mail: alex.middleton@btinternet.com]
01506 852645

Paxton, James
5 Main Street, Longridge, Bathgate EH47 8AE
[E-mail: jim_paxton@btinternet.com]
01501 772192

Salmon, Jeanie (Mrs)
81 Croftfoot Drive, Fauldhouse, Bathgate EH47 9EH
[E-mail: jeaniesalmon@aol.com]
01501 772468
(Work) 01501 828509

Scoular, Iain W.
15 Bonnyside Road, Bonnybridge FK4 2AD
[E-mail: iain@iwsconsultants.com]
01324 812395
(Mbl) 07717 131596

Wilkie, David — 53 Goschen Place, Broxburn EH52 5JH
[E-mail: david-fmu_09@tiscali.co.uk] — 01506 854777

3. LOTHIAN

Evans, W. John IEng MIIE(Elec) — Waterlily Cottage, 10 Fenton Steading, North Berwick EH39 5AF
[E-mail: jevans7is@hotmail.com] — 01620 842990

Hogg, David MA — 82 Eskhill, Penicuik EH26 8DQ
[E-mail: hogg-d2@sky.com] — 01968 676350 / (Mbl) 07821 693946

Millan, Mary (Mrs) — 33 Polton Vale, Loanhead EH20 9DF
[E-mail: marymillan@fsmail.net] — 0131-440 1624 / (Mbl) 07814 466104

Trevor, A. Hugh MA MTh — 29A Fidra Road, North Berwick EH39 4NE
[E-mail: htrevor@talktalk.net] — 01620 894924

Yeoman, Edward T.N. FSAScot — 75 Newhailes Crescent, Musselburgh EH21 6EF
[E-mail: edwardyeoman6@aol.com] — 0131-653 2291 / (Mbl) 07896 517666

4. MELROSE AND PEEBLES

Cashman, Margaret D. (Mrs) — 38 Abbotsford Road, Galashiels TD1 3HR
[E-mail: mcashman@tiscali.co.uk] — 01896 752711

Henderson-Howatt, David — Stoneyknowe, West Linton EH46 7BY
[E-mail: stoneyknowe@aol.com] — 01968 660677

Selkirk, Frances (Mrs) — 2 The Glebe, Ashkirk, Selkirk TD7 4PJ
[E-mail: f.selkirk@btinternet.com] — 01750 32204

5. DUNS

Landale, Alison (Mrs) — Green Hope Guest House, Ellemford, Duns TD11 3SG
[E-mail: alison@greenhope.co.uk] — 01361 890242

Taylor, Christine (Mrs) — Rowardennan, Main Street, Gavinton, Duns TD11 3QT
[E-mail: christine2751@btinternet.com] — 01361 882994

6. JEDBURGH

Findlay, Elizabeth (Mrs) — 10 Inch Park, Kelso TD5 7EQ
[E-mail: elizabeth@findlay8124.fsworld.co.uk] — 01573 226641

Knox, Dagmar (Mrs) — 3 Stichill Road, Ednam, Kelso TD5 7QQ
[E-mail: dagmar.knox.riding@btinternet.com] — 01573 224883

7. ANNANDALE AND ESKDALE

Boncey, David — Redbrae, Beattock, Moffat DG10 9RF
[E-mail: david.boncey613@btinternet.com] — 01683 300613

Brown, Martin J. — Lochhouse Farm, Beattock, Moffat DG10 9SG
[E-mail: martin@lochhousefarm.com] — 01683 300451

Brown, S. Jeffrey BA — Skara Brae, 8 Ballplay Road, Moffat DG10 9JU
[E-mail: sjbrown@btinternet.com] — 01683 220475

Chisholm, Dennis A.G. MA BSc — Moss-side, Hightae, Lockerbie DG11 1JR
[E-mail: dchis@talktalk.net] — 01387 811803

Dodds, Alan — Trinco, Battlehill, Annan DG12 6SN
[E-mail: alanandjen46@talktalk.net] — 01461 201235

Jackson, Susan (Mrs) — 48 Springbells Road, Annan DG12 6LQ
[E-mail: peter-jackson24@sky.com] — 01461 204159

Morton, Andrew A. BSc — 19 Sherwood Park, Lockerbie DG11 2DX
[E-mail: andrew.a.morton@btinternet.com]
[E-mail: andrew_morton@mac.com] — 01576 203164

Saville, Hilda A. (Mrs) — 32 Crosslaw Burn, Moffat DG10 9LP
[E-mail: saville.c@sky.com] — 01683 222854

8. DUMFRIES AND KIRKCUDBRIGHT

Carroll, J. Scott — 17 Downs Place, Heathhall, Dumfries DG1 3RF
[E-mail: scott.carroll@btinternet.com] — 01387 265350

Corson, Gwen (Mrs) — 7 Sunnybrae, Borgue, Kirkcudbright DG6 4SJ — 01557 870328

Ogilvie, D. Wilson MA FSAScot — Lingerwood, 2 Nelson Street, Dumfries DG2 9AY — 01387 264267

Paterson, Ronald M. (Dr) — Mirkwood, Ringford, Castle Douglas DG7 2AL
[E-mail: mirkwoodtyke@aol.com] — 01557 820202

9. WIGTOWN AND STRANRAER

McQuistan, Robert — Old Schoolhouse, Carsluith, Newton Stewart DG8 7DT
[E-mail: mcquistan@mcquistan.plus.com] — 01671 820327

Williams, Roy — 120 Belmont Road, Stranraer DG9 7BG
[E-mail: roywilliams84@hotmail.com] — 01776 705762

10. AYR

Anderson, James (Dr)
BVMS PhD DVM FRCPath FIBiol MRCVS — 67 Henrietta Street, Girvan KA26 9AN
[E-mail: jc.anderson@tesco.net] — 01465 710059 (Mbl) 07952 512720

Gowans, James — 2 Cochrane Avenue, Dundonald, Kilmarnock KA2 9EJ
[E-mail: jim@luker42.freeserve.co.uk] — 01563 850904 (Mbl) 07985 916814

Jamieson, Ian A. — 2 Whinfield Avenue, Prestwick KA9 2BH
[E-mail: ian@jamieson4189.freeserve.co.uk] — 01242 476898

Morrison, James — 27 Monkton Road, Prestwick KA9 1AP
[E-mail: jim.morrison@talktalk.net] — 01292 479313 (Mbl) 07773 287852

Murphy, Ian — 56 Lamont Crescent, Netherthird, Cumnock KA18 3DU
[E-mail: ianm_cumnock@yahoo.co.uk] — 01290 423675

Riome, Elizabeth (Mrs) — Monkwood Mains, Minishant, Maybole KA19 8EY
[E-mail: aj.riome@btinternet.com] — 01292 443440

11. IRVINE AND KILMARNOCK

Bircham, James F.
8 Holmlea Place, Kilmarnock KA1 1UU — 01563 532287

Cooper, Fraser
5 Balgray Way, Irvine KA11 1RP — 01294 211235
[E-mail: frasercooper@wightcablenorth.net]

Crosbie, Shona (Mrs)
4 Campbell Street, Darvel KA17 0DA — 01560 322229
[E-mail: fawltytowersdarvel@yahoo.co.uk]

Dempster, Ann (Mrs)
20 Graham Place, Kilmarnock KA3 7JN — 01563 529361
[E-mail: ademp99320@aol.com] (Work) 01563 534080 (Mbl) 07729 152945

Gillespie, Janice (Miss)
12 Jeffrey Street, Kilmarnock KA1 4EB — 01563 540009
[E-mail: janice.gillespie@tiscali.co.uk]

Hamilton, Margaret A. (Mrs)
59 South Hamilton Street, Kilmarnock KA1 2DT — 01563 534431
[E-mail: tomhnltn@sky.com]

Jamieson, John H. BSc DEP AFBPSS
22 Moorfield Avenue, Kilmarnock KA1 1TS — 01563 534065
[E-mail: johnhjamieson@tiscali.co.uk]

McGeever, Gerard
23 Kinloch Avenue, Stewarton, Kilmarnock KA3 3HQ — 01560 484331
[E-mail: gerard@gmcgeever.freeserve.co.uk] (Work) 0141-847 5717

MacLean, Donald
1 Four Acres Drive, Kilmaurs, Kilmarnock KA3 2ND — 01563 538475
[E-mail: donanmac@yahoo.co.uk]

Mills, Catherine (Mrs)
59 Crossdene Road, Crosshouse, Kilmarnock KA2 0JU — 01563 535305
[E-mail: cfmills5lib@hotmail.com]

Raleigh, Gavin
21 Landsborough Drive, Kilmarnock KA3 1RY — 01563 539377
[E-mail: gavin.raleigh@lineone.net]

Robertson, William
1 Archers Avenue, Irvine KA11 2GB — 01294 203577
[E-mail: willie.robert@yahoo.co.uk]

Whitelaw, David
9 Kirkhill, Kilwinning KA13 6NB — 01294 551695
[E-mail: whitelawfam@talktalk.net]

12. ARDROSSAN

Barclay, Elizabeth (Mrs)
2 Jacks Road, Saltcoats KA21 5NT — 01294 471855
[E-mail: mfiz98@dsl.pipex.com]

Clarke, Elizabeth (Mrs)
Swallowbrae, Torbeg, Isle of Arran KA27 8HE — 01770 860219
[E-mail: lizahclarke@gmail.com] (Mbl) 07780 574367

Currie, Archie BD
55 Central Avenue, Kilbirnie KA25 6JP — 01505 681474
[E-mail: archiecurrie@yahoo.co.uk] (Mbl) 07881 452115

Hunter, Jean C.Q. (Mrs) BD
Church of Scotland Manse, Shiskine, Isle of Arran KA27 3EP — 01770 860380
[E-mail: j.hunter744@btinternet.com]

McCool, Robert
17 McGregor Avenue, Stevenston KA20 4BA — 01294 466548

Mackay, Brenda H. (Mrs)
19 Eglinton Square, Ardrossan KA22 8LN — 01294 464491
[E-mail: bremac82@aol.com]

Macleod, Sharon (Mrs)
Creag Dhubh, Golf Course Road, Whiting Bay, Isle of Arran KA27 8QT — 01770 700353
[E-mail: macleodsharon@hotmail.com]

Nimmo, Margaret (Mrs)
12 Muirfield Place, Kilwinning KA13 6NL
[E-mail: margtmcmn@aol.com]
01294 553718

Ross, Magnus BA MEd
39 Beachway, Largs KA30 8QH
[E-mail: m.b.ross@btinternet.com]
(Work) 01292 220336
01475 689572

Smith, Nicola (Mrs)
5 Kames Street, Millport, Isle of Cumbrae KA28 0BN
[E-mail: nsasmith@fsmail.net]
01475 530747

13. LANARK

Grant, Alan
25 Moss-side Avenue, Carluke ML8 5UG
[E-mail: amgran25@aol.com]
01555 771419

Love, William
30 Barmore Avenue, Carluke ML8 4PE
[E-mail: janbill30@tiscali.co.uk]
01555 751243

14. GREENOCK AND PAISLEY

Allan, Douglas

Banks, Russell
18 Aboyne Drive, Paisley PA2 7SJ
[E-mail: margaret.banks2@ntlworld.com]
0141-884 6925

Bird, Mary Jane

Boag, Jennifer (Miss)
11 Madeira Street, Greenock PA16 7UJ
[E-mail: jenniferboag@hotmail.com]
01475 720125

Campbell, Tom BA DipCPC
3 Grahamston Place, Paisley PA2 7BY
[E-mail: tomcam38@googlemail.com]
0141-840 2273

Davey, Charles L.
16 Divert Road, Gourock PA19 1DT
[E-mail: charles.davey@talktalk.net]
01475 631544

Glenny, John C.
49 Cloch Road, Gourock PA19 1AT
[E-mail: jacklizg@aol.com]
01475 636415

Hood, Eleanor (Mrs)
12 Clochoderick Avenue, Kilbarchan, Johnstone PA10 2AY
[E-mail: eleanor.hood.kilbarchan@ntlworld.com]
01505 704208

MacDonald, Christine (Ms)
33 Collier Street, Johnstone PA5 8AG
[E-mail: christine.macdonald10@ntlworld.com]
01505 355779

McFarlan, Elizabeth (Miss)
20 Fauldswood Crescent, Paisley PA2 9PA
[E-mail: elizabeth.mcfarlan@ntlworld.com]
01505 358411

McHugh, Jack
'Earlshaugh', Earl Place, Bridge of Weir PA11 3HA
[E-mail: jackmchugh@tiscali.co.uk]
01505 612789

Marshall, Leon M.
'Glenisla', Gryffe Road, Kilmacolm PA13 4BA
[E-mail: lm@stevenson-kyles.co.uk]
01505 872417

Maxwell, Sandra A. (Mrs) BD
2 Grants Avenue, Paisley PA2 6AZ
[E-mail: sandra1.maxwell@virgin.net]
0141-884 3710

Munro, Irene (Mrs)
80 Bardrainney Avenue, Port Glasgow PA14 6HA
[E-mail: irenemunro906@hotmail.com]
01475 701213

Orry, Geoff
'Rhu Ellan', 4 Seaforth Crescent, Barrhead, Glasgow G78 1PL
[E-mail: geoff.orry@googlemail.com]
0141-881 9748

16. GLASGOW

Birchall, Edwin — Greenhill Lodge, 1 Old Humbie Road, Glasgow G77 5DF — 0141-639 1742

Bremner, David — [E-mail: david.bremner@tiscali.co.uk]

Campbell, Jack T. BD BEd — 40 Kenmure Avenue, Bishopbriggs, Glasgow G64 2DE — 0141-563 5837
[E-mail: jack.campbell@ntlworld.com]

Dickson, Hector M.K. — 'Gwito', 61 Whitton Drive, Giffnock, Glasgow G46 6EF — 0141-637 0080
[E-mail: hectordickson@hotmail.com]

Fullarton, Andrew — 8 Erskine Street, Stirling FK7 0QN — 0141-883 9518

Grant, George — [E-mail: georgegrant@gmail.com] (Mbl) 01786 609594 / 07921 168057

Grieve, Leslie — 23 Hertford Avenue, Glasgow G12 0LG — 0141-576 1376
[E-mail: leslie.grieve@gmail.com]

Horner, David J. — 20 Ledi Road, Glasgow G43 2AJ — 0141-637 7369
[E-mail: djhorner@btinternet.com]

Hunt, Roland BSc PhD CertEd — 4 Flora Gardens, Bishopbriggs, Glasgow G64 1DS — 0141-563 3257
[E-mail: roland.hunt@ntlworld.com] (Evenings and weekends) 0141-563 3257

Joansson, Tordur — 1/2, 18 Eglinton Court, Glasgow G5 9NE — 0141-429 6733
[E-mail: to4jo@yahoo.co.uk]

Kilpatrick, Mrs Joan — 39 Brent Road, Regent's Park, Glasgow G46 8JG — 0141-621 1809
[E-mail: je-kilpatrick@sky.com]

McChlery, Stuart — The Manse, Cheapside Street, Eaglesham, Glasgow G76 0NS — 01355 303495
[E-mail: s.mcchlery@gcu.ac.uk]

McColl, John — 2FL, 53 Aberfoyle Street, Glasgow G31 3RP — 0141-554 9881
[E-mail: solfolly11@gmail.com] (Mbl) 07757 303195

McFarlane, Robert — 25 Avenel Road, Glasgow G13 2PB — 0141-954 5540
[E-mail: robertmcfrln@yahoo.co.uk]

McInally, Gordon — 10 Melville Gardens, Bishopbriggs, Glasgow G64 3DF — 0141-563 2685
[E-mail: gmcinally@sky.com]

Mackenzie, Norman — Flat 3/2, 41 Kilmailing Road, Glasgow G44 5UH — 07780 733710
[E-mail: mackenzie799@btinternet.com] (Mbl)

MacLeod, John — 2 Shuna Place, Newton Mearns, Glasgow G77 6TN — 0141-639 6862
[E-mail: jmacleod2@sky.com]

Millar, Kathleen (Mrs) — 9 Glenbank Court, Thornliebank, Glasgow G46 7EJ — 0141-638 6250
[E-mail: kathleen.millar@tesco.net] (Mbl) 07793 203045

Montgomery, Hamish — 13 Avon Avenue, Bearsden, Glasgow G61 2PS — 0141-942 3640

Nairne, Elizabeth — 229 Southbrae Drive, Glasgow G13 1TT — 0141-959 5066

Nicolson, John — 2 Lindsaybeg Court, Chryston, Glasgow G69 9DD — 0141-779 2447
[E-mail: john.c.nicolson@btinternet.com]

Phillips, John B. — 2/3, 30 Handel Place, Glasgow G5 0TP — 0141-429 7716
[E-mail: johnphillips@fish.co.uk]

Robertson, Adam — 423 Amulree Street, Glasgow G32 7SS — 0141-573 6662

Roy, Mrs Shona	81 Busby Road, Clarkston, Glasgow G76 8BD [E-mail: theroyfamily@yahoo.co.uk]	0141-644 3713
Smith, Ann	52 Robslee Road, Thornliebank, Glasgow G46 7BX	0141-621 0638
Stead, Mrs Mary	9A Carrick Drive, Mount Vernon, Glasgow G32 0RW [E-mail: maystead@hotmail.co.uk]	0141-764 1016
Stewart, James	45 Airthrey Avenue, Glasgow G14 9LY [E-mail: jmstewart325@btinternet.com]	0141-959 5814
Tindall, Margaret (Mrs)	23 Ashcroft Avenue, Lennoxtown, Glasgow G65 7EN [E-mail: margarettindall@aol.com]	01360 310911
Wilson, George A.	46 Maxwell Drive, Garrowhill, Baillieston, Glasgow G69 6LS [E-mail: healthandsafety@talk21.com]	0141-771 3862

17. HAMILTON

Allan, Angus J.	Blackburn Mill, Chapelton, Strathaven ML10 6RR [E-mail: angus.allan@hotmail.com]	01357 528548
Beattie, Richard	4 Bent Road, Hamilton ML3 6QB [E-mail: richardbeattie1958@hotmail.com]	01698 420086
Bell, Sheena	2 Langdale, East Kilbride, Glasgow G74 4RP [E-mail: belljsheena@hotmail.co.uk]	01355 248217
Chirnside, Peter	141 Kyle Park Drive, Uddingston, Glasgow G71 7DB	01698 813769
Codona, Joy (Mrs)	Dykehead Farm, 300 Dykehead Road, Airdrie ML6 7SR [E-mail: jcodona772@btinternet.com]	01236 767063 07810 770609 (Mbl)
Cruickshanks, William	63 Progress Drive, Caldercruix, Airdrie ML6 7PU	01236 843352
Haggarty, Frank	46 Glen Road, Caldercruix, Airdrie ML6 7PZ	01236 842182
Hastings, William Paul	186 Glen More, East Kilbride, Glasgow G74 2AN [E-mail: wphastings@hotmail.co.uk]	01355 521228
Hewitt, Samuel	3 Corrie Court, Earnock, Hamilton ML3 9XE [E-mail: sambetty1@hotmail.com]	01698 457403
Hislop, Eric	1 Castlegait, Strathaven ML10 6FF [E-mail: eric.hislop@tiscali.co.uk]	01357 520003
Jardine, Lynette	32 Powburn Crescent, Uddingston, Glasgow G71 7SS [E-mail: lpjardine@blueyonder.co.uk]	01698 812404
Keir, Dickson	46 Brackenhill Drive, Hamilton ML3 8AY [E-mail: dickson.keir@btinternet.com]	01698 457351
Leckie, Elizabeth	8 Montgomery Place, Larkhall ML9 2EZ [E-mail: elizleckie@blueyonder.co.uk]	01698 308933
McCleary, Isaac	719 Coatbridge Road, Baillieston, Glasgow G69 7PH	01236 421073
Murphy, Jim	10 Hillview Crescent, Bellshill ML4 1NX [E-mail: jim.murphy5@btopenworld.com]	01698 740189
Preston, J. Steven	24 Glen Prosen, East Kilbride, Glasgow G74 3TA [E-mail: steven.preston1@btinternet.com]	01355 237359
Robertson, Rowan	68 Townhead Road, Coatbridge ML5 2HU	01236 425703
Stevenson, Thomas	34 Castle Wynd, Quarter, Hamilton ML3 7XD	01698 282263

Name	Address	Phone
White, Ian T.	21 Muirhead, Stonehouse, Larkhall ML9 3HG [E-mail: iantwhite@aol.com]	01698 792772

18. DUMBARTON

Foster, Peter	Flat 3 Templeton, 51 John Street, Helensburgh G84 8XN [E-mail: peterfostera39@btinternet.com]	01436 678226
Galbraith, Iain B. MA MPhil MTh ThD FTCL	Beechwood, Overton Road, Alexandria G83 0LJ	01389 753563
Giles, Donald (Dr)	Levern House, Stuckenduff, Shandon, Helensburgh G84 8NW [E-mail: don.giles@btopenworld.com]	01436 820565
Harold, Sandy	The Laurels, Risk Street, Clydebank G81 3LW [E-mail: harold996@btinternet.com]	0141-952 3673
Hart, R.J.M. BSc	7 Kidston Drive, Helensburgh G84 8QA [E-mail: rjm7k@yahoo.com]	01436 672039
Morgan, Richard	Annandale, School Road, Rhu, Helensburgh G84 8RS [E-mail: themorgans@hotmail.co.uk]	01436 821269
Rettie, Sara (Mrs)	86 Dennistoun Crescent, Helensburgh G84 7JF [E-mail: sarajayne.rettie@btinternet.com]	01436 677984

19. ARGYLL

Alexander, John	11 Cullipool Village, Isle of Luing, Oban PA34 4UB [E-mail: j.alexander42@btinternet.com]	01852 314242
Binner, Aileen (Mrs)	'Ailand', North Connel, Oban PA37 1QX [E-mail: binners@ailand.plus.com]	01631 710264
Hind, John Edwin	Kyle Cottage, Shore Street, Bowmore, Isle of Islay PA43 7LB [E-mail: eddieandsue2000@yahoo.co.uk]	01496 301494
Logue, David	3 Braeface, Tayvallich, Lochgilphead PA31 8PN [E-mail: david@loguenet.co.uk]	01546 870647
MacKellar, Janet BSc	Laurel Bank, 23 George Street, Dunoon PA23 8JT [E-mail: jkmackellar@aol.com]	01369 705549
McLellan, James A.	West Drimvore, Lochgilphead PA31 8SU [E-mail: james.mclellan8@btinternet.com]	01546 606403
Morrison, John L.	Tigh na Barnashaig, Tayvallich, Lochgilphead PA31 8PN [E-mail: jolomo@thejolomostudio.com]	01546 870637
Ramsay, Mathew M.	Portnastorm, Carradale, Campbeltown PA28 6SB [E-mail: portnastorm@iscali.co.uk]	01583 431381
Sinclair, Margaret (Mrs)	2 Quarry Place, Furnace, Inveraray PA32 8XW [E-mail: margaret_sinclair@btinternet.com]	01499 500633
Stather, Angela (Mrs)	9 Gartness Cottages, Ballygrant, Isle of Islay PA45 7QN [E-mail: angel.stather@virgin.net]	01496 840527
Thornhill, Christopher R.	4 Ardfern Cottages, Ardfern, Lochgilphead PA31 9QN [E-mail: c.thornhill@btinternet.com]	01852 500674
Waddell, Martin	2 Kilbrandon Cottages, Balvicar, Isle of Seil, Oban PA34 4RA [E-mail: waddell1715@btinternet.com]	01852 300395

Zielinski, Jennifer C. (Mrs) 26 Cromwell Street, Dunoon PA23 7AX
[E-mail: jczyefo@aol.com] 01369 706136

22. FALKIRK
Duncan, Lorna M. (Mrs) BA Richmond, 28 Solway Drive, Head of Muir, Denny FK6 5NS 01324 813020
[E-mail: ell.dee@blueyonder.co.uk]

Mathers, Sandra (Mrs) 10 Ercall Road, Brightons, Falkirk FK2 0RS 01324 872253
[E-mail: alexena@btinternet.com]

Stewart, Arthur MA 51 Bonnymuir Crescent, Bonnybridge FK4 1GD 01324 812667
[E-mail: arthur.stewart1@btinternet.com]

Struthers, Ivar B. 7 McVean Place, Bonnybridge FK4 1QZ 01324 841145
[E-mail: ivar.struthers@btinternet.com] (Mbl) 07921 778208

23. STIRLING
Durie, Alastair (Dr) 25 Forth Place, Stirling FK8 1UD 01786 451029
[E-mail: acdurie@btinternet.com]

Grier, Hunter 17 Station Road, Bannockburn, Stirling FK7 8LG 01786 815192
[E-mail: hunter@xaltmail.com]

Tilly, Patricia (Mrs) 25 Meiklejohn Street, Stirling FK9 5HQ 01786 446401
[E-mail: Trishatilly@aol.com] (Mbl) 07428 559554

Weir, Andrew (Dr) 16 The Oaks, Killearn, Glasgow G63 9SF 01360 550779
[E-mail: andrewweir@btinternet.com] (Mbl) 07534 506075

24. DUNFERMLINE
Adams, William 24 Foulford Street, Cowdenbeath KY4 0EQ 01383 510540
[E-mail: william.adams94@yahoo.co.uk]

Brown, Gordon Nowell, Fossoway, Kinross KY13 0UW 01577 840248
[E-mail: brown.nowell@hotmail.co.uk]

Conway, Bernard 4 Centre Street, Kelty KY4 0EQ 01383 830442
Grant, Allan 6 Normandy Place, Rosyth KY11 2HJ 01383 428760
[E-mail: allan75@btinternet.com]

McCafferty, Joyce (Mrs) 53 Foulford Street, Cowdenbeath KY4 9AS 01383 515775
McDonald, Elizabeth (Mrs) Parleyhill, Culross, Dunfermline KY12 8JD 01383 880231
Meiklejohn, Barry 40 Lilac Grove, Dunfermline KY11 8AP 01383 731550
[E-mail: barry.meiklejohn@btinternet.com]

Mitchell, Ian G. QC 17 Carlingnose Point, North Queensferry, Inverkeithing KY11 1ER 01383 416240
[E-mail: igmitchell@easynet.co.uk]

25. KIRKCALDY
Allardice, Michael 20 Parbroath Road, Glenrothes KY7 4TH 01592 772280
[E-mail: m.allardice@dundee.ac.uk] (Mbl) 07936 203465

Biernat, Ian — 2 Formonthills Road, Glenrothes KY6 3EF
[E-mail: ian.biernat@btinternet.com]
01592 655565

26. ST ANDREWS

Elder, Morag Anne (Ms) — 5 Provost Road, Tayport DD6 9JE
[E-mail: benuardin@tiscali.co.uk]
01382 552218

King, C.M. (Mrs) — 8 Bankwell Road, Anstruther KY10 3DA
01333 310017

Porteous, Brian — Kirkdene, Westfield Road, Cupar KY15 5DS
[E-mail: brian@porteousleisure.co.uk]
01334 653561

Smith, Elspeth (Mrs) — Whinstead, Dalgairn, Cupar KY15 4PH
[E-mail: elspeth.smith@btopenworld.com]
01334 653269

27. DUNKELD AND MEIGLE

Howat, David — Lilybank Cottage, Newton Street, Blairgowrie PH10 6HZ
[E-mail: david@thehowats.net]
01250 874715

Steele, Grace (Ms) — 12A Farragon Drive, Aberfeldy PH15 2BQ
[E-mail: gmfsteele@tiscali.co.uk]
01887 820025

Templeton, Elizabeth (Mrs) — Milton of Pitgur Farmhouse, Dalcapon, Pitlochry PH9 0ND
[E-mail: templeton.e@btinternet.com]
01796 472360

Theaker, Phillip — 5 Altamount Road, Blairgowrie PH10 6QL
[E-mail: ptheaker@talktalk.net]
01250 871162

28. PERTH

Archibald, Michael — Wychwood, Culdeesland Road, Methven, Perth PH1 3QE
[E-mail: michael.archibald@gmail.com]
01738 840995

Begg, James — 8 Park Village, Turretbank Road, Crieff PH7 4JN
[E-mail: Bjimmy37@aol.com]
01764 655907

Benneworth, Michael — 7 Hamilton Place, Perth PH1 1BB
[E-mail: mbenneworth@hotmail.com]
01738 628093

Davidson, Andrew — 95 Needless Road, Perth PH2 0LD
[E-mail: a.r.davidson.91@cantab.net]
01738 620839

Laing, John — 10 Graybank Road, Perth PH2 0GZ
[E-mail: johnandmarylaing@hotmail.co.uk]
01738 623888

Ogilvie, Brian — 67 Whitecraigs, Kinnesswood, Kinross KY13 9JN
[E-mail: brianj.ogilvie1@btopenworld.com]
01592 840823
(Mbl) 07815 759864

Stewart, Anne — Ballcraine, Murthly Road, Stanley, Perth PH1 4PN
[E-mail: anne.stewart13@btinternet.com]
01738 828637

Thorburn, Susan (Mrs) MTh — 3 Daleally Cottages, St Madoes Road, Errol, Perth PH2 7TJ
[E-mail: s_thor@yahoo.com]
01821 642681

Yellowlees, Deirdre (Mrs) — Ringmill House, Gannochy Farm, Perth PH2 7JH
[E-mail: d.yellowlees@btinternet.com]
01738 633773
(Mbl) 07920 805399

29. DUNDEE

Brown, Isobel (Mrs)	10 School Wynd, Muirhead, Dundee DD2 5LW	01382 580545
	[E-mail: isobel73@btinternet.com]	
Brown, Janet (Miss)	G2, 6 Baxter Park Terrace, Dundee DD4 6NL	01382 453066
	[E-mail: j.herries.brown@blueyonder.co.uk]	
Xenophontos-Hellen, Tim	Aspro Spiti, 23 Ancrum Drive, Dundee DD2 2JG	01382 630355
	[E-mail: tim.xsf@btinternet.com]	(Work) 01382 567756

30. ANGUS

Beedie, Alexander W.	62 Newton Crescent, Arbroath DD11 3JZ	01241 875001
	[E-mail: bill.beedie@hotmail.co.uk]	
Davidson, Peter I.	24 Kinnaird Place, Brechin DD9 7HF	
	[E-mail: mail@idavidson.co.uk]	
Gray, Linda (Mrs)	8 Inchgarth Street, Forfar DD8 3LY	01307 464039
	[E-mail: lindamgray@sky.com]	
Nicoll, Douglas	16 New Road, Forfar DD8 2AE	01307 463264

31. ABERDEEN

Cooper, Gordon	4 Springfield Place, Aberdeen AB15 7SF	01224 316667
	[E-mail: ga_cooper@hotmail.co.uk]	
Gray, Peter (Prof.)	165 Countesswells Road, Aberdeen AB15 7RA	01224 318172
	[E-mail: pmdgray165@btinternet.com]	

32. KINCARDINE AND DEESIDE

Bell, Robert	27 Mearns Drive, Stonehaven AB39 2DZ	01569 767173
	[E-mail: r.bell282@btinternet.com]	(Mbl) 07733 014826
Broere, Teresa (Mrs)	3 Balnastraid Cottages, Dinnet, Aboyne AB34 5NE	01339 880058
	[E-mail: broere@btinternet.com]	
Coles, Stephen	43 Mearns Walk, Laurencekirk AB30 1FA	01561 378400
	[E-mail: steve@sbcco.com]	
McCafferty, W. John	Lynwood, Cammachmore, Stonehaven AB39 3NR	01569 730281
	[E-mail: wjmcafferty@yahoo.co.uk]	
McLuckie, John	7 Monaltrie Close, Ballater AB35 5PT	01339 755489
	[E-mail: johnemcluckie@btinternet.com]	
Middleton, Robin B. (Capt.)	7 St Ternan's Road, Newtonhill, Stonehaven AB39 3PF	01569 730852
	[E-mail: robbiemiddleton7@hotmail.co.uk]	
Platt, David	2 St Michael's Road, Newtonhill, Stonehaven AB39 3RW	01569 730465
	[E-mail: daveplatt01@btinternet.com]	
Simpson, Elizabeth (Mrs)	Connemara, 33 Golf Road, Ballater AB35 5RS	01339 755597
	[E-mail: connemara33@yahoo.com]	

33. GORDON

Bichard, Susanna (Mrs)	Beechlee, Haddo Lane, Tarves, Ellon AB41 7JZ [E-mail: smbichard@aol.com]	01651 851345
Doak, Alan B.	17 Chievres Place, Ellon AB41 9WH [E-mail: alanbdoak@aol.com]	01358 721819
Findlay, Patricia (Mrs)	Douglas View, Tullynessle, Alford AB33 8QR [E-mail: p.a.findlay@btopenworld.com]	01975 562379
Mitchell, Jean (Mrs)	6 Cowgate, Oldmeldrum, Inverurie AB51 0EN [E-mail: j.g.mitchell@btinternet.com]	01651 872745
Robb, Margaret (Mrs)	Chrislouan, Keithhall, Inverurie AB51 0LN [E-mail: Robbminister1@aol.com]	01651 882310
Robertson, James Y. MA	1 Nicol Road, Kintore, Inverurie AB51 0QA [E-mail: j.robertson833@btinternet.com]	01467 633001

34. BUCHAN

Armitage, Rosaline (Mrs)	Whitecairn, Blackhills, Peterhead AB42 3LR [E-mail: r.r.armitage@btinternet.com]	01779 477267
Barker, Tim	South Silverford Croft, Longmanhill, Banff AB45 3SB [E-mail: tbarker05@aol.com]	01261 851839
Brown, Lillian (Mrs)	45 Main Street, Aberchirder, Huntly AB54 7ST	01466 780330
Davidson, James C.	19 Great Stuart Street, Peterhead AB42 1JX [E-mail: jim@jcdavidson.com]	01779 470242
Forsyth, Alicia (Mrs)	Rothie Inn Farm, Forgue Road, Rothienorman, Inverurie AB51 8YH [E-mail: a.forsyth@btinternet.com]	01651 821359
Givan, James	Zinra, Longmanhill, Banff AB45 3RP [E-mail: jim.givan@btinternet.com]	01261 833318 07753 458664 (Mbl)
Grant, Margaret (Mrs)	22 Elphin Street, New Aberdour, Fraserburgh AB43 6LH [E-mail: margaret@wilmar.demon.co.uk]	01346 561341
Higgins, Scott	St Ninian's, Manse Terrace, Turriff AB53 4BA [E-mail: mhairiandscott@btinternet.com]	01888 569103
Lumsden, Vera (Mrs)	8 Queen's Crescent, Portsoy, Banff AB45 2PX [E-mail: ivsd@lumsden77.freeserve.co.uk]	01261 842712
McColl, John	East Cairnchina, Lonmay, Fraserburgh AB43 8RH [E-mail: solfolly11@gmail.com]	01346 532558 07757 303195 (Mbl)
MacLeod, Ali (Ms)	11 Pitfour Crescent, Fetterangus, Peterhead AB42 4EL [E-mail: aliowl@hotmail.com]	01771 622992 07821 670705 (Mbl)
Macnee, Anthea (Mrs)	Wardend Cottage, Alvah, Banff AB45 3TR [E-mail: macneeiain4@googlemail.com]	01261 815647
Mair, Dorothy L.T. (Miss)	Flat F, 15 The Quay, Newburgh, Ellon AB41 6DA [E-mail: dorothymair2@aol.com]	01358 788832 07505 051305 (Mbl)
Noble, John M.	44 Henderson Park, Peterhead AB42 2WR [E-mail: john_m_noble@hotmail.co.uk]	01779 472522
Ogston, Norman	Rowandale, 6 Rectory Road, Turriff AB53 4SU [E-mail: norman.ogston@gmail.com]	01888 560342

Simpson, Andrew C.	10 Wood Street, Banff AB45 1JX [E-mail: andy.louise1@btinternet.com]	01261 812538
Smith, Ian M.G.	2 Hill Street, Cruden Bay, Peterhead AB42 0HF	01779 812698
Sneddon, Richard	100 West Road, Peterhead AB42 2AQ [E-mail: richard.sneddon@btinternet.com]	01779 480803
Stewart, William	Denend, Strichen, Fraserburgh AB43 6RN [E-mail: billandjunes@live.co.uk]	01771 637256
Taylor, Elaine (Mrs)	101 Cairntrodlie, Peterhead AB42 2AY [E-mail: elaine.taylor60@btinternet.com]	01779 472978
Williams, Paul	20 Soy Burn Gardens, Portsoy, Banff AB45 2QG [E-mail: paul.williams447@virgin.net]	01261 842338

35. MORAY

| Forbes, Jean (Mrs) | Greenmoss, Drybridge, Buckie AB56 2JB [E-mail: dancingfeet@tinyworld.co.uk] | 01542 831646 (Mbl) 07974 760337 |

36. ABERNETHY

| Bardgett, Alison (Mrs) | Tigh an Iasgair, Street of Kincardine, Boat of Garten PH24 3BY [E-mail: tigh@bardgett.plus.com] | 01479 831751 |

37. INVERNESS

Appleby, Jonathan	91 Cradlehall Park, Inverness IV2 5DB [E-mail: jon.wyvis@gmail.com]	01463 791470
Cazaly, Leonard	9 Moray Park Gardens, Culloden, Inverness IV2 7FY [E-mail: len_cazaly@lineone.net]	01463 794469
Cook, Arnett D.	66 Millerton Avenue, Inverness IV3 8RY [E-mail: arnett.cook@btinternet.com]	01463 224795
Dennis, Barry	50 Holm Park, Inverness IV2 4XU [E-mail: barry.dennis@tiscali.co.uk]	01463 225883 (Work) 01463 663448
Innes, Derek	Allanswell, Cawdor Road, Auldearn, Nairn IV12 5TQ [E-mail: dereklinnes@btinternet.com]	01463 230321
MacInnes, Ailsa (Mrs)	Kilmartin, 17 Southside Road, Inverness IV2 3BG [E-mail: ailsa.macinnes@btopenworld.com]	(Mbl) 07704 485055
Robertson, Hendry	Park House, 51 Glenurquhart Road, Inverness IV3 5PB [E-mail: hendry.robertson@connectfree.co.uk]	01463 231858 (Mbl) 07929 766102
Robertson, Stewart J.H.	21 Towerhill Drive, Cradlehall, Inverness IV2 5FD	01463 793144
Roden, Vivian (Mrs)	15 Old Mill Road, Tomatin, Inverness IV13 7YW [E-mail: vroden@btinternet.com]	01808 511355 (Mbl) 07887 704915
Todd, Iain	9 Leanach Gardens, Inverness IV2 5DD [E-mail: itoddyo@aol.com]	01463 791161

38. LOCHABER

Chalkley, Andrew BSc
41 Hillside Road, Campbeltown PA28 6NE
[E-mail: andrewjoan@googlemail.com]

Ogston, Jean (Mrs)
Church of Scotland Manse, Annie's Brae, Mallaig PH41 4RG
[E-mail: jeanogston@googlemail.com]
01687 460042

Walker, Eric
Tigh a' Chlann, Inverroy, Roy Bridge PH31 4AQ
[E-mail: line15@btinternet.com]
01397 712028

Walker, Pat (Mrs)
Tigh a' Chlann, Inverroy, Roy Bridge PH31 4AQ
[E-mail: pat.line15@btinternet.com]
01397 712028

39. ROSS

Finlayson, Michael R.
Amberlea, Glenskiach, Evanton, Dingwall IV16 9UU
[E-mail: finlayson935@btinternet.com]
01349 830598

Greer, Kathleen (Mrs) MEd
17 Duthac Wynd, Tain IV19 1LP
[E-mail: greer2@talktalk.net]
01862 892065

Gunstone, Ronald W.
20 Bellfield Road, North Kessock, Inverness IV1 3XU
[E-mail: ronald.gunstone@virgin.net]
(Mbl) 01463 731337
07974 443948

Jamieson, Patricia A. (Mrs)
9 Craig Avenue, Tain IV19 1JP
[E-mail: hapjam179@yahoo.co.uk]
01862 893154

McAlpine, James
5 Cromlet Park, Invergordon IV18 0RN
[E-mail: jmca1@tinyworld.co.uk]
01349 852801

McCreadie, Frederick
7 Castle Gardens, Dingwall IV15 9HY
[E-mail: fredmccreadie@tesco.net]
01349 862171

Munro, Irene (Mrs)
1 Wyvis Crescent, Conon Bridge, Dingwall IV15 9HY
[E-mail: irenemunro@rocketmail.com]
01349 865752

Riddell, Keith
2 Station Cottages, Fearn, Tain IV20 1RR
[E-mail: keithriddell@hotmail.co.uk]
01862 832867
(Mbl) 07719 645995

40. SUTHERLAND

Baxter, A. Rosie (Dr)
Creich Old Manse, Bonar Bridge, Ardgay IV24 3AB
[E-mail: drrosiereid@yahoo.co.uk]
01863 766257
(Mbl) 07748 761694

Roberts, Irene (Mrs)
Flat 4, Harbour Buildings, Main Street, Portmahomack, Tain IV20 1YG
[E-mail: ireneroberts43@hotmail.com]
01862 871166
(Mbl) 07854 436854

Weidner, Karl
6 St Vincent Road, Tain IV19 1JR
[E-mail: kweidner@btinternet.com]
01862 894202

41. CAITHNESS

42. LOCHCARRON – SKYE

Lamont, John H. BD
6 Tigh na Filine, Aultbea, Achnasheen IV22 2JE
[E-mail: jhlamont@btinternet.com]
(Mbl) 07714 720753

MacRae, Donald E. — Nethania, 52 Strath, Gairloch IV21 2DB
[E-mail: Dmgair@aol.com] 01445 712235

Murray, John W. — 1 Totescore, Kilmuir, Portree, Isle of Skye IV51 9YW 01470 542297
Ross, R. Ian — St Conal's, Invernate, Kyle IV40 8HB 01599 511371

43. UIST
Browning, Margaret (Miss) — 1 Middlequarter, Sollas, Lochmaddy, Isle of North Uist HS6 5BU
[E-mail: margaretckb@tiscali.co.uk] 01876 560392

Lines, Charles M.D. — Flat 1/02, 8 Queen Margaret Road, Glasgow G20 6DP
MacAulay, John — Fernhaven, 1 Flodabay, Isle of Harris HS3 3HA 01859 530340
MacNab, Ann (Mrs) — Druim Skilivat, Scolpaig, Lochmaddy, Isle of North Uist HS6 5DH 01876 510701
[E-mail: annabhan@hotmail.com]

44. LEWIS
Macleod, Donald — 14 Balmerino Drive, Stornoway, Isle of Lewis HS1 2TD
[E-mail: donaldmacleod25@btinternet.com] 01851 704516

Macmillan, Iain — 34 Scotland Street, Stornoway, Isle of Lewis HS1 2JR 01851 704826
[E-mail: macmillan@brocair.fsnet.co.uk] (Mbl) 07775 027987
Murray, Angus — 4 Ceann Chilleagraidh, Stornoway, Isle of Lewis HS1 2UJ 01851 703550
[E-mail: angydmurray@btinternet.com]

45. ORKNEY
Dicken, Marion (Mrs) — 6 Claymore Brae, Kirkwall, Orkney KW15 1UQ
[E-mail: mj44@hotmail.co.uk] 01856 879509

Robertson, Johan (Mrs) — Old Manse, Eday, Orkney KW17 2AA 01857 622251

46. SHETLAND
Greig, Diane (Mrs) MA — 6 Hayhoull Place, Bigton, Shetland ZE2 9GA
[E-mail: mrschm.greig@btinternet.com] 01950 422468

Harrison, Christine (Mrs) BA — Gerdavatn, Baltasound, Unst, Shetland ZE2 9DY 01957 711578
[E-mail: chris4242@btinternet.com]
Smith, M. Beryl (Mrs) DCE MSc — Vakterlee, Cumliewick, Sandwick, Shetland ZE2 9HH 01950 431280
[E-mail: beryl@brooniestaing.co.uk]

47. ENGLAND
Houghton, Mark (Dr) — Kentcliffe, Charney Road, Grange-over-Sands, Cumbria LA11 6BP
[E-mail: mark@chaplain.me.uk] 01539 525048
(Work) 01629 813505
Menzies, Rena (Mrs) — 49 Elizabeth Avenue, St Brelade's, Jersey JE3 8GR 01534 741095
[E-mail: menzfamily@jerseymail.co.uk]
Milligan, Elaine (Mrs) — 16 Surrey Close, Corby, Northants NN17 2TG 01536 205259
[E-mail: elainemilligan@ntlworld.com]
Munro, William — 35 Stour Road, Corby, Northants NN17 2HX 01536 504864

48. EUROPE
Ross, David

Urb. El Campanario, EDF Granada, Esc. 14, Baja B, Ctra Cadiz N-340, (Tel/Fax) 0034 952 88 26 34
Km 168, 29680 Estepona, Malaga, Spain
[E-mail: rosselcampanario@yahoo.co.uk]

49. JERUSALEM
Oakley-Levstein, Joanna

ASSOCIATE (Ireland)
Binnie, Jean (Miss)

2 Ailesbury Lawn, Dundrum, Dublin 16, Ireland   00353 1 298 7229
[E-mail: jeanbinnie@eircom.net]

LIST O – REPRESENTATIVES ON COUNCIL EDUCATION COMMITTEES

COUNCIL	NAME	ADDRESS	TEL
ABERDEEN	Rev. Eddie McKenna	The Manse, Kincorth Circle, Aberdeen AB12 5NX [E-mail: eddiemckenna@uwclub.net]	01224 872820
ABERDEENSHIRE	Dr Eleanor Anderson	Drumblair Cottage, Forgue, Huntly AB54 6DE [E-mail: edrumblair@hotmail.com]	01464 871329
ANGUS	Mr David Adams	Glebe House, Farnell, by Brechin DD9 6UH [E-mail: david.adams81@btinternet.com]	01674 820227
ARGYLL and BUTE CLACKMANNAN	Mr William Crossan Rev. Sang Y. Cha	Gowanbank, Kilkerran Road, Campbeltown PA26 6JL 37A Claremont, Alloa FK10 2DG [E-mail: syc@cantab.net]	01259 213872
DUMFRIES and GALLOWAY	Mr Robert McQuistan	Old Schoolhouse, Carsluith, Newton Stewart DG8 7DT [E-mail: mcquistan@mcquistan.plus.com]	01671 820327
DUNDEE	Miss Kathleen Mands	27 Noran Avenue, Dundee DD4 7LE [E-mail: kathmands@blueyonder.co.uk]	01382 451140
EAST AYRSHIRE	Mr Ian Rennie	46 Colonsay Place, Wardneuk, Kilmarnock KA3 2JU [E-mail: i.rennie@btinternet.com]	
EAST DUNBARTONSHIRE	Mrs Barbara Jarvie	18 Camerton Crescent, Milton of Campsie, Glasgow G66 8DR [E-mail: bj@bjarvie.fsnet.co.uk]	01360 319729
EAST LOTHIAN	Mrs Marjorie K. Goldsmith	20 St Lawrence, Haddington EH41 3RL	01620 823249
EAST RENFREWSHIRE	Ms Mary McIntyre	5 Buchanan Drive, Glasgow G77 6HT [E-mail: mmmcintyre@ntlworld.com]	
EDINBURGH CITY	Mr A. Craig Duncan	2 East Barnton Gardens, Edinburgh EH4 6AR [E-mail: acraigduncan@btinternet.com]	0131-336 4432

FALKIRK	Mrs Margaret Coutts	34 Pirleyhill Gardens, Falkirk FK1 5NB [E-mail: margaret.coutts03@btinternet.com]	01324 628732
FIFE GLASGOW	Rev. Graham R.G. Cartlidge	54 Mansewood Road, Eastwood, Glasgow G43 1TL [E-mail: cartlidge262@btinternet.com]	0141-649 0463
GLASGOW 2nd rep	Rev. David A. Keddie	21 Ilay Road, Bearsden, Glasgow G61 1QG [E-mail: revkeddie@gmail.com]	0141-942 5173
HIGHLAND	Mr Gordon Smith	Glenwood, Altour Road, Spean Bridge PH34 4EZ [E-mail: gordonsmith934@btinternet.com]	01397 712375
MIDLOTHIAN	Mr Paul Hayes	Kingsway Management Services Ltd, 127 Deanburn, Penicuik EH26 0JA [E-mail: paul.hayes@basilicon.com]	01968 673968
MORAY	Rev. Shuna M. Dicks	The Manse, Mary Avenue, Aberlour AB38 9QU [E-mail: revshuna@btinternet.com]	01340 871687
NORTH AYRSHIRE	Mrs Elizabeth Higton	Gorsebraehead, Darvel KA17 0LT [E-mail: elizabethigton@aol.com]	01560 321180
NORTH LANARKSHIRE	Mr John William Maddock	137 Manse Road, Motherwell ML1 2PS [E-mail: john@maddockfamily.plus.com]	01698 251137
ORKNEY PERTH and KINROSS	Mrs Pat Giles	190 Oakbank Road, Perth PH1 1EG [E-mail: patgiles190@yahoo.co.uk]	01738 625805
RENFREWSHIRE	Mr Ian Keith	5 Langside Drive, Kilbarchan PA10 2EL [E-mail: james.keith@fsmail.net]	
SCOTTISH BORDERS	Mr Graeme Donald	1 Upper Loan Park, Lauder TD2 6TR [E-mail: graeme.donald@btopenworld.com]	01578 722422
SHETLAND	Rev. Tom Macintyre	Lappideks, South Voxter, Cunningsburgh, Shetland ZE2 9HF [E-mail: the2macs.macintyre@btinternet.com]	01950 477549
SOUTH AYRSHIRE	Rev. David R. Gemmell	58 Monument Road, Ayr KA7 2UB [E-mail: drgemmell@hotmail.com]	01292 262580
SOUTH LANARKSHIRE	Rev. Sarah L. Ross	22 Lea Rig, Forth, Lanark ML11 8EA [E-mail: rev_sross@btinternet.com]	01555 812832
STIRLING	Mrs Jennifer Millar	5 Clifford Road, Stirling FK8 2AQ [E-mail: jmmillar@pkc.gov.uk]	01786 469979
WEST DUNBARTONSHIRE	Miss Sheila Rennie	128 Dumbuie Avenue, Dumbarton G82 2JW [E-mail: sheilarennie@tiscali.co.uk]	01389 763246
WEST LOTHIAN	Mrs Lynne McEwen	6 Fernlea, Uphall, Broxburn EH52 6DF [E-mail: lynnemcewen@hotmail.co.uk]	01506 855513

LIST P – RETIRED LAY AGENTS

Falconer, Alexander J.	84 Bridge Street, Dollar FK14 7DQ
	[E-mail: falconer59.freeserve.co.uk]
Forrester, Arthur A.	158 Lee Crescent North, Bridge of Don, Aberdeen AB22 8FR
Scott, John W.	15 Manor Court, Forfar DD8 1BR

LIST Q – MINISTERS ORDAINED FOR SIXTY YEARS AND UPWARDS

Until 1992, the *Year Book* contained each year a list of those ministers who had been ordained 'for fifty years and upwards'. Such a list was reinstated in the edition for 2002, including the names of those ordained for sixty years and upwards. With ministers, no less than the rest of society, living longer, it was felt reasonable to proceed on that basis. Correspondence made it clear that this list was welcomed, and it has been included in an appropriately revised form each year since then. Again this year, an updated version is offered following the best enquiries that could be made. The date of ordination is given in full where it is known.

1941	3 July	Donald William MacKenzie (Auchterarder: The Barony)
1943	3 September	George Cooper (Delting with Nesting and Lunnasting)
1945	4 February	James Shirra (St Martins with Scone: New)
	4 September	John Paul Tierney (Peterhead West: Associate)
1946	11 April	James Martin (Glasgow: High Carntyne)
	19 May	John McClymont Frew (Glasgow: Dennistoun)
	23 June	Ian Masson Fraser (Selly Oak Colleges)
	18 September	John Wilkinson (Kikuyu)
	3 October	John Henry Whyte (Gourock: Ashton)
	13 November	Ian Bruce Doyle (Department of National Mission)
1947	27 November	William Duncan Crombie (Glasgow: Calton New with Glasgow: St Andrew's)
1948	31 March	Gilbert Mollison Mowat (Dundee: Albany-Butterburn)
	20 April	Andrew Kerr (Kilbarchan: West)

	6 July	Alexander Chestnut (Greenock: St Mark's Greenbank)
	6 October	George Davidson Wilkie (Kirkcaldy: Viewforth)
1949	5 January	Andrew Queen Morton (Culross and Torryburn)
	14 February	Hamish Norman Mackenzie McIntosh (Fintry)
	17 July	Walter Vernon Stone (Langbank)
	1 September	John Anderson Macnaughton (Glasgow: Hyndland)
	18 December	James McMichael Orr (Aberfoyle with Port of Menteith)
1950	9 July	Alexander Craib Barr (Glasgow: St Nicholas' Cardonald)
	10 July	Kenneth MacVicar (Kenmore with Lawers with Fortingall and Glenlyon)
	5 September	James McLaren Ritchie (Coalsnaughton)
	28 December	Donald Stewart Wallace (Chaplain: RAF)
1951	28 January	William Henry Greenway Bristow (Chaplain: Army)
	12 June	Donald John Barker McAlister (North Berwick: Blackadder)
	26 July	Duncan Shaw (Edinburgh: Craigentinny St Christopher's)
	9 September	Alwyn James Cecil Macfarlane (Glasgow: Newlands South)
	6 November	Alexander Gordon McGillivray (Edinburgh: Presbytery Clerk)
	15 November	Andrew Whittingham Rae (Annan: St Andrew's Greenknowe Erskine)
	28 November	James Pringle Fraser (Strathaven: Avendale Old and Drumclog)
1952	April	William Frederick Laing (Selkirk: St Mary's West)
	11 June	Archibald Lamont (Kilcalmonell with Skipness)
	4 July	Charles Malcolm Henderson (Campbeltown: Highland)
	16 July	James Mercer Thomson (Elgin: St Giles' and St Columba's South: Associate)
1953	15 March	John Murrie (Kirkliston)
	4 June	George Dymock Goldie (Aberdeen: Greyfriars)
	21 June	Duncan Cameron McPhee (Department of National Mission)
	28 June	Ian Cameron (Kilbrandon and Kilchattan)
	12 July	John Donald Henderson (Cluny with Monymusk)
	19 August	Robert Bell Donaldson (Kilchoman with Portnahaven)
	3 September	David Courser Gordon (Gigha and Cara)
	30 September	David Peacock Munro (Bearsden: North)
	1 October	William James Gilmour McDonald (Edinburgh: Mayfield)
	7 October	Peter Brown (Holm)
	7 October	George Ivory Lithgow McCaskill (Religious Education)
	21 October	Donald Maciver Ross (Industrial Mission Organiser)
	25 October	George Mackenzie Philip (Glasgow: Sandyford Henderson Memorial)
	6 December	Mark Wilson

1954		
	17 January	Arthur William Alexander Main (University of Aberdeen)
	20 March	Ainslie Walton (University of Aberdeen)
	7 April	Joseph Ross Ingram (Chaplain: RAF)
	28 April	David Tindal Reid (Cleish with Fossoway: St Serf's and Devonside)
	2 May	Robert Alexander Stewart Barbour (University of Aberdeen)
	25 July	Joseph Brown (Linton with Hownam and Morebattle with Yetholm)
	29 September	James Marshall Buttery Scoular (Kippen)
	12 December	Eric William Sinclair Jeffrey (Edinburgh: Bristo Memorial)
	30 December	Alexander Glen Bowie (Principal Chaplain: RAF)

LIST R – DECEASED MINISTERS

The Editor has been made aware of the following ministers who have died since the publication of the previous volume of the *Year Book*.

Andrew, John (Teacher: Religious Education)
Bews, James (Dundee: Craigiebank)
Blane, Quintin Alexander (Bellshill: West)
Brown, Robert (Kilbrandon and Kilchattan)
Byers, Alan James (Gamrie with King Edward)
Campbell, George Houstoun (Stewarton: John Knox)
Carvalho, Jose Roberto (Cargill Burrelton with Collace)
Casebow, Brian Clifford (Edinburgh: Salisbury)
Charlton, Richard Malcolm Auxiliary Minister: Presbytery of Shetland
Cook, John Weir (Edinburgh: Portobello St Philip's Joppa)
Crawford, Joseph Frederick (Bowden with Newtown)
Cross, Brian Frank (Coalburn)
Duncan, Denis Macdonald (Editor: *The British Weekly*)
Edington, George Levack (Tayport)
Forsyth, David Stuart (Belhelvie)
Gauld, Ranald Stuart Robertson Keith: St Rufus, Botriphnie and Grange
Gibson, Michael (Giffnock: The Park)
Gillon, Charles Colin Campbell (Glasgow: Cathcart Old)
Heron, Alasdair Iain Campbell (Friedrich-Alexander University, Erlangen)
Hill, Stanley (Muiravonside)
Hudson, James Harrison (Dundee: St Peter's McCheyne)
Hughes, Clifford Eryl (Haddington: St Mary's)
Jones, Arthur John (Aberdeen: St Clement's)
Kelly, Alistair Francis (Edinburgh: Albany Deaf Church)
Lambie, Andrew Elliot (Carmichael with Covington and Thankerton with Pettinain)
Lawson, Alexander Hamilton (Clydebank: Kilbowie)

Learmonth, Walter	(Ceres with Springfield)
Leask, Rebecca McCrae	(Callander: St Bride's)
Linkens, Norman John	(Holytown)
Longmuir, Thomas Graeme	(Inverurie: St Andrew's)
Mackenzie, James Alexander Robertson	(Largo: St David's)
MacNeill, Charles Cecil	(Brussels)
Miller, John Robert	(Carsphairn with Dalry)
Morris, William James	(Glasgow: Cathedral)
Munroe, Henry	(Denny: Dunipace North with Old)
Musgrave, Clarence William	(Jerusalem: St Andrew's)
Rennie, Alistair McRae	(Kincardine Croick and Edderton)
Ritchie, Andrew	(Edinburgh: Craiglockhart)
Saunders, Campbell Milne	(Ayr: St Leonard's)
Simpson, David Christie Robertson	(Banchory-Devenick with Maryculter and Cookney)
Sinclair, Thomas Suter	(Stornoway: Martin's Memorial)
Smith, George Richmond Naismith Rendall Knight	(World Alliance of Reformed Churches)
Stewart, George Compton	(Drumblade with Huntly Strathbogie)
Tait, Henry Alexander Gardner	(Crieff: South and Monzievaird)
Thomson, Edward Peter Lindsay	(Cavers and Kirkton with Hawick: Trinity)
Walker, Alexander Leishman	(Glasgow: Trinity Possil and Henry Drummond)
Watson, James	(Bowden with Lilliesleaf)
Watt, John George Moncur	(Glasgow: Pollokshields East)
Wright, John Patrick	(Glasgow: New Govan)

SECTION 7

Legal Names and Scottish Charity Numbers for Individual Congregations

(All congregations in Scotland, and congregations furth of Scotland which are registered with OSCR, the Office of the Scottish Charity Regulator)

EXPLANATORY NOTE:
All documents, as defined in the Charities References in Documents (Scotland) Regulations 2007, must specify the Charity Number, Legal Name of the congregation, any other name by which the congregation is commonly known and the fact that it is a Charity.

For more information, please refer to the Law Department circular on the Regulations on the Church of Scotland website.

SCOTTISH CHARITY NUMBER	NEW LEGAL NAME
1.	**Presbytery of Edinburgh**
SC018012	Balerno Church of Scotland
SC001554	Edinburgh Currie Kirk (Church of Scotland)
SC010971	Dalmeny Parish Church of Scotland
SC018321	Albany Deaf Church, Edinburgh (Church of Scotland)
SC014757	Edinburgh Barclay Viewforth Church of Scotland
SC008756	Blackhall St Columba's Church of Scotland, Edinburgh
SC011625	Bristo Memorial Church of Scotland, Craigmillar, Edinburgh
SC012642	Edinburgh: Broughton St Mary's Parish Church (Church of Scotland)
SC015251	Canongate Parish Church of Scotland, Edinburgh
SC004783	Carrick Knowe Parish Church of Scotland, Edinburgh
SC010313	Colinton Parish Church of Scotland, Edinburgh
SC014719	Edinburgh: Corstorphine Craigsbank Parish Church (Church of Scotland)
SC016009	Corstorphine Old Parish Church, Church of Scotland, Edinburgh
SC006300	Edinburgh: Corstorphine St Anne's Parish Church (Church of Scotland)
SC016557	Edinburgh: Corstorphine St Ninian's Parish Church (Church of Scotland)
SC003466	Edinburgh: Craigentinny St Christopher's Parish Church of Scotland
SC010545	Craiglockhart Parish Church, Edinburgh (Church of Scotland)
SC017061	Craigmillar Park Church of Scotland, Edinburgh
SC003430	Cramond Kirk, Edinburgh (Church of Scotland)
SC009470	Davidsons Mains Parish Church of Scotland, Edinburgh
SC001692	Dean Parish Church, Edinburgh – The Church of Scotland
SC005744	Drylaw Parish Church of Scotland, Edinburgh
SC016610	Duddingston Kirk (Church of Scotland), Edinburgh
SC015967	Fairmilehead Parish Church of Scotland, Edinburgh
SC009146	Edinburgh: Gorgie Dalry Church of Scotland
SC011985	Granton Parish Church of Scotland, Edinburgh
SC011325	Edinburgh Greenbank Parish Church of Scotland
SC009749	Edinburgh Greenside Church of Scotland
SC003761	Edinburgh Greyfriars Kirk (Church of Scotland)
SC003565	St Giles' Cathedral, Edinburgh (Church of Scotland)
SC012562	Holy Trinity Church of Scotland, Edinburgh
SC000052	Holyrood Abbey Parish Church of Scotland, Edinburgh
SC015442	Edinburgh Inverleith St Serf's Church of Scotland
SC005197	Edinburgh Juniper Green Parish Church of Scotland
SC004950	Kaimes: Lockhart Memorial Church of Scotland, Edinburgh
SC014430	Kirk o' Field Parish Church, Edinburgh (Church of Scotland)
SC004932	Edinburgh Leith North Parish Church of Scotland
SC004695	South Leith Parish Church of Scotland, Edinburgh
SC012680	Leith St Andrew's Church of Scotland, Edinburgh
SC008710	Wardie Parish Church of Scotland, Edinburgh
SC011602	Edinburgh: Liberton Kirk (Church of Scotland)
SC008891	Liberton Northfield Parish Church of Scotland, Edinburgh
SC000896	London Road Church of Scotland, Edinburgh
SC009338	Marchmont St Giles Parish Church of Scotland, Edinburgh
SC000785	Mayfield Salisbury Parish (Edinburgh) Church of Scotland
SC034396	Morningside Parish Church of Scotland, Edinburgh
SC015552	Edinburgh: Morningside United Church
SC005198	Edinburgh Murrayfield Parish Church of Scotland
SC000963	New Restalrig Church of Scotland, Edinburgh
SC019117	Newhaven Church of Scotland, Edinburgh
SC006457	Edinburgh: The Old Kirk and Muirhouse (Church of Scotland)
SC004291	Edinburgh: Palmerston Place Church of Scotland
SC007277	Edinburgh: Pilrig St Paul's Church of Scotland
SC004183	Polwarth Parish Church, Edinburgh (Church of Scotland)
SC011728	Edinburgh: Portobello and Joppa Parish Church (Church of Scotland)
SC014499	Priestfield Parish Church of Scotland, Edinburgh
SC014027	Church of Scotland, Reid Memorial Church, Edinburgh
SC009035	Richmond Craigmillar Parish Church of Scotland, Edinburgh
SC030896	Slateford Longstone Parish Church of Scotland, Edinburgh
SC002748	Edinburgh: St Andrew's Clermiston Church of Scotland
SC009379	St Catherine's Argyle Parish Church of Scotland Edinburgh
SC010592	St Cuthberts Parish Church of Scotland, Edinburgh
SC004746	St Davids Broomhouse Church of Scotland, Edinburgh
SC008990	St Andrew's and St George's West Church of Scotland, Edinburgh
SC015982	Edinburgh: St John's Colinton Mains Church of Scotland
SC004779	St Margaret's Church of Scotland: Edinburgh
SC013918	St Martins Church of Scotland, Portobello, Edinburgh
SC009038	St Michaels Parish Church of Scotland, Edinburgh
SC007068	Edinburgh: St Nicholas' Sighthill Parish Church of Scotland
SC004487	St Stephen's Comely Bank Church of Scotland, Edinburgh
SC010004	Stenhouse St Aidan's Parish Church of Scotland: Edinburgh
SC002499	Stockbridge Parish Church of Scotland, Edinburgh
SC009274	Tron Kirk (Gilmerton and Moredun), Edinburgh, Church of Scotland
SC013924	Kirkliston Parish Church of Scotland
SC002329	Queensferry Parish Church of Scotland
SC001169	Ratho Church of Scotland
2.	**Presbytery of West Lothian**
SC013100	Abercorn Parish Church of Scotland
SC000791	Armadale Parish Church of Scotland
SC007454	Avonbridge Parish Church of Scotland

SC001881	Boghall Parish Church of Scotland, Bathgate
SC007418	Bathgate High Parish Church of Scotland
SC016755	St John's Parish Church of Scotland, Bathgate
SC024154	Blackburn and Seafield Parish Church of Scotland
SC006811	Blackridge Parish Church of Scotland
SC000800	Breich Valley Parish Church of Scotland
SC017180	Broxburn Parish Church of Scotland
SC016313	Fauldhouse St Andrews Parish Church of Scotland
SC007601	Harthill St Andrew's Parish Church of Scotland
SC013461	Kirk of Calder Parish (Church of Scotland)
SC006973	Kirknewton & East Calder Parish Church of Scotland
SC016185	St Michaels Parish Church of Scotland: Linlithgow
SC011348	St Ninians Craigmailen Parish Church of Scotland, Linlithgow
SC011826	Livingston Old Parish Church of Scotland
SC026230	Pardovan, Kingscavil and Winchburgh Parish Church of Scotland
SC017373	Polbeth Harwood Parish Church of Scotland
SC006336	Strathbrock Parish Church of Scotland, Uphall
SC021516	Torphichen Parish Church of Scotland
SC024255	Uphall South Parish Church of Scotland
SC004703	West Kirk of Calder (Church of Scotland)
SC003362	Brucefield Parish Church of Scotland, Whitburn
SC001053	Whitburn South Parish Church of Scotland

3.   Presbytery of Lothian

SC004580	Aberlady Parish Church (Church of Scotland)
SC009401	Athelstaneford Parish Church (Church of Scotland)
SC007231	Belhaven Parish Church (Church of Scotland)
SC032180	Bilston Parish Church (Church of Scotland)
SC003230	Bolton and Saltoun Parish Church (Church of Scotland)
SC003482	Bonnyrigg Parish Church (Church of Scotland)
SC004630	Cockenzie and Port Seton: Chalmers Memorial Parish Church (Church of Scotland)
SC007052	Cockenzie and Port Seton: Old Parish Church (Church of Scotland)
SC013139	Cockpen and Carrington Parish Church (Church of Scotland)
SC006926	Tyne Valley Parish (Church of Scotland)
SC008958	Dalkeith: St John's and King's Park Parish Church (Church of Scotland)
SC014158	Dalkeith: St Nicholas Buccleuch Parish Church (Church of Scotland)
SC004533	Dirleton Parish Church (Church of Scotland)
SC000455	Dunbar Parish Church (Church of Scotland)
SC014299	Dunglass Parish Church (Church of Scotland)
SC014972	Garvald and Morham Parish Church (Church of Scotland)
SC005996	Gladsmuir Parish Church (Church of Scotland)
SC030433	Glencorse Parish Church (Church of Scotland)
SC004673	Gorebridge Parish Church (Church of Scotland)
SC005237	Gullane Parish Church (Church of Scotland)
SC010614	Haddington: St Mary's Parish Church (Church of Scotland)
SC022183	Haddington: West Parish Church (Church of Scotland)
SC014364	Howgate Parish Church (Church of Scotland)
SC016765	Humbie Parish Church (Church of Scotland)
SC015878	Lasswade and Rosewell Parish Church (Church of Scotland)
SC014420	Loanhead Parish Church (Church of Scotland)

SC016556	Longniddry Parish Church (Church of Scotland)
SC004722	Musselburgh: Northesk Parish Church (Church of Scotland)
SC000129	Musselburgh: St Andrew's High Parish Church (Church of Scotland)
SC001726	Musselburgh: St Clement's and St Ninian's Parish Church (Church of Scotland)
SC013559	Musselburgh: St Michael's Inveresk Parish Church (Church of Scotland)
SC035087	Newbattle Parish Church (Church of Scotland)
SC030879	Newton Parish Church (Church of Scotland)
SC004761	Abbey Church, North Berwick, Church of Scotland
SC006421	St Andrew Blackadder, Church of Scotland, North Berwick
SC014810	Ormiston Parish Church (Church of Scotland)
SC004871	Pencaitland Parish Church (Church of Scotland)
SC010902	Penicuik: North Parish Church (Church of Scotland)
SC005838	Penicuik: St Mungo's Parish Church (Church of Scotland)
SC011871	Penicuik: South Parish Church (Church of Scotland)
SC031191	Prestonpans: Prestongrange Parish Church (Church of Scotland)
SC005457	Roslin Parish Church (Church of Scotland)
SC008667	Spott Parish Church (Church of Scotland)
SC017423	Tranent Parish Church (Church of Scotland)
SC012277	Traprain Parish Church (Church of Scotland)
SC000494	Whitekirk and Tyninghame Parish Church (Church of Scotland)
SC015414	Yester Parish Church (Church of Scotland)

4.   Presbytery of Melrose and Peebles

SC010768	Ashkirk Parish Church of Scotland
SC006480	Bowden and Melrose Church of Scotland
SC030062	Broughton, Glenholm and Kilbucho Church of Scotland
SC016990	Caddonfoot Parish Church of Scotland
SC001340	Carlops Parish Church of Scotland
SC009892	Channelkirk and Lauder Church of Scotland
SC003895	Earlston Parish Church of Scotland
SC010081	Eddleston Parish Church of Scotland
SC010389	Old Parish and St Paul's Church of Scotland: Galashiels
SC001386	Galashiels Trinity Church of Scotland
SC034662	Ettrick and Yarrow Parish (Church of Scotland)
SC000281	St John's Church of Scotland: Galashiels
SC001100	Innerleithen, Traquair and Walkerburn Parish Church of Scotland
SC021456	Lyne & Manor Church of Scotland
SC013481	Maxton and Mertoun Parish Church of Scotland
SC000575	Newtown Church of Scotland
SC013316	Peebles Old Parish Church of Scotland
SC009159	Church of Scotland St Andrews Leckie Parish: Peebles
SC010210	St Boswells Parish Church of Scotland
SC000228	Stow St Mary of Wedale & Heriot Church of Scotland
SC004728	Skirling Church of Scotland
SC001866	Stobo and Drumelzier Church of Scotland
SC013564	Tweedsmuir Kirk Church of Scotland
SC003938	St Andrews Parish Church of Scotland: West Linton
SC018087	Kirkurd and Newlands Parish Church of Scotland
SC014883	Selkirk Parish Church of Scotland

5. **Presbytery of Duns**
SC001208 Church of Scotland: Ayton and Burnmouth
Parish Church
SC000867 St Andrew's Wallace Green and Lowick
Church of Scotland, Berwick-upon-Tweed
SC000246 Bonkyl and Edrom Church of Scotland
SC006722 Chirnside Church of Scotland
SC009185 The Parish Church of Coldingham & St Abbs
[Church of Scotland]
SC001456 Coldstream Parish Church of Scotland
SC005161 Duns Parish Church of Scotland
SC000031 Eccles Parish Church of Scotland
SC006499 The Church of Scotland, Eyemouth Parish
Church
SC002789 Fogo & Swinton Church of Scotland
SC024535 Church of Scotland: Foulden and Mordington
Parish Church
SC022349 Gordon St Michael's Church of Scotland
SC016400 Church of Scotland: Grantshouse, Houndwood
and Reston Parish Church
SC013136 Greenlaw Parish, Church of Scotland
SC002216 Hutton, Fishwick and Paxton Church of
Scotland
SC010680 Langton and Lammermuir Kirk, Church of
Scotland
SC009995 Ladykirk and Whitsome Church of Scotland
SC004582 Legerwood Parish, Church of Scotland
SC005115 Leitholm Parish Church (Church of Scotland)
SC004903 Westruther Parish, Church of Scotland

6. **Presbytery of Jedburgh**
SC016457 Ale & Teviot United Church of Scotland
SC004550 Cavers and Kirkton Parish Church (Church of
Scotland)
SC004517 Hawick Burnfoot Church of Scotland
SC005574 St Mary's & Old Parish Church of Scotland,
Hawick
SC005191 Teviot and Roberton Church of Scotland
SC013892 Trinity Parish Church, Hawick (Church of
Scotland)
SC017381 Wilton Parish Church of Scotland
SC012830 Hobkirk & Southdean Parish Church of
Scotland
SC004530 Jedburgh Old and Trinity Parish Church of
Scotland
SC000958 Kelso Country Churches (Church of Scotland)
SC014039 Kelso North and Ednam Parish Church of
Scotland
SC010009 Kelso Old & Sprouston Parish Church of
Scotland
SC003023 Cheviot Churches: Church of Scotland
SC010593 Oxnam Parish Church of Scotland
SC034629 Ruberslaw Parish Church of Scotland
SC006917 Teviothead Parish Church of Scotland

7. **Presbytery of Annandale and Eskdale**
SC010555 Annan Old Parish Church of Scotland
SC010891 St Andrews Parish Church of Scotland, Annan
SC013947 Applegarth, Sibbaldbie & Johnstone Church of
Scotland
SC012516 Brydekirk Parish Church of Scotland
SC000717 Canonbie Parish Church of Scotland
SC006344 Dalton Parish Church of Scotland
SC004542 Dornock Parish Church of Scotland
SC016747 Gretna Old, Gretna St Andrew's, Half Morton
and Kirkpatrick Fleming Parish Church of
Scotland
SC022170 Hightae Parish Church of Scotland
SC005701 Kirkpatrick Juxta Church of Scotland
SC011946 Langholm, Eskdalemuir, Ewes and Westerkirk
Church of Scotland

SC006519 Liddesdale Parish Church of Scotland
SC004644 Lochmaben Church of Scotland
SC007116 Lockerbie Dryfesdale, Hutton and Corrie
Church of Scotland
SC000722 Hoddom, Kirtle-Eaglesfield and Middlebie
Church of Scotland
SC012236 St Andrews Church of Scotland, Moffat
SC001060 St Mungo Parish Church of Scotland,
Lockerbie
SC043454 The Border Kirk (Church of Scotland)
SC013190 Tundergarth Church of Scotland
SC007536 Wamphray Church of Scotland

8. **Presbytery of Dumfries and Kirkcudbright**
SC016053 Balmaclellan & Kells Church of Scotland
SC000498 Balmaghie Church of Scotland
SC004450 Borgue Parish Church of Scotland
SC008648 Caerlaverock Parish Church of Scotland
SC015242 Carsphairn Church of Scotland
SC011037 Castle Douglas Parish Church of Scotland
SC005624 Closeburn Parish Church of Scotland
SC009384 Colvend Southwick & Kirkbean Church of
Scotland
SC007152 Corsock & Kirkpatrick Durham Church of
Scotland
SC014901 Crossmichael & Parton Church of Scotland
SC002443 Dalbeattie and Kirkgunzeon Church of
Scotland
SC013121 Dalry Kirkcudbrightshire Church of Scotland
SC010748 Dumfries Northwest Church of Scotland
SC006404 St George's Church of Scotland, Dumfries
SC009432 St Mary's-Greyfriars' Parish Church, Dumfries
(Church of Scotland)
SC016201 St Michael's & South Church of Scotland,
Dumfries
SC000973 Troqueer Parish Church of Scotland, Dumfries
SC016060 Dunscore Parish Church of Scotland
SC014783 Durisdeer Church of Scotland
SC000961 Gatehouse of Fleet Parish Church of Scotland
SC014663 Glencairn & Moniaive Parish Church of
Scotland
SC033058 Irongray Lochrutton & Terregles Parish
Church of Scotland
SC014150 Kirkconnel Parish Church of Scotland
SC005883 Kirkcudbright Parish Church of Scotland
SC010508 Kirkmahoe Parish Church of Scotland
SC030785 Kirkmichael Tinwald & Torthorwald Church
of Scotland
SC014590 Lochend and New Abbey Church of Scotland
SC015925 Maxwelltown West Church of Scotland,
Dumfries
SC015087 Penpont Keir & Tynron Church of Scotland
SC015399 Cummertrees, Mouswald and Ruthwell Church
of Scotland
SC000845 St Bride's Parish Church of Scotland:
Sanquhar
SC004475 Tarff & Twynholm Church of Scotland
SC016850 The Bengairn Parishes (Church of Scotland)
SC012722 Thornhill Parish Church of Scotland
SC014465 Urr Parish Church of Scotland

9. **Presbytery of Wigtown and Stranraer**
SC003122 Ervie-Kirkcolm Church of Scotland
SC001705 Glasserton and the Isle of Whithorn Church of
Scotland
SC007375 Inch Church of Scotland
SC007136 Kirkcowan Parish Church (Church of Scotland)
SC001946 Kirkinner Church of Scotland
SC010150 Kirkmabreck Church of Scotland
SC007708 Kirkmaiden Parish Church (Church of
Scotland)

SC009412	Leswalt Parish Church (Church of Scotland)
SC003300	Mochrum Church of Scotland
SC006014	Monigaff Church of Scotland
SC006316	New Luce Church of Scotland
SC005302	Old Luce Church of Scotland
SC031847	Parish of Penninghame (Church of Scotland)
SC015452	Portpatrick Parish Church (Church of Scotland)
SC010621	Sorbie Parish Church of Scotland
SC007346	Stoneykirk Parish Church (Church of Scotland)
SC017312	High Kirk of Stranraer (Church of Scotland)
SC002247	Stranraer: St Ninian's Parish Church (Church of Scotland)
SC009905	Town Kirk of Stranraer (Church of Scotland)
SC016881	Whithorn: St Ninian's Priory Church of Scotland
SC014552	Wigtown Parish Church (Church of Scotland)

10.   **Presbytery of Ayr**

SC012456	Alloway Parish Church of Scotland
SC013225	Annbank Parish Church of Scotland
SC008536	Ballantrae Parish Church of Scotland
SC006707	Auchinleck Parish Church of Scotland
SC001792	Castlehill Parish Church of Scotland: Ayr
SC031474	Dalmellington Parish Church of Scotland
SC001994	Ayr: Newton Wallacetown Church of Scotland
SC001757	St Andrew's Parish Church of Scotland: Ayr
SC009336	St James' Parish Church of Scotland: Ayr
SC016860	St Leonard's Parish Church of Scotland: Ayr
SC015366	Barr Parish Church of Scotland
SC013689	Catrine Parish Church of Scotland
SC005283	Coylton Parish Church (Church of Scotland)
SC002144	Craigie Symington Parish Church (Church of Scotland)
SC017520	Crosshill Parish Church (Church of Scotland)
SC012591	Dailly Parish Church of Scotland
SC013503	Dalrymple Parish Church (Church of Scotland)
SC008482	Dundonald Church of Scotland
SC008226	Fisherton Church of Scotland
SC007347	Girvan: North Parish Church of Scotland
SC010381	Girvan South Parish Church of Scotland
SC031952	Kirkmichael Parish Church of Scotland: Maybole
SC000213	Kirkoswald Parish Church of Scotland
SC007714	Mauchline Parish Church of Scotland
SC014055	Lugar Parish Church of Scotland
SC004906	St Quivox Parish Church: Ayr (Church of Scotland)
SC014794	New Cumnock Parish Church (Church of Scotland)
SC010606	Muirkirk Parish Church of Scotland
SC003164	Maybole Parish Church of Scotland
SC034504	Church of Scotland Cumnock Trinity Church
SC000130	Ochiltree Parish Church of Scotland
SC006025	Old Cumnock Old Church of Scotland
SC001940	Kingcase Parish Church of Scotland: Prestwick
SC011750	St Nicholas Parish Church of Scotland: Prestwick
SC007403	Prestwick South Church of Scotland
SC004271	Monkton & Prestwick North Parish Church of Scotland
SC014381	St Colmon (Arnsheen Barrhill and Colmonell) Church of Scotland
SC015899	Sorn Parish Church of Scotland
SC035601	Stair Parish Church (Church of Scotland)
SC013366	Straiton (St Cuthbert's) Parish Church of Scotland: Maybole
SC014767	Tarbolton Parish Church of Scotland
SC030714	Drongan: The Schaw Kirk (Church of Scotland)

SC007246	Troon Old Parish Church of Scotland
SC003477	Portland Parish Church of Scotland: Troon
SC015019	Troon St Meddan's Parish Church of Scotland
SC016648	The Auld Kirk of Ayr Church of Scotland
SC008562	Patna Waterside Parish Church of Scotland
SC014338	Ayr St Columba Church of Scotland

11.   **Presbytery of Irvine and Kilmarnock**

SC011414	Crosshouse Parish Church (Church of Scotland)
SC012014	Darvel Parish Church of Scotland
SC008684	Dreghorn & Springside Parish Church of Scotland
SC000447	Dunlop Church of Scotland
SC010062	Fenwick Parish Church (Church of Scotland)
SC010370	Galston Parish Church of Scotland
SC001084	Hurlford Church of Scotland
SC005491	Girdle Toll Church of Scotland, Irvine New Town
SC008725	Fullarton Parish Church (Church of Scotland), Irvine
SC002299	Mure Parish Church of Scotland, Irvine
SC008345	Irvine Old Parish Church of Scotland
SC002469	Relief Church of Scotland, Irvine
SC010167	St Andrews Church of Scotland: Irvine
SC008154	Kilmarnock: Kay Park Parish Church of Scotland
SC031334	Kilmarnock: New Laigh Kirk (Church of Scotland)
SC006040	Kilmarnock Riccarton Church of Scotland
SC006345	St Andrew's and St Marnock's Parish Church of Scotland, Kilmarnock
SC033107	St Johns Parish Church of Scotland – Onthank: Kilmarnock
SC001324	St Kentigern's Parish Church of Scotland: Kilmarnock
SC012430	Kilmarnock South Parish Church of Scotland
SC009036	St Maurs Glencairn Church of Scotland, Kilmaurs
SC013880	Loudoun Church of Scotland, Newmilns
SC015890	John Knox Parish Church of Scotland, Stewarton
SC013595	St Columba's Parish Church of Scotland, Stewarton

12.   **Presbytery of Ardrossan**

SC004736	Ardrossan Park Parish Church of Scotland
SC023003	Ardrossan & Saltcoats Kirkgate Parish Church of Scotland
SC004660	Beith Parish Church of Scotland
SC012017	Brodick Church of Scotland
SC005030	Corrie Parish Church of Scotland
SC004919	Cumbrae Parish Church of Scotland
SC013170	Dalry St Margaret's Parish Church of Scotland
SC006882	Dalry Trinity Church of Scotland
SC017304	Fairlie Parish Church of Scotland
SC016024	Kilbirnie Auld Kirk (Church of Scotland)
SC013750	St Columbas Parish Church of Scotland: Kilbirnie
SC023602	Kilmory Parish Church of Scotland
SC016499	Kilwinning Mansefield Trinity Church of Scotland
SC001856	Kilwinning Old Parish Church of Scotland
SC015072	Lamlash Church of Scotland
SC002782	Largs Clark Memorial Church of Scotland
SC002294	The Church of Scotland, Largs: St Columba's Parish Church
SC009048	Largs St John's Church of Scotland
SC009377	Lochranza & Pirnmill Church of Scotland
SC003299	Saltcoats North Parish Church of Scotland

SC002905	Saltcoats St Cuthberts Parish Church of Scotland
SC005323	Shiskine Church of Scotland
SC015397	Stevenston Ardeer Parish Church of Scotland
SC009848	Stevenston High Church of Scotland
SC000452	Stevenston Livingstone Parish Church of Scotland
SC013464	West Kilbride Parish Church of Scotland
SC014005	Whiting Bay & Kildonan Church of Scotland

13.   **Presbytery of Lanark**

SC000333	Biggar Parish Church of Scotland
SC000603	Blackmount Parish Church (Church of Scotland)
SC017001	Cairngryffe Parish Church (Church of Scotland)
SC026539	Kirkton Parish Church, Carluke (Church of Scotland)
SC013968	St Andrews Parish Church of Scotland: Carluke
SC004066	St Johns Church of Scotland: Carluke
SC016360	Carnwath Parish Church of Scotland
SC028124	Carstairs & Carstairs Junction Church of Scotland
SC016493	Coalburn Parish Church (Church of Scotland)
SC014659	Crossford Church of Scotland
SC003080	Forth St Paul's Parish Church (Church of Scotland)
SC017506	The Upper Clyde Church of Scotland
SC011211	Kirkfieldbank Parish Church (Church of Scotland)
SC014451	Kirkmuirhill Parish Church (Church of Scotland)
SC016504	Greyfriars Parish Church, Lanark (Church of Scotland)
SC011368	St Nicholas Parish Church, Lanark (Church of Scotland)
SC013217	Law Parish Church (Church of Scotland)
SC006516	Lesmahagow Abbeygreen (Church of Scotland)
SC017014	Lesmahagow Old Parish Church (Church of Scotland)
SC016304	Libberton & Quothquan Parish Church (Church of Scotland)
SC009095	Symington Parish Church (Church of Scotland)
SC001718	The Douglas Valley Church (Church of Scotland)

14.   **Presbytery of Greenock and Paisley**

SC015730	Arthurlie Parish Church of Scotland Barrhead
SC016467	Barrhead Bourock Parish Church of Scotland
SC007776	Barrhead South and Levern Church of Scotland
SC006109	Bishopton Parish Church (Church of Scotland)
SC002293	Freeland Church of Scotland, Bridge of Weir
SC003766	Church of Scotland, St Machar's Ranfurly Church, Bridge of Weir
SC008214	Caldwell Parish Church of Scotland
SC015701	Elderslie Kirk (Church of Scotland)
SC017177	Erskine Parish Church of Scotland
SC007324	Old Gourock and Ashton Parish Church of Scotland
SC006412	St Johns Church of Scotland: Gourock
SC010818	Greenock: Lyle Kirk (Church of Scotland)
SC037023	Greenock East End Parish Church of Scotland

SC008357	Greenock The Mount Kirk (Church of Scotland)
SC004855	Old West Kirk, Greenock (Church of Scotland)
SC016711	St Margarets Church of Scotland: Greenock
SC008059	St Ninians Parish Church of Scotland: Greenock
SC001043	Wellpark Mid Kirk of Greenock (Church of Scotland)
SC005106	Greenock Westburn Church of Scotland
SC012822	Houston and Killellan Kirk (Church of Scotland)
SC003487	Howwood Parish Church of Scotland
SC011778	Inchinnan Parish Church (Church of Scotland)
SC001079	Inverkip Parish Church of Scotland
SC009588	Johnstone High Parish Church of Scotland
SC011696	St Andrews Trinity Parish Church of Scotland Johnstone
SC011747	St Pauls Church of Scotland: Johnstone
SC012123	Kilbarchan East Church of Scotland
SC017140	Kilbarchan West Church of Scotland
SC009291	Kilmacolm Old Kirk (Church of Scotland)
SC007992	St Columba Church of Scotland Kilmacolm
SC015085	Langbank Church of Scotland
SC020972	Linwood Parish Church of Scotland
SC014518	Lochwinnoch Parish Church of Scotland
SC035155	Neilston Parish Church of Scotland
SC007633	Paisley Abbey (Church of Scotland)
SC006718	Paisley: Glenburn Parish Church of Scotland
SC006437	Paisley: Stow Brae Kirk (Church of Scotland)
SC012648	Lylesland Parish Church of Scotland, Paisley
SC011798	Paisley: Martyrs Sandyford Church of Scotland
SC005362	Oakshaw Trinity Church, Paisley
SC007484	Sherwood Greenlaw Parish Church of Scotland, Paisley
SC005770	St Columba Foxbar Church of Scotland, Paisley
SC000949	St James's Paisley (Church of Scotland)
SC000558	St Luke's Church of Scotland: Paisley
SC011210	St Marks Church of Scotland (Oldhall): Paisley
SC004753	St Ninians Church of Scotland: Paisley
SC012650	Paisley Wallneuk North Church of Scotland
SC005421	Church of Scotland Port Glasgow: Hamilton Bardrainney Church
SC009018	Port Glasgow: St Andrew's Church of Scotland
SC002410	St Martins Church of Scotland: Port Glasgow
SC006605	Renfrew North Parish Church of Scotland
SC003785	Renfrew Trinity (Church of Scotland)
SC003309	Skelmorlie and Wemyss Bay Parish Church of Scotland

16.   **Presbytery of Glasgow**

SC017638	Banton Parish Church of Scotland
SC012329	Kenmure Parish Church of Scotland
SC005642	Springfield Cambridge Church of Scotland, Bishopbriggs
SC003290	Broom Parish Church of Scotland
SC006633	Burnside Blairbeth Church of Scotland
SC016612	Busby Parish Church of Scotland
SC015193	Cadder Parish Church of Scotland
SC006638	Flemington Hallside Parish Church of Scotland
SC000061	Cambuslang Parish Church of Scotland
SC023596	St Andrews Parish Church of Scotland Cambuslang: Glasgow
SC011456	Trinity St Pauls Church of Scotland, Cambuslang
SC000835	Campsie Parish Church of Scotland
SC006752	Chryston Church of Scotland
SC006377	Eaglesham Parish Church of Scotland

SC001077	Fernhill & Cathkin Church of Scotland
SC007541	Gartcosh Parish Church of Scotland
SC009774	Orchardhill Parish Church of Scotland, Giffnock
SC007807	Giffnock South Parish Church of Scotland
SC002965	Giffnock Park Church of Scotland
SC014631	Anderston Kelvingrove Church of Scotland, Glasgow
SC002220	Glasgow: Mure Memorial Church of Scotland
SC005625	Baillieston St Andrews Church of Scotland, Glasgow
SC000885	Balshagray Victoria Park Parish Church of Scotland, Glasgow
SC025730	Barlanark Greyfriars Parish Church of Scotland, Glasgow
SC006410	Blawarthill Parish Church of Scotland, Glasgow
SC012535	Bridgeton St Francis in the East Church of Scotland, Glasgow
SC007820	Broomhill Church of Scotland, Glasgow
SC006958	Calton Parkhead Parish Church of Scotland, Glasgow
SC010265	Cardonald Parish Church of Scotland, Glasgow
SC011224	Carmunnock Parish Church of Scotland, Glasgow
SC000532	Carmyle Church of Scotland, Glasgow
SC030150	Carnwadric Church of Scotland, Glasgow
SC015309	Glasgow: Castlemilk Parish Church of Scotland
SC002727	Cathcart Old Parish Church of Scotland, Glasgow
SC033802	Cathcart Trinity Church of Scotland, Glasgow
SC013966	Glasgow Cathedral (St Mungo's or High), Church of Scotland
SC012939	Colston Milton Parish Church of Scotland, Glasgow
SC005709	Colston Wellpark Parish Church of Scotland, Glasgow
SC009874	Cranhill Parish Church of Scotland, Glasgow
SC009761	Croftfoot Parish Church of Scotland, Glasgow
SC008824	Glasgow Dennistoun New Parish Church of Scotland
SC022128	Drumchapel St Andrews Parish Church of Scotland, Glasgow
SC008954	St Marks Parish Church of Scotland, Glasgow
SC004642	Glasgow Shettleston New Church of Scotland
SC003021	St Georges & St Peters Parish Church of Scotland: Easterhouse, Glasgow
SC000277	Eastwood Parish Church of Scotland, Glasgow
SC030168	Gairbraid Parish Church of Scotland, Glasgow
SC016862	Garthamlock & Craigend East Parish Church of Scotland, Glasgow
SC002214	Gorbals Parish Church of Scotland, Glasgow
SC004153	Glasgow Govan and Linthouse Parish Church of Scotland
SC006729	High Carntyne Church of Scotland, Glasgow
SC002614	Hillington Park Church of Scotland, Glasgow
SC007798	St Christophers Church of Scotland: Glasgow
SC002398	Hyndland Parish Church of Scotland, Glasgow
SC009841	Ibrox Parish Church of Scotland, Glasgow
SC027651	John Ross Memorial Church for Deaf People, Glasgow (Church of Scotland)
SC015683	Jordanhill Parish Church of Scotland, Glasgow
SC014414	Glasgow: Kelvinbridge Parish Church (Church of Scotland)
SC006629	Kelvinside Hillhead Parish Church of Scotland, Glasgow
SC008980	Kenmuir Mount Vernon Church of Scotland, Glasgow
SC017040	Kings Park Church of Scotland, Glasgow
SC014895	Kinning Park Parish Church of Scotland, Glasgow
SC007757	Knightswood St Margarets Parish Church of Scotland, Glasgow
SC007055	Langside Parish Church of Scotland, Glasgow
SC002161	Lochwood Parish Church of Scotland, Glasgow
SC002102	Maryhill Parish Church of Scotland, Glasgow
SC004016	Merrylea Parish Church of Scotland Newlands, Glasgow
SC013281	Mosspark Church of Scotland, Glasgow
SC010138	Glasgow: Clincarthill Church of Scotland
SC000042	Newlands South Church of Scotland, Glasgow
SC008315	Partick South Church of Scotland, Glasgow
SC007632	Partick Trinity Church of Scotland, Glasgow
SC022874	Penilee St Andrew Church of Scotland, Glasgow
SC006683	Pollokshaws Parish Church of Scotland, Glasgow
SC013690	Pollokshields Church of Scotland, Glasgow
SC003241	Possilpark Parish Church of Scotland, Glasgow
SC015858	Priesthill & Nitshill Church of Scotland, Glasgow
SC001575	Queens Park Govanhill Parish Church of Scotland, Glasgow
SC011423	Renfield St Stephens Parish Church of Scotland, Glasgow
SC032401	Robroyston Church of Scotland, Glasgow
SC003149	Ruchazie Parish Church of Scotland, Glasgow
SC014538	Glasgow: Ruchill Kelvinside Parish Church of Scotland
SC002155	Sandyford Henderson Memorial Church of Scotland, Glasgow
SC009460	Sandyhills Church of Scotland, Glasgow
SC030418	Scotstoun Parish Church of Scotland, Glasgow
SC012969	Shawlands Parish Church of Scotland, Glasgow
SC015155	Sherbrooke St Gilberts Church of Scotland, Glasgow
SC004642	Glasgow Shettleston New Church of Scotland
SC001070	Shettleston Old Parish Church of Scotland, Glasgow
SC010899	South Carntyne Church of Scotland, Glasgow
SC005196	South Shawlands Church of Scotland, Glasgow
SC004397	Springburn Parish Church of Scotland, Glasgow
SC009600	St Andrews East Parish Church, Glasgow (Church of Scotland)
SC006342	St Columbas Gaelic Church of Scotland, Glasgow
SC017297	St Davids Parish Church of Scotland: Glasgow
SC004918	St Enoch's – Hogganfield Parish Church of Scotland, Glasgow
SC004931	St Georges Tron Church of Scotland, Glasgow
SC013313	St James Pollok Parish Church of Scotland: Glasgow
SC012920	St Johns Renfield Church of Scotland, Glasgow
SC032738	Gallowgate Parish Church of Scotland, Glasgow
SC005764	St Margarets Tollcross Church of Scotland: Glasgow
SC011527	St Nicholas Parish Church of Scotland, Cardonald, Glasgow
SC016306	St Pauls Church of Scotland: Provanmill, Glasgow
SC015459	St Rollox Church of Scotland: Glasgow
SC015579	Temple Anniesland Parish Church of Scotland, Glasgow
SC009399	Toryglen Church of Scotland, Glasgow

SC009578	Trinity Possil & Henry Drummond Church of Scotland, Glasgow
SC017015	Tron St Marys Parish Church of Scotland, Glasgow
SC004821	Victoria Tollcross Church of Scotland, Glasgow
SC008840	Glasgow Wallacewell Church of Scotland New Charge
SC000289	Wellington Church of Scotland, Glasgow
SC030362	Whiteinch Church of Scotland, Glasgow
SC017408	Yoker Parish Church of Scotland, Glasgow
SC002834	Glenboig Parish Church of Scotland
SC011453	Greenbank Parish Church of Scotland
SC009866	Kilsyth Anderson Church of Scotland
SC009912	Kilsyth Burns & Old Parish Church of Scotland
SC002424	Kirkintilloch Hillhead Church of Scotland
SC008735	St Columba Parish Church of Scotland, Kirkintilloch
SC007427	St Davids Memorial Park Church of Scotland, Kirkintilloch
SC007260	St Marys Parish Church of Scotland, Kirkintilloch
SC008935	Lenzie Old Parish Church of Scotland
SC015287	Lenzie Union Church of Scotland
SC017317	Maxwell Mearns Church of Scotland
SC007125	Mearns Kirk (Church of Scotland)
SC014735	Milton of Campsie Parish Church of Scotland
SC015303	Netherlee Church of Scotland
SC004219	Newton Mearns Parish Church of Scotland
SC006856	Rutherglen Old Parish Church of Scotland
SC013558	Stonelaw Parish Church of Scotland, Rutherglen
SC007585	Rutherglen West and Wardlawhill Parish Church of Scotland
SC003155	Stamperland Parish Church of Scotland, Clarkston
SC014212	Stepps Parish Church of Scotland, Stepps
SC008426	Thornliebank Parish Church of Scotland
SC016058	Torrance Parish Church of Scotland
SC011672	Twechar Church of Scotland
SC009939	Williamwood Parish Church of Scotland

17.   Presbytery of Hamilton

SC016464	Airdrie Broomknoll Parish Church of Scotland
SC011239	Airdrie Clarkston Parish Church of Scotland
SC014555	Airdrie Flowerhill Parish Church of Scotland
SC024357	Airdrie High Parish Church of Scotland
SC004083	Airdrie Jackson Church of Scotland
SC011674	Airdrie New Monkland Parish Church of Scotland
SC002900	Airdrie St Columbas Parish Church of Scotland
SC004209	Bargeddie Parish Church of Scotland
SC012556	Bellshill: Central Parish Church of Scotland
SC008340	Bellshill West Parish Church of Scotland
SC005955	Blantyre St Andrew's Parish Church of Scotland
SC004084	Blantyre Livingstone Memorial Parish Church of Scotland
SC018492	Blantyre Old Parish Church of Scotland
SC012944	The New Wellwynd Parish Church of Scotland Airdrie
SC009819	Bothwell Parish Church of Scotland
SC015831	Calderbank Parish Church of Scotland
SC030492	Caldercruix and Longriggend Parish Church of Scotland
SC008486	Chapelhall Parish Church of Scotland
SC011817	Chapelton Parish Church of Scotland
SC017084	Cleland Parish Church of Scotland

SC009704	Coatbridge Blairhill Dundyvan Parish Church of Scotland
SC006854	Coatbridge Calder Parish Church of Scotland
SC016362	Coatbridge Middle Parish Church of Scotland
SC013521	Coatbridge New St Andrew's Parish Church of Scotland
SC010236	Coatbridge Old Monkland Parish Church of Scotland
SC008809	Coatbridge Townhead Parish Church of Scotland
SC016156	Dalserf Parish Church of Scotland
SC007396	East Kilbride Claremont Parish Church of Scotland
SC030300	East Kilbride Greenhills Parish Church of Scotland
SC016751	East Kilbride Moncreiff Parish Church of Scotland
SC000609	East Kilbride Old Parish Church of Scotland
SC008332	East Kilbride South Parish Church of Scotland
SC000250	East Kilbride West Kirk Church of Scotland
SC001857	East Kilbride Westwood Parish Church of Scotland
SC014716	Glassford Parish Church of Scotland
SC012692	East Kilbride Mossneuk Parish Church of Scotland
SC018154	Greengairs Parish Church of Scotland
SC006611	Cadzow Parish Church of Scotland, Hamilton
SC011571	Hamilton Gilmour & Whitehill Parish Church of Scotland
SC005376	Hamilton Hillhouse Parish Church of Scotland
SC010855	Hamilton Old Parish Church of Scotland
SC008779	Hamilton St John's Parish Church of Scotland
SC022166	Hamilton South Parish Church of Scotland
SC007051	Hamilton Trinity Parish Church of Scotland
SC008451	Hamilton West Parish Church of Scotland
SC012888	Holytown Parish Church of Scotland
SC013309	Chalmers Parish Church of Scotland Larkhall
SC002870	St Machan's Parish Church of Scotland Larkhall
SC008611	Trinity Parish Church of Scotland, Larkhall
SC034242	Church of Scotland Stewartfield New Charge Development East Kilbride
SC008810	Motherwell Crosshill Parish Church of Scotland
SC016821	Motherwell North Parish Church of Scotland
SC008601	Motherwell South Parish Church of Scotland
SC010924	Motherwell St Margaret's Parish Church of Scotland
SC012233	Motherwell St Marys Parish Church of Scotland
SC005427	Newarthill and Carfin Parish Church of Scotland
SC006540	Bonkle Parish Church of Scotland
SC001381	Newmains Coltness Memorial Parish Church of Scotland
SC004688	New Stevenston Wrangholm Parish Church of Scotland
SC007360	Overtown Parish Church of Scotland
SC009689	Quarter Parish Church of Scotland
SC015503	Motherwell Dalziel St Andrew's Parish Church of Scotland
SC013269	Kirk o' Shotts Parish Church of Scotland
SC003239	Stonehouse St Ninian's Parish Church of Scotland
SC001956	Strathaven Avendale Old and Drumclog Memorial Parish Church of Scotland
SC015591	Strathaven East Parish Church of Scotland
SC001020	Strathaven Rankin Parish Church of Scotland
SC010039	Uddingston Burnhead Parish Church of Scotland

SC006538	Shotts Calderhead – Erskine Parish Church of Scotland
SC009991	Uddingston Viewpark Parish Church of Scotland
SC013037	Wishaw: Cambusnethan North Parish Church of Scotland
SC011532	Wishaw Cambusnethan Old and Morningside Parish Church of Scotland
SC013841	Wishaw Craigneuk and Belhaven Church of Scotland
SC011253	Wishaw Old Parish Church of Scotland
SC012529	Wishaw St Marks Parish Church of Scotland
SC016893	Uddingston Old Parish Church of Scotland
SC010775	South Wishaw Parish Church of Scotland

18.   Presbytery of Dumbarton

SC001268	Alexandria Parish Church of Scotland
SC008929	Arrochar Parish Church of Scotland
SC006355	Baldernock Parish Church of Scotland
SC037739	Bearsden: Baljaffray Parish Church of Scotland
SC009748	Killermont Parish Church (Church of Scotland) Bearsden
SC012997	New Kilpatrick Parish Church of Scotland
SC009082	The Church of Scotland Bearsden Cross Church
SC004489	Westerton Fairlie Memorial Parish Church of Scotland, Bearsden
SC000886	Bonhill Church of Scotland
SC003494	Cardross Parish Church of Scotland
SC004596	Abbotsford, Church of Scotland, Clydebank
SC005108	Faifley Parish Church of Scotland, Clydebank
SC015005	Kilbowie St Andrews Church of Scotland, Clydebank
SC013242	Radnor Park Church of Scotland, Clydebank
SC003077	St Cuthberts Parish Church of Scotland: Clydebank
SC001725	Craigrownie Parish Church of Scotland
SC013599	Dalmuir Barclay Church of Scotland
SC002937	Riverside Parish Church of Scotland, Dumbarton
SC006235	St Andrews Church of Scotland: Dumbarton
SC010474	West Kirk, Dumbarton (Church of Scotland)
SC008854	Duntocher Trinity Parish Church of Scotland
SC016699	Garelochhead Parish Church of Scotland
SC007801	Park Church of Scotland, Helensburgh
SC012053	The Church of Scotland: Helensburgh: St Andrew's Kirk
SC012346	Jamestown Parish Church of Scotland
SC002145	Kilmaronock Gartocharn Church of Scotland
SC017192	Luss Parish Church of Scotland
SC009913	Cairns Church of Scotland, Milngavie
SC003870	St Lukes Church of Scotland: Milngavie
SC002737	St Pauls Parish Church of Scotland: Milngavie
SC011630	Old Kilpatrick Bowling Parish Church of Scotland
SC014833	Renton Trinity Parish Church of Scotland
SC010086	Rhu and Shandon Parish Church of Scotland
SC001510	Rosneath St Modans Church of Scotland

19.   Presbytery of Argyll

SC015795	Appin Parish Church (Church of Scotland)
SC000680	Ardchattan (Church of Scotland)
SC010713	Ardrishaig Parish Church (Church of Scotland)
SC003980	Barra Church of Scotland
SC002493	Campbeltown: Highland Parish Church of Scotland
SC011686	Campbeltown: Lorne and Lowland Church of Scotland
SC035582	Coll Parish Church (Church of Scotland)
SC031271	Colonsay & Oronsay Church of Scotland

SC006738	Connel Parish Church of Scotland
SC003718	Craignish Parish Church of Scotland
SC016097	Cumlodden, Lochfyneside and Lochgair (Church of Scotland)
SC003216	Dunoon: St John's Church (Church of Scotland)
SC017524	Dunoon: The High Kirk (Church of Scotland)
SC002567	Gigha & Cara Church (Church of Scotland)
SC002121	Glassary, Kilmartin & Ford Parish Church of Scotland
SC016665	Glenaray & Inveraray Parish Church (Church of Scotland)
SC003179	Glenorchy & Innishael Church of Scotland
SC013247	Innellan Church (Church of Scotland)
SC036399	Iona Parish Church (Church of Scotland)
SC002925	Jura Parish Church of Scotland
SC009853	Kilarrow Parish Church of Scotland
SC017005	Kilbrandon & Kilchattan Parish Church (Church of Scotland)
SC006948	Kilcalmonell Parish Church (Church of Scotland)
SC013203	Kilchoman Parish Church (Church of Scotland)
SC009417	Kilchrenan & Dalavich Parish Church (Church of Scotland)
SC006032	Kildalton & Oa Parish Church (Church of Scotland)
SC003483	Kilfinan Parish Church (Church of Scotland)
SC013473	Kilfinichen & Kilvickeon & the Ross of Mull Church of Scotland
SC016020	Killean & Kilchenzie Parish Church (Church of Scotland)
SC015317	Kilmeny Parish Church of Scotland
SC021449	Kilmodan & Colintraive Parish Church of Scotland
SC011171	Kilmore & Oban Church of Scotland
SC001694	Kilmun: St Munn's Church (Church of Scotland)
SC025506	Kilninian & Kilmore Church of Scotland
SC002458	Kilninver & Kilmelford Parish Church of Scotland
SC001976	Kirn Parish Church (Church of Scotland)
SC014928	Kyles Parish Church (Church of Scotland)
SC030972	Lismore Parish Church (Church of Scotland)
SC016311	Lochgilphead Church of Scotland
SC006458	Lochgoilhead & Kilmorich Church (Church of Scotland)
SC013377	Muckairn Parish Church (Church of Scotland)
SC001002	North Knapdale Parish Church of Scotland
SC004086	Portnahaven Parish Church of Scotland
SC006420	Rothesay: Trinity Church (Church of Scotland)
SC002609	Saddell & Carradale Church (Church of Scotland)
SC026099	Salen and Ulva Church of Scotland
SC006657	Sandbank Church (Church of Scotland)
SC004280	Skipness: St Brendan's Church (Church of Scotland)
SC005484	Southend Parish Church (Church of Scotland)
SC010782	South Knapdale Parish Church (Church of Scotland)
SC031790	South Uist Church of Scotland
SC001767	Strachur & Strathlachlan Church (Church of Scotland)
SC004088	Strathfillan Parish Church of Scotland
SC003410	Strone & Ardentinny Church (Church of Scotland)
SC002622	Tarbert, Loch Fyne and Kilberry (Church of Scotland)
SC030563	The United Church of Bute (Church of Scotland)

SC000878	Tiree Parish Church of Scotland
SC002878	Tobermory Parish Church of Scotland
SC003909	Torosay & Kinlochspelvie Church of Scotland
SC015531	Toward Church (Church of Scotland)

22.   Presbytery of Falkirk

SC029326	Cumbernauld Abronhill Church of Scotland
SC011038	Airth Parish Church of Scotland
SC008191	Bo'ness Old Kirk (Church of Scotland)
SC015225	Bonnybridge St Helen's Parish Church of Scotland
SC001385	Brightons Parish Church of Scotland
SC014816	Camelon Parish Church, Church of Scotland
SC011839	Cumbernauld: Condorrat Parish Church of Scotland
SC000877	Cumbernauld Old Parish Church of Scotland
SC016255	Denny Old Parish Church of Scotland
SC007072	Denny Westpark Church of Scotland
SC002943	Dunipace Parish Church of Scotland
SC000652	Falkirk Trinity Church of Scotland
SC000775	Grangemouth Abbotsgrange Church of Scotland
SC014536	Haggs Parish Church of Scotland
SC004564	Cumbernauld Kildrum Parish Church of Scotland
SC001603	Grangemouth, Kirk of the Holy Rood, Church of Scotland
SC006456	Larbert East Church of Scotland
SC000445	Larbert Old Church of Scotland
SC012251	Larbert West Parish Church of Scotland
SC007383	Laurieston Parish Church of Scotland
SC003421	Polmont Old Parish Church of Scotland
SC008787	Redding & Westquarter Church of Scotland
SC013602	Slamannan Parish Church of Scotland
SC005066	St Andrews West Church of Scotland, Falkirk
SC002263	Stenhouse & Carron Parish Church of Scotland: Stenhousemuir
SC013114	Grangemouth Zetland Parish Church of Scotland
SC036366	St Mungo's Church of Scotland, Cumbernauld
SC002512	Blackbraes & Shieldhill Parish Church of Scotland
SC007665	St James Church of Scotland, Falkirk
SC016991	Grahamston United Church
SC011448	St Andrew's Church of Scotland, Bo'ness
SC007571	Muiravonside Parish Church of Scotland
SC009754	Bothkennar & Carronshore Parish Church (Church of Scotland)
SC007811	Carriden Parish Church of Scotland
SC004142	Bainsford Parish Church of Scotland, Falkirk

23.   Presbytery of Stirling

SC001308	Aberfoyle Parish Church of Scotland
SC007821	St Mungo's Parish Church of Scotland, Alloa
SC007605	Alloa Ludgate Church of Scotland
SC000006	Alva Parish Church of Scotland
SC005335	Balfron Church of Scotland
SC012316	Balquhidder Parish Church of Scotland
SC002953	Allan Church of Scotland, Bannockburn
SC011345	Bannockburn Ladywell Church of Scotland
SC015171	Bridge of Allan Parish Church of Scotland
SC012927	Buchanan Parish Church of Scotland
SC000833	Buchlyvie Church of Scotland
SC000396	Callander Kirk Church of Scotland
SC019113	Cambusbarron Parish Church of Scotland Bruce Memorial
SC002324	Clackmannan Parish Church of Scotland
SC016296	Cowie and Plean Church of Scotland
SC009713	Dollar Parish Church of Scotland
SC004824	Drymen Church of Scotland
SC004454	Dunblane Cathedral Church of Scotland

SC005185	Dunblane: St Blane's Church of Scotland
SC028465	Fallin Parish Church of Scotland
SC012537	Fintry Church of Scotland
SC012154	Gargunnock Parish Church of Scotland
SC009788	Gartmore Parish Church of Scotland
SC003028	Glendevon Parish Church of Scotland
SC012140	Killearn Kirk (Church of Scotland)
SC010198	Killin & Ardeonaig Parish Church of Scotland
SC012031	Kilmadock Parish Church of Scotland, Doune
SC000802	Kincardine in Menteith Church of Scotland, Blair Drummond
SC004286	Kippen Parish Church of Scotland
SC014031	Lecropt Kirk Parish Church of Scotland
SC001298	Logie Kirk Stirling (Church of Scotland)
SC004778	Menstrie Parish Church of Scotland
SC009418	Muckhart Parish Church of Scotland
SC028719	Norrieston Parish Church of Scotland
SC001864	Port of Menteith Church of Scotland
SC018155	Sauchie and Coalsnaughton Parish Church of Scotland
SC001414	Allan Park South Church of Scotland, Stirling
SC011473	Church of the Holy Rude, Stirling (Church of Scotland)
SC011795	Stirling North Parish Church of Scotland
SC013444	St Columba's Church of Scotland Stirling
SC005432	St Marks Parish Church of Scotland: Stirling
SC016320	St Ninians Old Parish Church of Scotland, Stirling
SC007533	Viewfield Erskine Church of Scotland, Stirling
SC007261	Strathblane Parish Church of Scotland
SC016570	Tillicoultry Parish Church of Scotland
SC005918	St Serfs Church of Scotland, Tullibody

24.   Presbytery of Dunfermline

SC005851	St Fillans Church of Scotland: Aberdour
SC031695	Beath and Cowdenbeath North Church of Scotland
SC012892	Cairneyhill Parish Church of Scotland
SC010676	Carnock and Oakley Church of Scotland
SC003799	Cowdenbeath Trinity Church of Scotland
SC015149	Culross & Torryburn Church of Scotland
SC020926	Dalgety Parish Church of Scotland
SC016883	The Abbey Church of Dunfermline (Church of Scotland)
SC035690	Dunfermline East Church of Scotland
SC011659	Dunfermline Gillespie Memorial Church of Scotland
SC013226	Dunfermline North Parish Church of Scotland
SC007302	St Andrew's Erskine Church of Scotland, Dunfermline
SC007799	Dunfermline St Leonard's Parish Church of Scotland
SC007080	Dunfermline St Margaret's Parish Church of Scotland
SC007453	St Ninians Church of Scotland: Dunfermline
SC008085	Dunfermline Townhill & Kingseat Parish Church of Scotland
SC000968	Inverkeithing Parish Church of Scotland
SC011004	Kelty Church of Scotland
SC002435	Limekilns Church of Scotland
SC032353	Lochgelly and Benarty St Serf's Parish Church of Scotland
SC007414	North Queensferry Church of Scotland
SC013620	Rosyth Parish Church of Scotland
SC013688	Saline & Blairingone Parish Church of Scotland
SC002951	Tulliallan & Kincardine Parish Church of Scotland

25.   Presbytery of Kirkcaldy

SC031143	Auchterderran Kinglassie Parish Church, Church of Scotland

SC025310	Auchtertool Kirk (Church of Scotland)
SC009495	Buckhaven and Wemyss Parish Church of Scotland
SC016418	Burntisland Parish Church of Scotland
SC008991	Dysart St Clair Church of Scotland
SC007397	Glenrothes Christ's Kirk (Church of Scotland)
SC016386	St Columba's Parish Church of Scotland, Glenrothes
SC009845	St Margaret's Parish Church of Scotland: Glenrothes
SC002472	St Ninian's Parish Church of Scotland: Glenrothes
SC016733	Kennoway, Windygates and Balgonie: St Kenneth's Church of Scotland
SC007848	Kinghorn Parish Church of Scotland
SC002586	Abbotshall Parish Church of Scotland, Kirkcaldy
SC012039	Linktown Church of Scotland, Kirkcaldy
SC002858	Pathhead Parish Church of Scotland, Kirkcaldy
SC031064	St Bryce Kirk, Church of Scotland, Kirkcaldy
SC005628	Bennochy Parish Church of Scotland, Kirkcaldy
SC012756	Templehall Parish Church of Scotland, Kirkcaldy
SC015807	Torbain Parish Church of Scotland, Kirkcaldy
SC014025	Trinity Church of Scotland, Leslie
SC031969	Leven Parish Church of Scotland
SC003417	Markinch & Thornton Parish Church of Scotland
SC009581	Wellesley Parish Church of Scotland, Methil
SC007949	Methilhill and Denbeath Parish Church of Scotland
26.	**Presbytery of St Andrews**
SC004848	Abdie & Dunbog Parish Church of Scotland
SC012986	Anstruther Parish Church of Scotland
SC005402	Auchtermuchty Parish Church of Scotland
SC002542	Balmerino Parish Church of Scotland
SC001108	Boarhills and Dunino Parish Church of Scotland
SC005565	Cameron Parish Church (Church of Scotland)
SC016744	Carnbee Church of Scotland
SC000181	Cellardyke Parish Church of Scotland
SC017442	Ceres, Kemback & Springfield Church of Scotland
SC001601	Crail Parish Church of Scotland
SC001907	Creich, Flisk and Kilmany Church of Scotland
SC013123	Cupar Old & St Michael of Tarvit Parish Church (of Scotland)
SC015721	Cupar St John's and Dairsie United Parish Church of Scotland
SC015226	Edenshead and Strathmiglo Church of Scotland
SC003163	Elie, Kilconquhar and Colinsburgh Church of Scotland
SC012247	Falkland Parish Church of Scotland
SC016622	Freuchie Parish Church of Scotland
SC005381	Howe of Fife Parish Church (Church of Scotland)
SC002653	Kilrenny Parish Church of Scotland
SC012192	Kingsbarns Parish Church of Scotland
SC003465	Largo & Newburn Parish Church of Scotland
SC013075	Largo St David's Church of Scotland
SC009474	Largoward Church of Scotland
SC015677	Leuchars: St Athernase Church of Scotland
SC015182	Monimail Parish (Church of Scotland)
SC004607	Newburgh Parish Church of Scotland
SC006758	Newport-on-Tay Church of Scotland
SC015271	Pittenweem Church of Scotland
SC017173	The Parish Church of the Holy Trinity, St Andrews (Church of Scotland)

SC014934	Hope Park and Martyrs' Parish Church St Andrews (Church of Scotland)
SC013586	St Andrews: St Leonard's Parish Church of Scotland Congregation
SC005556	St Monans Church of Scotland
SC014710	Strathkinness Parish Church of Scotland
SC008659	Tayport Parish Church of Scotland
SC006447	Wormit Parish Church of Scotland
27.	**Presbytery of Dunkeld and Meigle**
SC007899	Aberfeldy Parish Church of Scotland
SC028023	Amulree and Strathbraan Parish Church of Scotland
SC001465	Dull and Weem Parish Church of Scotland
SC000540	Alyth Parish Church of Scotland
SC000098	Ardler Kettins & Meigle Parish Church of Scotland
SC004358	Bendochy Parish Church of Scotland
SC014438	Coupar Angus Abbey Church of Scotland
SC013516	Blair Atholl and Struan Church of Scotland
SC001984	Tenandry Parish Church of Scotland
SC033757	Blairgowrie Parish Church of Scotland
SC011351	Braes of Rannoch Church of Scotland
SC006570	Foss and Rannoch Church of Scotland
SC001957	Caputh and Clunie Church of Scotland
SC009251	Kinclaven Church of Scotland
SC009867	Dunkeld Parish Church of Scotland
SC003310	Fortingall & Glenlyon Church of Scotland
SC006260	Kenmore and Lawers Church of Scotland
SC004275	Grantully Logierait & Strathtay Church of Scotland
SC008021	Kirkmichael Straloch & Glenshee Church of Scotland
SC000323	Rattray Parish Church of Scotland
SC008361	Pitlochry Church of Scotland
28.	**Presbytery of Perth**
SC044503	Aberdalgie and Forteviot Church of Scotland
SC000586	Abernethy and Dron and Arngask Church of Scotland
SC030799	Aberuthven and Dunning Parish Church of Scotland
SC005203	Almondbank Tibbermore Parish Church of Scotland
SC000139	Ardoch Parish Church of Scotland
SC001688	Auchterarder Parish Church of Scotland
SC010247	Auchtergaven and Moneydie Parish Church of Scotland
SC005594	Blackford Parish Church of Scotland
SC007283	Cargill Burrelton Parish Church of Scotland
SC003168	Cleish Parish Church of Scotland
SC009031	Collace Church of Scotland
SC001878	Comrie Parish Church of Scotland
SC004304	Crieff Parish Church of Scotland
SC009638	Dunbarney and Forgandenny Parish Church (Church of Scotland)
SC010311	St Fillans Dundurn Parish Church of Scotland
SC015895	Errol Parish Church of Scotland
SC013157	Fossoway St Serf's & Devonside Parish Church of Scotland
SC002209	Fowlis Wester, Madderty and Monzie Parish Church of Scotland
SC009632	Gask Parish Church of Scotland
SC010838	Kilspindie & Rait Parish Church of Scotland
SC012555	Kinross Parish Church of Scotland
SC010807	Methven and Logiealmond Church of Scotland
SC004984	Muthill Parish Church of Scotland
SC015523	Orwell and Portmoak Parish Church of Scotland
SC001330	Perth: Craigie and Moncreiffe Church of Scotland

SC007509	Kinnoull Parish Church of Scotland, Perth
SC002467	Perth: Letham St Mark's Church of Scotland
SC013014	Perth North, Church of Scotland
SC011113	Perth Riverside Church of Scotland
SC017132	St John's Kirk of Perth (Church of Scotland)
SC002919	Perth St Leonard's-in-the-Fields Church of Scotland
SC016829	Perth: St Matthew's Church of Scotland
SC010629	Redgorton and Stanley Parish Church – Church of Scotland
SC007094	Scone and St Martins Parish Church of Scotland
SC014964	St Madoes and Kinfauns Church of Scotland, Glencarse
SC000004	Trinity Gask and Kinkell Church (Church of Scotland)

29.	**Presbytery of Dundee**
SC007847	Abernyte Parish Church of Scotland
SC016717	Auchterhouse Parish Church of Scotland
SC017449	Dundee: Balgay Parish Church of Scotland
SC007031	Broughty Ferry New Kirk (Church of Scotland)
SC003677	Dundee: Camperdown Parish Church of Scotland
SC021763	Chalmers-Ardler Parish Church of Scotland, Dundee
SC012089	Dundee: Coldside Parish Church of Scotland
SC016701	Dundee: Craigiebank Parish Church of Scotland
SC005707	Dundee: Downfield Mains Church of Scotland
SC010030	Dundee Douglas and Mid Craigie Church of Scotland
SC033313	Dundee Lochee Parish Church of Scotland
SC017136	Dundee: West Church of Scotland
SC002792	Fowlis & Liff Parish Church of Scotland
SC009839	Inchture & Kinnaird Parish Church of Scotland
SC009454	Invergowrie Parish Church of Scotland
SC009115	Dundee: Logie & St John's (Cross) Church of Scotland
SC012230	Longforgan Parish Church of Scotland
SC001085	Lundie and Muirhead Parish Church of Scotland
SC020742	Fintry Parish Church of Scotland, Dundee
SC013162	Dundee: Meadowside St Paul's Church of Scotland
SC004496	Dundee: Menzieshill Parish Church of Scotland
SC012137	Monikie & Newbigging and Murroes & Tealing Church of Scotland
SC011775	Dundee: St Andrew's Parish Church of Scotland
SC000723	St David's High Kirk Dundee (Church of Scotland)
SC005210	St James Church of Scotland: Broughty Ferry
SC000088	St Luke's and Queen Street Church of Scotland: Broughty Ferry
SC011017	Barnhill St Margaret's Parish Church of Scotland
SC002198	Dundee Parish Church (St Mary's) Church of Scotland
SC003714	St Stephen's & West Parish Church of Scotland: Broughty Ferry
SC000384	Stobswell Parish Church of Scotland: Dundee
SC018015	Strathmartine Church of Scotland: Dundee
SC011021	Dundee: Trinity Parish Church of Scotland
SC000316	Dundee: Whitfield Parish Church of Scotland
SC014314	The Steeple Church: Dundee (Church of Scotland)
SC008965	Monifieth Parish Church of Scotland

30.	**Presbytery of Angus**
SC018944	Aberlemno Parish Church of Scotland
SC002545	Barry Parish Church of Scotland
SC008630	Brechin Gardner Memorial Church of Scotland
SC015146	Carnoustie Church of Scotland
SC001293	Colliston Church of Scotland
SC007997	Farnell Parish Church of Scotland
SC000572	Dun and Hillside Church of Scotland
SC013105	Edzell Lethnot Glenesk Church of Scotland
SC009017	Inchbrayock Parish Church of Scotland
SC031461	The Isla Parishes Church of Scotland
SC013352	Eassie, Nevay and Newtyle Church of Scotland
SC017413	Airbirlot Parish Church of Scotland
SC006482	Arbroath West Kirk Church of Scotland
SC011361	Arbroath Knox's Parish Church of Scotland
SC005478	Arbroath: St Andrew's Church of Scotland
SC017424	Carmyllie Parish Church of Scotland
SC004594	Carnoustie Panbride Church of Scotland
SC003833	Dunnichen, Letham and Kirkden Church of Scotland
SC004921	Forfar East and Old Parish Church of Scotland
SC002417	Forfar Lowson Memorial Parish Church of Scotland
SC010332	Brechin Cathedral Church of Scotland
SC005085	Friockheim and Kinnell Parish Church of Scotland
SC017785	Inverkeilor and Lunan Church of Scotland
SC004395	Kirriemuir St Andrew's Parish Church of Scotland
SC015123	The Glens and Kirriemuir Old Parish Church of Scotland
SC009016	Montrose Melville South Church of Scotland
SC009934	Montrose: Old and St Andrew's Church of Scotland
SC003049	Arbroath St Vigeans Church of Scotland
SC006317	Oathlaw Tannadice Church of Scotland
SC001506	Forfar St Margaret's Church of Scotland
SC013052	Arbroath Old and Abbey Church of Scotland
SC011205	Glamis, Inverarity and Kinnettles Parish Church of Scotland
SC017327	Guthrie and Rescobie Church of Scotland
SC003236	Fern, Careston and Menmuir Church of Scotland

31.	**Presbytery of Aberdeen**
SC025324	Aberdeen Bridge of Don Oldmachar Church of Scotland
SC032413	Cove Church of Scotland, Aberdeen
SC017158	Craigiebuckler Church of Scotland, Aberdeen
SC010756	Aberdeen Ferryhill Parish Church of Scotland
SC022497	Garthdee Parish Church of Scotland, Aberdeen
SC003789	High Hilton Church of Scotland, Aberdeen
SC013318	Holburn West Church of Scotland, Aberdeen
SC001680	Mannofield Church of Scotland, Aberdeen
SC013459	Mastrick Parish Church of Scotland, Aberdeen
SC010643	Midstocket Parish Church of Scotland, Aberdeen
SC034441	Northfield Parish Church of Scotland, Aberdeen
SC014117	Queen Street Church of Scotland Aberdeen
SC002019	Queens Cross Church of Scotland Aberdeen
SC015841	Rubislaw Parish Church of Scotland, Aberdeen
SC013020	Ruthrieston West Church of Scotland, Aberdeen
SC017516	Aberdeen South Holburn Church of Scotland
SC027440	Aberdeen Bridge of Don St Columba's Church of Scotland

SC015451	Aberdeen St Marks Church of Scotland
SC018173	St Mary's Church of Scotland: Aberdeen
SC016043	South St Nicholas & Kincorth Church of Scotland, Aberdeen
SC014120	The Church of Scotland – Aberdeen: St Stephens Church
SC030587	New Stockethill Church of Scotland, Aberdeen
SC007076	Summerhill Parish Church of Scotland, Aberdeen
SC001966	Woodside Parish Church of Scotland, Aberdeen
SC017404	Bucksburn Stoneywood Parish Church of Scotland
SC017517	Cults Parish Church of Scotland
SC011204	Newhills Parish Church of Scotland
SC001452	Peterculter Parish Church of Scotland
SC009020	Torry St Fitticks Parish Church of Scotland, Aberdeen
SC006865	Kingswells Church of Scotland
SC031403	Middlefield Parish Church of Scotland, Aberdeen
SC016950	Dyce Parish Church of Scotland
SC024795	St Georges Tillydrone Church of Scotland, Aberdeen
SC008157	St Machar's Cathedral, Aberdeen, Church of Scotland
SC021283	St John's Church for Deaf People in the North of Scotland, Church of Scotland
SC008689	Kirk of St Nicholas Uniting

32.	**Presbytery of Kincardine and Deeside**
SC016449	Aberluthnott Church of Scotland
SC014112	Aboyne-Dinnet Parish Church of Scotland
SC009239	Arbuthnott, Bervie and Kinneff (Church of Scotland)
SC011251	Banchory-Ternan East Church of Scotland
SC003306	Banchory-Ternan West Parish Church of Scotland
SC013648	Banchory Devenick & Maryculter-Cookney Parish Church of Scotland
SC018517	Birse & Feughside Church of Scotland
SC012075	Braemar and Crathie Parish, The Church of Scotland
SC015856	Parish of Cromar Church of Scotland
SC033779	Drumoak-Durris Church of Scotland
SC005522	Glenmuick (Ballater) Parish Church of Scotland
SC007436	Kinneff Church of Scotland
SC014830	Laurencekirk Church of Scotland
SC011997	Mearns Coastal Parish Church of Scotland
SC012967	Mid Deeside Parish, Church of Scotland
SC005679	Newtonhill Parish Church (Church of Scotland)
SC007420	Portlethen Parish Church of Scotland
SC013165	Stonehaven Dunnottar Church of Scotland
SC011191	Stonehaven Fetteresso Church of Scotland
SC016565	Stonehaven South Church of Scotland
SC016193	West Mearns Parish Church of Scotland

33.	**Presbytery of Gordon**
SC010960	Barthol Chapel Church of Scotland
SC016387	Belhelvie Church of Scotland
SC000935	Insch-Leslie-Premnay-Oyne Church of Scotland
SC004050	Blairdaff and Chapel of Garioch Church of Scotland
SC003429	Cluny Church of Scotland
SC010911	Culsalmond and Rayne Church of Scotland
SC030817	Cushnie and Tough Parish Church of Scotland
SC003254	Daviot Parish Church of Scotland

SC003215	Echt Parish Church of Scotland
SC008819	Ellon Parish Church of Scotland
SC003115	Fintray Kinellar Keithhall Church of Scotland
SC011701	Foveran Church of Scotland
SC007979	Howe Trinity Parish Church of Scotland
SC001405	Huntly Cairnie Glass Church of Scotland
SC008791	St Andrews Parish Church of Scotland Inverurie
SC016907	Inverurie West Church of Scotland
SC014790	Kemnay Parish Church of Scotland
SC001406	Kintore Parish Church of Scotland
SC015960	Meldrum & Bourtie Parish Church of Scotland
SC016542	Methlick Parish Church of Scotland
SC009556	Midmar Parish Church of Scotland
SC004525	Monymusk Parish Church of Scotland
SC024017	Newmachar Parish Church of Scotland
SC007582	Parish of Noth Church of Scotland
SC009462	Skene Parish Church of Scotland
SC017161	Tarves Parish Church of Scotland
SC006056	Udny & Pitmedden Church of Scotland
SC014679	Upper Donside Parish Church of Scotland
SC000534	Strathbogie Drumblade Church of Scotland Huntly

34.	**Presbytery of Buchan**
SC007197	Aberdour Church of Scotland
SC017101	Auchaber United Parish Church of Scotland
SC009168	Auchterless Parish Church of Scotland
SC015501	Banff Parish Church of Scotland
SC006889	Crimond Parish Church of Scotland
SC006408	Cruden Parish Church of Scotland
SC012985	Deer Parish Church of Scotland
SC013119	Fraserburgh Old Church of Scotland
SC005714	Fraserburgh South Church of Scotland
SC016334	Fraserburgh West Parish Church of Scotland
SC001475	Fyvie Church of Scotland
SC012282	Gardenstown Church of Scotland
SC000375	Inverallochy & Rathen East Parish Church of Scotland
SC015077	King Edward Parish Church of Scotland
SC008873	Longside Parish Church of Scotland
SC008813	Lonmay Parish Church of Scotland
SC015786	Macduff Parish Church of Scotland
SC009773	Maud & Savoch Church of Scotland
SC010291	Monquhitter & New Byth Parish Church of Scotland
SC007917	New Deer St Kane's Church of Scotland
SC001107	Marnoch Church of Scotland
SC014620	New Pitsligo Parish Church of Scotland
SC001971	Ordiquhill & Cornhill Church of Scotland
SC011147	Peterhead Old Parish Church of Scotland
SC010841	Peterhead St Andrews Church of Scotland
SC009990	Peterhead Trinity Parish Church of Scotland
SC005498	Pitsligo Parish Church of Scotland
SC000522	Portsoy Church, Church of Scotland
SC015604	Rathen West Parish Church of Scotland
SC032016	Rothienorman Parish Church of Scotland
SC000710	St Fergus Parish Church of Scotland
SC024874	Sandhaven Parish Church of Scotland
SC007273	Strichen and Tyrie Parish Church of Scotland
SC015620	St Andrews Parish Church of Scotland, Turriff
SC007470	Turriff St Ninians and Forglen Parish Church of Scotland
SC002085	Whitehills Parish Church of Scotland

35.	**Presbytery of Moray**
SC001336	Aberlour Parish Church of Scotland
SC010330	Alves & Burghead Parish Church of Scotland
SC005310	Bellie Parish Church of Scotland
SC016720	Birnie and Pluscarden Church of Scotland
SC001235	Buckie North Church of Scotland

SC005608	Buckie South & West Church of Scotland
SC011231	Cullen & Deskford Church of Scotland
SC015881	St Michael's Parish Church of Scotland, Dallas
SC004853	Duffus Spynie & Hopeman Church of Scotland
SC000585	Dyke Parish Church of Scotland
SC009986	Edinkillie Church of Scotland
SC005240	Elgin High Church of Scotland
SC015164	St Giles & St Columbas Church of Scotland, Elgin
SC015093	Enzie Parish Church of Scotland
SC010045	Findochty Parish Church of Scotland
SC000711	St Laurence Parish Church of Scotland, Forres
SC005094	St Leonard's Church of Scotland, Forres
SC033804	Keith North Newmill Boharm & Rothiemay Church of Scotland
SC031791	Kirk of Keith: St Rufus, Botriphnie and Grange (Church of Scotland)
SC014557	Kinloss & Findhorn Parish Church of Scotland
SC014428	Knockando Elchies & Archiestown Parish Church of Scotland
SC009793	St Gerardine's High Church of Scotland, Lossiemouth
SC000880	St James Church of Scotland: Lossiemouth
SC010193	Mortlach and Cabrach Church of Scotland
SC014485	Portknockie Parish Church of Scotland
SC022567	Rafford Parish Church of Scotland
SC015906	Rathven Parish Church of Scotland
SC016116	Rothes Parish Church of Scotland
SC007113	Speymouth Parish Church of Scotland
SC008850	St Andrews Lhanbryd & Urquhart Parish Church of Scotland, Elgin

36.	**Presbytery of Abernethy**
SC003652	Abernethy Church of Scotland
SC002884	Cromdale & Advie Church of Scotland
SC010001	Grantown-on-Spey Church of Scotland
SC014015	Dulnain Bridge Church of Scotland
SC021546	Kingussie Church of Scotland
SC003282	Rothiemurchus & Aviemore Church of Scotland
SC001802	Tomintoul, Glenlivet and Inveravon Church of Scotland
SC000043	Alvie and Insh Church of Scotland
SC008346	Boat of Garten, Duthil and Kincardine Church of Scotland
SC008016	Laggan Church of Scotland
SC005490	Newtonmore Church of Scotland

37.	**Presbytery of Inverness**
SC015446	Ardersier Parish Church of Scotland
SC026653	Auldearn & Dalmore Parish Church of Scotland
SC001695	Cawdor Parish Church (Church of Scotland)
SC013601	Croy & Dalcross Parish Church (Church of Scotland)
SC000662	The Barn, Church of Scotland, Culloden
SC003301	Daviot & Dunlichity Church of Scotland
SC013579	Dores & Boleskine Church of Scotland
SC018159	Crown Church, Inverness (Church of Scotland)
SC011773	Dalneigh & Bona Parish Church of Scotland, Inverness
SC016866	East Church of Scotland Inverness
SC016775	Hilton Parish Church of Scotland, Inverness
SC005553	Inshes Church of Scotland, Inverness
SC010870	Ness Bank Church of Scotland, Inverness
SC035073	Old High St Stephen's Church of Scotland, Inverness
SC008109	Inverness: St Columba Church of Scotland New Charge

SC015432	Inverness Trinity Church of Scotland
SC008121	Kilmorack & Erchless Church of Scotland
SC014918	Kiltarlity Church of Scotland
SC020888	Kinmylies Church of Scotland, Inverness
SC003866	Kirkhill Church of Scotland
SC015653	Moy Dalarossie & Tomatin Church of Scotland
SC000947	Nairn Old Parish Church of Scotland
SC015361	St Ninians Church of Scotland, Nairn
SC004952	Petty Church of Scotland
SC016627	Urquhart & Glenmoriston Church of Scotland

38.	**Presbytery of Lochaber**
SC002916	Acharacle Parish Church of Scotland
SC008222	Ardgour and Kingairloch Parish Church of Scotland
SC030394	Ardnamurchan Parish Church of Scotland
SC021584	North West Lochaber Church of Scotland
SC018259	Duror Parish Church of Scotland
SC022635	Fort Augustus Parish Church of Scotland
SC013279	Fort William Duncansburgh MacIntosh Parish Church of Scotland
SC005211	Glencoe St Munda's Parish Church of Scotland
SC023413	Glengarry Parish Church of Scotland
SC005687	Kilmallie Parish Church of Scotland
SC014745	Kilmonivaig Parish Church of Scotland
SC030288	Kinlochleven Parish Church of Scotland
SC015532	Morvern Parish Church of Scotland
SC006700	Nether Lochaber Parish Church of Scotland
SC008982	Strontian Parish Church of Scotland

39.	**Presbytery of Ross**
SC015227	Alness Parish Church of Scotland
SC003921	Avoch Parish Church of Scotland
SC011897	Contin Parish Church of Scotland
SC006666	Cromarty Parish Church of Scotland
SC001167	Dingwall Castle Street Church of Scotland
SC001056	Dingwall St Clements Parish Church of Scotland
SC009309	Fearn Abbey & Nigg Church of Scotland
SC012675	Ferintosh Parish Church of Scotland
SC003499	Fodderty & Strathpeffer Parish Church of Scotland
SC004472	Fortrose & Rosemarkie Parish Church of Scotland
SC010964	Invergordon Church of Scotland
SC010319	Killearnan Parish Church of Scotland
SC013375	Kilmuir & Logie Easter Church of Scotland
SC009180	Kiltearn Parish Church of Scotland
SC014467	Knockbain Parish Church of Scotland
SC015631	Lochbroom & Ullapool Church of Scotland
SC013643	Resolis & Urquhart Church of Scotland
SC010093	Rosskeen Parish Church of Scotland
SC012425	Tain Parish Church of Scotland
SC021420	Tarbat Parish Church of Scotland
SC009902	Urray & Kilchrist Church of Scotland

40.	**Presbytery of Sutherland**
SC016038	Altnaharra & Farr Church of Scotland
SC010171	Assynt & Stoer Parish Church of Scotland
SC004973	Clyne Church of Scotland
SC003840	Creich Parish Church of Scotland
SC000315	Dornoch Cathedral (Church of Scotland)
SC005079	Durness & Kinlochbervie Church of Scotland
SC007326	Eddrachillis Parish Church of Scotland
SC004560	Golspie (St Andrews) Church of Scotland
SC004056	Kildonan & Loth Helmsdale Church of Scotland

SC016877	Kincardine Croick & Edderton Church of Scotland
SC020871	Lairg Church of Scotland
SC014066	Melness & Tongue Church of Scotland
SC010035	Rogart Church of Scotland
SC017558	Rosehall Church of Scotland

41.   Presbytery of Caithness

SC001363	Bower Church of Scotland
SC032164	Canisbay Parish Church of Scotland
SC030261	Dunnet Church of Scotland
SC008544	Halkirk & Westerdale Church of Scotland
SC010874	Keiss Parish Church of Scotland
SC034424	The Parish of Latheron Church of Scotland
SC010296	Olrig Church of Scotland
SC001815	North Coast Parish Church of Scotland
SC016691	Thurso St Peter's & St Andrew's Church of Scotland
SC007248	Thurso West Church of Scotland
SC003365	Watten Church of Scotland
SC013840	Wick St Fergus Church of Scotland
SC001291	Pulteneytown & Thrumster Church of Scotland

42.   Presbytery of Lochcarron – Skye

SC032334	Applecross, Lochcarron and Torridon Church of Scotland
SC022592	Bracadale and Duirinish Church of Scotland
SC015448	Gairloch and Dundonnell Church of Scotland
SC017510	Glenelg and Kintail Church of Scotland
SC014072	Kilmuir and Stenscholl Church of Scotland
SC016505	Lochalsh Church of Scotland
SC000416	Portree Church of Scotland
SC030117	Snizort Church of Scotland
SC001285	Strath and Sleat Church of Scotland

43.   Presbytery of Uist

SC002191	Benbecula Church of Scotland
SC016358	Berneray and Lochmaddy Church of Scotland
SC016461	Carinish Church of Scotland
SC030955	Kilmuir and Paible Church of Scotland
SC001770	Manish-Scarista Church of Scotland
SC004787	Tarbert Church of Scotland

44.   Presbytery of Lewis

SC006563	Barvas Church of Scotland
SC032250	Carloway Church of Scotland
SC000991	Cross Ness Church of Scotland
SC008004	Kinloch Church of Scotland
SC014492	Knock Church of Scotland
SC024236	Lochs Crossbost Parish Church of Scotland
SC008746	Lochs-in-Bernera Church of Scotland
SC010164	Stornoway High Church of Scotland
SC000753	Martins Memorial Church of Scotland, Stornoway

SC006777	St Columba Old Parish Church of Scotland, Stornoway
SC007879	Uig Parish Church of Scotland

45.   Presbytery of Orkney

SC035048	Birsay Harray & Sandwick Church of Scotland
SC019770	East Mainland Church of Scotland
SC005404	Eday Church of Scotland
SC005062	Evie Church of Scotland
SC013330	Firth Church of Scotland
SC016203	Flotta Parish Church of Scotland
SC023194	Hoy & Walls Parish Church of Scotland
SC018002	Kirkwall East Church, Church of Scotland
SC005322	Kirkwall St Magnus Cathedral (Church of Scotland)
SC030098	North Ronaldsay Parish Church of Scotland
SC016221	Orphir and Stenness Church of Scotland
SC013661	Papa Westray Church of Scotland
SC016806	Rendall Church of Scotland
SC001078	Rousay Church of Scotland
SC000271	Sanday Church of Scotland
SC006097	Shapinsay Church of Scotland
SC003298	South Ronaldsay & Burray Church of Scotland
SC003099	Stromness Church of Scotland
SC006572	Moncur Memorial Church of Scotland, Stronsay
SC025053	Westray Parish Church of Scotland

46.   Presbytery of Shetland

SC030483	Burra Church of Scotland
SC029873	Delting Parish Church (Church of Scotland)
SC015253	Dunrossness and St Ninian's Parish Church (incl. Fair Isle) (Church of Scotland)
SC038365	Fetlar Church of Scotland
SC017535	Lerwick and Bressay Parish Church (Church of Scotland)
SC031996	Nesting and Lunnasting Church of Scotland
SC002341	Northmavine Parish Church of Scotland
SC012345	Sandsting and Aithsting Parish Church of Scotland
SC014545	Sandwick, Cunningsburgh and Quarff Church of Scotland
SC030748	St Paul's Church of Scotland Walls: Shetland
SC032982	Tingwall Parish Church of Scotland
SC007954	Unst Church of Scotland
SC000293	Whalsay and Skerries Parish Church of Scotland
SC020628	Yell Parish Church of Scotland

47.   Presbytery of England

SC043458	Corby: St Andrew's Church of Scotland
SC043757	Corby: St Ninian's Church of Scotland
SC042648	Crown Court Church of Scotland London
SC042854	Liverpool: St Andrew's Church of Scotland

SECTION 8

Church Buildings: Ordnance Survey National Grid References

NOTE:
The placing of symbols denoting churches may vary according to the edition of published maps. The references which follow should be sufficiently accurate to allow church buildings to be located. The correction of any errors will always be welcomed, and appropriate details should be sent to the Editor of the *Year Book*.

The Churches are listed in the order in which they appear in the Presbytery Lists in the *Year Book*.

1. Presbytery of Edinburgh
Albany Deaf Church of Edinburgh, meets at 82 Montrose Terrace
Balerno, NT163664
Barclay Viewforth, NT249726
Blackhall St Columba's, NT219747
Bristo Memorial Craigmillar, NT287716
Broughton St Mary's, NT256748
Canongate, NT265738
Carrick Knowe, NT203721
Colinton, NT216692
Corstorphine Craigsbank, NT191730
Corstorphine Old, NT201728
Corstorphine St Anne's, NT204730
Corstorphine St Ninian's, NT198730
Craigentinny St Christopher's, NT292748
Craiglockhart, NT224705
Craigmillar Park, NT269714
Cramond, NT190768
Currie, NT183676
Dalmeny, NT144775
Davidson's Mains, NT207752
Dean, NT238742
Drylaw, NT221754
Duddingston, NT284726
Fairmilehead, NT248683
Gorgie Dalry, NT231724
Granton, NT237766
Greenbank, NT243702
Greenside, NT263745
Greyfriars Kirk, NT256734
High (St Giles'), NT257736
Holyrood Abbey, NT274744
Holy Trinity, NT201700
Inverleith St Serf's, NT248761
Juniper Green, NT199687
Kaimes Lockhart Memorial, NT277684
Kirkliston, NT125744
Leith North, NT263765
Leith St Andrew's, NT273757
Leith South, NT271761
Leith Wardie, NT246768
Liberton, NT275695
Liberton Northfield, NT280699
London Road, NT268745
Marchmont St Giles', NT256718
Mayfield Salisbury, NT266717
Morningside, NT246707
Morningside United, NT245719
Murrayfield, NT227733
Newhaven, NT254769
New Restalrig, NT284742
Palmerston Place, NT241734
Pilrig St Paul's, NT266752
Polwarth, NT236719
Portobello St Philip's Joppa, NT313736
Priestfield, NT271721
Queensferry, NT130782
Ratho, NT138710
Reid Memorial, NT261710
Richmond Craigmillar, NT296717
St Andrew's and St George's West, NT255741
St Andrew's Clermiston, NT201746
St Catherine's Argyle, NT257721
St Cuthbert's, NT248736
St David's Broomhouse, NT203714
St John's Colinton Mains, NT233692
St Margaret's, NT284745

St Martin's, NT305726
St Michael's, NT234722
St Nicholas' Sighthill, NT194707
St Stephen's Comely Bank, NT241748
Slateford Longstone, NT213707
Stenhouse St Aidan's, NT218716
Stockbridge, NT247748
The Old Kirk and Muirhouse, NT215763
The Tron Kirk (Gilmerton and Moredun):
    Gilmerton, NT293686
    Moredun, NT294697

2. Presbytery of West Lothian
Abercorn, NT082792
Armadale, NS935684
Avonbridge, NS910730
Bathgate: Boghall, NS996686
Bathgate: High, NS976691
Bathgate: St John's, NS977687
Blackburn and Seafield, NS991655
Blackridge, NS897671
Breich Valley, NS968622
Broxburn, NT085723
Fauldhouse: St Andrew's, NS931607
Harthill: St Andrew's, NS896643
Kirknewton and East Calder:
    Kirknewton, NT106670
    East Calder, NT086678
Kirk of Calder, NT074673
Linlithgow: St Michael's, NT002773
Linlithgow: St Ninian's Craigmailen, NS994771
Livingston Ecumenical Parish, NT027687
Livingston: Old, NT037669
    Deans, NT021686
Pardovan, Kingscavil and Winchburgh:
    Kingscavil, NT030764
    Winchburgh, NT087750
Polbeth Harwood, NT030641
Strathbrock, NT060722
    Ecclesmachan, NS059737
Torphichen, NS969725
Uphall: South, NT061718
West Kirk of Calder, NT014629
Whitburn: Brucefield, NS948650
Whitburn: South, NS947646

3. Presbytery of Lothian
Aberlady, NT462799
Athelstaneford, NT533774
Belhaven, NT668787
Bilston, NT262647
Bolton and Saltoun:
    Bolton, NT507701
    Saltoun, NT474678
Bonnyrigg, NT307654
Cockenzie and Port Seton: Chalmers Memorial, NT403757
Cockenzie and Port Seton: Old, NT401758
Cockpen and Carrington, NT319642
Dalkeith: St John's and King's Park, NT330670
Dalkeith: St Nicholas' Buccleuch, NT333674
Dirleton, NT513842
Dunbar, NT682786
Dunglass:
    Cockburnspath, NT774711
    Innerwick, NT721739
    Oldhamstocks, NT738707
Garvald and Morham:
    Garvald, NT591709
    Morham, NT557726
Gladsmuir, NT457733

Glencorse, NT247627
Gorebridge, NT343619
Gullane, NT483827
Haddington: St Mary's, NT519736
Haddington: West, NT512739
Howgate, NT248580
Humbie, NT461637
Lasswade and Rosewell:
  Lasswade, NT305661
  Rosewell, NT288624
Loanhead, NT278654
Longniddry, NT442763
Musselburgh: Northesk, NT340727
Musselburgh: St Andrew's High, NT345727
Musselburgh: St Clement's and St Ninian's, NT360727
  Wallyford, NT368722
Musselburgh: St Michael's Inveresk, NT344721
  St John's, Whitecraig, NT351701
Newbattle, NT331661:
  Newtongrange, NT334643
  Easthouses, NT348652
Newton, NT315693
North Berwick: Abbey, NT551853
North Berwick: St Andrew Blackadder, NT553853
Ormiston, NT414693
Pencaitland, NT443690
Penicuik: North, NT234603
Penicuik: St Mungo's, NT237599
Penicuik: South, NT236595
Prestonpans: Prestongrange, NT388746
Roslin, NT270631
Spott, NT673755
Tranent, NT403734
Traprain:
  Prestonkirk, NT592778
  Stenton, NT622743
  Whittingehame, NT603737
Tyne Valley Parish:
  Borthwick, NT369596
  Cranston, Crichton and Ford, NT386656
  Fala and Soutra, NT438609
Whitekirk and Tyninghame, NT596815
Yester, NT535681

4. Presbytery of Melrose and Peebles
Ashkirk, NT466220
Bowden and Melrose:
  Bowden, NT554301
  Melrose, NT544344
Broughton, Glenholm and Kilbucho, NT114357
Caddonfoot, NT451348
Carlops, NT161559
Channelkirk and Lauder:
  Channelkirk, NT482545
  Lauder, NT531475
Earlston, NT581388
Eddleston, NT244472
Ettrick and Yarrow:
  Ettrick, NT259145
  Yarrow, NT356278
  Kirkhope, NT390244
Galashiels: Old and St Paul's, NT492358
Galashiels: St John's, NT509357
Galashiels: Trinity, NT491363
Innerleithen, Traquair and Walkerburn:
  Innerleithen, NT332369
  Traquair, NT320335
Kirkurd and Newlands, NT162467
Lyne and Manor:
  Lyne, NT192405
  Manor, NT220380

Maxton and Mertoun:
  Maxton, NT610303
  Mertoun, NT615318
Newtown, NT581316
Peebles: Old, NT250404
Peebles: St Andrew's Leckie, NT253404
St Boswells, NT594310
Selkirk, NT472287
Skirling, NT075390
Stobo and Drumelzier:
  Stobo, NT183377
  Drumelzier, NT135343
Stow: St Mary of Wedale and Heriot:
  Stow: St Mary of Wedale, NT459444
  Heriot, NT390526
Tweedsmuir, NT101245
West Linton: St Andrew's, NT149516

5. Presbytery of Duns
Ayton and Burnmouth:
  Ayton, NT927609
  Burnmouth, NT956610
Berwick-upon-Tweed: St Andrew's Wallace Green
  and Lowick, NT999532
Bonkyl and Edrom:
  Bonkyl, NT808596
  Edrom, NT826558
Chirnside, NT869561
Coldingham and St Abbs, NT904659
Coldstream, NT843398
Duns, NT786539
Eccles, NT764413
Eyemouth, NT943640
Fogo and Swinton:
  Fogo, NT773492
  Swinton, NT838477
Foulden and Mordington, NT931558
Gordon: St Michael's, NT645432
Grantshouse and Houndwood and Reston:
  Reston, NT878621
  Grantshouse congregation meets in village hall
Greenlaw, NT712462
Hutton and Fishwick and Paxton:
  Hutton and Fishwick, NT907540
  Paxton, NT934532
Ladykirk and Whitsome, NT889477
Langton and Lammermuir:
  Cranshaws, NT692619
  Langton, NT767523
Legerwood, NT594434
Leitholm, NT791441
Westruther, NT633500

6. Presbytery of Jedburgh
Ale and Teviot United:
  Ancrum, NT627246
  Crailing, NT682250
  Lilliesleaf, NT539253
Cavers and Kirkton:
  Cavers, NT538159
  Kirkton, NT541140
Cheviot Churches:
  Linton, NT773262
  Hoselaw, NT802318
  Morebattle, NT772250
  Hownam, NT778193
  Yetholm, NT826281
Hawick: Burnfoot, NT510162
Hawick: St Mary's and Old, NT502143
Hawick: Teviot and Roberton:
  Hawick: Teviot, NT501144

Roberton, NT432142
Hawick: Trinity, NT505147
Hawick: Wilton, NT502153
Hobkirk and Southdean:
　Hobkirk, NT587109
　Southdean, NT624109
Jedburgh: Old and Trinity, NT651203
Kelso Country Churches:
　Makerstoun, NT669331
　Roxburgh, NT700307
　Smailholm, NT649364
　Stichill, NT711383
Kelso: North and Ednam:
　Kelso: North, NT725343
　Ednam, NT737372
Kelso: Old and Sprouston:
　Kelso: Old, NT725343
　Sprouston, NT757353
Oxnam, NT701190
Ruberslaw:
　Bedrule, NT599179
　Denholm, NT569186
　Minto, NT567201
　Teviothead, NT403052

7. Presbytery of Annandale and Eskdale
Annan: Old, NY197666
Annan: St Andrew's, NY193665
Applegarth, Sibbaldbie and Johnstone, NY104843
Brydekirk, NY183705
Canonbie United, NY395763
Dalton, NY114740
Dornock, NY231660
Gretna: Old, Gretna: St Andrew's, Half Morton and
　　Kirkpatrick Fleming:
　Gretna: Old, NY319680
　Gretna: St Andrew's, NY317670
　Kirkpatrick Fleming, NY277701
Hightae, NY090793
Hoddom, Kirtle-Eaglesfield and Middlebie:
　Eaglesfield, NY233743
　Middlebie, NY214762
Kirkpatrick Juxta, NT083009
Langholm Eskdalemuir Ewes and Westerkirk:
　Langholm, NY362844
　Eskdalemuir, NY253979
　Ewes, NY369908
　Westerkirk, NY312903
Liddesdale:
　Castleton, NY482877
　Saughtree, NY562968
Lochmaben, NY084823
Lockerbie: Dryfesdale, Hutton and Corrie
　Hutton and Corrie, NY171908
　Lockerbie: Dryfesdale, NY135818
Moffat: St Andrew's, NT084051
St Mungo, NY143771
The Border Kirk, NY402561
Tundergarth, NY175808
Wamphray, NY131965

8. Presbytery of Dumfries and Kirkcudbright
Balmaclellan and Kells:
　Balmaclellan, NX651791
　Kells, NX632784
Balmaghie, NX722663
Borgue, NX629483
Caerlaverock, NY025962
Carsphairn, NX563932
Castle Douglas, NX765622
Closeburn, NX904923

Colvend, Southwick and Kirkbean:
　Colvend, NX862541
　Southwick, NX927573
Corsock and Kirkpatrick Durham:
　Corsock, NX762760
　Kirkpatrick Durham, NX786699
Crossmichael and Parton:
　Crossmichael, NX729670
　Parton, NX697699
Cummertrees, Mouswald and Ruthwell, NY101683
Dalbeattie and Kirkgunzeon, NX831611
Dalry, NX618813
Dumfries: Maxwelltown West, NX967760
Dumfries: North West, NX958774
Dumfries: St George's, NX971764
Dumfries: St Mary's-Greyfriars', NX975763
Dumfries: St Michael's and South, NX975757
Dumfries: Troqueer, NX975751
Dunscore, NX867843
Durisdeer, NS894038
Gatehouse of Fleet, NX602566
Glencairn and Moniaive:
　Glencairn, NX809904
　Moniaive, NX777910
Irongray, Lochrutton and Terregles:
　Irongray, NX915794
　Terregles, NX931771
Kirkconnel, NS728123
Kirkcudbright, NX683509
Kirkmahoe, NX974815:
　Dalswinton, NX942850
Kirkmichael, Tinwald and Torthorwald:
　Kirkmichael, NY005884
　Tinwald, NY003816
　Torthorwald, NY035783
Lochend and New Abbey, NX965660
Penpont, Keir and Tynron, NX849944
Sanquhar: St Bride's, NS779102
Tarff and Twynholm, NX664542
The Bengairn Parishes:
　Auchencairn, NX799512
　Kelton, NX758603
Thornhill, NX883957
Urr, NX817658

9. Presbytery of Wigtown and Stranraer
Ervie Kirkcolm, NX026687
Glasserton and Isle of Whithorn:
　Glasserton, NX421381
　Isle of Whithorn, NX478363
Inch, NX101603
Kirkcowan, NX327610
Kirkinner, NX423514
Kirkmabreck, NX477585
Kirkmaiden, NX125369:
　Drummore, NX135366
Leswalt, NX020638
Mochrum, NX347463
Monigaff, NX410606
New Luce, NX175645
Old Luce, NX197574
Penninghame, NX410654
Portpatrick, NX002544
Sorbie, NX468463
Stoneykirk:
　Sandhead, NX097500
　Ardwell, NX101457
Stranraer: High Kirk, NX057609
Stranraer: Trinity, NX064606
Whithorn: St Ninian's Priory, NX444403
Wigtown, NX436555

10. Presbytery of Ayr
Alloway, NS332180
Annbank, NS407243
Auchinleck, NS552216
Ayr: Auld Kirk of Ayr, NS339219
Ayr: Castlehill, NS347203
Ayr: Newton Wallacetown, NS339224
Ayr: St Andrew's, NS338213
Ayr: St Columba, NS337209
Ayr: St James', NS342232
Ayr: St Leonard's, NS338204
Ayr: St Quivox:
　　Auchincruive, NS375241
　　Dalmilling, NS363229
Ballantrae, NX083825:
　　Glenapp, NX075746
Barr, NX275941
Catrine, NS528260
Coylton, NS422198
Craigie Symington, NS384314
Crosshill, NS327068
Dailly, NS271016
Dalmellington, NS481061:
　　Bellsbank, NS480046
Dalrymple, NS358144
Drongan: The Schaw Kirk, NS441185
Dundonald, NS366343
Fisherton, NS275175
Girvan: North (Old and St Andrew's), NX187982
Girvan: South, NX183977
Kirkmichael, NS345090
Kirkoswald, NS240073
Lugar, NS591213
Mauchline, NS498272
Maybole, NS299101
Monkton and Prestwick: North, NS353263
Muirkirk, NS701278
New Cumnock, NS617135
Ochiltree, NS504212
Old Cumnock: Old, NS568202
Old Cumnock: Trinity, NS567200
Patna Waterside, NS412106
Prestwick: Kingcase, NS348243
Prestwick: St Nicholas', NS351256
Prestwick: South, NS351259
St Colmon (Arnsheen Barrhill and Colmonell):
　　Colmonell, NX144857
　　Barrhill congregation meets in community centre
Sorn, NS550268
Stair, NS439236
Straiton: St Cuthbert's, NS381049
Tarbolton, NS430272
Troon: Old, NS321309
Troon: Portland, NS323308
Troon: St Meddan's, NS323309

11. Presbytery of Irvine and Kilmarnock
Caldwell, NS435552
Crosshouse, NS395384
Darvel, NS563375
Dreghorn and Springside, NS352383
Dunlop, NS405494
Fenwick, NS465435
Galston, NS500367
Hurlford, NS454372
Irvine: Fullarton, NS316389
Irvine: Girdle Toll, NS341409
Irvine: Mure, NS319390
Irvine: Old, NS322387
Irvine: Relief Bourtreehill, NS344392
Irvine: St Andrew's, NS325399

Kilmarnock: Kay Park, NS431380
Kilmarnock: New Laigh, NS428379
Kilmarnock: Riccarton, NS428364
Kilmarnock: St Andrew's and St Marnock's, NS427377
Kilmarnock: St John's Onthank, NS433399
Kilmarnock: St Kentigern's, NS442388
Kilmarnock: South, NS435359
Kilmaurs: St Maur's Glencairn, NS415408
Newmilns: Loudoun, NS537373
Stewarton: John Knox, NS421460
Stewarton: St Columba's, NS419457
Ayrshire Mission to the Deaf, Kilmarnock, NS430377

12. Presbytery of Ardrossan
Ardrossan and Saltcoats: Kirkgate, NS246414
Ardrossan: Park, NS233436
Beith: NS350539
Brodick, NS012359
Corrie, NS024437
Cumbrae, NS160550
Dalry: St Margaret's, NS291496
Dalry: Trinity, NS292494
Fairlie, NS209556
Kilbirnie: Auld Kirk, NS315536
Kilbirnie: St Columba's, NS314546
Kilmory, NR963218
Kilwinning: Mansefield Trinity, NS290432
Kilwinning: Old, NS303433
Lamlash, NS026309
Largs: Clark Memorial, NS202593
Largs: St Columba's, NS203596
Largs: St John's, NS201593
Lochranza and Pirnmill:
　　Lochranza, NR937503
　　Pirnmill, NR874447
Saltcoats: North, NS252423
Saltcoats: St Cuthbert's, NS244418
Shiskine, NR910295
Stevenson: Ardeer, NS269411
Stevenston: High, NS266422
Stevenson: Livingstone, NS268416
West Kilbride, NS207484
Whiting Bay and Kildonan, NS047273

13. Presbytery of Lanark
Biggar, NT040379
Black Mount, NT101464
Cairngryffe, NS923384
Carluke: Kirkton, NS844503
Carluke: St Andrew's, NS844508
Carluke: St John's, NS847503
Carnwath, NS976465
Carstairs and Carstairs Junction, The United Church of:
　　Carstairs, NS938461
　　Carstairs Junction, NS954450
Coalburn, NS813345
Crossford, NS827466
Culter, NT027342
Forth: St Paul's, NS942538
Kirkfieldbank, NS866438
Kirkmuirhill, NS799429
Lanark: Greyfriars, NS880437
Lanark: St Nicholas', NS881437
Law, NS821527
Lesmahagow: Abbeygreen, NS813402
Lesmahagow: Old, NS814399
Libberton and Quothquan, NS992428
Symington, NS999352
The Douglas Valley Church:
　　Douglas, NS835310
　　Douglas Water and Rigside, NS873347

Upper Clyde, NS930234

14. Presbytery of Greenock and Paisley
Barrhead: Bourock, NS499589
Barrhead: St Andrew's, NS501588
Bishopton, NS445721
Bridge of Weir: Freeland, NS387656
Bridge of Weir: St Machar's Ranfurly, NS392653
Elderslie Kirk, NS441631
Erskine, NS466707
Gourock: Old Gourock and Ashton, NS243775
Gourock: St John's, NS241778
Greenock: East End, meets at Crawfurdsburn Community
    Centre
Greenock: Lyle Kirk:
  Greenock: Ardgowan, NS271768
  Greenock: Finnart St Paul's, NS265774
  Greenock: Old West Kirk, NS273772
Greenock: Mount Kirk, NS271759
Greenock: St Margaret's, NS255764
Greenock: St Ninian's, NS242755
Greenock: Wellpark Mid Kirk, NS279762
Greenock: Westburn, NS273763
Houston and Killellan, NS410671
Howwood, NS396603
Inchinnan, NS479689
Inverkip, NS207720
Johnstone: High, NS426630
Johnstone: St Andrew's Trinity, NS434623
Johnstone: St Paul's, NS424626
Kilbarchan: East, NS403633
Kilbarchan: West, NS401632
Kilmacolm: Old, NS358700
Kilmacolm: St Columba, NS358697
Langbank, NS380734
Linwood, NS432645
Lochwinnoch, NS353587
Neilston, NS480574
Paisley: Abbey, NS486640
Paisley: Glenburn, NS473617
Paisley: Lylesland, NS488626
Paisley: Martyrs' Sandyford, NS474639
Paisley: Oakshaw Trinity, NS480641
Paisley: St Columba Foxbar, NS458622
Paisley: St James', NS477644
Paisley: St Luke's, NS482632
Paisley: St Mark's Oldhall, NS511640
Paisley: St Ninian's Ferguslie, NS464644
Paisley: Sherwood Greenlaw, NS492642
Paisley: Stow Brae Kirk, NS483634
Paisley: Wallneuk North, NS486643
Port Glasgow: Hamilton Bardrainney, NS337733
Port Glasgow: St Andrew's, NS319745
Port Glasgow: St Martin's, NS306747
Renfrew: North, NS508678
Renfrew: Old, NS509676
Renfrew: Trinity, NS505674
Skelmorlie and Wemyss Bay, NS192681

16. Presbytery of Glasgow
Banton, NS752788
Bishopbriggs: Kenmure, NS604698
Bishopbriggs: Springfield, NS615702
Broom, NS554563
Burnside Blairbeth:
  Burnside, NS622601
  Blairbeth, NS616603
Busby, NS577563
Cadder, NS616723
Cambuslang: Flemington Hallside, NS663595
Cambuslang Parish Church, NS645605

Campsie, NS629777
Chryston, NS688702:
  Moodiesburn, NS699708
Eaglesham, NS574519
Fernhill and Cathkin, NS624594
Gartcosh, NS698682
Giffnock: Orchardhill, NS563587
Giffnock: South, NS559582
Giffnock: The Park, NS559593
Glenboig, NS723687
Greenbank, NS574568
Kilsyth: Anderson, NS717782
Kilsyth: Burns and Old, NS716778
Kirkintilloch: Hillhead, NS663730
Kirkintilloch: St Columba's, NS664733
Kirkintilloch: St David's Memorial Park, NS653736
Kirkintilloch: St Mary's, NS654739
Lenzie: Old, NS655720
Lenzie: Union, NS654722
Maxwell Mearns Castle, NS553553
Mearns, NS533551
Milton of Campsie, NS652768
Netherlee, NS577590
Newton Mearns, NS537557
Rutherglen: Old, NS613617
Rutherglen: Stonelaw, NS617612
Rutherglen: West and Wardlawhill, NS609618
Stamperland, NS576581
Stepps, NS657686
Thornliebank, NS546588
Torrance, NS620744
Twechar, NS700753
Williamwood, NS566576
Glasgow: Anderston Kelvingrove, NS577655
Glasgow: Baillieston Mure Memorial, NS673643
Glasgow: Baillieston St Andrew's, NS681639
Glasgow: Balshagray Victoria Park, NS549671
Glasgow: Barlanark Greyfriars, NS667649
Glasgow: Blawarthill, NS522683
Glasgow: Bridgeton St Francis in the East, NS611639
Glasgow: Broomhill, NS549674
Glasgow: Calton Parkhead, NS624638
Glasgow: Cardonald, NS526639
Glasgow: Carmunnock, NS599575
Glasgow: Carmyle, NS649618
Glasgow: Carnwadric, NS544599
Glasgow: Castlemilk, NS596594
Glasgow: Cathcart Old, NS587606
Glasgow: Cathcart Trinity, NS582604
Glasgow: Cathedral (High or St Mungo's), NS603656
Glasgow: Clincarthill, NS586613
Glasgow: Colston Milton, NS592697
Glasgow: Colston Wellpark, NS606692
Glasgow: Cranhill, NS643658
Glasgow: Croftfoot, NS603602
Glasgow: Dennistoun New, NS613652
Glasgow: Drumchapel St Andrew's, NS523707
Glasgow: Drumchapel St Mark's, NS521719
Glasgow: Easterhouse St George's and St Peter's, NS678657
Glasgow: Eastwood, NS558607
Glasgow: Gairbraid, NS568688
Glasgow: Gallowgate, NS614646
Glasgow: Garthamlock and Craigend East, NS658667
Glasgow: Gorbals, NS593638
Glasgow: Govan and Linthouse, NS555658
Glasgow: High Carntyne, NS636653
Glasgow: Hillington Park, NS534639
Glasgow: Hyndland, NS559675
Glasgow: Ibrox, NS560642
Glasgow: John Ross Memorial Church for Deaf People,
    NS588644

Glasgow: Jordanhill, NS544682
Glasgow: Kelvinbridge, NS576673
Glasgow: Kelvinside Hillhead, NS567673
Glasgow: Kenmuir Mount Vernon, NS655626
Glasgow: King's Park, NS601608
Glasgow: Kinning Park, NS570648
Glasgow: Knightswood St Margaret's, NS536694
Glasgow: Langside, NS582614
Glasgow: Lochwood, NS685663
Glasgow: Maryhill, NS563695
Glasgow: Merrylea, NS575603
Glasgow: Mosspark, NS544633
Glasgow: Newlands South, NS573611
Glasgow: Partick South, NS559665
Glasgow: Partick Trinity, NS563668
Glasgow: Penilee St Andrew, NS518647
Glasgow: Pollokshaws, NS561612
Glasgow: Pollokshields, NS577635
Glasgow: Possilpark, NS592677
Glasgow: Queen's Park Govanhill:
   Govanhill, NS587627
   Queen's Park, NS579625
Glasgow: Renfield St Stephen's, NS582659
Glasgow: Robroyston, NS638688
Glasgow: Ruchazie, NS643662
Glasgow: Ruchill Kelvinside, NS573683
Glasgow: St Andrew's East, NS619656
Glasgow: St Christopher's Priesthill and Nitshill:
   Nitshill, NS522603
   Priesthill, NS531607
   St Christopher's, NS534616
Glasgow: St Columba, NS583657
Glasgow: St David's Knightswood, NS528689
Glasgow: St Enoch's Hogganfield, NS629660
Glasgow: St George's Tron, NS590655
Glasgow: St James' (Pollok), NS530626
Glasgow: St John's Renfield, NS558683
Glasgow: St Margaret's Tollcross Park, NS637631
Glasgow: St Nicholas' Cardonald, NS524646
Glasgow: St Paul's, NS631671
Glasgow: St Rollox, NS603668
Glasgow: Sandyford Henderson Memorial, NS570659
Glasgow: Sandyhills, NS658638
Glasgow: Scotstoun, NS533676
Glasgow: Shawlands, NS572621
Glasgow: Sherbrooke St Gilbert's, NS561636
Glasgow: Shettleston New, NS647642
Glasgow: Shettleston Old, NS649639
Glasgow: South Carntyne, NS630652
Glasgow: South Shawlands, NS569615
Glasgow: Springburn, NS607677
Glasgow: Temple Anniesland, NS547689
Glasgow: Toryglen, NS602615
Glasgow: Trinity Possil and Henry Drummond,
   NS593687
Glasgow: Tron St Mary's, NS618676
Glasgow: Victoria Tollcross, NS642632
Glasgow: Wallacewell, NS621690
Glasgow: Wellington, NS570667
Glasgow: Whiteinch, NS540668
Glasgow: Yoker, NS511689

17. Presbytery of Hamilton
Airdrie: Broomknoll, NS761653
Airdrie: Clarkston, NS783661
Airdrie: Flowerhill, NS765655
Airdrie: High, NS760658
Airdrie: Jackson, NS782647
Airdrie: New Monkland, NS753678
Airdrie: St Columba's, NS766665
Airdrie: The New Wellwynd, NS759654

Bargeddie, NS692648
Bellshill: Central, NS738602
Bellshill: West, NS727603
Blantyre: Livingstone Memorial, NS687577
Blantyre: Old, NS679565
Blantyre: St Andrew's, NS693573
Bothwell, NS705586
Calderbank, NS770631
Caldercruix and Longriggend, NS819677
Chapelhall, NS783627
Chapelton, NS685485
Cleland, NS805583
Coatbridge: Blairhill Dundyvan, NS726650
Coatbridge: Calder, NS738639
Coatbridge: Middle, NS723646
Coatbridge: Old Monkland, NS718633
Coatbridge: New St Andrew's, NS733653
Coatbridge: Townhead, NS718664
Dalserf, NS800507:
   Ashgill, NS783503
East Kilbride: Claremont, NS653543
East Kilbride: Greenhills, NS616525
East Kilbride: Moncreiff, NS647555
East Kilbride: Mossneuk, NS607532
East Kilbride: Old, NS635545
East Kilbride: South, NS633537
East Kilbride: Stewartfield, meets in a community
   centre at NS643561
East Kilbride: West, NS634547
East Kilbride: Westwood, NS618537
Glassford, NS726470
Greengairs, NS783705
Hamilton: Cadzow, NS723550
Hamilton: Gilmour and Whitehill, NS704563
Hamilton: Hillhouse, NS696554
Hamilton: Old, NS723555
Hamilton: St John's, NS724553
Hamilton: South, NS717538
Hamilton: Trinity, NS711543
Hamilton: West, NS712558
Holytown, NS773608
Kirk o' Shotts, NS843629
Larkhall: Chalmers, NS763499
Larkhall: St Machan's, NS763511
Larkhall: Trinity, NS762513
Motherwell: Crosshill, NS756566
Motherwell: Dalziel St Andrew's, NS752571
Motherwell: North, NS741577
Motherwell: St Margaret's, NS769549
Motherwell: St Mary's, NS750566
Motherwell: South, NS757560
Newarthill and Carfin, NS781597
Newmains: Bonkle, NS837571
Newmains: Coltness Memorial, NS819557
New Stevenston: Wrangholm Kirk, NS760596
Overtown, NS801527
Quarter, NS722512
Shotts: Calderhead Erskine, NS877600:
   Allanton, NS850578
Stonehouse: St Ninian's, NS752467
Strathaven: Avendale Old and Drumclog:
   Avendale Old, NS701443
   Drumclog, NS640389
Strathaven: East, NS702446
Strathaven: Rankin, NS701446
Uddingston: Burnhead, NS717614
Uddingston: Old, NS696603
Uddingston: Viewpark, NS702616
Wishaw: Cambusnethan North, NS808554
Wishaw: Cambusnethan Old, NS806553
Wishaw: Craigneuk and Belhaven, NS773561

Wishaw: Old, NS796552
Wishaw: St Mark's, NS801566
Wishaw: South Wishaw, NS797548

18. Presbytery of Dumbarton
Alexandria, NS387817
Arrochar, NM296037
Baldernock, NS577751
Bearsden: Baljaffray, NS534736
Bearsden: Cross, NS543719
Bearsden: Killermont, NS557713
Bearsden: New Kilpatrick, NS543723
Bearsden: Westerton Fairlie Memorial, NS543706
Bonhill, NS395796
Cardross, NS345775
Clydebank: Abbotsford, NS498703
Clydebank: Faifley, NS502732
Clydebank: Kilbowie St Andrew's, NS499712
Clydebank: Radnor Park, NS495713
Clydebank: St Cuthbert's, NS511704
Craigrownie, NS224811
Dalmuir: Barclay, NS479715
Dumbarton: Riverside, NS398752
Dumbarton: St Andrew's, NS407764
Dumbarton: West Kirk, NS390755
Duntocher, NS494727
Garelochhead, NS239912
Helensburgh: Park, NS300823
Helensburgh: St Andrew's Kirk, NS295825
Jamestown, NS397813
Kilmaronock Gartocharn, NS452875
Luss, NS361929
Milngavie: Cairns, NS556748
Milngavie: St Luke's, NS543747
Milngavie: St Paul's, NS557745
Old Kilpatrick Bowling, NS463731
Renton: Trinity, NS390780
Rhu and Shandon, NS267841
Rosneath: St Modan's, NS255832

19. Presbytery of Argyll
Appin, NM938459
Ardchattan, NM944360:
    Benderloch, NM905384
Ardrishaig, NR854852
Barra, NF670034
Campbeltown: Highland, NR720201
Campbeltown: Lorne and Lowland, NR718206
Coll, NM223573
Colonsay and Oronsay, NR390941
Connel, NM914343
Craignish, NM805042
Cumlodden, Lochfyneside and Lochgair:
    Cumlodden, NS015997
    Lochfyneside, NR979962
    Lochgair, NR922905
Dunoon: St John's, NS172769
Dunoon: The High Kirk, NS174765
Gigha and Cara, NR648489
Glassary, Kilmartin and Ford:
    Glassary, NR859935
    Kilmartin, NR834988
    Ford, NM869037
Glenaray and Inveraray, NN095085
Glenorchy and Innishael, NN168275
Innellan, NS151707
Iona, NM285243
Jura, NR527677
Kilarrow, NR312596
Kilbrandon and Kilchattan:
    Kilbrandon, NM758155

Kilchattan, NM743104
Kilcalmonell, NR763561
Kilchoman, NR257596
Kilchrenan and Dalavich:
    Kilchrenan, NN037229
    Dalavich, NM968124
Kildalton and Oa, NR368450
Kilfinan, NR934789
Kilfinichen and Kilvickeon and the Ross of Mull:
    Kilfinichen and Kilvickeon, NM383218
    The Ross of Mull, NM316232
Killean and Kilchenzie, NR681418
Kilmeny, NR390657
Kilmodan and Colintraive:
    Kilmodan, NR995842
    Colintraive, NS045735
Kilmore and Oban:
    Kilmore, NM872258
    Oban, NM861296
Kilmun (St Munn's), NS166821
Kilninian and Kilmore, NM432517
Kilninver and Kilmelford:
    Kilninver, NM825217
    Kilmelford, NM849130
Kirn, NS184783
Kyles, NR973713
Lismore, NM861435
Lochgilphead, NR863882
Lochgoilhead and Kilmorich:
    Lochgoilhead, NN198015
    Kilmorich, NN181108
Muckairn, NN005310
North Knapdale:
    Kilmichael Inverlussa, NR776859
    Bellanoch, NR797923
    Tayvallich, NR742871
Portnahaven, NR168523
Rothesay: Trinity, NS089645
Saddell and Carradale, NR796376
Salen and Ulva, NM573431
Sandbank, NS163803
Skipness, NR902579
Southend, NR698094
South Knapdale, NR781775
South Uist:
    Daliburgh, NF754214
    Howmore, NF758364
Strachur and Strathlachlan:
    Strachur, NN096014
    Strathlachlan, NS022958
Strathfillan:
    Crianlarich, NN387252
    Bridge of Orchy, NN297395
Strone and Ardentinny:
    Strone, NS193806
    Ardentinny, NS188876
Tarbert (Loch Fyne) and Kilberry:
    Kilberry, NR741620
    Tarbert, NR863686
The United Church of Bute, NS086637
Tiree:
    Heylipol, NL964432
    Kirkapol, NM041468
Tobermory, NM504554
Torosay and Kinlochspelvie, NM721367
Toward, NS135679

22. Presbytery of Falkirk
Airth, NS898878
Blackbraes and Shieldhill, NS899769
Bo'ness: Old, NS994813

Bo'ness: St Andrew's, NT007813
Bonnybridge: St Helen's, NS821804
Bothkennar and Carronshore, NS903834
Brightons, NS928778
Carriden, NT019812:
    Blackness, NT053798
Cumbernauld: Abronhill, NS781758
Cumbernauld: Condorrat, NS732730
Cumbernauld: Kildrum, NS767747
Cumbernauld: Old, NS764760
Cumbernauld: St Mungo's, NS757745
Denny: Old, NS812828
Denny: Westpark, NS809828
Dunipace, NS807833
Falkirk: Bainsford, NS887814
Falkirk: Camelon, NS873804
Falkirk: Grahamston United, NS889807
Falkirk: Laurieston, NS913794
Falkirk: St Andrew's West, NS887801
Falkirk: St James', NS893806
Falkirk: Trinity, NS887800
Grangemouth: Abbotsgrange, NS928817
Grangemouth: Kirk of the Holy Rood, NS931805
Grangemouth: Zetland, NS931818
Haggs, NS791793
Larbert: East, NS871829
Larbert: Old, NS856822
Larbert: West, NS863827
Muiravonside, NS956770
Polmont: Old, NS937793
Redding and Westquarter, NS921786
Slamannan, NS856734
Stenhouse and Carron, NS876831

23. Presbytery of Stirling
Aberfoyle, NN514013
Alloa: Ludgate, NS884927
Alloa: St Mungo's, NS883926
Alva, NS882970
Balfron, NS547893
Balquhidder, NN536209
Bannockburn: Allan, NS810903
Bannockburn: Ladywell, NS803907
Bridge of Allan, NS791974
Buchanan, NS443903
Buchlyvie, NS577939
Callander, NN629077:
    Trossachs, NN515066
Cambusbarron: The Bruce Memorial, NS778924
Clackmannan, NS910918
Cowie and Plean:
    Cowie, NS837892
    Plean, NS836867
Dollar, NS964980
Drymen, NS474881
Dunblane: Cathedral, NN782014
Dunblane: St Blane's, NN783014
Fallin, NS844913
Fintry, NS627862
Gargunnock, NS707943
Gartmore, NS521971
Glendevon, NN979051
Killearn, NS523861
Killin and Ardeonaig, NN573332:
    Morenish, NN607356
Kilmadock, NN727016
Kincardine-in-Menteith, NS719988
Kippen, NS650948
Lecropt, NS781979
Logie, NS818968
Menstrie, NS849969

Muckhart, NO001010
Norrieston, NN670001
Port of Menteith, NN583012
Sauchie and Coalsnaughton, NS897945
Stirling: Allan Park South, NS795933
Stirling: Church of the Holy Rude, NS792937
Stirling: North, NS802920
Stirling: St Columba's, NS796930
Stirling: St Mark's, NS791948
Stirling: St Ninian's Old, NS795916
Stirling: Viewfield, NS795938
Strathblane, NS557797
Tillicoultry, NS923968
Tullibody: St Serf's, NS860954

24. Presbytery of Dunfermline
Aberdour: St Fillan's, NT193855
Beath and Cowdenbeath: North, NT166925
Cairneyhill, NT052863
Carnock and Oakley:
    Carnock, NT043890
    Oakley, NT025890
Cowdenbeath: Trinity:
    Cowdenbeath, NT157908
    Crossgates, NT145893
Culross and Torryburn:
    Culross, NS989863
    Torryburn, NT027861
    Valleyfield, NT003866
Dalgety, NT155836
Dunfermline: Abbey, NT090873
Dunfermline: East, NT127864
Dunfermline: Gillespie Memorial, NT090876
Dunfermline: North, NT086879
Dunfermline: St Andrew's Erskine, NT107884
Dunfermline: St Leonard's, NT096869
Dunfermline: St Margaret's, NT114878
Dunfermline: St Ninian's, NT113868
Dunfermline: Townhill and Kingseat:
    Townhill, NT106894
    Kingseat, NT126904
Inverkeithing, NT131830
Kelty, NT144942
Limekilns, NT078833
Lochgelly and Benarty: St Serf's:
    Lochgelly, NT186933
    Ballingry, NT173977
North Queensferry, NT132808
Rosyth, NT114839
Saline and Blairingone, NT023924
Tulliallan and Kincardine, NS933879

25. Presbytery of Kirkcaldy
Auchterderran Kinglassie:
    Auchterderran, NT214960
    Kinglassie, NT227985
Auchtertool, NT207902
Buckhaven and Wemyss:
    Buckhaven, NT358981
    West Wemyss, NT328949
Burntisland, NT234857
Dysart: St Clair:
    Dysart, NT302931
    Kirkcaldy: Viewforth, NT294936
Glenrothes: Christ's Kirk, NO275023
Glenrothes: St Columba's, NO270009
Glenrothes: St Margaret's, NO285002
Glenrothes: St Ninian's, NO257007
Kennoway, Windygates and Balgonie: St Kenneth's:
    Kennoway, NO350027
    Windygates, NO345006

Kinghorn, NT272869
Kirkcaldy: Abbotshall, NT274913
Kirkcaldy: Bennochy, NT275925
Kirkcaldy: Linktown, NT278910
Kirkcaldy: Pathhead, NT291928
Kirkcaldy: St Bryce Kirk, NT279917
Kirkcaldy: Templehall, NT265934
Kirkcaldy: Torbain, NT259939
Leslie: Trinity, NO247015
Leven, NO383009
Markinch and Thornton:
    Markinch, NO297019
    Thornton, NT289976
Methil: Wellesley, NT370994
Methilhill and Denbeath, NT357999

26. Presbytery of St Andrews
Abdie and Dunbog, NO257167
Anstruther, NO567037
Auchtermuchty, NO238117
Balmerino, NO368245:
    Gauldry, NO379239
Boarhills and Dunino:
    Boarhills, NO562137
    Dunino, NO541109
Cameron, NO484116
Carnbee, NO532065
Cellardyke, NO574037
Ceres, Kemback and Springfield:
    Ceres, NO399117
    Kemback, NO419151
    Springfield, NO342119
Crail, NO613080
Creich, Flisk and Kilmany:
    Creich, NO328200
    Kilmany, NO388217
Cupar: Old and St Michael of Tarvit, NO373143
Cupar: St John's and Dairsie United:
    Cupar: St John's, NO373147
    Dairsie, NO413173
Edenshead and Strathmiglo, NO217103
Elie, Kilconquhar and Colinsburgh:
    Elie, NO491001
    Kilconquhar, NO485020
    Colinsburgh, NO475034
Falkland, NO252074
Freuchie, NO283067
Howe of Fife:
    Collessie, NO287133
    Cults, NO347099
    Kettle, NO310083
    Ladybank, NO302102
Kilrenny, NO575049
Kingsbarns, NO593121
Largo and Newburn, NO423035
Largo: St David's, NO419026
Largoward, NO469077
Leuchars: St Athernase, NO455214
Monimail, NO303142
Newburgh, NO240183
Newport-on-Tay, NO422280
Pittenweem, NO549026
St Andrews: Holy Trinity, NO509167
St Andrews: Hope Park and Martyrs', NO505167
St Andrews: St Leonard's, NO502164
St Monans, NO523014
Strathkinness, NO460163
Tayport, NO458286
Wormit, NO403267

27. Presbytery of Dunkeld and Meigle
Aberfeldy, NN854491
Alyth, NO243488
Amulree and Strathbraan, NN899366
Ardler, Kettins and Meigle:
    Kettins, NO238390
    Meigle, NO287446
Bendochy, NO218415
Blair Atholl, NN874654:
    Struan, NN808654
Blairgowrie, NO177454
Braes of Rannoch, NN507566
Caputh and Clunie:
    Caputh, NO088401
    Clunie, NO109440
Coupar Angus: Abbey, NO223398
Dull and Weem, NN844497
Dunkeld: Cathedral, NO024426:
    Little Dunkeld, NO028423
    Dowally, NO001480
Fortingall and Glenlyon:
    Fortingall, NN742471
    Glenlyon, NN588475
Foss and Rannoch:
    Foss, NN790581
    Rannoch, NN663585
Grantully, Logierait and Strathtay:
    Logierait, NN967520
    Strathtay, NN908532
Kenmore and Lawers, NN772454
Kinclaven, NO151385
Kirkmichael, Straloch and Glenshee:
    Kirkmichael, NO081601
    Glenshee, NO109702
Pitlochry, NO940582
Rattray, NO190457
Tenandry, NN911615

28. Presbytery of Perth
Aberdalgie and Forteviot:
    Aberdalgie, NO079203
    Forteviot, NO052175
Abernethy and Dron and Arngask:
    Abernethy, NO190164
    Arngask (Glenfarg), NO133104
Aberuthven and Dunning:
    Aberuthven, NN979155
    Dunning, NO020147
Almondbank and Tibbermore, NO065264
Ardoch, NO839098
Auchterarder, NN948129
Auchtergaven and Moneydie, NO061347
Blackford, NN899092
Cargill Burrelton, NO202377
Cleish, NT095981
Collace, NO197320
Comrie, NN770221
Crieff, NN867219
Dunbarney and Forgandenny:
    Dunbarney, NO130185
    Forgandenny, NO087183
Dundurn, NN697241
Errol, NO253230
Fossoway: St Serf's and Devonside, NO033001
Fowlis Wester, Madderty and Monzie:
    Fowlis Wester, NN928241
    Madderty, NN947217
    Monzie, NN879250
Gask, NO003203
Kilspindie and Rait, NO220258
Kinross, NO118023

Methven and Logiealmond, NO026260
Muthill, NN868171
Orwell and Portmoak:
  Orwell, NO121051
  Portmoak, NO183019
Perth: Craigie and Moncreiffe:
  Craigie, NO110228
  Moncreiffe, NO113218
Perth: Kinnoull, NO123235
Perth: Letham St Mark's, NO095243
Perth: North, NO116237
Perth: Riverside, NO110256
Perth: St John's Kirk of Perth, NO119235
Perth: St Leonard's-in-the-Fields, NO117232
Perth: St Matthew's, NO121235
Redgorton and Stanley, NO110329
St Madoes and Kinfauns, NO197212
Scone and St Martins:
  Scone, NO136262
  St David's Stormontfield, NO108298
  St Martins, NO154304
Trinity Gask and Kinkell, NN963183

29. Presbytery of Dundee
Abernyte, NO267311
Auchterhouse, NO342381
Dundee: Balgay, NO385309
Dundee: Barnhill St Margaret's, NO478316
Dundee: Broughty Ferry New Kirk, NO464309
Dundee: Broughty Ferry St James', NO460307
Dundee: Broughty Ferry St Luke's and Queen Street,
  NO457312
Dundee: Broughty Ferry St Stephen's and West, NO458309
Dundee: Camperdown, NO363320
Dundee: Chalmers Ardler, NO377333
Dundee: Coldside, NO403316
Dundee: Craigiebank, NO429315
Dundee: Douglas and Mid Craigie, NO444322
Dundee: Downfield Mains, NO389336
Dundee: Dundee (St Mary's), NO401301
Dundee: Fintry, NO423334
Dundee: Lochee, NO377318
Dundee: Logie and St John's Cross, NO386299
Dundee: Meadowside St Paul's, NO402300
Dundee: Menzieshill, NO362312
Dundee: St Andrew's, NO404307
Dundee: St David's High Kirk, NO394313
Dundee: Steeple, NO402301
Dundee: Stobswell, NO411315
Dundee: Strathmartine, NO384343
Dundee: Trinity, NO410310
Dundee: West, NO395297
Dundee: Whitfield, NO435334
Fowlis and Liff:
  Fowlis, NO322334
  Liff, NO333328
Inchture and Kinnaird:
  Inchture, NO281288
  Kinnaird, NO243287
Invergowrie, NO346304
Longforgan, NO309300
Lundie and Muirhead:
  Lundie, NO291366
  Muirhead, NO342345
Monifieth:
  Panmure, NO500327
  St Rule's, NO495323
  South, NO493324
Monikie and Newbigging and Murroes and Tealing:
  Monikie, NO518388
  Murroes, NO461351

30. Presbytery of Angus
Aberlemno, NO523555
Arbirlot, NO602406
Arbroath: Knox's, NO638414
Arbroath: Old and Abbey, NO644413
Arbroath: St Andrew's, NO643414
Arbroath: St Vigeans, NO638429
Arbroath: West Kirk, NO636410
Barry, NO541346
Brechin: Cathedral, NO595601:
  Stracathro, NO617657
Brechin: Gardner Memorial, NO601602
Carmyllie, NO549426
Carnoustie, NO559346
Carnoustie: Panbride, NO570347:
  Panbride, NO572358
Colliston, NO604453
Dun and Hillside:
  Dun, NO664600
  Hillside, NO709609
Dunnichen, Letham and Kirkden, NO528488
Eassie, Nevay and Newtyle, NO296413
Edzell Lethnot Glenesk:
  Edzell Lethnot, NO599693
  Glenesk, NO497795
Farnell, NO627554
Fern Careston Menmuir:
  Fern, NO484616
  Careston, NO528603
Forfar: East and Old, NO457506
Forfar: Lowson Memorial, NO465509
Forfar: St Margaret's, NO454505
Friockheim Kinnell, NO592497
Glamis, Inverarity and Kinnettles:
  Glamis, NO386469
  Inverarity, NO453443
Guthrie and Rescobie:
  Guthrie, NO568505
  Rescobie, NO509521
Inchbrayock, NO714567
Inverkeilor and Lunan, NO664496
Kirriemuir: St Andrew's, NO386535
Montrose: Melville South, NO713575
Montrose: Old and St Andrew's, NO715578
Oathlaw Tannadice, NO475581
The Glens and Kirriemuir: Old:
  Kirriemuir: Old, NO386539
  Cortachy, NO396597
  Glen Prosen, NO328657
  Memus, NO427590
The Isla Parishes:
  Glenisla, NO215604
  Kilry, NO246538

31. Presbytery of Aberdeen
Aberdeen: Bridge of Don Oldmachar, NJ928121
Aberdeen: Cove, meets in Loirston Primary School
Aberdeen: Craigiebuckler, NJ907053
Aberdeen: Ferryhill, NJ937051
Aberdeen: Garthdee, NJ918034
Aberdeen: High Hilton, NJ923078
Aberdeen: Holburn West, NJ926052
Aberdeen: Mannofield, NJ917045
Aberdeen: Mastrick, NJ902073
Aberdeen: Middlefield, NJ911088
Aberdeen: Midstocket, NJ919066
Aberdeen: Northfield, NJ903085
Aberdeen: Queen Street, NJ943064
Aberdeen: Queen's Cross, NJ925058
Aberdeen: Rubislaw, NJ924058
Aberdeen: Ruthrieston West, NJ924042

Aberdeen: St Columba's Bridge of Don, NJ935104
Aberdeen: St George's Tillydrone, NJ931090
Aberdeen: St John's Church for Deaf People, meets in
   Aberdeen: St Mark's
Aberdeen: St Machar's Cathedral, NJ939088
Aberdeen: St Mark's, NJ937063
Aberdeen: St Mary's, NJ943081
Aberdeen: St Nicholas Kincorth, South of, NJ934033
Aberdeen: St Nicholas Uniting, Kirk of, NJ941063
Aberdeen: St Stephen's, NJ936074
Aberdeen: South Holburn, NJ930042
Aberdeen: Stockethill, meets in community centre
Aberdeen: Summerhill, NJ904063
Aberdeen: Torry St Fittick's, NJ947050
Aberdeen: Woodside, NJ924088
Bucksburn Stoneywood, NJ897096
Cults, NJ886026
Dyce, NJ887130
Kingswells, NJ869063
Newhills, NJ876095
Peterculter, NJ841007

32. Presbytery of Kincardine and Deeside
Aberluthnott, NO687656:
   Luthermuir, NO655685
Aboyne and Dinnet, NO525983
Arbuthnott, Bervie and Kinneff:
   Arbuthnott, NO801746
   Bervie, NO830727
Banchory-Devenick and Maryculter/Cookney, NO857993
Banchory-Ternan: East, NO707958
Banchory-Ternan: West, NO693957
Birse and Feughside, NO605925
Braemar and Crathie:
   Braemar, NO150913
   Crathie, NO265949
Cromar:
   Coull, NJ512024
   Tarland, NJ485047
Drumoak-Durris:
   Drumoak, NO792993
   Durris, NO772965
Glenmuick (Ballater), NO369957
Laurencekirk, NO718717
Mearns Coastal:
   Johnshaven, NO798672
   St Cyrus, NO750648
Mid Deeside, NJ626021
Newtonhill, NO911934
Portlethen, NO924966
Stonehaven: Dunnottar, NO863853
Stonehaven: Fetteresso, NO869864
Stonehaven: South, NO872857
West Mearns:
   Fettercairn, NO651735
   Fordoun, NO726784
   Glenbervie, NO766807

33. Presbytery of Gordon
Barthol Chapel, NJ814339
Belhelvie, NJ957184
Blairdaff and Chapel of Garioch:
   Blairdaff, NJ704173
   Chapel of Garioch, NJ716242
Cluny, NJ685124
Culsalmond and Rayne, NJ698302
Cushnie and Tough:
   Cushnie, NJ530108
   Tough, NJ616129
Daviot, NJ750283
Echt, NJ739057

Ellon, NJ959304:
   Slains, NK042290
Fintray Kinellar Keithhall:
   Fintray, NJ841166
   Keithhall, NJ803210
Foveran, NJ999253
Howe Trinity, NJ582157
Huntly Cairnie Glass, NJ530398
Insch-Leslie-Premnay-Oyne,
   NJ631283
Inverurie: St Andrew's, NJ777211
Inverurie: West, NJ774215
Kemnay, NJ737162
Kintore, NJ793163
Meldrum and Bourtie:
   Meldrum, NJ813273
   Bourtie, NJ804248
Methlick, NJ858372
Midmar, NJ699065
Monymusk, NJ684152
New Machar, NJ887194
Noth, NJ497272
Skene, NJ803077:
   Westhill, NJ833072
Strathbogie Drumblade:
   Strathbogie, NJ531399
   Drumblade, NJ588402
Tarves, NJ868312
Udny and Pitmedden:
   Udny, NJ880264
   Pitmedden, NJ893274
Upper Donside:
   Strathdon, NJ355127
   Towie, NJ440129
   Lumsden, NJ475220

34. Presbytery of Buchan
Aberdour, NJ885634
Auchaber United, NJ632411
Auchterless, NJ713415
Banff, NJ689638
Crimond, NK054568
Cruden, NK071366
Deer, NJ979477:
   Fetterangus, NJ987508
Fraserburgh: Old, NJ998671
Fraserburgh: South, NJ998666
Fraserburgh: West, NJ994667
Fyvie, NJ768377
Gardenstown, NJ801648
Inverallochy and Rathen: East, NK043651
King Edward, NJ716579
Longside, NK037473
Lonmay, NK038602
Macduff, NJ701643
Marnoch, NJ628527
Maud and Savoch, NJ927478
Monquhitter and New Byth, NJ803506
New Deer: St Kane's, NJ886469
New Pitsligo, NJ880562
Ordiquhill and Cornhill, NJ587583
Peterhead: Old, NK131462
Peterhead: St Andrew's, NK131465
Peterhead: Trinity, NK132463:
   Boddam, NK133423
Pitsligo, NJ929673
Portsoy, NJ587659
Rathen: West, NK000609
Rothienorman, NJ723357
St Fergus, NK093519
Sandhaven, NJ963675

Strichen and Tyrie:
  Strichen, NJ945554
  Tyrie, NJ930631
Turriff: St Andrew's, NJ729497
Turriff: St Ninian's and Forglen, NJ723500
Whitehills, NJ655653

35. Presbytery of Moray
Aberlour, NJ264428:
  Craigellachie, NJ290451
Alves and Burghead:
  Alves, NJ125616
  Burghead, NJ114688
Bellie, NJ345588
Birnie and Pluscarden:
  Birnie, NJ207587
  Pluscarden, NJ149573
Buckie: North, NJ427657
Buckie: South and West, NJ426654
Cullen and Deskford, NJ507664
Dallas, NJ122518
Duffus, Spynie and Hopeman:
  Duffus, NJ168687
  Spynie, NJ183642
  Hopeman, NJ144693
Dyke, NH990584
Edinkillie, NJ020466
Elgin: High, NJ215627
Elgin: St Giles' and St Columba's South:
  St Giles', NJ217628
  St Columba's South, NJ219623
Enzie, NJ397643
Findochty, NJ464682
Forres: St Laurence, NJ035588
Forres: St Leonard's, NJ038591
Keith: North, Newmill, Boharm and Rothiemay:
  Keith: North, NJ433507
  Newmill, NJ439527
  Boharm, NJ355505
  Rothiemay, NJ547483
Keith: St Rufus, Botriphnie and Grange:
  Keith: St Rufus, NJ430508
  Botriphnie, NJ375441
  Grange, NJ481515
Kinloss and Findhorn:
  Kinloss, NJ063617
  Findhorn, NJ042642
Knockando, Elchies and Archiestown, NJ186429
Lossiemouth: St Gerardine's High, NJ233706
Lossiemouth: St James', NJ235707
Mortlach and Cabrach:
  Mortlach, NJ324393
  Lower Cabrach, NJ382313
Portknockie, NJ488684
Rafford, NJ061564
Rathven, NJ444657
Rothes, NJ278492
St Andrew's-Lhanbryd and Urquhart, NJ256622
Speymouth, NJ337607

36. Presbytery of Abernethy
Abernethy, NJ007218:
  Nethy Bridge, NJ003203
Alvie and Insh:
  Alvie, NH864093
  Insh, NH837053
Boat of Garten, Duthil and Kincardine:
  Boat of Garten, NH941190
  Duthil, NH908225
  Kincardine, NH938155
Cromdale and Advie, NJ067289

Dulnain Bridge, NH998249
Grantown-on-Spey, NJ032281
Kingussie, NH761007
Laggan, NN615943
Newtonmore: St Bride's, NN715993
Rothiemurchus and Aviemore:
  Rothiemurchus, NH903108
  Aviemore, NH896130
Tomintoul, Glenlivet and Inveraven:
  Tomintoul, NJ169185
  Inveraven, NJ183376

37. Presbytery of Inverness
Ardersier, NH781553
Auldearn and Dalmore, NH919556
Cawdor, NH844499
Croy and Dalcross, NH797498
Culloden: The Barn, NH719461
Daviot and Dunlichity:
  Daviot, NH722394
  Dunlichity, NH660330
Dores and Boleskine:
  Dores, NH601350
  Boleskine, NH507183
Inverness: Crown, NH671452
Inverness: Dalneigh and Bona:
  Dalneigh, NH655450
  Bona, NH595377
Inverness: East, NH666455
Inverness: Hilton, NH674436
Inverness: Inshes, NH688441
Inverness: Kinmylies, NH646446
Inverness: Ness Bank, NH665448
Inverness: Old High St Stephen's:
  Old High, NH665455
  St Stephen's, NH670447
Inverness: St Columba
Inverness: Trinity, NH661458
Kilmorack and Erchless:
  Beauly, NH525465
  Struy, NH402402
  Cannich, NH336318
Kiltarlity, NH513413
Kirkhill, NH553454
Moy, Dalarossie and Tomatin:
  Dalarossie, NH767242
  Tomatin, NH803290
Nairn: Old, NH879564
Nairn: St Ninian's, NH883563
Petty, NH767502
Urquhart and Glenmoriston,
  NH509294

38. Presbytery of Lochaber
Acharacle, NM674683
Ardgour and Kingairloch:
  Ardgour, NN011642
  Kingairloch, NM862526
Ardnamurchan, NM488638
Duror, NM993553
Fort Augustus, NH377090
Fort William: Duncansburgh MacIntosh, NN104741
Glencoe: St Munda's, NN083578
Glengarry, NH304012:
  Tomdoun, NH154011
Kilmallie:
  Achnacarry, NN181873
  Caol, NN106762
  Corpach, NN092770
Kilmonivaig, NN212819
Kinlochleven, NN187621

Morvern, NM672452
Nether Lochaber, NN031614
North West Lochaber:
  Arisaig, NM661866
  Canna, NG277054
  Eigg, NM481855
  Mallaig: St Columba, NM676967
Strontian, NM817617

39. Presbytery of Ross
Alness, NH647693
Avoch, NH701552
Contin, NH457557:
  Kinlochluichart, NH317622
Cromarty, NH786674
Dingwall: Castle Street, NH552588
Dingwall: St Clement's, NH548589
Fearn Abbey and Nigg:
  Fearn Abbey, NH837773
  Nigg, NH825736
Ferintosh, NH543556
Fodderty and Strathpeffer, NH482580
Fortrose and Rosemarkie:
  Fortrose, NH728568
  Rosemarkie, NH737576
Invergordon, NH707687
Killearnan, NH577494
Kilmuir and Logie Easter:
  Kilmuir, NH758732
  Logie Easter, NH779757
Kiltearn, NH607662
Knockbain, NH647530:
  Kessock, NH655479
Lochbroom and Ullapool:
  Lochbroom, NH177848
  Ullapool, NH130942
Resolis and Urquhart, NH608596
Rosskeen, NH658697
Tain, NH780820
Tarbat, NH917846
Urray and Kilchrist:
  Urray, NH509524
  Muir of Ord, NH528507

40. Presbytery of Sutherland
Altnaharra and Farr:
  Altnaharra, NC568355
  Farr, NC708622
  Strathnaver, NC694439
Assynt and Stoer, NC093225
Clyne, NC905044
Creich, NH611917
Dornoch Cathedral, NH797897
Durness and Kinlochbervie:
  Durness, NC404669
  Kinlochbervie, NC221564
Eddrachillis, NC151443
Golspie, NC837003
Kildonan and Loth Helmsdale, ND025154
Kincardine Croick and Edderton:
  Ardgay, NH595910
  Croick, NH457915
  Edderton, NH710847
Lairg, NC583065
Melness and Tongue:
  Melness, NC586634
  Tongue, NC591570
Rogart, Pitfure, NC715038:
  St Callan's, NC739035
Rosehall, NC484013

41. Presbytery of Caithness
Bower, ND238622
Canisbay, ND343728
Dunnet, ND220712
Halkirk Westerdale, ND131594
Keiss, ND348611
Olrig, ND191682
The North Coast Parish:
  Halladale, NC893558
  Reay, NC967648
  Strathy, NC843653
The Parish of Latheron:
  Lybster, ND248361
  Dunbeath, ND157295
Thurso: St Peter's and St Andrew's, ND115683
Thurso: West, ND114681
Watten, ND243547
Wick: Pulteneytown and Thrumster:
  Pulteneytown, ND365504
  Thrumster, ND333447
Wick: St Fergus, ND362512

42. Presbytery of Lochcarron – Skye
Applecross, Lochcarron and Torridon:
  Applecross, NG711417
  Lochcarron, NG893391
  Shieldaig, NG816542
  Torridon, NG864572
Bracadale and Duirinish:
  Bracadale, NG369331
  Duirinish, NG251479
Gairloch and Dundonnell:
  Gairloch, NG807756
  Aultbea, NG875886
  Dundonnell, NH019919
Glenelg and Kintail:
  Glenelg, NG813193
  Kintail, NG930213
Kilmuir and Stenscholl:
  Kilmuir, NG389694
  Stenscholl, NG489673
Lochalsh, NG761277
Portree, NG482436
Snizort:
  Arnisort, NG348532
  Kensaleyre, NG420517
  Uig, NG398642
Strath and Sleat:
  Broadford, NG642235
  Elgol, NG523143
  Kilmore, NG657069
  Kyleakin, NG751263

43. Presbytery of Uist
Benbecula, NF800519
Berneray and Lochmaddy:
  Berneray, NF920819
  Lochmaddy, NF918684
Carinish, NF811637
Kilmuir and Paible:
  Kilmuir, NF727703
  Sollas, NF802744
Manish-Scarista:
  Manish, NG102892
  Scaristabeg, NG007927
  Leverburgh, NG020868
Tarbert, NG159998

44. Presbytery of Lewis
Barvas, NB360494
Carloway, NB206424

Cross Ness, NB506619
Kinloch:
  Laxay, NB323220
  Lemreway, NB380118
Knock, NB522336
Lochs-Crossbost, NB382255
Lochs-in-Bernera, NB159366
Stornoway: High, NB427330
Stornoway: Martin's Memorial, NB424327
Stornoway: St Columba, NB426330
Uig, NB087347

45. Presbytery of Orkney
Birsay, Harray and Sandwick, HY296206
East Mainland, HY503019
Eday, HY562328
Evie, HY368255
Firth, HY359138
Flotta, ND366931
Hoy and Walls, ND312908
Kirkwall: East, HY451110
Kirkwall: St Magnus Cathedral, HY296206
North Ronaldsay, congregation meets in community
    school, HY758532
Orphir and Stenness:
  Orphir, HY343059
  Stenness, HY311125
Papa Westray, HY496516
Rendall, HY393206
Rousay, HY442278
Sanday, HY659408
Shapinsay, HY497173
South Ronaldsay and Burray:
  St Margaret's Hope, ND449934
  St Peter's Eastside, ND472908
Stromness, HY254090
Stronsay: Moncur Memorial, HY654252
Westray, HY457462

46. Presbytery of Shetland
Burra Isle, HU371330
Delting:
  Brae, HU359673

Togon, HU404637
Muckle Roe, HU342647
Dunrossness and St Ninian's:
  Bigton, HU384213
  Boddam, HU391151
  Fair Isle, HZ206706
Fetlar, HU607905
Lerwick and Bressay:
  Lerwick, HU478411
  Gulberwick, HU443389
  Bressay, HU493410
Nesting and Lunnasting:
  Nesting, HU487578
  Lunna, HU486690
Northmavine:
  Hillswick, HU282771
  North Roe, HU365895
  Ollaberry, HU366806
Sandsting and Aithsting, HU345556
Sandwick, Cunningsburgh and Quarff:
  Sandwick, HU432237
  Cunningsburgh, HU430293
  Quarff, HU429358
Tingwall:
  Scalloway, HU401395
  Veensgarth, HU419437
  Weisdale, HU394526
Unst:
  Baltasound, HP614088
  Uyeasound, HP601011
Walls and Sandness:
  Walls, HU240493
  Mid Walls, HU220502
  Sandness, HU195571
  Papa Stour, HU177600
  Foula, HT969378
Whalsay and Skerries:
  Whalsay, HU555654
  Skerries, HU680717
Yell:
  Cullivoe, HP544021
  Hamnavoe, HU494804
  Mid Yell, HU515907

SECTION 9

Discontinued Parish
and Congregational Names

The following list updates and corrects the 'Index of Discontinued Parish and Congregational Names' printed in the previous edition of the *Year Book*. As before, it lists the parishes of the Church of Scotland and the congregations of the United Presbyterian Church (and its constituent denominations), the Free Church (1843–1900) and the United Free Church (1900–29) whose names have completely disappeared, largely as a consequence of union.

It should be noted, as has been stressed in previous years, that this list is *not* intended to be 'a comprehensive guide to readjustment in the Church of Scotland'; that would require a considerably larger number of pages. Despite the annual reiteration of this statement, the Editor's attention continues to be drawn to the omission from the list of this or that now-vanished congregation whose name does not in fact fall within the criteria for inclusion given below.

The specific purpose of this list is to assist those who are trying to identify the present-day successor of some former parish or congregation whose name is now wholly out of use and which can therefore no longer be easily traced. Where the former name has not disappeared completely, and the whereabouts of the former parish or congregation may therefore be easily established by reference to the name of some existing parish, the former name has not been included in this list. Present-day names, in the right-hand column of this list, may be found in the 'Index of Parishes and Places' near the end of this book.

The following examples will illustrate some of the criteria used to determine whether a name should be included or not:

•   Where all the former congregations in a town have been united into one, as in the case of Melrose or Selkirk, the names of these former congregations have not been included; but in the case of towns with more than one congregation, such as Galashiels or Hawick, the names of the various constituent congregations are listed.

•   The same principle applies in the case of discrete areas of cities. For example, as Dundee: Lochee and Glasgow: Dennistoun New are now the only congregations in Lochee and Dennistoun respectively, there is no need to list Dundee: Lochee St Ninian's, Glasgow: Dennistoun South or any other congregations which had Lochee or Dennistoun in their names.

•   Where a prefix such as North, Old, Little, Mid or the like has been lost but the substantive part of the name has been retained, the former name has not been included: it is assumed that someone searching for Little Dalton or Mid Yell will have no difficulty in connecting these with Dalton or Yell.

•   Where the present name of a united congregation includes the names of some or all of its constituent parts, these former names do not appear in the list: thus, neither Glasgow: Anderston nor Glasgow: Kelvingrove appears, since both names are easily traceable to Glasgow: Anderston Kelvingrove.

Two other criteria for inclusion or exclusion may also be mentioned:

•   Some parishes and congregations have disappeared, and their names have been lost, as a consequence of suppression, dissolution or secession. The names of rural parishes in this category have been included, together with the names of their Presbyteries to assist with identification, but those in towns and cities have not been included, as there will clearly be no difficulty in establishing the general location of the parish or congregation in question.

•   Since 1929, a small number of rural parishes have adopted a new name (for example, Whitehills, formerly Boyndie). The former names of these parishes have been included, but it would have been too unwieldy to include either the vast numbers of such changes of name in towns and cities, especially those which occurred at the time of the 1900 and 1929 unions, or the very many older names of pre-Reformation parishes which were abandoned in earlier centuries (however fascinating a list of such long-vanished names as Fothmuref, Kinbathock and Toskertoun might have been).

In this list, the following abbreviations have been used:

C of S	Church of Scotland
FC	Free Church
R	Relief Church
RP	Reformed Presbyterian Church
UF	United Free Church
UP	United Presbyterian Church
US	United Secession Church

Name no longer used	Present name of parish
Abbey St Bathans	Langton and Lammermuir Kirk
Abbotrule	charge suppressed: Presbytery of Jedburgh
Aberargie	charge dissolved: Presbytery of Perth
Aberchirder	Marnoch
Aberdeen: Beechgrove	Aberdeen: Midstocket
Aberdeen: Belmont Street	Aberdeen: St Mark's
Aberdeen: Carden Place	Aberdeen: Queen's Cross
Aberdeen: Causewayend	Aberdeen: St Stephen's
Aberdeen: East	Aberdeen: St Mark's
Aberdeen: Gallowgate	Aberdeen: St Mary's
Aberdeen: Greyfriars	Aberdeen: Queen Street
Aberdeen: Hilton	Aberdeen: Woodside
Aberdeen: Holburn Central	Aberdeen: South Holburn
Aberdeen: John Knox Gerrard Street	Aberdeen: Queen Street
Aberdeen: John Knox's (Mounthooly)	Aberdeen: Queen Street
Aberdeen: King Street	Aberdeen: Queen Street
Aberdeen: Melville	Aberdeen: Queen's Cross
Aberdeen: Nelson Street	Aberdeen: Queen Street
Aberdeen: North	Aberdeen: Queen Street
Aberdeen: North of St Andrew	Aberdeen: Queen Street
Aberdeen: Pittodrie	Aberdeen: St Mary's
Aberdeen: Powis	Aberdeen: St Stephen's
Aberdeen: Ruthrieston (C of S)	Aberdeen: South Holburn
Aberdeen: Ruthrieston (FC)	Aberdeen: Ruthrieston West
Aberdeen: South (C of S)	Aberdeen: South of St Nicholas, Kincorth
Aberdeen: South (FC)	Aberdeen: St Mark's
Aberdeen: St Andrew's	Aberdeen: Queen Street
Aberdeen: St Columba's	Aberdeen: High Hilton
Aberdeen: St Mary's	Aberdeen: St Machar's Cathedral
Aberdeen: St Ninian's	Aberdeen: Midstocket
Aberdeen: Trinity (C of S)	Aberdeen: Kirk of St Nicholas Uniting
Aberdeen: Trinity (FC)	Aberdeen: St Mark's
Abington	Upper Clyde
Addiewell	Breich Valley
Afton	New Cumnock
Airdrie: West	Airdrie: New Wellwynd
Airlie	The Isla Parishes
Aldbar	Aberlemno
Aldcambus	Dunglass
Alford	Howe Trinity
Allanton	Bonkyl and Edrom
Alloa: Chalmers	Alloa: Ludgate
Alloa: Melville	Alloa: Ludgate
Alloa: North	Alloa: Ludgate
Alloa: St Andrew's	Alloa: Ludgate
Alloa: West	Alloa: Ludgate
Altries	charge dissolved: Presbytery of Kincardine and Deeside
Altyre	Rafford
Alvah	Banff
Ancrum	Ale and Teviot United
Annan: Erskine	Annan: St Andrew's
Annan: Greenknowe	Annan: St Andrew's
Anwoth	Gatehouse of Fleet
Arbroath: East	Arbroath: St Andrew's
Arbroath: Erskine	Arbroath: West Kirk
Arbroath: High Street	Arbroath: St Andrew's
Arbroath: Hopemount	Arbroath: St Andrew's
Arbroath: Ladyloan	Arbroath: West Kirk

Name no longer used	Present name of parish
Arbroath: Princes Street	Arbroath: West Kirk
Arbroath: St Columba's	Arbroath: West Kirk
Arbroath: St Margaret's	Arbroath: West Kirk
Arbroath: St Ninian's	Arbroath: St Andrew's
Arbroath: St Paul's	Arbroath: St Andrew's
Ardallie	Deer
Ardclach	charge dissolved: Presbytery of Inverness
Ardrossan: Barony	Ardrossan and Saltcoats: Kirkgate
Ardrossan: St John's	Ardrossan and Saltcoats: Kirkgate
Ardwell	Stoneykirk
Arisaig	North West Lochaber
Ascog	The United Church of Bute
Auchencairn	The Bengairn Parishes
Auchindoir	Upper Donside
Auchmithie	Arbroath: St Vigeans
Auldcathie	Dalmeny
Aultbea	Gairloch and Dundonnell
Ayr: Cathcart	Ayr: St Columba
Ayr: Darlington New	Ayr: Auld Kirk of Ayr
Ayr: Darlington Place	Ayr: Auld Kirk of Ayr
Ayr: Lochside	Ayr: St Quivox
Ayr: Martyrs'	Ayr: Auld Kirk of Ayr
Ayr: Sandgate	Ayr: St Columba
Ayr: St John's	Ayr: Auld Kirk of Ayr
Ayr: Trinity	Ayr: St Columba
Ayr: Wallacetown North	Ayr: Newton Wallacetown
Ayr: Wallacetown South	Ayr: Auld Kirk of Ayr
Back	charge dissolved: Presbytery of Lewis
Badcall	Eddrachillis
Balbeggie	Collace
Balfour	charge dissolved: Presbytery of Dundee
Balgedie	Orwell and Portmoak
Baliasta	Unst
Ballachulish	Nether Lochaber
Ballingry	Lochgelly and Benarty: St Serf's
Balmacolm	Howe of Fife
Balmullo	charge dissolved: Presbytery of St Andrews
Balnacross	Tarff and Twynholm
Baltasound	Unst
Banchory-Ternan: North	Banchory-Ternan: West
Banchory-Ternan: South	Banchory-Ternan: West
Bandry	Luss
Bara	Garvald and Morham
Bargrennan	Penninghame
Barnweil	Tarbolton
Barrhead: Arthurlie	Barrhead: St Andrew's
Barrhead: South	Barrhead: St Andrew's
Barrhead: Westbourne	Barrhead: St Andrew's
Barrock	Dunnet
Bearsden: North	Bearsden: Cross
Bearsden: South	Bearsden: Cross
Bedrule	Ruberslaw
Belkirk	Liddesdale
Bellshill: Macdonald Memorial	Bellshill: Central
Bellshill: Orbiston	Bellshill: Central
Benholm	Mearns Coastal
Benvie	Fowlis and Liff
Berriedale	The Parish of Latheron

Name no longer used	Present name of parish
Binny	Linlithgow: St Michael's
Blackburn	Fintray Kinellar Keithhall
Blackhill	Longside
Blairlogie	congregation seceded: Presbytery of Stirling
Blanefield	Strathblane
Blantyre: Anderson	Blantyre: St Andrew's
Blantyre: Burleigh Memorial	Blantyre: St Andrew's
Blantyre: Stonefield	Blantyre: St Andrew's
Blyth Bridge	Kirkurd and Newlands
Boddam	Peterhead: Trinity
Bonhill: North	Alexandria
Borthwick	Tyne Valley Parish
Bothwell: Park	Uddingston: Viewpark
Bourtreebush	Newtonhill
Bowmore	Kilarrow
Bow of Fife	Monimail
Boyndie	Whitehills
Brachollie	Petty
Braco	Ardoch
Braehead	Forth
Brechin: East	Brechin: Gardner Memorial
Brechin: Maison Dieu	Brechin: Cathedral
Brechin: St Columba's	Brechin: Gardner Memorial
Brechin: West	Brechin: Gardner Memorial
Breich	Breich Valley
Bridge of Teith	Kilmadock
Brora	Clyne
Bruan	The Parish of Latheron
Buccleuch	Ettrick and Yarrow
Buittle	The Bengairn Parishes
Burnhead	Penpont, Keir and Tynron
Cairnryan	charge dissolved: Presbytery of Wigtown and Stranraer
Cambuslang: Old	Cambuslang
Cambuslang: Rosebank	Cambuslang
Cambuslang: St Andrew's	Cambuslang
Cambuslang: St Paul's	Cambuslang
Cambuslang: Trinity	Cambuslang
Cambuslang: West	Cambuslang
Cambusmichael	Scone and St Martins
Campbeltown: Longrow	Campbeltown: Lorne and Lowland
Campsail	Rosneath: St Modan's
Canna	North West Lochaber
Carbuddo	Guthrie and Rescobie
Cardenden	Auchterderran Kinglassie
Carlisle	The Border Kirk
Carmichael	Cairngryffe
Carnoch	Contin
Carnousie	Turriff: St Ninian's and Forglen
Carnoustie: St Stephen's	Carnoustie
Carrbridge	Boat of Garten, Duthil and Kincardine
Carruthers	Hoddom, Kirtle-Eaglesfield and Middlebie
Castle Kennedy	Inch
Castleton	Liddesdale
Caterline	Arbuthnott, Bervie and Kinneff
Chapelknowe	congregation seceded: Presbytery of Annandale and Eskdale
Clatt	Noth
Clayshant	Stoneykirk
Climpy	charge dissolved: Presbytery of Lanark

Name no longer used	Present name of parish
Clola	Deer
Clousta	Sandsting and Aithsting
Clova	The Glens and Kirriemuir: Old
Clydebank: Bank Street	Clydebank: St Cuthbert's
Clydebank: Boquhanran	Clydebank: Kilbowie St Andrew's
Clydebank: Hamilton Memorial	Clydebank: St Cuthbert's
Clydebank: Linnvale	Clydebank: St Cuthbert's
Clydebank: St James'	Clydebank: Abbotsford
Clydebank: Union	Clydebank: Kilbowie St Andrew's
Clydebank: West	Clydebank: Abbotsford
Coatbridge: Clifton	Coatbridge: New St Andrew's
Coatbridge: Cliftonhill	Coatbridge: New St Andrew's
Coatbridge: Coatdyke	Coatbridge: New St Andrew's
Coatbridge: Coats	Coatbridge: New St Andrew's
Coatbridge: Dunbeth	Coatbridge: New St Andrew's
Coatbridge: Gartsherrie	Coatbridge: New St Andrew's
Coatbridge: Garturk	Coatbridge: Calder
Coatbridge: Maxwell	Coatbridge: New St Andrew's
Coatbridge: Trinity	Coatbridge: New St Andrew's
Coatbridge: Whifflet	Coatbridge: Calder
Cobbinshaw	charge dissolved: Presbytery of West Lothian
Cockburnspath	Dunglass
Coigach	charge dissolved: Presbytery of Lochcarron – Skye
Coldstone	Cromar
Collessie	Howe of Fife
Corgarff	Upper Donside
Cortachy	The Glens and Kirriemuir: Old
Coull	Cromar
Covington	Cairngryffe
Cowdenbeath: Cairns	Cowdenbeath: Trinity
Cowdenbeath: Guthrie Memorial	Beath and Cowdenbeath: North
Cowdenbeath: West	Cowdenbeath: Trinity
Craggan	Tomintoul, Glenlivet and Inveraven
Craig	Inchbrayock
Craigdam	Tarves
Craigend	Perth: Craigie and Moncreiffe
Crailing	Ale and Teviot United
Cranshaws	Langton and Lammermuir Kirk
Cranstoun	Tyne Valley Parish
Crawford	Upper Clyde
Crawfordjohn	Upper Clyde
Cray	Kirkmichael, Straloch and Glenshee
Creetown	Kirkmabreck
Crichton	Tyne Valley Parish
Crofthead	Fauldhouse: St Andrew's
Crombie	Culross and Torryburn
Crossgates	Cowdenbeath: Trinity
Cruggleton	Sorbie
Cuikston	Farnell
Culbin	Dyke
Cullicudden	Resolis and Urquhart
Culter	charge dissolved: Presbytery of Lanark
Cults	Howe of Fife
Cumbernauld: Baird	Cumbernauld: Old
Cumbernauld: Bridgend	Cumbernauld: Old
Cumbernauld: St Andrew's	Cumbernauld: Old
Dalgarno	Closeburn
Dalguise	Dunkeld

Name no longer used	Present name of parish
Daliburgh	South Uist
Dalkeith: Buccleuch Street	Dalkeith: St Nicholas Buccleuch
Dalkeith: West (C of S)	Dalkeith: St Nicholas Buccleuch
Dalkeith: West (UP)	Dalkeith: St John's and King's Park
Dalmeath	Huntly Cairnie Glass
Dalreoch	charge dissolved: Presbytery of Perth
Dalry: Courthill	Dalry: Trinity
Dalry: St Andrew's	Dalry: Trinity
Dalry: West	Dalry: Trinity
Deerness	East Mainland
Denholm	Ruberslaw
Denny: Broompark	Denny: Westpark
Denny: West	Denny: Westpark
Dennyloanhead	charge dissolved: Presbytery of Falkirk
Dolphinton	Black Mount
Douglas	The Douglas Valley Church
Douglas Water	The Douglas Valley Church
Dowally	Dunkeld
Drainie	Lossiemouth: St Gerardine's High
Drumdelgie	Huntly Cairnie Glass
Dumbarrow	charge dissolved: Presbytery of Angus
Dumbarton: Bridgend	Dumbarton: West
Dumbarton: Dalreoch	Dumbarton: West
Dumbarton: High	Dumbarton: Riverside
Dumbarton: Knoxland	Dumbarton: Riverside
Dumbarton: North	Dumbarton: Riverside
Dumbarton: Old	Dumbarton: Riverside
Dumfries: Lincluden	Dumfries: Northwest
Dumfries: Lochside	Dumfries: Northwest
Dumfries: Maxwelltown Laurieknowe	Dumfries: Troqueer
Dumfries: Townhead	Dumfries: St Michael's and South
Dunbeath	The Parish of Latheron
Dunblane: East	Dunblane: St Blane's
Dunblane: Leighton	Dunblane: St Blane's
Dundee: Albert Square	Dundee: Meadowside St Paul's
Dundee: Baxter Park	Dundee: Trinity
Dundee: Broughty Ferry East	Dundee: Broughty Ferry New Kirk
Dundee: Broughty Ferry St Aidan's	Dundee: Broughty Ferry New Kirk
Dundee: Broughty Ferry Union	Dundee: Broughty Ferry St Stephen's and West
Dundee: Chapelshade (FC)	Dundee: Meadowside St Paul's
Dundee: Clepington	Dundee: Coldside
Dundee: Douglas and Angus	Dundee: Douglas and Mid Craigie
Dundee: Downfield North	Dundee: Strathmartine
Dundee: Downfield South	Dundee: Downfield Mains
Dundee: Fairmuir	Dundee: Coldside
Dundee: Hawkhill	Dundee: Meadowside St Paul's
Dundee: Martyrs'	Dundee: Balgay
Dundee: Maryfield	Dundee: Stobswell
Dundee: McCheyne Memorial	Dundee: West
Dundee: Ogilvie	Dundee: Stobswell
Dundee: Park	Dundee: Stobswell
Dundee: Roseangle	Dundee: West
Dundee: Ryehill	Dundee: West
Dundee: St Andrew's (FC)	Dundee: Meadowside St Paul's
Dundee: St Clement's Steeple	Dundee: Steeple
Dundee: St David's (C of S)	Dundee: Steeple
Dundee: St Enoch's	Dundee: Steeple
Dundee: St George's	Dundee: Meadowside St Paul's

Name no longer used	Present name of parish
Dundee: St John's	Dundee: West
Dundee: St Mark's	Dundee: West
Dundee: St Matthew's	Dundee: Trinity
Dundee: St Paul's	Dundee: Steeple
Dundee: St Peter's	Dundee: West
Dundee: Tay Square	Dundee: Meadowside St Paul's
Dundee: Victoria Street	Dundee: Stobswell
Dundee: Wallacetown	Dundee: Trinity
Dundee: Wishart Memorial	Dundee: Steeple
Dundurcas	charge suppressed: Presbytery of Moray
Duneaton	Upper Clyde
Dunfermline: Chalmers Street	Dunfermline: St Andrew's Erskine
Dunfermline: Maygate	Dunfermline: Gillespie Memorial
Dunfermline: Queen Anne Street	Dunfermline: St Andrew's Erskine
Dungree	Kirkpatrick Juxta
Duninald	Inchbrayock
Dunlappie	Brechin: Cathedral
Dunoon: Gaelic	Dunoon: St John's
Dunoon: Old	Dunoon: The High Kirk
Dunoon: St Cuthbert's	Dunoon: The High Kirk
Dunrod	Kirkcudbright
Dunsyre	Black Mount
Dupplin	Aberdalgie and Forteviot
Ecclefechan	Hoddom, Kirtle-Eaglesfield and Middlebie
Ecclesjohn	Dun and Hillside
Ecclesmachan	Strathbrock
Ecclesmoghriodan	Abernethy and Dron and Arngask
Eckford	Ale and Teviot United
Edgerston	Jedburgh: Old and Trinity
Edinburgh: Abbey	Edinburgh: Greenside
Edinburgh: Abbeyhill	Edinburgh: Holyrood Abbey
Edinburgh: Arthur Street	Edinburgh: Greyfriars Kirk
Edinburgh: Barony	Edinburgh: Greenside
Edinburgh: Belford	Edinburgh: Palmerston Place
Edinburgh: Braid	Edinburgh: Morningside
Edinburgh: Bruntsfield	Edinburgh: Barclay Viewforth
Edinburgh: Buccleuch	Edinburgh: Greyfriars Kirk
Edinburgh: Cairns Memorial	Edinburgh: Gorgie Dalry
Edinburgh: Candlish	Edinburgh: Polwarth
Edinburgh: Canongate (FC, UP)	Edinburgh: Holy Trinity
Edinburgh: Chalmers	Edinburgh: Barclay Viewforth
Edinburgh: Charteris Memorial	Edinburgh: Greyfriars Kirk
Edinburgh: Cluny	Edinburgh: Morningside
Edinburgh: College	Edinburgh: The Old Kirk and Muirhouse
Edinburgh: College Street	Edinburgh: The Old Kirk and Muirhouse
Edinburgh: Cowgate (FC)	Edinburgh: The Old Kirk and Muirhouse
Edinburgh: Cowgate (R)	Edinburgh: Barclay Viewforth
Edinburgh: Cowgate (US)	Edinburgh: Mayfield Salisbury
Edinburgh: Davidson	Edinburgh: Stockbridge
Edinburgh: Dean (FC)	Edinburgh: Palmerston Place
Edinburgh: Dean Street	Edinburgh: Stockbridge
Edinburgh: Fountainhall Road	Edinburgh: Mayfield Salisbury
Edinburgh: Grange (C of S)	Edinburgh: Marchmont St Giles'
Edinburgh: Grange (FC)	Edinburgh: St Catherine's Argyle
Edinburgh: Guthrie Memorial	Edinburgh: Greenside
Edinburgh: Haymarket	Edinburgh: Gorgie Dalry
Edinburgh: Henderson (C of S)	Edinburgh: Craigmillar Park
Edinburgh: Henderson (UP)	Edinburgh: Richmond Craigmillar

Name no longer used	Present name of parish
Edinburgh: Hillside	Edinburgh: Greenside
Edinburgh: Holyrood	Edinburgh: Holyrood Abbey
Edinburgh: Hope Park	Edinburgh: Mayfield Salisbury
Edinburgh: Hopetoun	Edinburgh: Greenside
Edinburgh: John Ker Memorial	Edinburgh: Polwarth
Edinburgh: Kirk o' Field	Edinburgh: Greyfriars Kirk
Edinburgh: Knox's	Edinburgh: Holy Trinity
Edinburgh: Lady Glenorchy's North	Edinburgh: Greenside
Edinburgh: Lady Glenorchy's South	Edinburgh: Holy Trinity
Edinburgh: Lady Yester's	Edinburgh: Greyfriars Kirk
Edinburgh: Lauriston	Edinburgh: Barclay Viewforth
Edinburgh: Lochend	Edinburgh: St Margaret's
Edinburgh: Lothian Road	Edinburgh: Palmerston Place
Edinburgh: Mayfield North	Edinburgh: Mayfield Salisbury
Edinburgh: Mayfield South	Edinburgh: Craigmillar Park
Edinburgh: McCrie	Edinburgh: Greyfriars Kirk
Edinburgh: McDonald Road	Edinburgh: Broughton St Mary's
Edinburgh: Moray	Edinburgh: Holy Trinity
Edinburgh: Morningside High	Edinburgh: Morningside
Edinburgh: New North (C of S)	Edinburgh: Marchmont St Giles'
Edinburgh: New North (FC)	Edinburgh: Greyfriars Kirk
Edinburgh: Newington East	Edinburgh: Greyfriars Kirk
Edinburgh: Newington South	Edinburgh: Mayfield Salisbury
Edinburgh: Nicolson Street	Edinburgh: Greyfriars Kirk
Edinburgh: North Morningside	Edinburgh: Morningside United
Edinburgh: North Richmond Street	Edinburgh: Richmond Craigmillar
Edinburgh: Pleasance (FC)	Edinburgh: The Old Kirk and Muirhouse
Edinburgh: Pleasance (UF)	Edinburgh: Greyfriars Kirk
Edinburgh: Prestonfield	Edinburgh: Priestfield
Edinburgh: Queen Street (FC)	Edinburgh: St Andrew's and St George's West
Edinburgh: Queen Street (UP)	Edinburgh: Stockbridge
Edinburgh: Restalrig (C of S)	Edinburgh: St Margaret's
Edinburgh: Restalrig (FC)	Edinburgh: New Restalrig
Edinburgh: Rosehall	Edinburgh: Priestfield
Edinburgh: Roxburgh	Edinburgh: Greyfriars Kirk
Edinburgh: Roxburgh Terrace	Edinburgh: Greyfriars Kirk
Edinburgh: South Morningside	Edinburgh: Morningside
Edinburgh: St Bernard's	Edinburgh: Stockbridge
Edinburgh: St Bride's	Edinburgh: Gorgie Dalry
Edinburgh: St Colm's	Edinburgh: Gorgie Dalry
Edinburgh: St Columba's	Edinburgh: Greyfriars Kirk
Edinburgh: St David's (C of S)	Edinburgh: Barclay Viewforth
Edinburgh: St David's (FC)	Edinburgh: St David's Broomhouse
Edinburgh: St James' (C of S)	Edinburgh: Greenside
Edinburgh: St James' (FC)	Edinburgh: Inverleith St Serf's
Edinburgh: St James' Place	Edinburgh: Greenside
Edinburgh: St John's	Edinburgh: Greyfriars Kirk
Edinburgh: St John's Oxgangs	Edinburgh: St John's Colinton Mains
Edinburgh: St Luke's	Edinburgh: St Andrew's and St George's West
Edinburgh: St Matthew's	Edinburgh: Morningside
Edinburgh: St Oran's	Edinburgh: Greyfriars Kirk
Edinburgh: St Oswald's	Edinburgh: Barclay Viewforth
Edinburgh: St Paul's	Edinburgh: Greyfriars Kirk
Edinburgh: St Stephen's (C of S)	Edinburgh: Stockbridge
Edinburgh: St Stephen's (FC)	Edinburgh: St Stephen's Comely Bank
Edinburgh: The Highland	Edinburgh: Greyfriars Kirk
Edinburgh: Tolbooth (C of S)	Edinburgh: Greyfriars Kirk
Edinburgh: Tolbooth (FC)	Edinburgh: St Andrew's and St George's West

Name no longer used	Present name of parish
Edinburgh: Trinity College	Edinburgh: Holy Trinity
Edinburgh: Tynecastle	Edinburgh: Gorgie Dalry
Edinburgh: Warrender	Edinburgh: Marchmont St Giles'
Edinburgh: West St Giles	Edinburgh: Marchmont St Giles'
Eigg	North West Lochaber
Eilean Finain	Ardnamurchan
Elgin: Moss Street	Elgin: St Giles' and St Columba's South
Elgin: South Street	Elgin: St Giles' and St Columba's South
Ellem	Langton and Lammermuir Kirk
Elsrickle	Black Mount
Eshaness	Northmavine
Essie	Noth
Essil	Speymouth
Ethie	Inverkeilor and Lunan
Ettiltoun	Liddesdale
Ewes Durris	Langholm Eskdalemuir Ewes and Westerkirk
Fala	Tyne Valley Parish
Falkirk: Erskine	Falkirk: Trinity
Falkirk: Graham's Road	Falkirk: Grahamston United
Falkirk: Old	Falkirk: Trinity
Falkirk: St Modan's	Falkirk: Trinity
Farnua	Kirkhill
Fergushill	Kilwinning: Mansfield Trinity
Ferryden	Inchbrayock
Fetterangus	Deer
Fettercairn	West Mearns
Fetternear	Blairdaff and Chapel of Garioch
Finzean	Birse and Feughside
Fochabers	Bellie
Forbes	Howe Trinity
Ford	Tyne Valley Parish
Fordoun	West Mearns
Fordyce	Portsoy
Forfar: South	Forfar: St Margaret's
Forfar: St James'	Forfar: St Margaret's
Forfar: West	Forfar: St Margaret's
Forgan	Newport-on-Tay
Forgue	Auchaber United
Forres: Castlehill	Forres: St Leonard's
Forres: High	Forres: St Leonard's
Forvie	Ellon
Foula	Walls and Sandness
Galashiels: East	Galashiels: Trinity
Galashiels: Ladhope	Galashiels: Trinity
Galashiels: South	Galashiels: Trinity
Galashiels: St Aidan's	Galashiels: Trinity
Galashiels: St Andrew's	Galashiels: Trinity
Galashiels: St Columba's	Galashiels: Trinity
Galashiels: St Cuthbert's	Galashiels: Trinity
Galashiels: St Mark's	Galashiels: Trinity
Galashiels: St Ninian's	Galashiels: Trinity
Galtway	Kirkcudbright
Gamrie	charge dissolved: Presbytery of Buchan
Garmouth	Speymouth
Gartly	Noth
Garvell	Kirkmichael, Tinwald and Torthorwald
Garvock	Mearns Coastal
Gauldry	Balmerino

Name no longer used	Present name of parish
Gelston	The Bengairn Parishes
Giffnock: Orchard Park	Giffnock: The Park
Girthon	Gatehouse of Fleet
Girvan: Chalmers	Girvan: North (Old and St Andrew's)
Girvan: Trinity	Girvan: North (Old and St Andrew's)
Glasgow: Abbotsford	Glasgow: Gorbals
Glasgow: Albert Drive	Glasgow: Pollokshields
Glasgow: Auldfield	Glasgow: Pollokshaws
Glasgow: Baillieston Old	Glasgow: Baillieston St Andrew's
Glasgow: Baillieston Rhinsdale	Glasgow: Baillieston St Andrew's
Glasgow: Balornock North	Glasgow: Wallacewell
Glasgow: Barmulloch	Glasgow: Wallacewell
Glasgow: Barrowfield (C of S)	Glasgow: Bridgeton St Francis in the East
Glasgow: Barrowfield (RP)	Glasgow: Gallowgate
Glasgow: Bath Street	Glasgow: Renfield St Stephen's
Glasgow: Battlefield East	Glasgow: Clincarthill
Glasgow: Battlefield West	Glasgow: Langside
Glasgow: Bellahouston	Glasgow: Ibrox
Glasgow: Bellgrove	Glasgow: Dennistoun New
Glasgow: Belmont	Glasgow: Kelvinside Hillhead
Glasgow: Berkeley Street	Glasgow: Renfield St Stephen's
Glasgow: Blackfriars	Glasgow: Dennistoun New
Glasgow: Bluevale	Glasgow: Dennistoun New
Glasgow: Blythswood	Glasgow: Renfield St Stephen's
Glasgow: Bridgeton East	Glasgow: Bridgeton St Francis in the East
Glasgow: Bridgeton West	Glasgow: Gallowgate
Glasgow: Buccleuch	Glasgow: Renfield St Stephen's
Glasgow: Burnbank	Glasgow: Kelvinbridge
Glasgow: Calton New	Glasgow: Gallowgate
Glasgow: Calton Old	Glasgow: Calton Parkhead
Glasgow: Calton Relief	Glasgow: Gallowgate
Glasgow: Cambridge Street	Bishopbriggs: Springfield Cambridge
Glasgow: Candlish Memorial	Glasgow: Queen's Park Govanhill
Glasgow: Carntyne Old	Glasgow: Shettleston New
Glasgow: Cathcart South	Glasgow: Cathcart Trinity
Glasgow: Central	Glasgow: Gallowgate
Glasgow: Cessnock	Glasgow: Kinning Park
Glasgow: Chalmers (C of S)	Glasgow: Gallowgate
Glasgow: Chalmers (FC)	Glasgow: Gorbals
Glasgow: Claremont	Glasgow: Anderston Kelvingrove
Glasgow: College	Glasgow: Anderston Kelvingrove
Glasgow: Copland Road	Glasgow: Govan and Linthouse
Glasgow: Cowcaddens	Glasgow: Renfield St Stephen's
Glasgow: Cowlairs	Glasgow: Springburn
Glasgow: Crosshill	Glasgow: Queen's Park Govanhill
Glasgow: Dalmarnock (C of S)	Glasgow: Calton Parkhead
Glasgow: Dalmarnock (UF)	Rutherglen: Old
Glasgow: Dean Park	Glasgow: Govan and Linthouse
Glasgow: Dowanhill	Glasgow: Partick Trinity
Glasgow: Dowanvale	Glasgow: Partick South
Glasgow: Drumchapel Old	Glasgow: Drumchapel St Andrew's
Glasgow: East Campbell Street	Glasgow: Dennistoun New
Glasgow: East Park	Glasgow: Kelvinbridge
Glasgow: Eastbank	Glasgow: Shettleston New
Glasgow: Edgar Memorial	Glasgow: Gallowgate
Glasgow: Eglinton Street	Glasgow: Queen's Park Govanhill
Glasgow: Elder Park	Glasgow: Govan and Linthouse
Glasgow: Elgin Street	Glasgow: Queen's Park Govanhill

Name no longer used	Present name of parish
Glasgow: Erskine	Glasgow: Langside
Glasgow: Fairbairn	Rutherglen: Old
Glasgow: Fairfield	Glasgow: Govan and Linthouse
Glasgow: Finnieston	Glasgow: Anderston Kelvingrove
Glasgow: Garnethill	Glasgow: Renfield St Stephen's
Glasgow: Garscube Netherton	Glasgow: Knightswood St Margaret's
Glasgow: Gillespie	Glasgow: Gallowgate
Glasgow: Gordon Park	Glasgow: Whiteinch
Glasgow: Grant Street	Glasgow: Renfield St Stephen's
Glasgow: Greenhead	Glasgow: Gallowgate
Glasgow: Hall Memorial	Rutherglen: Old
Glasgow: Hamilton Crescent	Glasgow: Partick South
Glasgow: Highlanders' Memorial	Glasgow: Knightswood St Margaret's
Glasgow: Househillwood St Christopher's	Glasgow: St Christopher's Priesthill and Nitshill
Glasgow: Hyndland (UF)	Glasgow: St John's Renfield
Glasgow: John Knox's	Glasgow: Gorbals
Glasgow: Johnston	Glasgow: Springburn
Glasgow: Jordanvale	Glasgow: Whiteinch
Glasgow: Kelvin	Glasgow: Kelvinbridge
Glasgow: Kelvinhaugh	Glasgow: Anderston Kelvingrove
Glasgow: Kelvinside Botanic Gardens	Glasgow: Kelvinside Hillhead
Glasgow: Kelvinside Old	Glasgow: Kelvinbridge
Glasgow: Kingston	Glasgow: Carnwadric
Glasgow: Lancefield	Glasgow: Anderston Kelvingrove
Glasgow: Langside Avenue	Glasgow: Shawlands
Glasgow: Langside Hill	Glasgow: Clincarthill
Glasgow: Langside Old	Glasgow: Langside
Glasgow: Lansdowne	Glasgow: Kelvinbridge
Glasgow: Laurieston (C of S)	Glasgow: Gorbals
Glasgow: Laurieston (FC)	Glasgow: Carnwadric
Glasgow: London Road	Glasgow: Bridgeton St Francis in the East
Glasgow: Lyon Street	Glasgow: Renfield St Stephen's
Glasgow: Macgregor Memorial	Glasgow: Govan and Linthouse
Glasgow: Macmillan	Glasgow: Gallowgate
Glasgow: Martyrs' East	Glasgow: Cathedral
Glasgow: Martyrs' West	Glasgow: Cathedral
Glasgow: Milton	Glasgow: Renfield St Stephen's
Glasgow: Mount Florida	Glasgow: Clincarthill
Glasgow: Netherton St Matthew's	Glasgow: Knightswood St Margaret's
Glasgow: New Cathcart	Glasgow: Cathcart Trinity
Glasgow: Newhall	Glasgow: Bridgeton St Francis in the East
Glasgow: Newton Place	Glasgow: Partick South
Glasgow: Nithsdale	Glasgow: Queen's Park Govanhill
Glasgow: North Kelvinside	Glasgow: Ruchill Kelvinside
Glasgow: Old Partick	Glasgow: Partick Trinity
Glasgow: Paisley Road	Glasgow: Kinning Park
Glasgow: Partick Anderson	Glasgow: Partick South
Glasgow: Partick East	Glasgow: Partick Trinity
Glasgow: Partick High	Glasgow: Partick South
Glasgow: Phoenix Park	Glasgow: Springburn
Glasgow: Plantation	Glasgow: Kinning Park
Glasgow: Pollok St Aidan's	Glasgow: St James' Pollok
Glasgow: Pollok Street	Glasgow: Kinning Park
Glasgow: Polmadie	Glasgow: Queen's Park Govanhill
Glasgow: Queen's Cross	Glasgow: Ruchill Kelvinside
Glasgow: Renfield (C of S)	Glasgow: Renfield St Stephen's
Glasgow: Renfield (FC)	Glasgow: St John's Renfield
Glasgow: Renfield Street	Glasgow: Renfield St Stephen's

Name no longer used	Present name of parish
Glasgow: Renwick	Glasgow: Gorbals
Glasgow: Robertson Memorial	Glasgow: Cathedral
Glasgow: Rockcliffe	Rutherglen: Old
Glasgow: Rockvilla	Glasgow: Possilpark
Glasgow: Rose Street	Glasgow: Langside
Glasgow: Rutherford	Glasgow: Dennistoun New
Glasgow: Shamrock Street	Glasgow: Renfield St Stephen's
Glasgow: Shawholm	Glasgow: Pollokshaws
Glasgow: Shawlands Cross	Glasgow: Shawlands
Glasgow: Shawlands Old	Glasgow: Shawlands
Glasgow: Sighthill	Glasgow: Springburn
Glasgow: Somerville	Glasgow: Springburn
Glasgow: Springbank	Glasgow: Kelvinbridge
Glasgow: St Andrew's (C of S)	Glasgow: Gallowgate
Glasgow: St Andrew's (FC)	Glasgow: St Andrew's East
Glasgow: St Clement's	Glasgow: Bridgeton St Francis in the East
Glasgow: St Columba Gaelic	Glasgow: Govan and Linthouse
Glasgow: St Cuthbert's	Glasgow: Ruchill Kelvinside
Glasgow: St Enoch's (C of S)	Glasgow: St Enoch's Hogganfield
Glasgow: St Enoch's (FC)	Glasgow: Anderston Kelvingrove
Glasgow: St George's (C of S)	Glasgow: St George's Tron
Glasgow: St George's (FC)	Glasgow: Anderston Kelvingrove
Glasgow: St George's Road	Glasgow: Renfield St Stephen's
Glasgow: St James' (C of S)	Glasgow: St James' Pollok
Glasgow: St James' (FC)	Glasgow: Gallowgate
Glasgow: St John's (C of S)	Glasgow: Gallowgate
Glasgow: St John's (FC)	Glasgow: St John's Renfield
Glasgow: St Kenneth's	Glasgow: Govan and Linthouse
Glasgow: St Kiaran's	Glasgow: Govan and Linthouse
Glasgow: St Luke's	Glasgow: Gallowgate
Glasgow: St Mark's	Glasgow: Anderston Kelvingrove
Glasgow: St Mary's Partick	Glasgow: Partick South
Glasgow: St Matthew's (C of S)	Glasgow: Renfield St Stephen's
Glasgow: St Matthew's (FC)	Glasgow: Knightswood St Margaret's
Glasgow: St Ninian's	Glasgow: Gorbals
Glasgow: St Peter's	Glasgow: Anderston Kelvingrove
Glasgow: St Thomas'	Glasgow: Gallowgate
Glasgow: Steven Memorial	Glasgow: Ibrox
Glasgow: Stevenson Memorial	Glasgow: Kelvinbridge
Glasgow: Strathbungo	Glasgow: Queen's Park Govanhill
Glasgow: Summerfield	Rutherglen: Old
Glasgow: Summertown	Glasgow: Govan and Linthouse
Glasgow: Sydney Place	Glasgow: Dennistoun New
Glasgow: The Martyrs'	Glasgow: Cathedral
Glasgow: The Park	Giffnock: The Park
Glasgow: Titwood	Glasgow: Pollokshields
Glasgow: Tradeston	Glasgow: Gorbals
Glasgow: Trinity	Glasgow: Gallowgate
Glasgow: Trinity Duke Street	Glasgow: Dennistoun New
Glasgow: Tron St Anne's	Glasgow: St George's Tron
Glasgow: Union	Glasgow: Carnwadric
Glasgow: Victoria	Glasgow: Queen's Park Govanhill
Glasgow: Wellfield	Glasgow: Springburn
Glasgow: Wellpark	Glasgow: Dennistoun New
Glasgow: West Scotland Street	Glasgow: Kinning Park
Glasgow: White Memorial	Glasgow: Kinning Park
Glasgow: Whitehill	Glasgow: Dennistoun New
Glasgow: Whitevale (FC)	Glasgow: Gallowgate

Name no longer used	Present name of parish
Glasgow: Whitevale (UP)	Glasgow: Dennistoun New
Glasgow: Wilton	Glasgow: Kelvinbridge
Glasgow: Woodlands	Glasgow: Wellington
Glasgow: Woodside	Glasgow: Kelvinbridge
Glasgow: Wynd (C of S)	Glasgow: Gallowgate
Glasgow: Wynd (FC)	Glasgow: Gorbals
Glasgow: Young Street	Glasgow: Dennistoun New
Glenapp	Ballantrae
Glenbervie	West Mearns
Glenbuchat	Upper Donside
Glenbuck	Muirkirk
Glencaple (Dumfries and Kirkcudbright)	Caerlaverock
Glencaple (Lanark)	Upper Clyde
Glen Convinth	Kiltarlity
Glendoick	St Madoes and Kinfauns
Glenfarg	Abernethy and Dron and Arngask
Glengairn	Glenmuick (Ballater)
Glengarnock	Kilbirnie: Auld Kirk
Glenisla	The Isla Parishes
Glenluce	Old Luce
Glenmoriston (FC)	Fort Augustus
Glenprosen	The Glens and Kirriemuir: Old
Glenrinnes	Mortlach and Cabrach
Glenshiel	Glenelg and Kintail
Glentanar	Aboyne and Dinnet
Glen Ussie	Fodderty and Strathpeffer
Gogar	Edinburgh: Corstorphine Old
Gordon	Monquhitter and New Byth
Graemsay	Stromness
Grangemouth: Dundas	Grangemouth: Abbotsgrange
Grangemouth: Grange	Grangemouth: Zetland
Grangemouth: Kerse	Grangemouth: Abbotsgrange
Grangemouth: Old	Grangemouth: Zetland
Greenloaning	Ardoch
Greenock: Ardgowan	Greenock: Lyle Kirk
Greenock: Augustine	Greenock: East End
Greenock: Cartsburn	Greenock: East End
Greenock: Cartsdyke	Greenock: East End
Greenock: Crawfordsburn	Greenock: East End
Greenock: Finnart	Greenock: Lyle Kirk
Greenock: Gaelic	Greenock: Westburn
Greenock: Greenbank	Greenock: Westburn
Greenock: Martyrs'	Greenock: Westburn
Greenock: Middle	Greenock: Westburn
Greenock: Mount Park	Greenock: Mount Kirk
Greenock: Mount Pleasant	Greenock: Mount Kirk
Greenock: North (C of S)	Greenock: Lyle Kirk
Greenock: North (FC)	Greenock: Westburn
Greenock: Old West	Greenock: Lyle Kirk
Greenock: Sir Michael Street	Greenock: Lyle Kirk
Greenock: South	Greenock: Mount Kirk
Greenock: South Park	Greenock: Mount Kirk
Greenock: St Andrew's	Greenock: Lyle Kirk
Greenock: St Columba's Gaelic	Greenock: Lyle Kirk
Greenock: St George's	Greenock: Westburn
Greenock: St Luke's	Greenock: Westburn
Greenock: St Mark's	Greenock: Westburn
Greenock: St Paul's	Greenock: Lyle Kirk

Name no longer used	Present name of parish
Greenock: St Thomas'	Greenock: Westburn
Greenock: The Old Kirk	Greenock: Westburn
Greenock: The Union Church	Greenock: Lyle Kirk
Greenock: Trinity	Greenock: Lyle Kirk
Greenock: Union Street	Greenock: Lyle Kirk
Greenock: West	Greenock: Westburn
Gress	Stornoway: St Columba
Guardbridge	Leuchars: St Athernase
Haddington: St John's	Haddington: West
Hamilton: Auchingramont North	Hamilton: Old
Hamilton: Burnbank	Hamilton: Gilmour and Whitehill
Hamilton: North	Hamilton: Old
Hamilton: Saffronhall Assoc. Anti-Burgher	Hamilton: Old
Hardgate	Urr
Hassendean	Ruberslaw
Hawick: East Bank	Hawick: Trinity
Hawick: Orrock	Hawick: St Mary's and Old
Hawick: St Andrew's	Hawick: Trinity
Hawick: St George's	Hawick: Teviot
Hawick: St George's West	Hawick: Teviot
Hawick: St John's	Hawick: Trinity
Hawick: St Margaret's	Hawick: Teviot
Hawick: West Port	Hawick: Teviot
Hawick: Wilton South	Hawick: Teviot
Haywood	Forth
Helensburgh: Old	Helensburgh: St Andrew's Kirk
Helensburgh: St Bride's	Helensburgh: St Andrew's Kirk
Helensburgh: St Columba	Helensburgh: St Andrew's Kirk
Helensburgh: The West Kirk	Helensburgh: St Andrew's Kirk
Heylipol	Tiree
Hillside	Unst
Hillswick	Northmavine
Hilton	Ladykirk and Whitsome
Holm	East Mainland
Holywell	The Border Kirk
Holywood	Dumfries: Northwest
Hope Kailzie	charge suppressed: Presbytery of Melrose and Peebles
Horndean	Ladykirk and Whitsome
Howford	charge dissolved: Presbytery of Inverness
Howmore	South Uist
Hownam	Cheviot Chuches
Hume	Kelso Country Churches
Huntly: Princes Street	Strathbogie Drumblade
Inchkenneth	Kilfinichen and Kilvickeon and the Ross of Mull
Inchmartin	Errol
Innerleven: East	Methil: Wellesley
Innerwick	Dunglass
Inverallan	Grantown-on-Spey
Inverchaolain	Toward
Inverkeithny	Auchaber United
Inverness: Merkinch St Mark's	Inverness: Trinity
Inverness: Queen Street	Inverness: Trinity
Inverness: St Mary's	Inverness: Dalneigh and Bona
Inverness: West	Inverness: Inshes
Irving	Gretna, Half Morton and Kirkpatrick Fleming
Johnshaven	Mearns Coastal
Johnstone: East	Johnstone: St Paul's
Johnstone: West	Johnstone: St Paul's

Name no longer used	Present name of parish
Kames	Kyles
Kearn	Upper Donside
Keig	Howe Trinity
Keith Marischal	Humbie
Keith: South	Keith: North, Newmill, Boharm and Rothiemay
Kelso: East	Kelso: North and Ednam
Kelso: Edenside	Kelso: North and Ednam
Kelso: St John's	Kelso: North and Ednam
Kelso: Trinity	Kelso: North and Ednam
Kelton	The Bengairn Parishes
Kennethmont	Noth
Kettle	Howe of Fife
Kilbirnie: Barony	Kilbirnie: Auld Kirk
Kilbirnie: East	Kilbirnie: St Columba's
Kilbirnie: West	Kilbirnie: St Columba's
Kilblaan	Southend
Kilblane	Kirkmahoe
Kilbride (Cowal)	Kyles
Kilbride (Dumfries and Kirkcudbright)	Sanquhar
Kilbride (Lorn)	Kilmore and Oban
Kilbride (Stirling)	Dunblane: Cathedral
Kilchattan Bay	The United Church of Bute
Kilchousland	Campbeltown: Highland
Kilcolmkill (Kintyre)	Southend
Kilcolmkill (Lochaber)	Morvern
Kildrummy	Upper Donside
Kilkerran	Campbeltown: Highland
Kilkivan	Campbeltown: Highland
Killintag	Morvern
Kilmacolm: St James'	Kilmacolm: St Columba
Kilmahew	Cardross
Kilmahog	Callander
Kilmarnock: Grange	Kilmarnock: New Laigh Kirk
Kilmarnock: Henderson	Kilmarnock: Kay Park
Kilmarnock: High (C of S)	Kilmarnock: Kay Park
Kilmarnock: High (FC)	Kilmarnock: New Laigh Kirk
Kilmarnock: Howard	Kilmarnock: St Andrew's and St Marnock's
Kilmarnock: King Street	Kilmarnock: St Andrew's and St Marnock's
Kilmarnock: Old High	Kilmarnock: Kay Park
Kilmarnock: Portland Road	Kilmarnock: St Andrew's and St Marnock's
Kilmarnock: St Ninian's Bellfield	Kilmarnock: South
Kilmarnock: Shortlees	Kilmarnock: South
Kilmarrow	Killean and Kilchenzie
Kilmichael (Inverness)	Urquhart and Glenmoriston
Kilmichael (Kintyre)	Campbeltown: Highland
Kilmoir	Brechin: Cathedral
Kilmore	Urquhart and Glenmoriston
Kilmoveonaig	Blair Atholl and Struan
Kilmun: St Andrew's	Strone and Ardentinny
Kilpheder	South Uist
Kilry	The Isla Parishes
Kilwinning: Abbey	Kilwinning: Old
Kilwinning: Erskine	Kilwinning: Old
Kinairney	Midmar
Kincardine O'Neil	Mid Deeside
Kincraig	Alvie and Insh
Kinedar	Lossiemouth: St Gerardine's High
Kingarth	The United Church of Bute

Name no longer used	Present name of parish
Kingoldrum	The Isla Parishes
Kininmonth	charge dissolved: Presbytery of Buchan
Kinkell	Fintray Kinellar Keithhall
Kinloch	Caputh and Clunie
Kinlochewe	Applecross, Lochcarron and Torridon
Kinlochluichart	Contin
Kinlochrannoch	Foss and Rannoch
Kinneil	Bo'ness: Old
Kinnettas	Fodderty and Strathpeffer
Kinnoir	Huntly Cairnie Glass
Kinrossie	Collace
Kirkandrews	Borgue
Kirkapol	Tiree
Kirkcaldy: Abbotsrood	Kirkcaldy: Bennochy
Kirkcaldy: Bethelfield	Kirkcaldy: Linktown
Kirkcaldy: Dunnikier	Kirkcaldy: Bennochy
Kirkcaldy: Gallatown	Dysart: St Clair
Kirkcaldy: Invertiel	Kirkcaldy: Linktown
Kirkcaldy: Old	Kirkcaldy: St Bryce Kirk
Kirkcaldy: Raith	Kirkcaldy: Abbotshall
Kirkcaldy: Sinclairtown	Dysart: St Clair
Kirkcaldy: St Andrew's	Kirkcaldy: Bennochy
Kirkcaldy: St Brycedale	Kirkcaldy: St Bryce Kirk
Kirkcaldy: St John's	Kirkcaldy: Bennochy
Kirkcaldy: Victoria Road	Kirkcaldy: Bennochy
Kirkcaldy: Viewforth	Dysart: St Clair
Kirkchrist	Tarff and Twynholm
Kirkconnel	Gretna, Half Morton and Kirkpatrick Fleming
Kirkcormick	The Bengairn Parishes
Kirkdale	Kirkmabreck
Kirkforthar	Markinch and Thornton
Kirkhope	Ettrick and Yarrow
Kirkintilloch: St Andrew's	Kirkintilloch: St Columba's
Kirkintilloch: St David's	Kirkintilloch: St Columba's
Kirkmadrine (Machars)	Sorbie
Kirkmadrine (Rhinns)	Stoneykirk
Kirkmaiden	Glasserton and Isle of Whithorn
Kirkmichael	Tomintoul, Glenlivet and Inveraven
Kirkpottie	Abernethy and Dron and Arngask
Kirkwall: King Street	Kirkwall: East
Kirkwall: Paterson	Kirkwall: East
Kirriemuir: Bank Street	The Glens and Kirriemuir: Old
Kirriemuir: Barony	The Glens and Kirriemuir: Old
Kirriemuir: Livingstone	Kirriemuir: St Andrew's
Kirriemuir: South	Kirriemuir: St Andrew's
Kirriemuir: St Ninian's	The Glens and Kirriemuir: Old
Kirriemuir: West	The Glens and Kirriemuir: Old
Knoydart	North West Lochaber
Ladybank	Howe of Fife
Lagganallochie	Dunkeld
Lamberton	Foulden and Mordington
Lamington	Upper Clyde
Lanark: Broomgate	Lanark: Greyfriars
Lanark: Cairns	Lanark: Greyfriars
Lanark: St Kentigern's	Lanark: Greyfriars
Lanark: St Leonard's	Lanark: St Nicholas'
Largieside	Killean and Kilchenzie
Lassodie	Dunfermline: Townhill and Kingseat

Name no longer used	Present name of parish
Lathones	Largoward
Laurieston	Balmaghie
Laxavoe	Delting
Leadhills	Upper Clyde
Leith: Bonnington	Edinburgh: Leith North
Leith: Claremont	Edinburgh: Leith St Andrew's
Leith: Dalmeny Street	Edinburgh: Pilrig St Paul's
Leith: Elder Memorial	Edinburgh: St John's Colinton Mains
Leith: Harper Memorial	Edinburgh: Leith North
Leith: Junction Road	Edinburgh: Leith St Andrew's
Leith: Kirkgate	Edinburgh: Leith South
Leith: South (FC)	Edinburgh: Leith St Andrew's
Leith: St Andrew's Place	Edinburgh: Leith St Andrew's
Leith: St John's	Edinburgh: St John's Colinton Mains
Leith: St Nicholas	Edinburgh: Leith North
Leith: St Ninian's	Edinburgh: Leith North
Leith: St Thomas'	Edinburgh: Leith St Andrew's
Lemlair	Kiltearn
Lempitlaw	Kelso: Old and Sprouston
Leny	Callander
Leochel	Cushnie and Tough
Lesmahagow: Cordiner	Lesmahagow: Abbey Green
Lethendy	Caputh and Clunie
Levern	Barrhead: St Andrew's
Lilliesleaf	Ale and Teviot United
Lindowan	Craigrownie
Linlithgow: East	Linlithgow: St Ninian's Craigmailen
Linlithgow: Trinity	Linlithgow: St Ninian's Craigmailen
Linton	Cheviot Churches
Lintrathen	The Isla Parishes
Livingston: Tulloch	Livingston: Old
Livingston: West	Livingston: Old
Lochaline	Morvern
Lochcraig	Lochgelly and Benarty: St Serf's
Lochdonhead	Torosay and Kinlochspelvie
Lochearnhead	Balquhidder
Lochlee	Edzell Lethnot Glenesk
Lochryan	Inch
Logie (Dundee)	Fowlis and Liff
Logie (St Andrews)	charge dissolved: Presbytery of St Andrews
Logiebride	Auchtergaven and Moneydie
Logie Buchan	Ellon
Logie Mar	Cromar
Logie Pert	charge dissolved: Presbytery of Angus
Logie Wester	Ferintosh
Longcastle	Kirkinner
Longformacus	Langton and Lammermuir Kirk
Longnewton	Ale and Teviot United
Longridge	Breich Valley
Longtown	The Border Kirk
Lowther	Upper Clyde
Luce	Hoddom, Kirtle-Eaglesfield and Middlebie
Lude	Blair Atholl and Struan
Lumphanan	Mid Deeside
Lumphinnans	Beath and Cowdenbeath: North
Lumsden	Upper Donside
Luncarty	Redgorton and Stanley
Lund	Unst

Name no longer used	Present name of parish
Lybster	The Parish of Latheron
Lynturk	Cushnie and Tough
Mailor	Aberdalgie and Forteviot
Mainsriddle	Colvend, Southwick and Kirkbean
Makerstoun	Kelso Country Churches
Mallaig	North West Lochaber
Maryburgh	Ferintosh
Marykirk	Aberluthnott
Maryton	Inchbrayock
Meadowfield	Caldercruix and Longriggend
Meathie	Glamis, Inverarity and Kinnettles
Megget	Ettrick and Yarrow
Melville	charge suppressed: Presbytery of Lothian
Memus	The Glens and Kirriemuir: Old
Mid Calder: Bridgend	Kirk of Calder
Mid Calder: St John's	Kirk of Calder
Midholm	congregation seceded: Presbytery of Jedburgh
Migvie	Cromar
Millbrex	Fyvie
Millerston	charge dissolved: Presbytery of Glasgow
Millport	Cumbrae
Milnathort	Orwell and Portmoak
Minto	Ruberslaw
Monecht	charge dissolved: Presbytery of Gordon
Monifieth: North	Monikie and Newbigging and Murroes and Tealing
Montrose: Knox's	Montrose: Melville South
Montrose: St George's	Montrose: Old and St Andrew's
Montrose: St John's	Montrose: Old and St Andrew's
Montrose: St Luke's	Montrose: Old and St Andrew's
Montrose: St Paul's	Montrose: Melville South
Montrose: Trinity	Montrose: Old and St Andrew's
Monzievaird	Crieff
Moonzie	charge dissolved: Presbytery of St Andrews
Morebattle	Cheviot Churches
Morton	Thornhill
Mossbank	Delting
Mossgreen	Cowdenbeath: Trinity
Motherwell: Brandon	Motherwell: Crosshill
Motherwell: Cairns	Motherwell: Crosshill
Motherwell: Manse Road	Motherwell: South
Motherwell: South Dalziel	Motherwell: South
Moulin	Pitlochry
Mount Kedar	Cummertrees, Mouswald and Ruthwell
Mow	Linton, Morebattle, Hownam and Yetholm
Moy	Dyke
Moyness	charge dissolved: Presbytery of Moray
Muckersie	Aberdalgie and Forteviot
Muirton	Aberluthnott
Murthly	Caputh and Clunie
Musselburgh: Bridge Street	Musselburgh: St Andrew's High
Musselburgh: Millhill	Musselburgh: St Andrew's High
Nairn: High	Nairn: St Ninian's
Nairn: Rosebank	Nairn: St Ninian's
Navar	Edzell Lethnot Glenesk
Nenthorn	Kelso Country Churches
New Leeds	charge dissolved: Presbytery of Buchan
New Liston	Edinburgh: Kirkliston
Newcastleton	Liddesdale

Name no longer used	Present name of parish
Newdosk	Edzell Lethnot Glenesk
Newmills	Culross and Torryburn
Newseat	Rothienorman
Newtongrange	Newbattle
Newton Stewart	Penninghame
Nigg	charge dissolved: Presbytery of Aberdeen
Nisbet	Ale and Teviot United
North Bute	The United Church of Bute
Norwick	Unst
Ogston	Lossiemouth: St Gerardine's High
Old Cumnock: Crichton Memorial	Old Cumnock: Trinity
Old Cumnock: St Ninian's	Old Cumnock: Trinity
Old Cumnock: West	Old Cumnock: Trinity
Oldhamstocks	Dunglass
Old Kilpatrick: Barclay	Dalmuir: Barclay
Ollaberry	Northmavine
Olnafirth	Delting
Ord	Ordiquhill and Cornhill
Paisley: Canal Street	Paisley: Stow Brae Kirk
Paisley: Castlehead	Paisley: Stow Brae Kirk
Paisley: George Street	Paisley: Glenburn
Paisley: High	Paisley: Oakshaw Trinity
Paisley: Laigh Kirk	Paisley: Stow Brae Kirk
Paisley: Merksworth	Paisley: Wallneuk North
Paisley: Middle	Paisley: Stow Brae Kirk
Paisley: Mossvale	Paisley: Wallneuk North
Paisley: New Street	Paisley: Glenburn
Paisley: North	Paisley: Wallneuk North
Paisley: Oakshaw West	Paisley: St Luke's
Paisley: Orr Square	Paisley: Oakshaw Trinity
Paisley: South	Paisley: St Luke's
Paisley: St Andrew's	Paisley: Stow Brae Kirk
Paisley: St George's	Paisley: Stow Brae Kirk
Paisley: St John's	Paisley: Oakshaw Trinity
Paisley: Thread Street	Paisley: Martyrs' Sandyford
Papa Stour	Walls and Sandness
Park	Kinloch
Pathhead	Ormiston
Pathstruie	Aberdalgie and Forteviot
Pearston	Dreghorn and Springside
Peebles: West	Peebles: St Andrew's Leckie
Pennersaughs	Hoddom, Kirtle-Eaglesfield and Middlebie
Pentland	Lasswade and Rosewell
Persie	Kirkmichael, Straloch and Glenshee
Perth: Bridgend	Perth: St Matthew's
Perth: East	Perth: St Leonard's-in-the-Fields
Perth: Knox's	Perth: St Leonard's-in-the-Fields
Perth: Middle	Perth: St Matthew's
Perth: St Andrew's	Perth: Riverside
Perth: St Columba's	Perth: North
Perth: St Leonard's	Perth: North
Perth: St Stephen's	Perth: Riverside
Perth: West	Perth: St Matthew's
Perth: Wilson	Perth: St Matthew's
Perth: York Place	Perth: St Leonard's-in-the-Fields
Peterhead: Charlotte Street	Peterhead: Trinity
Peterhead: East	Peterhead: St Andrew's
Peterhead: South	Peterhead: St Andrew's

Name no longer used	Present name of parish
Peterhead: St Peter's	Peterhead: Trinity
Peterhead: West Associate	Peterhead: Trinity
Pettinain	Cairngryffe
Pitcairn (C of S)	Redgorton and Stanley
Pitcairn (UF)	Almondbank Tibbermore
Pitlessie	Howe of Fife
Pitroddie	St Madoes and Kinfauns
Plockton	Lochalsh
Polmont South	Brightons
Polwarth	Langton and Lammermuir Kirk
Poolewe	Gairloch and Dundonnell
Port Bannatyne	The United Church of Bute
Port Ellen	Kildalton and Oa
Port Glasgow: Clune Park	Port Glasgow: St Andrew's
Port Glasgow: Newark	Port Glasgow: St Andrew's
Port Glasgow: Old	Port Glasgow: St Andrew's
Port Glasgow: Princes Street	Port Glasgow: St Andrew's
Port Glasgow: West	Port Glasgow: St Andrew's
Portsonachan	Glenorchy and Innishael
Port William	Mochrum
Preston	Bonkyl and Edrom
Prestonkirk	Traprain
Prinlaws	Leslie: Trinity
Quarrier's Mount Zion	Kilmacolm: St Columba
Raasay	Portree
Rathillet	Creich, Flisk and Kilmany
Rathmuriel	Noth
Reay	The North Coast Parish
Redcastle	Killearnan
Rerrick	The Bengairn Parishes
Restenneth	Forfar: East and Old
Rhynd	Perth: Craigie and Moncreiffe
Rhynie	Noth
Rickarton	charge dissolved: Presbytery of Kincardine and Deeside
Rigg	Gretna, Half Morton and Kirkpatrick Fleming
Rigside	The Douglas Valley Church
Rinpatrick	Gretna, Half Morton and Kirkpatrick Fleming
Roberton	Upper Clyde
Rosehearty	Pitsligo
Rossie	Inchture and Kinnaird
Rothesay: Bridgend	The United Church of Bute
Rothesay: Craigmore High	Rothesay: Trinity
Rothesay: Craigmore St Brendan's	The United Church of Bute
Rothesay: High	The United Church of Bute
Rothesay: New	The United Church of Bute
Rothesay: St James'	Rothesay: Trinity
Rothesay: St John's	The United Church of Bute
Rothesay: West	Rothesay: Trinity
Roxburgh	Kelso Country Churches
Rutherglen: East	Rutherglen: Old
Rutherglen: Greenhill	Rutherglen: Old
Rutherglen: Munro	Rutherglen: West and Wardlawhill
Ruthven (Angus)	The Isla Parishes
Ruthven (Gordon)	Huntly Cairnie Glass
St Andrew's (Orkney)	East Mainland
St Cyrus	Mearns Coastal
St Ola	Kirkwall: St Magnus Cathedral
Saltcoats: Erskine	Ardrossan and Saltcoats: Kirkgate

Name no longer used	Present name of parish
Saltcoats: Landsborough	Ardrossan and Saltcoats: Kirkgate
Saltcoats: Middle	Ardrossan and Saltcoats: Kirkgate
Saltcoats: New Trinity	Ardrossan and Saltcoats: Kirkgate
Saltcoats: South Beach	Saltcoats: St Cuthbert's
Saltcoats: Trinity	Ardrossan and Saltcoats: Kirkgate
Saltcoats: West	Ardrossan and Saltcoats: Kirkgate
Sandhead	Stoneykirk
Saughtree	Liddesdale
Saulseat	Inch
Scalloway	Tingwall
Scatsta	Delting
Sclattie	Blairdaff and Chapel of Garioch
Scoonie	Leven
Scourie	Eddrachillis
Seafield	Portknockie
Sennick	Borgue
Seton	Tranent
Shawbost	Carloway
Shebster	The North Coast Parish
Sheuchan	Stranraer: High
Shieldaig	Applecross, Lochcarron and Torridon
Shiels	Belhelvie
Shottsburn	Kirk o' Shotts
Shurrery	The North Coast Parish
Simprin	Fogo and Swinton
Skerrols	Kilarrow
Skinnet	Halkirk Westerdale
Slains	Ellon
Smailholm	Kelso Country Churches
Small Isles	North West Lochaber
South Ballachulish	charge dissolved: Presbytery of Lochaber
Soutra	Tyne Valley Parish
Spittal (Caithness)	Halkirk Westerdale
Spittal (Duns)	charge dissolved: Presbytery of Duns
Springfield	Gretna, Half Morton and Kirkpatrick Fleming
Stenton	Traprain
Stewartfield	Deer
Stewarton: Cairns	Stewarton: St Columba's
Stewarton: Laigh	Stewarton: St Columba's
Stichill	Kelso Country Churches
Stirling: Craigs	Stirling: St Columba's
Stirling: North (FC)	Stirling: St Columba's
Stobhill	Gorebridge
Stockbridge	Dunglass
Stonehaven: North	Stonehaven: South
Stoneyburn	Breich Valley
Stornoway: James Street	Stornoway: Martin's Memorial
Stracathro	Brechin: Cathedral
Strachan	Birse and Feughside
Stranraer: Bellevilla	Stranraer: Trinity
Stranraer: Bridge Street	Stranraer: Trinity
Stranraer: Ivy Place	Stranraer: Trinity
Stranraer: Old	Stranraer: Trinity
Stranraer: St Andrew's	Stranraer: Trinity
Stranraer: St Margaret's	Stranraer: High
Stranraer: St Mark's	Stranraer: Trinity
Stranraer: St Ninian's	Stranraer: Trinity
Stranraer: Town Kirk	Stranraer: Trinity

Name no longer used	Present name of parish
Strathaven: West	Strathaven: Avendale Old and Drumclog
Strathconon	Contin
Strathdeveron	Mortlach and Cabrach
Strathdon	Upper Donside
Stratherrick	Dores and Boleskine
Strathgarve	Contin
Strathglass	Kilmorack and Erchless
Strathmartine (C of S)	Dundee: Downfield Mains
Strathy	The North Coast Parish
Strowan	Comrie
Suddie	Knockbain
Tarfside	Edzell Lethnot Glenesk
Tarland	Cromar
Tarvit	Cupar: Old and St Michael of Tarvit
Temple	Gorebridge
Thankerton	Cairngryffe
The Bass	North Berwick: St Andrew Blackadder
The Stewartry of Strathearn	Aberdalgie and Forteviot; Aberuthven and Dunning
Tighnabruaich	Kyles
Tongland	Tarff and Twynholm
Torphins	Mid Deeside
Torrance	East Kilbride: Old
Towie	Upper Donside
Trailflat	Kirkmichael, Tinwald and Torthorwald
Trailtrow	Cummertrees, Mouswald and Ruthwell
Trefontaine	Langton and Lammermuir Kirk
Trossachs	Callander
Trumisgarry	Berneray and Lochmaddy
Tullibole	Fossoway: St Serf's and Devonside
Tullich	Glenmuick (Ballater)
Tullichetil	Comrie
Tullynessle	Howe Trinity
Tummel	Foss and Rannoch
Tushielaw	Ettrick and Yarrow
Uddingston: Aitkenhead	Uddingston: Viewpark
Uddingston: Chalmers	Uddingston: Old
Uddingston: Trinity	Uddingston: Old
Uig	Snizort
Uphall: North	Strathbrock
Uyeasound	Unst
Walston	Black Mount
Wandel	Upper Clyde
Wanlockhead	Upper Clyde
Waterbeck	charge dissolved: Presbytery of Annandale and Eskdale
Waternish	Bracadale and Duirinish
Wauchope	Langholm Eskdalemuir Ewes and Westerkirk
Waulkmill	Insch-Leslie-Premnay-Oyne
Weisdale	Tingwall
Wheelkirk	Liddesdale
Whitehill	New Pitsligo
Whiteness	Tingwall
Whittingehame	Traprain
Wick: Bridge Street	Wick: St Fergus
Wick: Central	Wick: Pulteneytown and Thrumster
Wick: Martyrs'	Wick: Pulteneytown and Thrumster
Wick: Old	Wick: St Fergus
Wick: St Andrew's	Wick: Pulteneytown and Thrumster
Wilkieston	Edinburgh: Ratho

Name no longer used	Present name of parish
Wilsontown	Forth
Wishaw: Chalmers	Wishaw: South Wishaw
Wishaw: Thornlie	Wishaw: South Wishaw
Wiston	Upper Clyde
Wolfhill	Cargill Burrelton
Wolflee	Hobkirk and Southdean
Woomet	Newton
Yetholm	Cheviot Churches
Ythan Wells	Auchaber United

SECTION 10

Congregational
Statistics
2013

CHURCH OF SCOTLAND
Comparative Statistics: 1973–2013

	2013	2003	1993	1983	1973
Communicants	398,389	553,248	732,936	902,714	1,088,873
Elders	32,834	42,071	46,268	47,441	50,963

NOTES ON CONGREGATIONAL STATISTICS

Com   Number of communicants at 31 December 2013.

Eld   Number of elders at 31 December 2013.

G   Membership of the Guild including Young Woman's Group and others as recorded on the 2013 annual return submitted to the Guild Office.

In 13   Ordinary General Income for 2013. Ordinary General Income consists of members' offerings, contributions from congregational organisations, regular fund-raising events, income from investments, deposits and so on. This figure does not include extraordinary or special income, or income from special collections and fund-raising for other charities.

M&M   Final amount allocated to congregations after allowing for Presbytery-approved amendments up to 31 December 2013, but before deducting stipend endowments and normal allowances given for stipend purposes in a vacancy.

–18   This figure shows 'the number of children and young people aged 17 years and under who are involved in the life of the congregation'.

(NB: Figures may not be available for new charges created or for congregations which have entered into readjustment late in 2013 or during 2014. Figures might also not be available for congregations which failed to submit the appropriate schedule.)

Congregation	Com	Eld	G	In 13	M&M	–18

1. Edinburgh

Congregation	Com	Eld	G	In 13	M&M	–18
Albany Deaf Church of Edinburgh	73	–	–	–	–	–
Balerno	609	70	35	132,170	77,721	72
Barclay Viewforth	323	34	–	155,712	111,959	40
Blackhall St Columba's	890	74	27	205,129	103,516	51
Bristo Memorial Craigmillar	72	5	14	55,394	25,457	44
Broughton St Mary's	216	28	–	71,492	51,741	33
Canongate	361	47	–	130,347	65,732	15
Carrick Knowe	400	49	73	59,533	37,114	323
Colinton	906	72	–	199,341	127,778	96
Colinton Mains	167	15	–	45,342	33,722	54
Corstorphine Craigsbank	500	28	–	93,079	61,477	69
Corstorphine Old	461	45	56	98,596	69,156	59
Corstorphine St Anne's	365	51	69	101,058	63,825	39
Corstorphine St Ninian's	749	75	46	162,895	95,575	55
Craigentinny St Christopher's	89	–	–	28,063	19,627	–
Craiglockhart	448	49	29	154,257	101,338	56
Craigmillar Park	220	19	24	70,439	53,439	4
Cramond	1,060	91	–	204,855	157,782	83
Currie	573	40	73	182,958	90,266	69
Dalmeny	109	12	–	23,285	18,710	8
Queensferry	675	43	60	117,400	56,546	125
Davidson's Mains	636	13	39	–	106,115	77
Dean	165	22	–	61,414	36,438	7
Drylaw	104	14	–	18,444	13,754	5
Duddingston	548	43	44	110,051	68,913	164
Fairmilehead	657	60	35	90,159	69,178	58
Gorgie Dalry	242	26	–	97,531	57,350	50
Granton	207	17	–	47,822	24,102	30
Greenbank	770	82	35	263,649	142,157	84
Greenside	145	30	–	–	34,252	16
Greyfriars Kirk	397	39	–	220,062	114,449	37
High (St Giles')	507	35	–	296,006	167,678	7
Holyrood Abbey	212	29	–	134,266	86,836	76
Holy Trinity	209	19	–	199,805	77,776	60
Inverleith St Serf's	398	43	22	96,895	98,386	25
Juniper Green	330	23	–	98,336	63,760	30
Kaimes Lockhart Memorial	46	6	–	10,681	3,879	10
Liberton	728	80	51	221,862	112,145	90
Kirkliston	273	32	49	94,299	61,537	52
Leith North	304	33	–	82,915	49,584	70
Leith St Andrew's	262	33	–	73,222	57,070	176
Leith South	393	63	–	156,691	76,200	104
Leith Wardie	532	69	34	168,997	83,985	166
Liberton Northfield	214	8	19	57,272	31,877	18
London Road	194	30	25	57,323	32,165	10
Marchmont St Giles'	231	35	29	96,903	62,249	54
Mayfield Salisbury	537	52	–	240,713	139,248	74
Morningside	477	66	21	187,343	116,789	120

Congregation	Com	Eld	G	In 13	M&M	–18
Morningside United	226	40	–	89,036	–	14
Muirhouse St Andrew's	50	11	–	16,233	275	20
Murrayfield	541	78	–	160,962	92,859	59
Newhaven	177	15	37	–	56,017	111
New Restalrig	75	3	14	40,248	81,489	–
Old Kirk	100	8	–	19,582	11,828	6
Palmerston Place	394	37	–	174,577	97,836	117
Pilrig St Paul's	237	15	24	40,291	34,084	23
Polwarth	206	23	15	67,955	57,581	25
Portobello Old	281	43	36	66,003	49,680	63
Portobello St James'	226	40	–	39,434	29,096	22
Portobello St Philip's Joppa	537	44	61	170,453	104,151	245
Priestfield	178	20	22	61,691	40,017	18
Ratho	197	18	–	49,024	24,642	12
Reid Memorial	313	20	–	–	65,914	12
Richmond Craigmillar	91	11	–	–	2,546	11
St Andrew's and St George's West	327	48	–	223,347	162,979	16
St Andrew's Clermiston	227	14	–	49,687	36,659	11
St Catherine's Argyle	351	25	–	–	90,570	220
St Cuthbert's	348	50	–	150,297	98,444	15
St David's Broomhouse	130	13	–	29,257	18,452	69
St John's Oxgangs	183	12	31	14,219	14,955	–
St Margaret's	361	38	20	52,331	36,070	50
St Martin's	100	–	–	15,476	4,921	–
St Michael's	352	26	29	71,148	39,831	12
St Nicholas' Sighthill	349	26	16	45,361	28,073	16
St Stephen's Comely Bank	245	18	–	119,355	81,555	100
Slateford Longstone	225	16	40	50,885	31,150	20
Stenhouse St Aidan's	77	9	–	21,010	18,037	3
Stockbridge	219	25	–	96,019	57,335	33
Tron Kirk (Gilmerton and Moredun)	92	13	–	27,913	3,626	137

2. West Lothian

Abercorn	75	9	–	15,208	10,580	–
Pardovan, Kingscavil and Winchburgh	272	29	16	61,488	37,339	87
Armadale	543	44	31	72,588	43,624	224
Avonbridge	82	8	–	13,033	6,871	8
Torphichen	239	16	–	52,491	28,220	68
Bathgate: Boghall	250	30	24	79,266	42,557	51
Bathgate: High	520	35	32	91,698	58,411	30
Bathgate: St John's	358	25	35	63,994	38,429	100
Blackburn and Seafield	404	37	–	61,166	43,018	105
Blackridge	72	5	–	24,590	11,818	–
Harthill: St Andrew's	194	8	30	51,978	37,327	52
Breich Valley	194	11	25	26,661	23,572	11
Broxburn	381	36	44	71,819	48,124	156
Fauldhouse: St Andrew's	205	15	–	49,766	31,460	18
Kirknewton and East Calder	334	36	29	108,329	65,711	85
Kirk of Calder	578	46	18	75,676	47,554	43
Linlithgow: St Michael's	1,374	113	60	–	166,655	241

Congregation	Com	Eld	G	In 13	M&M	–18
Linlithgow: St Ninian's Craigmailen	433	42	53	68,046	40,939	80
Livingston Ecumenical Parish	522	27	–	–	–	231
Livingston: Old	372	38	20	86,582	56,909	40
Polbeth Harwood	174	25	–	25,175	17,573	5
West Kirk of Calder	260	17	18	49,594	36,904	22
Strathbrock	305	36	18	95,979	69,602	100
Uphall: South	210	23	–	43,635	40,833	58
Whitburn: Brucefield	241	22	22	84,086	49,671	7
Whitburn: South	376	22	26	73,912	47,094	108

3. Lothian

Congregation	Com	Eld	G	In 13	M&M	–18
Aberlady	230	24	–	36,884	20,931	10
Gullane	367	27	25	57,636	39,004	26
Athelstaneford	205	13	–	23,906	14,448	15
Whitekirk and Tyninghame	140	14	–	–	19,576	15
Belhaven	666	39	62	74,154	48,028	30
Spott	109	8	–	10,180	8,043	5
Bilston	94	5	15	12,762	3,694	–
Glencorse	302	13	–	26,373	15,975	4
Roslin	241	9	–	23,725	18,444	31
Bolton and Saltoun	139	18	–	29,602	16,340	20
Humbie	70	8	–	20,937	11,853	12
Yester	181	16	18	23,737	14,946	9
Bonnyrigg	680	58	48	109,744	67,039	25
Cockenzie and Port Seton: Chalmers Memorial	206	29	35	–	53,530	10
Cockenzie and Port Seton: Old	377	20	17	–	25,423	–
Cockpen and Carrington	233	23	42	28,786	19,531	40
Lasswade and Rosewell	338	21	–	30,144	20,811	8
Dalkeith: St John's and King's Park	511	40	24	94,700	59,518	65
Dalkeith: St Nicholas' Buccleuch	394	21	–	68,600	35,922	10
Dirleton	236	15	–	–	36,076	12
North Berwick: Abbey	300	30	44	86,530	47,809	22
Dunbar	409	20	34	108,851	60,061	92
Dunglass	305	16	–	25,287	17,272	–
Garvald and Morham	45	10	–	–	5,773	16
Haddington: West	437	23	33	54,066	39,020	29
Gladsmuir	180	12	–	–	17,219	35
Longniddry	367	45	39	74,330	49,967	46
Gorebridge	108	10	–	106,232	56,189	76
Haddington: St Mary's	546	39	–	–	67,033	76
Howgate	41	6	–	22,456	8,264	10
Penicuik: South	125	15	–	–	41,092	28
Loanhead	321	26	35	65,030	28,248	35
Musselburgh: Northesk	345	28	42	63,400	41,656	92
Musselburgh: St Andrew's High	337	31	21	68,973	33,786	14
Musselburgh: St Clement's and St Ninian's	210	13	–	20,119	18,329	–
Musselburgh: St Michael's Inveresk	413	39	–	76,421	43,895	10
Newbattle	474	34	25	81,122	40,759	205
Newton	124	9	–	13,837	10,990	20
North Berwick: St Andrew Blackadder	617	39	30	140,851	76,268	95

Congregation	Com	Eld	G	In 13	M&M	–18
Ormiston	179	10	24	39,676	25,284	18
Pencaitland	231	8	–	40,370	33,030	32
Penicuik: North	538	33	–	75,005	56,389	71
Penicuik: St Mungo's	363	23	26	68,698	42,880	7
Prestonpans: Prestongrange	327	27	22	53,440	33,325	30
Tranent	229	16	31	48,507	36,200	17
Traprain	445	30	31	64,222	46,663	61
Tyne Valley Parish	352	30	–	65,727	54,193	40

4. Melrose and Peebles

Congregation	Com	Eld	G	In 13	M&M	–18
Ashkirk	61	4	8	9,446	4,236	1
Selkirk	496	23	–	70,339	41,864	20
Bowden and Melrose	892	70	39	117,275	79,001	45
Broughton, Glenholm and Kilbucho	149	10	26	17,633	10,509	–
Skirling	67	6	–	8,242	5,494	2
Stobo and Drumelzier	–	–	–	18,195	10,644	–
Tweedsmuir	–	–	–	8,918	4,304	–
Caddonfoot	–	–	–	17,373	8,934	–
Galashiels: Trinity	468	44	40	63,581	46,755	6
Carlops	–	–	–	24,125	7,744	–
Kirkurd and Newlands	89	13	14	24,839	13,169	5
West Linton: St Andrew's	218	21	–	42,492	22,641	114
Channelkirk and Lauder	418	25	28	56,590	37,952	17
Earlston	411	21	12	58,730	30,081	24
Eddleston	108	7	10	12,037	7,401	33
Peebles: Old	503	42	–	111,931	65,081	27
Ettrick and Yarrow	195	18	–	43,803	28,326	10
Galashiels: Old and St Paul's	267	20	29	61,806	40,904	33
Galashiels: St John's	200	12	–	50,832	32,601	81
Innerleithen, Traquair and Walkerburn	387	28	37	57,147	39,215	60
Lyne and Manor	108	7	–	28,240	18,800	16
Peebles: St Andrew's Leckie	618	33	–	103,291	59,255	94
Maxton and Mertoun	129	12	–	11,357	12,171	12
Newtown	143	10	–	16,827	8,250	3
St Boswells	208	25	26	33,906	24,817	9
Stow: St Mary of Wedale and Heriot	185	14	–	29,169	22,735	19

5. Duns

Congregation	Com	Eld	G	In 13	M&M	–18
Ayton and Burnmouth	–	–	–	–	12,341	–
Foulden and Mordington	75	8	–	4,234	7,087	–
Grantshouse and Houndwood and Reston	98	7	14	–	10,505	3
Berwick-upon-Tweed: St Andrew's Wallace Green and Lowick	380	23	29	48,874	34,916	12
Bonkyl and Preston	65	6	–	8,939	5,418	–
Duns	509	28	37	53,107	28,254	30
Edrom Allanton	65	5	–	6,213	5,639	–
Chirnside	198	9	13	15,937	10,262	–
Hutton and Fishwick and Paxton	71	8	12	21,650	9,031	–
Coldingham and St Abbs	82	9	–	41,080	22,409	36
Eyemouth	181	23	32	37,235	24,475	32

Congregation	Com	Eld	G	In 13	M&M	–18
Coldstream	367	26	–	48,193	31,637	38
Eccles	77	12	15	16,860	6,717	6
Fogo and Swinton	99	2	–	8,386	9,194	2
Ladykirk and Whitsome	54	9	–	16,551	10,143	–
Leitholm	71	7	–	12,407	5,958	–
Gordon: St Michael's	64	7	–	8,358	6,216	9
Greenlaw	101	9	12	19,950	11,503	–
Legerwood	63	6	–	6,510	4,631	7
Westruther	44	8	12	6,547	4,479	41
Langton and Lammermuir Kirk	148	15	21	39,227	31,779	–

6. Jedburgh

Congregation	Com	Eld	G	In 13	M&M	–18
Ale and Teviot United	410	26	14	28,669	44,141	18
Cavers and Kirkton	122	8	–	11,179	9,536	–
Hawick: Trinity	752	29	50	48,998	31,308	69
Hawick: Burnfoot	107	14	11	28,568	19,003	121
Hawick: St Mary's and Old	444	22	24	37,878	29,138	101
Hawick: Teviot and Roberton	303	9	12	50,438	35,914	18
Hawick: Wilton	367	25	–	47,725	31,150	51
Teviothead	73	4	–	5,333	4,110	1
Hobkirk and Southdean	165	14	16	12,017	16,538	15
Ruberslaw	254	20	19	35,007	22,074	20
Jedburgh: Old and Trinity	685	17	34	78,190	52,920	4
Kelso Country Churches	213	18	15	28,043	31,604	15
Kelso: Old and Sprouston	518	34	–	51,862	35,218	8
Kelso: North and Ednam	1,170	74	42	149,932	79,217	107
Linton, Morebattle, Hownam and Yetholm	379	25	38	66,940	45,937	50
Oxnam	124	11	–	12,409	5,329	6

7. Annandale and Eskdale

Congregation	Com	Eld	G	In 13	M&M	–18
Annan: Old	390	43	40	67,985	47,570	40
Dornock	116	10	–	–	7,434	7
Annan: St Andrew's	641	45	52	58,643	36,463	90
Brydekirk	53	6	–	9,154	3,857	5
Applegarth, Sibbaldbie and Johnstone	164	8	8	8,915	10,361	–
Lochmaben	435	22	43	60,105	36,875	7
Canonbie United	104	15	–	27,986	–	13
Liddesdale	133	8	22	–	25,254	18
Dalton	107	9	–	13,832	6,619	2
Hightae	83	5	11	10,203	5,300	12
St Mungo	90	12	13	16,766	7,936	10
Gretna: Old, Gretna: St Andrew's Half Morton and Kirkpatrick Fleming	355	31	27	–	30,978	91
Hoddom, Kirtle-Eaglesfield and Middlebie	213	–	27	15,799	19,978	20
Kirkpatrick Juxta	113	7	–	10,457	8,835	–
Moffat: St Andrew's	379	33	27	62,860	43,569	60
Wamphray	55	6	–	8,983	3,242	4
Langholm Eskdalemuir Ewes and Westerkirk	464	43	16	59,120	37,263	243
Lockerbie: Dryfesdale, Hutton and Corrie	795	45	33	62,315	44,256	22
The Border Kirk	319	45	49	67,134	37,735	45

Congregation	Com	Eld	G	In 13	M&M	–18
Tundergarth	49	8	–	13,328	3,982	–
8. Dumfries and Kirkcudbright						
Auchencairn and Rerrick	70	7	–	8,547	7,375	–
Buittle and Kelton	154	16	–	19,778	16,472	–
Balmaclellan and Kells	72	7	15	16,353	15,027	5
Carsphairn	96	12	–	8,585	5,904	6
Dalry	147	11	14	19,497	9,288	2
Balmaghie	69	8	6	13,702	7,956	–
Tarff and Twynholm	154	14	22	28,444	18,713	8
Borgue	46	4	–	4,429	5,225	1
Gatehouse of Fleet	266	16	15	–	30,289	6
Caerlaverock	110	7	–	11,326	6,719	2
Dumfries: St Mary's-Greyfriars	458	34	36	70,538	46,966	7
Castle Douglas	390	28	14	55,459	37,044	9
Closeburn	196	12	–	24,368	18,454	9
Colvend, Southwick and Kirkbean	228	21	23	86,872	53,952	–
Corsock and Kirkpatrick Durham	90	14	11	18,977	15,347	17
Crossmichael and Parton	162	10	14	22,225	14,480	6
Cummertrees, Mouswald and Ruthwell	201	19	14	–	19,359	5
Dalbeattie and Kirkgunzeon	527	–	38	50,216	36,261	–
Urr	187	11	–	–	12,380	8
Dumfries: Maxwelltown West	623	44	47	92,153	62,757	139
Dumfries: Northwest	398	15	20	41,349	25,574	18
Dumfries: St George's	531	49	36	122,246	65,000	26
Dumfries: St Michael's and South	830	44	34	97,330	61,678	137
Dumfries: Troqueer	279	26	34	106,638	60,352	67
Dunscore	218	19	10	35,580	25,947	7
Glencairn and Moniaive	176	14	–	41,555	23,598	12
Durisdeer	149	6	12	19,555	11,790	8
Penpont, Keir and Tynron	168	9	–	17,982	21,683	15
Thornhill	168	10	13	25,416	23,852	–
Irongray, Lochrutton and Terregles	214	26	–	–	23,161	–
Kirkconnel	282	12	–	–	24,259	45
Kirkcudbright	543	28	–	86,125	51,541	82
Lochend and New Abbey	199	17	13	20,816	19,363	6
Kirkmahoe	306	17	13	23,109	20,792	7
Kirkmichael, Tinwald and Torthorwald	450	40	35	38,966	42,687	12
Sanquhar: St Bride's	418	24	15	45,094	26,627	25
9. Wigtown and Stranraer						
Ervie Kirkcolm	206	14	–	22,235	14,792	29
Leswalt	303	15	–	26,466	17,489	13
Glasserton and Isle of Whithorn	103	6	–	–	9,739	–
Whithorn: St Ninian's Priory	321	9	23	40,908	23,613	27
Inch	222	15	10	13,226	13,098	56
Portpatrick	221	9	25	21,844	15,031	–
Stranraer: Trinity	566	44	48	–	80,211	65
Kirkcowan	120	9	–	32,957	20,273	5
Wigtown	176	14	15	33,878	22,213	–

Congregation	Com	Eld	G	In 13	M&M	–18
Kirkinner	131	8	13	13,497	8,453	–
Sorbie	128	12	–	20,084	12,355	–
Kirkmabreck	146	12	21	17,135	11,584	–
Monigaff	269	17	–	29,766	27,180	70
Kirkmaiden	210	19	–	24,045	20,042	11
Stoneykirk	311	25	15	38,443	23,752	–
Mochrum	254	20	26	28,368	18,937	30
New Luce	91	–	–	7,803	7,546	3
Old Luce	146	–	27	37,237	25,850	–
Penninghame	424	21	22	77,149	46,988	21
Stranraer: High Kirk	577	–	25	75,376	48,733	–

10. Ayr

Congregation	Com	Eld	G	In 13	M&M	–18
Alloway	1,125	102	–	228,269	117,709	465
Annbank	275	17	18	38,237	22,097	12
Tarbolton	458	–	22	54,097	31,535	–
Auchinleck	335	20	27	–	31,687	22
Catrine	122	12	23	24,287	17,419	–
Ayr: Auld Kirk of Ayr	517	58	36	77,199	53,578	–
Ayr: Castlehill	616	35	48	95,015	68,063	212
Ayr: Newton Wallacetown	423	–	58	111,764	76,716	–
Ayr: St Andrew's	312	22	12	90,063	42,140	105
Ayr: St Columba	1,316	121	79	282,552	124,599	50
Ayr: St James'	429	42	48	66,663	45,173	181
Ayr: St Leonard's	525	53	33	74,809	45,106	11
Dalrymple	244	12	–	34,368	16,085	–
Ayr: St Quivox	251	24	13	48,312	31,006	11
Ballantrae	224	19	24	29,248	25,105	16
St Colmon (Arnsheen Barrhill and Colmonell)	1,242	11	–	24,458	17,590	3
Barr	66	–	–	3,179	3,471	–
Dailly	138	9	–	14,841	10,833	–
Girvan: South	308	25	30	30,848	23,691	12
Coylton	323	–	–	40,671	22,080	–
Drongan: The Schaw Kirk	187	19	16	42,518	18,501	86
Craigie	119	8	–	12,219	7,677	11
Symington	338	–	20	50,870	35,208	–
Crosshill	177	12	20	12,873	11,379	–
Maybole	352	31	27	–	38,198	16
Dalmellington	226	20	10	30,181	32,742	45
Patna Waterside	133	9	–	20,544	15,010	10
Dundonald	441	49	54	–	54,319	105
Fisherton	113	10	10	10,512	9,831	–
Kirkoswald	224	–	10	26,695	19,761	–
Girvan: North (Old and St Andrew's)	703	49	–	75,524	48,191	68
Kirkmichael	208	18	18	21,352	14,995	5
Straiton: St Cuthbert's	173	–	16	17,880	15,406	–
Lugar	159	12	14	19,137	8,147	–
Old Cumnock: Old	359	17	32	60,918	46,220	45
Mauchline	447	24	43	76,801	55,862	45
Sorn	150	13	15	19,538	13,992	10

Congregation	Com	Eld	G	In 13	M&M	–18
Monkton and Prestwick: North	356	–	38	–	61,693	–
Muirkirk	181	13	–	19,961	15,665	6
Old Cumnock: Trinity	358	18	36	55,433	38,831	15
New Cumnock	488	34	30	85,031	47,248	140
Ochiltree	243	21	20	33,026	23,696	30
Stair	216	16	17	33,736	22,121	40
Prestwick: Kingcase	683	–	72	129,381	78,791	–
Prestwick: St Nicholas'	640	71	63	117,103	71,047	183
Prestwick: South	294	37	37	92,751	52,755	85
Troon: Old	926	62	–	140,448	85,187	200
Troon: Portland	547	52	33	132,011	73,684	42
Troon: St Meddan's	865	97	40	186,634	97,936	111

11. Irvine and Kilmarnock

Caldwell	232	16	–	65,058	42,413	25
Dunlop	398	42	26	72,111	46,077	40
Crosshouse	287	34	16	65,236	33,430	90
Darvel	358	27	41	46,981	28,072	30
Dreghorn and Springside	494	44	30	81,715	50,252	43
Fenwick	328	23	28	–	41,369	22
Galston	653	60	60	97,966	69,412	56
Hurlford	372	26	33	72,331	38,910	13
Irvine: Fullarton	391	42	47	103,500	62,982	178
Irvine: Girdle Toll	166	15	26	–	20,013	78
Irvine: Mure	327	25	22	64,519	46,436	54
Irvine: Old	399	25	20	–	56,676	12
Irvine: Relief Bourtreehill	240	26	31	45,610	27,718	8
Irvine: St Andrew's	275	–	31	38,951	41,096	–
Kilmarnock: Kay Park	575	78	56	141,971	84,569	22
Kilmarnock: New Laigh Kirk	889	89	70	208,391	121,374	143
Kilmarnock: Riccarton	264	29	19	65,952	44,937	63
Kilmarnock: St Andrew's and St Marnock's	865	101	45	174,734	107,217	484
Kilmarnock: St John's Onthank	264	22	21	58,740	28,275	112
Kilmarnock: St Kentigern's	277	27	–	57,280	33,721	91
Kilmarnock: South	269	13	25	36,531	27,097	30
Kilmaurs: St Maur's Glencairn	297	16	23	46,045	31,185	20
Newmilns: Loudoun	231	7	–	–	41,332	7
Stewarton: John Knox	281	32	18	89,222	49,120	40
Stewarton: St Columba's	413	42	48	76,902	51,061	131

12. Ardrossan

Ardrossan: Park	410	31	44	69,381	45,085	36
Ardrossan and Saltcoats: Kirkgate	–	–	64	104,189	68,221	–
Beith	811	59	35	99,323	74,000	33
Brodick	140	18	–	53,558	33,312	85
Corrie	47	5	–	19,854	10,352	2
Lochranza and Pirnmill	67	12	11	24,317	9,843	4
Shiskine	71	10	17	34,009	13,970	17
Cumbrae	254	21	48	50,280	36,724	72
Dalry: St Margaret's	642	58	33	147,998	82,880	96

Congregation	Com	Eld	G	In 13	M&M	−18
Dalry: Trinity	207	17	–	81,988	54,647	34
Fairlie	241	35	45	–	42,973	17
Kilbirnie: Auld Kirk	322	32	–	64,634	33,339	10
Kilbirnie: St Columba's	542	30	–	61,549	36,422	63
Kilmory	37	7	–	13,864	6,773	5
Lamlash	100	16	26	33,915	23,931	14
Kilwinning: Mansefield Trinity	244	13	25	–	27,573	11
Kilwinning: Old	587	49	60	107,882	66,542	20
Largs: Clark Memorial	806	101	75	140,676	86,194	33
Largs: St Columba's	400	45	75	98,940	57,260	30
Largs: St John's	752	47	61	125,062	91,742	28
Saltcoats: North	300	24	28	41,647	33,106	70
Saltcoats: St Cuthbert's	275	34	13	71,276	53,008	112
Stevenston: Ardeer	273	27	28	38,463	30,435	196
Stevenston: Livingstone	298	35	23	42,083	33,930	12
Stevenston: High	243	20	20	81,359	58,428	31
West Kilbride	491	47	35	122,762	82,919	50
Whiting Bay and Kildonan	96	8	–	50,237	29,601	10

13. Lanark

Congregation	Com	Eld	G	In 13	M&M	−18
Biggar	561	29	30	–	49,885	15
Black Mount	65	8	13	15,449	9,203	–
Cairngryffe	168	15	15	24,900	19,427	12
Libberton and Quothquan	86	11	–	17,376	5,853	11
Symington	193	22	22	31,502	20,421	7
Carluke: Kirkton	813	51	22	107,793	65,005	355
Carluke: St Andrew's	218	12	20	50,801	33,821	30
Carluke: St John's	731	44	30	89,994	55,787	33
Carnwath	143	12	18	23,245	26,605	–
Carstairs and Carstairs Junction	213	22	20	42,710	30,991	60
Coalburn	127	9	16	20,030	10,959	17
Lesmahagow: Old	429	24	17	71,797	51,409	12
Crossford	176	7	–	31,094	20,288	24
Kirkfieldbank	82	6	–	16,197	10,097	–
Forth: St Paul's	351	24	45	62,609	39,711	28
Kirkmuirhill	281	18	51	116,982	66,626	60
Lanark: Greyfriars	571	43	34	94,150	53,884	192
Lanark: St Nicholas'	518	47	25	–	67,212	104
Law	191	14	30	–	26,052	125
Lesmahagow: Abbeygreen	226	15	–	93,056	54,708	180
The Douglas Valley Church	336	25	41	56,875	35,886	7
Upper Clyde	215	16	20	23,852	19,649	9

14. Greenock and Paisley

Congregation	Com	Eld	G	In 13	M&M	−18
Barrhead: Bourock	449	39	45	92,266	59,053	201
Barrhead: St Andrew's	–	–	60	142,834	103,490	–
Bishopton	647	46	–	92,940	61,171	71
Bridge of Weir: Freeland	395	57	–	126,049	70,225	46
Bridge of Weir: St Machar's Ranfurly	377	36	31	96,331	60,116	54
Elderslie Kirk	494	55	54	110,810	71,655	195

Congregation	Com	Eld	G	In 13	M&M	−18
Erskine	328	31	55	90,973	65,838	308
Gourock: Old Gourock and Ashton	696	58	34	126,422	76,137	194
Gourock: St John's	572	68	16	115,845	66,233	342
Greenock: East End	56	6	–	12,869	4,000	15
Greenock: Lyle Kirk	836	59	25	158,223	109,467	282
Greenock: Mount Kirk	310	30	–	62,223	43,211	150
Greenock: St Margaret's	155	25	–	29,809	13,635	16
Greenock: St Ninian's	220	18	–	30,467	16,482	122
Greenock: Wellpark Mid Kirk	540	48	18	134,506	65,742	91
Greenock: Westburn	710	94	32	–	78,730	113
Houston and Killellan	664	57	77	155,771	91,871	230
Howwood	157	11	18	40,864	30,732	72
Inchinnan	340	30	32	63,233	40,622	32
Inverkip	375	28	25	57,584	34,856	15
Skelmorlie and Wemyss Bay	327	41	–	85,481	51,905	–
Johnstone: High	236	31	35	–	57,708	117
Johnstone: St Andrew's Trinity	233	25	22	42,101	32,038	102
Johnstone: St Paul's	415	65	–	78,887	49,658	170
Kilbarchan: East	346	40	29	69,459	45,290	70
Kilbarchan: West	407	46	28	–	61,951	39
Kilmacolm: Old	480	44	–	132,738	71,536	20
Kilmacolm: St Columba	200	30	–	91,805	60,682	100
Langbank	144	14	–	–	20,655	9
Port Glasgow: St Andrew's	510	–	34	75,819	48,686	382
Linwood	307	21	19	64,957	40,365	14
Lochwinnoch	148	15	–	39,244	26,572	130
Neilston	502	34	16	107,081	60,831	126
Paisley: Abbey	724	44	–	209,356	96,862	108
Paisley: Glenburn	238	22	–	50,130	30,567	11
Paisley: Lylesland	344	45	28	93,149	57,700	25
Paisley: Martyrs' Sandyford	574	66	20	120,134	67,039	122
Paisley: Oakshaw Trinity	511	67	34	–	–	43
Paisley: St Columba Foxbar	168	20	–	33,007	21,693	108
Paisley: St James'	208	31	–	67,388	40,434	9
Paisley: St Luke's	227	27	–	–	35,611	9
Paisley: St Mark's Oldhall	492	60	79	114,604	67,877	36
Paisley: St Ninian's Ferguslie	56	–	–	13,656	3,500	10
Paisley: Sherwood Greenlaw	613	82	40	108,165	77,516	195
Paisley: Stow Brae Kirk	460	69	69	96,974	68,593	73
Paisley: Wallneuk North	395	34	–	64,715	44,612	30
Port Glasgow: Hamilton Bardrainney	–	–	13	42,904	25,242	–
Port Glasgow: St Martin's	165	14	–	–	13,303	16
Renfrew: North	712	65	34	118,080	70,379	179
Renfrew: Trinity	398	29	53	100,608	58,150	248

16. Glasgow

Banton	68	11	–	12,439	8,537	10
Twechar	72	4	–	20,734	9,432	9
Bishopbriggs: Kenmure	275	24	55	90,336	62,301	146
Bishopbriggs: Springfield Cambridge	665	45	92	122,739	69,952	168

Congregation	Com	Eld	G	In 13	M&M	–18
Broom	574	58	35	128,842	94,124	412
Burnside Blairbeth	616	44	98	269,403	151,432	184
Busby	245	34	26	77,872	43,548	35
Cadder	773	84	45	–	90,943	176
Cambuslang: Flemington Hallside	299	27	27	53,401	28,787	80
Cambuslang Parish Church	720	61	40	159,503	98,839	224
Campsie	157	15	21	61,062	36,214	62
Chryston	625	32	18	193,469	114,882	95
Eaglesham	552	50	67	150,312	76,631	150
Fernhill and Cathkin	270	27	34	57,893	33,466	115
Gartcosh	137	14	–	27,964	10,983	78
Glenboig	116	10	11	14,832	8,842	16
Giffnock: Orchardhill	440	46	22	156,293	85,099	246
Giffnock: South	636	87	44	191,288	104,477	80
Giffnock: The Park	261	31	–	69,308	39,412	178
Greenbank	896	81	51	211,850	123,983	250
Kilsyth: Anderson	307	16	52	75,901	51,336	125
Kilsyth: Burns and Old	397	29	45	67,001	49,851	72
Kirkintilloch: Hillhead	108	7	12	12,712	9,527	22
Kirkintilloch: St Columba's	453	38	40	91,396	56,683	10
Kirkintilloch: St David's Memorial Park	588	45	32	74,224	70,228	128
Kirkintilloch: St Mary's	732	46	42	132,556	83,816	–
Lenzie: Old	449	44	–	122,000	70,118	–
Lenzie: Union	669	64	86	189,124	102,136	280
Maxwell Mearns Castle	303	30	–	173,727	89,785	109
Mearns	852	57	–	–	120,706	53
Milton of Campsie	339	36	50	68,992	47,561	106
Netherlee	713	64	30	210,612	116,159	305
Newton Mearns	449	45	17	112,878	73,547	126
Rutherglen: Old	305	27	–	63,161	36,469	20
Rutherglen: Stonelaw	344	40	32	145,849	80,842	30
Rutherglen: West and Wardlawhill	476	52	52	84,175	64,824	161
Stamperland	355	36	24	69,266	43,995	212
Stepps	317	24	–	–	32,496	163
Thornliebank	109	10	37	42,390	32,051	3
Torrance	312	14	–	96,014	57,775	160
Williamwood	431	66	34	105,714	77,165	595
Glasgow: Anderston Kelvingrove	50	7	14	–	20,682	12
Glasgow: Baillieston Mure Memorial	452	38	86	90,509	53,555	162
Glasgow: Baillieston St Andrew's	281	18	36	56,236	39,669	138
Glasgow: Balshagray Victoria Park	190	32	17	98,164	62,388	39
Glasgow: Barlanark Greyfriars	90	10	12	–	27,408	214
Glasgow: Blawarthill	172	29	27	–	17,419	85
Glasgow: Bridgeton St Francis in the East	83	16	15	32,802	21,423	3
Glasgow: Broomhill	436	56	50	150,676	84,250	228
Glasgow: Calton Parkhead	86	12	–	13,006	10,963	49
Glasgow: Cardonald	377	28	68	115,568	72,916	253
Glasgow: Carmunnock	301	27	24	50,283	33,768	6
Glasgow: Carmyle	93	5	16	22,041	14,008	23
Glasgow: Kenmuir Mount Vernon	131	10	24	59,044	34,859	63

Congregation	Com	Eld	G	In 13	M&M	–18
Glasgow: Carnwadric	148	16	–	32,950	21,829	32
Glasgow: Castlemilk	147	21	8	31,143	28,069	10
Glasgow: Cathcart Old	272	–	38	91,975	61,726	–
Glasgow: Cathcart Trinity	452	52	56	143,546	110,233	130
Glasgow: Cathedral (High or St Mungo's)	402	45	–	91,562	64,203	40
Glasgow: Clincarthill	269	34	46	105,574	71,577	139
Glasgow: Colston Milton	64	8	–	13,031	16,454	19
Glasgow: Colston Wellpark	107	–	–	27,684	19,944	–
Glasgow: Cranhill	43	7	–	–	4,371	45
Glasgow: Croftfoot	270	41	43	78,429	45,946	60
Glasgow: Dennistoun New	294	38	22	89,100	61,588	86
Glasgow: Drumchapel St Andrew's	194	38	–	47,399	41,471	40
Glasgow: Drumchapel St Mark's	69	–	–	14,268	2,214	–
Glasgow: Easterhouse St George's and St Peter's	58	6	–	–	212	14
Glasgow: Eastwood	234	45	18	89,854	55,692	82
Glasgow: Gairbraid	128	13	17	34,906	23,075	5
Glasgow: Gallowgate	51	16	–	30,503	9,561	6
Glasgow: Garthamlock and Craigend East	87	14	–	–	3,732	85
Glasgow: Gorbals	90	12	–	28,566	17,509	27
Glasgow: Govan and Linthouse	220	48	43	–	43,796	316
Glasgow: Govanhill Trinity	81	18	–	23,424	20,850	4
Glasgow: High Carntyne	268	23	43	54,153	38,473	117
Glasgow: Hillington Park	298	30	35	75,160	42,870	118
Glasgow: Hyndland	238	33	22	92,349	52,831	50
Glasgow: Ibrox	136	21	23	53,775	33,654	90
Glasgow: John Ross Memorial (for Deaf People)	57	4	–	–	–	–
Glasgow: Jordanhill	409	67	28	177,904	103,943	156
Glasgow: Kelvinbridge	189	29	11	34,716	39,377	82
Glasgow: Kelvinside Hillhead	164	29	–	73,325	55,868	99
Glasgow: King's Park	639	75	48	144,524	90,223	65
Glasgow: Kinning Park	134	12	–	31,398	22,696	9
Glasgow: Knightswood St Margaret's	215	23	30	55,136	34,429	88
Glasgow: Langside	208	54	19	87,185	48,489	170
Glasgow: Lochwood	64	5	8	–	7,181	116
Glasgow: Maryhill	151	15	12	–	25,258	119
Glasgow: Merrylea	306	66	29	76,781	51,808	100
Glasgow: Mosspark	126	27	36	53,863	33,290	148
Glasgow: Newlands South	490	64	24	157,003	98,943	28
Glasgow: Partick South	141	24	–	65,876	36,766	20
Glasgow: Partick Trinity	167	25	–	87,370	45,819	44
Glasgow: Penilee St Andrew's	120	20	–	38,920	27,215	100
Glasgow: Pollokshaws	125	21	24	38,956	30,076	23
Glasgow: Pollokshields	194	31	21	–	60,210	102
Glasgow: Possilpark	115	22	12	28,250	17,704	15
Glasgow: Queen's Park	200	27	38	85,705	54,894	9
Glasgow: Renfield St Stephen's	143	21	29	–	49,286	18
Glasgow: Robroyston	39	–	–	34,514	2,000	43
Glasgow: Ruchazie	26	6	–	8,385	5,240	158
Glasgow: Ruchill Kelvinside	91	17	–	57,318	51,913	15
Glasgow: St Andrew's East	69	15	16	36,455	22,142	55

Congregation	Com	Eld	G	In 13	M&M	–18
Glasgow: St Christopher's Priesthill and Nitshill	228	24	–	43,833	30,545	15
Glasgow: St Columba	140	17	13	41,266	17,629	12
Glasgow: St David's Knightswood	283	19	33	93,248	55,766	27
Glasgow: St Enoch's Hogganfield	149	16	30	40,675	22,570	6
Glasgow: St George's Tron	380	–	–	3,729	–	–
Glasgow: St James' (Pollok)	158	25	27	52,167	34,462	92
Glasgow: St John's Renfield	339	43	–	143,658	95,109	203
Glasgow: St Margaret's Tollcross Park	132	–	–	–	13,338	–
Glasgow: St Nicholas' Cardonald	267	24	11	51,852	36,270	385
Glasgow: St Paul's	64	6	–	10,301	4,981	171
Glasgow: St Rollox	74	8	–	36,756	21,818	30
Glasgow: Sandyford Henderson Memorial	261	27	15	200,119	102,060	20
Glasgow: Sandyhills	290	29	50	–	46,385	29
Glasgow: Scotstoun	173	6	–	58,423	43,008	20
Glasgow: Shawlands	256	19	32	84,640	59,638	53
Glasgow: Sherbrooke St Gilbert's	251	45	–	159,564	77,694	132
Glasgow: Shettleston New	232	35	34	76,720	49,249	87
Glasgow: Shettleston Old	231	28	20	58,311	30,315	100
Glasgow: South Carntyne	55	7	–	–	20,285	48
Glasgow: South Shawlands	167	27	–	63,823	48,017	100
Glasgow: Springburn	212	32	28	–	44,933	76
Glasgow: Temple Anniesland	297	25	70	88,705	58,245	111
Glasgow: Toryglen	93	13	–	18,027	12,996	7
Glasgow: Trinity Possil and Henry Drummond	72	8	–	58,988	36,673	2
Glasgow: Tron St Mary's	120	17	–	–	31,630	71
Glasgow: Victoria Tollcross	88	13	22	29,562	16,815	101
Glasgow: Wallacewell	126	–	–	–	–	–
Glasgow: Wellington	168	24	–	79,058	64,242	29
Glasgow: Whiteinch	47	5	–	–	32,537	76
Glasgow: Yoker	97	10	–	25,113	18,227	24

17. Hamilton

Congregation	Com	Eld	G	In 13	M&M	–18
Airdrie: Broomknoll	246	31	27	51,160	29,306	97
Calderbank	115	9	17	25,314	12,172	3
Airdrie: Clarkston	355	34	25	63,759	39,530	104
Airdrie: Flowerhill	567	37	–	114,334	72,449	212
Airdrie: High	317	34	–	67,748	40,458	139
Airdrie: Jackson	339	50	20	81,113	47,833	204
Airdrie: New Monkland	298	30	18	60,305	33,254	132
Greengairs	128	9	–	23,481	12,982	10
Airdrie: St Columba's	236	–	–	16,490	10,469	–
Airdrie: The New Wellwynd	749	89	–	145,420	79,039	65
Bargeddie	105	8	–	–	37,357	14
Bellshill: Macdonald Memorial	249	–	20	45,446	26,608	–
Bellshill: Orbiston	190	–	–	10,921	8,242	–
Bellshill: West	511	38	24	65,800	46,402	20
Blantyre: Livingstone Memorial	222	22	20	53,221	35,821	160
Blantyre: Old	270	18	27	53,968	41,976	24
Blantyre: St Andrew's	222	22	–	56,710	37,180	25
Bothwell	480	58	33	–	65,602	163

Congregation	Com	Eld	G	In 13	M&M	–18
Caldercruix and Longriggend	223	–	–	48,652	29,892	–
Chapelhall	225	24	41	42,088	29,504	655
Chapelton	164	17	19	22,235	12,519	24
Strathaven: Rankin	542	59	32	84,030	50,217	160
Cleland	180	14	–	26,570	17,603	12
Coatbridge: Blairhill Dundyvan	273	23	21	57,404	39,579	125
Coatbridge: Calder	341	–	30	59,711	34,372	–
Coatbridge: Old Monkland	292	–	21	46,733	31,776	70
Coatbridge: Middle	365	39	33	60,210	35,036	189
Coatbridge: New St Andrew's	734	76	24	126,078	75,553	241
Coatbridge: Townhead	129	17	–	39,048	29,727	27
Dalserf	227	11	29	77,720	55,248	57
East Kilbride: Claremont	599	52	–	123,234	65,654	270
East Kilbride: Greenhills	172	15	35	39,488	17,859	16
East Kilbride: Moncreiff	669	69	58	113,986	69,288	230
East Kilbride: Mossneuk	260	15	–	30,747	22,675	190
East Kilbride: Old	698	62	41	117,142	67,325	145
East Kilbride: South	293	36	30	70,639	52,368	8
East Kilbride: Stewartfield	–	–	–	–	5,000	–
East Kilbride: West	402	–	49	59,199	42,230	–
East Kilbride: Westwood	533	44	–	82,418	51,554	231
Glassford	124	8	15	20,039	11,801	–
Strathaven: East	303	31	36	63,209	34,202	34
Hamilton: Cadzow	458	61	56	125,496	78,878	184
Hamilton: Gilmour and Whitehill	164	35	–	45,121	37,026	100
Hamilton: Hillhouse	378	48	31	89,126	46,575	40
Hamilton: Old	517	39	61	–	95,560	62
Hamilton: St Andrew's	193	–	27	–	37,807	–
Hamilton: St John's	513	51	60	114,436	69,244	230
Hamilton: South	218	27	26	65,154	33,399	22
Quarter	106	16	17	25,520	16,824	12
Hamilton: Trinity	300	25	–	58,080	31,641	103
Hamilton: West	269	28	–	64,481	49,296	20
Holytown	178	19	30	48,365	27,978	85
New Stevenston: Wrangholm Kirk	97	13	14	36,414	27,181	42
Kirk o' Shotts	171	11	9	27,841	21,279	20
Larkhall: Chalmers	112	13	29	–	16,923	10
Larkhall: St Machan's	448	49	43	–	63,840	76
Larkhall: Trinity	182	22	28	43,354	30,632	201
Motherwell: Crosshill	454	–	58	87,687	52,161	–
Motherwell: St Margaret's	359	–	20	48,139	24,067	–
Motherwell: Dalziel St Andrew's	524	72	41	128,913	81,206	200
Motherwell: North	201	21	–	–	33,414	180
Motherwell: St Mary's	799	94	67	1,406	73,435	227
Motherwell: South	429	–	88	108,916	70,061	–
Newarthill and Carfin	375	29	20	–	37,060	194
Newmains: Bonkle	138	18	–	34,961	26,320	14
Newmains: Coltness Memorial	207	24	18	–	39,699	79
Overtown	273	38	52	52,328	31,743	170
Shotts: Calderhead Erskine	464	36	24	87,947	51,762	19

Congregation	Com	Eld	G	In 13	M&M	–18
Stonehouse: St Ninian's	359	39	38	–	47,254	35
Strathaven: Avendale Old and Drumclog	685	60	52	131,329	76,400	33
Uddingston: Burnhead	254	25	10	48,442	24,715	82
Uddingston: Old	583	64	49	116,201	73,174	45
Uddingston: Viewpark	442	55	30	93,771	57,821	250
Wishaw: Cambusnethan North	467	31	–	68,610	50,227	130
Wishaw: Cambusnethan Old and Morningside	427	32	25	84,674	49,067	215
Wishaw: Craigneuk and Belhaven	156	26	26	51,056	32,566	16
Wishaw: Old	226	28	–	43,459	28,705	64
Wishaw: St Mark's	335	30	46	67,243	51,206	120
Wishaw: South Wishaw	460	34	38	78,745	58,303	109

18. Dumbarton

Congregation	Com	Eld	G	In 13	M&M	–18
Alexandria	300	36	23	71,544	47,627	34
Arrochar	61	9	14	17,648	12,687	47
Luss	99	20	29	60,121	39,949	20
Baldernock	186	19	–	41,180	23,441	26
Bearsden: Baljaffray	365	30	55	89,488	43,775	80
Bearsden: Cross	868	98	39	180,832	104,781	65
Bearsden: Killermont	626	59	59	147,393	86,065	60
Bearsden: New Kilpatrick	1,502	132	123	303,695	151,886	170
Bearsden: Westerton Fairlie Memorial	384	46	47	–	51,863	34
Bonhill	839	67	–	54,434	45,386	82
Renton: Trinity	252	20	–	34,643	19,532	–
Cardross	391	36	30	84,290	51,544	12
Clydebank: Abbotsford	260	15	–	46,747	33,270	39
Dalmuir: Barclay	212	16	18	40,248	26,992	15
Clydebank: Faifley	182	16	34	47,531	24,953	22
Clydebank: Kilbowie St Andrew's	274	27	17	48,674	31,061	129
Clydebank: Radnor Park	166	22	23	46,733	31,000	–
Clydebank: St Cuthbert's	120	12	17	13,353	10,445	6
Duntocher	231	32	38	41,057	35,472	2
Craigrownie	153	18	27	44,614	27,288	8
Rosneath: St Modan's	118	9	22	24,123	16,336	3
Dumbarton: Riverside	516	66	53	110,745	63,612	252
Dumbarton: St Andrew's	115	22	–	26,813	19,596	–
Old Kilpatrick Bowling	241	26	22	51,371	35,972	90
Dumbarton: West Kirk	289	35	–	–	25,738	6
Garelochhead	183	17	–	61,057	39,239	40
Helensburgh: Park	359	38	13	60,782	47,767	4
Helensburgh: St Andrew's Kirk	969	66	45	204,054	127,777	30
Rhu and Shandon	277	23	33	61,966	44,199	14
Jamestown	350	24	18	–	31,066	8
Kilmaronock Gartocharn	219	12	–	27,296	17,054	–
Milngavie: Cairns	465	39	–	167,628	77,738	18
Milngavie: St Luke's	385	33	30	81,543	45,800	36
Milngavie: St Paul's	951	90	86	218,043	117,108	153

19. Argyll

Congregation	Com	Eld	G	In 13	M&M	–18
Appin	103	14	22	18,105	12,098	12

Congregation	Com	Eld	G	In 13	M&M	–18
Lismore	50	4	15	13,165	7,823	8
Ardchattan	110	8	–	–	14,308	23
Ardrishaig	139	20	30	37,501	22,136	11
South Knapdale	34	6	–	9,377	3,862	1
Barra	45	5	–	17,652	7,906	50
Campbeltown: Highland	410	36	–	51,225	36,981	–
Campbeltown: Lorne and Lowland	810	60	40	82,694	53,882	134
Coll	15	3	–	3,338	1,394	–
Connel	121	16	14	45,865	26,785	11
Colonsay and Oronsay	13	2	–	–	6,214	–
Craignish	48	4	–	8,937	6,513	–
Kilbrandon and Kilchattan	97	18	–	28,200	16,353	20
Kilninver and Kilmelford	61	6	–	–	7,215	12
Cumlodden, Lochfyneside and Lochgair	93	17	14	27,109	14,064	3
Glenaray and Inveraray	107	18	–	27,032	17,372	6
Dunoon: St John's	176	23	45	43,601	32,403	8
Kirn	291	30	–	60,447	50,610	17
Sandbank	–	–	–	11,268	11,078	–
Dunoon: The High Kirk	324	34	43	–	41,353	–
Innellan	82	10	–	19,285	12,989	6
Toward	92	9	–	21,112	12,842	13
Gigha and Cara	34	7	–	9,605	5,559	12
Kilcalmonell	51	13	14	11,877	3,930	5
Killean and Kilchenzie	152	14	24	20,286	16,277	3
Glassary, Kilmartin and Ford	100	13	–	20,406	18,225	12
North Knapdale	51	6	–	22,685	23,315	4
Glenorchy and Innishael	60	6	–	13,955	5,137	4
Strathfillan	45	6	–	12,563	5,462	–
Iona	15	6	–	5,307	3,494	4
Kilfinichen and Kilvickeon and the Ross of Mull	30	6	–	9,625	6,288	4
Jura	27	7	–	8,260	6,061	–
Kilarrow	50	16	–	30,730	20,417	7
Kildalton and Oa	106	16	–	42,651	23,109	9
Kilchoman	83	–	–	14,226	17,247	–
Kilmeny	35	4	–	11,015	5,456	–
Portnahaven	26	5	9	11,690	2,521	–
Kilchrenan and Dalavich	23	4	8	12,635	8,215	–
Muckairn	144	19	8	35,983	16,271	12
Kilfinan	29	4	–	6,819	2,681	–
Kilmodan and Colintraive	80	10	–	16,240	13,509	10
Kyles	110	18	19	–	19,105	7
Kilmore and Oban	514	47	35	85,941	57,419	49
Kilmun (St Munn's)	88	8	15	16,449	10,240	3
Strone and Ardentinny	113	10	18	30,263	20,163	5
Kilninian and Kilmore	29	4	–	9,956	6,706	–
Salen and Ulva	35	5	–	15,525	6,525	19
Tobermory	57	11	–	23,076	13,651	7
Torosay and Kinlochspelvie	25	4	–	7,690	3,250	2
Lochgilphead	–	–	21	46,482	17,331	–
Lochgoilhead and Kilmorich	64	10	–	19,888	17,560	–

Congregation	Com	Eld	G	In 13	M&M	–18
Strachur and Strachlachlan	91	16	16	25,074	23,252	3
Rothesay: Trinity	389	43	28	67,935	40,825	49
Saddell and Carradale	203	15	21	36,898	18,492	13
Southend	228	12	19	30,267	18,134	12
Skipness	19	6	–	6,978	3,806	–
South Uist	53	11	–	20,863	17,988	5
Tarbert, Loch Fyne and Kilberry	149	18	20	–	24,817	3
The United Church of Bute	549	43	50	70,595	45,800	44
Tiree	84	14	18	–	16,530	4

22. Falkirk

Congregation	Com	Eld	G	In 13	M&M	–18
Airth	153	6	20	–	29,107	30
Blackbraes and Shieldhill	166	23	20	31,584	18,260	7
Muiravonside	199	24	–	40,319	26,741	7
Bo'ness: Old	371	33	12	53,186	42,763	36
Bo'ness: St Andrew's	508	27	–	86,882	56,982	116
Bonnybridge: St Helen's	347	17	–	58,305	38,241	18
Bothkennar and Carronshore	222	22	–	34,018	20,965	14
Brightons	635	39	59	–	82,855	256
Carriden	452	45	25	55,165	33,350	6
Cumbernauld: Abronhill	230	21	32	49,440	45,151	117
Cumbernauld: Condorrat	401	28	38	67,705	45,215	106
Cumbernauld: Kildrum	298	40	–	66,176	37,470	187
Cumbernauld: Old	340	41	–	66,585	58,018	115
Cumbernauld: St Mungo's	214	32	–	47,103	26,940	20
Denny: Old	376	44	30	81,757	48,412	80
Denny: Westpark	513	34	38	86,724	56,048	120
Dunipace	372	28	–	57,379	38,514	73
Falkirk: Bainsford	146	12	–	34,640	23,802	80
Falkirk: Camelon	303	21	–	–	55,017	25
Falkirk: Erskine	351	38	28	67,518	48,217	17
Falkirk: Grahamston United	342	42	37	57,202	–	21
Falkirk: Laurieston	220	21	28	–	27,086	17
Redding and Westquarter	159	13	22	31,011	18,141	8
Falkirk: Old and St Modan's	501	60	9	118,507	68,513	90
Falkirk: St Andrew's West	454	35	–	76,351	66,223	50
Falkirk: St James'	236	22	–	30,634	20,305	45
Grangemouth: Abbotsgrange	474	55	26	65,165	43,498	54
Grangemouth: Kirk of the Holy Rood	394	40	–	51,618	40,481	48
Grangemouth: Zetland	768	69	70	114,984	72,562	182
Haggs	264	28	16	41,419	24,403	64
Larbert: East	659	49	50	122,840	68,351	271
Larbert: Old	352	17	–	77,806	57,520	115
Larbert: West	392	41	34	69,976	48,536	122
Polmont: Old	368	26	40	–	55,163	196
Slamannan	218	7	–	–	22,191	10
Stenhouse and Carron	383	36	19	68,841	47,692	15

23. Stirling

Congregation	Com	Eld	G	In 13	M&M	–18
Aberfoyle	110	7	20	19,765	14,847	10

Congregation	Com	Eld	G	In 13	M&M	–18
Port of Menteith	57	8	–	13,400	6,964	3
Alloa: Ludgate	312	23	22	73,334	48,387	14
Alloa: St Mungo's	373	46	62	74,709	45,013	21
Alva	508	54	25	70,622	46,183	60
Balfron	142	18	18	52,501	34,097	15
Fintry	125	15	22	19,620	14,826	9
Balquhidder	66	2	–	16,090	13,436	6
Killin and Ardeonaig	104	6	6	21,110	14,783	6
Bannockburn: Allan	389	31	–	56,415	36,368	15
Bannockburn: Ladywell	395	17	–	–	18,998	9
Bridge of Allan	735	56	64	127,336	83,973	250
Buchanan	96	8	–	27,229	12,044	9
Drymen	264	26	–	68,844	40,008	60
Buchlyvie	215	14	14	23,825	18,201	5
Gartmore	68	10	–	16,293	13,971	8
Callander	567	25	32	–	73,906	40
Cambusbarron: The Bruce Memorial	329	16	–	55,545	32,468	52
Clackmannan	419	29	37	–	46,716	22
Cowie and Plean	188	10	6	23,608	13,611	–
Fallin	249	7	–	–	19,813	65
Dollar	396	31	61	100,704	55,821	8
Glendevon	44	3	–	4,832	3,201	–
Muckhart	115	7	–	19,176	11,904	10
Dunblane: Cathedral	866	77	58	222,259	126,761	317
Dunblane: St Blane's	326	39	37	98,077	62,275	35
Gargunnock	153	14	–	25,013	20,475	20
Kilmadock	95	13	–	17,008	10,151	1
Kincardine-in-Menteith	81	7	–	18,631	9,027	10
Killearn	402	28	39	94,258	59,841	148
Kippen	223	17	21	27,882	21,699	–
Norrieston	115	11	9	19,063	13,690	3
Lecropt	167	15	–	44,620	30,731	19
Logie	535	58	33	96,297	61,593	20
Menstrie	374	20	25	64,604	45,024	6
Sauchie and Coalsnaughton	611	29	15	56,124	37,506	8
Stirling: Allan Park South	176	24	–	36,160	28,557	65
Stirling: Church of the Holy Rude	150	23	–	40,586	32,934	8
Stirling: Viewfield Erskine	294	21	30	41,382	29,116	14
Stirling: North	377	32	22	89,891	52,629	78
Stirling: St Columba's	498	67	–	117,851	58,395	24
Stirling: St Mark's	201	7	–	27,501	19,571	70
Stirling: St Ninian's Old	711	61	–	95,748	53,532	45
Strathblane	201	19	43	97,644	46,610	80
Tillicoultry	660	60	38	85,703	58,216	107
Tullibody: St Serf's	396	17	24	51,076	35,870	60

24. Dunfermline

Aberdour: St Fillan's	390	24	–	68,213	48,373	118
Beath and Cowdenbeath: North	215	23	15	59,844	34,979	37
Cairneyhill	113	20	–	29,578	15,163	8

Congregation	Com	Eld	G	In 13	M&M	–18
Limekilns	256	46	–	81,369	40,822	10
Carnock and Oakley	186	18	22	53,537	32,817	36
Cowdenbeath: Trinity	316	26	15	65,471	39,425	11
Culross and Torryburn	129	18	–	47,560	33,262	24
Dalgety	521	41	24	114,637	66,955	78
Dunfermline: Abbey	677	72	–	131,386	81,296	160
Dunfermline: East	–	–	–	30,413	3,000	60
Dunfermline: Gillespie Memorial	262	42	21	77,652	60,235	25
Dunfermline: North	175	14	–	42,913	21,494	9
Dunfermline: St Andrew's Erskine	191	24	19	45,068	28,143	42
Dunfermline: St Leonard's	336	30	31	70,464	45,895	20
Dunfermline: St Margaret's	252	43	19	80,892	41,981	68
Dunfermline: St Ninian's	194	26	32	–	26,397	88
Dunfermline: Townhill and Kingseat	340	27	28	68,444	41,878	16
Inverkeithing	322	35	–	61,824	42,632	105
North Queensferry	61	8	–	18,063	10,025	16
Kelty	296	–	55	60,024	44,755	–
Lochgelly and Benarty: St Serf's	420	49	–	62,026	40,987	22
Rosyth	245	30	–	35,672	21,818	42
Saline and Blairingone	161	14	16	41,566	26,668	35
Tulliallan and Kincardine	419	20	35	49,180	32,224	62

25. Kirkcaldy

Congregation	Com	Eld	G	In 13	M&M	–18
Auchterderran Kinglassie	364	30	13	47,525	40,217	5
Auchtertool	68	7	–	9,580	4,900	6
Kirkcaldy: Linktown	268	33	33	57,405	37,888	23
Buckhaven and Wemyss	259	26	25	50,271	32,811	8
Burntisland	331	35	18	60,289	42,242	12
Dysart: St Clair	497	33	14	–	49,317	5
Glenrothes: Christ's Kirk	215	19	40	67,351	20,826	12
Glenrothes: St Columba's	477	34	8	63,331	36,815	27
Glenrothes: St Margaret's	313	30	37	64,916	38,363	70
Glenrothes: St Ninian's	252	38	13	71,232	41,242	22
Kennoway, Windygates and Balgonie: St Kenneth's	655	46	63	89,539	54,143	50
Kinghorn	377	–	–	73,336	46,674	–
Kirkcaldy: Abbotshall	520	23	–	74,905	47,578	15
Kirkcaldy: Bennochy	484	42	46	89,696	68,208	6
Kirkcaldy: Pathhead	360	35	38	78,409	53,715	110
Kirkcaldy: St Bryce Kirk	406	25	37	82,890	70,016	62
Kirkcaldy: Templehall	180	12	16	41,328	23,085	11
Kirkcaldy: Torbain	234	29	20	37,597	25,423	84
Leslie: Trinity	189	18	16	26,386	22,850	4
Leven	505	34	39	112,924	68,332	5
Markinch	501	39	–	91,761	48,319	47
Methil: Wellesley	334	26	21	55,060	17,821	175
Methilhill and Denbeath	205	19	38	30,234	20,902	13
Thornton	149	7	–	18,238	11,983	8

26. St Andrews

Congregation	Com	Eld	G	In 13	M&M	–18
Abdie and Dunbog	162	14	–	21,304	14,088	–

Congregation	Com	Eld	G	In 13	M&M	–18
Newburgh	–	–	–	19,447	14,863	–
Anstruther	215	23	–	48,378	29,390	5
Cellardyke	257	21	54	49,109	29,377	8
Kilrenny	119	16	–	30,089	19,183	12
Auchtermuchty	271	21	22	43,128	22,263	6
Edenshead and Strathmiglo	163	12	–	–	14,041	6
Balmerino	130	13	17	24,052	16,598	–
Wormit	252	19	38	40,790	23,421	9
Boarhills and Dunino	142	9	–	18,953	15,165	–
Cameron	92	13	13	18,165	12,421	14
St Andrews: St Leonard's	590	45	27	145,507	77,119	50
Carnbee	–	–	19	15,492	10,992	–
Pittenweem	253	14	16	20,643	20,040	14
Ceres, Kemback and Springfield	409	36	23	57,810	68,984	6
Crail	379	29	39	–	41,782	15
Kingsbarns	76	8	–	16,258	11,084	–
Creich, Flisk and Kilmany	107	12	11	22,308	13,821	5
Monimail	100	15	–	18,223	16,099	3
Cupar: Old and St Michael of Tarvit	602	36	28	146,978	73,125	80
Cupar: St John's and Dairsie United	737	49	41	–	63,978	15
Elie Kilconquhar and Colinsburgh	453	38	71	83,033	62,415	11
Falkland	249	17	–	33,406	21,706	7
Freuchie	198	14	14	24,055	12,343	12
Howe of Fife	502	28	–	48,654	37,393	28
Largo and Newburn	261	18	–	54,162	31,817	12
Largo: St David's	142	18	28	34,729	23,435	3
Largoward	73	6	–	11,536	5,556	8
St Monans	273	15	39	–	40,582	30
Leuchars: St Athernase	335	32	36	50,984	42,100	5
Newport-on-Tay	384	43	–	74,548	42,796	20
St Andrews: Holy Trinity	461	35	51	117,144	69,722	48
St Andrews: Hope Park and Martyrs'	647	53	32	128,077	86,114	2
Strathkinness	95	11	–	18,276	11,740	–
Tayport	361	26	27	47,523	33,815	10
27. Dunkeld and Meigle						
Aberfeldy	200	13	–	40,516	32,081	159
Amulree and Strathbraan	19	3	–	–	2,543	–
Dull and Weem	107	12	14	18,588	14,806	10
Alyth	702	34	26	89,568	43,215	16
Ardler, Kettins and Meigle	408	21	35	40,073	34,715	20
Bendochy	90	12	–	24,810	13,976	2
Coupar Angus: Abbey	300	19	–	40,446	24,007	90
Blair Atholl and Struan	135	16	13	18,517	19,334	–
Tenandry	53	11	–	19,351	15,968	1
Blairgowrie	899	48	30	120,046	71,509	46
Braes of Rannoch	27	7	–	17,433	8,539	–
Foss and Rannoch	90	11	13	15,335	14,290	–
Caputh and Clunie	158	18	18	22,518	16,736	–
Kinclaven	150	15	18	21,626	15,122	–

Congregation	Com	Eld	G	In 13	M&M	–18
Dunkeld	381	26	18	90,244	57,356	30
Fortingall and Glenlyon	47	9	–	16,616	15,279	–
Kenmore and Lawers	76	7	24	25,371	23,720	20
Grantully, Logierait and Strathtay	138	11	9	31,617	30,913	16
Kirkmichael, Straloch and Glenshee	107	5	–	16,836	11,046	7
Rattray	362	28	23	33,469	20,186	1
Pitlochry	386	30	25	84,704	53,970	70

28. Perth

Congregation	Com	Eld	G	In 13	M&M	–18
Abernethy and Dron and Arngask	312	25	–	33,084	38,722	15
Almondbank Tibbermore	284	17	35	–	27,276	8
Methven and Logiealmond	274	17	15	–	21,332	–
Ardoch	167	16	26	24,450	18,460	30
Blackford	110	15	–	27,711	13,041	50
Auchterarder	594	27	44	114,776	54,699	32
Auchtergaven and Moneydie	504	28	32	48,515	34,679	115
Redgorton and Stanley	349	23	33	42,995	30,622	26
Cargill Burrelton	274	11	28	31,458	22,953	6
Collace	115	8	14	21,927	11,214	8
Cleish	223	16	22	54,145	32,465	–
Fossoway: St Serf's and Devonside	243	20	–	46,839	27,860	26
Comrie	429	25	23	82,857	53,430	25
Dundurn	56	9	–	15,883	12,477	–
Crieff	758	48	35	101,690	67,918	100
Dunbarney and Forgandenny	570	32	12	85,848	51,257	15
Errol	281	16	20	43,013	29,522	18
Kilspindie and Rait	66	6	–	10,400	8,245	–
Fowlis Wester, Madderty and Monzie	305	23	12	49,736	33,048	26
Gask	85	9	13	19,619	19,737	2
Kinross	657	38	50	105,573	59,667	145
Muthill	262	24	17	37,554	26,009	12
Trinity Gask and Kinkell	53	4	–	8,665	4,371	–
Orwell and Portmoak	458	37	32	67,593	45,221	16
Perth: Craigie and Moncrieffe	734	46	37	74,213	51,624	49
Perth: Kinnoull	435	39	22	–	42,391	38
Perth: Letham St Mark's	516	10	27	106,864	61,184	90
Perth: North	1,066	89	35	196,801	115,979	94
Perth: Riverside	56	7	–	–	17,500	21
Perth: St John's Kirk of Perth	500	34	–	87,955	59,934	–
Perth: St Leonard's-in-the-Fields	470	30	–	–	55,426	8
Perth: St Matthew's	816	33	20	–	71,890	172
St Madoes and Kinfauns	295	31	22	48,227	29,092	63
Scone and St Martins	870	69	123	131,758	85,716	–
The Stewartry of Strathearn	383	24	–	45,179	61,116	–

29. Dundee

Congregation	Com	Eld	G	In 13	M&M	–18
Abernyte	91	8	–	17,809	8,645	10
Inchture and Kinnaird	201	28	–	37,650	17,548	10
Longforgan	190	22	27	–	18,424	15
Auchterhouse	144	14	15	24,547	15,740	–

Congregation .... Com	Eld	G	In 13	M&M	–18
Monikie and Newbigging and Murroes and Tealing 551	28	17	52,963	41,604	27
Dundee: Balgay 394	31	19	74,801	49,489	29
Dundee: Barnhill St Margaret's 786	54	67	162,784	87,198	57
Dundee: Broughty Ferry New Kirk 784	51	52	116,275	70,071	18
Dundee: Broughty Ferry St James' 252	9	27	51,103	39,888	40
Dundee: Broughty Ferry St Luke's and Queen Street 441	54	31	76,638	48,679	17
Dundee: Broughty Ferry St Stephen's and West 322	26	–	51,617	27,255	27
Dundee: Camperdown 143	12	11	–	22,447	9
Dundee: Chalmers-Ardler 229	21	32	82,557	52,326	96
Dundee: Coldside 318	23	–	58,101	32,689	8
Dundee: Craigiebank 193	15	–	31,775	26,353	130
Dundee: Douglas and Mid Craigie 132	13	17	52,563	18,391	95
Dundee: Downfield Mains 398	33	31	92,308	59,393	27
Dundee: Dundee (St Mary's) 553	45	24	92,297	60,724	10
Dundee: Fintry Parish Church 93	7	–	54,099	34,422	22
Dundee: Lochee 566	34	28	79,390	47,007	208
Dundee: Logie and St John's Cross 223	11	21	112,436	65,135	16
Dundee: Meadowside St Paul's 481	17	21	74,762	47,550	41
Dundee: Menzieshill 273	17	–	42,565	28,282	160
Dundee: St Andrew's 499	60	30	123,013	59,867	26
Dundee: St David's High Kirk 283	48	25	66,526	35,859	40
Dundee: Steeple 317	32	–	114,093	79,182	20
Dundee: Stobswell 471	41	–	–	44,081	–
Dundee: Strathmartine 287	21	26	51,064	33,554	4
Dundee: Trinity 481	36	36	64,757	32,952	78
Dundee: West 309	29	24	81,645	49,800	–
Dundee: Whitfield 50	7	–	–	5,221	67
Fowlis and Liff 146	14	14	27,193	27,811	20
Lundie and Muirhead 312	26	–	45,832	26,310	25
Invergowrie 420	57	48	72,545	40,636	112
Monifieth 1,144	62	47	170,573	84,861	95
30. Angus					
Aberlemno 198	10	–	19,082	12,737	12
Guthrie and Rescobie 223	10	12	21,522	13,334	12
Arbirlot 167	12	–	–	17,446	5
Carmyllie 121	12	–	–	16,096	–
Arbroath: Knox's 312	22	29	42,723	26,986	9
Arbroath: St Vigeans 558	42	26	74,570	47,060	16
Arbroath: Old and Abbey 524	46	33	103,239	65,953	30
Arbroath: St Andrew's 625	–	36	152,563	78,797	–
Arbroath: West Kirk 793	74	44	86,374	59,951	50
Barry 202	12	10	28,801	15,716	5
Carnoustie 363	24	28	66,209	46,019	15
Brechin: Cathedral 759	–	18	–	54,118	–
Brechin: Gardner Memorial 505	18	–	47,729	35,882	35
Farnell 112	11	–	8,752	9,858	11
Carnoustie: Panbride 703	34	–	69,613	38,934	43
Colliston 182	–	9	20,268	10,668	–
Friockheim Kinnell 149	13	19	17,938	12,066	1

Congregation	Com	Eld	G	In 13	M&M	–18
Inverkeilor and Lunan	141	–	22	21,671	16,663	–
Dun and Hillside	424	47	40	71,379	41,965	35
Dunnichen, Letham and Kirkden	288	17	25	39,322	27,877	9
Eassie, Nevay and Newtyle	297	16	18	27,715	25,395	26
Edzell Lethnot Glenesk	340	–	29	39,714	33,375	–
Fern Careston Menmuir	96	7	–	13,382	14,997	7
Forfar: East and Old	842	58	44	90,219	58,277	35
Forfar: Lowson Memorial	910	38	28	79,446	50,165	135
Forfar: St Margaret's	531	31	17	–	47,322	105
Glamis, Inverarity and Kinnettles	378	26	–	49,689	38,216	50
Inchbrayock	195	10	–	28,346	28,075	16
Montrose: Melville South	288	–	–	34,282	20,865	–
Kirriemuir: St Andrew's	301	23	33	47,437	37,208	9
Oathlaw Tannadice	161	8	–	18,666	17,825	9
Montrose: Old and St Andrew's	732	48	27	101,835	64,006	55
The Glens and Kirriemuir: Old	1,019	75	40	–	84,088	–
The Isla Parishes	253	23	17	37,445	27,868	12

31. Aberdeen

Aberdeen: Bridge of Don Oldmachar	226	11	–	58,729	47,580	60
Aberdeen: Cove	74	5	–	29,902	5,000	32
Aberdeen: Craigiebuckler	780	75	47	–	69,289	130
Aberdeen: Ferryhill	379	53	27	78,210	58,469	40
Aberdeen: Garthdee	211	13	12	–	19,210	9
Aberdeen: Ruthrieston West	356	33	17	69,491	48,468	10
Aberdeen: Gilcomston South	326	–	–	–	106,322	–
Aberdeen: High Hilton	367	21	30	58,172	48,880	93
Aberdeen: Holburn West	437	44	26	100,013	65,674	24
Aberdeen: Mannofield	1,187	121	55	166,116	103,386	179
Aberdeen: Mastrick	271	15	12	53,370	30,042	42
Aberdeen: Middlefield	113	7	–	13,506	1,971	5
Aberdeen: Midstocket	601	49	42	106,735	76,854	26
Aberdeen: Northfield	245	12	15	25,236	19,649	100
Aberdeen: Queen Street	467	54	41	92,570	60,209	60
Aberdeen: Queen's Cross	428	48	30	140,071	86,633	160
Aberdeen: Rubislaw	490	69	37	135,532	87,496	108
Aberdeen: St Columba's Bridge of Don	262	15	–	–	56,006	80
Aberdeen: St George's Tillydrone	103	11	–	15,558	8,009	7
Aberdeen: St John's Church for Deaf People	95	–	–	–	–	–
Aberdeen: St Machar's Cathedral	524	49	–	–	66,528	8
Aberdeen: St Mark's	358	37	32	97,837	61,947	30
Aberdeen: St Mary's	340	33	–	61,115	38,992	74
Aberdeen: St Nicholas Kincorth, South of	351	32	28	68,043	39,583	40
Aberdeen: St Nicholas Uniting, Kirk of	377	42	16	–	–	8
Aberdeen: St Stephen's	172	24	14	–	40,036	51
Aberdeen: South Holburn	600	49	52	99,721	69,535	39
Aberdeen: Stockethill	93	7	–	25,835	5,000	17
Aberdeen: Summerhill	137	19	–	23,861	20,356	6
Aberdeen: Torry St Fittick's	375	21	19	66,155	35,305	1
Aberdeen: Woodside	281	31	31	44,009	28,359	–

Congregation	Com	Eld	G	In 13	M&M	–18
Buscksburn Stoneywood	440	19	7	40,112	30,028	–
Cults	775	69	38	170,520	88,719	36
Dyce	1,035	51	34	–	52,249	261
Kingswells	390	27	24	56,012	33,158	20
Newhills	456	43	54	132,747	72,494	30
Peterculter	621	48	–	114,273	62,964	250

32. Kincardine and Deeside

Congregation	Com	Eld	G	In 13	M&M	–18
Aberluthnott	194	7	13	14,113	12,224	3
Laurencekirk	451	9	34	34,024	24,692	14
Aboyne-Dinnet	324	8	28	51,619	34,990	30
Cromar	232	12	–	32,681	20,618	–
Arbuthnott, Bervie and Kinneff	691	35	29	71,326	53,152	30
Banchory-Devenick and Maryculter/Cookney	177	10	10	31,153	25,545	3
Banchory-Ternan: East	566	37	28	94,407	72,445	70
Banchory-Ternan: West	586	30	30	136,970	65,523	130
Birse and Feughside	234	20	20	32,285	32,771	36
Braemar and Crathie	215	36	10	77,414	43,688	16
Drumoak-Durris	401	23	37	58,699	51,516	60
Glenmuick (Ballater)	279	21	29	47,310	23,934	–
Mearns Coastal	280	14	15	25,288	19,767	14
Mid Deeside	670	45	22	60,722	52,326	25
Newtonhill	354	12	14	25,604	19,359	84
Portlethen	313	21	–	69,118	45,652	125
Stonehaven: Dunnottar	630	31	26	79,173	57,668	14
Stonehaven: South	266	18	–	41,059	25,878	19
Stonehaven: Fetteresso	801	32	30	149,595	97,112	150
West Mearns	504	18	31	51,841	35,806	13

33. Gordon

Congregation	Com	Eld	G	In 13	M&M	–18
Barthol Chapel	91	11	10	–	3,955	90
Tarves	398	18	33	36,612	22,173	–
Belhelvie	373	34	26	91,472	56,567	35
Blairdaff and Chapel of Garioch	389	34	15	–	28,196	41
Cluny	202	9	6	28,867	17,188	23
Monymusk	113	5	–	21,084	10,676	9
Culsalmond and Rayne	175	7	–	11,516	9,434	21
Daviot	138	9	–	14,698	11,101	18
Cushnie and Tough	266	17	9	26,525	20,058	20
Echt	230	11	–	29,194	16,073	4
Midmar	143	6	–	13,624	9,328	3
Ellon	1,519	91	–	135,658	106,257	168
Fintray Kinellar Keithhall	191	13	14	–	25,558	4
Foveran	316	15	–	53,441	25,833	40
Howe Trinity	586	23	24	63,954	37,732	26
Huntly Cairnie Glass	643	10	15	39,760	33,452	–
Insch-Leslie-Premnay-Oyne	328	28	19	28,370	24,244	18
Inverurie: St Andrew's	1,011	34	31	–	66,733	10
Inverurie: West	674	50	32	92,465	53,867	40
Kemnay	513	40	–	63,179	50,247	135

Congregation	Com	Eld	G	In 13	M&M	–18
Kintore	711	45	24	–	65,987	40
Meldrum and Bourtie	450	30	34	66,350	46,682	14
Methlick	355	24	21	48,216	36,760	13
New Machar	438	20	16	48,382	52,935	36
Noth	253	13	–	22,216	23,271	6
Skene	1,310	92	61	154,920	81,634	212
Strathbogie Drumblade	532	39	34	72,615	49,448	67
Udny and Pitmedden	262	29	19	57,281	40,964	80
Upper Donside	384	23	–	37,813	31,544	53

34. Buchan

Congregation	Com	Eld	G	In 13	M&M	–18
Aberdour	107	8	9	10,519	6,957	7
Pitsligo	97	10	–	–	10,036	–
Auchaber United	151	13	12	16,811	12,684	10
Auchterless	185	18	17	23,044	15,544	10
Banff	621	32	16	66,930	48,196	138
King Edward	148	17	10	–	12,682	10
Crimond	206	11	–	–	11,612	–
Lonmay	106	12	13	12,999	9,661	57
Cruden	414	26	–	55,384	31,905	30
Deer	732	25	24	56,454	44,086	10
Fordyce	399	14	30	38,191	36,117	40
Fraserburgh: Old	594	59	73	123,818	73,827	203
Fraserburgh: South	284	20	–	–	26,397	5
Inverallochy and Rathen: East	87	10	–	18,392	6,634	10
Fraserburgh: West	524	44	–	71,619	44,964	128
Rathen: West	103	10	–	12,192	4,947	26
Fyvie	268	20	14	35,123	24,762	–
Rothienorman	130	8	11	15,734	7,393	10
Gardenstown	64	9	24	52,929	33,208	60
Longside	501	29	–	55,874	41,149	97
Macduff	665	32	44	92,284	52,644	146
Marnoch	393	14	15	34,486	22,618	1
Maud and Savoch	191	13	21	25,984	19,797	–
New Deer: St Kane's	353	19	14	53,927	38,419	50
Monquhitter and New Byth	318	19	12	21,684	21,007	14
Turriff: St Andrew's	551	30	10	49,920	31,221	63
New Pitsligo	280	6	–	26,064	18,223	28
Strichen and Tyrie	522	19	25	48,729	28,161	60
Ordiquhill and Cornhill	136	8	12	10,959	7,722	16
Whitehills	282	20	25	43,870	27,265	6
Peterhead: Old	385	23	29	69,778	38,333	41
Peterhead: St Andrew's	477	37	35	68,755	35,972	28
Peterhead: Trinity	280	20	24	95,618	68,834	1
St Fergus	174	12	14	14,068	6,840	8
Sandhaven	69	6	–	6,977	4,522	48
Turriff: St Ninian's and Forglen	787	24	37	79,312	47,638	27

35. Moray

Congregation	Com	Eld	G	In 13	M&M	–18
Aberlour	283	19	26	49,330	30,500	40

Congregation	Com	Eld	G	In 13	M&M	–18
Alves and Burghead	154	17	41	37,533	18,677	7
Kinloss and Findhorn	93	15	13	23,257	15,432	–
Bellie	226	20	32	50,196	36,296	76
Speymouth	141	11	14	17,239	13,882	10
Birnie and Pluscarden	265	23	39	41,710	26,915	3
Elgin: High	534	42	–	69,937	48,595	38
Buckie: North	399	37	59	56,113	39,625	11
Rathven	88	18	20	18,300	15,083	8
Buckie: South and West	237	22	37	38,327	27,496	–
Enzie	75	4	12	9,382	11,057	–
Cullen and Deskford	316	24	23	53,508	37,711	–
Dallas	52	6	10	10,942	8,047	–
Forres: St Leonard's	189	11	42	45,120	35,531	42
Rafford	67	6	–	20,083	7,146	28
Duffus, Spynie and Hopeman	261	28	9	48,794	29,032	34
Dyke	127	11	13	35,479	14,331	15
Edinkillie	78	9	–	12,962	14,784	–
Elgin: St Giles' and St Columba's South	650	56	45	128,969	83,656	8
Findochty	43	6	8	–	9,696	3
Portknockie	65	11	16	18,325	13,468	32
Forres: St Laurence	399	26	46	89,072	52,264	10
Keith: North, Newmill, Boharm and Rothiemay	547	43	27	52,230	79,332	25
Keith: St Rufus, Botriphnie and Grange	963	66	35	100,971	60,535	125
Knockando, Elchies and Archiestown	234	15	13	36,030	25,028	4
Rothes	302	18	13	41,017	25,979	14
Lossiemouth: St Gerardine's High	271	14	28	43,787	32,556	–
Lossiemouth: St James'	307	21	33	51,730	34,089	41
Mortlach and Cabrach	344	14	12	28,589	25,231	–
St Andrew's-Lhanbryd and Urquhart	373	40	31	75,273	45,283	66

36. Abernethy

Congregation	Com	Eld	G	In 13	M&M	–18
Abernethy	146	11	–	41,697	24,385	75
Boat of Garten, Duthil and Kincardine	149	15	32	32,276	21,201	2
Alvie and Insh	70	6	–	27,811	17,563	34
Rothiemurchus and Aviemore	80	–	–	16,959	10,288	–
Cromdale and Advie	60	2	–	15,234	16,606	–
Dulnain Bridge	34	6	–	14,322	8,946	–
Grantown-on-Spey	160	18	12	41,377	26,611	12
Kingussie	93	18	–	23,596	19,024	5
Laggan	37	8	–	17,282	8,781	9
Newtonmore: St Bride's	79	12	–	32,237	16,417	35
Tomintoul, Glenlivet and Inveraven	138	11	–	158,110	22,632	6

37. Inverness

Congregation	Com	Eld	G	In 13	M&M	–18
Ardersier	53	11	–	16,882	10,641	18
Petty	68	9	10	15,820	10,535	–
Auldearn and Dalmore	60	5	–	15,747	9,094	–
Nairn: St Ninian's	208	15	27	51,412	27,208	11
Cawdor	157	18	–	30,694	21,310	5
Croy and Dalcross	56	7	13	15,782	8,697	8

Congregation	Com	Eld	G	In 13	M&M	–18
Culloden: The Barn	242	20	28	93,644	53,515	130
Daviot and Dunlichity	57	11	9	17,498	10,869	6
Moy, Dalarossie and Tomatin	32	5	12	11,021	8,616	10
Dores and Boleskine	70	9	–	13,344	12,450	–
Inverness: Crown	565	72	40	136,725	78,138	129
Inverness: Dalneigh and Bona	254	23	20	86,970	55,226	126
Inverness: East	260	30	–	115,363	71,729	120
Inverness: Hilton	253	11	–	80,543	51,105	56
Inverness: Inshes	212	16	–	136,807	77,016	78
Inverness: Kinmylies	100	9	–	37,384	24,013	85
Inverness: Ness Bank	582	66	30	157,797	68,717	206
Inverness: Old High St Stephen's	434	41	–	–	72,359	28
Inverness: St Columba	92	–	–	40,921	2,000	23
Inverness: Trinity	234	32	22	68,827	49,274	56
Kilmorack and Erchless	102	7	16	–	30,952	10
Kiltarlity	48	5	–	21,746	13,293	15
Kirkhill	74	10	14	25,524	8,181	–
Nairn: Old	547	46	21	103,195	67,605	40
Urquhart and Glenmoriston	118	6	–	53,247	34,696	40

38. Lochaber

Acharacle	40	5	–	23,066	9,621	18
Ardnamurchan	18	5	–	11,149	4,419	8
Ardgour and Kingairloch	51	6	19	13,418	8,752	1
Morvern	45	6	9	9,520	8,005	10
Strontian	30	5	–	9,670	4,301	3
Duror	36	6	12	10,821	7,197	12
Glencoe: St Munda's	48	10	–	18,608	8,191	3
Fort Augustus	72	8	6	21,723	14,856	6
Glengarry	27	5	9	10,503	8,903	15
Fort William: Duncansburgh MacIntosh	374	29	25	84,089	62,162	50
Kilmonivaig	71	7	13	17,064	18,279	14
Kilmallie	118	14	25	33,529	28,002	13
Kinlochleven	56	5	16	21,904	12,001	17
Nether Lochaber	47	9	–	19,908	12,643	2
North West Lochaber	98	9	16	31,428	23,824	14

39. Ross

Alness	80	7	–	31,241	17,355	28
Avoch	15	4	–	18,846	10,342	12
Fortrose and Rosemarkie	102	12	–	39,519	28,877	8
Contin	54	11	–	17,225	15,747	–
Fodderty and Strathpeffer	107	16	–	31,877	19,498	32
Cromarty	43	2	–	12,243	3,350	3
Resolis and Urquhart	67	7	–	39,121	21,295	7
Dingwall: Castle Street	136	23	27	47,378	34,330	10
Dingwall: St Clement's	220	–	29	59,663	35,177	–
Fearn Abbey and Nigg	53	9	–	–	18,717	–
Tarbat	43	6	–	14,214	9,816	1
Ferintosh	159	23	17	47,969	31,987	28

Congregation	Com	Eld	G	In 13	M&M	–18
Invergordon	144	10	–	53,981	33,722	20
Killearnan	118	17	–	23,779	32,724	6
Knockbain	53	10	–	–	14,399	–
Kilmuir and Logie Easter	77	9	26	31,927	21,108	6
Kiltearn	55	8	–	30,343	19,751	24
Lochbroom and Ullapool	38	6	11	30,525	19,872	9
Rosskeen	128	10	20	59,329	36,680	68
Tain	111	7	18	50,217	36,661	8
Urray and Kilchrist	78	14	14	–	28,913	125

40. Sutherland

Congregation	Com	Eld	G	In 13	M&M	–18
Altnaharra and Farr	22	2	–	–	9,008	1
Assynt and Stoer	11	1	–	12,143	5,233	5
Clyne	66	11	–	–	15,676	5
Kildonan and Loth Helmsdale	36	5	–	11,331	6,147	6
Dornoch Cathedral	333	35	54	–	76,490	116
Durness and Kinlochbervie	18	2	–	–	12,890	1
Eddrachillis	9	2	–	15,592	7,363	3
Golspie	72	15	15	44,016	25,616	3
Kincardine Croick and Edderton	45	10	16	21,249	16,832	9
Creich	18	7	–	13,884	16,395	2
Rosehall	23	4	–	10,262	5,370	5
Lairg	48	6	20	18,712	15,117	–
Rogart	16	3	–	17,863	11,063	1
Melness and Tongue	50	7	–	–	13,003	15

41. Caithness

Congregation	Com	Eld	G	In 13	M&M	–18
Bower	36	–	12	12,115	6,215	–
Halkirk Westerdale	59	–	12	12,679	11,581	–
Watten	40	4	–	13,788	8,601	7
Canisbay	45	–	11	13,149	7,396	–
Dunnet	17	3	7	–	4,315	22
Keiss	27	–	10	8,477	4,733	–
Olrig	51	–	10	6,718	5,904	–
Thurso: St Peter's and St Andrew's	192	–	29	41,080	38,349	–
The North Coast Parish	53	–	15	20,001	15,320	–
The Parish of Latheron	71	–	12	26,571	17,179	–
Thurso: West	218	–	18	53,635	30,319	–
Wick: Pulteneytown and Thrumster	241	–	28	45,629	33,233	–
Wick: St Fergus	265	39	28	59,457	40,131	14

42. Lochcarron – Skye

Congregation	Com	Eld	G	In 13	M&M	–18
Applecross, Lochcarron and Torridon	89	–	21	34,649	30,362	–
Bracadale and Duirinish	70	–	20	34,268	21,160	–
Gairloch and Dundonnell	85	–	–	56,252	46,171	–
Glenelg and Kintail	51	7	–	25,340	21,571	30
Kilmuir and Stenscholl	44	–	–	27,300	26,994	–
Lochalsh	48	–	11	32,976	26,321	–
Portree	82	–	–	58,445	38,098	–
Snizort	41	–	–	31,460	25,837	–

Congregation	Com	Eld	G	In 13	M&M	–18
Strath and Sleat	172	–	19	86,327	62,506	–
43. Uist						
Benbecula	63	9	8	34,781	24,434	37
Berneray and Lochmaddy	46	4	14	24,728	20,054	–
Carinish	69	6	15	42,503	33,700	8
Kilmuir and Paible	28	4	–	27,538	21,644	10
Manish-Scarista	28	3	–	36,648	26,723	11
Tarbert	138	16	–	74,856	49,465	50
44. Lewis						
Barvas	85	12	–	64,566	52,256	24
Carloway	50	–	–	21,811	19,373	–
Cross Ness	65	3	–	58,118	34,926	62
Kinloch	37	9	–	36,859	22,883	16
Knock	52	–	–	–	25,999	–
Lochs-Crossbost	26	–	–	23,053	15,324	–
Lochs-in-Bernera	24	–	–	–	12,815	–
Uig	29	3	–	23,209	19,004	2
Stornoway: High	243	15	–	103,644	80,517	80
Stornoway: Martin's Memorial	270	–	–	159,066	50,213	–
Stornoway: St Columba	129	16	49	90,779	49,127	80
45. Orkney						
Birsay, Harray and Sandwick	329	–	33	32,700	26,928	–
East Mainland	240	11	17	42,909	17,749	3
Eday	10	–	–	3,459	1,416	–
Stronsay: Moncur Memorial	81	6	–	14,202	8,842	15
Evie	23	3	–	6,083	8,491	5
Firth	94	–	–	–	16,388	–
Rendall	51	5	–	11,420	5,870	25
Rousay	17	2	–	2,061	2,612	–
Flotta	25	7	–	4,659	1,620	–
Hoy and Walls	55	–	13	7,251	2,649	–
Orphir and Stenness	154	13	16	20,632	13,556	10
Kirkwall: East	378	27	31	63,699	47,166	29
Shapinsay	47	6	–	7,836	4,947	12
Kirkwall: St Magnus Cathedral	560	–	27	52,323	45,073	–
North Ronaldsay	12	–	–	–	1,079	–
Sanday	64	4	11	7,993	6,663	–
Papa Westray	5	4	–	4,621	1,829	7
Westray	78	10	27	19,818	16,620	13
South Ronaldsay and Burray	147	10	15	19,152	10,847	8
Stromness	312	22	24	35,024	27,905	37
46. Shetland						
Burra Isle	37	6	20	10,366	4,294	14
Tingwall	134	16	13	26,309	19,813	–
Delting	75	7	14	19,419	9,128	18
Northmavine	65	8	–	10,320	6,009	10

Congregation	Com	Eld	G	In 13	M&M	–18
Dunrossness and St Ninian's	50	11	–	21,110	12,972	44
Sandwick, Cunningsburgh and Quarff	74	10	6	22,730	14,602	21
Fetlar	16	5	–	1,082	870	–
Unst	114	7	21	21,226	12,612	–
Yell	107	12	14	11,410	8,737	–
Lerwick and Bressay	373	27	9	–	48,984	39
Nesting and Lunnasting	34	6	16	5,646	6,807	–
Whalsay and Skerries	187	15	15	24,708	14,893	10
Sandsting and Aithsting	42	9	–	6,719	3,666	16
Walls and Sandness	34	10	–	5,780	4,189	2

47. England

Congregation	Com	Eld	G	In 13	M&M	–18
Corby: St Andrew's	252	12	37	62,225	29,482	4
Corby: St Ninian's	196	17	–	35,428	27,973	–
Guernsey: St Andrew's in the Grange	186	22	–	69,636	43,549	19
Jersey: St Columba's	121	16	–	65,616	44,042	19
Liverpool: St Andrew's	24	4	–	24,742	11,756	4
London: Crown Court	249	–	6	–	60,038	–
London: St Columba's	981	56	–	–	178,973	30
Newcastle: St Andrew's	99	–	–	–	1,585	–

INDEX OF ADVERTISERS

458

INDEX OF MINISTERS

NOTE: Ministers who are members of a Presbytery are designated 'A' if holding a parochial appointment in that Presbytery, or 'B' if otherwise qualifying for membership.

'A-1, A-2' etc. indicate the numerical order of congregations in the Presbyteries of Edinburgh, Glasgow and Hamilton.

Also included are:
    (1) Ministers who have resigned their seat in Presbytery (List 6-H)
    (2) Ministers who hold a Practising Certificate (List 6-I)
    (3) Ministers serving overseas (List 6-K)
    (4) Auxiliary Ministers (List 6-A)
    (5) Ministers ordained for sixty years and upwards (List 6-Q)
    (6) Ministers who have died since the publication of the last *Year Book* (List 6-R)
    NB *For a list of the Diaconate, see List 6-G.*

Abeledo, B.J.A.	Stirling 23B	
Abernethy, W.	Edinburgh 1B	
Acklam, C.R.	Argyll 19A	
Adams, D.G.	Kirkcaldy 25B	
Adams, J.	Moray 35A	
Adamson, A.	Ardrossan 12A	
Adamson, H.M.	List 6-I	
Addis, Mrs R.A.	Edinburgh 1A-1	
Aiken, P.W.I.	Wigtown/Stranraer 9B	
Aitchison, J.W.	List 6-J	
Aitken, A.R.	Edinburgh 1B	
Aitken, E.D.	Stirling 23B	
Aitken, E.R.	List 6-I	
Aitken, F.R.	Ayr 10A	
Aitken, I.M.	Aberdeen 31A	
Aitken, J.D.	Edinburgh 1A-69	
Albon, D.A.	Ayr 10A	
Alexander, D.N.	G'ock/Paisley 14B	
Alexander, E.J.	Glasgow 16B	
Alexander, H.J.R.	Edinburgh 1A-30	
Alexander, I.W.	Edinburgh 1B	
Alexander, J.S.	St Andrews 26B	
Alexander, W.M.	List 6-I	
Allan, R.T.	Falkirk 22A	
Allen, M.A.W.	Glasgow 16B	
Allen, Ms V.L.	Stirling 23B	
Allison, A.	St Andrews 26A	
Allison, Mrs M.M.	Glasgow 16B	
Allison, R.N.	G'ock/Paisley 14A	
Almond, D.M.	Dum'/K'cudbright 8A	
Alston, C.M.	Dunfermline 24A	
Alston, W.G.	Glasgow 16B	
Amed, P.	Lewis 44A	
Anderson, A.F.	England 47B	
Anderson, D.	List 6-I	
Anderson, D.M.	Lochaber 38B	
Anderson, D.P.	Europe 48B	
Anderson, Mrs D.U.	Dundee 29A	
Anderson, J.F.	Angus 30B	
Anderson, K.G.	List 6-I	
Anderson, R.A.	West Lothian 2A	
Anderson, R.J.M.	Moray 35A	
Anderson, R.S.	Edinburgh 1B	
Anderson, Mrs S.M.	List 6-I	
Andrew, J.	List 6-R	
Andrews, J.E.	Lothian 3B	
Annand, J.M.	Annandale/Eskdale 7B	
Arbuthnott, Mrs J.E.	List 6-J	
Archer, Mrs M.	Inverness 37B	
Archer, N.D.C.	Ross 39B	
Armitage, W.L.	Edinburgh 1B	
Armstrong, G.B.	G'ock/Paisley 14A	
Armstrong, W.R.	G'ock/Paisley 14B	
Arnott, A.D.K.	Melrose/Peebles 4B	
Ashley-Emery, S.	Dum'/K'cud' 8A	
Astles, G.D.	Jedburgh 6A	
Atkins, Mrs Y.E.S.	Lothian 3A	
Atkinson, G.T.	Glasgow 16A-116	
Attenburrow, A.	Moray 35A	
Auffermann, M.	Aberdeen 31A	
Auld, A.G.	Jedburgh 6B	
Austin, G.	Hamilton 17A-76	
Baader, T.	Lochaber 38A	
Bain, B.	Moray 35B	
Baird, K.S.	Edinburgh 1B	
Baker, Mrs C.M.	Wig'/Stranraer 9B	
Balaj, N.I.	Angus 30A	
Ballentine, Miss A.M.	Perth 28B	
Barber, P.I.	Edinburgh 1A-25	
Barbour, R.A.S.	List 6-I	
Barclay, N.W.	List 6-I	
Barclay, S.G.	Irvine/Kilmarnock 11A	
Bardgett, F.D.	List 6-I	
Barge, N.L.	Glasgow 16A-39	
Barlow, R.D.	Perth 28A	
Barr, A.C.	Glasgow 16B	
Barr, G.K.	Perth 28B	
Barr, G.R.	Edinburgh 1A-17	
Barr, J.	Stirling 23B	
Barr, T.L.	Perth 28B	
Barrett, L.	Dundee 29B	
Barrie, A.	Argyll 19A	
Barrie, A.	Inverness 37A	
Barrie, A.P.	Hamilton 17A-17	
Barrington, C.W.H.	Edinburgh 1B	
Barron, Mrs J.L.	Aberdeen 31B	
Bartholomew, D.S.	Dum'/K'cud' 8A	
Bartholomew, Mrs J.	List 6-I	
Baxendale, Mrs G.M.	Hamilton 17B	
Baxter, R.	Kirkcaldy 25B	
Bayne, A.L.	Lothian 3B	
Beaton, D.	Lochcarron/Skye 42B	
Beattie, Mrs C.J.	Glasgow 16A-16	
Beattie, W.G.	Aberdeen 31B	
Beattie, W.R.	List 6-I	
Beautyman, P.H.	Argyll 19B	
Beck, J.C.	List 6-J	
Beckett, D.M.	Edinburgh 1B	
Beebee, G.W.	England 47A	
Begg, R.	Stirling 23A	
Bell, D.W.	Argyll 19B	
Bell, G.K.	Glasgow 16A-54	
Bell, I.W.	Greenock/Paisley 14B	
Bell, J.L.	Glasgow 16B	
Bell, Mrs M.	Greenock/Paisley 14B	
Bellis, P.A.	Wigtown/Stranraer 9B	
Bennett, A.G.	Melrose/Peebles 4A	
Bennett, D.K.P.	Dum'/K'cudbright 8B	
Benzie, I.W.	Irvine/Kilmarnock 11A	
Berry, G.T.	Lothian 3B	
Bertram, T.A.	Perth 28B	
Beveridge, S.E.P.	Annan'/Eskdale 7B	
Bews, J.	List 6-R	
Bezuidenhout, L.C.	Moray 35A	
Bezuidenhout, W.J.	Dum'/K'cud' 8A	
Bicket, M.S.	Angus 30A	
Biddle, L.	List 6-I	
Billes, R.H.	Edinburgh 1A-9	
Binks, M.	Wigtown/Stranraer 9B	
Birch, J.	Glasgow 16B	
Bircham, M.F.	Perth 28A	
Birrell, Mrs I.	List 6-J	
Birrell, J.M.	List 6-I	
Birse, G.S.	Ayr 10B	
Birss, A.D.	Greenock/Paisley 14A	
Bjarnason, S.	Abernethy 36B	
Black, A.G.	Lothian 3B	
Black, A.R.	Irvine/Kilmarnock 11A	
Black, A.T.	Inverness 37B	
Black, D.R.	Glasgow 16A-96	
Black, D.W.	West Lothian 2B	
Black, G.W.G.	Hamilton 17A-52	
Black, I.W.	Falkirk 22B	
Black, Mrs J.M.K.	G'ock/Paisley 14B	

INDEX OF PARISHES AND PLACES

NOTE: Numbers on the right of the column refer to the Presbytery in which the district lies. Names in brackets are given for ease of identification. They may refer to the name of the parish, which may be different from that of the district, or they distinguish places with the same name, or they indicate the first named charge in a union.

INDEX OF SUBJECTS

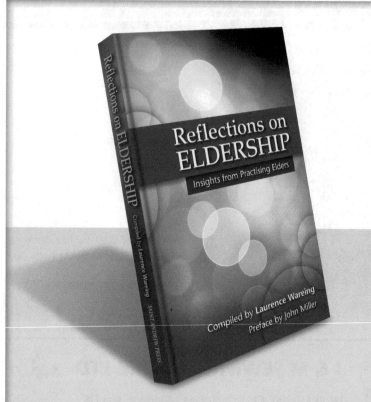

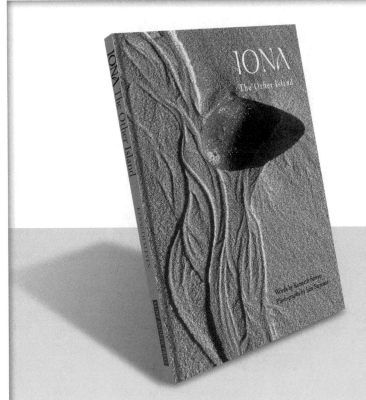

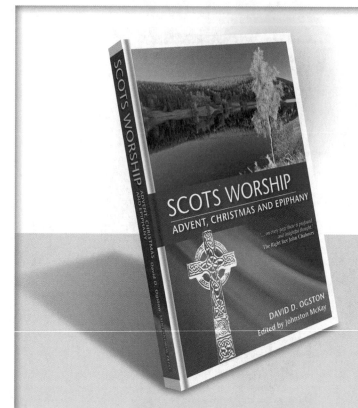